1,001 BEST SLOW-COOKER RECIPES

The Only Slow-Cooker Cookbook You'll Ever Need

SUE SPITLER

WITH LINDA R. YOAKAM, R.D., M.S.

S

SURREY BOOKS

CHICAGO

First edition

ISBN-13: 978-1-57284-098-0
ISBN-10: 1-57284-098-6

Cover design: Joan Sommers Design, Chicago
Nutritional analyses: Linda R. Yoakam, R.D., M.S.

Printed in the United States

Surrey Books is an imprint of Agate Publishing, Inc.

Library of Congress Cataloging-in-Publication Data

Spitler, Sue.
  1,001 best slow-cooker recipes / by Sue Spitler with Linda R. Yoakam.
     p. cm.
  Includes index.
  Summary: "Over 1000 recipes for slow-cookers, from appetizers to desserts. Includes nutritional data and exchanges for all recipes and designations for vegetarian dishes"--Provided by publisher.
  ISBN-13: 978-1-57284-098-0 (pbk. : alk. paper)
  ISBN-10: 1-57284-098-6 (pbk. : alk. paper)
  1. Electric cookery, Slow. 2. Low-fat diet--Recipes. I. Yoakam, Linda R. II. Title. III. Title: One thousand one best slow-cooker recipes. IV. Title: One thousand and one best slow-cooker recipes.

TX827.S694 2008
641'5'884--dc22

                    2008031301

13 12 11   10 9 8 7 6

Agate and Surrey books are available in bulk at discount prices. For more information, go to agatepublishing.com.

CONTENTS

ACKNOWLEDGMENTS

Many thanks to Perrin Davis, the dedicated editor of this book. The 1,001 series of cookbooks would not have been possible without my first Surrey Books publisher, Susan Schwartz. Current publisher Doug Seibold's continued enthusiasm for the series is greatly appreciated. Thanks also to the creative team that was invaluable in testing the recipes that went into this book—Susan Barnes, Jane Ellis, Jean Ann Morton, Carol Roessler, Chef Kevin Stantz, and Fran Wagner. And to Pat Molden, for her help in recipe editing.

INTRODUCTION

The advent of today's slow cooking was 1971, when Rival introduced its Crock-Pot® brand slow cooker. Since then, the term "crock-pot" has become a generic term for slow cookers. As slow cooker use has continued to expand over the past 20 years, many other manufacturers have developed slow cookers. We thank Rival, West Bend, Kitchen Aid, Hamilton Beach and Proctor Silex for providing the slow cookers we used to test recipes for *1,001 Best Slow Cooker Recipes*.

By 2002, about 72% of U.S. households owned one or more slow cookers, up from 60% ownership in 2000. The use of slow cookers continues to increase rapidly. Some 60% of slow cooker users have purchased a new slow cooker in the past few years; close to 30% own 2 or more slow cookers. By 2007, slow cooker cooking started to appear on television's Food Network, featuring recipes by celebrity chefs. The Food Network has forecast slow cooking as one of the fastest-growing cooking trends.

Manufacturers have added technological advances to make slow cookers easier and more convenient to use. Among the recent innovations are digital displays, multiple settings, dual dials to set both cooking time and heat level, programmable timers to turn heat to warm when the cooking time is up, divided crocks for cooking more than one kind of food at a time, and cookers with multiple crock sizes, enhancing versatility and saving storage space. Stylish designs allow slow cookers to go to the table or buffet for serving.

These are welcome improvements for the average American lifestyle, with people working more than 40 hours a week, and many working multiple jobs. Slow-cooker meals are versatile and easier on the budget. Less expensive cuts of meat become perfectly tender and delicious when cooked in a slow cooker and less expensive fresh foods can replace more expensive packaged and processed foods.

Slow-Cooking Benefits
- Hands-free all-day cooking
- Safe to leave plugged in all day
- Saves cooking time and energy
- Portable for potluck occasions, use in campers, etc.

- All-in-one-pot convenience
- Easy cleanup and no other pots and pans needed
- Versatile for many kinds of foods from appetizers to desserts
- Meets multiple cooking needs -poaching, stewing, braising, roasting, and baking
- Warm setting keeps food ready for family members' varying dinner times

Frequently Asked Questions About Slow Cookers

1. *Do I need to stir ingredients while cooking?* No. Valuable heat is lost every time the lid is lifted, requiring an increase in cooking time.

2. *What size slow cooker should I buy?* This depends on the number of people you're cooking for and the type of cooking you're doing. For a couple and small families, a 3- to 3½-quart cooker is adequate. Larger families will want a 5- to 6-quart size. If you want to have leftovers to freeze and serve again, the larger size slow cookers will hold bigger quantities. Most roasts will fit best in a 6-quart or larger cooker. If you entertain a lot, a 1- to 1½-quart slow cooker is perfect for making and serving dips, snack mixes, meatballs, etc.

3. *Can slow cookers be left unattended?* Yes. One of the main benefits of a slow cooker is that you can put in your ingredients, leave home and come back to a delicious meal. Slow cookers operate on a low 120 wattage, just slightly more than light bulbs, which generally use 100 watts. Ovens use about 220 watts of electricity, small stovetop burners use about 300 watts and large burners require about 1,500 watts.

4. *Can I use my slow cooker to prepare roasts, whole chickens and other meats so that they can be sliced, rather cooked to falling-apart doneness?* Yes. To cook meat to perfect doneness for slicing and serving, use a meat thermometer and cook to the temperature recommended for the type of meat. See the Other Entrées chapter (pg. 453) for recipes of this type. The use of foil handles facilitates removal of whole roasts and chicken from the slow cooker. Cut 2 long strips of heavy duty foil that will fit into the slow cooker, going across the bottom and extending to the top of the sides of the crock. Fold the strips in half 2 or 3 times to increase their strength; fit into slow cooker and add the roast or chicken.

5. *Sometimes my recipe is done cooking but it is too watery. How can I thicken the juices?* If you want to thicken the juices, turn the slower cooker to high and cook, covered, for 10 minutes. Stir in 1 tablespoon cornstarch or 2 tablespoons flour with ¼ cup cold water for every cup of juices.

Stir 2 or 3 minutes, until thickened. Or, the dish can be uncovered and cooked on high to the desired consistency, 20 to 30 minutes.

6. *What if I don't have all day to cook food—can I still use my slow cooker?* Higher cooking temperatures can be used to cook foods faster. The following conversion chart compares cooking times for high and low settings:

High	Low
3 hours	7 hours
4 hours	8 hours
5 hours	9 hours
6 hours	10 hours
7 hours	11 hours
8 hours	12 hours

Manufacturers' recommendations on times can vary and should be checked in the instruction manual.

Tips for General Use

- In general, the order in which ingredients go into the slow cooker makes little difference. If a certain order is required it will be stated in the recipe. Assume a 3½- to 4-quart slow cooker is being used unless a specific size is stated in the recipe.
- When cooking soups and stews, slow cookers need to be at least half full to cook properly. If less than half full, cooking time will be less, so check for doneness sooner.
- Never fill a slow cooker to the top; leave at least a 2-inch space between the top of the crock and the lid to allow space for simmering.
- Stirring is not necessary in a slow cooker unless specified in the recipe. In fact, each time the lid is removed to stir, there is a loss of heat, thus increasing cooking time.
- If cooking cakes or breads, do not lift the lid during the first 1½ to 2 hours of cooking time.
- Most manufacturers do not recommend cooking frozen foods. For food safety, thaw meat and vegetables completely before adding to the slow cooker. Add thawed, frozen vegetables during the last 15 to 20 minutes of cooking time so that they will not overcook.

Tips for Using Specific Foods

Dried beans—Will cook in soups and stews with ample liquid in 7 to 8 hours on high; they do not need to be presoaked. Acid ingredients, such as tomatoes and vinegar, prevent beans from becoming tender, so add near the end of cooking time when the beans are already tender.

Dried lentils and split peas—Do not require soaking and can be added to the recipe at the beginning of cooking time.

Rice—Only converted long-grain rice (like Uncle Ben's) can be cooked successfully in the slow cooker; be sure the recipe has plenty of liquid and add the uncooked rice during the last 1½ to 2 hours of cooking time. Other types of rice, such as jasmine, basmati, or brown, should be cooked and added near the end of cooking time.

Pasta—Dried pasta should be cooked al dente and added to the slow cooker during the last 15 to 20 minutes cooking time; small soup pasta, such as acini de pepe or orzo can be added, uncooked, during the last 20 to 30 minutes cooking time. Fresh pastas can be added, uncooked, during the last 15 to 20 minutes of cooking time.

Liquid (stock, water, wine)—Aids in heat transfer and facilitates even cooking. When doubling recipes for stews, increasing the liquid by 1 ½ times is usually sufficient.

Dairy products—Full-fat dairy products are more stable and don't curdle as easily as lower fat milk products. In this book, milk products are added near the end of cooking time and combined with cornstarch to increase stability. Evaporated milk and canned cream soups are very stable and can be added to the slow cooker at the beginning of cooking time.

Meats—Less tender cuts of meat, such as pork shoulder, beef rump, and chuck roast, are perfect for long, slow cooking. Ground meats need to be browned and crumbled with a fork before adding to the slow cooker, otherwise they will cook into a "clump" in the slow cooker. Other cuts do not need to be browned; the difference in appearance and flavor is minimal, and not browning saves time and dirty pots and pans.

Seafood—Add shellfish (shrimp, scallops, clams) and pieces of fish (salmon, red snapper, tuna, haddock) during the last 10 to 15 minutes of cooking time, depending upon the quantity and thickness of the fish.

Vegetables—High-moisture vegetables, such as yellow winter squash or zucchini, cook more quickly than root vegetables, so cut into larger pieces or add during the last 30 minutes of cooking time.

Frozen vegetables—Thaw and add to the slow cooker during the last 15 to 20 minutes of cooking time to retain best texture.

Herbs—Add fresh herbs at the end for optimum color and flavor. Add ground and dried herbs at beginning, adding more to taste at the end, if needed.

Thickening agents—Cornstarch and flour can be used for thickening soups, stews, and gravies. Not every slow cooker achieves boiling in a reasonable amount of time, so cornstarch is used thicken recipes in this book; it thickens more quickly at less than a boiling temperature than flour does and leaves no "aftertaste."

Tips for Making Desserts and Breads in the Slow Cooker

- A variety of delicious desserts and breads can be made in the slow cooker—creamy, perfect cheesecakes, cakes, breads, bar cookies, bread puddings, custards, and poached fruit are some examples.
- Making most breads and desserts requires a 6- to 7-quart slow cooker to accommodate the various sizes of pans and dishes used. You may need to experiment with recipe times a little, as various slow cookers cook a little differently. The shape and dimensions of the crock do influence cooking times; recipes will indicate a range of possible cooking times.
- Cakes and other baked goods may be a little "sticky" on top, but they can be frosted, glazed, or sprinkled with powdered sugar or cocoa.
- Test doneness of cakes and breads with a toothpick; test as quickly as possible so the lid of the slow cooker can be replaced to prevent loss of heat. If the cover is removed often, cooking time will be increased.
- Baked goods are best eaten the day they are made. They can be "refreshed" the next day with minimal microwave heating before serving.
- Most cake recipes can be cooked directly in a greased and floured crock in a 3-quart slow cooker. The cooking time will be less than if cooked in a pan, the edges may be a little dry, and if the slow cooker heats unevenly, one side of the cake may be more brown. You'll need to experiment a little!
- Many desserts are baked in a 7-inch springform pan. Fill the pan with water to make sure it doesn't leak or wrap the outside of the pan in aluminum foil.
- Place baking pans, casseroles, and souffle dishes on a small rack for best heat circulation and more even cooking. A tuna can, with both ends cut out, can be used as a rack.
- Some cakes and cheesecakes are cooked with 3 layers of paper toweling placed under the lid, which absorbs unneeded moisture and assures best quality.

- There are no general rules for adapting conventional cakes, cheesecakes, or breads to slow cooker cooking. Each item cooks differently, so it's best to use recipes that have been developed for the slow cooker.

Nutritional Information

In keeping with today's trend of healthy eating, we've emphasized use of lower-fat ingredients. In fact, most of the recipes in this book have less than 30 percent calories from fat, as recommended by the American Heart Association.

Nutritional analysis and food exchanges are given for each recipe. The nutritional analyses are derived with computer software that is highly regarded by nutritionists and dietitians. But nutritional data are intended as guidelines only, and are not infallible. The figures are based on actual laboratory values of ingredients, so results may vary slightly depending upon the brand or manufacturer of ingredients used. Any ingredients noted as "optional," "to taste," or "as garnish" are not included in the nutritional analyses.

When alternate choices or amounts of ingredients are given, the ingredient or amount listed first is used for analysis. Other factors that can affect the accuracy of nutritional data include variability in sizes, weights, and measures of fruits, vegetables, and other foods. Nutritional labels on prepared foods can have a possible error factor of 20 percent.

If you have any health problems requiring strict dietary requirements, it's important to consult a physician, dietitian, or nutritionist before using recipes in this or any other cookbook. For example, if you are a diabetic or require a diet that restricts calories, fat, or sodium, remember that the nutritional data for the recipe as written might not be precisely accurate for the food you cooked.

The book includes vegetarian chapters for soups and stews; vegetarian recipes also appear in other chapters. Any vegetarian recipes are coded as follows:

V   (vegan)—Recipes contain only plant-based food, with no dairy products or eggs.
LO (lacto-ovo vegetarian)—Recipes contain dairy products and eggs.
L   (lacto vegetarian)—Recipes contain dairy products, but no eggs.
O   (ovo vegetarian)—Recipes contain eggs, but no dairy products.

INGREDIENT INFORMATION

The ingredients in this book are readily available in supermarkets and health food stores. Following is helpful information on some of the ingredients we've used.

Butter—Butter is suggested as an alternate for margarine for its lack of trans-fats and improved flavor, except in Vegan recipes.

Cream Cheese—The block-type of reduced-fat and fat-free cream cheese is usually specified in the recipes in this book; the tub type is much softer in texture and does not always work the same in recipes. If substituting fat-free cream cheese in your favorite recipes for dips, use the block type and add any liquid ingredients gradually, as the cream cheese thins much more quickly than full-fat or reduced-fat cream cheese. Fat-free cream cheese can be used to make cake glaze but not frosting, as it thins with the addition of powdered sugar and cannot be thickened.

Cooking Sprays—Vegetable and olive oil cooking sprays are used to greatly reduce the amounts of oil or fat needed in recipes.

Herbs and Spices—In most recipes, dried herbs are called for, but where fresh are used, an amount for dried is also given. As a general rule, fresh herbs may be substituted for dried by using two to three times as much as indicated for the dried version.

Margarine—Use an all-vegetable product that is trans-fat free. Use regular rather than diet or "soft" margarine, as they do not perform well in baking.

Shortening—The manufacturing process of shortening usually creates trans-fats; shop carefully for one of the new trans-fat free brands.

Enjoy your slow cooking adventures!

ONE

Appetizers and Beverages

Garlic-Rosemary Cashews

This recipe is delicious made with any type of nut. Store in airtight container.

24 servings (¼ cup each)

6 cups cashews
3 tablespoons margarine or butter, melted
1 tablespoon sugar
3 tablespoons crushed dried rosemary leaves
¾ teaspoon cayenne pepper
½ teaspoon garlic powder

Per Serving:
Calories: 212
% of calories from fat: 69
Fat (gm): 17.3
Saturated fat (gm): 3.4
Cholesterol (mg): 0.0
Sodium (mg): 22
Protein (gm): 5
Carbohydrate (gm): 12.0
Exchanges:
Milk: 0.0
Vegetable: 0.0
Fruit: 0.0
Bread: 1.0
Meat: 0.0
Fat: 3.0

1. Heat slow cooker on high 15 minutes; add cashews. Drizzle margarine over cashews and toss; sprinkle with combined remaining ingredients and toss. Cover and cook on low 2 hours, stirring every hour. Turn heat to high; uncover and cook 30 minutes, stirring after 15 minutes. Turn heat to low to keep warm for serving or remove from slow cooker and cool.

Garlic-Pepper Almonds

Try a mixture of coarsely ground black, red, and green peppercorns for a gourmet touch!

24 servings (about ¼ cup each)

6 cups whole unblanched almonds
4 tablespoons margarine or butter, melted
3 cloves garlic, minced
2–3 teaspoons coarse ground pepper

Per Serving:
Calories: 155
% of calories from fat: 76
Fat (gm): 13.9
Saturated fat (gm): 1.3
Cholesterol (mg): 0.0
Sodium (mg): 23
Protein (gm): 5
Carbohydrate (gm): 4.9
Exchanges:
Milk: 0.0
Vegetable: 0.0
Fruit: 0.0
Bread: 0.0
Meat: 1.0
Fat: 3.0

1. Heat slow cooker on high 15 minutes; add almonds. Drizzle margarine over almonds and toss; sprinkle with garlic and pepper and toss. Cover and cook on low 2 hours, stirring every 30 minutes. Turn heat to high; uncover and cook 30 minutes, stirring after 15 minutes. Turn heat to low to keep warm for serving or remove from slow cooker and cool.

Sugar-Glazed Five-Spice Pecans

V *A sugar-glazed treat that's hard to resist!!*

24 servings (about ¼ cup each)

8 tablespoons margarine or butter, melted
½ cup powdered sugar
1 teaspoon ground cinnamon
¾ teaspoon five-spice powder
6 cups pecan halves

Per Serving:
Calories: 230
% of calories from fat: 86
Fat (gm): 23.4
Saturated fat (gm): 2.4
Cholesterol (mg): 0.0
Sodium (mg): 44
Protein (gm): 3
Carbohydrate (gm): 6.0
Exchanges:
Milk: 0.0
Vegetable: 0.0
Fruit: 0.0
Bread: 0.0
Meat: 0.0
Fat: 5.0

1. Heat slow cooker on high 15 minutes. Mix margarine, sugar, and spices; pour over pecans in large bowl and toss. Transfer mixture to slow cooker; cover and cook on high 30 minutes; uncover and cook until pecans are crisply glazed, 45 to 60 minutes, stirring every 20 minutes. Pour pecans in single layer on jelly roll pans and cool.

Variation

Pumpkin-Glazed Nuts—Make recipe as above, substituting 1 teaspoon pumpkin pie spice for the five-spice powder and mixed nuts for the pecans.

Curry-Spiced Mixed Nuts

V *The blend of sweet and savory flavors is delicious.*

24 servings (about ¼ cup each)

6 cups mixed nuts
4 tablespoons margarine or butter, melted
2 tablespoons sugar
1½ teaspoons curry powder
1 teaspoon each: garlic powder, ground cinnamon

Per Serving:
Calories: 225
% of calories from fat: 73
Fat (gm): 19.5
Saturated fat (gm): 2.7
Cholesterol (mg): 0.0
Sodium (mg): 26
Protein (gm): 6
Carbohydrate (gm): 19.5
Exchanges:
Milk: 0.0
Vegetable: 0.0
Fruit: 0.0
Bread: 0.5
Meat: 0.0
Fat: 4.0

1. Heat slow cooker on high 15 minutes; add nuts. Drizzle margarine over nuts and toss; sprinkle with combined remaining ingredients and toss. Cover and cook on low 2 hours, stirring every 20 minutes. Turn heat to high; uncover and cook 30 minutes, stirring after 15 minutes. Turn heat to low to keep warm for serving or remove from slow cooker and cool.

Sweet Curried Soy Nuts

V *Peanuts, walnuts, blanched almonds, or pecans can be substituted for the soy nuts.*

24 servings (¼ cup each)

4 tablespoons margarine or butter, melted
6 cups roasted soy nuts
1½ tablespoons sugar
1 tablespoon curry powder
Salt, to taste

Per Serving:
Calories: 186
% of calories from fat: 46
Fat (gm): 9.5
Saturated fat (gm): 1.6
Cholesterol (mg): 0.3
Sodium (mg): 26
Protein (gm): 16
Carbohydrate (gm): 9.5
Exchanges:
Milk: 0.0
Vegetable: 0.0
Fruit: 0.0
Bread: 0.0
Meat: 2.0
Fat: 2.0

1. Heat slow cooker on high 15 minutes. Drizzle margarine over soy nuts in large bowl and toss; sprinkle with combined remaining ingredients, except salt, and toss. Transfer to slow cooker; cover and cook on low 2 hours, stirring every 15 minutes. Turn heat to high; remove lid and cook 30 minutes, stirring after 15 minutes. Season to taste with salt. Turn heat to low to keep warm for serving or remove from slow cooker and cool.

Soy Noshers

V *Healthy soy beans and dried cranberries star in this savory-sweet snack mix.*

8 servings (about ⅓ cup each)

1½ cups roasted soy beans
½ cup each: wheat squares cereal, mini pretzel twists
1 cup dried cranberries or blueberries
Vegetable cooking spray
¾ teaspoon each: crushed dried rosemary and
    thyme leaves
Garlic salt, to taste

Per Serving:
Calories: 196
% of calories from fat: 28
Fat (gm): 6.4
Saturated fat (gm): 1
Cholesterol (mg): 0.0
Sodium (mg): 93
Protein (gm): 12
Carbohydrate (gm): 25
Exchanges:
Milk: 0.0
Vegetable: 0.0
Fruit: 0.5
Bread: 1.0
Meat: 1.0
Fat: 1.0

1. Heat slow cooker on high 15 minutes; add soy beans, cereal, pretzels, and cranberries. Spray mixture generously with cooking spray and toss; sprinkle with herbs and toss. Cover and cook on low 2 hours, stirring every 20 minutes. Turn heat to high; uncover and cook 30 minutes, stirring after 15 minutes. Season to taste with garlic salt. Turn heat to low to keep warm for serving or remove from slow cooker and cool.

Gorp, by Golly!

 A great snack mix for curing the munchies or for sharing with a gathering of friends.

16 servings (about ½ cup each)

3 cups low-fat granola
2 cups pretzel goldfish
½ cup sesame sticks, broken into halves
3 cups coarsely chopped mixed dried fruit
Butter-flavored cooking spray
1 teaspoon ground cinnamon
½ teaspoon ground nutmeg

Per Serving:
Calories: 172
% of calories from fat: 13
Fat (gm): 2.6
Saturated fat (gm): 0.2
Cholesterol (mg): 0
Sodium (mg): 82
Protein (gm): 2.7
Carbohydrate (gm): 37.8
Exchanges:
Milk: 0.0
Vegetable: 0.0
Fruit: 2.0
Bread: 0.5
Meat: 0.0
Fat: 0.5

1. Heat slow cooker on high 15 minutes; add granola, goldfish, sesame sticks, and dried fruit. Spray mixture generously with cooking spray and toss; sprinkle with combined spices and toss. Cook, uncovered, on high 1½ hours, stirring every 30 minutes. Turn slow cooker to low to keep warm for serving or remove from slow cooker and cool.

Hot Stuff!

 If this snack mix is not hot enough for you, add a few sprinkles of red pepper sauce!

16 servings (about ½ cup each)

4 cups baked pita chips
2 cups oyster crackers
½ cup dry-roasted smoked almonds
1 cup each: coarsely chopped mixed dried fruit, dried pineapple chunks
Butter-flavored cooking spray
1 teaspoon each: dried oregano leaves, garlic powder, chili powder, cayenne pepper, black pepper

Per Serving:
Calories: 120
% of calories from fat: 22
Fat (gm): 3.2
Saturated fat (gm): 0.2
Cholesterol (mg): 0
Sodium (mg): 160
Protein (gm): 3.2
Carbohydrate (gm): 21.7
Exchanges:
Milk: 0.0
Vegetable: 0.0
Fruit: 0.5
Bread: 1.0
Meat: 0.0
Fat: 0.5

1. Heat slow cooker on high for 15 minutes; add pita chips, crackers, almonds, and dried fruit. Spray mixture generously with cooking spray and toss; sprinkle with combined herbs and pepper and toss. Cook, uncovered, on high 1½ hours, stirring every 30 minutes. Turn slow cooker to low to keep warm for serving or remove from slow cooker and cool.

Favorite Party Mix

Choose cereals with different shapes to make this snack interesting.

16 servings (about ½ cup each)

5 cups assorted cereal (rice, oats, and wheat)
1½ cups each: small pretzels, sesame sticks,
   mixed nuts
¼ cup margarine or butter, melted
3 tablespoons Worcestershire sauce
1 teaspoon hot pepper sauce
1 tablespoon dried minced onion
½ teaspoon garlic powder
Salt, to taste

Per Serving:
Calories: 175
% of calories from fat: 54
Fat (gm): 10.8
Saturated fat (gm): 1.6
Cholesterol (mg): 0.0
Sodium (mg): 245
Protein (gm): 4
Carbohydrate (gm): 17.0
Exchanges:
Milk: 0.0
Vegetable: 0.0
Fruit: 0.0
Bread: 0.0
Meat: 0.0
Fat: 2.0

1. Heat slow cooker on high 15 minutes; add cereal, pretzels, sesame sticks, and mixed nuts; drizzle with combined remaining ingredients, except salt, and toss. Cook, uncovered, on high 1½ hours, stirring every 30 minutes. Season to taste with salt. Turn slow cooker to low to keep warm for serving or remove from slow cooker and cool.

Hot Curried Party Mix

v *Lots of crunch and lots of flavor!!*

10 servings (about ½ cup each)

3 cups rice cereal squares
1 cup sesame sticks
½ cup each: cashews, honey roasted peanuts,
   wasabi peas
2 tablespoons margarine or butter, melted
1½ teaspoons each: soy sauce, curry powder, sugar

Per Serving:
Calories: 147
% of calories from fat: 55
Fat (gm): 9.1
Saturated fat (gm): 1.7
Cholesterol (mg): 0.0
Sodium (mg): 215
Protein (gm): 3
Carbohydrate (gm): 13.9
Exchanges:
Milk: 0.0
Vegetable: 0.0
Fruit: 0.0
Bread: 1.0
Meat: 0.0
Fat: 2.0

1. Heat slow cooker on high 15 minutes; add cereal, sesame sticks, nuts, and wasabi peas. Drizzle mixture with combined margarine and soy sauce and toss; sprinkle with combined curry powder and sugar and toss. Cook, uncovered, on high 1½ hours, stirring every 30 minutes. Turn slow cooker to low to keep warm for serving or remove from slow cooker and cool.

"Go Fish" Party Mix

V *A colorful snack mix, with lots of variety!*

16 servings (about ½ cup each)

3 cups each: corn cereal squares, colored
    goldfish crackers
1½ cups each: potato sticks, peanuts
¼ cup margarine or butter, melted
½ teaspoon hot pepper sauce
1 tablespoon dried Italian seasoning
½–1 teaspoon garlic salt

Per Serving:
Calories: 179
% of calories from fat: 60
Fat (gm): 12.4
Saturated fat (gm): 2.2
Cholesterol (mg): 1.3
Sodium (mg): 199
Protein (gm): 5
Carbohydrate (gm): 14.3
Exchanges:
Milk: 0.0
Vegetable: 0.0
Fruit: 0.0
Bread: 1.0
Meat: 0.0
Fat: 2.5

1. Heat slow cooker on high 15 minutes; add cereal,
crackers, potato sticks, and peanuts. Drizzle with
combined remaining ingredients and toss. Cook,
uncovered, on high 1½ hours, stirring every 30 minutes. Turn slow cooker
to low to keep warm for serving or remove from slow cooker and cool.

Chutney Cheese Dip

L *Enjoy these Indian-inspired flavors.*

16 servings (about ¼ cup each)

1 pound reduced-fat cream cheese, room temperature
2 cups (8 ounces) shredded reduced-fat Cheddar
    cheese
½ cup chopped mango chutney, divided
⅓ cup finely chopped onion
¼ cup chopped raisins
2–4 teaspoons each: finely chopped gingerroot,
    garlic
1–2 teaspoons curry powder
Dippers: baked pita chips, assorted vegetables

Per Serving:
Calories: 116
% of calories from fat: 52
Fat (gm): 7.0
Saturated fat (gm): 4.4
Cholesterol (mg): 23.3
Sodium (mg): 274
Protein (gm): 6.4
Carbohydrate (gm): 8.1
Exchanges:
Milk: 0.0
Vegetable: 0.0
Fruit: 0.0
Bread: 1.0
Meat: 1.0
Fat: 2.5

1. Place cheeses in 1½-quart slow cooker; cover and cook until cheese is
melted, about 30 minutes. Mix in remaining ingredients, except dippers;
cover and cook until hot, 1 to 1½ hours. Serve with dippers (not included
in nutritional data).

Hot Artichoke Dip

LO

Everyone's favorite party dip!

16 servings (about 3 tablespoons each)

1 can (15 ounces) artichoke hearts, drained,
   finely chopped
4 ounces reduced-fat cream cheese, room temperature
½ cup each: grated Parmesan cheese, reduced-fat
   mayonnaise and sour cream
1–2 teaspoons lemon juice
1 green onion, thinly sliced
2 teaspoons minced garlic
Salt and cayenne pepper, to taste
Dippers: assorted vegetables, bread sticks, crackers

Per Serving:
Calories: 60
% of calories from fat: 62
Fat (gm): 4.2
Saturated fat (gm): 1.6
Cholesterol (mg): 7.6
Sodium (mg): 214
Protein (gm): 2
Carbohydrate (gm): 3.7
Exchanges:
Milk: 0.0
Vegetable: 1.0
Fruit: 0.0
Bread: 0.0
Meat: 0.0
Fat: 1.0

1. Place cheese in 1½-quart slow cooker; cover and cook until cheese is melted, about 30 minutes. Mix in remaining ingredients, except salt, cayenne pepper, and dippers; cover and cook until hot, 1 to 1½ hours. Season to taste with salt and cayenne pepper. Serve with dippers (not included in nutritional data).

Variations

Spinach and Artichoke Dip—Make recipe as above, adding ½ cup well drained, thawed, frozen chopped spinach and ¼ cup chopped roasted red pepper.

Artichoke and Shrimp Dip—Make recipe as above, adding ½ cup chopped shrimp and 1 to 2 tablespoons drained capers.

Hot Crab and Artichoke Dip—Make recipe as above, adding 12 ounces coarsely chopped crab and 2 tablespoons chopped pickled jalapeño chili.

Pepperoni Cheese Dip

Salami, ham, or smoked turkey can be substituted for the pepperoni.

10 servings (about 3 tablespoons each)

1 package (8 ounces) soft-style cream cheese
with onions and chives
1½ cups (6 ounces) shredded reduced-fat Swiss cheese
1 package (3½ ounces) sliced pepperoni, chopped
½ cup chopped green pepper
¼ teaspoon cayenne pepper
½–⅔ cup whole milk
Dippers: assorted vegetables, crackers, bread sticks

Per Serving:
Calories: 165
% of calories from fat: 70
Fat (gm): 12.2
Saturated fat (gm): 7.3
Cholesterol (mg): 41.3
Sodium (mg): 331
Protein (gm): 8
Carbohydrate (gm): 4.0
Exchanges:
Milk: 0.0
Vegetable: 0.0
Fruit: 0.0
Bread: 0.0
Meat: 1.0
Fat: 2.0

1. Place cheeses in 1½-quart slow cooker; cover and cook until cheeses are melted, about 30 minutes. Mix in remaining ingredients, except dippers; cover and cook until hot, about 1½ hours. Serve with dippers (not included in nutritional data).

Pizza Dip

All the flavors of pizza in a creamy dip!

12 servings (about ¼ cup each)

1 pound reduced-fat processed cheese, cubed
2 cups (8 ounces) shredded reduced-fat mozzarella
cheese
1½ cups pizza sauce
⅓ cup sliced ripe olives
2 teaspoons dried Italian seasoning
1 package (3½ ounces) sliced pepperoni, chopped
Dippers: tortilla chips, carrot and celery sticks

Per Serving:
Calories: 180
% of calories from fat: 53
Fat (gm): 10.5
Saturated fat (gm): 5.8
Cholesterol (mg): 35.6
Sodium (mg): 985
Protein (gm): 13
Carbohydrate (gm): 8.1
Exchanges:
Milk: 0.0
Vegetable: 0.0
Fruit: 0.0
Bread: 0.0
Meat: 2.0
Fat: 2.0

1. Place cheeses in 1½-quart slow cooker; cover and cook until cheese is melted, about 30 minutes. Mix in remaining ingredients, except dippers; cover and cook until hot, 1 to 1½ hours. Serve with dippers (not included in nutritional data).

Variation

Pizza Dip Supreme—Make recipe as above, adding 1 cup cooked crumbled ground beef or Italian sausage and ⅓ cup each chopped onion and green bell pepper.

Reuben Dip

All the favorite sandwich flavors, ready for dipping!

24 servings (about ¼ cup each)

12 ounces reduced-fat cream cheese, room
   temperature
1 cup (8 ounces) shredded reduced-fat Swiss cheese
1½ cups fresh sauerkraut, rinsed, drained
1 cup chopped lean corned beef
¼ cup reduced-fat 1,000 island salad dressing
2 tablespoons snipped fresh or dried chives
2 teaspoons caraway seeds, lightly crushed
Dippers: halved rye cocktail bread, assorted vegetables

Per Serving:
Calories: 58
% of calories from fat: 50
Fat (gm): 3.2
Saturated fat (gm): 1.8
Cholesterol (mg): 13.1
Sodium (mg): 230
Protein (gm): 5
Carbohydrate (gm): 2.2
Exchanges:
Milk: 0.0
Vegetable: 0.0
Fruit: 0.0
Bread: 0.0
Meat: 1.0
Fat: 0.0

1. Place cheeses in 1½-quart slow cooker; cover and cook until cheeses are melted, about 30 minutes. Mix in remaining ingredients, except dippers; cover and cook until hot, 1 to 1½ hours. Serve with dippers (not included in nutritional data).

Dried Beef and Onion Dip

This warm, creamy dip can also be served cold—just beat cream cheese and sour cream until smooth and mix in remaining ingredients.

16 servings (about 3 tablespoons each)

12 ounces reduced-fat cream cheese, room
   temperature
¾ cup reduced-fat mayonnaise
1 package (4½ ounces) dried beef, chopped
⅓ cup thinly sliced green onions
2 tablespoons dried onion flakes
1 teaspoon garlic salt
Dippers: crackers, assorted vegetables, bread sticks

Per Serving:
Calories: 86
% of calories from fat: 62
Fat (gm): 6.0
Saturated fat (gm): 2.2
Cholesterol (mg): 16.3
Sodium (mg): 468
Protein (gm): 4.6
Carbohydrate (gm): 3.8
Exchanges:
Milk: 0.0
Vegetable: 0.0
Fruit: 0.0
Bread: 0.0
Meat: 1.0
Fat: 0.5

1. Place cream cheese in 1½-quart slow cooker; cover and cook until cheese is melted, about 30 minutes. Mix in remaining ingredients, except dippers; cover and cook until hot, 1 to 1½ hours. Serve with dippers (not included in nutritional data).

Toasted Onion Dip

This dip brings back memories of the popular dip made with onion soup mix! Toasting the dried onion flakes is the flavor secret. The dip can also be served at room temperature.

24 servings (about 2 tablespoons each)

6–8 tablespoons dried onion flakes
1 pound reduced-fat cream cheese, room temperature
⅔ cup each: reduced-fat plain yogurt and
    mayonnaise
4 small green onions, chopped
3 cloves garlic, minced
½ teaspoon beef bouillon crystals
½–¾ cup 2% reduced-fat milk, divided
1–2 teaspoons lemon juice
4–6 drops red pepper sauce
Salt and white pepper, to taste
Dippers: assorted vegetable relishes, bread sticks

Per Serving:
Calories: 66
% of calories from fat: 60
Fat (gm): 4.5
Saturated fat (gm): 2.0
Cholesterol (mg): 9.5
Sodium (mg): 166
Protein (gm): 2
Carbohydrate (gm): 4.2
Exchanges:
Milk: 0.0
Vegetable: 0.0
Fruit: 0.0
Bread: 0.0
Meat: 0.0
Fat: 1.0

1. Cook onion flakes in small skillet over medium to medium-low heat until toasted, 3 to 4 minutes, stirring frequently; remove from heat. Place cream cheese in 1½-quart slow cooker; cover and cook until cheese is melted, about 30 minutes. Mix in yogurt, mayonnaise, green onions, garlic, bouillon, onion flakes, and ½ cup milk; cover and cook until hot, 1 to 1½ hours. Season to taste with lemon juice, pepper sauce, salt, and white pepper; stir in remaining ¼ cup milk if desired for consistency. Serve with dippers (not included in nutritional data).

Roasted Garlic and Three-Cheese Dip

L

Using roasted garlic in jars makes this recipe extra easy. This dip can also be a spread; beat cheeses until blended and mix in garlic, pepper, and milk.

24 servings (about 2 tablespoons each)

1 pound reduced-fat cream cheese, room temperature
4 ounces goat cheese
½ cup (2 ounces) grated Parmesan cheese
2–3 tablespoons minced roasted garlic
¼ teaspoon white pepper
½–¾ cup 2% reduced-fat milk, divided
Dippers: vegetable relishes and assorted crackers

Per Serving:
Calories: 43
% of calories from fat: 28
Fat (gm): 1.3
Saturated fat (gm): 0.9
Cholesterol (mg): 3.8
Sodium (mg): 142
Protein (gm): 4.7
Carbohydrate (gm): 2.5
Exchanges:
Milk: 0.0
Vegetable: 0.0
Fruit: 0.0
Bread: 0.0
Meat: 0.5
Fat: 0.5

1. Place cream cheese and goat cheese in 1½-quart slow cooker; cover and cook until cheese is melted, about 30 minutes. Mix in Parmesan cheese, roasted garlic, white pepper, and ½ cup milk; cover and cook until hot, 1 to 1½ hours. Stir in remaining ¼ cup milk, if desired for consistency. Serve with dippers (not included in nutritional data).

Chili con Queso

L

If you prefer a dip that is less "hot," substitute green bell peppers and 2 to 3 teaspoons minced jalapeño chili for the poblano chilies.

12 servings (about ¼ cup each)

2 small poblano chilies, halved
2 cups (8 ounces) shredded reduced-fat processed cheese
1 cup (4 ounces) shredded reduced-fat sharp Cheddar cheese
⅓ cup each: finely chopped onion, tomato
½ teaspoon dried oregano leaves
2–4 tablespoons 2% reduced-fat milk
Tortilla chips

Per Serving:
Calories: 72
% of calories from fat: 26
Fat (gm): 2.8
Saturated fat (gm): 1.8
Cholesterol (mg): 9.1
Sodium (mg): 412
Protein (gm): 7.4
Carbohydrate (gm): 5.7
Exchanges:
Milk: 0.0
Vegetable: 0.0
Fruit: 0.0;
Bread: 0.5
Meat: 1.0
Fat: 0.0

1. Place chilies, skin sides up, on baking pan. Bake at 425 degrees until chilies are browned and soft, about 20 minutes. Cool; discard seeds and stems and chop coarsely.
2. Place cheeses in 1½-quart slow cooker; cover and cook until cheeses are melted, about 30 minutes. Add remaining ingredients, except tortilla chips; cover and cook until hot, 1 to 1½ hours. Serve with tortilla chips (not included in nutritional data).

Black Bean and Green Chili con Queso

LO *This dip is fiery! Reduce the amount of crushed red pepper and/or omit the red pepper sauce for a milder dip.*

16 servings (about ¼ cup each)

8 ounces each: cubed reduced-fat pepper-Jack
  cheese and cream cheese, room temperature
1 cup reduced-fat mayonnaise
½ cup (2 ounces) grated Parmesan cheese
¾ cup drained, canned black beans
1 can (4 ounces) diced green chilies, undrained
2 cloves garlic, minced
2 teaspoons crushed red pepper
½–1 teaspoon red pepper sauce
Dippers: tortilla chips, assorted vegetables

Per Serving:
Calories: 125
% of calories from fat: 61
Fat (gm): 8.8
Saturated fat (gm): 3.5
Cholesterol (mg): 16.3
Sodium (mg): 377
Protein (gm): 7
Carbohydrate (gm): 5.8
Exchanges:
Milk: 0.0
Vegetable: 0.0
Fruit: 0.0
Bread: 0.0
Meat: 1.0
Fat: 1.0

1. Place cheeses in 1½-quart slow cooker; cover and cook until cheeses are melted, about 30 minutes. Mix in remaining ingredients, except dippers; cover and cook until hot, 1 to 1½ hours. Serve with dippers (not included in nutritional data).

Variation

Black Bean and Chorizo con Queso—Make recipe as above, omitting green chilies, crushed red pepper, and red pepper sauce. Add ¼ recipe Chorizo (see p. 166) and 1 to 2 teaspoons pickled jalapeño chilies.

Queso Fundido

The Chorizo can be used in many Mexican recipes; for best flavor, make Chorizo several hours in advance and refrigerate, so flavors meld.

16 servings (about 3 tablespoons each)

1½ cups (6 ounces) shredded reduced-fat Cheddar
  cheese
1 cup (4 ounces) cubed reduced-fat processed cheese
½ roasted red pepper, chopped
½–⅔ cup 2% reduced-fat milk
1 cup Chorizo (¼ recipe) (see p. 166)
16 flour or corn tortillas (6-inch), warm
Thinly sliced green onion and chopped cilantro, as
  garnish

Per Serving:
Calories: 182
% of calories from fat: 33
Fat (gm): 6.6
Saturated fat (gm): 2.9
Cholesterol (mg): 22.8
Sodium (mg): 459
Protein (gm): 12
Carbohydrate (gm): 18.6
Exchanges:
Milk: 0.0
Vegetable: 0.0
Fruit: 0.0
Bread: 2.0
Meat: 2.0
Fat: 0.0

1. Place cheeses in 1½-quart slow cooker; cover and cook until cheeses are melted, about 30 minutes. Mix in remaining ingredients, except tortillas and garnishes; cover and cook until hot, 1 to 1½ hours. Spoon about 3 tablespoons cheese mixture in the center of each tortilla. Sprinkle with green onion and cilantro, and roll up.

Refried Bean Dip

L

Refried black beans can also be used in this south-of-the border dip.

16 servings (about ¼ cup each)

2 cups (8 ounces) cubed mild Mexican-style
  processed cheese
2 cans (16 ounces each) refried beans
¼ cup each: taco sauce, chopped green onions
1–2 tablespoons chopped pickled jalapeño chilies
Dippers: tortilla chips, assorted vegetables

1. Place cheese in 1½-quart slow cooker; cover and cook until cheese is melted, about 30 minutes. Mix in remaining ingredients, except dippers; cover and cook until hot, 1 to 1½ hours. Serve with dippers (not included in nutritional data).

Per Serving:
Calories: 101
% of calories from fat: 34
Fat (gm): 3.8
Saturated fat (gm): 2.3
Cholesterol (mg): 17.0
Sodium (mg): 406
Protein (gm): 6
Carbohydrate (gm): 10.8
Exchanges:
Milk: 0.0
Vegetable: 0.0
Fruit: 0.0
Bread: 1.0
Meat: 0.0
Fat: 1.0

Spicy Cheese and Seafood Dip

Pepper-Jack cheese adds a definite hot accent to this very easy dip.

8 servings (about 3 tablespoons each)

8 ounces each: cubed reduced-fat pepper-Jack cheese
  and room-temperature cream cheese
¾ cup whole milk
1 cup each: chopped, cooked shrimp and crab
¼ cup chopped pitted green olives
Dippers: assorted vegetables, crackers, bread sticks

1. Place cheeses in 1½-quart slow cooker; cover and cook until cheese is melted, about 30 minutes. Mix in remaining ingredients, except dippers; cover and cook until hot, 1 to 1½ hours. Serve with dippers (not included in nutritional data).

Per Serving:
Calories: 179
% of calories from fat: 57
Fat (gm): 11.6
Saturated fat (gm): 6.7
Cholesterol (mg): 70.7
Sodium (mg): 667
Protein (gm): 16
Carbohydrate (gm): 3.8
Exchanges:
Milk: 0.0
Vegetable: 0.0
Fruit: 0.0
Bread: 0.0
Meat: 2.0
Fat: 1.0

Variation

Easy Jack Shrimp Dip—Make recipe as above, substituting reduced-fat pepper-Jack cheese for the cream cheese, shrimp for the crab, and black olives for the green olives.

Smoked Salmon Dip

Any smoked fish can be substituted for the salmon in this recipe.

16 servings (about 3 tablespoons each)

8 ounces reduced-fat cream cheese, room
  temperature
1½ cups reduced-fat mayonnaise
1 can (14 ounces) artichoke hearts, drained, chopped
12 ounces packaged or canned smoked salmon
½ cup (2 ounces) grated Parmesan cheese
¼ cup drained capers
1 tablespoon minced garlic
3–4 dashes hot pepper sauce
Dippers: assorted vegetables, crackers

Per Serving:
Calories: 145
% of calories from fat: 66
Fat (gm): 11.0
Saturated fat (gm): 2.3
Cholesterol (mg): 13.7
Sodium (mg): 576
Protein (gm): 6
Carbohydrate (gm): 6.4
Exchanges:
Milk: 0.0
Vegetable: 0.0
Fruit: 0.0
Bread: 0.5
Meat: 1.0
Fat: 1.0

1. Place cream cheese in 1½-quart slow cooker; cover and cook until cheese is melted, about 30 minutes. Mix in remaining ingredients, except dippers; cover and cook until hot, 1 to 1½ hours. Serve with dippers (not included in nutritional data).

Variation

Smoked Whitefish Dip—Make recipe as above, omitting artichoke hearts; substitute 4 ounces goat cheese for the cream cheese, ¾ cup reduced-fat sour cream for ¾ cup mayonnaise, and smoked whitefish for the salmon.

Eggplant Caviar

L

Middle Eastern flavors will tempt you to second helpings!

6 servings (about 2 tablespoons each)

1 large eggplant (about 1½ pounds)
½ cup finely chopped tomato
¼ cup each: finely chopped onion,
    reduced-fat yogurt
3 cloves garlic, minced
2 tablespoons olive oil
½ teaspoon dried oregano leaves
1–2 tablespoons lemon juice
Salt and pepper, to taste
Dippers: lavosh or pita bread wedges

Per Serving:
Calories: 59
% of calories from fat: 28
Fat (gm): 2.1
Saturated fat (gm): 0.3
Cholesterol (mg): 0.2
Sodium (mg): 19.1
Protein (gm): 1.8
Carbohydrate (gm): 10.1
Exchanges:
Milk: 0.0
Vegetable: 1.5
Fruit: 0.0
Bread: 0.0
Meat: 0.0
Fat: 0.5

1. Pierce eggplant in several places with fork and place in slow cooker; cover and cook on low until tender, 4 to 5 hours. Cool to room temperature.
2. Cut eggplant in half; scoop out pulp with spoon. Mash eggplant and mix with remaining ingredients, except lemon juice, salt, pepper, and dippers. Season to taste with lemon juice, salt, and pepper. Serve with dippers (not included in nutritional data).

Cheese Fondue

L

Substitute other cheeses for the Swiss, if you like.

12 servings (about ¼ cup each)

2 cups (8 ounces) shredded reduced-fat Swiss cheese
1 tablespoon flour
8 ounces reduced-fat cream cheese, room temperature
¾ cup dry white wine or apple juice
1 clove garlic, minced
Cayenne pepper, to taste
Dippers: cubed French bread, assorted vegetables

Per Serving:
Calories: 83
% of calories from fat: 44
Fat (gm): 3.6
Saturated fat (gm): 2.4
Cholesterol (mg): 15.2
Sodium (mg): 136
Protein (gm): 7
Carbohydrate (gm): 2.8
Exchanges:
Milk: 0.0
Vegetable: 0.0
Fruit: 0.0
Bread: 0.0
Meat: 1.0
Fat: 0.5

1. Toss Swiss cheese with flour. Combine cheeses, wine, and garlic in 1½-quart slow cooker; cover and cook until cheeses are melted and fondue is hot, 1 to 1½ hours. Season to taste with cayenne pepper; serve with dippers (not included in nutritional data). If fondue becomes too thick, stir in additional wine or milk.

Variations

Bacon-Chipotle Fondue—Make recipe as above, adding ¼ to ½ cup crisply cooked, crumbled bacon and 1 to 2 teaspoons finely chopped chipotle chilies in adobo sauce.

Blue Cheese Fondue—Make recipe as above, substituting 3 ounces crumbled blue cheese for 3 ounces of the cream cheese; add ¼ cup thinly sliced green onions and 2 cloves minced garlic.

Shrimp Fondue—Make recipe as above, substituting 1 cup shredded Cheddar cheese for the Swiss cheese. Stir 8 ounces chopped cooked shrimp into the fondue during last 15 minutes of cooking time.

Tomato Cheddar Fondue

L *For extra spiciness, use Rotel brand tomatoes.*

16 servings (about 3 tablespoons each)

1 pound mild Mexican-style processed cheese, cubed
1 can (14½ ounces) stewed tomatoes, undrained
½ cup sliced black or green olives
1 large clove garlic, minced
Dippers: tortilla chips, assorted vegetables

1. Place cheese in 1½-quart slow cooker; cover and cook until cheese is melted, about 30 minutes. Mix in remaining ingredients, except dippers; cover and cook until hot, about 1½ hours. Serve with dippers (not included in nutritional data).

Per Serving:
Calories: 102
% of calories from fat: 58
Fat (gm): 6.4
Saturated fat (gm): 4.1
Cholesterol (mg): 25.0
Sodium (mg): 513
Protein (gm): 5
Carbohydrate (gm): 5.2
Exchanges:
Milk: 0.0
Vegetable: 0.0
Fruit: 0.0
Bread: 0.0
Meat: 1.0
Fat: 1.0

Black Bean Cheesecake with Salsa

LO

This fabulous appetizer can also be served in larger pieces as a brunch or supper entrée—sauté wedges of cheesecake in lightly greased large skillet over medium-low heat until warm and browned on both sides. Serve with salsa.

24 servings

⅓ cup unseasoned dry bread crumbs
24 ounces reduced-fat cream cheese, room
  temperature
6 eggs
1 can (15 ounces) black beans, rinsed, drained
½ jalapeño chili, finely chopped
2 tablespoons finely chopped onion
2 cloves garlic, minced
2 teaspoons dried cumin
½ teaspoon each: dried oregano leaves, chili powder,
  salt, cayenne pepper
1 cup salsa

Per Serving:
Calories: 251
% of calories from fat: 18
Fat (gm): 5.1
Saturated fat (gm): 1.6
Cholesterol (mg): 212
Sodium (mg): 715
Protein (gm): 15
Carbohydrate (gm): 35.1
Exchanges:
Milk: 0.0
Vegetable: 0.0
Fruit: 0.0
Bread: 2.5
Meat: 1.0
Fat: 0.5

1. Grease 7-inch springform pan and coat with bread crumbs. Beat cream cheese in large bowl until fluffy; beat in eggs. Mix in remaining ingredients, except salsa; pour into prepared pan and place on rack in 6-quart slow cooker. Place 3 layers of paper toweling over top of slow cooker; cover and cook on high until cheesecake is set and sharp knife inserted halfway between center and edge of cheesecake comes out almost clean, about 4 hours. Transfer crock to wire rack and cool 1 hour; remove cheesecake from crock and cool completely on wire rack. Refrigerate 8 hours or overnight.

Chicken Liver Pâté

This superb pate has a velvety texture and a hint of sweetness from the apple.

16 servings (about 3 tablespoons each)

1 pound chicken livers
¼ cup finely chopped onion
1 small apple, peeled, finely chopped
2–4 tablespoons brandy (optional)
½ cup unsalted margarine or butter, room
 temperature
Salt and cayenne pepper, to taste

Per Serving:
Calories: 89
% of calories from fat: 71
Fat (gm): 7.0
Saturated fat (gm): 1.5
Cholesterol (mg): 97.8
Sodium (mg): 20
Protein (gm): 5
Carbohydrate (gm): 1.5
Exchanges:
Milk: 0.0
Vegetable: 0.0
Fruit: 0.0
Bread: 0.0
Meat: 1.0
Fat: 2.0

1. Combine livers, onion, and apple in slow cooker; cover and cook on high until livers are no longer pink in the center, about 3 hours. Process liver mixture and brandy in food processor or blender until very smooth, adding margarine 2 tablespoons at a time. Season to taste with salt and cayenne pepper. Spoon into crock and refrigerate until chilled.

Ginger-Soy Chicken Wings

Five-spice powder, soy sauce, maple syrup, and fresh gingerroot combine for spectacular flavor.

8 servings

3 pounds disjointed chicken wings with tips
 removed (about 16)
⅓ cup soy sauce
1 tablespoon maple syrup
1 tablespoon minced gingerroot
3 cloves garlic, minced
1½ teaspoons five-spice powder
3 tablespoons sliced green onions
1 tablespoon sesame seeds, toasted

Per Serving:
Calories: 265
% of calories from fat: 9
Fat (gm): 2.8
Saturated fat (gm): 0.7
Cholesterol (mg): 33.2
Sodium (mg): 2158
Protein (gm): 15
Carbohydrate (gm): 45.3
Exchanges:
Milk: 0.0
Vegetable: 0.0
Fruit: 0.0
Bread: 3.0
Meat: 2.0
Fat: 0.0

1. Combine all ingredients, except green onions and sesame seeds in slow cooker; cover and cook on high 3 to 4 hours, draining off fat after 2 hours. Arrange chicken wings on platter; garnish with green onions and sesame seeds.

Teriyaki Chicken Wings

Cooked chicken wings can be broiled briefly after cooking if you want them to be browned.

8 servings

3 pounds chicken wings with wing tips removed, halved (about 16)
1½ cups packed light brown sugar
1 cup soy sauce
2 tablespoons hoisin sauce
1 teaspoon ground ginger
½ teaspoon garlic powder
1 tablespoon each: chopped parsley, toasted sesame seeds

Per Serving:
Calories: 95
% of calories from fat: 26
Fat (gm): 2.6
Saturated fat (gm): 0.6
Cholesterol (mg): 33.1
Sodium (mg): 724
Protein (gm): 14
Carbohydrate (gm): 3.5
Exchanges:
Milk: 0.0
Vegetable: 0.0
Fruit: 0.0
Bread: 0.0
Meat: 2.0
Fat: 0.0

1. Place chicken wings in slow cooker; pour combined remaining ingredients, except parsley and sesame seeds, over chicken wings. Cover and cook on high 3 to 4 hours. Sprinkle with parsley and sesame seeds.

Buffalo Chicken Wings

Everybody's favorite!

8 servings

4 tablespoons each: margarine or butter, hot pepper sauce
1 tablespoon white distilled vinegar
3 pounds chicken wings with wing tips removed, halved (about 16)
Salt and pepper, to taste
Blue Cheese Dressing (recipe follows)

Per Serving:
Calories: 159
% of calories from fat: 54
Fat (gm): 9.4
Saturated fat (gm): 2.4
Cholesterol (mg): 37.6
Sodium (mg): 552
Protein (gm): 14
Carbohydrate (gm): 4.1
Exchanges:
Milk: 0.0
Vegetable: 0.0
Fruit: 0.0
Bread: 0.0
Meat: 2.0
Fat: 1.0

1. Combine margarine, hot pepper sauce, and vinegar in slow cooker; turn heat to high and cook until margarine is melted, about 15 minutes.
2. Sprinkle chicken wings with salt and pepper; broil 6 inches from heat source until lightly browned, about 5 minutes on each side. Add to slow cooker and toss with margarine mixture; cover and cook on high 3 to 4 hours. Serve with Blue Cheese Dressing.

Blue Cheese Dressing

Makes about 1 cup

¾ cup reduced-fat mayonnaise or salad dressing
3 tablespoons crumbled blue cheese
1½ tablespoons red wine vinegar
1 teaspoon celery seeds
½ teaspoon salt
⅛ teaspoon each: cayenne and black pepper

1. Mix all ingredients.

Meatballs in Tomato Pasilla Chili Sauce

The meatballs can be made in advance and frozen; thaw before using.
Pasilla chilies are picante—use three only if you enjoy a truly hot sauce!

12 servings (2 meatballs each)

2–3 pasilla chilies
2 cans (16 ounces each) diced tomatoes, undrained
Salt, to taste
Jalapeño Meatballs (recipe follows)

Per Serving:
Calories: 96
% of calories from fat: 20
Fat (gm): 2.0
Saturated fat (gm): 0.8
Cholesterol (mg): 41.5
Sodium (mg): 325
Protein (gm): 10
Carbohydrate (gm): 8.5
Exchanges:
Milk: 0.0
Vegetable: 0.0
Fruit: 0.0
Bread: 0.5
Meat: 1.0
Fat: 0.0

1. Cook pasilla chilies in large lightly greased saucepan over medium heat until softened; discard stems, seeds, and veins. Process chilies and tomatoes with liquid in blender until smooth; season to taste with salt. Combine tomato mixture and meatballs in slow cooker; cover and cook on high until meatballs are cooked, about 4 hours. Turn heat to low to keep warm for serving.

Jalapeño Meatballs

Makes 24

8 ounces each: ground pork tenderloin, lean ground beef
1 egg
¼ cup each: seasoned dry bread crumbs, finely chopped onion
2 cloves garlic, minced
1 teaspoon each: minced jalapeño chili, dried oregano leaves
½ teaspoon salt

1. Mix all ingredients; shape into 24 meatballs.

Sweet–Sour Meatballs

This recipe can be made substituting 1 pound kielbasa, smoked sausage, or hot dogs for the Appetizer Meatballs.

12 servings (2 meatballs each)

Appetizer Meatballs (recipe follows)
2 cups chili sauce
1 cup apricot jelly
1 tablespoon each: Dijon mustard, lemon juice

1. Combine Appetizer Meatballs and remaining ingredients in slow cooker; cover and cook on high until meatballs are cooked, about 4 hours. Turn heat to low to keep warm for serving.

Per Serving:
Calories: 192
% of calories from fat: 12
Fat (gm): 2.6
Saturated fat (gm): 1.0
Cholesterol (mg): 41.1
Sodium (mg): 717
Protein (gm): 10
Carbohydrate (gm): 30.8
Exchanges:
Milk: 0.0
Vegetable: 0.0
Fruit: 0.0
Bread: 2.0
Meat: 1.0
Fat: 0.0

Appetizer Meatballs

Makes 24

1 pound lean ground beef
¼ cup unseasoned dry bread crumbs
1 egg
2 tablespoons dried minced onion
1 teaspoon garlic powder
½ teaspoon each: salt, pepper

1. Mix all ingredients; shape into 24 meatballs.

Island Barbecue Meatballs

Use your favorite barbecue sauce in this orange and pineapple accented appetizer.

12 servings (2 meatballs each)

Appetizer Meatballs (see p. 22)
2 cups barbecue sauce
1½ cups orange marmalade
¾ teaspoon ground allspice
1 can (8 ounces) pineapple tidbits, drained

Per Serving:
Calories: 208
% of calories from fat: 12
Fat (gm): 2.9
Saturated fat (gm): 1.1
Cholesterol (mg): 41.1
Sodium (mg): 1709
Protein (gm): 11
Carbohydrate (gm): 36.1
Exchanges:
Milk: 0.0
Vegetable: 0.0
Fruit: 0.0
Bread: 2.0
Meat: 1.0
Fat: 0.0

1. Combine Appetizer Meatballs and remaining ingredients in slow cooker; cover and cook on high until meatballs are cooked, about 4 hours. Turn heat to low to keep warm for serving.

Hot Mulled Cider

v *Slow cookers are great for making warm beverages and keeping them at a perfect serving temperature.*

16 servings (about ½ cup each)

2 quarts apple cider
½ cup packed light brown sugar
1½ teaspoons whole cloves
1 teaspoon whole allspice
2 whole cinnamon sticks
1 medium orange, sliced

Per Serving:
Calories: 93
% calories from fat: 2
Fat (gm): 0.2
Saturated fat (gm): 0
Cholesterol (mg): 0
Sodium (mg): 7
Protein (gm): 0.2
Carbohydrate (gm): 25
Exchanges:
Milk: 0.0
Vegetable: 0.0
Fruit: 1.5
Bread: 0.0
Meat: 0.0
Fat: 0.0

1. Combine all ingredients in slow cooker, tying spices in a cheesecloth bag; cover and cook on high 2 to 3 hours (if mixture begins to boil, turn heat to low). Remove spice bag; turn heat to low to keep warm for serving.

Variations
Ginger-Spiced Cider—Make recipe as above omitting brown sugar, spices, and orange slices; add eight ¼-inch slices gingerroot. Remove gingerroot with slotted spoon.

Herb-Scented Cider—Make recipe as above, omitting brown sugar, spices, and orange slices; add two four-inch sprigs fresh rosemary or lavender or 1 tablespoon dried rosemary or lavender leaves tied in a cheesecloth bag.

Apricot–Apple Cider—Make recipe as above, substituting 5 cups apricot nectar for 5 cups of the cider. At the end of cooking time, stir in ¼ to ½ cup apricot brandy (optional).

Cranberry Cider—Make recipe as above, omitting brown sugar and substituting 3 cups cranberry juice for 3 cups of the cider. Sweeten to taste with brown sugar or maple syrup.

Hot Spiced Wine—Make recipe as above, substituting 8 cups sweet red wine or sweet sherry for the apple cider.

Fruit Wassail

V *A warming hot drink, made with a blending of fruit juices, spiked with rum.*

12 servings (about ½ cup each)

2 cups each: cranberry juice, pineapple juice, orange juice
1 small orange, sliced
½ cup sugar
1 cinnamon stick
1 teaspoon whole allspice
¼–½ cup lemon juice
½ cup light rum (optional)

Per Serving:
Calories: 101
% of calories from fat: 1
Fat (gm): 0.1
Saturated fat (gm): 0.0
Cholesterol (mg): 0.0
Sodium (mg): 7
Protein (gm): 0.5
Carbohydrate (gm): 25.3
Exchanges:
Milk: 0.0
Vegetable: 0.0
Fruit: 1.5
Bread: 0.0
Meat: 0.0
Fat: 0.0

1. Combine all ingredients, except lemon juice and rum, in slow cooker; cover and cook on high 2 to 3 hours (if mixture begins to boil, turn heat to low). Season to taste with lemon juice; stir in rum. Turn heat to low to keep warm for serving.

Variation

Five-Spice Fruit Punch—Make recipe as above, omitting rum and lemon juice; substitute apple cider for the cranberry juice and 1 tablespoon five-spice powder for the cinnamon and allspice.

Glogg

V *This hot wine punch is traditionally made with raisins and whole almonds.*

12 servings (about ½ cup each)

1 bottle (25 ounces) each: Bordeaux and port wine
2 tablespoons grated orange zest
4 each: small cinnamon sticks, cardamom pods,
   whole cloves
1 cup each: blanched almonds, raisins
½–1 cup cognac or brandy

Per Serving:
Calories: 274
% of calories from fat: 30
Fat (gm): 6.2
Saturated fat (gm): 0.5
Cholesterol (mg): 0.0
Sodium (mg): 9
Protein (gm): 3
Carbohydrate (gm): 21.9
Exchanges:
Milk: 0.0
Vegetable: 0.0
Fruit: 1.5
Bread: 0.0
Meat: 0.0
Fat: 2.0

1. Combine all ingredients, except almonds, raisins, and cognac, in slow cooker, tying orange zest and spices in cheesecloth bag; cover and cook on high 2 to 3 hours (if mixture begins to boil, turn heat to low), adding almonds and raisins during last hour. Remove spice bag and stir in cognac; turn to low to keep warm for serving.

Hot Ginger Lemonade

 V *Yes, there is lemonade for every season! Enjoy this gingery version hot, or chill and serve over ice in the summer.*

12 servings (about ½ cup each)

5 cups water
¾ cup each: lemon juice, sugar
2-inch piece gingerroot, sliced

Per Serving:
Calories: 53
% of calories from fat: 0.0
Fat (gm): 0.0
Saturated fat (gm): 0.0
Cholesterol (mg): 0.0
Sodium (mg): 0
Protein (gm): 0
Carbohydrate (gm): 13.9
Exchanges:
Milk: 0.0
Vegetable: 0.0
Fruit: 1.0
Bread: 0.0
Meat: 0.0
Fat: 0.0

1. Combine all ingredients in slow cooker; cover and cook on high 2 to 3 hours (if mixture begins to boil, turn heat to low); turn to low to keep warm for serving.

Variation

Hot Cranberry Mint Lemonade—Make recipe as above, substituting 2½ cups cranberry juice for 2½ cups of the water; omit ginger-root. Add 1 tablespoons dried mint leaves, tied in cheesecloth bag, during last hour of cooking.

Sweet Cinnamon Java

V

This spiced coffee is also refreshing served chilled over crushed ice.

12 servings (about 6 ounces cup each)

2 quarts water
½ cup dark roast regular grind coffee
½–⅔ cup packed light brown sugar
2 small cinnamon sticks
8 whole cloves

1. Combine all ingredients in slow cooker, tying spices in cheesecloth bag; cover and cook until hot and steaming (do not boil), about 2 hours. Remove spice bag; turn to low to keep warm for serving.

Per Serving:
Calories: 37
% of calories from fat: 0
Fat (gm): 0
Saturated fat (gm): 0
Cholesterol (mg): 0
Sodium (mg): 6
Protein (gm): 0.1
Carbohydrate (gm): 9.4
Exchanges:
Milk: 0.0
Vegetable: 0.0
Fruit: 0.0
Bread: 0.5
Meat: 0.0
Fat: 0.0

Variation
Honey–Orange Coffee—Make recipe as above, substituting ¼ cup honey for the brown sugar and adding grated orange zest from ¼ medium orange, tied in cheesecloth bag.

Honey Chai

L

This aromatic spiced tea is sweetened with honey.

12 servings (about 6 ounces each)

1½ quarts water
2 cups whole milk
2 cinnamon sticks
1 teaspoon ground cardamom
1-inch piece gingerroot, sliced
½ cup honey
12 black tea bags or ¼ cup loose black tea

1. Combine all ingredients in slow cooker; cover and cook on high until hot and steaming (do not boil) about 2 hours. Remove tea bags and gingerroot with a slotted spoon; turn heat to low to keep warm for serving.

Per Serving:
Calories: 69
% of calories from fat: 17
Fat (gm): 1.3
Saturated fat (gm): 0.8
Cholesterol (mg): 4.1
Sodium (mg): 20
Protein (gm): 1
Carbohydrate (gm): 13.9
Exchanges:
Milk: 0.0
Vegetable: 0.0
Fruit: 0.0
Bread: 1.0
Meat: 0.0
Fat: 0.0

Variation
Green Tea–Soy Chai—Make recipe above, substituting green tea for the black tea and vanilla soy milk for the milk. Sweeten with ¼ to ½ cup honey.

Hot Chocolate

L *Add marshmallows or dollops of marshmallow crème to each cup of Hot Chocolate.*

12 servings (about 6 ounces each)

½ cup each: Dutch process cocoa, sugar
½ teaspoon ground cinnamon
Pinch salt
2 quarts whole milk
½ teaspoon vanilla

Per Serving:
Calories: 144
% of calories from fat: 35
Fat (gm): 5.6
Saturated fat (gm): 3.0
Cholesterol (mg): 16.1
Sodium (mg): 65
Protein (gm): 6
Carbohydrate (gm): 17.9
Exchanges:
Milk: 0.5
Vegetable: 0.0
Fruit: 0.0
Bread: 0.5
Meat: 0.0
Fat: 1.0

1. Combine cocoa, sugar, cinnamon, and salt in slow cooker; whisk in enough milk to make a smooth paste. Whisk in remaining milk and vanilla. Cover and cook on high until hot and steaming (do not boil), about 2 hours. Turn heat to low to keep warm for serving.

Variation

Brazilian Mocha—Make recipe above, omitting cinnamon and vanilla and decreasing milk to 5 cups; add 3 cups strong brewed coffee.

Spiced White Chocolate

L *For a richer hot chocolate, substitute half-and-half for part of the milk—if you're not counting calories!*

12 servings (about 6 ounces each)

1½ cups white chocolate morsels
8 cups whole milk
¼ teaspoon each: ground cinnamon and nutmeg

Per Serving:
Calories: 219
% of calories from fat: 51
Fat (gm): 12.1
Saturated fat (gm): 7.6
Cholesterol (mg): 20.1
Sodium (mg): 89
Protein (gm): 7
Carbohydrate (gm): 19.6
Exchanges:
Milk: 0.5
Vegetable: 0.0
Fruit: 0.0
Bread: 1.0
Meat: 0.0
Fat: 2.5

1. Place chocolate morsels in slow cooker; cover and cook on low until chocolate is melted, about 30 minutes. Gradually whisk in milk and spices; cover and cook on high until hot and steaming (do not boil), about 2 hours. Turn heat to low to keep warm for serving.

Variation

Peppermint Cocoa—Make recipe above, omitting spices; add ½ to 1 teaspoon peppermint extract with the milk. Top each cup of cocoa with whipped cream and crushed peppermint candy.

TWO

Stocks and First-Course Soups

Chicken Stock

You'll have many uses for this delicious stock.

Makes about 1½ quarts

1 quart water
3 pounds chicken pieces
2 ribs celery, thickly sliced
3 each: thickly sliced small onions, medium carrots
1 small turnip, quartered
5 cloves garlic
2 bay leaves
½ teaspoon whole peppercorns
1 teaspoon dried sage leaves
Salt and pepper, to taste

Per Cup:
Calories: 32
% calories from fat: 20
Protein (g): 4.9
Carbohydrate (g): 1.3
Fat (g): 0.7
Saturated fat (g): 0.2
Cholesterol (mg): 17
Sodium (mg): 26
Exchanges:
Milk: 0.0
Vegetable: 0.0
Fruit: 0.0
Bread: 0.0
Meat: 0.5
Fat: 0.0

1. Combine all ingredients, except salt and pepper, in slow cooker; cover and cook on low 6 to 8 hours. Strain, discarding meat, vegetables, and seasonings; season to taste with salt and pepper. Refrigerate stock overnight; skim fat from surface of stock.

Rich Chicken Stock

Veal knuckle adds richness to this stock.

Makes about 4 quarts

4 quarts water
1 cup dry white wine or water
1 chicken (about 3 pounds), cut up, fat trimmed
1 veal knuckle, cracked (optional)
2 each: thickly sliced medium onions, leeks
  (white parts only)
4 each: thickly sliced medium carrots, ribs celery
1 clove garlic, peeled
½ teaspoon each: dried basil, thyme, and
  tarragon leaves
10 black peppercorns
4 whole cloves
Salt and pepper, to taste

Per Cup:
Calories: 39
% calories from fat: 18
Protein (g): 4.9
Carbohydrate (g): 0.8
Fat (g): 0.8
Saturated fat (g): 0.2
Cholesterol (mg): 1
Sodium (mg): 36
Exchanges:
Milk: 0.0
Vegetable: 0.0
Fruit: 0.0
Bread: 0.0
Meat: 0.5
Fat: 0.0

1. Combine all ingredients, except salt and pepper, in 6-quart slow cooker; cover and cook on low 6 to 8 hours. Strain stock through double layer of

cheesecloth, discarding solids; season to taste with salt and pepper. Refrigerate until chilled; remove fat from surface of stock.

Turkey Stock

The perfect ending for a Thanksgiving turkey, this stock can be used for Turkey Noodle Soup (see p. 86) or as a substitute in recipes calling for chicken stock.

Makes about 4 quarts

4 quarts water
1 cup dry white wine or water
1 turkey carcass, cut up
2 each: thickly sliced medium onions,
    leeks (white parts only)
4 each: thickly sliced medium carrots, ribs celery
1 teaspoon dried thyme leaves
10 black peppercorns
6 sprigs parsley
Salt and pepper, to taste

Per Cup:
Calories: 29
% calories from fat: 28
Protein (g): 2
Carbohydrate (g): 0.9
Fat (g): 0.9
Saturated fat (g): 0.2
Cholesterol (mg): 5.6
Sodium (mg): 7
Exchanges:
Milk: 0.0
Vegetable: 0.0
Fruit: 0.0
Bread: 0.0
Meat: 0.0
Fat: 0.0

1. Combine all ingredients, except salt and pepper, in 6-quart slow cooker; cover and cook on low 6 to 8 hours. Strain stock through double layer of cheesecloth, discarding solids; season to taste with salt and pepper. Refrigerate until chilled; remove fat from surface of stock.

Beef Stock

A flavorful stock that's easy to prepare.

Makes about 2 quarts

2½ quarts water
2 ribs from cooked beef rib roast, fat trimmed
4 each: thickly sliced large onions, medium carrots,
    small ribs celery
1 parsnip, halved
2 bay leaves
8 black peppercorns
5 sage leaves
Salt, to taste

Per Cup:
Calories: 8
% calories from fat: 31
Protein (g): 0.2
Carbohydrate (g): 1.3
Fat (g): 0.3
Saturated fat (g): 0
Cholesterol (mg): 0.3
Sodium (mg): 4
Exchanges:
Milk: 0.0
Vegetable: 0.0
Fruit: 0.0
Bread: 0.0
Meat: 0.0
Fat: 0.0

1. Combine all ingredients, except salt, in 6-quart slow cooker; cover and cook on low 6 to 8 hours. Strain stock through double layer of cheesecloth, discarding solids; season to taste with salt. Refrigerate until chilled; remove fat from surface of stock.

Fragrant Beef Stock

Dried mushrooms, red wine, and herbs give a rich flavor to this stock. Brown the beef, if you like, for an even richer stock.

Makes about 3½ quarts

3 quarts water
1 cup dry red wine (optional)
2 pounds each: short ribs of beef (fat trimmed),
   beef marrow bones
1 pound cubed beef chuck, fat trimmed
1 large onion, chopped
3 each: thickly sliced medium carrots, ribs celery
½ cup dried mushrooms
1 clove garlic, halved
10 black peppercorns
1 bay leaf
1 teaspoon each: dried basil and thyme leaves
1 tablespoon soy sauce
Salt, to taste

Per Cup:
Calories: 16
% calories from fat: 28
Protein (g): 2.7
Carbohydrate (g): 0.6
Fat (g): 0.5
Saturated fat (g): 0.3
Cholesterol (mg): 3
Sodium (mg): 42
Exchanges:
Milk: 0.0
Vegetable: 0.0
Fruit: 0.0
Bread: 0.0
Meat: 0.0
Fat: 0.0

1. Combine all ingredients, except salt, in 6-quart slow cooker; cover and cook on low 6 to 8 hours. Strain stock through double layer of cheesecloth, discarding solids; season to taste with salt. Refrigerate until chilled; remove fat from surface of stock.

Veal Stock

Veal bones can be difficult to find, so make this delicately flavored stock when you can find the ingredients and freeze it. Brown the veal for a richer flavored stock.

Makes about 2 quarts

2 quarts water
1½ pounds veal cubes for stew
½ cup each: chopped onion, carrot, celery
1 veal knuckle or veal bones (about 1¾ pounds)
2 bay leaves
6 black peppercorns
3 whole cloves
Salt and pepper, to taste

Per Cup:
Calories: 17
% calories from fat: 36
Protein (g): 2.4
Carbohydrate (g): 0.2
Fat (g): 0.6
Saturated fat (g): 0.1
Cholesterol (mg): 8.9
Sodium (mg): 6
Exchanges:
Milk: 0.0
Vegetable: 0.0
Fruit: 0.0
Bread: 0.0
Meat: 0.0
Fat: 0.0

1. Combine all ingredients, except salt and pepper, in 6-quart slow cooker; cover and cook on low 6 to 8 hours. Strain through double layer of cheesecloth, discarding solids; season to taste with salt and pepper. Refrigerate until chilled; remove fat from surface of stock.

Fish Stock

Ask the fish department of your supermarket to save fish bones for you.

Makes about 1½ quarts

1½ quarts water
2–3 pounds fish bones (from non-oily fish)
1 each: chopped large onion, rib celery
2 bay leaves
7–8 black peppercorns
½ teaspoon each: kosher or sea salt, white pepper

Per Cup:
Calories: 17
% calories from fat: 0
Protein (g): 2.8
Carbohydrate (g): 0.3
Fat (g): 0.1
Saturated fat (g): 0
Cholesterol (mg): 0
Sodium (mg): 191
Exchanges:
Milk: 0.0
Vegetable: 0.0
Fruit: 0.0
Bread: 0.0
Meat: 0.0
Fat: 0.0

1. Combine all ingredients in slow cooker; cook on low 4 to 6 hours. Strain through double layer of cheesecloth, discarding solids.

Easy Fish Stock

Any mildly-flavored fish will make a delicious stock; avoid strongly flavored fish, such as salmon or tuna. Stock will keep in refrigerator for 2 days or up to 2 months in the freezer.

Makes about 1 quart

3½ cups water
¾ cup dry white wine or water
1½ pounds fresh or frozen fish steaks, cubed (1-inch)
1 each: finely chopped medium onion, carrot
3 ribs celery with leaves, halved
3 sprigs parsley
3 slices lemon
8 black peppercorns
Salt, to taste

Per Cup:
Calories: 10
% calories from fat: 3
Protein (g): 0.7
Carbohydrate (g): 0.2
Fat (g): 0
Saturated fat (g): 0
Cholesterol (mg): 2
Sodium (mg): 3
Exchanges:
Milk: 0.0
Vegetable: 0.0
Fruit: 0.0
Bread: 0.0
Meat: 0.0
Fat: 0.0

1. Combine all ingredients, except salt, in slow cooker; cover and cook on low 4 to 6 hours. Strain stock through double layer of cheesecloth, discarding solids; season to taste with salt.

Basic Vegetable Stock

v *As vegetables used in stocks are later discarded, they should be scrubbed but do not need to be peeled.*

Makes about 2 quarts

2 quarts water
1 cup dry white wine or water
1 each: thickly sliced large onion, leek
   (white part only), carrot, rib celery
4 cups mixed chopped vegetables
   (broccoli, green beans, cabbage, potatoes,
   tomatoes, summer or winter squash, bell
   peppers, mushrooms, etc.)
6–8 parsley sprigs
1 bay leaf
4 whole allspice
1 tablespoon black peppercorns
2 teaspoons dried bouquet garni
Salt, to taste

Per Cup:
Calories: 4
% calories from fat: 3
Protein (g): 0.1
Carbohydrate (g): 1.0
Fat (g): 0.0
Saturated fat (g): 0.0
Cholesterol (mg): 0.0
Sodium (mg): 3
Exchanges:
Milk: 0.0
Vegetable: 0.0
Fruit: 0.0
Bread: 0.0
Meat: 0.0
Fat: 0.0

1. Combine all ingredients, except salt, in 6-quart slow cooker; cover and cook on high 3 to 4 hours or low 6 to 8 hours. Strain stock, discarding solids; season to taste with salt.

Roasted Vegetable Stock

v

Roasting vegetables intensifies their flavors, adding richness to the stock. The beet adds a subtle sweetness to the stock, but use only if you don't object to the pink color it creates!

Makes about 2 quarts

2 quarts water
1 cup dry white wine or water
1 each: coarsely chopped medium
   onion, leek (white part only), carrot,
   zucchini, turnip, beet, tomato
½ small butternut or acorn squash, cubed (2-inch)
1 bulb garlic, cut crosswise in half
3 cups coarsely chopped kale
6 sprigs parsley
1 bay leaf
1–2 teaspoons dried bouquet garni
1 teaspoon black peppercorns
4 whole allspice
Salt and pepper, to taste

Per Cup:
Calories: 25
% calories from fat: 1
Protein (g): 0.2
Carbohydrate (g): 1.5
Fat (g): 0
Saturated fat (g): 0
Cholesterol (mg): 0
Sodium (mg): 12
Exchanges:
Milk: 0.0
Vegetable: 0.0
Fruit: 0.0
Bread: 0.0
Meat: 0.0
Fat: 0.0

1. Arrange vegetables, except kale, in single layer on greased, foil-lined jelly roll pan; bake at 425 degrees until tender and browned, 35 to 40 minutes. Transfer vegetables to 6-quart slow cooker and add remaining ingredients, except salt and pepper; cover and cook on low 4 to 6 hours. Strain, discarding solids; season to taste with salt and pepper.

Mediterranean Stock

v

A lovely stock scented with orange and fennel.

Makes about 2 quarts

2 quarts water
1 cup dry white wine or water
Juice of 1 orange
1 each: thickly sliced large onion,
   leek (white part only), carrot,
   sweet potato, zucchini, rib celery
½ each: sliced small fennel bulb, red bell pepper
2 medium tomatoes, quartered
1 medium bulb garlic, cut crosswise in half
3 cups coarsely chopped spinach or romaine lettuce
6 sprigs parsley
1 each: strip orange zest (3 x 1-inch), bay leaf
1–2 teaspoons bouquet garni
1 teaspoon black peppercorns
4 whole allspice
Salt, to taste

Per Cup:
Calories: 43
% calories from fat: 24
Protein (g): 0.5
Carbohydrate (g): 3.3
Fat (g): 1.2
Saturated fat (g): 0.2
Cholesterol (mg): 0
Sodium (mg): 15
Exchanges:
Milk: 0.0
Vegetable: 0.5
Fruit: 0.0
Bread: 0.0
Meat: 0.0
Fat: 0.5

1. Combine all ingredients, except salt, in 6-quart slow cooker; cover and cook on low 4 to 6 hours. Strain, discarding solids; season to taste with salt.

Oriental Stock

v

A light, fragrant stock that can be used in Asian soups and entrées.

Makes about 2 quarts

2 quarts water
6 cups shredded bok choy or Chinese cabbage
1¼ cups coarsely chopped loosely packed cilantro
1 each: sliced large onion, carrot, small red bell pepper
⅓ cup sliced gingerroot
1 tablespoon minced garlic
3 dried shiitake mushrooms
4 teaspoons reduced-sodium tamari soy sauce
2 star anise
2 teaspoons five-spice powder
1½ teaspoons Szechuan peppercorns, toasted
Salt and pepper, to taste

Per Cup:
Calories: 8
% calories from fat: 11
Protein (g): 0.6
Carbohydrate (g): 1.1
Fat (g): 0.1
Saturated fat (g): 0
Cholesterol (mg): 0
Sodium (mg): 110
Exchanges:
Milk: 0.0
Vegetable: 0.0
Fruit: 0.0
Bread: 0.0
Meat: 0.0
Fat: 0.0

1. Combine all ingredients, except salt and pepper, in 6-quart slow cooker; cover and cook on low 4 to 6 hours. Strain, discarding solids; season to taste with salt and pepper.

Rich Mushroom Stock

v *Dried shiitake mushrooms, also known as Chinese black mushrooms, add richness and depth of flavor to this stock.*

Makes about 2 quarts

1 quarts water
¾ cup dry white wine (optional)
1 each: sliced large onion, leek
   (white part only), rib celery
12 ounces cremini or white mushrooms
1 tablespoon minced garlic
1½–2 ounces dried shiitake mushrooms
6 sprigs parsley
¾ teaspoon each: dried sage and thyme leaves
1½ teaspoons black peppercorns
Salt, to taste

Per Cup:
Calories: 27
% calories from fat: 22
Protein (g): 0.4
Carbohydrate (g): 1.6
Fat (g): 0.7
Saturated fat (g): 0.1
Cholesterol (mg): 0
Sodium (mg): 9
Exchanges:
Milk: 0.0
Vegetable: 0.0
Fruit: 0.0
Bread: 0.0
Meat: 0.0
Fat: 0.0

1. Combine all ingredients, except salt, in 6-quart slow cooker; cover and cook on low 6 to 8 hours. Strain, discarding solids; season to taste with salt and pepper.

Cream of Broccoli Soup

Eat broccoli often—it's high in antioxidants and packed with nutrients.

6 first-course servings

3 cups reduced-sodium fat-free chicken broth
2 pounds broccoli, cut into pieces (1-inch)
1 cup chopped onion
3 cloves garlic, minced
½ teaspoon dried thyme leaves
⅛ teaspoon ground nutmeg
½ cup 2% reduced-fat milk
Salt and white pepper, to taste
6 tablespoons reduced-fat sour cream
Croutons (recipe follows)

Per Serving:
Calories: 99
% calories from fat: 9
Protein (g): 6.8
Carbohydrate (g): 17.6
Fat (g): 1.1
Saturated fat (g): 0.2
Cholesterol (mg): 0
Sodium (mg): 110
Exchanges:
Milk: 0.0
Vegetable: 2.0
Fruit: 0.0
Bread: 0.5
Meat: 0.0
Fat: 0.0

1. Combine all ingredients, except milk, salt, white pepper, sour cream, and Croutons, in slow cooker; cover and cook on high 3 to 4 hours. Process soup and milk in food processor or blender until smooth; season to taste with salt and white pepper. Serve warm or refrigerate and serve chilled; top each bowl of soup with dollop of sour cream and sprinkle with Croutons.

Croutons

Makes 1½ cups

1½ cups cubed firm or day-old French or Italian bread (½–¾-inch)
Vegetable cooking spray

1. Spray bread cubes with cooking spray; arrange in single layer on jelly roll pan. Bake at 375 degrees until browned, 8 to 10 minutes, stirring occasionally. Cool; store in airtight container up to 2 weeks.

Variations

Dilled Broccoli Soup—Make recipe as above, omitting thyme, nutmeg, and Croutons. Add ⅔ cup loosely packed fresh dill weed to soup when puréeing.

Broccoli-Kale Soup—Make recipe as above, omitting the milk, Croutons, and nutmeg. Stir 2 cups lightly packed kale into soup during the last 15 minutes of cooking time.

Broccoli and Cucumber Soup—Make recipe as above, adding a thickly sliced medium cucumber and omitting thyme, nutmeg, and Croutons. Stir 1 cup lightly packed cilantro into soup during last 15 minutes of cooking.

Cream of Asparagus Soup—Make recipe as above, substituting 2 pounds asparagus for the broccoli, and reserving 18 small asparagus tips for garnish. Omit thyme leaves. Add 1 teaspoon dried marjoram leaves and 1 teaspoon grated lemon zest. Steam reserved asparagus tips until crisp-tender, and use to garnish soup.

Creamy Broccoli-Potato Soup

For a colorful touch, garnish each bowl of soup with a lemon slice.

6 first-course servings

3 cups Chicken Stock (see p. 30) or chicken broth
1 quart chopped broccoli
3½ cups peeled diced potatoes
4 medium leeks (white parts only), sliced
1 cup whole milk
2 tablespoons cornstarch
Salt and white pepper, to taste

Per Serving:
Calories: 148
% calories from fat: 15
Protein (g): 6.3
Carbohydrate (g): 26.9
Fat (g): 2.5
Saturated fat (g): 1
Cholesterol (mg): 5.2
Sodium (mg): 175
Exchanges:
Milk: 0.0
Vegetable: 0.0
Fruit: 0.0
Bread: 1.5
Meat: 0.0
Fat: 0.5

1. Combine all ingredients, except milk, cornstarch, salt, and pepper, in slow cooker and cook on high 3 to 4 hours. Stir in combined milk and cornstarch, stirring until thickened, 2 to 3 minutes. Process soup in food processor or blender until smooth. Season to taste with salt and white pepper.

Herbed Broccoli-Cauliflower Bisque

This healthful soup is so delicious, you'll want to make enough for the freezer!

6 first-course servings

3 cups Chicken Stock (see p. 30) or chicken broth
2 medium stalks broccoli, coarsely chopped
½ small head cauliflower, coarsely chopped
1½ cups peeled coarsely chopped potatoes
1 cup thinly sliced green onions
1 tablespoon dried basil leaves
1 cup whole milk, divided
Salt and pepper, to taste

Per Serving:
Calories: 121
% calories from fat: 19
Protein (g): 7
Carbohydrate (g): 18.6
Fat (g): 2.7
Saturated fat (g): 1
Cholesterol (mg): 4.5
Sodium (mg): 230
Exchanges:
Milk: 0.0
Vegetable: 1.0
Fruit: 0.0
Bread: 1.0
Meat: 0.0
Fat: 0.5

1. Combine all ingredients, except milk, salt, and pepper, in slow cooker; cover and cook on high 4 to 5 hours. Process soup and 1 cup milk in food processor or blender until smooth. Season to taste with salt and pepper.

Hot-and-Sour Cabbage Soup

The flavor of this soup is reminiscent of classic Chinese hot-and-sour soup.

8 first-course servings

2 quarts reduced-fat chicken broth
3 cups shredded green cabbage
1 large carrot, chopped
¼ cup finely chopped red bell pepper
4 green onions, thinly sliced, divided
1 large clove garlic, minced
2 teaspoons minced gingerroot
3 tablespoons soy sauce
1½ tablespoons apple cider vinegar
¼ teaspoon Oriental hot chili oil
2 tablespoons cornstarch
1 tablespoon light brown sugar

Per Serving:
Calories: 81
% calories from fat: 21
Protein (g): 6.2
Carbohydrate (g): 10.8
Fat (g): 2
Saturated fat (g): 0 3
Cholesterol (mg): 0
Sodium (mg): 635
Exchanges:
Milk: 0.0
Vegetable: 2.0
Fruit: 0.0
Bread: 0.0
Meat: 0.0
Fat: 0.0

1. Combine broth, vegetables, garlic, and gingerroot in 6-quart slow cooker; cover and cook on high 3 to 4 hours. Stir in combined remaining ingredients during last 2 to 3 minutes.

Dilled Carrot Soup

Carrots team with dill for a fresh, clean flavor.

6 first-course servings

3 cups reduced-sodium fat-free chicken broth
1 can (14½ ounces) diced tomatoes, undrained
1 pound carrots, thickly sliced
1½ cups chopped onions
1 medium Idaho potato, peeled, cubed
2 cloves garlic, minced
1–1½ teaspoons dried dill weed
2–3 tablespoons lemon juice
Salt and white pepper, to taste
6 tablespoons reduced-fat plain yogurt

Per Serving:
Calories: 108
% calories from fat: 2.3
Protein (g): 4.8
Carbohydrate (g): 22.4
Fat (g): 2.3
Saturated fat (g): 0.1
Cholesterol (mg): 0.3
Sodium (mg): 457
Exchanges:
Milk: 0.0
Vegetable: 0.0
Fruit: 0.0
Bread: 1.5
Meat: 0.0
Fat: 0.0

1. Combine all ingredients, except lemon juice, salt, white pepper, and yogurt, in slow cooker; cover and cook on high 3 to 4 hours. Process soup in food processor or blender until smooth; season to taste with lemon juice, salt, and white pepper. Serve soup warm or refrigerate and serve chilled. Garnish each bowl of soup with a dollop of yogurt.

Cream of Cauliflower Soup with Cheese

This pureed soup has a velvety texture.

6 first-course servings

3½ cups reduced-sodium fat-free chicken broth
12 ounces cauliflower, cut into florets
1 large Idaho potato, peeled, cubed
½ cup chopped onion
2 cloves garlic, minced
½ cup 2% reduced-fat milk
1 tablespoon cornstarch
¾ cup (3 ounces) shredded reduced-fat Cheddar cheese
Salt and white pepper, to taste
Ground mace or nutmeg, as garnish

Per Serving:
Calories: 98
% calories from fat: 22
Protein (g): 5.5
Carbohydrate (g): 13.6
Fat (g): 2.4
Saturated fat (g): 1.1
Cholesterol (mg): 7.6
Sodium (mg): 214
Exchanges:
Milk: 0.0
Vegetable: 1.0
Fruit: 0.0
Bread: 0.5
Meat: 0.5
Fat: 0.0

1. Combine broth, cauliflower, potato, onion, and garlic in slow cooker; cover and cook on high 3 to 4 hours. Remove about half the vegetables from the soup with a slotted spoon and reserve. Purée remaining soup in food processor or blender until smooth; return to slow cooker. Add reserved vegetables; cover and cook on high 10 minutes. Stir in combined milk and cornstarch, stirring 2 to 3 minutes. Add cheese, stirring until melted. Season to taste with salt and white pepper; sprinkle each bowl of soup with mace.

Variations

Chilled Cauliflower Soup—Make soup as above, omitting Cheddar cheese, mace, and cornstarch. Process soup, milk, and 1 tablespoon dried dill weed in food processor until smooth, without reserving any vegetables. Garnish each bowl of soup with chopped dill or parsley.

Fennel Bisque with Walnuts—Make soup as above, substituting 1 large sliced leek for the onion, and 12 ounces sliced fennel bulbs for the cauliflower. Omit Cheddar cheese, mace, and cornstarch. Process soup and milk in food processor until smooth, without reserving any vegetables. Sprinkle each bowl of soup with crumbled blue cheese and chopped toasted walnuts.

Cream of Turnip Soup—Make soup as above, substituting 12 ounces chopped turnips for the cauliflower and reduced-fat Swiss, Gouda, or Havarti cheese for the Cheddar; add ½ teaspoon dried thyme leaves.

Garlic Soup with Toasted Bread

Long, slow cooking mellows the garlic flavor. A beaten egg is often stirred into this Mexican soup before serving.

4 first-course servings

1 quart chicken broth
6–8 cloves garlic, finely chopped
½ teaspoon each: ground cumin, dried oregano leaves
Salt and cayenne pepper, to taste
4 slices French or sourdough bread
Vegetable cooking spray
Chopped cilantro, as garnish

Per Serving:
Calories: 162
% calories from fat: 28
Protein (g): 3.2
Carbohydrate (g): 20.6
Fat (g): 5
Saturated fat (g): 0.7
Cholesterol (mg): 0
Sodium (mg): 202
Exchanges:
Milk: 0.0
Vegetable: 1.0
Fruit: 0.0
Bread: 1.5
Meat: 0.0
Fat: 0.5

1. Combine broth, garlic, and herbs in slow cooker; cover and cook on high 4 hours; season to taste with salt and cayenne pepper.
2. Spray both sides of bread slices generously with cooking spray; cook in large skillet, over medium heat, until golden, about 2 minutes on each side. Place slices of bread in bottoms of soup bowls; ladle soup over and sprinkle with cilantro.

Fragrant Mushroom Soup

You'll love this delicately flavored mushroom soup.

4 first-course servings

1¼ pounds mushrooms, divided
3 cups Fragrant Beef Stock (see p. 32) or beef broth
1 tablespoon light soy sauce
2 tablespoons cornstarch
¼ cup cold water
2 tablespoons dry sherry (optional)
½ teaspoon lemon juice
Salt and pepper, to taste

Per Serving:
Calories: 86
% calories from fat: 28
Protein (g): 6
Carbohydrate (g): 9.2
Fat (g): 2.9
Saturated fat (g): 0.7
Cholesterol (mg): 3
Sodium (mg): 245
Exchanges:
Milk: 0.0
Vegetable: 2.0
Fruit: 0.0
Bread: 0.0
Meat: 0.0
Fat: 0.5

1. Slice 4 ounces mushrooms and reserve; coarsely chop remaining mushrooms and stems. Combine chopped mushrooms, stock, and soy sauce in slow cooker; cover and cook on low 4 to 6 hours. Process soup in food processor or blender until smooth; return to slow cooker. Add sliced mushrooms; cover and cook on high 30 minutes. Stir in combined cornstarch and water, stirring 2 to 3 minutes. Stir in sherry and lemon juice; season to taste with salt and pepper.

Lemon Mushroom Soup

Fresh and dried mushrooms combine in this richly flavored, lemon-accented soup.

6 first-course servings

1½ cups hot water
1 ounce dried porcini or other dried mushrooms
3 cups Rich Chicken Stock (see p. 30) or
   chicken broth
¼ cup dry white wine (optional)
8 ounces cremini mushrooms, quartered
¾ cup thinly sliced onion
1½ tablespoons minced garlic
1 teaspoon dried rosemary leaves
¼ cup each: chopped lemon pulp, parsley
¼ cup water
2 tablespoons cornstarch
Salt and pepper, to taste
Bruschetta (recipe follows)

Per Serving:
Calories: 90
% calories from fat: 10
Protein (g): 3.7
Carbohydrate (g): 14.9
Fat (g): 1
Saturated fat (g): 0.1
Cholesterol (mg): 0
Sodium (mg): 86
Exchanges:
Milk: 0.0
Vegetable: 2.0
Fruit: 0.0
Bread: 0.5
Meat: 0.0
Fat: 0.0

1. Pour hot water over porcini mushrooms in bowl; let stand until softened, about 20 minutes. Remove mushrooms with slotted spoon; strain liquid through double layer of cheesecloth and reserve. Inspect mushrooms carefully, rinsing if necessary, to remove grit. Chop coarsely.
2. Combine porcini mushrooms and reserved liquid, and remaining ingredients, except lemon pulp, parsley, water, cornstarch, salt, pepper, and Bruschetta in slow cooker; cover and cook on high 3 to 4 hours, adding lemon pulp and parsley during last 5 minutes. Stir in combined water and cornstarch, stirring 2 to 3 minutes. Season to taste with salt and pepper. Place Bruschetta in bottoms of soup bowls; ladle soup over.

Bruschetta

Makes 6

6 slices French bread (¾-inch)
Olive oil cooking spray
1 clove garlic, halved

1. Spray both sides of bread lightly with cooking spray. Broil on cookie sheet 4 inches from heat source, until browned, 2 to 3 minutes on each side. Rub top sides of bread slices with cut sides of garlic.

Vidalia Onion Soup

The mild sweetness of Vidalia onions makes this soup special, but try it with other onion varieties too. For richer flavor, brown onions in a skillet before adding to the slow cooker.

8 first-course servings

6 cups reduced-sodium fat-free chicken or
   vegetable broth
6 cups thinly sliced Vidalia onions
2 cloves garlic, minced
1 teaspoon sugar
1½ teaspoons dried sage leaves
2 bay leaves
2–3 tablespoons cornstarch
¼ cup cold water
Salt and white pepper, to taste
Snipped chives or sliced green onions, as garnish

Per Serving:
Calories: 88
% calories from fat: 3
Protein (g): 2.2
Carbohydrate (g): 16.4
Fat (g): 0.3
Saturated fat (g): 0.1
Cholesterol (mg): 0
Sodium (mg): 13
Exchanges:
Milk: 0.0
Vegetable: 2.
Fruit: 0.0
Bread: 0.5
Meat: 0.0
Fat: 0.0

1. Combine all ingredients, except cornstarch, water, salt, white pepper, and chives, in 6-quart slow cooker; cover and cook on high 5 to 6 hours. Discard bay leaves; stir in combined cornstarch and water, stirring 2 to 3 minutes. Process soup in food processor or blender until smooth. Season to taste with salt and white pepper. Serve warm or chilled; sprinkle each bowl of soup with chives.

Three-Onion Soup with Mushrooms

For a soup with a richer flavor, sprinkle onions, leeks, and shallots with 1 teaspoon sugar and cook in 1 tablespoon margarine in large skillet over medium low heat until onions are golden, about 15 minutes.

6 first-course servings

6½ cups reduced-sodium fat-free chicken broth
3 cups thinly sliced onions
1½ cups thinly sliced leeks
½ cup chopped shallots or green onions
2 cups sliced mushrooms
1 teaspoon sugar
Salt and pepper, to taste

Per Serving:
Calories: 119
% calories from fat: 21
Protein (g): 2.7
Carbohydrate (g): 18.5
Fat (g): 3
Saturated fat (g): 0.5
Cholesterol (mg): 0
Sodium (mg): 218
Exchanges:
Milk: 0.0
Vegetable: 3.0
Fruit: 0.0
Bread: 0.0
Meat: 0.0
Fat: 0.5

1. Combine all ingredients, except salt and pepper, in 6-quart slow cooker; cover and cook on low 6 to 8 hours. Season to taste with salt and pepper.

Red Onion and Apple Soup with Curry

Red onions, slow cooked until sweet and tender, lend a special flavor to this autumn soup.

6 first-course servings

1½ quarts Rich Chicken Stock (see p. 30) or
  chicken broth
1¼ pounds red onions (about 4 medium),
  thinly sliced
2 cups coarsely grated peeled tart cooking apples,
  divided
½ cup cubed carrots (½ inch)
1 large bay leaf
1 teaspoon each: curry and chili powder
¼ teaspoon each: dried thyme leaves, ground allspice
Salt and pepper, to taste
Mango chutney, as garnish

Per Serving:
Calories: 106
% calories from fat: 18
Protein (g): 6.4
Carbohydrate (g): 16.4
Fat (g): 2.3
Saturated fat (g): 0.4
Cholesterol (mg): 0
Sodium (mg): 393
Exchanges:
Milk: 0.0
Vegetable: 2.0
Fruit: 0.5
Bread: 0.0
Meat: 0.0
Fat: 0.5

1. Combine all ingredients, except salt, pepper, and mango chutney, in slow cooker; cover and cook on high 4 to 5 hours. Discard bay leaf; season to taste with salt and pepper. Serve with chutney to stir into soup.

Onion and Leek Soup with Pasta

Soup pasta, small shells, or bow ties can be alternate pasta choices.

6 first-course servings

7 cups reduced-sodium fat-free chicken broth
4 cups sliced onions
2 cups sliced leeks (white parts only)
6 cloves garlic, minced
1 teaspoon sugar
4 ounces pasta, cooked
Salt and white pepper, to taste
6 teaspoons grated Parmesan cheese

Per Serving:
Calories: 211
% calories from fat: 3
Protein (g): 12.9
Carbohydrate (g): 37.1
Fat (g): 0.8
Saturated fat (g): 0.1
Cholesterol (mg): 0
Sodium (mg): 234
Exchanges:
Milk: 0.0
Vegetable: 2.0
Fruit: 0.0
Bread: 2.0
Meat: 0.0
Fat: 0.0

1. Combine all ingredients, except pasta, salt, white pepper, and Parmesan cheese, in slow cooker; cover and cook on high 4 to 5 hours, adding pasta during the last 20 minutes. Season to taste with salt and white pepper. Sprinkle each bowl of soup with 1 teaspoon Parmesan cheese.

Hot Chili Vichyssoise

Potato soup will never be boring if served Tex-Mex style. This version, prepared with chilies, packs a punch!

6 first-course servings

4 cups reduced-sodium fat-free chicken broth, divided
1 pound new red potatoes, unpeeled, halved
1 each: medium leek (white part only), poblano and jalapeño chili
6 cloves garlic, peeled
1½ teaspoons ground cumin
½ teaspoon each: chili powder, dried oregano leaves
½–¾ cup 2% reduced-fat milk
1 tablespoon cornstarch
¼ cup chopped cilantro
Salt, to taste

Per Serving:
Calories: 113
% calories from fat: 2
Protein (g): 6.6
Carbohydrate (g): 20.9
Fat (g): 0.3
Saturated fat (g): 0
Cholesterol (mg): 0
Sodium (mg): 169
Exchanges:
Milk: 0.0
Vegetable: 1.0
Fruit: 0.0
Bread: 1.0
Meat: 0.0
Fat: 0.0

1. Combine all ingredients, except milk, cornstarch, cilantro, and salt, in 6-quart slow cooker; cover and cook on high 4 to 5 hours. Stir in combined milk and cornstarch, stirring 2 to 3 minutes. Process soup in food processor or blender until smooth. Stir in cilantro; season with salt. Serve warm or chilled.

Acorn Squash Soup

Sweet spices complement this fall soup.

6 first-course servings

2 cups reduced-fat chicken broth
2 medium acorn squash, peeled, cubed
½ cup chopped onion
½ teaspoon ground cinnamon
¼ teaspoon each: ground coriander and cumin
½ cup 2% reduced-fat milk
1 tablespoon cider vinegar
Salt and pepper, to taste

Per Serving:
Calories: 90
% calories from fat: 5
Protein (g): 4.0
Carbohydrate (g): 19.2
Fat (g): 0.6
Saturated fat (g): 0.3
Cholesterol (mg): 1.6
Sodium (mg): 317
Exchanges:
Milk: 0.0
Vegetable: 0.0
Fruit: 0.0
Bread: 1.5
Meat: 0.0
Fat: 0.0

1. Combine all ingredients, except milk, vinegar, salt, and pepper, in slow cooker; cover and cook on high 3 to 4 hours. Process soup, milk, and vinegar in food processor or blender until smooth. Season to taste with salt and pepper.

Apple Squash Soup

This soup is the perfect autumn offering.

8 first-course servings

3 cups Chicken Stock (see p. 30) or chicken broth
1⅓ cups apple cider
1 large butternut squash (about 2½ pounds), peeled, seeded, cubed
2 tart cooking apples, peeled, cored, chopped
1½ cups chopped onions
2 teaspoons ground cinnamon
¼ teaspoon each: ground ginger, cloves
⅛ teaspoon ground nutmeg
Salt and pepper, to taste
Spiced Sour Cream (recipe follows)

Per Serving:
Calories: 155
% calories from fat: 15
Protein (g): 3.3
Carbohydrate (g): 32.6
Fat (g): 2.8
Saturated fat (g): 0.5
Cholesterol (mg): 1.3
Sodium (mg): 48
Exchanges:
Milk: 0.0
Vegetable: 0.0
Fruit: 0.0
Bread: 2.0
Meat: 0.0
Fat: 0.5

1. Combine all ingredients, except salt, pepper, and sour cream, in slow cooker; cover and cook on high 4 to 5 hours. Process soup in food processor or blender until smooth; season to taste with salt and pepper. Serve with Spiced Sour Cream.

Spiced Sour Cream

Makes about 1 cup

½ cup reduced-fat sour cream
1 teaspoon sugar
½ teaspoon ground cinnamon
⅛ teaspoon ground ginger
1–2 teaspoons lemon juice

1. Combine all ingredients.

Summer Squash Soup

Use any summer squash in this soup.

6 first-course servings

3 cups reduced-sodium fat-free chicken broth
4 medium zucchini, chopped
1 cup peeled cubed Idaho potato
⅓ cup each: chopped shallots, green onions
2 cloves garlic, minced
1½ teaspoons dried tarragon leaves
1 cup chopped kale or spinach
¼–½ cup 2% reduced-fat milk
1 tablespoon cornstarch
Salt and white pepper, to taste
Cayenne pepper, as garnish
Garlic Croutons (see p. 51)

Per Serving:
Calories: 100
% calories from fat: 7
Protein (g): 3.8
Carbohydrate (g): 20.6
Fat (g): 0.8
Saturated fat (g): 0.1
Cholesterol (mg): 0
Sodium (mg): 65
Exchanges:
Milk: 0.0
Vegetable: 1.0
Fruit: 0.0
Bread: 1.0
Meat: 0.0
Fat: 0.0

1. Combine all ingredients, except kale, milk, cornstarch, salt, white and cayenne pepper, and Garlic Croutons, in slow cooker; cover and cook on high 4 to 5 hours, adding kale during the last 15 minutes. Process soup, milk, and cornstarch in food processor or blender until smooth; season to taste with salt and white pepper. Serve warm or chilled; sprinkle each bowl of soup with cayenne pepper and top with Garlic Croutons.

Variation

Squash and Fennel Bisque—Make soup as above, adding 1 sliced fennel bulb and ½ cup sliced celery, and substituting spinach for kale. Omit tarragon. Thin with additional broth if necessary.

Ginger Pumpkin Soup

Yellow winter squash, such as hubbard or acorn, can be substituted for the pumpkin.

6 first-course servings

3 cups Chicken Stock (see p. 30) or chicken broth
1 small pumpkin (about 2 pounds), peeled, seeded, cubed
1 cup chopped onion
1 tablespoon chopped gingerroot
1 teaspoon minced garlic
½ cup dry white wine or chicken stock
½ teaspoon ground cloves
Salt and pepper, to taste

Per Serving:
Calories: 83
% calories from fat: 6
Protein (g): 2.8
Carbohydrate (g): 15.3
Fat (g): 0.6
Saturated fat (g): 0.2
Cholesterol (mg): 1.7
Sodium (mg): 8
Exchanges:
Milk: 0.0
Vegetable: 0.0
Fruit: 0.0
Bread: 1.0
Meat: 0.0
Fat: 0.0

1. Combine all ingredients, except salt and pepper, in slow cooker; cover and cook on high 4 to 5 hours. Process soup in food processor or blender until smooth; season to taste with salt and pepper.

Spinach-Pasta Soup with Basil

Serve this fragrant soup with garlic bread or foccacia.

4 first-course servings

1½ quarts Chicken Stock (see p. 30) or chicken broth
1 each: finely chopped small onion, minced garlic clove
1–1½ teaspoons dried basil leaves
1 cup each: chopped plum tomatoes, rinsed drained canned garbanzo beans
1 package (10 ounces) frozen chopped spinach, thawed
¾ cup cooked broken vermicelli
Salt and pepper, to taste
2 tablespoons grated Parmesan cheese, as garnish

Per Serving:
Calories: 193
% calories from fat: 18
Protein (g): 13.3
Carbohydrate (g): 27.6
Fat (g): 3.9
Saturated fat (g): 0.9
Cholesterol (mg): 2
Sodium (mg): 563
Exchanges:
Milk: 0.0
Vegetable: 0.0
Fruit: 0.0
Bread: 2.0
Meat: 1.0
Fat: 0.0

1. Combine all ingredients, except spinach, pasta, salt, pepper, and cheese, in slow cooker; cover and cook on high 4 to 6 hours, adding spinach and pasta during the last 30 minutes. Season to taste with salt and pepper. Sprinkle each bowl of soup with Parmesan cheese.

Variation

Spinach-Pasta Soup with Ham and Beans—Make recipe as above, adding 8 to 12 ounces cubed boneless pork loin and substituting navy or Great Northern beans for the garbanzo beans.

Cream of Tomato Soup

A soup similar to the favorite brand-name canned tomato soup we all remember eating as kids! Canned tomatoes are necessary for the flavor, so don't substitute fresh.

4 first-course servings

2 cups whole milk, divided
1 can (14½ ounces each) diced tomatoes, undrained
1–2 teaspoons beef bouillon crystals
3 tablespoons cornstarch
⅛ teaspoon baking soda
2 teaspoons sugar
1–2 tablespoons margarine or butter
Salt and pepper, to taste

Per Cup:
Calories: 39
% calories from fat: 18
Protein (g): 4.9
Carbohydrate (g): 0.8
Fat (g): 0.8
Saturated fat (g): 0.2
Cholesterol (mg): 1
Sodium (mg): 36
Exchanges:
Milk: 0.0
Vegetable: 0.0
Fruit: 0.0
Bread: 0.0
Meat: 0.5
Fat: 0.0

1. Combine 1 cup milk, tomatoes with liquid, and bouillon crystals in slow cooker; cover and cook on low 3 to 4 hours. Process in food processer or blender until smooth; return to slow cooker. Cover and cook on high 10 minutes; stir in combined remaining 1 cup milk and cornstarch, stirring 2 to 3 minutes. Stir in baking soda, sugar, and margarine; season to taste with salt and pepper.

Winter Gazpacho

This hot version of gazpacho brings vegetable-garden flavors and a bright assortment of garnishes to the winter dinner table.

6 first-course servings

4 cups tomato juice
½ cup each: chopped carrots, celery, green bell pepper
2 teaspoons Worcestershire sauce
1 teaspoon beef bouillon crystals
¼ teaspoon dried tarragon leaves
1 cup packed spinach
Salt and cayenne pepper, to taste
1 each: chopped small onion, hard-cooked egg, cubed
  small avocado
Garlic Croutons (recipe follows)

Per Serving:
Calories: 115
% calories from fat: 27
Protein (g): 4.2
Carbohydrate (g): 18.3
Fat (g): 3.8
Saturated fat (g): 0.7
Cholesterol (mg): 35.3
Sodium (mg): 221
Exchanges:
Milk: 0.0
Vegetable: 2.0
Fruit: 0.0
Bread: 0.5
Meat: 0.0
Fat: 0.5

1. Combine tomato juice, carrots, celery, bell pepper, Worcestershire sauce, bouillon crystals, and tarragon in slow cooker; cover and cook on high 4 to 5 hours adding spinach during last 15 minutes. Process soup in food processor or blender until smooth. Season to taste with salt and cayenne pepper. Serve in shallow bowls; sprinkle with chopped onion, egg, avocado, and Garlic Croutons.

Garlic Croutons

Makes 1½ cups

1½ cups cubed firm or day-old French bread (½-inch)
Vegetable cooking spray
1 teaspoon garlic powder

1. Spray bread cubes with cooking spray; sprinkle with garlic powder and toss. Arrange in single layer in baking pan; bake at 375 degrees until browned, 8 to 10 minutes, stirring occasionally.

Smoky Tomato Bisque

Smoked pork hocks give a rich flavor to this tomato soup.

8 first-course servings

2½ cups Beef Stock (see p. 31) or beef broth
1 can (28 ounces) crushed tomatoes
1 can (6 ounces) tomato paste
2 small smoked pork hocks
1 each: chopped large onion, cubed medium potato,
    sliced carrot, small red bell pepper
2 each: sliced ribs celery, minced garlic cloves
1 teaspoon dried thyme leaves
½ teaspoon each: ground allspice, curry powder
1½ cups whole milk, divided
2 tablespoons cornstarch
1 teaspoon sugar
Salt and pepper, to taste

Per Serving:
Calories: 123
% calories from fat: 13
Protein (g): 6.5
Carbohydrate (g): 20.1
Fat (g): 1.8
Saturated fat (g): 0.6
Cholesterol (mg): 4.1
Sodium (mg): 500
Exchanges:
Milk: 0.0
Vegetable: 0.0
Fruit: 0.5
Bread: 1.5
Meat: 0.0
Fat: 0.5

1. Combine all ingredients, except milk, cornstarch, sugar, salt, and pepper, in slow cooker; cover and cook on high 4 to 5 hours. Discard pork hocks. Process soup and 1 cup milk in food processor or blender until smooth; return to slow cooker. Cover and cook on high 10 minutes. Stir in combined remaining ½ cup milk, cornstarch, and sugar, stirring 2 to 3 minutes. Season to taste with salt and pepper.

Two-Tomato Soup

The concentrated flavor of sun-dried tomatoes enhances the taste of garden-ripe tomato soup.

6 first-course servings

4 cups each: reduced-sodium fat-free chicken
    broth, chopped ripe or canned tomatoes
1 cup chopped onion
½ cup each: chopped celery, carrot
2 teaspoons minced roasted garlic
1 large Idaho potato, peeled, cubed
½ cup sun-dried tomatoes (not in oil),
    room temperature
½ teaspoon dried basil leaves
½ cup 2% reduced-fat milk
2–3 teaspoons sugar
Salt and pepper, to taste

Per Serving:
Calories: 117
% calories from fat: 5
Protein (g): 3.7
Carbohydrate (g): 22.6
Fat (g): 0.8
Saturated fat (g): 0.1
Cholesterol (mg): 0
Sodium (mg): 150
Exchanges:
Milk: 0.0
Vegetable: 2.0
Fruit: 0.0
Bread: 1.0
Meat: 0.0
Fat: 0.0

1. Combine all ingredients, except milk, sugar, salt, and pepper, in slow cooker; cover and cook on high 4 to 5 hours. Process soup, milk, and sugar in food processor or blender until smooth; season to taste with sugar, salt, and pepper.

Variation

Baked Two-Tomato Soup—Make soup as above. Ladle into oven-proof bowls. Thaw 1 sheet (½ package) frozen puff pastry according to package directions. Cut 6 rounds the size of tops of bowls and place on top of soup, pressing gently to rims of bowls. Brush with beaten egg, and sprinkle each with 1 to 2 teaspoons grated Parmesan cheese. Bake at 375 degrees until dough is puffed and golden, about 20 minutes.

Zesty Tomato-Vegetable Soup

Italian tomatoes make this flavorful vegetable soup especially good.

6 first-course servings

2 cups reduced-sodium beef broth
1 can (28 ounces) Italian plum tomatoes,
    undrained
¼ cup dry white wine or beef broth
1 teaspoon lemon juice
1 each: chopped medium onion, large rib celery,
    medium carrot, red bell pepper
¾ teaspoon celery salt
Pinch crushed red pepper
Salt and pepper, to taste

Per Serving:
Calories: 81
% calories from fat: 15
Protein (g): 3.1
Carbohydrate (g): 11.6
Fat (g): 1.3
Saturated fat (g): 0.2
Cholesterol (mg): 0
Sodium (mg): 608
Exchanges:
Milk: 0.0
Vegetable: 2.0
Fruit: 0.0
Bread: 0.0
Meat: 0.0
Fat: 0.5

1. Combine all ingredients, except salt and pepper, in slow cooker; cover and cook on high 4 to 5 hours. Process soup in food processor or blender until smooth; season to taste with salt and pepper. Serve warm or refrigerate and serve chilled.

Zucchini Soup

Make this soup when your garden is overflowing with zucchini!

8 first-course servings

4 cups each: reduced-fat chicken broth, sliced zucchini
2 cups chopped onions
4 cloves garlic, minced
2 tablespoons tarragon vinegar
2 teaspoons curry powder
1 teaspoon dried marjoram leaves
¼ teaspoon celery seeds
½ cup reduced-fat plain yogurt
Salt and cayenne pepper, to taste
Paprika, as garnish

Per Serving:
Calories: 84
% calories from fat: 4
Protein (g): 8.5
Carbohydrate (g): 11.9
Fat (g): 0.4
Saturated fat (g): 0.1
Cholesterol (mg): 1.4
Sodium (mg): 144
Exchanges:
Milk: 0.5
Vegetable: 2.0
Fruit: 0.0
Bread: 0.0
Meat: 0.0
Fat: 0.0

1. Combine all ingredients, except yogurt, salt, cayenne pepper, and paprika in slow cooker; cover and cook on high 3 to 4 hours. Process soup and yogurt in food processor or blender until smooth; season to taste with salt and cayenne pepper. Serve warm or refrigerate and serve chilled; sprinkle each bowl of soup with paprika.

Garden Soup

A light, colorful soup showcasing an appealing blend of vegetables and herbs.

6 first-course servings

4 cups Chicken Stock (see p. 30) or chicken broth
1 cup chopped onion
1 cup canned cannellini beans, rinsed, drained
½ cup each: diced red bell pepper, celery, carrots
2 cloves garlic, minced
1 bay leaf
1½ teaspoons dried Italian seasoning
½ cup each: diced yellow summer squash, zucchini
2 medium tomatoes, diced
Salt and pepper, to taste

Per Serving:
Calories: 124
% calories from fat: 19
Protein (g): 8.8
Carbohydrate (g): 17.8
Fat (g): 2.7
Saturated fat (g): 0.4
Cholesterol (mg): 0
Sodium (mg): 366
Exchanges:
Milk: 0.0
Vegetable: 1.0
Fruit: 0.0
Bread: 1.0
Meat: 0.0
Fat: 0.5

1. Combine all ingredients, except squash, zucchini, tomatoes, salt, and pepper, in slow cooker; cover and cook on high 3 to 4 hours, adding squash and tomatoes during last 30 minutes. Discard bay leaf; season to taste with salt and pepper.

Many-Vegetable Soup

Any combination of vegetables may be used for this soup.

4 first-course servings

2 cups reduced-fat chicken broth
½ cup each: coarsely chopped carrot, celery, onion,
   mushrooms, small broccoli florets
½ teaspoon dried tarragon leaves
1½ cups sliced asparagus (1-inch)
1 cup reduced-fat plain yogurt
2 tablespoons cornstarch
Salt and pepper, to taste

Per Serving:
Calories: 63
% calories from fat: 4
Protein (g): 6.3
Carbohydrate (g): 9.3
Fat (g): 0.3
Saturated fat (g): 0.1
Cholesterol (mg): 1
Sodium (mg): 102
Exchanges:
Milk: 0.0
Vegetable: 2.0
Fruit: 0.0
Bread: 0.0
Meat: 0.0
Fat: 0.0

1. Combine broth and vegetables, except asparagus,
in slow cooker; cover and cook on high 3 to 4 hours,
adding asparagus during last 20 minutes. Stir in combined yogurt and
cornstarch, stirring 2 to 3 minutes; season to taste with salt and pepper.

Stracciatelle with Tiny Meatballs

*Stracciatelle means "torn rags," which is what the egg whites look like when
you stir them into the hot soup.*

4 first-course servings

1 quart Chicken Stock (see p. 30) or
   chicken broth
4 ounces spinach, sliced
Turkey Meatballs (recipe follows)
½ cup each: chopped celery, onion, sliced
   carrot, pastina or other small soup pasta
1 egg white, lightly beaten
Salt and pepper, to taste
Shredded Parmesan cheese, as garnish

Per Serving:
Calories: 220
% calories from fat: 25
Protein (g): 21.5
Carbohydrate (g): 19.2
Fat (g): 6.0
Saturated fat (g): 1.7
Cholesterol (mg): 46.1
Sodium (mg): 296
Exchanges:
Milk: 0.0
Vegetable: 0.0
Fruit: 0.0
Bread: 1.5
Meat: 2.0
Fat: 0.0

1. Combine all ingredients, except pastina, egg white,
salt, pepper, and Parmesan cheese, in slow cooker; cover and cook on low
6 to 8 hours, adding pastina during last 30 minutes. Slowly stir egg white
into soup; season to taste with salt and pepper. Garnish each bowl of soup
with Parmesan cheese.

Turkey Meatballs

Makes 24 small meatballs

8 ounces ground lean turkey
½ small onion, minced
2 tablespoons seasoned dry bread crumbs
1 tablespoon grated Parmesan cheese
2 tablespoons tomato paste

1. Mix all ingredients; shape into 24 meatballs.

Vegetable-Barley Soup

Any vegetables you like can be substituted in this versatile soup.

8 first-course servings

2 quarts Beef Stock (see p. 31) or beef broth
1 can (15 ounces) tomato sauce
2 cups each: cubed potatoes, cut green beans,
    thinly sliced cabbage
½ cup finely chopped parsley
1 tablespoon dried Italian seasoning
1–2 teaspoons chili powder
⅓ cup quick-cooking barley
Salt and pepper, to taste

Per Serving:
Calories: 108
% calories from fat: 9
Protein (g): 3.5
Carbohydrate (g): 22.7
Fat (g): 1.1
Saturated fat (g): 0.2
Cholesterol (mg): 0.3
Sodium (mg): 111
Exchanges:
Milk: 0.0
Vegetable: 0.0
Fruit: 0.0
Bread: 1.5
Meat: 0.0
Fat: 0.0

1. Combine all ingredients, except barley, salt, and pepper, in 6-quart slow cooker; cover and cook on high 3 to 4 hours, adding barley during the last 30 minutes. Season to taste with salt and pepper.

Bean and Barley Soup with Kale

This nutritious soup is a great beginning to any meal.

8 first-course servings

7 cups Fragrant Beef Stock (see p. 32) or beef broth
2 cans (15 ounces each) Great Northern beans,
   rinsed, drained
1½ cups chopped onions
1 cup chopped carrots
8 ounces mushrooms, sliced
1 teaspoon minced garlic
⅛–¼ teaspoon crushed red pepper
2 teaspoons dried thyme leaves
½ cup quick-cooking barley
3–4 cups sliced kale
1 tablespoon lemon juice
Salt and pepper, to taste

Per Serving:
Calories: 183
% calories from fat: 10
Protein (g): 11.7
Carbohydrate (g): 35.6
Fat (g): 2.3
Saturated fat (g): 0.5
Cholesterol (mg): 2.6
Sodium (mg): 350
Exchanges:
Milk: 0.0
Vegetable: 1.0
Fruit: 0.0
Bread: 2.0
Meat: 0.0
Fat: 0.5

1. Combine all ingredients, except barley, kale, lemon juice, salt, and pepper, in 6-quart slow cooker; cover and cook on high 4 to 5 hours, adding barley and kale during last 30 minutes. Stir in lemon juice; season to taste with salt and pepper.

Navy Bean and Spinach Soup

A delicious, hearty soup with the meaty taste of smoked pork.

6 first-course servings

2 quarts chicken broth
1 smoked pork hock (optional)
1½ cups dried navy beans
1 large chopped onion
2 cloves garlic, minced
2 each: sliced large carrots, ribs celery, bay leaves
¾ teaspoon each: dried marjoram, thyme, and
   basil leaves
1 can (14½ ounces) stewed tomatoes
1 package (10 ounces) frozen chopped spinach,
   thawed
¼ cup quick-cooking barley
Salt and cayenne pepper, to taste

Per Serving:
Calories: 225
% calories from fat: 8
Protein (g): 16
Carbohydrate (g): 37.6
Fat (g): 2.2
Saturated fat (g): 0.4
Cholesterol (mg): 1.3
Sodium (mg): 385
Exchanges:
Milk: 0.0
Vegetable: 1.0
Fruit: 0.0
Bread: 2.0
Meat: 1.0
Fat: 0.0

1. Combine all ingredients, except tomatoes, spinach, barley, salt, and cayenne pepper, in 6-quart slow cooker; cover and cook on low until beans are tender, 8 to 10 hours, adding tomatoes, spinach, and barley during last 30 minutes. Discard pork hock and bay leaves; season to taste with salt and cayenne pepper.

Lentil Soup

This satisfying soup is good on a cold, snowy day.

6 first-course servings

2 quarts water
1 large smoked pork hock
1 pound dried brown lentils
1 cup finely chopped onion
½ cup each: finely chopped celery and carrot
2 teaspoons each: sugar, beef bouillon crystals
¼ teaspoon dry mustard
½ teaspoon dried thyme leaves
Salt and cayenne pepper, to taste

Per Serving:
Calories: 89
% calories from fat: 12
Protein (g): 6.7
Carbohydrate (g): 16.5
Fat (g): 1.4
Saturated fat (g): 0.3
Cholesterol (mg): 6.5
Sodium (mg): 277
Exchanges:
Milk: 0.0
Vegetable: 0.0
Fruit: 0.0
Bread: 1.0
Meat: 0.0
Fat: 0.5

1. Combine all ingredients, except salt and pepper, in 6-quart slow cooker; cover and cook on low 6 to 8 hours. Discard pork hock; season to taste with salt and pepper.

Lentil Soup with Orzo

For a hearty vegetarian dinner, make this soup with Roasted Vegetable Stock (see p. 35).

6 first-course servings

2 cups Beef Stock (see p. 31) or beef broth
2 cans (14½ ounces each) Italian-style stewed tomatoes
1 cup water
8 ounces dried lentils
1½ cups minced onions
¾ cup each: chopped carrot, celery
1 tablespoon minced garlic
1 teaspoon dried oregano leaves
⅛–¼ teaspoon crushed red pepper
4 ounces uncooked orzo or other small soup pasta
2 cups sliced packed spinach
Salt and pepper, to taste

Per Serving:
Calories: 212
% calories from fat: 9
Protein (g): 12.3
Carbohydrate (g): 45 7
Fat (g): 24
Saturated fat (g): 0.3
Cholesterol (mg): 0
Sodium (mg): 293
Exchanges:
Milk: 0.0
Vegetable: 2.0
Fruit: 0.0
Bread: 2.0
Meat: 1.0
Fat: 0.0

1. Combine all ingredients, except orzo, spinach, salt, and pepper, in 6-quart slow cooker; cover and cook on high 4 to 5 hours, adding orzo and spinach during last 30 minutes. Season to taste with salt and pepper.

Sausage and Lentil Soup

Thick, hearty, and accented with the robust flavor of Italian sausage.

10 first-course servings

8–12 ounces reduced-fat Italian-style turkey sausage, casing removed
3 quarts Beef Stock (see p. 31) or beef broth
1 can (28 ounces) crushed tomatoes
1 pound dried lentils
1½ cups chopped onions
¾ cup chopped carrots
½ teaspoon each: dried marjoram and thyme leaves
1 bay leaf
2–3 teaspoons lemon juice
Salt and pepper, to taste

Per Serving:
Calories: 192
% calories from fat: 15
Protein (g): 14.3
Carbohydrate (g): 28.8
Fat (g): 3.4
Saturated fat (g): 0.8
Cholesterol (mg): 12.5
Sodium (mg): 202
Exchanges:
Milk: 0.0
Vegetable: 0.0
Fruit: 0.0
Bread: 2.0
Meat: 1.0
Fat: 0.0

1. Cook sausage in medium skillet over medium heat until browned, about 8 minutes, and crumble with a fork. Combine sausage and remaining ingredients, except lemon juice, salt, and pepper, in 6-quart slow cooker; cover and cook on high 4 to 5 hours. Discard bay leaf; season to taste with lemon juice, salt, and pepper.

Variation
Lentil Soup with Fennel—Make recipe as above, omitting Italian sausage and adding ½ cup sliced fennel bulb. Substitute 1 teaspoon lightly crushed fennel seeds for the marjoram and thyme. Process soup in food processor or blender until smooth; garnish each bowl of soup with finely chopped fennel tops.

Split-Pea Soup Jardiniere

This "gardener's style" split pea soup is flavored the old-fashioned way with a ham bone, leeks, turnips, and carrots.

8 first-course servings

2½ quarts water
1 pound dried split green peas
1 each: meaty ham bone, quartered small onion
2 each: sliced leeks (white parts only), ribs celery, carrots, cubed small turnips, chopped large tomatoes, minced cloves garlic
4 whole cloves
2 teaspoons dried thyme leaves
1 bay leaf
Salt and pepper, to taste

Per Serving:
Calories: 175
% calories from fat: 6
Protein (g): 11.6
Carbohydrate (g): 31.5
Fat (g): 1.2
Saturated fat (g): 0.3
Cholesterol (mg): 4.8
Sodium (mg): 156
Exchanges:
Milk 0.0
Vegetable: 2.0
Fruit: 0.0
Bread: 1.0
Meat: 1.0
Fat: 0.0

1. Combine all ingredients, except salt and pepper, in 6-quart slow cooker; cover and cook on low 6 to 8 hours. Remove ham bone; remove and shred meat. Return shredded meat to soup; discard bones and bay leaf. Season to taste with salt and pepper.

Variations

Canadian Pea Soup—Make soup as above, substituting yellow split peas for the green split peas, 2 to 4 ounces diced lean salt pork for the ham bone, and 2 parsnips for the turnip. Omit celery.

Dutch Split-Pea Soup—Make soup as above, omitting onion and cloves; substitute an 8-ounce link reduced-fat smoked sausage for the ham bone and ½ cup diced celery root for the turnips. Remove sausage; process soup in food processor or blender until smooth. Slice sausage and stir into soup; season to taste with salt and pepper.

THREE

Lunch and Supper Soups

Asparagus-Tomato Soup with Cheese

This delicious soup combines flavors of asparagus, tomatoes, and Cheddar cheese, accented with mustard.

6 first-course servings

3 cups reduced-sodium fat-free chicken broth
1 can (14½ ounces) diced tomatoes, undrained
1 each: chopped medium onion, carrot
½ teaspoon dried marjoram leaves
¼ teaspoon each: dry mustard, white pepper
½ cup uncooked converted long-grain rice
1¼ pounds asparagus spears, sliced, cooked
1 cup (4 ounces) shredded reduced-fat Cheddar cheese
Salt, to taste

Per Serving:
Calories: 141
% calories from fat: 26
Protein (g): 10.2
Carbohydrate (g): 17.3
Fat (g): 4.2
Saturated fat (g): 2
Cholesterol (mg): 12.7
Sodium (mg): 558
Exchanges:
Milk: 0.0
Vegetable: 2.0
Fruit: 0.0
Bread: 0.5
Meat: 1.0
Fat: 0.0

1. Combine all ingredients, except rice, asparagus, cheese, and salt, in slow cooker; cover and cook on high 4 to 6 hours, stirring in rice during last 2 hours, and asparagus during last 20 minutes. Add cheese and stir until melted. Season to taste with salt.

Cheesy Broccoli-Potato Soup

For variation, cauliflower can be substituted for part or all of the broccoli.

6 entrée servings

1 quart reduced-sodium fat-free chicken or beef broth
1 cup chopped onion
½ cup each: finely chopped celery, carrots
2 cups unpeeled cubed Idaho potatoes
½ teaspoon each: celery seeds, dried thyme leaves
2 cups small broccoli florets
1 cup 2% reduced-fat milk
2 tablespoons cornstarch
2 cups (8 ounces) shredded reduced-fat mild
   Cheddar cheese
Salt and pepper, to taste

Per Serving:
Calories: 233
% calories from fat: 31
Protein (g): 15.2
Carbohydrate (g): 26
Fat (g): 8.3
Saturated fat (g): 4.7
Cholesterol (mg): 33.3
Sodium (mg): 757
Exchanges:
Milk: 0.0
Vegetable: 1.0
Fruit: 0.0
Bread: 1.5
Meat: 1.0
Fat: 1.0

1. Combine all ingredients, except broccoli, milk, cornstarch, cheese, salt, and pepper, in slow cooker; cover and cook on low 6 to 8 hours, adding broccoli during last 30 minutes. Turn heat to high and cook 10 minutes; stir in combined milk and cornstarch, stirring 2 to 3 minutes. Add cheese, stirring until melted, 2 to 3 minutes. Season to taste with salt and pepper.

Sweet-and-Sour Cabbage Soup

This rich, tangy cabbage soup is made with both beef and turkey.

8 entrée servings

8 ounces each: ground beef round, turkey breast
2 quarts Fragrant Beef Stock (see p. 32) or beef broth
1 can (15 ounces) tomato sauce
4 cups thinly sliced green cabbage
1 large onion, chopped
½ cup sliced carrot
2 cloves garlic, minced
2 tablespoons each: cider vinegar, brown sugar
1 bay leaf
1 teaspoon dried thyme leaves
⅛ teaspoon ground cinnamon
⅓ cup raisins
½ cup uncooked converted long-grain rice
Salt and pepper, to taste

Per Serving:
Calories: 202
% calories from fat: 18
Protein (g): 16.1
Carbohydrate (g): 26.2
Fat (g): 4.2
Saturated fat (g): 1.7
Cholesterol (mg): 25.8
Sodium (mg): 425
Exchanges:
Milk: 0.0
Vegetable: 1.0
Fruit: 0.0
Bread: 1.0
Meat: 2.0
Fat: 0.0

1. Cook ground beef and turkey in lightly greased large skillet over medium heat until browned, about 5 minutes, crumbling meat with a fork. Combine meats and remaining ingredients, except rice, salt, and pepper, in 6-quart slow cooker; cover and cook on low 6 to 8 hours, adding rice during last 2 hours. Discard bay leaf; season to taste with salt and pepper.

Creamy Carrot Soup

Orange and ginger flavor this delicious soup. The soup is also excellent served chilled.

8 first-course servings

4 cups each: reduced-sodium fat-free chicken
   broth, sliced carrots
½ cup frozen orange juice concentrate
1 teaspoon chopped gingerroot
½ teaspoon each: dried tarragon and thyme leaves
1½ cups 2% reduced-fat milk, divided
1 tablespoon cornstarch
Salt and pepper, to taste
Sour cream, as garnish

Per Serving:
Calories: 104
% calories from fat: 22
Protein (g): 7.3
Carbohydrate (g): 12.7
Fat (g): 2.6
Saturated fat (g): 0.3
Cholesterol (mg): 1.9
Sodium (mg): 159
Exchanges:
Milk: 0.5
Vegetable: 1.0
Fruit: 0.0
Bread: 0.0
Meat: 0.0
Fat: 0.5

1. Combine broth, carrots, orange juice concentrate,

gingerroot, and herbs in slow cooker; cover and cook on low 4 to 6 hours, adding 1 cup milk during last 30 minutes. Turn slow cooker to high and cook 10 minutes; stir in combined remaining ½ cup milk and cornstarch, stirring 2 to 3 minutes. Process soup in food processor or blender until smooth. Season to taste with salt and pepper; garnish each bowl of soup with a dollop of sour cream.

Cauliflower Soup

This velvety soup is flavored with a combination of curry powder, and crushed red pepper—delicious!

4–6 first-course servings

3 cups reduced-sodium fat-free chicken broth
4 cups cauliflower florets
⅔ cup each: diced carrot, onion, sliced celery
1 teaspoon curry powder
⅛–¼ teaspoon crushed red pepper
1 cup 2% reduced-fat milk
Juice of ½ lemon
Salt and pepper, to taste
Paprika, as garnish

Per Serving:
Calories: 67
% calories from fat: 10
Protein (g): 4.3
Carbohydrate (g): 12.4
Fat (g): 0.8
Saturated fat (g): 0.1
Cholesterol (mg): 0.8
Sodium (mg): 316
Exchanges:
Milk: 0.0
Vegetable: 2.0
Fruit: 0.0
Bread: 0.0
Meat: 0.0
Fat: 0.0

1. Combine all ingredients, except milk, lemon juice, salt, pepper, and paprika, in slow cooker; cover and cook on high 4 to 6 hours. Process soup and milk in food processor or blender until smooth; season to taste with lemon juice, salt, and pepper; sprinkle each bowl of soup with paprika.

Curried Corn Soup

A variety of spices and coconut milk make this soup an exotic treat.

6 first-course servings

2 cups each: reduced-sodium fat-free chicken
  broth, whole kernel corn
1½ cups chopped onions
1 jalapeño chili, finely chopped
1 tablespoon each: minced garlic, gingerroot
½ teaspoon each: ground cumin, cinnamon
1 cup 2% reduced-fat milk
1 can (14 ounces) light coconut milk
2 tablespoons cornstarch
Salt and pepper, to taste
Chopped cilantro, as garnish

Per Serving:
Calories: 161
% calories from fat: 27
Protein (g): 6.2
Carbohydrate (g): 23.5
Fat (g): 4.9
Saturated fat (g): 0.3
Cholesterol (mg): 0
Sodium (mg): 117
Exchanges:
Milk: 0.0
Vegetable: 1.0
Fruit: 0.0
Bread: 1.0
Meat: 0.0
Fat: 1.0

1. Combine chicken broth, corn, onions, jalapeño chili, garlic, and gingerroot in slow cooker; cover and cook on high 3 to 4 hours, stirring in milk during last 30 minutes. Turn heat to high and cook 10 minutes; add combined coconut milk and cornstarch, stirring 2 to 3 minutes. Season to taste with salt and pepper. Sprinkle each bowl of soup with cilantro.

Eggplant Soup with Roasted Red Pepper Sauce

The swirl of Roasted Red Pepper Sauce is attractive, as well as flavorful.

4 entrée servings

4–5 cups reduced-sodium fat-free chicken broth
2 medium eggplants, peeled, cubed (¾-inch)
¾ cup chopped onion
¼ cup chopped green bell pepper
2 cloves garlic, minced
Salt and white pepper, to taste
Roasted Red Pepper Sauce (recipe follows)

Per Serving:
Calories: 250
% calories from fat: 19
Protein (g): 6.8
Carbohydrate (g): 44.8
Fat (g): 6
Saturated fat (g): 0.7
Cholesterol (mg): 0
Sodium (mg): 25
Exchanges:
Milk: 0.0
Vegetable: 2.0
Fruit: 0.0
Bread: 2.0
Meat: 0.0
Fat: 1.0

1. Combine all ingredients, except salt, white pepper, and Roasted Red Pepper Sauce, in slow cooker; cover and cook on high 4 to 5 hours. Process soup in food processor or blender until smooth. Season to taste with salt and white pepper. Serve warm or refrigerate and serve chilled; swirl about ¼ cup Roasted Red Pepper Sauce into each bowl of soup.

Roasted Red Pepper Sauce

Makes about ¾ cup

2 large red bell peppers, halved
1 teaspoon sugar

1. Place peppers, skin sides up, on broiler pan. Broil 4 to 6 inches from heat source until skins are blistered and blackened. Place peppers in plastic bag for 5 minutes; remove and peel off skins. Process peppers and sugar in food processor or blender until smooth.

Note: 1 jar (12 ounces) roasted red peppers, drained, can be substituted for the peppers in the recipe.

Cream of Mushroom Soup

For richer flavor, use whole milk or light cream instead of reduced-fat milk.

4 first-course servings

3 cups reduced-sodium fat-free chicken broth
1 pound mushrooms, sliced
1 cup chopped onion
1½ cups 2% reduced-fat milk, divided
2 tablespoons cornstarch
Salt and pepper, to taste

1. Combine all ingredients, except milk, cornstarch, salt, and pepper, in slow cooker; cover and cook on low 5 to 6 hours, stirring in 1 cup milk during last 30 minutes. Turn heat to high and cook 10 minutes; stir in combined remaining ½ cup milk and cornstarch, stirring 2 to 3 minutes. Season to taste with salt and pepper.

Per Serving:
Calories: 207
% calories from fat: 29
Protein (g): 8.6
Carbohydrate (g): 25.3
Fat (g): 7
Saturated fat (g): 1.4
Cholesterol (mg): 2.5
Sodium (mg): 185
Exchanges:
Milk: 0.5
Vegetable: 2.5
Fruit: 0.0
Bread: 0.5
Meat: 0.0
Fat: 1.5

Brandied Onion Soup

This soup is wonderful because slow cooking melds flavors. If desired, onions can be cooked in 1 tablespoon margarine or butter in a large skillet over medium-low heat until golden before assembling ingredients in the slow cooker.

8 first-course servings

4 cups thinly sliced onions
2 quarts Fragrant Beef Stock (see p. 32) or beef broth
2–4 tablespoons brandy (optional)
Salt and pepper, to taste

1. Combine all ingredients in 6-quart slow cooker; cover and cook on low 6 to 8 hours. Add brandy; season to taste with salt and pepper.

Per Serving:
Calories: 186
% calories from fat: 30
Protein (g): 10.2
Carbohydrate (g): 22.4
Fat (g): 6.5
Saturated fat (g): 2.7
Cholesterol (mg): 10.9
Sodium (mg): 394
Exchanges:
Milk: 0.0
Vegetable: 1.0
Fruit: 0.0
Bread: 1.0
Meat: 1.0
Fat: 0.5

Variation

Onion and Potato Soup—Make recipe as above, adding 3 cups cubed peeled potatoes, and ¼ teaspoon each dried marjoram and thyme leaves with the stock; sprinkle each bowl of soup with 2 tablespoons shredded Swiss cheese.

Curried Onion-Potato Soup

Enjoy this delicious soup warm in the winter; sip it chilled from soup cups in the summer.

4 first-course servings

1 quart Chicken Stock (see p. 30) or chicken broth
3 cups coarsely chopped onions
2 cups peeled diced potatoes
1 clove garlic, minced
1¼ teaspoons each: ground cumin and turmeric,
   curry powder
¾ cup 2% reduced-fat milk
Salt and pepper, to taste

Per Serving:
Calories: 206
% calories from fat: 21
Protein (g): 7.5
Carbohydrate (g): 31.9
Fat (g): 4.7
Saturated fat (g): 1.6
Cholesterol (mg): 14.6
Sodium (mg): 61
Exchanges:
Milk: 0.0
Vegetable: 0.0
Fruit: 0.0
Bread: 2.0
Meat: 0.0
Fat: 1.0

1. Combine all ingredients, except milk, cornstarch, salt, and pepper, in slow cooker; cover and cook on high 3 to 4 hours. Process soup and milk in food processor or blender until smooth. Season to taste with salt and pepper; serve warm or refrigerate and serve chilled.

Easy Curried Potato Soup

Very simple ingredients make wonderful soup!

4 entrée servings

1 quart reduced-sodium fat-free chicken broth
4 cups peeled cubed baking potatoes
1 each: chopped large onion, diced peeled apple
2 teaspoons minced gingerroot
2 large cloves garlic, minced
½ teaspoon caraway seeds
2–3 teaspoons curry powder
1 can (14½ ounces) stewed tomatoes
Salt and pepper, to taste

Per Serving:
Calories: 254
% calories from fat: 9
Protein (g): 8.8
Carbohydrate (g): 52
Fat (g): 2.7
Saturated fat (g): 1.3
Cholesterol (mg): 5.1
Sodium (mg): 1049
Exchanges:
Milk: 0.0
Vegetable: 1.0
Fruit: 0.0
Bread: 3.0
Meat: 0.0
Fat: 0.5

1. Combine all ingredients, except stewed tomatoes,
salt, and pepper, in slow cooker; cover and cook on high until potatoes are
tender, about 4 hours. Process half the potato mixture in food processor or
blender until smooth. Return to slow cooker and add tomatoes; cover and
cook on high 15 minutes. Season to taste with salt and pepper.

Variation

Smoky Cheese and Potato Soup—Make recipe above, omitting gingerroot,
caraway seeds, and curry powder. At end of cooking time, stir in combined
¾ cup reduced-fat sour cream and 1 tablespoon cornstarch, stirring 2 to
3 minutes. Stir in 1 cup (4 ounces) shredded smoked Gouda or Cheddar
cheese, stirring until melted.

Velvet Vichyssoise

Although typically served chilled, this soup is also delicious served warm.

6 first-course servings

2 cups reduced-sodium fat-free chicken broth
3½ cups peeled cubed Idaho potatoes
½ cup each: chopped onion, leek
2 cups 2% reduced-fat milk, divided
2 tablespoons cornstarch
Salt and pepper, to taste
Minced chives, as garnish

Per Serving:
Calories: 227
% calories from fat: 16
Protein (g): 8.3
Carbohydrate (g): 39.4
Fat (g): 4.2
Saturated fat (g): 0.9
Cholesterol (mg): 1.5
Sodium (mg): 151
Exchanges:
Milk: 0.0
Vegetable: 2.0
Fruit: 0.0
Bread: 2.0
Meat: 0.0
Fat: 1.0

1. Combine broth, potatoes, onion, and leek, in slow cooker; cover and cook on low 6 to 8 hours, stirring in 1½ cups milk during last ½ hour. Turn slow cooker to high and cook 10 minutes; stir in combined remaining ½ cup milk and cornstarch, stirring 2 to 3 minutes. Season to taste with salt and pepper. Process soup in food processor or blender until smooth. Serve hot, or refrigerate and serve chilled. Sprinkle each bowl of soup with chives.

Variations:

Creamy Cauliflower Soup—Make recipe as above, substituting 2½ cups coarsely chopped cauliflower for 2½ cups of the potatoes; add ½ cup (2 ounces) grated Parmesan cheese to the soup with the milk. Omit chives; sprinkle each bowl of soup with ground nutmeg.

Sweet Potato Vichyssoise—Make recipe as above, substituting ¾ cup chopped green onions for the leeks, sweet potatoes for the Idaho potatoes, ½ cup orange juice for the ½ cup milk, and adding ½ teaspoon each ground cinnamon and mace. Sprinkle each bowl of soup with grated orange zest.

Two-Season Squash Soup

Winter butternut squash and summer garden zucchini are combined in this perfect soup.

6 first-course servings

3 cups Beef Stock (see p. 31) or beef broth
1 can (28 ounces) diced tomatoes, undrained
1 can (15 ounces) Great Northern beans, drained, rinsed
1 medium butternut squash, peeled, seeded, cubed
2 medium zucchini, sliced
1 cup chopped onion
2 cloves garlic, minced
1 teaspoon each: Worcestershire sauce, dried marjoram leaves
½ teaspoon dried rosemary leaves
Salt and pepper, to taste

Per Serving:
Calories: 136
% calories from fat: 9
Protein (g): 83
Carbohydrate (g): 27.3
Fat (g): 1.7
Saturated fat (g): 0.3
Cholesterol (mg): 0
Sodium (mg): 296
Exchanges:
Milk: 0.0
Vegetable: 3.0
Fruit: 0.0
Bread: 0.5
Meat: 0.0
Fat: 0.5

1. Combine all ingredients, except 6-quart salt and pepper, in slow cooker; cover and cook on high 4 to 6 hours. Season to taste with salt and pepper.

Ripe Tomato and Leek Soup

Here's a perfect soup for summer's ripest tomatoes.

6 first-course servings

1 quart reduced-sodium fat-free chicken broth
6 large tomatoes, chopped
2 cups sliced leeks (white parts only)
3 cloves garlic, minced
1 teaspoon dried basil leaves
Salt and white pepper, to taste
6 tablespoons reduced-fat sour cream
Basil sprigs, as garnish

Per Serving:
Calories: 120
% calories from fat: 19
Protein (g): 7.3
Carbohydrate (g): 17.7
Fat (g): 2.6
Saturated fat (g): 0.5
Cholesterol (mg): 0
Sodium (mg): 173
Exchanges:
Milk: 0.0
Vegetable: 3.0
Fruit: 0.0
Bread: 0.0
Meat: 0.5
Fat: 0.5

1. Combine all ingredients, except, salt, pepper, sour cream, and basil, in slow cooker; cover and cook on high 3 to 4 hours. Process soup in food processor or blender until smooth; season to taste with salt and white pepper. Serve warm or refrigerate and serve chilled. Garnish each bowl of soup with a dollop of sour cream and a basil sprig.

Creamy Tomato Soup with Chunky Vegetables

A grown-up version of that comforting soup we know so well.

4 first-course servings

1 quart Chicken Stock (see p. 30) or chicken broth
1 can (8 ounces) tomato sauce
1½ cups small cauliflower florets
1 cup each: diced zucchini, green bell pepper,
    onion, cubed unpeeled new potatoes
1 large clove garlic, minced
¾ teaspoon dried basil leaves
¼ teaspoon each: dried thyme and marjoram leaves
⅛ teaspoon dry mustard
¾ cup 2% reduced-fat milk
1 tablespoon cornstarch
2 tablespoons dry sherry (optional)
Salt and pepper, to taste

Per Serving:
Calories: 207
% calories from fat: 22
Protein (g): 8.6
Carbohydrate (g): 31.6
Fat (g): 5.1
Saturated fat (g): 1.6
Cholesterol (mg): 14.6
Sodium (mg): 356
Exchanges:
Milk: 0.0
Vegetable: 0.0
Fruit: 0.0
Bread: 2.0
Meat: 0.0
Fat: 1.0

1. Combine all ingredients, except milk, cornstarch, sherry, salt, and pepper, in slow cooker; cover and cook on high 4 to 6 hours. Stir in combined milk and cornstarch, stirring 2 to 3 minutes. Stir in sherry; season to taste with salt and pepper.

Tomato Soup with Pasta

Freeze ripe tomatoes from your garden for making this soup in the winter, too.

6 first-course servings

3 cups Rich Chicken Stock (see p. 30) or chicken
  broth
3 pounds tomatoes, coarsely chopped
½ cup each: chopped onion, carrot
¼ cup chopped celery
1 clove garlic, minced
1 teaspoon each: dried basil and oregano leaves
½ teaspoon anise seeds, lightly crushed
1 cup small soup pasta (stelline, orzo, or rings)
Salt and pepper, to taste
Shredded Parmesan cheese, as garnish

Per Serving:
Calories: 164
% calories from fat: 20
Protein (g): 7
Carbohydrate (g): 26.3
Fat (g): 3.8
Saturated fat (g): 0.6
Cholesterol (mg): 0.5
Sodium (mg): 45
Exchanges:
Milk: 0.0
Vegetable: 2.0
Fruit: 0.0
Bread: 1.0
Meat: 0.0
Fat: 0.5

1. Combine all ingredients, except pasta, salt, pepper, and cheese, in 6-quart slow cooker; cover and cook on high 3 to 4 hours. Process soup in food processor or blender until smooth. Return soup to slow cooker; cover and cook on high 10 minutes. Stir in pasta and cook until al dente, about 20 minutes. Season to taste with salt and pepper. Sprinkle each bowl of soup with Parmesan cheese.

Garden Harvest Soup

Vary the vegetables according to your garden's or greengrocer's bounty.

6 first-course servings

1¼ quarts reduced-sodium fat-free chicken broth
1 cup each: cut green beans, sliced onion, zucchini,
    yellow summer squash
¾ cup each: sliced carrots, red and yellow bell pepper
½ cup whole kernel corn
2 cloves garlic, minced
½ teaspoon each: dried basil and oregano leaves
⅓ cup 2% reduced-fat milk
Salt and pepper, to taste

Per Serving:
Calories: 136
% calories from fat: 17
Protein (g): 8.4
Carbohydrate (g): 21.3
Fat (g): 2.8
Saturated fat (g): 0.4
Cholesterol (mg): 0
Sodium (mg): 161
Exchanges:
Milk: 0.0
Vegetable: 4.0
Fruit: 0.0
Bread: 0.0
Meat: 0.0
Fat: 0.5

1. Combine all ingredients, except milk, salt, and
pepper, in 6-quart slow cooker; cover and cook on high 4 to 6 hours, adding milk during last 10 minutes. Season to taste with salt and pepper.

Light Minestrone

*Minestrone does not always contain pasta, nor is it always a heavy, hearty
soup. Enjoy this light version of an old favorite.*

8 first-course servings

1¼ quarts reduced-sodium fat-free beef broth
1 cup each: snap peas, broccoli florets, sliced zucchini,
    carrots, halved cherry tomatoes
½ cup each: chopped onion, celery, sliced fennel bulb
2 cloves garlic, minced
1 teaspoon each: dried basil and oregano leaves
Salt and pepper, to taste
Parmesan Croutons (recipe follows)

Per Serving:
Calories: 146
% calories from fat: 21
Protein (g): 7.3
Carbohydrate (g): 4.9
Fat (g): 3.5
Saturated fat (g): 0.6
Cholesterol (mg): 0.5
Sodium (mg): 447
Exchanges:
Milk: 0.0
Vegetable: 1.0
Fruit: 0.0
Bread: 1.0
Meat: 0.0
Fat: 0.5

1. Combine all ingredients, except salt, pepper, and
Parmesan Croutons, in 6-quart slow cooker; cover
and cook on high 3 to 4 hours. Season to taste with salt and pepper;
sprinkle each bowl of soup with Parmesan Croutons.

Parmesan Croutons

Makes 1½ cups

1½ cups cubed firm or day-old Italian bread (½–¾–inch)
Vegetable cooking spray
2 tablespoons Parmesan cheese, finely grated

1. Spray bread cubes with cooking spray; sprinkle with Parmesan cheese and toss. Arrange in single layer on jelly roll pan. Bake at 375 degrees until browned, 8 to 10 minutes, stirring occasionally.

Minestrone with Basil Pesto

In the basil-loving town of Genoa, the addition of aromatic Basil Pesto distinguishes the local version of minestrone.

12 entrée servings

3 quarts Chicken Stock (see p. 30) or chicken broth
2 cans (15 ounces each) cannellini beans, rinsed,
    drained
¾ cup each: chopped leeks (white parts only), carrots,
    celery, chopped yellow bell pepper
2 large cloves garlic, minced
1 pound yellow summer squash, cubed
1 cup frozen peas, thawed
2 cups cooked elbow macaroni
Basil Pesto (recipe follows)
Salt and pepper, to taste
Shredded Parmesan cheese, as garnish

Per Serving:
Calories: 222
% calories from fat: 20
Protein (g): 14
Carbohydrate (g): 32.2
Fat (g): 5.2
Saturated fat (g): 0.8
Cholesterol (mg): 17.4
Sodium (mg): 248
Exchanges:
Milk: 0.0
Vegetable: 0.0
Fruit: 0.0
Bread: 2.0
Meat: 1.0
Fat: 0.5

1. Combine all ingredients, except summer squash, peas, macaroni, Basil Pesto, salt, pepper, and cheese, in 6-quart slow cooker; cover and cook on high 4 to 5 hours, adding summer squash during last hour and peas, marcaroni, and Basil Pesto during last 20 minutes. Season to taste with salt and pepper; sprinkle each bowl of soup with Parmesan cheese.

Basil Pesto

Makes about ½ cup

¾ cup packed basil leaves
3 cloves garlic
2–3 tablespoons each: grated Parmesan cheese, pine nuts or slivered
   almonds, olive oil
2 teaspoons lemon juice
Salt and pepper, to taste

1. Process basil, garlic, Parmesan cheese, and pine nuts in food processor,
adding oil and lemon juice gradually, until mixture is very finely chopped.
Season to taste with salt and pepper.

Summer Soup with Tomato Relish

A fresh tomato relish adds flavor highlights to this colorful soup.

4 first-course servings

1 quart Chicken Stock (see p. 30) or chicken broth
1 pound yellow summer squash, chopped
2 large onions, coarsely chopped
1½ cups whole kernel corn, divided
½ cup diced peeled potato
1 large clove garlic, chopped
¼ teaspoon dry mustard
½ cup 2% reduced-fat milk
1–2 teaspoons lemon juice
Salt and pepper, to taste
Chopped cilantro, as garnish
Fresh Tomato Relish (recipe follows)

Per Serving:
Calories: 169
% calories from fat: 18
Protein (g): 7.6
Carbohydrate (g): 29.7
Fat (g): 3.7
Saturated fat (g): 1.1
Cholesterol (mg): 3.3
Sodium (mg): 357
Exchanges:
Milk: 0.0
Vegetable: 2.0
Fruit: 0.0
Bread: 2.0
Meat: 0.0
Fat: 0.5

1. Combine stock, squash, onions, 1 cup corn, potato, garlic, and dry mustard in slow cooker; cover and cook on high 4 to 6 hours. Process soup and
milk in food processor or blender until smooth; return to slow cooker and
add remaining ½ cup corn. Cover and cook on high 10 minutes; season to
taste with lemon juice, salt, and pepper. Sprinkle each bowl of soup with
cilantro; serve with Fresh Tomato Relish to stir into soup.

Fresh Tomato Relish

1 large, ripe tomato, peeled, finely diced
¼ cup chopped cilantro
1 tablespoon red wine vinegar
¼ teaspoon salt

1. Combine all ingredients.

Easy Tortilla Soup

This simple tortilla soup uses many canned ingredients to speed preparation.

6 first-course servings

2 cans (14½ ounces each) reduced-sodium fat-
free chicken broth
1 can (14½ ounces) diced tomatoes, undrained
1 can (15 ounces) spicy chili beans, undrained
1 can (4 ounces) chopped green chilies, drained
¾ cup chopped onion
1 clove garlic, minced
2 teaspoons red wine vinegar
⅛–¼ teaspoon crushed red pepper
¼ cup chopped cilantro
Salt, to taste
6 corn tortillas (6-inch), cut into ½-inch strips
Vegetable cooking spray
½ small avocado, peeled, cubed

Per Serving:
Calories: 181
% calories from fat: 18
Protein (g): 10
Carbohydrate (g): 30.2
Fat (g): 4.1
Saturated fat (g): 0.6
Cholesterol (mg): 0
Sodium (mg): 530
Exchanges:
Milk: 0.0
Vegetable: 0.0
Fruit: 0.0
Bread: 2.0
Meat: 0.0
Fat: 1.0

1. Combine all ingredients, except cilantro, salt, tortillas, cooking spray, and avocado, in 6-quart slow cooker; cover and cook on high 3 to 4 hours. Stir in cilantro and season to taste with salt.
2. Place tortilla strips on baking sheet. Spray with cooking spray and toss; bake at 375 degrees until crisp, about 5 minutes. Place tortilla strips and avocado in each soup bowl; ladle soup over.

Old-Fashioned Chicken-Vegetable Soup

A homey, heartwarming soup like Grandma used to make.

6 entrée servings

5 cups Chicken Stock (see p. 30)
1 pound boneless, skinless chicken breast, cubed
   (¾-inch)
1 cup each: diced, peeled red potatoes, thinly
   sliced cabbage
¾ cup each: sliced carrots, cubed peeled rutabaga
   or parsnips
⅓ cup each: sliced celery and green onions
2 cups small cauliflower florets
2 ounces medium egg noodles, cooked
Salt and pepper, to taste

Per Serving:
Calories: 197
% calories from fat: 18
Protein (g): 18.2
Carbohydrate (g): 22.9
Fat (g): 3.9
Saturated fat (g): 0.9
Cholesterol (mg): 38.2
Sodium (mg): 401
Exchanges:
Milk: 0.0
Vegetable: 0.0
Fruit: 0.0
Bread: 2.0
Meat: 1.0
Fat: 0.0

1. Combine all ingredients, except cauliflower, noodles, salt, and pepper, in 6-quart slow cooker; cover and cook on low 6 to 8 hours, adding cauliflower and noodles during last 30 minutes. Season to taste with salt and pepper.

Classic Chicken Noodle Soup

Comfort food at its best!

4 entrée servings

2 cans (14½ ounces each) reduced-sodium fat-free
   chicken broth
4 ounces each: boneless, skinless chicken breast
   and thighs, cubed (¾-inch)
1 cup each: sliced celery, carrots, chopped onion
1 teaspoon dried marjoram leaves
1 bay leaf
1 cup cooked wide noodles
Salt and pepper, to taste

Per Serving:
Calories: 307
% calories from fat: 14
Protein (g): 22.8
Carbohydrate (g): 44.3
Fat (g): 5
Saturated fat (g): 0.8
Cholesterol (mg): 32.9
Sodium (mg): 409
Exchanges:
Milk: 0.0
Vegetable: 1.0
Fruit: 0.0
Bread: 2.5
Meat: 2.0
Fat: 0.0

1. Combine all ingredients, except noodles, salt, and pepper, in slow cooker; cover and cook on high 4 to 6 hours, adding noodles during last 20 minutes. Discard bay leaf; season to taste with salt and pepper.

Chicken-Vegetable Noodle Soup

This chicken noodle soup is loaded with vegetables for extra goodness and nutrition.

6 entrée servings

2 quarts Rich Chicken Stock (see p. 30) or chicken broth
8 ounces boneless, skinless chicken breast, cubed (½-inch)
1 cup each: chopped onion, celery, carrots, parsnip, cut green beans
¾ teaspoon each: dried thyme and rosemary leaves
1–2 teaspoons balsamic vinegar
1 cup small broccoli florets
½ cup frozen peas, thawed
4 ounces noodles, cooked
Salt and pepper, to taste

Per Serving:
Calories: 262
% calories from fat: 18
Protein (g): 22.2
Carbohydrate (g): 28.7
Fat (g): 4.9
Saturated fat (g): 1.1
Cholesterol (mg): 28.3
Sodium (mg): 147
Exchanges:
Milk: 0.0
Vegetable: 3.0
Fruit: 0.0
Bread: 1.0
Meat: 2.0
Fat: 0.0

1. Combine all ingredients, except broccoli, peas, noodles, salt, and pepper, in 6-quart slow cooker; cover and cook on high 4 to 6 hours, stirring in broccoli, peas, and noodles during last 20 to 30 minutes. Season to taste with salt and pepper.

Country Chicken Noodle Soup

Made with a stewing hen and homemade egg noodles, this chicken soup tastes just like the one Grandma used to make.

10 entrée servings

1 stewing chicken (about 4 pounds), cut up
3 quarts water
2 cups each: sliced carrots, whole kernel corn
¾ cup chopped onion
1 teaspoon dried marjoram leaves
1 cup frozen peas, thawed
Country Noodles (recipe follows), cooked
¼ cup chopped parsley
Salt and pepper, to taste

Per Serving:
Calories: 232
% calories from fat: 22
Protein (g): 23.2
Carbohydrate (g): 22.1
Fat (g): 5.6
Saturated fat (g): 1.5
Cholesterol (mg): 79
Sodium (mg): 138
Exchanges:
Milk 0.0
Fruit: 0.0
Vegetable: 2.0
Bread: 1.0
Meat: 2.0
Fat: 0.0

1. Combine chicken, water, carrots, corn, onion, and marjoram in 6-quart slow cooker; cover and cook on low 6 to 8 hours. Remove chicken; cut meat into small pieces and return to slow cooker. Cover and cook on high 30 minutes, adding peas, Country Noodles, and parsley during last 5 minutes; season to taste with salt and pepper.

Country Noodles

1 cup all-purpose flour
1 egg
1 tablespoon water
¼ teaspoon salt

1. Place flour on medium cutting board; make a well in the center and add egg, water, and salt. Gradually mix flour into egg with a fork until dough is formed. Knead dough on floured surface until smooth, kneading in additional flour if dough is sticky. Let dough stand, covered, at room temperature 1 hour.
2. Roll dough on lightly floured surface to ⅛-inch thickness. Loosely roll up dough; cut into ¼-inch slices. Unroll noodles and cook in large saucepan of boiling water until tender, about 3 minutes.

Alphabet Chicken Soup

Kids like the alphabet letters in this traditional chicken soup!

4 entrée servings

2 quarts Chicken Stock (see p. 30) or chicken broth
1 pound skinless chicken breast, cubed (½-inch)
½ cup each: chopped onion, carrots, celery
1 large clove garlic, minced
1 large bay leaf
½ teaspoon dried thyme leaves
⅛ teaspoon celery seeds
½ cup uncooked alphabet pasta
Salt and pepper, to taste

Per Serving:
Calories: 303
% calories from fat: 19
Protein (g): 36.5
Carbohydrate (g): 19.2
Fat (g): 5.9
Saturated fat (g): 1.2
Cholesterol (mg): 88.4
Sodium (mg): 139
Exchanges:
Milk: 0.0
Vegetable: 1.0
Fruit: 0.0
Bread: 1.0
Meat: 4.0
Fat: 0.0

1. Combine all ingredients, except pasta, salt, and pepper, in slow cooker; cover and cook on low 6 to 8 hours, adding pasta during last 20 minutes. Discard bay leaf. Season to taste with salt and pepper.

Chunky Chicken and Pasta Soup

This colorful soup will always get an enthusiastic reception!

4 entrée servings

3½ cups reduced-sodium fat-free chicken broth
1 can (14½ ounces) diced tomatoes, undrained
8 ounces boneless, skinless chicken breast, cubed
1 cup chopped onion
½ cup each: diced green and red bell pepper
1 clove garlic, minced
¾ teaspoon each: dried basil and oregano leaves
1 cup uncooked ditalini
¼ cup chopped parsley
Salt and pepper, to taste

Per Serving:
Calories: 305
% calories from fat: 15
Protein (g): 22.8
Carbohydrate (g): 41.7
Fat (g): 5.1
Saturated fat (g): 0.7
Cholesterol (mg): 32.9
Sodium (mg): 650
Exchanges:
Milk: 0.0
Vegetable: 0.0
Fruit: 0.0
Bread: 3.0
Meat: 2.0
Fat: 0.0

1. Combine all ingredients, except pasta, parsley, salt, and pepper, in slow cooker; cover and cook on high 4 to 6 hours, stirring in pasta and parsley during last 20 to 30 minutes. Season to taste with salt and pepper.

Chicken-Rice Soup

The combination of tarragon, turnip, and parsnip gives this soup its great flavor.

6 entrée servings

2 quarts Chicken Stock (see p. 30) or chicken broth
1 pound boneless, skinless chicken breast, cubed
   (½-inch)
1 cup finely chopped onion
½ cup each: coarsely chopped parsnip, turnip,
   carrots, celery
1 clove garlic, chopped
2 bay leaves
½ teaspoon each: dried thyme and tarragon leaves
½ cup uncooked converted long-grain rice
Salt and pepper, to taste

Per Serving:
Calories: 283
% calories from fat: 15
Protein (g): 32.7
Carbohydrate (g): 23.4
Fat (g): 4.4
Saturated fat (g): 0.9
Cholesterol (mg): 79.0
Sodium (mg): 116
Exchanges:
Milk: 0.0
Vegetable: 0.0
Fruit: 0.0
Bread: 1.5
Meat: 4.0
Fat: 0.0

1. Combine all ingredients, except rice, salt, and pepper, in 6-quart slow cooker; cover and cook on low 6 to 8 hours, adding rice during last 2 hours. Discard bay leaves; season to taste with salt and pepper.

Chicken and Barley Soup

Quick-cooking barley requires about 30 minutes to cook in the slow cooker, compared to pearl barley, which can cook in the slow cooker 6 to 8 hours.

6 entrée servings

1 quart Chicken Stock (see p. 30) or chicken broth
1 cup water
12 ounces boneless, skinless chicken breast, cubed
  (¾-inch)
1 cup chopped onion
⅓ cup each: coarsely chopped carrot, celery
1 clove garlic, minced
¼ cup chopped parsley
½ teaspoon dried thyme leaves
1 bay leaf
⅓ cup quick-cooking barley
Salt and pepper, to taste

Per Serving:
Calories: 145
% calories from fat: 16
Protein (g): 18.1
Carbohydrate (g): 12
Fat (g): 2.5
Saturated fat (g): 0.7
Cholesterol (mg): 45.9
Sodium (mg): 327
Exchanges:
Milk: 0.0
Vegetable: 0.0
Fruit: 0.0
Bread: 0.5
Meat: 2.0
Fat: 0.0

1. Combine all ingredients, except barley, salt, and pepper, in slow cooker; cover and cook on high 4 to 6 hours, adding barley during last 30 minutes. Discard bay leaf; season to taste with salt and pepper.

Chunky Chicken Soup

Try other grains in this soup—millet, wheat berries, or bulgur would be delicious!

6 entrée servings

1½ quarts reduced-sodium fat-free chicken broth
1 can (14½ ounces) stewed tomatoes
1 pound boneless, skinless chicken breast, cubed
  (1-inch)
2 cups each: rinsed, drained canned garbanzo beans,
  coarsely chopped cauliflower
1 large chopped onion
⅓ cup each: thinly sliced celery, carrots
1 teaspoon each: dried basil, thyme, and marjoram
  leaves
½ cup uncooked converted long-grain rice
Salt and pepper, to taste

Per Serving:
Calories: 293
% calories from fat: 8
Protein (g): 28.5
Carbohydrate (g): 39.4
Fat (g): 2.8
Saturated fat (g): 0.5
Cholesterol (mg): 43.8
Sodium (mg): 855
Exchanges:
Milk: 0.0
Vegetable: 2.0
Fruit: 0.0
Bread: 2.0
Meat: 2.0
Fat: 0.0

1. Combine all ingredients, except rice, salt, and pepper, in 6-quart slow cooker; cover and cook on low 6 to 8 hours, adding rice during last 2 hours. Season to taste with salt and pepper.

Chicken-Vegetable Soup with Endive

Kale, Swiss chard, watercress, or spinach can be substituted for the endive.

6 entrée servings

1½ quarts reduced-sodium fat-free chicken broth
1½ pounds boneless, skinless chicken breast,
    cubed (¾-inch)
1 can (14½ ounces) diced tomatoes, undrained
2 medium red potatoes, peeled, diced
1 each: chopped large onion, rib celery, carrot
2 large cloves garlic, minced
1½ teaspoons dried marjoram leaves
½ teaspoon dried basil leaves
¼ cup uncooked orzo
4 cups coarsely chopped curly endive
Salt and pepper, to taste

Per Serving:
Calories: 256
% calories from fat: 16
Protein (g): 33.1
Carbohydrate (g): 20.3
Fat (g): 4.4
Saturated fat (g): 1.0
Cholesterol (mg): 67.2
Sodium (mg): 689
Exchanges:
Milk: 0.0
Vegetable: 1.0
Fruit: 0.0
Bread: 1.0
Meat: 3.0
Fat: 0.0

1. Combine all ingredients, except orzo, endive, salt, and pepper, in 6-quart slow cooker; cover and cook on low 6 to 8 hours, adding orzo and endive during last 20 minutes. Season to taste with salt and pepper.

Chicken and Chilies Soup

The green chilies add spicy south-of-the-border flavor.

6 first-course servings

1 quart Chicken Stock (see p. 30) or chicken broth
8 ounces boneless, skinless chicken breast, cubed
    (¾-inch)
1 can (4 ounces) chopped green chilies, drained
1 cup canned kidney beans, rinsed, drained
1½ cups small cauliflower florets
½ cup each: finely chopped onion, celery
1 large clove garlic, minced
2 tablespoons cornstarch
¼ cup cold water
1 cup (4 ounces) shredded reduced-fat Cheddar cheese
Salt and pepper, to taste

Per Serving:
Calories: 139
% calories from fat: 22
Protein (g): 12.5
Carbohydrate (g): 14.2
Fat (g): 3.4
Saturated fat (g): 1.8
Cholesterol (mg): 17.9
Sodium (mg): 471
Exchanges:
Milk: 0.0
Vegetable: 0.0
Fruit: 0.0
Bread: 1.0
Meat: 1.0
Fat: 0.0

1. Combine all ingredients, except cornstarch, water, cheese, salt, and pepper, in slow cooker; cover and cook on high 3 to 4 hours. Add combined cornstarch and water, stirring 2 to 3 minutes. Add cheese, stirring until melted. Season to taste with salt and pepper.

Herbed Chicken Soup with Split Peas

This easy variation of split pea soup uses chicken instead of the more traditional ham.

8 entrée servings

2 quarts reduced-sodium fat-free chicken broth
1 pound dried green split peas
12 ounces boneless, skinless chicken breast, cubed
   (¾-inch)
¼ cup each: sliced green onions, carrots, celery
½ teaspoon each: dried savory and marjoram leaves
Salt and pepper, to taste

1. Combine all ingredients, except salt and pepper, in 6-quart slow cooker; cover and cook on high 4 to 6 hours. Season to taste with salt and pepper.

Per Serving:
Calories: 282
% calories from fat: 5
Protein (g): 28.6
Carbohydrate (g): 37.8
Fat (g): 1.6
Saturated fat (g): 0.3
Cholesterol (mg): 21.8
Sodium (mg): 203
Exchanges:
Milk: 0.0
Vegetable: 0.0
Fruit: 0.0
Bread: 2.5
Meat: 2.0
Fat: 0.0

Chicken and Corn Soup

This soup makes an easy workday meal.

6 entrée servings

1½ cups fat-free reduced-sodium fat-free
   chicken broth
1 can (16 ounces) cream-style corn
8 ounces boneless, skinless chicken breast, cubed
2 cups peeled diced potatoes
¾ cup chopped onion
1½ cups 2% reduced-fat milk, divided
2 tablespoons cornstarch
Salt and pepper, to taste

Per Serving:
Calories: 194
% calories from fat: 12.5
Protein (g): 15
Carbohydrate (g): 29.1
Fat (g): 2.8
Saturated fat (g): 1.1
Cholesterol (mg): 33
Sodium (mg): 506
Exchanges:
Milk: 0.0
Vegetable: 0.0
Fruit: 0.0
Bread: 2.0
Meat: 1.0
Fat: 0.0

1. Combine all ingredients, except milk, cornstarch, salt, and pepper, in slow cooker; cover and cook on high 4 to 6 hours, stirring in 1 cup milk during last 30 minutes. Stir in combined remaining ½ cup milk and cornstarch, stirring 2 to 3 minutes. Season to taste with salt and pepper.

Hearty Meatball and Vegetable Soup

If meatballs are browned in a lightly greased large skillet, or baked at 350 degrees until browned, they will be less fragile and more attractive. Add meatballs to slow cooker carefully, so they don't break apart.

6 entrée servings

Hearty Meatballs (recipe follows)
1 cup reduced-sodium fat-free beef broth
1 can (28 ounces) diced tomatoes, undrained
3 carrots, thickly sliced
1 teaspoon dried basil leaves
2 small zucchini, sliced
½ cup frozen peas, thawed
2 tablespoons cornstarch
¼ cup cold water
Salt and pepper, to taste
12 ounces noodles or fettuccine, cooked, warm

Per Serving:
Calories: 554
% calories from fat: 26
Protein (g): 35.8
Carbohydrate (g): 65.3
Fat (g): 16
Saturated fat (g): 5.8
Cholesterol (mg): 105.8
Sodium (mg): 536
Exchanges:
Milk: 0.0
Vegetable: 2.0
Fruit: 0.0
Bread: 4.0
Meat: 3.0
Fat: 1.0

1. Combine all ingredients, except zucchini, peas, cornstarch, water, salt, pepper, and noodles, in slow cooker, making sure meatballs are submerged; cover and cook on low 6 to 8 hours, adding zucchini and peas during last 20 minutes. Turn heat to high and cook 10 minutes; stir in combined cornstarch and water, stirring 2 to 3 minutes. Season to taste with salt and pepper; serve over noodles.

Hearty Meatballs

Makes 18

1½ pounds lean ground beef
⅓ cup finely chopped onion
1 egg
½ cup unseasoned dry bread crumbs
2 cloves garlic, minced
1–2 teaspoons beef-flavor bouillon crystals
½ teaspoon salt
¼ teaspoon pepper

1. Mix all ingredients in bowl; shape mixture into 18 meatballs.

Variation

Italian-Style Meatball Stew—Make recipe as above, substituting dried Italian seasoning for the basil, adding 1 cup halved small mushrooms, and substituting Italian Turkey Meatballs (see p. 198) for the Hearty Meatballs.

Chicken Meatball Soup

Chicken Meatballs can be prepared in advance and refrigerated, covered, several hours before making the soup.

8 entrée servings

2 quarts reduced-sodium fat-free chicken broth
1 cup each: chopped onion, thickly sliced carrots, zucchini
Chicken Meatballs (recipe follows)
Salt and pepper, to taste

1. Combine all ingredients, except salt and pepper, in 6-quart slow cooker; cover and cook on high 3 to 4 hours. Season to taste with salt and pepper.

Per Serving:
Calories: 238
% calories from fat: 23
Protein (g): 35.4
Carbohydrate (g): 6.6
Fat (g): 5.5
Saturated fat (g): 1.9
Cholesterol (mg): 72.9
Sodium (mg): 545
Exchanges:
Milk: 0.0
Vegetable: 0.0
Fruit: 0.0
Bread: 0.5
Meat: 3.5
Fat: 0.0

Chicken Meatballs

Makes 40 meatballs

2 pounds ground chicken breast
1½ cups fresh whole-wheat bread crumbs
¼ cup (1 ounce) grated Parmesan cheese
1 egg
2 teaspoons minced garlic
1½ teaspoons dried Italian seasoning
½ teaspoon each: salt, pepper

1. Combine all ingredients; shape into 40 meatballs.

Variation
Garden Meatball Soup—Make soup as above, substituting beef broth for the chicken broth and adding 1 cup sliced cabbage and 1 can (15 ounces each) rinsed, drained kidney beans and stewed tomatoes. Substitute lean ground beef for the chicken in the meatballs.

Home-Style Turkey-Vegetable Soup

A great soup for a crowd!

12 entrée servings

1¾ quarts reduced-sodium fat-free chicken broth
3 cups water
4 pounds turkey wings
2 cups coarsely chopped onions
¼ teaspoon each: dried marjoram and thyme leaves
1 can (14½ ounces) diced tomatoes, undrained
1 can (16 ounces) Great Northern beans, rinsed,
   drained
1 cup each: chopped peeled rutabaga or turnip,
   celery, cabbage, carrots
1½ cups whole kernel corn
¼ cup quick-cooking barley
¼ cup uncooked ditalini
Salt and pepper, to taste

Per Serving:
Calories: 336
% calories from fat: 28
Protein (g): 31
Carbohydrate (g): 29.9
Fat (g): 10.6
Saturated fat (g): 2.8
Cholesterol (mg): 65.1
Sodium (mg): 610
Exchanges:
Milk: 0.0
Vegetable: 2.0
Fruit: 0.0
Bread: 1.0
Meat: 4.0
Fat: 0.0

1. Combine broth, water, turkey, onions, and herbs in 6-quart slow cooker; cover and cook on high 4 to 5 hours. Remove turkey wings; remove and shred meat and reserve. Discard bones; skim fat from soup.
2. Add remaining ingredients, except barley, pasta, salt, and pepper, to slow cooker; cover and cook on high 3 to 4 hours, adding reserved turkey, barley, and pasta during last 20 minutes. Season to taste with salt and pepper.

Turkey Noodle Soup

The perfect soup for using that leftover holiday turkey!

6 entrée servings

2½ quarts Turkey Stock (see p. 31) or chicken broth
1 cup each: chopped carrots, celery, onion, sliced
   mushrooms
1 tablespoon minced garlic
¾ teaspoon each: dried marjoram and thyme leaves
4 ounces egg noodles, cooked
4 cups cooked diced turkey
1 cup frozen peas, thawed
Salt and pepper, to taste

Per Serving:
Calories: 376
% calories from fat: 26
Protein (g): 36.7
Carbohydrate (g): 28.5
Fat (g): 10.4
Saturated fat (g): 2.7
Cholesterol (mg): 80.1
Sodium (mg): 182
Exchanges:
Milk: 0.0
Vegetable: 0.0
Fruit: 0.0
Bread: 1.0
Meat: 4.0
Fat: 0.0

1. Combine all ingredients, except noodles, turkey,
peas, salt, and pepper, in 6-quart slow cooker; cover and cook on high 3 to
4 hours, adding noodles, turkey, and peas during last 15 minutes. Season
to taste with salt and pepper.

Variation

Turkey-Wild Rice Soup—Make soup as above, adding 1 cup cubed turnips
or parsnips. Omit noodles and peas; add 2 cups cooked wild rice during
last 20 minutes of cooking time.

Turkey Soup with Tarragon

This chunky, mustard-spiked soup makes a great one-dish meal.

4 entrée servings

1 quart reduced-sodium fat-free chicken broth
1 pound boneless, skinless turkey breast, cubed
   (¾-inch)
2 large potatoes, cubed
1 cup coarsely chopped onion
⅓ cup each: thinly sliced celery, carrots
1 tablespoon dried tarragon leaves
1–1½ tablespoons Dijon mustard
Salt and pepper, to taste

Per Serving:
Calories: 229
% calories from fat: 26
Protein (g): 21.7
Carbohydrate (g): 20.9
Fat (g): 6.6
Saturated fat (g): 1.2
Cholesterol (mg): 35.2
Sodium (mg): 381
Exchanges:
Milk: 0.0
Vegetable: 0.0
Fruit: 0.0
Bread: 1.5
Meat: 2.0
Fat: 0.0

1. Combine all ingredients, except salt and pepper,
in slow cooker; cover and cook on high 4 to 6 hours.
Season to taste with salt and pepper.

Beef Soup with Red Wine

The flavor of this soup is reminiscent of the classic Beef Burgundy.

6 entrée servings

1 quart Beef Stock (see p. 31) or beef broth
1 pound lean beef stew meat, cubed
6 ounces Canadian bacon, diced
1 can (8 ounces) tomato sauce
½ cup dry red wine (optional)
4 cups cubed red potatoes
1 cup each: chopped onion, sliced mushrooms
½ cup each: sliced carrots, celery
1 clove garlic, minced
1½ teaspoon dried thyme leaves
2 bay leaves
Salt and pepper, to taste

Per Serving:
Calories: 336
% calories from fat: 17
Protein (g): 28.1
Carbohydrate (g): 32.5
Fat (g): 6.2
Saturated fat (g): 1.8
Cholesterol (mg): 51.8
Sodium (mg): 280
Exchanges:
Milk: 0.0
Vegetable: 1.0
Fruit: 0.0
Bread: 1.5
Meat: 4.0
Fat: 0.0

1. Combine all ingredients, except salt and pepper, in 6-quart slow cooker; cover and cook on low 6 to 8 hours. Discard bay leaves; season to taste with salt and pepper.

Beefy Bean Soup

Meaty beef shanks flavor this bean soup. You can substitute 1 pound cubed lean beef for the beef shanks to turn it into a stew.

8 entrée servings

2 quarts water
1 pound meaty beef shanks
2 cans (15 ounces each) kidney beans, rinsed,
    drained
1 can (14½ ounces) stewed tomatoes
1 cup each: sliced carrots, onion, diced turnips, cut
    green beans
1 each: rib celery, halved onion
1 teaspoon each: dried oregano and thyme leaves
1 bay leaf
Salt and pepper, to taste

Per Serving:
Calories: 158
% calories from fat: 10
Protein (g): 10.2
Carbohydrate (g): 26.8
Fat (g): 2
Saturated fat (g): 0.6
Cholesterol (mg): 8.7
Sodium (mg): 510
Exchanges:
Milk: 0.0
Vegetable: 1.0
Fruit: 0.0
Bread: 2.0
Meat: 0.0
Fat: 1.0

1. Combine all ingredients, except salt and pepper, in 6-quart slow cooker; cover and cook on low 6 to 8 hours. Remove beef shanks; cut meat from bones and return to soup. Discard bones and bay leaf; season to taste with salt and pepper.

Smoky Bean and Spinach Soup

Canadian bacon lends a subtle smoky flavor to this soup.

6 entrée servings

1½ quarts chicken broth
1 can (15 ounces) each: tomato sauce, rinsed
    drained cannellini beans
6 ounces Canadian bacon, thinly sliced
1 clove garlic, minced
1 tablespoon dried Italian seasoning
1 package (10 ounces) frozen chopped spinach,
    thawed, drained
½ cup uncooked orzo
Salt and pepper, to taste

Per Serving:
Calories: 207
% calories from fat: 11
Protein (g): 12.8
Carbohydrate (g): 30.5
Fat (g): 2.5
Saturated fat (g): 0.6
Cholesterol (mg): 16.4
Sodium (mg): 1524
Exchanges:
Milk 0.0
Vegetable: 0.0
Fruit: 0.0
Bread: 2.0
Meat: 1.0
Fat: 0.0

1. Combine all ingredients, except spinach, orzo, salt, and pepper, in slow cooker; cover and cook on high 3 to 4 hours, adding spinach and orzo during last 20 minutes. Season to taste with salt and pepper.

Navy Bean Soup with Ham

Beans can be cooked in the slow cooker without soaking as long as the recipe is cooked 8 to 10 hours. For a shorter cooking time, beans should be soaked overnight.

6 entrée servings

1½ quarts reduced-sodium fat-free chicken broth
8 ounces dried navy or Great Northern beans
1½ cups cubed lean smoked ham
⅔ cup each: chopped onion, carrot, celery
1 clove garlic, minced
¼ teaspoon dried thyme leaves
1 bay leaf
Salt and pepper, to taste

Per Serving:
Calories: 223
% calories from fat: 16
Protein (g): 20.1
Carbohydrate (g): 29.5
Fat (g): 4.0
Saturated fat (g): 0.9
Cholesterol (mg): 21.6
Sodium (mg): 639
Exchanges:
Milk: 0.0
Vegetable: 0.0
Fruit: 0.0
Bread: 2.0
Meat: 2.0
Fat: 0.0

1. Combine all ingredients, except salt and pepper, in slow cooker; cover and cook on low until beans are tender, 8 to 10 hours. Discard bay leaf; season to taste with salt and pepper.

Workday Bean Soup

This easy, economical soup is designed to fit into a busy work schedule.

6 entrée servings

1½ quarts reduced-sodium fat-free beef broth
1 cup each: dried pinto or cranberry beans, Great
   Northern beans
½ cup each: finely diced red or green bell pepper,
   onion, sliced celery
1 bay leaf
2 tablespoons sugar
2 teaspoons chili powder
¼ teaspoon each: dried thyme leaves, dry mustard,
   ground allspice, pepper
1 can (8 ounces) tomato paste
1 tablespoon apple cider vinegar
Salt and pepper, to taste

Per Serving:
Calories: 325
% calories from fat: 4
Protein (g): 19
Carbohydrate (g): 61.7
Fat (g): 1.5
Saturated fat (g): 0.4
Cholesterol (mg): 0.9
Sodium (mg): 422
Exchanges:
Milk: 0.0
Vegetable: 0.0
Fruit: 0.0
Bread: 4.0
Meat: 1.0
Fat: 0.0

1. Combine all ingredients, except tomato paste, vinegar, salt, and pepper, in 6-quart slow cooker; cover and cook on low until beans are tender, 8 to 10 hours, adding tomato paste and vinegar during last 30 minutes. Discard bay leaf; season to taste with salt and pepper.

Beef, Vegetable, and Barley Soup

Thick and hearty, this soup will warm you on a cold winter day.

6 entrée servings

12 ounces ground beef round
1½ quarts Fragrant Beef Stock (see p. 32) or beef broth
1 can (14½ ounces) stewed tomatoes
3 cups coarsely shredded cabbage
1 cup each: cubed, peeled potato, chopped onion
½ cup each: sliced celery, carrots
2 large cloves garlic, minced
1 teaspoon each: dried thyme and basil leaves,
   chili powder, paprika
½ teaspoon dry mustard
2 bay leaves
⅓ cup quick-cooking barley
Salt and pepper, to taste

Per Serving:
Calories: 116
% calories from fat: 11
Protein (g): 16.2
Carbohydrate (g): 24.3
Fat (g): 2.2
Saturated fat (g): 0.7
Cholesterol (mg): 23.4
Sodium (mg): 118
Exchanges:
Milk: 0.0
Vegetable: 2.0
Fruit: 0.0
Bread: 1.0
Meat: 1.0
Fat: 0.0

1. Cook beef in lightly greased skillet over medium heat until browned, about 5 minutes, crumbling with a fork. Combine beef and remaining ingredients, except barley, salt, and pepper, in 6-quart slow cooker; cover and cook on low 6 to 8 hours, adding barley during last 30 minutes. Discard bay leaves; season to taste with salt and pepper.

Beef-Barley Soup

This hearty, rib-sticking soup is even better if made a day or so in advance.

8 entrée servings

4 cups water
1 can (14½ ounces) each: reduced-sodium beef broth, undrained diced tomatoes
1 pound lean beef stew meat, cubed
1 cup each: cut green beans, cubed parsnips or potatoes, chopped onion, celery, carrots
1 clove garlic, minced
½ teaspoon each: dried marjoram and thyme leaves
1 bay leaf
½ cup each: frozen thawed peas, quick-cooking barley
Salt and pepper, to taste

Per Serving:
Calories: 187
% calories from fat: 16
Protein (g): 18.8
Carbohydrate (g): 21.1
Fat (g): 3.3
Saturated fat (g): 1.1
Cholesterol (mg): 35.4
Sodium (mg): 153
Exchanges:
Milk: 0.0
Vegetable: 2.0
Fruit: 0.0
Bread: 0.5
Meat: 2.0
Fat: 0.0

1. Combine all ingredients, except peas, barley, salt, and pepper, in 6-quart slow cooker; cover and cook on low 6 to 8 hours, adding peas and barley during last 20 minutes. Discard bay leaf; season to taste with salt and pepper.

Stuffed Green Pepper Soup

Susan Barnes's recipe for this zesty soup has the flavors of everyone's favorite baked stuffed green peppers!

Makes 6 entrée servings

1 pound lean ground beef, browned, crumbled
1 quart tomato juice
1 can (14 ½ ounces) each: diced and crushed
  tomatoes, undrained
2 each: chopped medium onions and green peppers
⅔ cup uncooked converted long-grain rice
Salt and pepper, to taste

1. Combine all ingredients, except rice, salt, and pepper, in slow cooker; cover and cook on low 6 to 8 hours, stirring in rice during last 2 hours. Season to taste with salt and pepper.

Per Serving:
Calories: 260
% calories from fat: 15
Protein (g): 21.1
Carbohydrate (g): 34.0
Fat (g): 4.0
Saturated fat (g): 1.7
Cholesterol (mg): 46.2
Sodium (mg): 781
Exchanges:
Milk: 0.0
Vegetable: 2.5
Fruit: 0.0
Bread: 1.5
Meat: 1.5
Fat: 0.0

Hamburger Goulash Soup

This is a great entrée soup the whole family will enjoy.

6 entrée servings

12–16 ounces lean ground beef
3 cups reduced-sodium fat-free beef broth
1 cup canned stewed tomatoes
3 cups cubed potatoes
⅔ cup each: chopped onion, red or green bell pepper
3 tablespoons paprika
¾ teaspoon each: chili and garlic powder
½ teaspoon each: caraway seeds, dried thyme leaves
1 tablespoon Worcestershire sauce
¼ cup catsup
Salt and pepper, to taste

1. Cook beef in lightly greased large saucepan over medium heat until is browned, about 5 minutes, crumbling with a fork. Add beef and remaining ingredients, except salt and pepper to slow cooker; cover and cook on low 6 to 8 hours. Season to taste with salt and pepper.

Per Serving:
Calories: 202
% calories from fat: 16
Protein (g): 16.6
Carbohydrate (g): 27
Fat (g): 3.6
Saturated fat (g): 1.4
Cholesterol (mg): 35.2
Sodium (mg): 259
Exchanges:
Milk: 0.0
Vegetable: 0.0
Fruit: 0.0
Bread: 1.5
Meat: 2.0
Fat: 0.0

Hamburger and Vegetable Soup

This favorite simmers to sweet-sour goodness.

4–6 entrée servings

12 ounces ground beef round
1 large finely chopped onion
2 large cloves garlic, minced
1¼ quarts reduced-sodium fat-free beef broth
1 can (15 ounces) tomato sauce
1 cup each: diced potato, thinly sliced carrot,
    whole kernel corn, baby lima beans
⅓ cup sliced celery
2 tablespoons each: pearl barley, packed light
    brown sugar, apple cider vinegar
¾ teaspoon each: dry mustard, dried thyme leaves
1 large bay leaf
Salt and pepper, to taste

Per Serving:
Calories: 347
% calories from fat: 13
Protein (g): 25.3
Carbohydrate (g): 50
Fat (g): 5.1
Saturated fat (g): 2.1
Cholesterol (mg): 52.7
Sodium (mg): 596
Exchanges:
Milk: 0.0
Vegetable: 0.0
Fruit: 0.0
Bread: 3.0
Meat: 2.0
Fat: 0.0

1. Cook beef, onion, and garlic in lightly greased large skillet over medium heat until beef is browned, about 5 minutes, crumbling beef with a fork. Combine beef mixture and remaining ingredients, except salt and pepper, in 6-quart slow cooker; cover and cook on low 6 to 8 hours. Discard bay leaf; season to taste with salt and pepper.

Vegetable Soup with Chili Meatballs

Lightly spiced meatballs add the perfect touch to this simple vegetable soup.

8 entrée servings

2 quarts Chicken Stock (see p. 30) or chicken broth
Chili Meatballs (recipe follows)
1 cup each: thinly sliced onion, Mexican-style
    whole kernel corn
¾ cup thinly sliced carrots
1 package (10 ounces) frozen chopped spinach,
    thawed, drained
2–4 tablespoons dry sherry (optional)
Salt and pepper, to taste

Per Serving:
Calories: 192
% calories from fat: 28
Protein (g): 20.6
Carbohydrate (g): 14.8
Fat (g): 6
Saturated fat (g): 1.6
Cholesterol (mg): 71.2
Sodium (mg): 279
Exchanges:
Milk: 0.0
Vegetable: 0.0
Fruit: 0.0
Bread: 1.0
Meat: 2.0
Fat: 0.0

1. Combine all ingredients, except spinach, sherry, salt, and pepper, in 6-quart slow cooker; cover and cook on high 3 to 4 hours, adding spinach and sherry during last 20 minutes. Season to taste with salt and pepper.

Chili Meatballs

Makes 32 meatballs

1½ pounds ground beef round
⅓ cup each: finely chopped onion, unseasoned dry bread crumbs
1 teaspoon minced garlic
1 tablespoon chili powder
2 teaspoons ground cumin
1 egg
½ teaspoon salt

1. Combine all ingredients; shape into 32 balls.

Vegetable Soup with Cabbage Rolls

Stuffed cabbage leaves are cooked in this vegetable soup for a hearty dinner treat!

4 entrée servings

Cabbage Rolls (recipe follows)
1¼ quarts Chicken Stock (see p. 30)
   or chicken broth
4 ribs celery, sliced
1 each: peeled cubed large potato, chopped onion,
   carrot, tomato
1 cup whole kernel corn
Salt and pepper, to taste
6 tablespoons shredded Gruyère or Swiss cheese

Per Serving:
Calories: 373
% calories from fat: 22
Protein (g): 35.4
Carbohydrate (g): 37.3
Fat (g): 9.6
Saturated fat (g): 3.4
Cholesterol (mg): 200.2
Sodium (mg): 765
Exchanges:
Milk: 0.0
Vegetable: 2.0
Fruit: 0.0
Bread: 2.0
Meat: 3.0
Fat: 0.0

1. Place Cabbage Rolls, seam sides down, in 6-quart slow cooker; add remaining ingredients, except salt, pepper, and cheese. Cover and cook on high 4 to 5 hours; season to taste with salt and pepper. Spoon Cabbage Rolls into shallow soup bowls; ladle soup over and sprinkle with cheese.

Cabbage Rolls

Makes 8

12 medium cabbage leaves
12 ounces lean ground veal
½ cup fresh bread crumbs
2 eggs
¾–1 teaspoon each: dried marjoram and thyme leaves
½ teaspoon salt

1. Place cabbage leaves in boiling water until softened, about 1 minute; drain well. Trim thick veins from leaves so they lay flat. Mix remaining ingredients and divide into 8 equal parts. Place on cabbage leaves and fold sides and ends in to make packets.

Corned Beef and Cabbage Soup

This unusual soup duplicates the flavor of a New England boiled dinner.

6 entrée servings

1¾ quarts reduced-sodium fat-free chicken broth
8 ounces deli corned beef, fat trimmed, cubed
  (½-inch)
4 cups each: cubed red potatoes, thinly sliced
  cabbage
12 baby carrots, halved
1 large onion, chopped
2 each: large minced garlic cloves, bay leaves
1 tablespoon apple cider vinegar
2 teaspoons each: Dijon mustard, caraway seeds
Salt and pepper, to taste

Per Serving:
Calories: 209
% calories from fat: 22
Protein (g): 14.1
Carbohydrate (g): 26.9
Fat (g): 5.3
Saturated fat (g): 1.8
Cholesterol (mg): 21.3
Sodium (mg): 1216
Exchanges:
Milk: 0.0
Vegetable: 2.0
Fruit: 0.0
Bread: 1.0
Meat: 1.0
Fat: 0.0

1. Combine all ingredients, except salt and pepper, in 6-quart slow cooker; cover and cook on high 3 to 4 hours. Discard bay leaves; season to taste with salt and pepper.

Vegetable Oxtail Soup

Slow cooking brings out the rich flavor of oxtails, making this vegetable soup a real treat. The oxtails can be browned first, if you prefer.

6 entrée servings

1½ quarts Beef Stock (see p. 31) or beef broth
1 pound oxtails, sliced (2-inch)
2 large tomatoes, chopped
1 cup sliced celery
¾ cup each: chopped onion, sliced carrot, diced
    parsnip, diced potato
1 teaspoon dried thyme leaves
1 bay leaf
⅓ cup quick-cooking barley
Salt and pepper, to taste

Per Serving:
Calories: 219
% calories from fat: 28
Protein (g): 12.4
Carbohydrate (g): 28.1
Fat (g): 17
Saturated fat (g): 0.4
Cholesterol (mg): 0.3
Sodium (mg): 35
Exchanges:
Milk: 0.0
Vegetable: 2.0
Fruit: 0.0
Bread: 1.0
Meat: 1.0
Fat: 1.0

1. Combine all ingredients, except barley, salt, and pepper, in 6-quart slow cooker; cover and cook on high 6 to 8 hours, adding barley during last 30 minutes. Remove oxtails from soup. Remove meat from bones and return to soup; discard bones and bay leaf. Season to taste with salt and pepper.

Lamb and White Bean Soup

If you like bean soup, try this version with lamb shanks.

6 entrée servings

2 quarts Beef Stock (see p. 31) or beef broth
1½ cups dried Great Northern or navy beans
2 lamb shanks (about 1¾ pounds)
3 cups thinly sliced cabbage
2 each: sliced large carrots, ribs celery, minced garlic
    cloves
1 large finely chopped onion
3 bay leaves
1½ teaspoons dried thyme and marjoram leaves
½ teaspoon each: crushed celery seeds, dry mustard
Salt and pepper, to taste

Per Serving:
Calories: 371
% calories from fat: 29
Protein (g): 28.8
Carbohydrate (g): 37.4
Fat (g): 11.8
Saturated fat (g): 5.4
Cholesterol (mg): 61.6
Sodium (mg): 110
Exchanges:
Milk: 0.0
Vegetable: 0.0
Fruit: 0.0
Bread: 2.5
Meat: 3.0
Fat: 0.5

1. Combine all ingredients, except salt and pepper, in 6-quart slow cooker; cover and cook on low until beans are tender, 7 to 8 hours. Remove lamb shanks; cut meat into bite-sized pieces and return to soup. Discard bones and bay leaves; season to taste with salt and pepper.

Lamb Soup with Barley

This vegetable soup can also be made with lean pork or beef.

8 entrée servings

1½ quarts Chicken Stock (see p. 30) or chicken broth
1½ pounds lean lamb stew meat, cubed
1 quart water
1½ cups each: sliced onions, carrots, turnips
1 cup sliced celery
1 tablespoon minced garlic
1 teaspoon each: dried oregano and rosemary leaves
1 bay leaf
½ cup each: dry white wine (optional), quick-cooking
    barley
Salt and pepper, to taste

Per Serving:
Calories: 241
% calories from fat: 20
Protein (g): 16.1
Carbohydrate (g): 27.9
Fat (g): 5.5
Saturated fat (g): 1.5
Cholesterol (mg): 38.9
Sodium (mg): 70
Exchanges:
Milk: 0.0
Vegetable: 2.0
Fruit: 0.0
Bread: 1.0
Meat: 2.0
Fat: 0.0

1. Combine all ingredients, except barley, salt, and pepper, in 6-quart slow cooker; cover and cook on low 6 to 8 hours, adding barley during last 20 minutes. Discard bay leaf; season to taste with salt and pepper.

Lamb, Split-Pea, Bean, and Barley Soup

If you like split pea soup made with a ham bone, try this slightly different version using lamb shanks.

8 entrée servings

2¾ quarts water
2–4 beef bouillon cubes
2 pounds lamb shanks
2 cups dried green split peas
¾ cup dried navy or Great Northern beans
¼ cup pearl barley
1 cup chopped onion
⅓ cup each: sliced carrots, celery
1 clove garlic, minced
1 teaspoon each: dried thyme and basil leaves
½ teaspoon crushed celery seeds
3 bay leaves
Salt and pepper, to taste

Per Serving:
Calories: 331
% calories from fat: 11
Protein (g): 29
Carbohydrate (g): 46
Fat (g): 4.1
Saturated fat (g): 1.3
Cholesterol (mg): 41
Sodium (mg): 253
Exchanges:
Milk 0.0
Vegetable: 1.0
Fruit: 0.0
Bread: 2.5
Meat: 2.5
Fat: 0.0

1. Combine all ingredients, except salt and pepper, in 6-quart slow cooker; cover and cook on low until beans are tender, 8 to 10 hours. Remove lamb shanks; remove meat, cut into bite-sized pieces and return to soup. Discard bones and bay leaves. Season to taste with salt and pepper.

Four-Bean Soup with Sausage

This hearty soup has a Mexican accent and spicy flavor!

8 entrée servings

8 ounces reduced-sodium reduced-fat smoked sausage, sliced
1 can (14½ ounces) each: stewed tomatoes, reduced-sodium fat-free chicken broth
1 can (15 ounces) each: rinsed drained garbanzo, pinto and black beans
1 jar (8 ounces) mild salsa
1 can (6 ounces) spicy vegetable juice cocktail
8 ounces green beans, halved
1 cup chopped onion
½ cup each: chopped green bell pepper, celery
1 teaspoon minced garlic
1 small jalapeño chili, chopped
2–3 teaspoons chili powder
1 teaspoon dried oregano leaves
Salt and hot pepper sauce, to taste

Per Serving:
Calories: 245
% calories from fat: 13
Protein (g): 15.3
Carbohydrate (g): 42.6
Fat (g): 4.1
Saturated fat (g): 0.7
Cholesterol (mg): 13.2
Sodium (mg): 911
Exchanges:
Milk: 0.0
Vegetable: 2.0
Fruit: 0.0
Bread: 2.0
Meat: 1.0
Fat: 0.0

1. Combine all ingredients, except salt and hot pepper sauce, in 6-quart slow cooker; cover and cook on high 4 to 6 hours. Season to taste with salt and hot pepper sauce.

Rice and Adzuki Bean Soup with Vegetables

In this easy soup, an Indian-style grain-and-bean stew, slightly sweet adzuki beans replace the usual dal or legume.

6 entrée servings

2 cans (14½ ounces each) reduced-sodium fat-free chicken broth
1 can (15 ounces) adzuki beans, rinsed, drained
2 cups each: sliced carrots, cut waxed beans, chopped plum tomatoes
1 small jalapeño chili, minced
1 teaspoon each: ground cumin, turmeric, minced gingerroot
½ cup uncooked converted long-grain rice
Salt and pepper, to taste
¼ cup toasted sunflower seeds

Per Serving:
Calories: 323
% calories from fat: 10
Protein (g): 10.3
Carbohydrate (g): 62.4
Fat (g): 3.5
Saturated fat (g): 04
Cholesterol (mg): 0
Sodium (mg): 209
Exchanges:
Milk: 0.0
Vegetable: 3.0
Fruit: 0.0
Bread: 3.0
Meat: 0.0
Fat: 0.0

1. Combine all ingredients, except rice, salt, pepper, and sunflower seeds, in 6-quart slow cooker; cover and cook on high 4 to 6 hours, adding rice during last 2 hours. Season to taste with salt and pepper; sprinkle each bowl of soup with sunflower seeds.

Roasted Red Pepper, Corn, and Black Bean Soup

Jarred roasted red peppers and canned black beans are great time-savers in this hearty, colorful soup.

4 entrée servings

1 quart reduced-sodium fat-free chicken broth
1 can (15 ounces) black beans, rinsed, drained
1 jar (12 ounces) roasted red peppers, drained, diced
1 cup whole kernel corn
2 cups chopped onions
¾ teaspoon dried thyme leaves
⅛ teaspoon each: crushed red pepper, ground allspice
½ cup diced lean ham
⅔ cup uncooked converted long-grain rice
Salt and pepper, to taste

Per Serving:
Calories: 286
% calories from fat: 13
Protein (g): 13.3
Carbohydrate (g): 55.2
Fat (g): 4.4
Saturated fat (g): 0.7
Cholesterol (mg): 8.4
Sodium (mg): 1325
Exchanges:
Milk: 0.0
Vegetable: 0.0
Fruit: 0.0
Bread: 3.5
Meat: 1.0
Fat: 0.0

1. Combine all ingredients, except rice, salt, and pepper, in slow cooker, cover and cook on high 4 to 6 hours, adding rice during last 2 hours. Season to taste with salt and pepper.

Black Bean Soup with Rice and Ham

Serve this flavorful soup with salsa, sour cream, and tortilla chips.

6 entrée servings

3 cans (14½ ounces each) chicken broth
1 can (15 ounces each) black beans, rinsed, drained
1 medium onion, chopped
3 cloves garlic, minced
2 each: sliced carrots, ribs celery
1 small green bell pepper, sliced
2 cups cubed lean smoked ham
1 teaspoon ground cumin
½ teaspoon crushed red pepper
⅓ cup each: uncooked converted long-grain rice, chopped cilantro
Salt and pepper to taste

Per Serving:
Calories: 215
% calories from fat: 11
Protein (g): 17.7
Carbohydrate (g): 34.0
Fat (g): 2.7
Saturated fat (g): 0.7
Cholesterol (mg): 22.9
Sodium (mg): 1887
Exchanges:
Milk: 0.0
Vegetable: 0.0
Fruit: 0.0
Bread: 2.0
Meat: 1.5
Fat: 0.0

1. Combine all ingredients, except rice, cilantro, salt, and pepper, in 6-quart slow cooker; cover and cook on low 6 to 8 hours, adding rice during last 2 hours. Stir in cilantro; season to taste with salt and pepper.

Sausage and Black Bean Soup

Smoked sausage flavors this hearty black bean soup.

6 entrée servings

2½ quarts Chicken Stock (see p. 30) or chicken
  broth
1 pound dried black beans
8 ounces smoked turkey sausage, sliced
1 cup each: sliced carrots, chopped onion
½ cup chopped celery
2 tablespoons Worcestershire sauce
2 teaspoons dried marjoram leaves
1 bay leaf
Salt and pepper, to taste
Lemon wedges

Per Serving:
Calories: 370
% calories from fat: 16
Protein (g): 24.9
Carbohydrate (g): 55.7
Fat: (g): 6.7
Saturated fat (g): 1.7
Cholesterol (mg): 28.2
Sodium (mg): 403
Exchanges:
Milk 0.0
Vegetable: 1.0
Fruit: 0.0
Bread: 3.0
Meat: 2.0
Fat: 0.0

1. Combine all ingredients, except salt, pepper, and lemon wedges, in 6-quart slow cooker; cover and cook on low until beans are tender, 7 to 8 hours. Discard bay leaf; season to taste with salt and pepper. Serve with lemon wedges.

Variation

Sherried Black Bean Soup—Make recipe as above, substituting crushed cumin seeds for the marjoram and adding 1 teaspoon dried oregano leaves and 1 to 2 teaspoons brown sugar. Before serving, season to taste with 1 to 2 tablespoons dry sherry.

Garbanzo and Pasta Soup

This soup makes a delicious luncheon entrée.

4 entrée servings

1 quart Chicken Stock (see p. 30) or chicken broth
1 can (15 ounces) garbanzo beans, rinsed, drained
1 can (8 ounces) tomato sauce
1 each: chopped medium onion, minced clove garlic
½ cup each: finely chopped celery, carrot
1 bay leaf
½ teaspoon each: dried thyme and basil leaves
1 small zucchini, chopped
⅓ cup uncooked ditalini or orzo
Salt and pepper, to taste

Per Serving:
Calories: 209
% calories from fat: 16
Protein (g): 12.4
Carbohydrate (g): 32.5
Fat (g): 3.8
Saturated fat (g): 0.4
Cholesterol (mg): 0
Sodium (mg): 333
Exchanges:
Milk: 0.0
Vegetable: 0.0
Fruit: 0.0
Bread: 2.0
Meat: 1.0
Fat: 0.0

1. Combine all ingredients, except zucchini, pasta,
salt, and pepper, in slow cooker; cover and cook on high 4 to 6 hours, adding zucchini and pasta during last 20 minutes. Discard bay leaf; season to taste with salt and pepper.

Pay Day Soup

Use up what's on hand today—pay day is tomorrow!!

8 entrée servings

1½ quarts reduced-sodium fat-free chicken broth
1 can (15 ounces) garbanzo beans, rinsed, drained
2 cups cubed peeled potatoes
1 cup chopped onion
2 cloves garlic, minced
⅓ cup uncooked converted long-grain rice
2 tablespoons grated Parmesan cheese
Salt and pepper, to taste

Per Serving:
Calories: 359
% calories from fat: 21
Protein (g): 9.5
Carbohydrate (g): 61
Fat (g): 8.5
Saturated fat (g): 2
Cholesterol (mg): 4.3
Sodium (mg): 206
Exchanges:
Milk: 0.0
Vegetable: 3.0
Fruit: 0.0
Bread: 3.0
Meat: 0.0
Fat: 1.5

1. Combine all ingredients, except rice, cheese, salt,
and pepper, in 6-quart slow cooker; cover and cook on
high 4 to 5 hours, adding rice during last 2 hours. Stir in
Parmesan cheese; season to taste with salt and pepper.

Curried Bean Soup

Use any white bean, such as cannellini, navy, soy, lima, or garbanzo, in this creamy, rich soup.

6 entrée servings

3½ cups reduced-sodium vegetable broth
2 cans (15 ounces each) Great Northern beans, rinsed, drained
1 cup each: chopped onion, sliced leek
1 tablespoon each: minced garlic, curry powder
½ cup 2% reduced-fat milk
Salt and pepper, to taste
6 tablespoons reduced-fat sour cream
Chopped cilantro, as garnish

Per Serving:
Calories: 263
% calories from fat: 16
Protein (g): 13.7
Carbohydrate (g): 42.5
Fat (g): 4.9
Saturated fat (g): 1
Cholesterol (mg): 0
Sodium (mg): 393
Exchanges:
Milk: 0.0
Vegetable: 1.5
Fruit: 0.0
Bread: 2.5
Meat: 0.5
Fat: 0.5

1. Combine all ingredients, except milk, salt, pepper, sour cream, and cilantro, in slow cooker; cover and cook on high 4 to 6 hours. Process soup and milk in food processor or blender until smooth; season to taste with salt and pepper. Top each bowl of soup with a tablespoon of sour cream and sprinkle with cilantro.

Lima Bean and Barley Soup

An excellent winter soup, with robust seasonings.

4 entrée servings

1½ quarts Chicken Stock (see p. 30) or chicken broth
1 can (14½ ounces) diced tomatoes, undrained
1 cup each: chopped onion, frozen thawed lima beans
½ cup each: thinly sliced celery, cubed turnip
1 medium ham hock
¾ teaspoon each: dried thyme and marjoram leaves
1 bay leaf
¼ cup quick-cooking barley
½–1 teaspoon sugar
Salt and pepper, to taste

Per Serving:
Calories: 226
% calories from fat: 18
Protein (g): 11.4
Carbohydrate (g): 33.1
Fat (g): 4.4
Saturated fat (g): 0.8
Cholesterol (mg): 16.4
Sodium (mg): 281
Exchanges:
Milk: 0.0
Vegetable: 1.0
Fruit: 0.0
Bread: 2.0
Meat: 1.0
Fat: 0.0

1. Combine all ingredients, except barley, sugar, salt, and pepper, in slow cooker; cover and cook on high 4 to 6 hours, adding barley during last 20 minutes. Discard ham hock and bay leaf; skim fat from soup. Season to taste with sugar, salt, and pepper.

White Bean Soup

Great Northern or navy beans can be substituted for the cannellini beans.

4 first-course servings

2 cups Chicken Stock (see p. 30) or chicken broth
2 cans (15 ounces each) cannellini beans, rinsed,
  drained
2 cups chopped celery
1 medium onion, chopped
3 green onions, sliced
1–2 cloves garlic, minced
½ teaspoon each: dried dill weed and thyme leaves
⅛ teaspoon ground allspice
Juice of 1 lemon
Salt and cayenne pepper, to taste

Per Serving:
Calories: 238
% calories from fat: 17
Protein (g): 11
Carbohydrate (g): 38.3
Fat (g): 4.6
Saturated fat (g): 0.3
Cholesterol (mg): 0
Sodium (mg): 399
Exchanges:
Milk: 0.0
Vegetable: 0.0
Fruit: 0.0
Bread: 2.5
Meat: 0.0
Fat: 1.0

1. Combine all ingredients, except salt and cayenne pepper, in slow cooker; cover and cook on high 3 to 4 hours. Process soup in food processor or blender until smooth; season to taste with salt and pepper.

White Bean and Pasta Soup

Enjoy the combination of beans and pasta in this Italian-seasoned soup.

6 entrée servings

2 cans (15 ounces each) Great Northern beans,
  rinsed, drained
2 quarts Chicken Stock (see p. 30) or chicken broth
1 can (8 ounces) tomato sauce
1 large onion, chopped
½ cup each: sliced carrots, celery, chopped parsley
2 cloves garlic, chopped
1 tablespoon dried Italian seasoning
2 cups broken angel hair pasta (3-inch)
Salt and pepper, to taste

Per Serving:
Calories: 401
% calories from fat: 10
Protein (g): 21.2
Carbohydrate (g): 66.7
Fat (g): 4.6
Saturated fat (g): 1.0
Cholesterol (mg): 15.2
Sodium (mg): 251
Exchanges:
Milk: 0.0
Vegetable: 1.0
Fruit: 0.0
Bread: 4.0
Meat: 1.0
Fat: 0.0

1. Combine all ingredients, except pasta, salt, and pepper, in 6-quart slow cooker; cover and cook on low 6 to 8 hours, adding pasta during last 15 minutes. Season to taste with salt and pepper.

White Bean Soup with Spinach

This soup is a meal in a bowl. Serve with warm crusty bread and a crisp green salad.

8 first-course servings

2 quarts Chicken Stock (see p. 30) or chicken broth
1½ cups dried Great Northern beans
¼ cup pearl barley
1 large onion, chopped
⅓ cup each: sliced carrots, celery
2 cloves garlic, minced
2 bay leaves
1 teaspoon each: dried marjoram and basil leaves
½ teaspoon dried thyme leaves
1 can (14½ ounces) diced tomatoes, undrained
1 package (10 ounces) frozen chopped spinach,
  thawed, drained
Salt and pepper, to taste

Per Serving:
Calories: 115
% calories from fat: 14
Protein (g): 5.4
Carbohydrate (g): 20.9
Fat (g): 1.9
Saturated fat (g): 1
Cholesterol (mg): 0
Sodium (mg): 806
Exchanges:
Milk: 0.0
Vegetable: 3.0
Fruit: 0.0
Bread: 0.5
Meat: 0.0
Fat: 0.0

1. Combine all ingredients, except tomatoes and liquid, spinach, salt, and pepper, in 6-quart slow cooker; cover and cook on low until beans are tender, 7 to 8 hours, adding tomatoes with liquid and spinach during last 30 minutes. Discard bay leaves; season to taste with salt and pepper.

Hearty Bean and Barley Soup

Bean and barley soup is hard to beat on a chilly evening.

8 entrée servings

2½ quarts reduced-sodium beef broth
2 cups dried Great Northern beans
¼ cup pearl barley
1 meaty ham bone
3 cups thinly sliced cabbage
2 cups chopped onions
⅓ cup each: sliced carrots, celery
2 cloves garlic, minced
3 bay leaves
1½ teaspoons dried thyme leaves
1 can (8 ounces) tomato sauce
Salt and pepper, to taste

Per Serving:
Calories: 225
% calories from fat: 4
Protein (g): 12.2
Carbohydrate (g): 43.1
Fat (g): 1.1
Saturated fat (g): 0.3
Cholesterol (mg): 1.4
Sodium (mg): 378
Exchanges:
Milk: 0.0
Vegetable: 0.0
Fruit: 0.0
Bread: 3.0
Meat: 1.0
Fat: 0.0

1. Combine all ingredients, except tomato sauce, salt, and pepper, in 6-quart slow cooker; cover and cook on low until beans are tender, 8 to 10 hours, adding tomato sauce during last 30 minutes. Discard bay leaves; season to taste with salt and pepper.

Vegetable Soup with Country Ham

Country ham, beef broth, and chicken are a unique combination in this delicious soup.

6 entrée servings

2 quarts reduced-sodium fat-free beef broth
1 can (15 ounces) lima or navy beans, rinsed, drained
12 ounces boneless, skinless chicken breast, cubed
8 ounces country ham, fat trimmed, diced
1 cup each: cubed red potatoes, cut green beans
½ cup each: chopped onion, leek, sliced carrot, celery
2 large cloves garlic, minced
1 teaspoon dried thyme leaves
1 cup asparagus spears
Salt and pepper, to taste

Per Serving:
Calories: 263
% calories from fat: 20
Protein (g): 31
Carbohydrate (g): 20.7
Fat (g): 5.7
Saturated fat (g): 1.5
Cholesterol (mg): 59.3
Sodium (mg): 1406
Exchanges:
Milk: 0.0
Vegetable: 1.0
Fruit: 0.0
Bread: 1.0
Meat: 3.0
Fat: 0.0

1. Combine all ingredients, except asparagus, salt, and pepper, in 6-quart slow cooker; cover and cook on low 6 to 8 hours, adding asparagus during last 30 minutes. Season to taste with salt and pepper.

Ham, Spinach, and Pasta Soup

Be sure to add leafy greens, like spinach, and small pasta, like orzo, near the end of the cooking time, as they cook quickly.

4 entrée servings

1¼ quarts reduced-sodium fat-free chicken broth
1 can (15 ounces) tomato sauce
6 ounces lean reduced-sodium ham, cubed
1 medium onion, chopped
2 teaspoons dried Italian seasoning
1 cup uncooked orzo or other small soup pasta
3 cups sliced loosely packed spinach
Salt and pepper to taste

Per Serving:
Calories: 188
% calories from fat: 10
Protein (g): 14.7
Carbohydrate (g): 29.5
Fat (g): 2.3
Saturated fat (g): 0.3
Cholesterol (mg): 19.1
Sodium (mg): 653
Exchanges:
Milk: 0.0
Vegetable: 2.0
Fruit: 0.0
Bread: 1.0
Meat: 1.0
Fat: 0.0

1. Combine all ingredients, except pasta, spinach, salt, and pepper, in slow cooker; cover and cook on high 4 to 6 hours, stirring in orzo and spinach during last 20 to 30 minutes. Season to taste with salt and pepper.

Split-Pea Soup with Ham

Serve this hearty soup with thick slices of garlic bread.

8 entrée servings

1½ quarts water
1 can (14½ ounces) reduced-sodium fat-free chicken broth
1 pound dried split peas
1½ cups each: cubed lean ham, chopped onions
1 cup chopped carrots
½ cup sliced celery
1–2 teaspoons beef bouillon crystals
1 teaspoon dried marjoram leaves
Salt and pepper, to taste

Per Serving:
Calories: 264
% calories from fat: 11
Protein (g): 21.6
Carbohydrate (g): 39.9
Fat (g): 3.4
Saturated fat (g): 0.6
Cholesterol (mg): 16.2
Sodium (mg): 513
Exchanges:
Milk: 0.0
Vegetable: 1.0
Fruit: 0.0
Bread: 2.0
Meat: 2.0
Fat: 0.0

1. Combine all ingredients, except salt and pepper, in 6-quart slow cooker; cover and cook on high 4 to 6 hours. Season to taste with salt and pepper.

Variations

Savory Pea Soup with Smoked Sausage—Make soup as above, substituting 8 ounces smoked turkey sausage, halved lengthwise and sliced, for the ham, and adding 2 cups diced potato, 1 teaspoon dried thyme leaves, and 1 bay leaf. Discard bay leaf; season to taste with hot pepper sauce.
Split-Pea Soup with Barley—Make soup as above, omitting ham. Increase water to 2 quarts, and add ½ cup pearl barley with the split peas.

Hearty Split-Pea, Bean, and Barley Soup

We love this stick-to-the-ribs soup for its variety of textures.

12 entrée servings

4 quarts water
1 meaty ham bone
2 cups dried green split peas
½ cup each: pearl barley, dried black-eyed peas,
   navy beans
2–4 beef bouillon cubes
1 cup coarsely chopped onions
½ cup each: thinly sliced carrots, celery
2 cloves garlic, minced
½ teaspoon each: dried thyme leaves,
   crushed celery seeds
3 bay leaves
Salt and pepper, to taste

Per Serving:
Calories: 153
% calories from fat: 10
Protein (g): 8.4
Carbohydrate (g): 27.4
Fat (g): 1.8
Saturated fat (g): 0.5
Cholesterol (mg): 5.9
Sodium (mg): 205
Exchanges:
Milk: 0.0
Vegetable: 0.0
Fruit: 0.0
Bread: 2.0
Meat: 0.0
Fat: 0.0

1. Combine all ingredients, except salt and pepper, in 6-quart slow cooker; cover and cook on low 6 to 8 hours. Remove ham bone, cut meat into bite-sized pieces, and return to soup; discard bone. Discard bay leaves; season to taste with salt and pepper.

Down-Home Soup

Ham hock, black-eyed peas, and barley combine to give this soup its homey flavor and richness.

6 entrée servings

2 quarts Chicken Stock (see p. 30) or chicken broth
½ cup dried black-eyed peas
¼ cup pearl barley
2 small ham hocks
2½ cups cut green beans
1 cup chopped onion
¼ cup each: sliced carrot, chopped celery
1 clove garlic, minced
2 teaspoons dried basil leaves
½ teaspoon dried thyme leaves
1 bay leaf
1 can (14½ ounces) diced tomatoes, undrained
Pinch crushed red pepper
Salt and pepper, to taste

Per Serving:
Calories: 146
% calories from fat: 22
Protein (g): 7.8
Carbohydrate (g): 19.2
Fat (g): 3.4
Saturated fat (g): 0.8
Cholesterol (mg): 15.2
Sodium (mg): 61
Exchanges:
Milk: 0.0
Vegetable: 0.0
Fruit: 0.0
Bread: 1.0
Meat: 1.0
Fat: 0.5

1. Combine all ingredients, except tomatoes, crushed red pepper, salt, and pepper, in 6-quart slow cooker; cover and cook on low 6 to 8 hours, adding tomatoes with liquid and red pepper during last 45 minutes. Discard bay leaf and ham hocks; season to taste with salt and pepper.

Black-Eyed Pea and Lentil Soup

This soup is flavorful, economical, and full of protein.

10 entrée servings

2 quarts Beef Stock (see p. 31) or beef broth
1½ cups dried lentils
1 cup dried black-eyed peas
8 ounces lean smoked ham, cubed
½ cup each: chopped carrots, celery, onion
2 cloves garlic, minced
½ teaspoon each: dried thyme and rosemary leaves
1 can (14½ ounces) diced tomatoes, undrained
Salt and pepper, to taste

Per Serving:
Calories: 219
% calories from fat: 12
Protein (g): 15.4
Carbohydrate (g): 33.9
Fat (g): 3
Saturated fat (g): 0.7
Cholesterol (mg): 12.3
Sodium (mg): 300
Exchanges:
Milk: 0.0
Vegetable: 1.0
Fruit: 0.0
Bread: 2.0
Meat: 1.0
Fat: 0.0

1. Combine all ingredients, except tomatoes, salt, and pepper, in 6-quart slow cooker; cover and cook on low 6 to 8 hours, adding tomatoes and liquid during last 45 minutes. Season to taste with salt and pepper.

Lentil-Vegetable Soup with Ham

Lentils lend a wonderful homey flavor and heartiness to this simple soup.

4 entrée servings

1 quart Rich Chicken Stock (see p. 30) or chicken broth
1 small ham hock
⅔ cup dried lentils
½ cup each: chopped onion, carrot, celery, ham
⅛–¼ teaspoon crushed red pepper
1 can (14½ ounce) stewed tomatoes
Salt and pepper, to taste

Per Serving:
Calories: 237
% calories from fat: 24
Protein (g): 16.9
Carbohydrate (g): 27.3
Fat (g): 6.4
Saturated fat (g): 1.4
Cholesterol (mg): 11.6
Sodium (mg): 414
Exchanges:
Milk: 0.0
Vegetable: 2.0
Fruit: 0.0
Bread: 1.0
Meat: 2.0
Fat: 0.0

1. Combine all ingredients, except stewed tomatoes, salt, and pepper, in slow cooker; cover and cook on high 4 to 6 hours, adding tomatoes during last 45 minutes. Discard ham hock; season to taste with salt and pepper.

Beef and Lentil Soup

Beef adds richness to a favorite lentil soup.

10 entrée servings

3 quarts reduced-sodium fat-free beef broth
¼ cup dry white wine (optional)
1 pound cubed lean beef stew meat
3 cups dried lentils
1½ cups finely chopped onions
½ cup each: finely chopped leeks, carrots, celery
Salt and pepper, to taste

Per Serving:
Calories: 313
% calories from fat: 12
Protein (g): 31.7
Carbohydrate (g): 37.3
Fat (g): 4.2
Saturated fat (g): 1.1
Cholesterol (mg): 28.4
Sodium (mg): 234
Exchanges:
Milk: 0.0
Vegetable: 1.0
Fruit: 0.0
Bread: 2.0
Meat: 2.5
Fat: 0.0

1. Combine all ingredients, except salt and pepper, in 6-quart slow cooker; cover and cook on low 6 to 8 hours. Season to taste with salt and pepper.

Spicy Lentil-Tomato Soup With Ham

This easy, spicy lentil soup is seasoned with ham, tomatoes, and a lively blend of herbs.

6 entrée servings

1½ quarts Chicken Stock (see p. 30) or chicken broth
1 can (28 ounces) Italian plum tomatoes, coarsely
  chopped, undrained
½ cup each: finely diced lean ham, dried red or
  brown lentils
2 cups chopped onions
1 cup each: shredded green cabbage, finely
  chopped celery, carrots, rinsed drained canned
  garbanzo beans
2 large cloves garlic, minced
1 tablespoon dried basil leaves
½ teaspoon each: dried oregano and thyme leaves
Salt and cayenne pepper, to taste

Per Serving:
Calories: 204
% calories from fat: 16
Protein (g): 14.3
Carbohydrate (g): 28.6
Fat (g): 3.7
Saturated fat (g): 0.6
Cholesterol (mg): 5
Sodium (mg): 671
Exchanges:
Milk: 0.0
Vegetable: 3.0
Fruit: 0.0
Bread: 1.0
Meat: 1.0
Fat: 0.0

1. Combine all ingredients, except salt and cayenne pepper, in 6-quart slow cooker; cover and cook on high 4 to 6 hours. Season to taste with salt and cayenne pepper.

Easy Barley and Garbanzo Soup

Dry mustard, celery seed, thyme, and cayenne pepper combine for great flavor in this soup.

6 first-course servings

1½ quarts beef broth
1 can (15 ounces) each: rinsed drained garbanzo
  beans, tomato sauce
¼ cup each: finely chopped celery, carrot, onion
2 teaspoons sugar
½ teaspoon each: dry mustard, dried thyme leaves
⅓ cup quick-cooking barley
1 can (16 ounces) cut green beans, drained
Salt and pepper, to taste

Per Serving:
Calories: 122
% calories from fat: 5
Protein (g): 5.8
Carbohydrate (g): 26.9
Fat (g): 0.8
Saturated fat (g): 0.1
Cholesterol (mg): 0
Sodium (mg): 738
Exchanges:
Milk: 0.0
Vegetable: 0.0
Fruit: 0.0
Bread: 1.5
Meat: 0.0
Fat: 0.0

1. Combine all ingredients, except barley, green beans, salt, and pepper, in 6-quart slow cooker; cover and cook on high 4 to 5 hours, adding barley and green beans during last 30 minutes. Season to taste with salt and pepper.

FOUR

Chowders

Florida Avocado and Tomato Chowder

In this easy recipe, colorful ingredients create a kaleidoscope of fresh colors and flavors.

4 entrée servings

1 can (14 ounces) reduced-sodium fat-free chicken broth
3 cups peeled cubed potatoes
1 cup each: whole kernel corn, chopped plum tomatoes
8 ounces smoked turkey breast, cubed
1 teaspoon dried thyme leaves
1 cup cubed avocado
Juice of 1 lime
3 slices bacon, cooked, crumbled
Salt and pepper, to taste

Per Serving:
Calories: 333
% calories from fat: 26
Protein (g): 21
Carbohydrate (g): 44.7
Fat (g): 10.2
Saturated fat (g): 2.4
Cholesterol (mg): 51.1
Sodium (mg): 765
Exchanges:
Milk: 0.0
Vegetable: 2.0
Fruit: 0.0
Bread: 2.0
Meat: 2.0
Fat: 1.5

1. Combine all ingredients, except avocado, lime, bacon, salt, and pepper, in slow cooker; cover and cook on high 4 to 5 hours. Stir in avocado, lime, and bacon; season to taste with salt and pepper.

Cheesy Corn Chowder

A satisfying whole-meal chowder, rich with sausage, cheese, and the flavor of corn.

6 entrée servings

2 cups reduced-sodium fat-free chicken broth
8 ounces reduced-fat smoked sausage, sliced
1 can (16 ounces) each: whole kernel corn, cream-style corn
1½ cups chopped tomatoes
1 each: medium chopped onion, red bell pepper, potato, minced clove garlic
2 cups whole milk, divided
2 tablespoons cornstarch
½–¾ cup (2–3 ounces) shredded reduced-fat Cheddar cheese
Salt and pepper, to taste
Garlic Croutons (see p. 51)

Per Serving:
Calories: 326
% calories from fat: 16
Protein (g): 18
Carbohydrate (g): 54.7
Fat (g): 6.2
Saturated fat (g): 2.8
Cholesterol (mg): 29.8
Sodium (mg): 786
Exchanges:
Milk: 0.0
Vegetable: 2.0
Fruit: 0.0
Bread: 3.0
Meat: 1.0
Fat: 0.0

1. Combine all ingredients, except milk, cornstarch cheese, salt, pepper, and Garlic Croutons, in slow cooker; cover and cook on high 4 to 5 hours, adding 1 cup milk during last 30 minutes. Stir in remaining combined 1 cup milk and cornstarch, stirring 2 to 3 minutes. Add cheese, stirring until melted. Season to taste with salt and pepper. Sprinkle each bowl of soup with Garlic Croutons.

Hearty Corn and Potato Chowder

A thick, hearty, and comforting cold-weather chowder.

4 entrée servings

2 cups each: reduced-sodium fat-free chicken broth, cubed potatoes
2 cups whole kernel corn
1 medium onion, chopped
½ cup sliced celery
½ teaspoon dried thyme leaves
1¾ cups whole milk, divided
2 tablespoons cornstarch
Salt and pepper, to taste

Per Serving:
Calories: 248
% calories from fat: 19
Protein (g): 8.2
Carbohydrate (g): 44.7
Fat (g): 5.6
Saturated fat (g): 1.5
Cholesterol (mg): 5.3
Sodium (mg): 447
Exchanges:
Milk: 0.0
Vegetable: 0.0
Fruit: 0.0
Bread: 3.0
Meat: 0.0
Fat: 1.0

1. Combine all ingredients, except milk, cornstarch, salt, and pepper, in slow cooker; cover and cook on high 4 to 5 hours, adding 1¼ cups milk during last 30 minutes. Stir in combined ½ cup milk and cornstarch, stirring 2 to 3 minutes; season to taste with salt and pepper.

Sweet Onion and Bean Chowder

The onions can be caramelized to enhance flavor, if desired. Sauté onions in 2 tablespoons butter in large skillet 2 minutes; reduce heat to medium-low and cook until golden, about 10 minutes.

8 entrée servings

2 cups each: reduced-sodium fat-free chicken and beef broth
1 can (15½ ounces) Great Northern beans, rinsed, drained
1½ pounds onions, thinly sliced
¾ teaspoon dried thyme leaves
¼ cup dry sherry (optional)
Salt and pepper, to taste
Garlic Croutons (see p. 51)

Per Serving:
Calories: 159
% calories from fat: 17
Protein (g): 10.1
Carbohydrate (g): 25
Fat (g): 3.2
Saturated fat (g): 0.6
Cholesterol (mg): 0
Sodium (mg): 443
Exchanges:
Milk: 0.0
Vegetable: 2.0
Fruit: 0.0
Bread: 1.0
Meat: 0.0
Fat: 0.5

1. Combine all ingredients, except sherry, salt, pepper, and Garlic Croutons, in slow cooker; cover and cook on high 5 to 6 hours, adding sherry during last 15 minutes. Season to taste with salt and pepper; sprinkle each bowl of chowder with Garlic Croutons.

Potato Chowder

Substitute any desired vegetables in this versatile soup, such as carrots, zucchini, green beans, or corn, for a delectable vegetable chowder.

6 entrée servings

3 cups reduced-sodium fat-free chicken broth
3½ cups peeled cubed Idaho potatoes
1 cup chopped onion
¼ cup thinly sliced celery
¼–½ teaspoon celery seeds
1 cup whole milk
2 tablespoons cornstarch
Salt and pepper, to taste

Per Serving:
Calories: 212
% calories from fat: 17
Protein (g): 7.5
Carbohydrate (g): 37.1
Fat (g): 4.2
Saturated fat (g): 0.9
Cholesterol (mg): 1.3
Sodium (mg): 210
Exchanges:
Milk: 0.0
Vegetable: 1.0
Fruit: 0.0
Bread: 2.0
Meat: 0.0
Fat: 1.0

1. Combine all ingredients, except milk, cornstarch, salt, and pepper, in slow cooker; cover and cook on high 3 to 4 hours. Stir in combined milk and cornstarch during last 20 minutes. Season to taste with salt and pepper.

Variations

Easy Vichyssoise—Make recipe as above, substituting chopped leeks for half the onion and omitting celery and celery seeds. Process soup in food processor or blender until smooth. Serve warm, or refrigerate and serve chilled. Sprinkle each bowl of soup with minced fresh chives.

Potato au Gratin Chowder—Make recipe as above. Process half the chowder in food processor or blender until almost smooth; return to slow cooker and cook on high 10 minutes. Add ¾ cup (3 ounces) shredded reduced-fat Cheddar cheese, stirring until melted. Sprinkle each bowl of chowder with ground nutmeg.

Potato Curry Chowder

The curry flavor in this chowder is subtle; increase the amount if you prefer.

4 entrée servings

1 quart Chicken Stock (see p. 30) or chicken broth
1 cup chopped green onions
3 each: cubed large potatoes, minced cloves garlic
¾ teaspoon curry powder
½ teaspoon ground cumin
1 cup 2% reduced-fat milk
2 tablespoons cornstarch
Salt and pepper, to taste

Per Serving:
Calories: 183
% calories from fat: 6
Protein (g): 12.2
Carbohydrate (g): 33.1
Fat (g): 1.2
Saturated fat (g): 0.3
Cholesterol (mg): 8
Sodium (mg): 186
Exchanges:
Milk: 1.0
Vegetable: 0.0
Fruit: 0.0
Bread: 1.5
Meat: 0.0
Fat: 0.0

1. Combine all ingredients, except milk, cornstarch, salt, and pepper, in slow cooker; cover and cook on low 6 to 8 hours. Turn heat to high and cook 10 minutes; stir in combined milk and cornstarch, stirring 2 to 3 minutes. Season to taste with salt and pepper.

Idaho Chowder with Cheese

Rosemary gives this soup an aromatic flavor.

8 entrée servings

1 quart Chicken Stock (see p. 30) or chicken broth
6 large Idaho potatoes, peeled, cubed (½-inch)
4 cups chopped onions
1 cup chopped celery
2 tablespoons minced garlic
½ teaspoon dried rosemary leaves
2 cups whole milk, divided
2 tablespoons cornstarch
2 teaspoons Worcestershire sauce
⅛ teaspoon ground nutmeg
1 cup (4 ounces) shredded reduced-fat Swiss cheese
Salt and white pepper, to taste

Per Serving:
Calories: 241
% calories from fat: 17
Protein (g): 11.9
Carbohydrate (g): 38
Fat (g): 4.7
Saturated fat (g): 2.8
Cholesterol (mg): 18.1
Sodium (mg): 111
Exchanges:
Milk: 0.0
Vegetable: 1.0
Fruit: 0.0
Bread: 2.0
Meat: 0.5
Fat: 1.0

1. Combine stock, potatoes, onions, celery, garlic, and rosemary in 6-quart slow cooker; cover and cook on high 4 to 5 hours, adding 1 cup milk during last 30 minutes. Stir in combined remaining 1 cup milk and cornstarch, nutmeg, and Worcestershire sauce, stirring 2 to 3 minutes. Add cheese, stirring until melted; season to taste with salt and white pepper.

Variation

Three-Cheese and Potato Chowder—Make recipe as above, substituting ½ cup (2 ounces) each shredded reduced-fat mozzarella and Cheddar cheese and 2 to 4 tablespoons crumbled blue cheese for the Swiss cheese. Sprinkle each bowl of soup with chopped chives.

Potato, Corn, and Canadian Bacon Chowder

If desired, the Canadian bacon can be sautéed in 1 teaspoon margarine or butter or sautéed until crisp and "frizzled," then sprinkled on the chowder as a garnish.

6 entrée servings

3 cups each: reduced-sodium fat-free chicken broth,
    cubed peeled red potatoes
2 cups whole kernel corn
1 each: chopped large onion, minced garlic clove
6 ounces Canadian bacon, julienned
1 large bay leaf
¾ teaspoon dried thyme leaves
¼ teaspoon dry mustard
2 cups whole milk, divided
2 tablespoons cornstarch
Salt and white pepper, to taste

Per Serving:
Calories: 282
% calories from fat: 19
Protein (g): 13.8
Carbohydrate (g): 45.9
Fat (g): 6
Saturated fat (g): 1.7
Cholesterol (mg): 19.3
Sodium (mg): 824
Exchanges:
Milk: 0.0
Vegetable: 0.0
Fruit: 0.0
Bread: 3.0
Meat: 1.0
Fat: 0.5

1. Combine all ingredients, except milk, cornstarch, salt, and white pepper, in slow cooker; cover and cook on high 4 to 5 hours, adding 1½ cups milk during last 30 minutes. Discard bay leaf. Process half the soup in food processor or blender until smooth; return to slow cooker. Cover and cook on high 10 minutes; stir in combined ½ cup milk and cornstarch, stirring 2 to 3 minutes. Season to taste with salt and white pepper.

Variation

Colcannon Chowder—Make recipe as above, adding 2 cups thinly sliced cabbage, omitting corn, and decreasing milk to 1½ cups. Do not purée the soup. Stir combined ½ cup reduced-fat sour cream and 2 tablespoons cornstarch into chowder at end of cooking time.

Fresh Tomato-Zucchini Chowder

Savor summer's bounty in this lively chowder of basil, tomatoes, and zuc-chini. Bacon adds a delightful smoky accent.

4 first-course servings

1 can (14½ ounces) vegetable broth
1 pound plum tomatoes, chopped
1 cup chopped onion
1 medium potato, cubed
1 cup cubed zucchini
¼ cup whole kernel corn
1 tablespoon dried basil leaves
Salt and cayenne pepper, to taste
2 slices bacon, fried crisp, crumbled

Per Serving:
Calories: 138
% calories from fat: 12
Protein (g): 4.9
Carbohydrate (g): 28.8
Fat (g): 2
Saturated fat (g): 0.4
Cholesterol (mg): 5
Sodium (mg): 463
Exchanges:
Milk: 0.0
Vegetable: 1.0
Fruit: 0.0
Bread: 1.5
Meat: 0.0
Fat: 0.0

1. Combine all ingredients, except salt, cayenne pepper, and bacon, in slow cooker; cover and cook on high 4 to 5 hours. Season to taste with salt and cayenne pepper; sprinkle each bowl of soup with crumbled bacon.

Variation

Green Garden Chowder—Make chowder as above, omitting corn. Add 1 cup each small broccoli florets, cut green beans, and sliced spinach or kale during last 30 minutes of cooking time. Sprinkle each bowl of soup with crumbled bacon and grated Parmesan cheese.

Black-Eyed Pea and Corn Chowder

Roasted red peppers and bacon enliven this fuss-free chowder.

4 first-course servings

1½ cups each: fat-free chicken broth, chopped onion
1 can (15 ounces) black-eyed peas, rinsed, drained
1 can (14 ounces) cream-style corn
2 teaspoons minced garlic
1 teaspoon dried savory leaves
1 cup coarsely chopped roasted red peppers
Salt and pepper, to taste
4 slices bacon, cooked, drained, crumbled

Per Serving:
Calories: 153
% calories from fat: 14
Protein (g): 11.3
Carbohydrate (g): 25.5
Fat (g): 2.7
Saturated fat (g): 0.6
Cholesterol (mg): 10
Sodium (mg): 576
Exchanges:
Milk: 0.0
Vegetable: 1.0
Fruit 0.0
Bread: 1.0
Meat: 1.0
Fat: 1.0

1. Combine all ingredients, except roasted red peppers, salt, pepper, and bacon, in slow cooker; cover and cook on high 2 to 3 hours, adding roasted peppers during the last 15 minutes. Season to taste with salt and pepper; sprinkle each bowl of soup with bacon.

Variation

Red Beans 'n' Greens Chowder—Make recipe as above, substituting red beans for the black-eyed peas, 1½ cups frozen cut okra for the corn, and 1 cup sliced turnip greens or kale for the roasted red peppers.

Navy Bean and Bacon Chowder

Milk adds a creamy smoothness to this bean soup.

8 entrée servings

1½ quarts Chicken Stock (see p. 30) or chicken broth
1½ cups dried navy beans, rinsed
½ cup each: chopped carrots, onion
2 large cloves garlic, minced
½ teaspoon each: dried oregano, basil, and rosemary
  leaves
1 cup whole milk
2 tablespoons cornstarch
Salt and pepper, to taste
8 slices bacon, cooked, crumbled

Per Serving:
Calories: 216
% calories from fat: 18
Protein (g): 13.2
Carbohydrate (g): 31.4
Fat (g): 4.2
Saturated fat (g): 1.3
Cholesterol (mg): 7.9
Sodium (mg): 153
Exchanges:
Milk: 0.0
Vegetable: 0.0
Fruit: 0.0
Bread: 2.0
Meat: 1.0
Fat: 0.5

1. Combine stock, beans, vegetables, and herbs in 6-quart slow cooker; cover and cook on low until beans are tender, 6 to 8 hours. Turn heat to high and cook 10 minutes; stir in combined milk and cornstarch, stirring 2 to 3 minutes. If desired, process half the soup in food processor or blender until smooth; stir back into slow cooker. Season to taste with salt and pepper. Sprinkle each bowl of chowder with bacon.

Variation

Mixed Bean Chowder—Make recipe as above, substituting ½ cup each dried Great Northern, pinto, and kidney beans for the navy beans.

Tex-Mex Chicken and Cheese Chowder

For less heat, plain Jack cheese can be substituted for all or part of the pepper-Jack cheese.

4 entrée servings

1½ cups reduced-sodium fat-free chicken broth
2 cans (17 ounces) cream-style corn
1 pound boneless, skinless chicken breast, cubed
   (½-inch)
½ cup finely chopped onion
1 cup cubed zucchini
1½ cups 2% reduced-fat milk
2 tablespoons cornstarch
1½ cups (6 ounces) shredded reduced-fat
   pepper-Jack cheese
Salt and pepper, to taste

Per Serving:
Calories: 358
% calories from fat: 20
Protein (g): 25.9
Carbohydrate (g): 50.3
Fat (g): 8.6
Saturated fat (g): 4.1
Cholesterol (mg): 49.4
Sodium (mg): 816
Exchanges:
Milk: 0.0
Vegetable: 0.0
Fruit: 0.0
Bread: 3.0
Meat: 2.0
Fat: 0.5

1. Combine broth, corn, chicken, and onion in slow cooker. Cover and cook on high 4 to 5 hours, adding zucchini during last 30 minutes. Stir in combined milk and cornstarch, stirring 2 to 3 minutes; add cheese, stirring until melted. Season to taste with salt and pepper.

Variation

Chicken and Creamed Chowder—Make recipe as above, substituting ½ cup each thinly sliced celery and carrots for the zucchini and Colby cheese for the pepper-Jack cheese; increase cream-style corn to 2 cans.

Chicken Corn Chowder

Nicely seasoned, with a piquant hint of jalapeño!

8 entrée servings

1 quart Chicken Stock (see p. 30) or chicken broth
1 pound boneless skinless chicken breast, cubed
  (½-inch)
3 cups whole kernel corn, thawed
2 medium tomatoes, chopped
½ cup each: chopped onion, green bell pepper, carrots
1–2 teaspoons each: minced jalapeño chili, garlic
½ teaspoon each: dried savory and thyme leaves
1 cup 2% reduced-fat milk
2 tablespoons cornstarch
Salt and pepper, to taste

Per Serving:
Calories: 171
% calories from fat: 11
Protein (g): 17.6
Carbohydrate (g): 22
Fat (g): 2.1
Saturated fat (g): 0.8
Cholesterol (mg): 37.7
Sodium (mg): 130
Exchanges:
Milk: 0.0
Vegetable: 1.0
Fruit: 0.0
Bread: 1.0
Meat: 2.0
Fat: 0.0

1. Combine all ingredients, except milk, cornstarch, salt, and pepper, in 6-quart slow cooker; cover and cook on low 6 to 8 hours. Turn heat to high and cook 10 minutes; stir in combined milk and cornstarch, stirring 2 to 3 minutes. Season to taste with salt and pepper.

Hearty Chicken Corn Chowder

Salsa and black olives are surprising flavor accents in this hearty chowder.

6 entrée servings

2 cups reduced-sodium fat-free chicken broth
2 cans (15 ounces each) cream-style corn
1 pound boneless, skinless chicken breast, cubed
2 cups peeled cubed potatoes
½ cup each: chopped onion, red bell pepper
2 teaspoons minced garlic
⅓ cup mild or hot salsa
Salt and pepper, to taste
Chopped black olives, as garnish

Per Serving:
Calories: 291
% calories from fat: 17
Protein (g): 22
Carbohydrate (g): 45.6
Fat (g): 3.9
Saturated fat (g): 0.7
Cholesterol (mg): 46
Sodium (mg): 536
Exchanges:
Milk: 0.0
Vegetable: 0.0
Fruit: 0.0
Bread: 2.5
Meat: 2.0
Fat: 0.0

1. Combine all ingredients, except salt, pepper, and olives, in 6-quart slow cooker; cover and cook on high 3 to 4 hours. Season to taste with salt and pepper. Sprinkle each serving with olives.

Variation
Mediterranean-Style Chicken and Shrimp Chowder—Make recipe as above, using 8 ounces chicken and substituting 1 can (19 ounces) garbanzo beans for 1 can of corn, and 1 chopped roasted red pepper for the bell pepper. Omit salsa. Add ¾ teaspoon dried oregano leaves and 8 ounces peeled deveined shrimp.

Chicken-Vegetable Chowder

A delicious chowder that uses canned and frozen ingredients for convenience.

6 entrée servings

2 cups Chicken Stock (see p. 30) or chicken broth
1 can (10¼ ounces) reduced-sodium 98% fat-free
  cream of potato soup
1 pound boneless, skinless chicken breast, cubed
  (¾-inch)
1 cup sliced carrots
½ cup Mexican-style whole kernel corn
½ cup chopped onion
2 cloves garlic, minced
1 teaspoon dried thyme leaves
2 cups small broccoli florets
½ cup 2% reduced-fat milk
Salt and pepper, to taste

Per Serving:
Calories: 207
% calories from fat: 21
Protein (g): 21.3
Carbohydrate (g): 19.1
Fat (g): 4.8
Saturated fat (g): 1.3
Cholesterol (mg): 47.1
Sodium (mg): 107
Exchanges:
Milk: 0.0
Vegetable: 1.0
Fruit: 0.0
Bread: 2.0
Meat: 2.0
Fat: 0.0

1. Combine all ingredients, except broccoli, milk, salt, and pepper, in slow cooker; cover and cook on low 6 to 8 hours, adding broccoli and milk during last 20 minutes. Season to taste with salt and pepper.

Chicken and Fresh Vegetable Chowder

This delicious chowder is very easy to prepare; use a food processor to chop all the vegetables quickly.

8 entrée servings

1 quart Chicken Stock (see p. 30) or chicken broth
1½ pounds boneless, skinless chicken breast, cubed (1-inch)
½ cup each: chopped onion, green bell pepper, celery, carrots, zucchini
2 cloves garlic, minced
¾ teaspoon each: dried thyme and marjoram leaves
1 bay leaf
¾ cup 2% reduced-fat milk
2 tablespoons cornstarch
Salt and pepper, to taste

Per Serving:
Calories: 188
% calories from fat: 27
Protein (g): 21.8
Carbohydrate (g): 11.3
Fat (g): 5.6
Saturated fat (g): 1.3
Cholesterol (mg): 53.5
Sodium (mg): 118
Exchanges:
Milk: 0.0
Vegetable: 3.0
Fruit: 0.0
Bread: 0.0
Meat: 2.0
Fat: 0.0

1. Combine all ingredients, except milk, cornstarch, salt, and pepper, in slow cooker; cover and cook on low 6 to 8 hours. Turn heat to high and cook 10 minutes; stir in combined milk and cornstarch, stirring 2 to 3 minutes. Discard bay leaf; season to taste with salt and pepper.

Chicken Chowder Hispaniola

This enticing chowder boasts sofrito, a popular Cuban seasoning found in the ethnic section of many supermarkets.

4 entrée servings

1 can (14½ ounces) each: undrained diced tomatoes, reduced-sodium fat-free chicken broth
1 can (15 ounces) garbanzo beans, rinsed, drained
12 ounces boneless, skinless chicken breast, cubed (¾-inch)
1 medium onion, chopped
2 cups packed spinach
2 tablespoons sofrito sauce (optional)
Salt and pepper, to taste
¼ cup slivered almonds, toasted

Per Serving:
Calories: 346
% calories from fat: 29
Protein (g): 30.5
Carbohydrate (g): 28.2
Fat (g): 10.5
Saturated fat (g): 1.9
Cholesterol (mg): 54.3
Sodium (mg): 639
Exchanges:
Milk: 0.0
Vegetable: 3.0
Fruit: 0.0
Bread: 1.0
Meat: 3.0
Fat: 1.0

1. Combine all ingredients, except spinach, sofrito sauce, salt, pepper, and almonds, in slow cooker; cover and cook on high 4 to 5 hours, stirring in spinach and sofrito sauce during the last 15 minutes. Season to taste with salt and pepper. Sprinkle each bowl with almonds.

Chicken and Shrimp Chowder with Lime

Lime provides the flavor accent in this soup, while tomatoes and avocados contribute crisp color contrasts.

4 entrée servings

2 cans (14½ ounces each) reduced-sodium fat-free chicken broth
8 ounces boneless, skinless chicken breast, cubed (¾-inch)
4 each: sliced green onions, chopped plum tomatoes
⅛–¼ teaspoon crushed red pepper
⅛ teaspoon celery seeds
½ cup uncooked converted long-grain rice
8 ounces shrimp, peeled, deveined, halved crosswise
1 avocado, cubed
Juice of 1 lime
1 teaspoon grated lime zest
Salt and pepper, to taste

Per Serving:
Calories: 331
% calories from fat: 25
Protein (g): 30.9
Carbohydrate (g): 30.9
Fat (g): 9.2
Saturated fat (g): 2
Cholesterol (mg): 121.2
Sodium (mg): 290
Exchanges:
Milk: 0.0
Vegetable: 0.0
Fruit: 0.0
Bread: 2.0
Meat: 3.5
Fat: 0.0

1. Combine broth, chicken, green onions, tomatoes, crushed red pepper, and celery seeds in slow cooker; cover and cook on high 4 to 5 hours, adding rice during last 2 hours and shrimp during last 20 minutes. Stir in avocado, lime juice, and zest; season to taste with salt and pepper.

Shrimp and Vegetable Chowder

The rich flavor of this chowder comes from a combination of herbs, spices, and tomato sauce.

6 entrée servings

3 cups each: reduced-sodium fat-free chicken broth, whole kernel corn
1 can (8 ounces) tomato sauce
2 cups peeled diced red potatoes
1 cup each: chopped onion, green or red bell pepper
2 cloves garlic, minced
¼ cup dry sherry (optional)
1–2 teaspoons dried Italian seasoning
¼ teaspoon each: chili powder, dry mustard
3–4 drops hot pepper sauce
1½ cups cooked peeled deveined halved shrimp
½ cup whole milk
Salt and pepper, to taste

Per Serving:
Calories: 270
% calories from fat: 9
Protein (g): 15.9
Carbohydrate (g): 45.2
Fat (g): 2.9
Saturated fat (g): 0.8
Cholesterol (mg): 72
Sodium (mg): 455
Exchanges:
Milk: 0.0
Vegetable: 3.0
Fruit: 0.0
Bread: 2.0
Meat: 1.0
Fat: 0.0

1. Combine all ingredients, except shrimp, milk, salt, and pepper, in 6-quart slow cooker; cover and cook on high 4 to 5 hours, adding shrimp and milk during last 10 minutes. Season to taste with salt and pepper.

Bean and Shrimp Chowder

You can make a great meal out of this chowder; just add a slice of warm crusty bread and a green salad.

8 entrée servings

2 cans (15½ ounces each) Great Northern beans, rinsed, drained
1½ cups Chicken Stock (see p. 30) or chicken broth
1 can (16 ounces) cream-style corn
¼ cup chopped onion
½–¾ teaspoon dried thyme leaves
¼ teaspoon dry mustard
1½ pounds medium shrimp, peeled, deveined
1–1½ cups 2% reduced-fat milk
2 tablespoons cornstarch
Salt and cayenne pepper, to taste

Per Serving:
Calories: 218
% calories from fat: 10
Protein (g): 22.9
Carbohydrate (g): 30.9
Fat (g): 2.7
Saturated fat (g): 0.6
Cholesterol (mg): 131.8
Sodium (mg): 658
Exchanges:
Milk: 0.0
Vegetable: 0.0
Fruit: 0.0
Bread: 2.0
Meat: 2.0
Fat: 0.0

1. Combine beans, stock, corn, onion, thyme, and dry mustard in slow cooker; cover and cook on high 3 to 4 hours, stirring in shrimp and combined milk and cornstarch during last 15 to 20 minutes. Season to taste with salt and cayenne pepper.

Lobster and Shrimp Chowder

For easiest preparation, purchase cooked lobster and shrimp in the seafood department of your supermarket.

4 entrée servings

1½ cups clam juice
1 can (14½ ounces) diced tomatoes, undrained
2 large Yukon gold potatoes, cubed
1 medium onion, chopped
1 teaspoon dried tarragon leaves
8 ounces lobster tail, cooked, cut into small chunks
4 ounces small shrimp, cooked, peeled, deveined
1 cup 2% reduced-fat milk
¼ cup chopped parsley
Salt and pepper, to taste

Per Serving:
Calories: 210
% calories from fat: 9
Protein (g): 22.4
Carbohydrate (g): 25.7
Fat (g): 2.1
Saturated fat (g): 0.9
Cholesterol (mg): 100.7
Sodium (mg): 519
Exchanges:
Milk: 0.0
Vegetable: 1.0
Fruit: 0.0
Bread: 1.0
Meat: 2.0
Fat: 0.0

1. Combine clam juice, tomatoes with liquid, potatoes, onion, and tarragon in slow cooker; cover and cook on high 3 to 4 hours, adding remaining ingredients, except salt and pepper, during last 10 to 15 minutes. Season to taste with salt and pepper.

Variation

Crabmeat Chowder—Make recipe as above, substituting 1½ cups Fish Stock (see p. 33) for the clam juice, ½ teaspoon dried thyme leaves for the tarragon, and 3 cans (4 ounces each) lump crabmeat for the lobster and shrimp; drain crabmeat and remove any shells.

Curried Scallop and Potato Chowder

This chowder has a lively curry flavor and a bright yellow color!

4 entrée servings

1½ cups clam juice
½ cup dry white wine or water
1 pound potatoes, peeled, cubed
1 teaspoon curry powder
½ teaspoon minced garlic
1 pound bay scallops
1 cup frozen peas, thawed
¼–½ cup 2% reduced-fat milk
Salt and pepper, to taste

Per Serving:
Calories: 251
% calories from fat: 7
Protein (g): 25.6
Carbohydrate (g): 29.4
Fat (g): 1.8
Saturated fat (g): 0.2
Cholesterol (mg): 49.3
Sodium (mg): 482
Exchanges:
Milk: 0.0
Vegetable: 0.0
Fruit: 0.0
Bread: 2.0
Meat: 3.0
Fat: 0.0

1. Combine clam juice, wine, potatoes, curry powder, and garlic in slow cooker; cover and cook on high 3 to 4 hours. Process mixture in food processor or blender until smooth; return to slow cooker. Stir in scallops, peas, and milk. Cover and cook on high until scallops are cooked, about 10 minutes. Season to taste with salt and pepper.

Sherried Crab and Mushroom Chowder

Succulent, sweet crabmeat and fresh mushrooms complement one another in this elegant dish.

4 entrée servings

2½ cups Chicken Stock (see p. 30) or chicken broth
1 pound mushrooms, sliced
¾ cup each: diced peeled red potato, chopped onion
¼ cup each: finely chopped celery, carrot
⅛ teaspoon dried thyme leaves
1 tablespoon tomato paste
1½ teaspoons soy sauce
1⅓ cups whole milk, divided
6 ounces fresh lump crabmeat, coarsely chopped
2 tablespoons dry sherry or water
1 tablespoon cornstarch
Salt and white pepper, to taste

Per Serving:
Calories: 159
% calories from fat: 27
Protein (g): 10.8
Carbohydrate (g): 18.1
Fat (g): 5
Saturated fat (g): 1.7
Cholesterol (mg): 33.8
Sodium (mg): 371
Exchanges:
Milk: 0.0
Vegetable: 0.0
Fruit: 0.0
Bread: 1.0
Meat: 1.0
Fat: 0.5

1. Combine stock, vegetables, thyme, tomato paste, and soy sauce in slow cooker; cover and cook on high 4 to 5 hours, adding 1 cup milk and crabmeat during last 30 minutes. Stir in combined remaining ⅓ cup milk, sherry, and cornstarch, stirring 2 to 3 minutes. Season to taste with salt and white pepper.

Spicy Crab and Scallop Chowder

The flavor kick in this seafood chowder comes from pickling spice!

4 entrée servings

1½ cups clam juice
1 can (14½ ounces) stewed tomatoes
1 medium onion, chopped
1 rib celery, chopped
2 teaspoons pickling spice
1 can (4 ounces) lump crabmeat, drained
8 ounces bay scallops
½ cup 2% reduced-fat milk
Salt and pepper, to taste

Per Serving:
Calories: 144
% calories from fat: 26
Protein (g): 18.2
Carbohydrate (g): 8.9
Fat (g): 4.3
Saturated fat (g): 0.8
Cholesterol (mg): 50.4
Sodium (mg): 485
Exchanges:
Milk: 0.0
Vegetable: 1.0
Fruit: 0.0
Bread: 0.0
Meat: 2.0
Fat: 0.0

1. Combine clam juice, tomatoes, onion, celery, and pickling spice tied in a cheesecloth bag in slow cooker; cover and cook on high 3 to 4 hours, adding crabmeat, scallops, and milk during last 15 minutes. Discard spice bag. Season to taste with salt and pepper.

Seafood Sampler Chowder

This delicately seasoned chowder is great with Croutons (see p. 38).

4 entrée servings

1 can (14½ ounces) diced tomatoes, undrained
1 cup clam juice or chicken broth
2 medium potatoes, cubed
½ cup each: chopped yellow bell pepper, onion,
   dry white wine or water
½ teaspoon celery seeds
1 teaspoon herbes de Provence or dried Italian
   seasoning
8 ounces haddock or halibut, cubed (1-inch)
4 ounces each: bay scallops, peeled deveined shrimp
½ teaspoon hot pepper sauce
Salt, to taste

Per Serving:
Calories: 231
% calories from fat: 10
Protein (g): 23.7
Carbohydrate (g): 24.7
Fat (g): 2.5
Saturated fat (g): 0.4
Cholesterol (mg): 88
Sodium (mg): 172
Exchanges:
Milk: 0.0
Vegetable: 1.0
Fruit: 0.0
Bread: 1.0
Meat: 3.0
Fat: 0.0

1. Combine tomatoes with liquid, clam juice, potatoes, bell pepper, onion, wine, celery seeds, and herbs in slow cooker; cover and cook on high 3 to 4 hours, adding seafood during last 20 minutes. Stir in hot pepper sauce; season to taste with salt.

Seafood Chowder

If you prefer, Fish Stock (see p. 33) can be used in place of the clam juice.

8 entrée servings

2 cups clam juice
1 can (28 ounces) diced tomatoes, undrained
½–1 cup tomato sauce
4 cups peeled chopped potatoes
1 cup each: sliced onions, celery
1 tablespoon Worcestershire sauce
1 teaspoon dried rosemary leaves
1½ pounds halibut or whitefish steaks, cubed (1-inch)
1 cup whole milk
3 tablespoons cornstarch
Salt and pepper, to taste
4 slices bacon, cooked crisp, crumbled

Per Serving:
Calories: 300
% calories from fat: 12
Protein (g): 24.2
Carbohydrate (g): 41.6
Fat (g): 3.9
Saturated fat (g): 0.9
Cholesterol (mg): 29.8
Sodium (mg): 395
Exchanges:
Milk: 0.0
Vegetable: 2.0
Fruit: 0.0
Bread: 2.0
Meat: 2.0
Fat: 0.0

1. Combine clam juice, tomatoes with liquid, tomato sauce, potatoes, onions, celery, Worcestershire sauce, and rosemary in 6-quart slow cooker; cover and cook on high 4 to 5 hours, adding fish during last 15 minutes. Stir in combined milk and cornstarch, stirring 2 to 3 minutes. Season to taste with salt and pepper. Sprinkle each bowl of chowder with bacon.

Variation
Rich Shrimp Chowder—Make recipe as above, substituting 1½ pounds peeled, deveined shrimp for the halibut. Decrease potatoes to 2 cups and add 1 cup frozen peas.

Fresh Salmon Chowder with Potatoes

Salmon is a good choice for fine chowders.

4 entrée servings

3 cups Fish Stock (see p. 33) or clam juice, divided
3¼ cups peeled cubed potatoes
1 cup chopped onion
½ teaspoon each: dry mustard, dried marjoram leaves
1 pound salmon steaks, cubed (1-inch)
1 cup whole milk
2 tablespoons cornstarch
Salt and white pepper, to taste

Per Serving:
Calories: 418
% calories from fat: 20
Protein (g): 30.1
Carbohydrate (g): 50.1
Fat (g): 9.1
Saturated fat (g): 2.5
Cholesterol (mg): 70.3
Sodium (mg): 158
Exchanges:
Milk: 0.0
Vegetable: 0.0
Fruit: 0.0
Bread: 3.5
Meat: 3.0
Fat: 0.0

1. Combine stock, potatoes, onion, dry mustard, and marjoram in slow cooker; cover and cook on high 5 to 6 hours. Process chowder in food processor or blender until smooth; return to slow cooker. Stir in salmon; cover and cook on high until fish is cooked, 10 to 15 minutes. Stir in combined milk and cornstarch, stirring 2 to 3 minutes. Season to taste with salt and white pepper.

Salmon and Roasted Pepper Chowder

Salmon is paired with corn and seasoned with jalapeño chilies, cumin, and oregano for a fabulous feast.

4 entrée servings

2 cups each: whole kernel corn, reduced-sodium
   vegetable broth
2 medium potatoes, peeled, cubed
1 cup chopped roasted red pepper
½–1 jalapeño chili, minced
2 teaspoons minced garlic
1 teaspoon each: cumin seeds, dried oregano leaves
12 ounces salmon steaks, cubed (1-inch)
Salt and pepper, to taste

Per Serving:
Calories: 259
% calories from fat: 12
Protein (g): 20.5
Carbohydrate (g): 36.4
Fat (g): 3.4
Saturated fat (g): 0.5
Cholesterol (mg): 42.8
Sodium (mg): 197
Exchanges:
Milk: 0.0
Vegetable: 0.0
Fruit: 0.0
Bread: 2.0
Meat: 2.0
Fat: 0.0

1. Combine all ingredients, except salmon, salt, and pepper, in slow cooker; cover and cook on high 4 to 5 hours, adding salmon during last 15 minutes. Season to taste with salt and pepper.

Bermuda Fish Chowder

Like Manhattan-style chowders, Bermuda chowders typically contain toma-toes. They have a wonderful flavor and robustness all their own.

6 entrée servings

1 quart Fish Stock (see p. 33) or clam juice
1 can (14½ ounces) Italian plum tomatoes, undrained,
   chopped
⅓ cup catsup
2 small smoked pork hocks
3¼ cups peeled cubed potatoes
1 cup each: chopped onion, celery, carrots
½ cup chopped green bell pepper
2½ teaspoons Worcestershire sauce
2 large bay leaves
½–¾ teaspoon dried thyme leaves
1 teaspoon curry powder
1 pound lean fish fillets (whitefish, flounder, haddock, cod), cubed (1-inch)
Salt and pepper, to taste

Per Serving:
Calories: 282
% calories from fat: 23
Protein (g): 20.2
Carbohydrate (g): 32.8
Fat (g): 7.2
Saturated fat (g): 1
Cholesterol (mg): 45.5
Sodium (mg): 742
Exchanges:
Milk: 0.0
Vegetable: 0.0
Fruit: 0.0
Bread: 2.0
Meat: 2.0
Fat: 0.5

1. Combine all ingredients, except fish, salt, and pepper, in 6-quart slow cooker; cover and cook on low 6 to 8 hours, adding fish during last 15 minutes. Discard pork hocks and bay leaves; season to taste with salt and pepper.

Flounder Chowder

Although this dish calls for flounder, orange roughy or halibut may be substituted.

6 entrée servings

2 cups each: Fish Stock (see p. 33) or vegetable broth, cubed peeled potatoes (¾-inch)
1 cup each: chopped onion, carrot, celery, lima beans
½ cup whole kernel corn
1 clove garlic, minced
1½ teaspoons dried basil leaves
½ teaspoon dried marjoram leaves
¼ teaspoon each: dry mustard, crushed celery seeds
2 cups 2% reduced-fat milk, divided
1 pound skinless flounder fillets, cubed (1-inch)
1 tablespoon cornstarch
Salt and pepper, to taste

Per Serving:
Calories: 252
% calories from fat: 28
Protein (g): 21.2
Carbohydrate (g): 23.7
Fat (g): 7.9
Saturated fat (g): 2.4
Cholesterol (mg): 48
Sodium (mg): 179
Exchange:
Milk: 0.0
Vegetable: 0.0
Fruit: 0.0
Bread: 1.5
Meat: 3.0
Fat: 0.0

1. Combine all ingredients, except milk, flounder, cornstarch, salt, and pepper, in 6-quart slow cooker; cover and cook on low 6 to 8 hours, adding 1½ cups milk during last 30 minutes. Add fish; cover and cook on high 10 to 15 minutes. Stir in combined remaining ½ cup milk and cornstarch, stirring 2 to 3 minutes. Season to taste with salt and pepper.

Canadian Fish Chowder

Mace is the secret flavor in this easy chowder.

6 entrée servings

1 can (28 ounces) crushed tomatoes
2 cups water
1 cup each: finely chopped onion, carrots, celery
2 leeks (white parts only), thinly sliced
1 pound cod or halibut, cubed (1-inch)
1 cup 2% reduced-fat milk
¼–½ teaspoon ground mace
Salt and white pepper, to taste
¼ cup thinly sliced green onions

Per Serving:
Calories: 176
% calories from fat: 8
Protein (g): 18.4
Carbohydrate (g): 22.3
Fat (g): 1.6
Saturated fat (g): 0.6
Cholesterol (mg): 35.4
Sodium (mg): 311
Exchanges:
Milk: 0.0
Vegetable: 2.0
Fruit: 0.0
Bread: 0.0
Meat: 2.0
Fat: 0.0

1. Combine tomatoes, water, and vegetables in slow cooker; cover and cook on high 4 to 5 hours, adding fish, milk, and mace during last 15 minutes. Season to taste with salt and white pepper. Sprinkle each bowl of chowder with green onions.

Monkfish-Cheddar Chowder

Use any favorite firm-textured fish in this creamy, cheesy chowder.

4 entrée servings

1 can (14 ounces) reduced-sodium fat-free chicken broth
1 pound potatoes, peeled, cubed
½ cup each: chopped onion, sliced carrots
1 pound monkfish, cubed (¾-inch)
½ cup each: 2% reduced-fat milk, shredded reduced-fat Cheddar cheese (2 ounces)
½–1 teaspoon hot pepper sauce
Salt, to taste

Per Serving:
Calories: 274
% calories from fat: 19
Protein (g): 24.9
Carbohydrate (g): 29.5
Fat (g): 5.9
Saturated fat (g): 1.8
Cholesterol (mg): 35.4
Sodium (mg): 344
Exchanges:
Milk: 0.0
Vegetable: 0.0
Fruit: 0.0
Bread: 1.5
Meat: 3.0
Fat: 0.0

1. Combine broth and vegetables in slow cooker; cover and cook on low 6 to 8 hours. Process chowder in food processor or blender until smooth; return to slow cooker. Cover and cook on high 25 minutes, adding fish and milk during last 15 minutes. Add cheese and hot pepper sauce, stirring until cheese is melted. Season to taste with salt.

Variation
Cod and Vegetable Chowder—Make recipe as above, substituting cod for the monkfish. Decrease potatoes to 2 cups; add 1 cup small broccoli florets, ½ cup frozen thawed peas, and ½ cup cut green beans.

Nova Scotia Seafood Chowder

Hearty chowders are a hallmark of the cuisine in Canada's Atlantic provinces. The type and combination of seafood used depends on the day's catch.

4 entrée servings

2 cups each: Fish Stock (see p. 33) or clam juice,
   cubed peeled potatoes, small cauliflower florets
1 each: chopped large onion, carrot, rib celery,
   garlic clove
1½ teaspoons dried basil leaves
½ teaspoon dried marjoram leaves
¼ teaspoon dry mustard
2 cups whole milk, divided
1 tablespoon cornstarch
8 ounces skinless flounder or whitefish fillets, cubed
4 ounces each: peeled deveined shrimp, crabmeat
Salt and white pepper, to taste

Per Serving:
Calories: 255
% calories from fat: 19
Protein (g): 20.3
Carbohydrate (g): 31.1
Fat (g): 5.3
Saturated fat (g): 2.2
Cholesterol (mg): 80
Sodium (mg): 317
Exchanges:
Milk: 0.0
Vegetable: 0.0
Fruit: 0.0
Bread: 2.0
Meat: 2.0
Fat: 0.0

1. Combine stock, vegetables, garlic, herbs, and dry mustard in slow cooker; cover and cook on low 6 to 8 hours, adding 1½ cups milk during last 30 minutes. Turn heat to high and add seafood; cover and cook 10 minutes. Stir in combined remaining ½ cup milk and cornstarch, stirring 2 to 3 minutes. Season to taste with salt and white pepper.

Potato Seafood Chowder

Saffron adds a subtle flavor and beautiful color to this soup.

4 entrée servings

2 cups Fish Stock (see p. 33) or clam juice
3 medium russet potatoes, unpeeled, cubed
1 cup sliced onion
½ cup sliced celery
⅛ teaspoon crushed saffron (optional)
2 cups 2% reduced-fat milk, divided
8 ounces each: haddock or cod fillets
½ cup peeled deveined small shrimp
1 tablespoon cornstarch
Salt and white pepper, to taste

Per Serving:
Calories: 254
% calories from fat: 7
Protein (g): 22.8
Carbohydrate (g): 36.2
Fat (g): 2
Saturated fat (g): 0.6
Cholesterol (mg): 37
Sodium (mg): 245
Exchanges:
Milk: 1.0
Vegetable: 0.0
Fruit: 0.0
Bread: 1.0
Meat: 2.0
Fat: 0.0

1. Combine stock, vegetables, and saffron in slow cooker; cover and cook on high 4 to 5 hours, adding 1½ cups milk during last 30 minutes and seafood during last 15 minutes. Stir in combined remaining ½ cup milk and cornstarch, stirring 2 to 3 minutes. Season to taste with salt and white pepper.

Halibut and Potato Chowder

This chunky chowder has a thick, flavorful base of puréed vegetables.

4 entrée servings

1½ cups clam juice
4 cups peeled cubed potatoes
1 each: chopped large onion, rib celery, carrot
1 teaspoon dried savory leaves
1 cup 2% reduced-fat milk
1 pound halibut, cubed (¾-inch)
½–1 teaspoons hot pepper sauce
Salt, to taste
2 slices bacon, cooked crisp, crumbled

Per Serving:
Calories: 394
% calories from fat: 12
Protein (g): 31.4
Carbohydrate (g): 55.4
Fat (g): 5.4
Saturated fat (g): 1.4
Cholesterol (mg): 45.7
Sodium (mg): 430
Exchanges:
Milk: 0.0
Vegetable: 1.0
Fruit: 0.0
Bread: 3.0
Meat: 3.0
Fat: 0.0

1. Combine clam juice, vegetables, and savory in slow cooker; cover and cook on high 4 to 5 hours. Process soup and milk in food processor or blender until smooth; return to slow cooker. Add halibut and hot pepper sauce; cover and cook on high 10 to 15 minutes. Season to taste with salt; sprinkle each bowl of soup with bacon.

Fish and Sweet Potato Chowder

Cod, orange roughy, and red snapper are other possible fish choices for this herb-scented chowder.

8 entrée servings

2 cans (14½ ounces each) diced tomatoes, undrained
2 cups reduced-sodium fat-free chicken broth
½ cup dry white wine or chicken broth
4 cups cubed cooked sweet potatoes
½ cup each: chopped onion, green bell pepper, whole
   kernel corn
2 cloves garlic, minced
1 teaspoon each: dried basil and oregano leaves
¼ teaspoon dried thyme leaves
12 ounces each: cubed salmon steaks (1-inch), peeled
   deveined shrimp
Salt and pepper, to taste

Per Serving:
Calories: 261
% calories from fat: 23
Protein (g): 19.8
Carbohydrate (g): 25.3
Fat (g): 6.7
Saturated fat (g): 1.7
Cholesterol (mg): 85.7
Sodium (mg): 184
Exchanges:
Milk: 0.0
Vegetable: 0.0
Fruit: 0.0
Bread: 2.0
Meat: 2.0
Fat: 0.0

1. Combine all ingredients, except salmon, shrimp, salt, and pepper, in 6-quart slow cooker; cover and cook on low 6 to 8 hours, adding shrimp and salmon during last 15 to 20 minutes. Season to taste with salt and pepper.

Scandinavian Fish Chowder

This fish soup features cod, with accents of dill, cucumber, and hard-cooked eggs.

8 entrée servings

2 cups each: water, diced peeled potatoes
1 cup chopped celery
½ cup chopped onion
1 teaspoon dried dill weed
½ teaspoon paprika
¼ teaspoon ground allspice
2 cups 2% reduced-fat milk, divided
1 pound skinless cod fillets, sliced
1 cup seeded chopped cucumber
2 tablespoons each: cornstarch, lemon juice
Salt and pepper, to taste
Hard-cooked egg slices, as garnish

Per Serving:
Calories: 159
% calories from fat: 11
Protein (g): 14.2
Carbohydrate (g): 21
Fat (g): 2.1
Saturated fat (g): 0.5
Cholesterol (mg): 25.4
Sodium (mg): 99
Exchanges:
Milk: 0.0
Vegetable: 1.0
Fruit: 0.0
Bread 1.0
Meat: 1.0
Fat: 0.0

1. Combine water, potatoes, celery, onion, dill weed, paprika, and allspice in 6-quart slow cooker; cover and cook on low 6 to 8 hours, stirring in 1½ cups milk during last 30 minutes. Stir in cod and cucumber; cover and cook on high 10 minutes. Stir in combined remaining ½ cup milk and cornstarch, stirring 2 to 3 minutes. Stir in lemon juice; season to taste with salt and pepper. Garnish bowls of soup with egg slices.

Red Clam Chowder

For variation, sweet potatoes can be substituted for the white potatoes.

8 first-course servings

2 cups each: clam juice, tomato juice, diced peeled
  potatoes
1 can (14½ ounces) diced tomatoes, undrained
1 cup each: chopped onion, sliced carrots
½ cup each: chopped green bell pepper, celery
1 clove garlic
1 bay leaf
1 teaspoon dried basil leaves
½ teaspoon each: dried oregano leaves, sugar
2 cans (6½ ounces each) chopped clams, drained,
  liquor reserved
Salt and cayenne pepper, to taste

Per Serving:
Calories: 154
% calories from fat: 20
Protein (g): 6.3
Carbohydrate (g): 26.1
Fat (g): 3.7
Saturated fat (g): 0.5
Cholesterol (mg): 7.6
Sodium (mg): 651
Exchanges:
Milk: 0.0
Vegetable: 2.0
Fruit: 0.0
Bread: 2.0
Meat: 0.0
Fat: 0.5

1. Combine all ingredients, except clams, salt, and cayenne pepper, in 6-quart slow cooker; cover and cook on high 4 to 5 hours, adding clams during last 30 minutes. Discard bay leaf; season to taste with salt and cayenne pepper.

Manhattan-Style Clam Chowder with Corn

The mild smokiness of Canadian bacon adds subtle flavor to this chowder.

4 entrée servings

2 cans (14½ ounces each) diced tomatoes, undrained
1 cup each: reduced-sodium fat-free chicken broth,
  peeled cubed potatoes, finely chopped onion,
  whole kernel corn
½ cup each: chopped celery, green bell pepper
2 ounces Canadian bacon, julienned
1 clove garlic, minced
1 bay leaf
½ teaspoon each: dried thyme and basil leaves, sugar
2 cans (6½ ounces each) chopped clams, undrained
Salt, and cayenne pepper, to taste

Per Serving:
Calories: 206
% calories from fat: 14
Protein (g): 9.8
Carbohydrate (g): 37.3
Fat (g): 3.6
Saturated fat (g): 0.8
Cholesterol (mg): 9.5
Sodium (mg): 488
Exchanges:
Milk: 0.0
Vegetable: 1.0
Fruit: 0.0
Bread: 2.0
Meat: 0.5
Fat: 0.0

1. Combine all ingredients, except clams, salt, and cayenne pepper, in slow cooker; cover and cook on high 4 to 6 hours, adding clams during last 45 minutes. Discard bay leaf; season to taste with salt and cayenne pepper.

Manhattan-Style Fish and Vegetable Chowder

A delicious chowder with a flavor of the sea and a vegetable-rich texture.

6 entrée servings

1 quart tomato juice
2 cups reduced-sodium fat-free chicken broth
1 cup each: frozen French-style green beans,
  whole kernel corn, cubed potato, chopped onion
½ cup each: chopped celery, carrot
1 bay leaf
½ teaspoon each: dried thyme and marjoram leaves
¼ teaspoon each: dry mustard, black pepper
12 ounces skinless flounder or halibut fillets, cubed
  (¾-inch)
Salt and cayenne pepper, to taste

Per Serving:
Calories: 198
% calories from fat: 20
Protein (g): 17.9
Carbohydrate (g): 24.4
Fat (g): 4.8
Saturated fat (g): 1.2
Cholesterol (mg): 39
Sodium (mg): 692
Exchanges:
Milk: 0.0
Vegetable: 0.0
Fruit: 0.0
Bread: 1.5
Meat: 2.0
Fat: 0.0

1. Combine all ingredients, except fish, salt, and pepper, in 6-quart slow cooker; cover and cook on low 6 to 8 hours, adding fish during last 15 to 20 minutes. Discard bay leaf; season to taste with salt and pepper.

White Clam and Corn Chowder

This hearty chowder is savory and rich in flavor.

4 entrée servings

1 cup clam juice or fat-free chicken broth
2 cups peeled cubed red potatoes (½-inch)
1 cup whole kernel corn
1 each: chopped medium onion, large rib celery
1 large bay leaf
½ teaspoon dried marjoram leaves
1 cup 2% reduced-fat milk, divided
1 can (10½ ounces) minced clams, undrained
2 teaspoons cornstarch
Salt and pepper, to taste

Per Serving:
Calories: 281
% calories from fat: 18
Protein (g): 27.9
Carbohydrate (g): 33.5
Fat (g): 5.9
Saturated fat (g): 1.5
Cholesterol (mg): 54.7
Sodium (mg): 554
Exchanges:
Milk: 0.0
Vegetable: 0.0
Fruit: 0.0
Bread: 2.0
Meat: 3.0
Fat: 0.0

1. Combine all ingredients, except milk, clams, cornstarch, salt, and pepper, in slow cooker; cover and cook on high 4 to 5 hours. Discard bay leaf. Process chowder in food processor or blender until smooth; return to slow cooker. Stir in ¾ cup milk and clams; cover and cook on high 15 minutes. Stir in combined remaining ¼ cup milk and cornstarch, stirring 2 to 3 minutes. Season to taste with salt and pepper.

FIVE

Chilis

- - - - - - - - - - - - -

Chicken Chili with Orange Cilantro Rice

An aromatic chili, with a perfect rice accompaniment.

6 entrée servings

1 pound boneless, skinless chicken breast, cubed
1 can (28 ounces) diced tomatoes, undrained
1 can (15 ounces) Great Northern beans, rinsed,
   drained
½ cup chopped onion
1 clove garlic, minced
2 teaspoons chili powder
½ teaspoon ground cumin
¼ teaspoon ground allspice
1 strip orange zest (2 x ½-inch)
Salt and pepper, to taste
Orange Cilantro Rice (recipe follows)
Chopped cilantro, as garnish

Per Serving:
Calories: 295
% calories from fat: 14
Protein (g): 24.1
Carbohydrate (g): 41.3
Fat (g): 4.8
Saturated fat (g): 0.9
Cholesterol (mg): 46
Sodium (mg): 765
Exchanges:
Milk: 0.0
Vegetable: 2.0
Fruit: 0.0
Bread: 2.0
Meat: 2.0
Fat: 0.0

1. Combine all ingredients, except salt, pepper, Orange Cilantro Rice, and cilantro, in slow cooker; cover and cook on low 6 to 8 hours. Season to taste with salt and pepper. Serve over Orange Cilantro Rice; sprinkle with cilantro.

Orange Cilantro Rice

Makes 6 servings

½ cup sliced green onions
1 cup long-grain rice
Grated zest of 1 small orange
2¼ cups water
2 tablespoons finely chopped cilantro
Salt and pepper, to taste

1. Sauté onions in lightly greased medium saucepan until tender, 3 to 5 minutes. Add rice and orange zest; stir over medium heat until rice is lightly browned, 2 to 3 minutes. Add water and heat to boiling; reduce heat and simmer, covered, until rice is tender, 20 to 25 minutes. Stir in cilantro; season to taste with salt and pepper.

White Chili

Although the Tomatillo Salsa is terrific and easy to make, you can substitute a purchased salsa if you prefer.

8 entrée servings

1 pound boneless, skinless chicken breast, cubed (¾-inch)
2 cups Chicken Stock (see p. 30) or chicken broth, divided
2 cans (15 ounces each) Great Northern beans, rinsed, drained
1 cup each: chopped red or green bell pepper, onion
2 teaspoons each: minced garlic, jalapeño chili, gingerroot
1 teaspoon each: dried thyme and oregano leaves
1 tablespoon cornstarch
Salt and pepper, to taste
Tomatillo Salsa (recipe follows)
Reduced-fat sour cream, as garnish

Per Serving:
Calories: 195
% calories from fat: 16
Protein (g): 19.6
Carbohydrate (g): 25.1
Fat (g): 4
Saturated fat (g): 0.8
Cholesterol (mg): 35.4
Sodium (mg): 322
Exchanges:
Milk: 0.0
Vegetable: 2.0
Fruit: 0.0
Bread: 1.0
Meat: 1.5
Fat: 0.0

1. Combine all ingredients, except ½ cup stock, cornstarch, salt, pepper, Tomatillo Salsa, and sour cream, in slow cooker; cover and cook on low 6 to 8 hours. Cook on high 10 minutes; stir in combined remaining ½ cup stock and cornstarch, stirring 2 to 3 minutes. Season to taste with salt and pepper. Serve with Tomatillo Salsa and sour cream.

Tomatillo Salsa

Makes about 1 cup

12 ounces tomatillos, husked
½ small onion, chopped
1 tablespoon finely chopped cilantro
1 teaspoon each: minced jalapeño chili, garlic
¼ teaspoon ground cumin
⅛ teaspoon sugar
Salt, to taste

1. Simmer tomatillos in water to cover in large saucepan until tender, 5 to 8 minutes. Cool; drain, reserving liquid. Process tomatillos, and remaining ingredients, except salt, in food processor or blender until almost smooth, adding enough reserved liquid to make medium dipping consistency. Season to taste with salt.

Sweet and Spicy Chili

Sweet potatoes and sweet spices, combined with jalapeño chili and ginger-root, make a chili that is sure to please.

6 entrée servings

1 pound boneless, skinless chicken breast, cubed
  (¾-inch)
2–3 cups reduced-sodium fat-free chicken broth
2 cans (15 ounces each) Great Northern beans, rinsed,
  drained
1½ cups chopped onions
8 ounces mushrooms, quartered
2 medium sweet potatoes, peeled, cubed (¾-inch)
2 teaspoons each: minced garlic, gingerroot, jalapeño
  chili
1 teaspoon each: dried oregano leaves, ground cumin
½ teaspoon ground coriander and cinnamon
Salt and white pepper, to taste
Reduced-fat sour cream, as garnish

Per Serving:
Calories: 274
% calories from fat: 16
Protein (g): 26.5
Carbohydrate (g): 36.7
Fat (g): 5.2
Saturated fat (g): 1
Cholesterol (mg): 46
Sodium (mg): 716
Exchanges:
Milk: 0.0
Vegetable: 0.0
Fruit: 0.0
Bread: 2.5
Meat: 2.0
Fat: 0.0

1. Combine all ingredients, except salt, white pepper, and sour cream in 6-quart slow cooker; cover and cook on low 6 to 8 hours. Season to taste with salt and white pepper. Serve with sour cream.

Roasted Pepper Chili

Here's a mild-mannered chili with a lean and healthful profile. For crunch, serve it topped with crumbled tortilla chips.

4 entrée servings

1 pound ground turkey
2 cans (14½ ounces) stewed tomatoes
1 can (15 ounces) rinsed drained black beans
1 cup chopped red onion
½ cup coarsely chopped roasted red pepper
1 small jalapeño chili, minced
1 tablespoon chili powder
½ teaspoon ground cumin
¼ teaspoon ground allspice
Salt and pepper, to taste

Per Serving:
Calories: 316
% calories from fat: 27
Protein (g): 26.3
Carbohydrate (g): 35.2
Fat (g): 9.9
Saturated fat (g): 2.7
Cholesterol (mg): 89.7
Sodium (mg): 919
Exchanges:
Milk: 0.0
Vegetable: 0.0
Fruit: 0.0
Bread: 2.0
Meat: 3.0
Fat: 0.0

1. Cook turkey in lightly greased skillet over medium heat until browned, about 5 minutes, crumbling with a fork. Combine turkey and remaining ingredients, except salt and pepper, in slow cooker; cover and cook on low 6 to 8 hours. Season to taste with salt and pepper.

California Chili

This zesty chili sports familiar West Coast ingredients.

6 entrée servings

1 pound boneless, skinless chicken breast, cubed (1-inch)
4 cups sliced plum tomatoes
1 cup each: diced softened sun-dried tomatoes (not in oil), dry red wine or chicken broth
1–2 tablespoons chili powder
1 teaspoon crushed mixed peppercorns
¼–½ teaspoon crushed red pepper
1 avocado, chopped
2 tablespoons sunflower seeds, toasted
Salt, to taste
6 tablespoons chopped basil, as garnish

Per Serving:
Calories: 258
% calories from fat: 30
Protein (g): 21.5
Carbohydrate (g): 19.7
Fat (g): 9.2
Saturated fat (g): 1.8
Cholesterol (mg): 46
Sodium (mg): 272
Exchanges:
Milk: 0.0
Vegetable: 4.0
Fruit: 0.0
Bread: 0.0
Meat: 2.0
Fat: 1.0

1. Combine all ingredients, except avocado, sunflower seeds, salt, and basil, in slow cooker; cover and cook on low 6 to 8 hours. Stir in avocado and sunflower seeds; season to taste with salt. Sprinkle each bowl of chili with basil.

Big Red Chili

A spicy chili that sports red onions, red kidney beans, red bell peppers, and crushed tomatoes.

4 entrée servings

8 ounces ground beef sirloin
1 can (28 ounces) crushed tomatoes
1 can (15 ounces) red kidney beans, rinsed, drained
1 each: chopped large red onion, red bell pepper
2 tablespoons each: red wine vinegar, chili powder
¼ teaspoon ground allspice
⅔ cup mild or medium picante sauce
Salt and pepper, to taste

Per Serving:
Calories: 197
% calories from fat: 16
Protein (g): 17.5
Carbohydrate (g): 25.3
Fat (g): 3.6
Saturated fat (g): 1.1
Cholesterol (mg): 29.7
Sodium (mg): 652
Exchanges:
Milk: 0.0
Vegetable: 2.0
Fruit: 0.0
Bread: 1.0
Meat: 1.0
Fat: 0.5

1. Cook beef in lightly greased large skillet over medium heat until browned, about 5 minutes, crumbling with a fork. Combine beef and remaining ingredients, except salt and pepper, in slow cooker; cover and cook on low 6 to 8 hours. Season to taste with salt and pepper.

Variation

Farmhouse Chili—Make recipe as above, substituting turkey breakfast sausage for the ground beef and tomato juice for the picante sauce. Decrease chili powder to 1 tablespoon. Omit allspice; add 1 to 2 tablespoons maple syrup and ¾ teaspoon each ground cumin and dried sage leaves.

Corn and Bean con Carne

Cornmeal Crisps are a perfect chili complement!

8 entrée servings

12 ounces ground beef round
2 cans (14½ ounces each) diced tomatoes, undrained
2 cans (15 ounces each) kidney beans, rinsed, drained
1 quart reduced-sodium fat-free beef broth
2 cups whole kernel corn
1 large onion, finely chopped
1–2 tablespoons chili powder
1 teaspoon each: ground cumin, sugar
Salt and pepper, to taste
Cornmeal Crisps (recipe follows)

Per Serving:
Calories: 364
% calories from fat: 21
Protein (g): 22.2
Carbohydrate (g): 52.2
Fat (g): 8.8
Saturated fat (g): 2
Cholesterol (mg): 21.6
Sodium (mg): 422
Exchanges:
Milk: 0.0
Vegetable: 1.0
Fruit: 0.0
Bread: 3.0
Meat: 2.0
Fat: 0.5

1. Cook beef in lightly greased large skillet over medium heat until browned, about 8 minutes, crumbling with a fork. Combine beef and remaining ingredients, except salt, pepper, and Cornmeal Crisps, in 6-quart slow cooker; cover and cook on low 6 to 8 hours. Season to taste with salt and pepper. Serve with Cornmeal Crisps.

Cornmeal Crisps

Makes about 12

1 cup self-rising flour
⅓ cup yellow cornmeal
1 tablespoon sugar
4 tablespoons cold margarine or butter, cut into pieces
1 tablespoon distilled white vinegar
¼ cup ice water
1 egg white, beaten
2–3 tablespoons grated Parmesan cheese

1. Combine flour, cornmeal, and sugar in small bowl; cut in margarine with pastry cutter until mixture resembles coarse crumbs. Mix in vinegar and enough ice water for mixture to form a dough. Roll dough on floured surface to scant ¼ inch thickness; cut into rounds and place on greased cookie sheet. Brush with egg white and sprinkle with Parmesan cheese. Bake at 375 degrees until golden, 7 to 10 minutes. Cool on wire rack.

Chili with Squash and Beans

A squeeze of lime adds a cooling touch to this spicy chili.

6 entrée servings

1 pound lean ground beef
3 cups tomato juice
1 can (15 ounces) each: chunky tomato sauce,
    rinsed drained red kidney beans
2 cups each: sliced onions, chopped celery, cubed
    butternut squash (1-inch)
1 cup each: sliced red bell pepper, zucchini,
    mushrooms
½ jalapeño chili, finely chopped
2 cloves garlic, minced
1½ teaspoons each: chili powder, ground cumin
Salt and pepper, to taste
6 lime wedges

Per Serving:
Calories: 317
% calories from fat: 30
Protein (g): 21.2
Carbohydrate (g): 36.1
Fat (g): 10.8
Saturated fat (g): 4
Cholesterol (mg): 46.6
Sodium (mg): 357
Exchanges:
Milk: 0.0
Vegetable: 1.0
Fruit: 0.0
Bread: 2.0
Meat: 2.0
Fat: 1.0

1. Cook ground beef in lightly greased large skillet over medium heat until browned, about 8 minutes, crumbling with a fork. Combine beef and remaining ingredients, except salt, pepper, and lime wedges, in 6-quart slow cooker; cover and cook on low 6 to 8 hours. Season to taste with salt and pepper. Serve with lime wedges.

Blizzard Chili

A great chili for snowbound winter evenings.

6 entrée servings

1 pound lean ground beef
2 cans (15 ounces each) tomato sauce
2 cups each: cooked dry or rinsed drained canned
    kidney, black, and cannellini beans, finely
    chopped onions
1 clove garlic, minced
1 bay leaf
1 tablespoon chili powder
2 teaspoons sugar
1 teaspoon ground cumin
Salt and pepper, to taste

Per Serving:
Calories: 457
% calories from fat: 10.4
Protein (g): 33
Carbohydrate (g): 59
Fat (g): 10.4
Saturated fat (g): 3.8
Cholesterol (mg): 47
Sodium (mg): 98
Exchanges:
Milk: 0.0
Vegetable: 3.0
Fruit: 0.0
Bread: 2.5
Meat: 3.0
Fat: 0.5

1. Cook ground beef in lightly greased large skillet over medium heat until browned, 8 to 10 minutes, crumbling with a fork. Combine beef and remaining ingredients, except salt and pepper, in 6-quart slow cooker; cover and cook on low 6 to 8 hours. Discard bay leaf; season to taste with salt and pepper.

Family-Favorite Chili

This very easy chili will appeal to all ages.

8 entrée servings

1½ pounds lean ground beef or turkey
2 cans (15 ounces each) pinto beans, rinsed, drained
2 cans (14½ ounces each) stewed tomatoes
2 cups whole kernel corn
1 cup chopped onion
½ cup chopped green bell pepper
2 tablespoons taco seasoning mix
1 tablespoon ranch salad dressing mix
Salt and pepper, to taste
Reduced-fat sour cream
Tortilla chips

Per Serving:
Calories: 268
% calories from fat: 13
Protein (g): 23.3
Carbohydrate (g): 36.4
Fat (g): 4.1
Saturated fat (g): 1.2
Cholesterol (mg): 41.2
Sodium (mg): 566
Exchanges:
Milk: 0.0
Vegetable: 1.0
Fruit: 0.0
Bread: 2.0
Meat: 2.0
Fat: 0.0

1. Cook ground beef in lightly greased large skillet over medium heat until browned, about 10 minutes, crumbling with a fork. Combine beef and remaining ingredients, except salt, pepper, sour cream, and tortilla chips, in 6-quart slow cooker; cover and cook on low 6 to 8 hours. Season to taste with salt and pepper. Serve with sour cream and tortilla chips.

Cincinnati Chili

5-Way Cincinnati Chili gained fame in the chili parlors of Cincinnati. The sauce is seasoned with sweet spices and a hint of dark chocolate. The chili is served alone (1-way), over spaghetti (2-ways), with added beans (3-ways), with chopped onions (4-ways), and with shredded cheese (5-ways).

8 entrée servings

12 ounces lean ground turkey or beef
1 can (28 ounces) crushed tomatoes
1 can (8 ounces) tomato sauce
½ cup each: water, chopped onion
4 cloves garlic, minced
2–3 tablespoons chili powder
1 tablespoon cocoa
2 teaspoons dried oregano leaves
1 teaspoon each: ground cinnamon, allspice
Salt and pepper, to taste
1 pound spaghetti, cooked, warm
Toppings: cooked pinto beans, chopped onions,
   shredded reduced-fat Cheddar cheese

Per Serving:
Calories: 381
% calories from fat: 13
Protein (g): 19.6
Carbohydrate (g): 62
Fat (g): 5.7
Saturated fat (g): 1.3
Cholesterol (mg): 31.6
Sodium (mg): 454
Exchanges:
Milk: 0.0
Vegetable: 3.0
Fruit: 0.0
Bread: 3.0
Meat: 1.0
Fat: 0.5

1. Cook turkey in lightly greased large skillet over medium heat until browned, about 5 minutes, crumbling with a fork. Combine turkey and remaining ingredients, except salt, pepper, spaghetti and toppings, in slow cooker; cover and cook on low 6 to 8 hours. Season to taste with salt and pepper. Serve with spaghetti and Toppings (not included in nutritional data).

Chunky Chili for a Crowd

Make this big batch of chili for a party, and serve it with a do-it-yourself array of garnishes. Or make it for dinner, and freeze some for later use.

16 entrée servings

4 pounds lean beef stew meat, cubed (1-inch)
1½ cups each: sliced onions, green bell peppers
¼ cup each: minced garlic, chopped jalapeño chili
2 cans (28 ounces each) diced tomatoes, undrained
2 cans (15 ounces each) pinto beans, rinsed, drained
1 can (6 ounces) tomato paste
3–4 tablespoons chili powder
1 teaspoon beef bouillon crystals
½ cup water
¼ cup cornstarch
Salt and pepper, to taste
Hot pepper sauce, to taste
Toppings: baked tortilla chips, grated reduced-fat Cheddar cheese, reduced-fat sour cream, chopped tomatoes, diced avocado, sliced black olives

Per Serving:
Calories: 301
% calories from fat: 22
Protein (g): 34.3
Carbohydrate (g): 24.5
Fat (g): 7.4
Saturated fat (g): 2.3
Cholesterol (mg): 70.9
Sodium (mg): 304
Exchanges:
Milk: 0.0
Vegetable: 2.0
Fruit: 0.0
Bread: 1.0
Meat: 3.0
Fat: 0.0

1. Combine all ingredients, except salt, pepper, hot pepper sauce, and toppings, in 6-quart slow cooker; cover and cook on low 6 to 8 hours. Turn heat to high; cook 10 minutes. Stir in combined water and cornstarch, stirring 2 to 3 minutes. Season to taste with salt, pepper, and hot pepper sauce. Serve with toppings (not included in nutritional data).

Male Chauvinist Chili

A real man's chili—but women will love it too!

8 entrée servings

8 ounces each: sliced Italian-style turkey sausage,
   lean ground beef
1½ quarts chopped tomatoes
1 can (15 ounces) each: rinsed drained pinto and
   black beans, chickpeas
1 cup dry red wine or tomato juice
1½ cups coarsely chopped onions
1 green bell pepper, coarsely chopped
2 cloves garlic, minced
1 small jalapeño chili, minced
¼–½ cup Worcestershire sauce
1 teaspoon each: dry mustard, celery seeds
1–2 tablespoons chili powder
½ teaspoon ground cumin
8 slices bacon, fried crisp, crumbled
Salt and pepper, to taste

Per Serving:
Calories: 332
% calories from fat: 21
Protein (g): 21.8
Carbohydrate (g): 43.4
Fat (g): 8.4
Saturated fat (g): 2.2
Cholesterol (mg): 33.9
Sodium (mg): 789
Exchanges:
Milk: 0.0
Vegetable: 2.0
Fruit: 0.0
Bread: 2.0
Meat: 2.0
Fat: 0.5

1. Cook Italian sausage and ground beef in lightly greased large skillet over medium heat until browned, about 10 minutes, crumbling beef with a fork. Combine meat and remaining ingredients, except bacon, salt, and pepper, in 6-quart slow cooker; cover and cook on low 6 to 8 hours. Stir in bacon; season to taste with salt and pepper.

Chili con Carne

A flavorful chili that will satisfy the heartiest of appetites!

8 entrée servings

1 pound lean ground beef
1 cup each: chopped onions, green bell pepper
2 cloves garlic, minced
1–2 tablespoons chili powder
2 teaspoons each: ground cumin, dried oregano leaves
2 cans (14½ ounces each) diced tomatoes, undrained
1 can (15 ounces) red kidney beans, rinsed, drained
1 can (6 ounces) tomato paste
¾ cup beer or water
1 tablespoon each: packed light brown sugar,
 unsweetened cocoa
Salt and pepper, to taste
½ cup each: shredded reduced-fat Cheddar cheese (2 ounces), sliced green
 onions, reduced-fat sour cream

Per Serving:
Calories: 220
% calories from fat: 13
Protein (g): 21.9
Carbohydrate (g): 28.7
Fat (g): 3.6
Saturated fat (g): 1
Cholesterol (mg): 32.5
Sodium (mg): 224
Exchanges:
Milk: 0.0
Vegetable: 2.0
Fruit: 0.0
Bread: 1.0
Meat: 2.0
Fat: 0.0

1. Cook ground beef in lightly greased large skillet over medium heat until meat is browned, about 10 minutes, crumbling with a fork. Combine beef and remaining ingredients, except salt, pepper, cheese, green onions, and sour cream, in slow cooker; cover and cook on low 6 to 8 hours. Season to taste with salt and pepper. Sprinkle each bowl of chili with cheese, green onions, and sour cream.

Variations

Chili Mac—Make chili as above. Turn heat to high and add 1 cup cooked elbow macaroni or chili mac pasta and ½ cup water. Cook 15 minutes.
Southwestern Chili—Make recipe as above, substituting black or pinto beans for the red kidney beans, and adding 1 minced jalapeño chili. Garnish each bowl with chopped cilantro.

Tenderloin Chili

This super-easy chili sports tender, lean pork and fresh tomatoes.

4 entrée servings

1 pound pork tenderloin, cubed (½-inch)
1 can (15 ounces) each: reduced-sodium fat-free
   beef broth, rinsed drained pinto beans
1 pound plum tomatoes, sliced
2 jalapeño chilies, minced
1 tablespoon chili powder
1 teaspoon each: toasted cumin seeds,
   Worcestershire sauce
Salt and pepper, to taste

Per Serving:
Calories: 274
% calories from fat: 19
Protein (g): 32.7
Carbohydrate (g): 23.4
Fat (g): 5.8
Saturated fat (g): 1.7
Cholesterol (mg): 67.1
Sodium (mg): 475
Exchanges:
Milk: 0.0
Vegetable: 2.0
Fruit: 0.0
Bread: 1.0
Meat: 3.0
Fat: 0.0

1. Combine all ingredients, except salt and pepper,
in slow cooker; cover and cook on high 4 to 6 hours.
Season to taste with salt and pepper.

Pork Chili with Greens

Kale adds nutrients and color to this tasty chili.

8 entrée servings

1½ pounds lean ground pork or turkey
2 cans (15 ounces each) kidney beans, rinsed, drained
2 cans (14½ ounces each) petite-diced tomatoes,
   undrained
½ cup chopped onion
½ teaspoon each: ground cinnamon, cumin
8 ounces kale or spinach, coarsely chopped
Salt and pepper, to taste

Per Serving:
Calories: 261
% calories from fat: 21
Protein (g): 28
Carbohydrate (g): 23.8
Fat (g): 6.1
Saturated fat (g): 2
Cholesterol (mg): 48.3
Sodium (mg): 332
Exchanges:
Milk: 0.0
Vegetable: 2.0
Fruit: 0.0
Bread: 1.0
Meat: 2.5
Fat: 0.0

1. Cook pork in lightly greased large skillet until
browned, about 10 minutes, crumbling with fork.
Combine pork and remaining ingredients, except kale, salt, and pepper,
in slow cooker; cover and cook on low 6 to 8 hours, stirring in kale during
the last 20 minutes. Season to taste with salt and pepper.

Variation

Chili with Rajas—Make chili as above, substituting lean ground beef for the pork. Omit cinnamon and kale; add 1 to 2 tablespoons chili powder. Cook 2 thinly sliced poblano chilies and 1 sliced medium onion in 1 to 2 tablespoons olive oil in large skillet over medium to medium-low heat until chilies are very tender and onions are caramelized, 15 to 20 minutes; season to taste with salt. Serve chili in bowls; top with chili and onion mixture.

Habanero Chili

This chili gets its firepower from the habanero chili; substitute jalapeño chili for a milder flavor.

4 entrée servings

4 ounces turkey sausage, casing removed
1 can (14½ ounces) diced tomatoes, undrained
2 cups refried beans
1 each: chopped large onion, medium green
  bell pepper
¼–½ habanero chili, chopped
1 tablespoon chili powder
1 teaspoon ground cumin
Salt, to taste
1 cup reduced-fat sour cream

Per Serving:
Calories: 293
% calories from fat: 18
Protein (g): 17.1
Carbohydrate (g): 43.8
Fat (g): 5.9
Saturated fat (g): 1
Cholesterol (mg): 25.6
Sodium (mg): 767
Exchanges:
Milk: 0.0
Vegetable: 0.0
Fruit: 0.0
Bread: 3.0
Meat: 1.0
Fat: 0.5

1. Cook sausage in lightly greased small skillet until browned, about 5 minutes, crumbling with a fork. Combine sausage and remaining ingredients, except salt and sour cream, in slow cooker; cover and cook on low 4 to 5 hours. Season to taste with salt. Serve with sour cream.

Chili Rio Grande

Lots of onions, and a combination of ground and cubed meats give this chili loads of flavor and texture.

12 entrée servings

1 pound lean ground beef
2 pounds lean pork, cubed (¾-inch)
1¾ cups Beef Stock (see p. 31) or beef broth
1 can (28 ounces) red kidney beans, rinsed, drained
2 cans (14½ ounces each) diced tomatoes, undrained
1 can (12 ounces) beer or tomato juice
1 can (4 ounces) green chilies, chopped
4 cups chopped onions
2 tablespoons minced garlic
¼ cup chili powder
1 tablespoon ground cumin
2 teaspoons dried oregano leaves
Salt and pepper, to taste
¾ cup Cilantro-Chili Sour Cream (1½ recipes) (see p. 165)

Per Serving:
Calories: 344
% calories from fat: 30
Protein (g): 32.7
Carbohydrate (g): 25.3
Fat (g): 11.5
Saturated fat (g): 3.8
Cholesterol (mg): 66.4
Sodium (mg): 352
Exchanges:
Milk: 0.0
Vegetable: 2.0
Fruit: 0.0
Bread: 1.0
Meat: 4.0
Fat: 0.0

1. Cook ground beef in lightly greased large skillet over medium heat until browned, crumbling with a fork. Combine beef and remaining ingredients, except salt, pepper, and Cilantro-Chili Sour Cream, in 6-quart slow cooker; cover and cook on low 6 to 8 hours. Season to taste with salt and pepper; serve with dollops of Cilantro-Chili Sour Cream.

Texas Hot Chili

Hot sausage, hot chilies, and lots of spices make this chili extra good.

8 entrée servings

12 ounces hot Italian-style turkey sausage, casing removed
1¼ pounds coarsely ground lean beef
1 can (14½ ounces) each: undrained diced tomatoes, reduced-sodium fat-free beef broth
1 can (15 ounces) each: tomato sauce, rinsed drained red kidney and garbanzo beans
1 can (4 ounces) chopped green chilies, undrained
1 large chopped onion
1 jalapeño chili, chopped
2 tablespoons hot chili powder
½ teaspoon each: ground cumin and coriander
1 tablespoon low-sodium Worcestershire sauce
Salt and cayenne pepper, to taste
Hot pepper sauce, to taste

Per Serving:
Calories: 300
% calories from fat: 24
Protein (g): 28.9
Carbohydrate (g): 29.8
Fat (g): 8.3
Saturated fat (g): 2.2
Cholesterol (mg): 57.1
Sodium (mg): 744
Exchanges:
Milk: 0.0
Vegetable: 0.0
Fruit: 0.0
Bread: 2.0
Meat: 3.0
Fat: 0.0

1. Cook sausage and ground beef in lightly greased large skillet over medium heat until browned, about 10 minutes, crumbling with a fork. Combine meat and remaining ingredients, except salt, cayenne pepper, and hot pepper sauce, in 6-quart slow cooker; cover and cook on low 6 to 8 hours. Season to taste with salt, cayenne pepper, and hot pepper sauce.

Variation

Italian-Style Chili—Make recipe as above, omitting green chilies and jalapeño chilies and substituting 4 ounces sliced pepperoni for 4 ounces of the ground beef and 1 to 1½ teaspoons dried Italian seasoning for the cumin and coriander.

Mesquite Chicken Chili

This differently delicious Tex-Mex dish will appeal to the adventurous!

4 entrée servings

12 ounces boneless, skinless chicken breast, cubed
1 can (28 ounces) crushed tomatoes
1 can (15 ounces) red beans, rinsed, drained
8 ounces tomatillos, husked, coarsely chopped
¾ cup each: chopped onion, poblano chili
2 tablespoons chili powder
2 teaspoons minced garlic
1 teaspoon mesquite smoke flavoring
Salt and pepper, to taste

Per Serving:
Calories: 293
% calories from fat: 15
Protein (g): 28.1
Carbohydrate (g): 36.3
Fat (g): 5.3
Saturated fat (g): 1.1
Cholesterol (mg): 51.7
Sodium (mg): 469
Exchanges:
Milk: 0.0
Vegetable: 2.0
Fruit: 0.0
Bread: 2.0
Meat: 2.0
Fat: 0.0

1. Combine all ingredients, except salt and pepper, in slow cooker; cover and cook on low 6 to 8 hours. Season to taste with salt and pepper.

Variation

Hominy Chili—Make chili as above, substituting boneless lean beef for the chicken and 1 can (15 ounces) hominy, drained, for the tomatillos; omit mesquite smoke flavoring. Sprinkle each bowl of chili with shredded reduced-fat Cheddar cheese and dollops of reduced-fat sour cream.

Veal Chili Poblano

Ground veal, poblano chili, and purchased seasoning mix make this fast-track chili a busy-day favorite.

4 entrée servings

1 pound ground lean veal or turkey
1 can (14½ ounces) crushed tomatoes
1 can (15 ounces) Great Northern beans, rinsed, drained
1 each: chopped large onion, small poblano chili, rib celery
½–1 package (1¼ ounce-size) chili seasoning mix
Tortilla Wedges (recipe follows)

Per Serving:
Calories: 282
% calories from fat: 18
Protein (g): 34.2
Carbohydrate (g): 26.4
Fat (g): 6.1
Saturated fat (g): 1.6
Cholesterol (mg): 99.5
Sodium (mg): 659
Exchanges:
Milk: 0.0
Vegetable: 0.0
Fruit: 0.0
Bread: 2.0
Meat: 3.0
Fat: 0.0

1. Combine all ingredients, except Tortilla Wedges, in slow cooker; cover and cook on low 6 to 8 hours. Serve with Tortilla Wedges.

Tortilla Wedges

Makes 12 wedges

2 flour tortillas (6-inch)
¼ cup (1 ounce) each: shredded reduced-fat pepper-Jack and
   Cheddar cheese, sliced green onions, mild or hot salsa
Reduced-fat sour cream, as garnish

1. Place tortillas on baking sheet; sprinkle with combined cheeses and
green onions. Bake at 450 degrees until edges of tortillas are browned and
cheese is melted, 5 to 7 minutes. Cut each tortilla into 6 wedges; top each
with 1 teaspoon salsa and small dollop of sour cream.

Texas Two-Step Chili

Get Texas-size flavor in this recipe. Cilantro adds a captivating pungency.

4 entrée servings

8 ounces each: lean ground pork, and turkey breast
1 cup sliced green onions
1 can (15 ounces) chili beans, undrained
1 pound tomatoes, chopped
1 small cayenne or jalapeño chili, seeded, chopped
Salt, to taste
Finely chopped cilantro, as garnish

Per Serving:
Calories: 262
% calories from fat: 19
Protein (g): 30.5
Carbohydrate (g): 25.3
Fat (g): 5.9
Saturated fat (g): 1.6
Cholesterol (mg): 54.9
Sodium (mg): 404
Exchanges:
Milk: 0.0
Vegetable: 2.0
Fruit: 0.0
Bread: 1.0
Meat: 2.5
Fat: 0.0

1. Cook pork, turkey, and green onions in lightly
greased large skillet over medium heat until meat is
browned, about 8 minutes, crumbling with a fork.
Combine meat mixture and remaining ingredients, except salt and
cilantro, in slow cooker; cover and cook on low 5 to 6 hours. Season to
taste with salt; sprinkle each bowl of soup with cilantro.

Easy Tortilla Chili

Baked tortilla chips add crunch and texture to this flavorful chili.

8 entrée servings

8 ounces ground beef round
3¾ cups reduced-sodium fat-free beef broth
1 jar (16 ounces) reduced-sodium mild or
   medium salsa
1 can (15 ounces) kidney beans, rinsed, drained
2 cups chopped onions
1½ cups whole kernel corn
1 teaspoon chili powder
2 cups crushed tortilla chips
Salt and pepper, to taste
½ cup (2 ounces) shredded reduced-fat Cheddar
   cheese

Per Serving:
Calories: 280
% calories from fat: 12
Protein (g): 20
Carbohydrate (g): 42
Fat (g): 3.9
Saturated fat (g): 1.1
Cholesterol (mg): 23.3
Sodium (mg): 622
Exchanges:
Milk: 0.0
Vegetable: 2.0
Fruit: 0.0
Bread: 2.0
Meat: 1.5
Fat: 0.0

1. Cook beef in lightly greased large skillet over medium heat until browned, about 5 minutes, crumbling with a fork. Combine beef, broth, salsa, beans, onions, corn, and chili powder in 6-quart slow cooker; cover and cook on low 6 to 8 hours. Stir in tortilla chips; season to taste with salt and pepper. Sprinkle each bowl of chili with cheese.

Taco Chili

A favorite recipe from my friend RayMona Dunn, who graciously shared it with us—enjoy!

8 entrée servings

1–2 pounds lean ground beef
1 can (15 ounces) each: hominy and pinto beans,
   rinsed, drained
1 can (14½ ounces) diced tomatoes, undrained
1 can (10 ounces) diced Rotel-brand tomatoes,
   undrained
1 can (8 ounces) whole kernel corn, drained
1 large onion, chopped
2 ribs celery, chopped
1 package (1.25 ounces) taco seasoning mix
1 package (1 ounce) ranch seasoning mix
Garnishes: sour cream, shredded Cheddar cheese,
   taco chips

Per Serving:
Calories: 301
% calories from fat: 16
Protein (g): 17.0
Carbohydrate (g): 31.3
Fat (g): 4.1
Saturated fat (g): 1.5
Cholesterol (mg): 35.2
Sodium (mg): 1337
Exchanges:
Milk: 0.0
Vegetable: 1.0
Fruit: 0.0
Bread: 2.0
Meat: 2.0
Fat: 0.0

1. Cook ground beef in lightly greased large skillet until browned, about 10 minutes, crumbling with a fork. Combine beef and remaining ingredients, except garnishes, in slow cooker. Cover and cook on low 6 to 8 hours. Serve with garnishes.

South-of-the-Border Chili

A chili that's a little different, made with canned soup!

6 entrée servings

1 pound boneless, skinless chicken breast, cubed (¾-inch)
1 can (10¾ ounces) reduced-sodium 98% fat-free cream of chicken soup
½ cup each: tomato sauce, chopped onion, green onions, red bell pepper
1 small jalapeño chili, seeded, finely chopped
2 cloves garlic, minced
1 can (4 ounces) chopped green chilies, drained
1 tablespoon chili powder
½ teaspoon ground cumin
1 cup 2% reduced-fat milk
Salt and pepper, to taste
½ cup (2 ounces) shredded reduced-fat Monterey Jack cheese
Baked Tortilla Chips (recipe follows)

Per Serving:
Calories: 259
% calories from fat: 27
Protein (g): 24.4
Carbohydrate (g): 23.5
Fat (g): 7.8
Saturated fat (g): 2.6
Cholesterol (mg): 59.8
Sodium (mg): 467
Exchanges:
Milk: 0.0
Vegetable: 2.0
Fruit: 0.0
Bread: 1.0
Meat: 2.5
Fat: 0.0

1. Combine all ingredients, except milk, salt, pepper, cheese, and Baked Tortilla Chips, in slow cooker; cover and cook on low 6 to 8 hours, adding milk during last 20 minutes. Season to taste with salt and pepper. Sprinkle each bowl of chili with cheese; serve with Baked Tortilla Chips.

Baked Tortilla Chips

Makes 6 servings (8 chips each)

6 corn tortillas (6-inch)
Vegetable cooking spray
⅛ teaspoon each: ground cumin, chili powder, dried oregano leaves, paprika
Salt and cayenne pepper, to taste

1. Cut each tortilla into 8 wedges; arrange in single layer on jelly roll pan. Spray tortillas with cooking spray; sprinkle lightly with combined herbs, salt, and cayenne pepper. Bake at 350 degrees until lightly browned, 5 to 7 minutes.

Chili Mole

This chili boasts the intriguing flavor of traditional Mexican mole; use chicken, pork, beef, or a combination of all three meats.

6 entrée servings

1 pound lean pork, fat trimmed, cubed
1 cup reduced-sodium fat-free chicken broth
1 can (14½ ounces) diced tomatoes, undrained
1 can (15 ounces) black beans, rinsed, drained
Mole Sauce (see p. 479)
Salt and pepper, to taste
Guacamole (recipe follows)
Finely chopped cilantro, as garnish

Per Serving:
Calories: 328
% calories from fat: 28
Protein (g): 28.8
Carbohydrate (g): 32.5
Fat (g): 10.6
Saturated fat (g): 3
Cholesterol (mg): 42.9
Sodium (mg): 671
Exchanges:
Milk: 0.0
Vegetable: 1.0
Fruit: 0.0
Bread: 2.0
Meat: 2.0
Fat: 1.0

1. Combine all ingredients, except salt, pepper, Guacamole, and cilantro, in slow cooker; cover and cook on low 6 to 8 hours. Season to taste with salt and pepper. Top each bowl of chili with Guacamole; sprinkle generously with cilantro.

Guacamole

Makes about ⅔ cup

1 medium avocado, coarsely mashed
½ each: small finely chopped onion, seeded minced jalapeño chili
1 tablespoon finely chopped cilantro
Hot pepper sauce, to taste
Salt, to taste

1. Mix avocado, onion, jalapeño chili, and cilantro; season to taste with hot pepper sauce and salt.

Chili Verde

This "green chili" is made with tomatillos, which are also called Mexican green tomatoes. Use canned tomatillos if fresh are not available.

8 entrée servings

1 pound boneless lean pork, cubed (½-inch)
2 cans (14½ ounces each) reduced-sodium
   fat-free chicken broth
2 cans (15 ounces each) Great Northern beans,
   rinsed, drained
2 cans (4 ounces each) diced green chilies
1 cup water
2 pounds tomatillos, husked, quartered
2 large onions, thinly sliced
6–8 cloves garlic, chopped
2 teaspoons ground cumin
½ cup chopped lightly packed cilantro
Cilantro-Chili Sour Cream (recipe follows)

Per Serving:
Calories: 276
% calories from fat: 19
Protein (g): 24.4
Carbohydrate (g): 31.2
Fat (g): 5.8
Saturated fat (g): 1.6
Cholesterol (mg): 32.2
Sodium (mg): 550
Exchanges:
Milk: 0.0
Vegetable: 1.0
Fruit: 0.0
Bread: 2.0
Meat: 2.0
Fat: 0.0

1. Combine all ingredients, except cilantro and Cilantro-Chili Sour Cream, in 6-quart slow cooker; cover and cook on low 6 to 8 hours. Stir in cilantro; serve with Cilantro-Chili Sour Cream.

Cilantro-Chili Sour Cream

Makes about ½ cup

½ cup reduced-fat sour cream
1 tablespoon chopped cilantro
1 teaspoon chopped pickled jalapeño chili

1. Combine all ingredients.

Chorizo Chili

This chili begins with our flavorful low-fat version of Chorizo, to which beans, tomatoes, and onions are added. The Chorizo can be used in many of your favorite Mexican recipes, or formed into patties and cooked for a dinner entrée.

6 entrée servings

Chorizo (recipe follows)
½ cup chopped onion
2 cans (14½ ounces each) diced tomatoes, undrained
2 cans (15 ounces each) pinto or black beans, rinsed, drained
Salt and pepper to taste

Per Serving:
Calories: 229
% calories from fat: 17
Protein (g): 24.4
Carbohydrate (g): 24.2
Fat (g): 4.3
Saturated fat (g): 1.3
Cholesterol (mg): 49.3
Sodium (mg): 414
Exchanges:
Milk: 0.0
Vegetable: 2.0
Fruit: 0.0
Bread: 1.0
Meat: 2.0
Fat: 0.0

1. Cook Chorizo and onion in lightly greased large skillet over medium heat until browned, 8 to 10 minutes, crumbling with a fork. Combine chorizo and remaining ingredients, except salt and pepper, in slow cooker; cover and cook on low 4 to 6 hours. Season to taste with salt and pepper.

Chorizo

Makes 1½ pounds

½ teaspoon each: crushed coriander and cumin seeds
2 dried ancho chilies
1½ pounds pork tenderloin, finely chopped or ground
4 cloves garlic, minced
2 tablespoons each: paprika, cider vinegar, water
1 teaspoon dried oregano leaves
½ teaspoon salt

1. Cook coriander and cumin seeds in lightly greased small skillet over medium heat, stirring frequently until toasted, 2 to 3 minutes. Remove from skillet; reserve. Add ancho chilies to skillet; cook over medium heat until softened, about 1 minute on each side, turning chilies often so they do not burn. Remove and discard stems, veins, and seeds; chop finely. Combine all ingredients, mixing well.

Cheesy Chili Blanco with Red Tomato Salsa

This white chili is made extra-creamy with the addition of sour cream and Monterey Jack cheese.

8 entrée servings

1½ pounds boneless, skinless chicken breasts, cubed
2 cans (15 ounces each) Great Northern beans, rinsed, drained
1 can (14½ ounces) reduced-sodium fat-free chicken broth
1 can (4 ounces) diced green chilies, drained
2 cups chopped onions
1 tablespoon chopped garlic
1 tablespoon dried oregano leaves
1 teaspoon ground cumin
1 cup reduced-fat sour cream
2 cups (8 ounces) shredded reduced-fat Monterey Jack cheese
Salt and cayenne pepper, to taste
Red Tomato Salsa (recipe follows)

Per Serving:
Calories: 331
% calories from fat: 24
Protein (g): 37.5
Carbohydrate (g): 27.7
Fat (g): 9.3
Saturated fat (g): 4.4
Cholesterol (mg): 72
Sodium (mg): 674
Exchanges:
Milk: 0.0
Vegetable: 0.0
Fruit: 0.0
Bread: 2.0
Meat: 3.5
Fat: 0.0

1. Combine all ingredients, except sour cream, cheese, salt, cayenne pepper, and Red Tomato Salsa, in slow cooker; cover and cook on low 6 to 8 hours. Stir in sour cream and cheese, stirring until cheese is melted. Season to taste with salt and cayenne pepper. Serve with Red Tomato Salsa.

Red Tomato Salsa

Makes about 2 cups

2 large tomatoes, chopped
⅓ cup each: finely chopped onion, poblano chili
1 clove garlic, minced
2 tablespoons finely chopped cilantro
Salt, to taste

1. Mix all ingredients, except salt; season to taste with salt.

Yellow Squash and White Bean Chili

Your family will enjoy this vegetable-packed chili.

6 entrée servings

1 pound lean ground pork
1 quart reduced-sodium fat-free chicken broth
½ cup dry white wine or chicken broth
⅔ cup each: dried Great Northern and garbanzo
   beans
1 cup each: chopped onion, yellow bell pepper,
   thinly sliced leeks, cubed yellow summer squash,
   red potatoes
2 teaspoons each: minced garlic, jalapeño chili,
   cumin seeds
1 teaspoon each: dried oregano leaves, chili powder
½ teaspoon each: ground coriander, cinnamon
1 bay leaf
Salt and pepper, to taste
1 small tomato, finely chopped
2 green onions, thinly sliced
3 tablespoons finely chopped cilantro

Per Serving:
Calories: 350
% calories from fat: 23
Protein (g): 32.7
Carbohydrate (g): 41.2
Fat (g): 10
Saturated fat (g): 2.7
Cholesterol (mg): 49.3
Sodium (mg): 719
Exchanges:
Milk: 0.0
Vegetable: 2.0
Fruit: 0.0
Bread: 2.0
Meat: 3.0
Fat: 0.0

1. Cook pork in lightly greased large skillet until browned, about 8
minutes, crumbling with a fork. Combine pork and remaining ingredients,
except salt, pepper, chopped tomato, green onions, and cilantro, in
6-quart slow cooker; cover and cook on low until beans are tender, 7 to 8
hours. Season to taste with salt and pepper; discard bay leaf. Sprinkle each
bowl of soup with tomato, green onions, and cilantro.

Variation

Med-Rim Chili—Make chili as above, substituting ground lamb or beef for
the pork and adding ¼ cup sliced Greek or ripe olives. Make 1 package
(5.6 ounces) couscous according to package directions. Serve chili over
couscous; sprinkle each serving with 1 tablespoon crumbled feta cheese.

Old Hickory Chili with White Beans

This hickory-smoked turkey chili is made without wood chips or a grill. The cook's flavor trick—natural hickory seasoning.

4 entrée servings

8 ounces ground turkey
1 can (15 ounces) white kidney beans, rinsed, drained
2 cups coarsely chopped tomatoes
1 cup each: chopped onion, mild or medium salsa
1 tablespoon white wine vinegar
2 tablespoons each: chili powder, finely chopped
   fresh cilantro
1 teaspoon natural hickory seasoning (optional)
Salt and pepper, to taste

Per Serving:
Calories: 212
% calories from fat: 10
Protein (g): 17.3
Carbohydrate (g): 31.4
Fat (g): 2.5
Saturated fat (g): 0.6
Cholesterol (mg): 22.4
Sodium (mg): 630
Exchanges:
Milk: 0.0
Vegetable: 0.0
Fruit: 0.0
Bread: 2.0
Meat: 1.0
Fat: 0.0

1. Cook turkey in lightly greased large skillet over medium heat until browned, about 5 minutes, crumbling with a fork. Combine turkey and remaining ingredients, except cilantro, hickory seasoning, salt, and pepper, in slow cooker; cover and cook on low 5 to 6 hours, stirring in cilantro and hickory seasoning during last 5 minutes. Season to taste with salt and pepper.

Chili with Beans

Great to come home to on those tired mid-week evenings.

8 entrée servings

1 pound each: lean ground beef, ground turkey
2 large onions, chopped
3 cloves garlic, minced
1 can (6 ounces) tomato paste
2 cans (10½ ounces each) zesty tomato sauce
2 cans (15½ ounces each) kidney beans, rinsed, drained
2 tablespoons chili powder
1 teaspoon dried oregano leaves
Salt and pepper, to taste

Per Serving:
Calories: 293
% calories from fat: 14
Protein (g): 33.6
Carbohydrate (g): 29.2
Fat (g): 4.4
Saturated fat (g): 1.7
Cholesterol (mg): 57.7
Sodium (mg): 902
Exchanges:
Milk: 0.0
Vegetable: 0.0
Fruit: 0.0
Bread: 2.0
Meat: 3.0
Fat: 0.0

1. Cook ground beef and turkey in lightly greased large skillet over medium heat until meat is browned, about 10 minutes, crumbling meat with a fork. Combine meat and remaining ingredients, except salt and pepper, in slow cooker; cover and cook on low 6 to 8 hours. Season to taste with salt and pepper.

Black and White Bean Chili

Made with black and white beans, this chili is uniquely accented in flavor and color with sun-dried tomatoes.

4 entrée servings

12 ounces lean ground beef
2 cans (14½ ounces) each: diced tomatoes,
  undrained
1 can (15 ounces) each: Great Northern and black
  beans, rinsed, drained
1 cup chopped onion
½ cup chopped green bell pepper
¼ cup chopped sun-dried tomatoes (not in oil)
1 medium jalapeño chili, finely chopped
2 teaspoons minced garlic
2–3 tablespoons chili powder
1–1½ teaspoons each: ground cumin, dried oregano leaves
1 bay leaf
Salt and pepper, to taste
¼ cup finely chopped cilantro

Per Serving:
Calories: 386
% calories from fat: 14
Protein (g): 34
Carbohydrate (g): 55.2
Fat (g): 6.5
Saturated fat (g): 2.2
Cholesterol (mg): 52.7
Sodium (mg): 604
Exchanges:
Milk: 0.0
Vegetable: 2.0
Fruit: 0.0
Bread: 3.0
Meat: 2.0
Fat: 0.0

1. Cook beef in lightly greased large skillet over medium heat until browned, 8 to 10 minutes, crumbling with a fork. Combine beef and remaining ingredients, except salt, pepper, and cilantro, in slow cooker; cover and cook on low 6 to 8 hours. Discard bay leaf; season to taste with salt and pepper. Stir in cilantro.

Chili with Beans and Beer

This chili is very easy to make—the longer it cooks, the better the flavor.

6 entrée servings

1 pound lean ground beef
2 cans (10½ ounces each) reduced-sodium fat-free
   beef broth
1 cup beer or beef broth
1 can (16 ounces) petite-diced tomatoes, undrained
1 can (15 ounces) each: undrained chili beans in chili
   sauce, rinsed drained pinto beans
1 tablespoon each: minced garlic, ground cumin
3 tablespoons chili powder
1 teaspoon dried oregano leaves
Salt and pepper, to taste

Per Serving:
Calories: 320
% calories from fat: 29
Protein (g): 25
Carbohydrate (g): 30.8
Fat (g): 10.7
Saturated fat (g): 3.9
Cholesterol (mg): 47
Sodium (mg): 609
Exchanges:
Milk: 0.0
Vegetable: 0.0
Fruit: 0.0
Bread: 2.0
Meat: 2.5
Fat: 1.0

1. Cook ground beef in lightly greased large skillet over medium heat until browned, about 8 minutes, crumbling with a fork. Combine ground beef and remaining ingredients, except salt and pepper, in slow cooker; cover and cook on low 6 to 8 hours. Season to taste with salt and pepper.

Variation

Ranchero Chili—Make recipe as above, cooking 4 ounces sliced reduced-fat smoked sausage with the ground beef and adding ½ cup each chopped onion and green bell pepper and 1 small minced jalapeño chili to the slow cooker. Serve bowls of chili with dollops of sour cream.

Spiced Bean Chili with Fusilli

Use your favorite beans and any shaped pasta in this versatile chili.

8 entrée servings

1 pound lean ground beef
2 cans (14½ ounces each) diced tomatoes with
  roasted garlic, undrained
1 can (15 ounces) each: garbanzo and dark red
  kidney beans, rinsed, drained
2 cups chopped onions
1 cup sliced cremini or white mushrooms
½ cup each: sliced celery, dry white wine or water
2 tablespoons chili powder
¾ teaspoon each: dried oregano and thyme leaves,
  ground cumin
8 ounces fusilli, cooked
Salt and pepper, to taste
3–4 tablespoons sliced green or ripe olives

Per Serving:
Calories: 367
% calories from fat: 26
Protein (g): 21.3
Carbohydrate (g): 47.3
Fat (g): 10.6
Saturated fat (g): 3.2
Cholesterol (mg): 35.2
Sodium (mg): 759
Exchanges:
Milk: 0.0
Vegetable: 1.0
Fruit: 0.0
Bread: 3.0
Meat: 1.0
Fat: 1.5

1. Cook beef in lightly greased large skillet over medium heat until browned, 8 to 10 minutes, crumbling with a fork. Combine beef and remaining ingredients, except fusilli, salt, pepper, and olives, in 6-quart slow cooker; cover and cook on low 6 to 8 hours, adding pasta during last 20 minutes. Season to taste with salt and pepper; sprinkle each bowl of soup with olives.

Lentil Chili with Bacon and Beer

Lime, beer, and bacon make this chili differently delicious. So give it a try; it's a snap to make.

4 entrée servings

3 cups beef broth
1 cup beer or beef broth
½ cup each: dried lentils, dried black beans
1 medium onion, chopped
1 tablespoon each: minced garlic, jalapeno, chili powder
1 teaspoon each: ground cumin, crushed dried rosemary leaves
1 cup each: canned crushed tomatoes
Juice of 1 lime
Salt and pepper, to taste
4 slices bacon, cooked crisp, crumbled

Per Serving:
Calories: 244
% calories from fat: 1
Protein (g): 15
Carbohydrate (g): 43
Fat (g): 3.7
Saturated fat (g): 0.9
Cholesterol (mg): 5
Sodium (mg): 631
Exchanges:
Milk: 0.0
Vegetable: 0.0
Fruit: 0.0
Bread: 3.0
Meat: 0.0
Fat: 0.5

1. Combine all ingredients, except tomatoes, lime juice, salt, pepper, and bacon, in slow cooker; cover and cook on high until beans are tender, 5 to 6 hours, adding tomatoes during last 30 minutes. Stir in lime juice; season to taste with salt and pepper. Sprinkle each bowl of chili with bacon.

SIX

Melting-Pot Soups

Yankee Bean Soup

Bean soup doesn't get any better than this!

6 entrée servings

1 quart Chicken Stock (see p. 30) or chicken broth
2 cans (15 ounces each) navy beans, rinsed, drained
1 pound lean lamb for stew, cubed (½-inch)
8–12 ounces smoked ham, cubed (½-inch)
1 each: chopped large onion, rib celery
2 each: chopped carrots, minced cloves garlic
1 teaspoon dried Italian seasoning
1 can (14½ ounces) diced tomatoes, undrained
Salt and pepper, to taste

Per Serving:
Calories: 284
% calories from fat: 17
Protein (g): 20.9
Carbohydrate (g): 39.2
Fat (g): 5.7
Saturated fat (g): 1.3
Cholesterol (mg): 22.4
Sodium (mg): 836
Exchanges:
Milk: 0.0
Vegetable: 2.0
Fruit: 0.0
Bread: 2.0
Meat: 2.0
Fat: 0.0

1. Combine all ingredients, except salt and pepper, in 6-quart slow cooker; cover and cook on low 6 to 8 hours. Season to taste with salt and pepper.

Southern Gumbo

To please all palates, serve this soup with an assortment of hot sauces.

12 entrée servings

1½ quarts Rich Chicken Stock (see p. 30) or chicken broth
1 can (28 ounces) diced tomatoes, undrained
12 ounces boneless, skinless chicken breast, cubed
2 cups each: cubed lean ham, chopped onions
1 cup each: chopped celery, green bell pepper
1 tablespoon minced garlic
2 teaspoons each: Worcestershire sauce, gumbo file powder
1 teaspoon dried thyme leaves
2 bay leaves
1 cup uncooked converted long-grain rice
12 ounces small shrimp, peeled, deveined
Salt and hot pepper sauce, to taste

Per Serving:
Calories: 212
% calories from fat: 15
Protein (g): 21.2
Carbohydrate (g): 22.6
Fat (g): 3.3
Saturated fat (g): 0.5
Cholesterol (mg): 71.2
Sodium (mg): 353
Exchanges:
Milk: 0.0
Vegetable: 0.0
Fruit: 0.0
Bread: 1.5
Meat: 2.0
Fat: 0.0

1. Combine all ingredients, except rice, shrimp, salt, and hot pepper sauce, in 6-quart slow cooker; cover and cook on low 6 to 8 hours, adding rice during last 2 hours and shrimp during last 20 minutes. Discard bay leaves; season to taste with salt and hot pepper sauce.

Bourbon Street Soup

Okra, rice, tomatoes, and crushed red pepper add Southern accents to this vegetable beef soup.

6 entrée servings

1 quart water
1 pound lean beef stew meat, cubed (1-inch)
1 can (28 ounces) diced tomatoes, undrained
1 can (14½ ounces) stewed tomatoes
1½ cups chopped onions
¾ cup chopped green bell pepper
3 cloves garlic, minced
1 teaspoon dried thyme leaves
¼–½ teaspoon crushed red pepper
1 bay leaf
⅓ cup uncooked converted long-grain rice
1½ cups each: whole kernel corn, sliced fresh or frozen thawed okra
Salt and pepper, to taste
Hot pepper sauce, to taste

Per Serving:
Calories: 264
% calories from fat: 15
Protein (g): 24.1
Carbohydrate (g): 34.5
Fat (g): 4.4
Saturated fat (g): 1.4
Cholesterol (mg): 47.3
Sodium (mg): 77
Exchanges:
Milk: 0.0
Vegetable: 1.0
Fruit: 0.0
Bread: 2.0
Meat: 2.0
Fat: 0.0

1. Combine all ingredients, except rice, corn, okra, salt, and pepper, in 6-quart slow cooker; cover and cook on low 6 to 8 hours, adding rice during last 2 hours and corn and okra during last 30 minutes. Discard bay leaf; season to taste with salt, pepper, and hot pepper sauce.

Southern Corn and Bean Soup with Bean Biscuits

Smoky chipotle chilies give this soup a unique flavor; biscuits made with puréed beans are extra moist.

6 entrée servings

1½ quarts Rich Chicken Stock (see p. 30) or chicken broth
2 cans (15 ounces each) Great Northern beans, rinsed, drained, coarsely mashed
2 cups whole kernel corn
1 cup each: chopped onion, red bell pepper
1 teaspoon chopped garlic
¼–½ small chipotle chili in adobo, chopped
1 teaspoon dried thyme leaves
Salt and pepper, to taste
½ cup reduced-fat sour cream
Bean Biscuits (recipe follows)

Per Serving:
Calories: 361
% calories from fat: 23
Protein (g): 18.3
Carbohydrate (g): 55.2
Fat (g): 10
Saturated fat (g): 2.4
Cholesterol (mg): 1.1
Sodium (mg): 789
Exchanges:
Milk: 0.0
Vegetable: 1.0
Fruit: 0.0
Bread: 3.0
Meat: 1.0
Fat: 1.5

1. Combine all ingredients, except salt, pepper, sour cream, and Bean Biscuits, in 6-quart slow cooker; cover and cook on high 4 to 5 hours. Season to taste with salt and pepper. Garnish each bowl of soup with dollops of sour cream and serve with Bean Biscuits.

Bean Biscuits

Makes 6

¾ cup all-purpose flour
2 teaspoons baking powder
1½ teaspoons sugar
¼ teaspoon salt
¼ cup vegetable shortening
½ can (15 ounces) Great Northern beans, rinsed, drained
3 tablespoons fat-free milk

1. Combine flour, baking powder, sugar, and salt in medium bowl; cut in shortening until mixture resembles coarse crumbs. Process beans and milk in food processor or blender until almost smooth; add to flour mixture and mix just until dough comes together. Drop dough by spoonfuls onto ungreased baking sheet. Bake at 375 degrees until light brown, about 12 minutes.

Red Beans, Rice, and Sausage Soup

Sausage gives this easy but satisfying soup its distinctive flavor.

6 entrée servings

1¼ quarts chicken broth
2 cans (15 ounces each) dark red kidney beans, rinsed, drained
1 can (15 ounces) tomato sauce
6 ounces reduced-fat smoked sausage, sliced
⅓ cup each: diced carrot, celery, red bell pepper
1 each: large finely chopped onion, minced garlic clove
¼ teaspoon dried thyme leaves
1 bay leaf
⅓ cup uncooked converted long-grain rice
Salt and pepper, to taste

Per Serving:
Calories: 221
% calories from fat: 221
Protein (g): 15.4
Carbohydrate (g): 34.7
Fat (g): 2.7
Saturated fat (g): 0.5
Cholesterol (mg): 13.5
Sodium (mg): 417
Exchanges:
Milk: 0.0
Vegetable: 1.0
Fruit: 0.0
Bread: 2.0
Meat: 1.0
Fat: 0.0

1. Combine all ingredients, except rice, salt, and pepper, in 6-quart slow cooker; cover and cook on high 4 to 5 hours, adding rice during last 2 hours. Discard bay leaf and season to taste with salt and pepper.

Creole-Style Lamb Soup

Let this luscious soup cook all day while you're away.

6 entrée servings

1 quart fat-free beef broth
2 cans (15 ounces each) tomato sauce
1 pound lean lamb for stew, cubed (½-inch)
1 cup each: chopped onion, zucchini
½ cup each: chopped green bell pepper, celery
2 large cloves garlic, minced
1 bay leaf
1 teaspoon dried marjoram leaves
½ teaspoon each: dried thyme and basil leaves
¼ teaspoon dry mustard
⅓ cup uncooked converted long-grain rice
Salt and pepper, to taste
Hot pepper sauce, to taste

Per Serving:
Calories: 217
% calories from fat: 10
Protein (g): 16.1
Carbohydrate (g): 34.6
Fat (g): 2.5
Saturated fat (g): 0.7
Cholesterol (mg): 27.4
Sodium (mg): 383
Exchanges:
Milk: 0.0
Vegetable: 0.0
Fruit: 0.0
Bread: 2.5
Meat: 1.0
Fat: 0.0

1. Combine all ingredients, except rice, salt, pepper, and hot pepper sauce, in 6-quart slow cooker; cover and cook on low 6 to 8 hours, adding rice during last 2 hours. Discard bay leaf; season to taste with salt and pepper. Serve with hot pepper sauce.

Pinto Soup with Chili Crisps

The flavor of this vegetable soup is enhanced with a garnish of fresh tomatoes and chili-flavored tortilla strips.

8 entrée servings

2 quarts reduced-sodium fat-free chicken broth
2 cups each: sliced onions, carrots, mushrooms,
   cubed unpeeled red potatoes, chopped tomatoes
1 tablespoon minced garlic
2 teaspoons dried oregano leaves
1 teaspoon ground cumin
⅛–¼ teaspoon crushed red pepper
Salt and pepper, to taste
Chili Crisps (recipe follows)
¼ cup chopped cilantro

Per Serving:
Calories: 206
% calories from fat: 7
Protein (g): 8.1
Carbohydrate (g): 38.2
Fat (g): 1.6
Saturated fat (g): 0.3
Cholesterol (mg): 0
Sodium (mg): 277
Exchanges:
Milk: 0.0
Vegetable: 2.0
Fruit: 0.0
Bread: 2.0
Meat: 0.0
Fat: 0.0

1. Combine all ingredients, except Chili Crisps and cilantro, in 6-quart slow cooker; cover and cook on high 4 to 5 hours. Season to taste with salt and pepper. Sprinkle each bowl of soup with Chili Crisps and cilantro.

Chili Crisps

Makes about 3 cups

3 corn tortillas (6-inch)
Olive oil cooking spray
½ teaspoon each: garlic powder, chili powder

1. Spray both sides of tortillas with cooking spray; sprinkle tops with garlic and chili powder. Cut tortillas in half; cut halves into thin strips. Arrange on cookie sheet and bake at 425 degrees until crisp, about 10 minutes.

Mexican-Style Chicken and Lime Soup

Lightly seasoned with lime, this soup has an abundance of chicken and vegetables.

8 entrée servings

2 quarts Chicken Stock (see p. 30) or chicken broth
1½ pounds boneless, skinless chicken breast, cubed
2 large tomatoes, peeled, seeded, chopped
1 cup each: whole kernel corn, diced zucchini
½ cup each: chopped onion, green bell pepper
¼ cup each: chopped cilantro, lime juice
Salt and pepper, to taste
4 each: corn tortillas (6-inch), each cut into 10 wedges
Vegetable cooking spray
Thin lime slices, as garnish

Per Serving:
Calories: 185
% calories from fat: 13
Protein (g): 24.9
Carbohydrate (g): 15.5
Fat (g): 2.8
Saturated fat (g): 0.5
Cholesterol (mg): 49.3
Sodium (mg): 609
Exchanges:
Milk: 0.0
Vegetable: 0.0
Fruit: 0.0
Bread: 1.0
Meat: 2.0
Fat: 0.0

1. Combine broth, chicken, and vegetables in 6-quart slow cooker; cover and cook on low 6 to 8 hours, stirring in cilantro and lime juice during last 30 minutes. Season to taste with salt and pepper.
2. Spray tortillas lightly with cooking spray and toss; cook in lightly greased large skillet over medium heat until browned and crisp, about 5 minutes. Add tortilla wedges to soup bowls; ladle soup over. Float lime slices on top of soup.

Shrimp and Black Bean Soup

In Mexico, leaves from the avocado tree are used for seasoning this favorite Oaxacan soup; we've substituted a bay leaf.

6 entrée servings

3 cans (14½ ounces each) reduced-sodium fat-free
   chicken broth, divided
2 cans (15 ounces each) black beans, rinsed, drained
2 each: medium chopped onions, wedged tomatoes
4 cloves garlic, minced
1 teaspoon each: dried oregano and thyme leaves,
   ground cumin
1 bay leaf
8 ounces shrimp, peeled, deveined
Salt and pepper, to taste
Chopped cilantro, as garnish

Per Serving:
Calories: 162
% calories from fat: 4
Protein (g): 17.0
Carbohydrate (g): 26.6
Fat (g): 0.9
Saturated fat (g): 0.2
Cholesterol (mg): 57.5
Sodium (mg): 1071
Exchanges:
Milk: 0.0
Vegetable: 0.0
Fruit: 0.0
Bread: 1.5
Meat: 1.0
Fat: 0.0

1. Combine all ingredients, except shrimp, salt, pepper, and cilantro, in slow cooker; cover and cook on high 4 to 5 hours, adding shrimp during last 15 minutes. Discard bay leaf. Season to taste with salt and pepper; sprinkle each bowl of soup with cilantro.

Sopa de Casa

Chicken, green chilies, and Monterey Jack cheese offer a pleasing flavor combination.

6 entrée servings

1 can (14½ ounces) reduced-sodium fat-free
  chicken broth
3 cups whole kernel corn, thawed, divided
1 can (4 ounces) chopped green chilies, undrained
1 pound boneless, skinless chicken breast, cubed
  (¾-inch)
1 cup chopped onion
1 large tomato, chopped
½ jalapeño chili, minced
2 large cloves garlic, minced
¾ teaspoon dried oregano leaves
½ teaspoon ground cumin
1 cup whole milk
1 cup (4 ounces) shredded reduced-fat Monterey Jack cheese
Salt and pepper, to taste

Per Serving:
Calories: 281
% calories from fat: 24
Protein (g): 28.8
Carbohydrate (g): 24.5
Fat (g): 7.7
Saturated fat (g): 3.4
Cholesterol (mg): 59.5
Sodium (mg): 376
Exchanges:
Milk: 0.0
Vegetable: 2.0
Fruit: 0.0
Bread: 1.0
Meat: 3.0
Fat: 0.0

1. Process chicken broth and 1½ cups corn in food processor or blender until smooth. Combine puréed corn and remaining ingredients, except milk, cheese, salt, and pepper, in slow cooker; cover and cook on low 6 to 8 hours, adding milk during last 30 minutes. Stir in cheese, stirring until melted; season to taste with salt and pepper.

Pozole

This Mexican soup traditionally contains hominy, but you can substitute black or pinto beans, if you prefer.

4 entrée servings

2 ancho chilies, stems, seeds, and veins discarded
1 cup boiling water
2 cans (14½ ounces each) reduced-sodium fat-free chicken broth
8 ounces each: cubed pork loin, boneless skinless chicken breast
1 can (14½ ounces) diced tomatoes, undrained
1 can (15 ounces) hominy, drained
1 cup chopped onion
1 clove garlic, minced
½ teaspoon each: dried oregano and thyme leaves
Salt and pepper, to taste
6 lime wedges
Garnishes: thinly sliced lettuce, cabbage, green onion, radish, shredded carrot

Per Serving:
Calories: 181
% calories from fat: 16
Protein (g): 21.2
Carbohydrate (g): 16.7
Fat (g): 3.2
Saturated fat (g): 0.9
Cholesterol (mg): 44.8
Sodium (mg): 244
Exchanges:
Milk: 0.0
Vegetable: 1.0
Fruit: 0.0
Bread: 1.0
Meat: 2.5
Fat: 0.0

1. Cover chilies with boiling water in small bowl; let stand until softened, about 10 minutes. Process chilies and water in food processor or blender until smooth.
2. Combine chili mixture and remaining ingredients, except salt, pepper, lime wedges, and garnishes in slow cooker; cover and cook on low 6 to 8 hours. Season to taste with salt and pepper. Serve with lime wedges and garnishes (not included in nutritional data).

Mexican Chicken-Corn Soup

Monterey Jack cheese gives this chicken-based soup a rich flavor; use pepper-Jack cheese for a spicier soup.

8 entrée servings

1 quart Rich Chicken Stock (see p. 30) or
   chicken broth
1 pound boneless, skinless chicken breasts, cubed
2 cups whole kernel corn
1½ cups chopped onions
1 cup chopped red or green bell pepper
1 each: chopped small jalapeño chili, clove garlic
1 teaspoon ground cumin
Salt and pepper, to taste
1–1½ cups (4–6 ounces) shredded reduced-fat
   Monterey Jack cheese

Per Serving:
Calories: 194
% calories from fat: 30
Protein (g): 21.4
Carbohydrate (g): 12.3
Fat (g): 6.4
Saturated fat (g): 2.6
Cholesterol (mg): 45.1
Sodium (mg): 163
Exchanges:
Milk: 0.0
Vegetable: 0.0
Fruit: 0.0
Bread: 1.0
Meat: 2.0
Fat: 0.0

1. Combine all ingredients, except salt, pepper, and cheese, in slow cooker; cover and cook on low 6 to 8 hours. Season to taste with salt and pepper; add cheese, stirring until melted.

Variation

El Paso Pork and Hominy Soup—Make recipe as above, substituting lean pork for the chicken, rinsed drained canned hominy for the corn, and 1 small poblano chili for the bell pepper. Omit Monterey Jack cheese; sprinkle each serving of soup with 1 tablespoon crumbled Mexican white cheese or feta cheese.

Mexican Meatball Soup

A great favorite in Mexico, this soup is traditionally seasoned with mint; we've offered oregano as an addition or alternative, if you like.

4 entrée servings

2 cans (14½ ounces each) reduced-sodium fat-free chicken broth
2 cups each: tomato juice, water
Mexican Meatballs (recipe follows)
2 medium zucchini, sliced
½ cup each: chopped onion, sliced carrots
2 cloves garlic, minced
1 small jalapeño chili, seeds and veins discarded, minced
1½ teaspoons dried mint and/or oregano leaves
Salt and pepper, to taste

Per Serving:
Calories: 227
% calories from fat: 16
Protein (g): 28
Carbohydrate (g): 20.2
Fat (g): 4.1
Saturated fat (g): 1.4
Cholesterol (mg): 54.7
Sodium (mg): 426
Exchanges:
Milk: 0.0
Vegetable: 3.0
Fruit: 0.0
Bread: 0.0
Meat: 3.0
Fat: 0.0

1. Combine all ingredients, except salt and pepper, in slow cooker; cover and cook on high 4 to 5 hours. Season to taste with salt and pepper.

Mexican Meatballs

Makes 24

1 pound ground beef eye of round
¼ cup cooked rice
⅓ cup finely chopped onion
1 clove garlic, minced
½ teaspoon each: dried mint and oregano leaves, ground cumin, salt
¼ teaspoon pepper

1. Mix all ingredients; shape into 24 small meatballs.

French Vegetable Soup

Made with veal stock, cubes of veal, and lots of fresh vegetables, this soup is a special treat.

8 entrée servings

2 quarts Veal Stock (see p. 33) or chicken broth
1 can (14½ ounces) diced tomatoes, undrained
1 pound lean veal, cubed
1½ cups peeled cubed potatoes
1 cup each: cut green beans, cauliflower florets
½ cup each: chopped onion, sliced celery, carrot
1 teaspoon dried thyme leaves
½ teaspoon dried savory leaves
1 cup each: small broccoli florets, frozen thawed peas
Salt and pepper, to taste

Per Serving:
Calories: 199
% calories from fat: 18
Protein: (g): 21.5
Carbohydrate (g): 19.4
Fat (g): 4.2
Saturated fat (g): 1.2
Cholesterol (mg): 66.1
Sodium (mg): 84
Exchanges:
Milk: 0.0
Vegetable: 1.0
Fruit: 0.0
Bread: 1.0
Meat: 2.0
Fat: 0.0

1. Combine all ingredients, except broccoli, peas, salt, and pepper, in 6-quart slow cooker; cover and cook on low 6 to 8 hours, adding broccoli and peas during last 20 to 30 minutes. Season to taste with salt and pepper.

French Onion Soup

The soup can be made without browning the onions, but the flavor will not be as rich.

4 entrée servings

1 pound onions, thinly sliced
1–2 tablespoons margarine or butter
½ teaspoon dry mustard
2 teaspoons flour
1 quart Fragrant Beef Stock (see p. 32) or beef broth
½ cup dry white wine (optional)
Salt and pepper, to taste
4 slices French bread, toasted
½ cup (2 ounces) shredded Parmesan cheese

Per Serving:
Calories: 243
% calories from fat: 30
Protein (g): 10.7
Carbohydrate (g): 25.2
Fat (g): 8.3
Saturated fat (g): 3.1
Cholesterol (mg): 10.9
Sodium (mg): 430
Exchanges:
Milk: 0.0
Vegetable: 2.0
Fruit: 0.0
Bread: 1.0
Meat: 0.5
Fat: 2.0

1. Cook onions in margarine in large saucepan over medium to medium-low heat until golden, 15 to 20 minutes; stir in mustard and flour and cook 1 to 2 minutes.

2. Combine onion mixture and remaining ingredients, except salt, pepper, bread, and cheese, in slow cooker; cover and cook on low 6 to 8 hours. Season to taste with salt and pepper. Sprinkle bread with cheese; broil until melted, 1 to 2 minutes. Top each bowl of soup with bread slices.

Variation

Onion and White Bean Soup—Make recipe as above, adding 1 can (15 ounces) rinsed drained navy or Great Northern beans, ½ teaspoon dried savory leaves, and ¼ teaspoon dried thyme leaves. Omit French bread and Parmesan cheese. Sprinkle top of each serving with 1 tablespoon grated Manchego or Romano cheese.

White Bean Soup Provençal

Serve warm focaccia as a perfect accompaniment to this herb-infused soup.

8 entrée servings

1½ quarts Chicken Stock (see p. 30) or chicken broth
2 cups water
1 pound dried cannellini or navy beans
1 cup each: chopped onion, celery
3 cloves garlic, minced
2 teaspoons dried sage leaves
3 large plum tomatoes, chopped
2 teaspoons lemon juice
Salt and pepper, to taste
Mixed Herb Pesto (recipe follows)

Per Serving:
Calories: 283
% calories from fat: 21
Protein (g): 16.2
Carbohydrate (g): 41.9
Fat (g): 6.9
Saturated fat (g): 1.2
Cholesterol (mg): 3.6
Sodium (mg): 199
Exchanges:
Milk: 0.0
Vegetable: 2.0
Fruit: 0.0
Bread: 2.0
Meat: 1.0
Fat: 1.0

1. Combine all ingredients, except tomatoes, lemon juice, salt, pepper, and Mixed Herb Pesto, in 6-quart slow cooker; cover and cook on low until beans are tender, 7 to 8 hours, adding tomatoes and lemon juice during last 30 minutes. Season to taste with salt and pepper. Stir 1 tablespoon Mixed Herb Pesto into each bowl of soup.

Mixed Herb Pesto

Makes about ½ cup

½ cup each: packed basil leaves, parsley sprigs
¼ cup packed oregano leaves
3 cloves garlic
2–3 tablespoons each: grated Parmesan cheese, walnut pieces, olive oil
2 teaspoons lemon juice
Salt and pepper, to taste

1. Process herbs, garlic, Parmesan cheese, and walnuts in food processor, adding oil and lemon juice gradually, until mixture is very finely chopped. Season to taste with salt and pepper.

Minestrone

Make this chunky soup the centerpiece of an Italian-style family supper. Serve with a tossed salad and crusty bread.

8 entrée servings

2 quarts Beef Stock (see p. 31) or beef broth
1 can (19 ounces) cannellini beans, rinsed, drained
1 can (6 ounces) tomato paste
1 pound lean beef round, cubed (¾-inch)
2 cups each: coarsely diced zucchini, chopped cabbage
1 large onion, chopped
2 each: sliced medium carrots, minced garlic cloves
2 bay leaves
1 tablespoon dried Italian seasoning
3 cups cooked elbow macaroni
Salt and pepper, to taste

Per Serving:
Calories: 220
% calories from fat: 13
Protein (g): 22.1
Carbohydrate (g): 31.2
Fat (g): 3.4
Saturated fat (g): 0.8
Cholesterol (mg): 27.4
Sodium (mg): 388
Exchanges:
Milk: 0.0
Vegetable: 2.0
Fruit: 0.0
Bread: 1.0
Meat: 2.0
Fat: 0.0

1. Combine all ingredients, except macaroni, salt, and pepper, in 6-quart slow cooker; cover and cook on low 6 to 8 hours, adding macaroni during last 15 minutes. Discard bay leaves; season to taste with salt and pepper.

Minestrone Primavera

This chunky soup, chock full of vegetables, often opens an Italian meal.

8 entrée servings

1¼ quarts reduced-sodium fat-free chicken broth, divided
1 can (15 ounces) rinsed, drained garbanzo beans
2 cups each: coarsely shredded cabbage, chopped tomatoes
1 cup cut green beans
6 small new potatoes, quartered
¾ cup each: chopped onion, thinly sliced leeks (white part only), sliced carrots
1 teaspoon dried Italian seasoning
¾ cup each: small broccoli florets, frozen thawed peas
4 ounces macaroni, cooked
½ cup finely chopped parsley (optional)
Salt and pepper, to taste
Grated Parmesan cheese, as garnish

Per Serving:
Calories: 259
% calories from fat: 4
Protein (g): 11.7
Carbohydrate (g): 53.5
Fat (g): 1.2
Saturated fat (g): 0.2
Cholesterol (mg): 0.0
Sodium (mg): 471
Exchanges:
Milk: 0.0
Vegetable: 2.0
Fruit: 0.0
Bread: 3.0
Meat: 0.0
Fat: 0.0

1 Combine all ingredients, except broccoli, peas, macaroni, parsley, salt, pepper, and cheese, in 6-quart slow cooker; cover and cook on low 6 to 8 hours, adding broccoli, peas, and macaroni during last 30 minutes. Stir in parsley; season to taste with salt and pepper. Sprinkle each bowl of soup with Parmesan cheese.

Chickpea and Pasta Minestrone

Substantial and wonderfully flavorful, this interesting minestrone is simple to make.

6 entrée servings

1½ quarts reduced-sodium fat-free chicken broth
1 can (15 ounces) chickpeas, rinsed, drained
1 can (14½ ounces) tomatoes with Italian herbs, undrained, coarsely chopped
4–5 ounces reduced-sodium smoked ham, diced
2 cups chopped cabbage
1 large onion, chopped
2 each: peeled thinly sliced large carrots, ribs celery, minced garlic cloves
1 tablespoon dried Italian seasoning
¼ cup uncooked orzo
Salt and pepper, to taste

Per Serving:
Calories: 220
% calories from fat: 11
Protein (g): 14.0
Carbohydrate (g): 34.8
Fat (g): 2.7
Saturated fat (g): 0.7
Cholesterol (mg): 11.7
Sodium (mg): 998
Exchanges:
Milk: 0.0
Vegetable: 2.0
Fruit: 0.0
Bread: 2.5
Meat: 1.0
Fat: 0.0

1. Combine all ingredients, except orzo, salt, and pepper, in 6-quart slow cooker; cover and cook on low 6 to 8 hours, adding orzo during last 20 minutes. Season to taste with salt and pepper.

Meaty Minestrone

The combination of beef and Italian sausage make this easy vegetable soup extra-hearty.

8 entrée servings

1½ quarts Beef Stock (see p. 31) or beef broth
1 can (15 ounces) Great Northern beans, rinsed, drained
1 can (14½ ounces) diced tomatoes, undrained
1¼ pounds lean beef stew meat, cubed
4 ounces Italian-style turkey sausage
1 each: chopped large onion, sliced rib celery
2 each: sliced carrots, minced cloves garlic
2 teaspoons dried basil leaves
1 teaspoon dried oregano leaves
1 bay leaf
1 package (10 ounces) frozen Italian green beans, thawed
2 ounces rotini or shell pasta, cooked
Salt and pepper, to taste
Shredded Parmesan cheese, as garnish

Per Serving:
Calories: 235
% calories from fat: 30
Protein (g): 24
Carbohydrate (g): 19
Fat (g): 8.5
Saturated fat (g): 2.6
Cholesterol (mg): 52
Sodium (mg): 280
Exchanges:
Milk: 0.0
Vegetable: 1.0
Fruit: 0.0
Bread: 1.0
Meat: 2.0
Fat: 0.5

1. Combine all ingredients, except green beans, pasta, salt, pepper, and cheese in 6-quart slow cooker; cover and cook on low 6 to 8 hours, adding green beans and pasta during last 15 minutes. Discard bay leaf; season to taste with salt and pepper. Sprinkle each bowl of soup with Parmesan cheese.

Variation

Vegetarian Minestrone Gratin—Make recipe as above, adding 1 can (15 ounces) rinsed drained kidney beans and 1 large cubed zucchini, omitting turkey sausage, and substituting vegetable broth for the Beef Stock. Toast 8 slices (½-inch) French bread under broiler; sprinkle each with 2 tablespoons shredded reduced-fat mozzarella cheese and broil until melted, 1 to 2 minutes. Top each bowl of soup with a bread slice and sprinkle with chopped parsley.

Hearty Minestrone with Pepperoni

Pepperoni adds great flavor to this full-bodied soup. Serve with crusty bread and a salad for an easy, satisfying supper.

4 entrée servings

1½ quarts reduced-sodium fat-free chicken broth
1 can (28 ounces) Italian plum tomatoes, undrained
1 can (15 ounces) cannellini beans or Great Northern beans, rinsed, drained
1 each: chopped large onion, coarsely diced rib celery, red bell pepper
2 each: coarsely chopped medium carrots, zucchini, minced garlic cloves
¼ cup finely diced pepperoni or hard salami
1 tablespoon dried Italian seasoning
½ cup cooked elbow macaroni
Salt and pepper, to taste

Per Serving:
Calories: 327
% calories from fat: 21
Protein (g): 15.5
Carbohydrate (g): 48.1
Fat (g): 7.7
Saturated fat (g): 1.7
Cholesterol (mg): 5.6
Sodium (mg): 1067
Exchanges:
Milk: 0.0
Vegetable: 0.0
Fruit: 0.0
Bread: 3.0
Meat: 2.0
Fat: 0.0

1. Combine all ingredients, except macaroni, salt, and pepper, in 6-quart slow cooker; cover and cook on low 6 to 8 hours, adding macaroni during last 15 minutes. Season to taste with salt and pepper.

Italian-Style Vegetable Soup

Convenience foods make this soup a snap to assemble.

8 entrée servings

1½ quarts Rich Chicken Stock (see p. 30) or chicken broth
1 can (19 ounces) cannellini beans, rinsed, drained
1 can (15 ounces) tomato sauce
1½ cups chopped cabbage
1 cup each: chopped onion, sliced carrots
1 clove garlic, minced
1 teaspoon dried Italian seasoning
1 package (16 ounces) frozen mixed broccoli, corn, and red bell peppers, thawed
Salt and pepper, to taste
2 cups seasoned crouton stuffing mix

Per Serving:
Calories: 178
% calories from fat: 9
Protein (g): 12.5
Carbohydrate (g): 33.9
Fat (g): 2.1
Saturated fat (g): 0.2
Cholesterol (mg): 0
Sodium (mg): 529
Exchanges:
Milk: 0.0
Vegetable: 3.0
Fruit: 0.0
Bread: 1.0
Meat: 0.0
Fat: 0.5

1. Combine all ingredients, except thawed vegetables, salt, pepper, and stuffing mix, in 6-quart slow cooker; cover and cook on high 4 to 5 hours, adding thawed vegetables during last 20 minutes. Season to taste with salt and pepper. Spoon ¼ cup stuffing mix into each soup bowl; ladle soup over.

Garbanzo and Couscous Soup

The addition of couscous enhances this flavorful soup.

6 entrée servings

1¼ quarts reduced-sodium fat-free chicken broth
1 can (14½ ounces) diced tomatoes, undrained
1 can (15 ounces) garbanzo beans, rinsed, drained
1 cup each: diced zucchini, small cauliflower florets
½ medium green bell pepper, diced
1 each: chopped medium onion, rib celery, large carrot
1 bay leaf
1 clove garlic, minced
¾ teaspoon each: ground cumin, dried thyme leaves
Generous pinch ground cloves
⅓ cup uncooked couscous
Salt and pepper, to taste

Per Serving:
Calories: 202
% calories from fat: 15
Protein (g): 11.8
Carbohydrate (g): 33
Fat (g): 3.4
Saturated fat (g): 0.4
Cholesterol (mg): 0
Sodium (mg): 413
Exchanges:
Milk: 0.0
Vegetable: 1.0
Fruit: 0.0
Bread: 2.0
Meat: 0.0
Fat: 0.5

1. Combine all ingredients, except couscous, salt, and pepper, in 6-quart slow cooker; cover and cook on high 4 to 5 hours. Turn heat to off and stir in couscous; cover and let stand 5 to 10 minutes. Discard bay leaf; season to taste with salt and pepper.

Portuguese Soup

This flavorful kale soup is a simplified version of the Portuguese favorite Caldo Verde. Use linguiça, a Portuguese sausage, for the most authentic flavor; brown it in a skillet, if you like, and drain well.

4 entrée servings

1 quart Beef Stock (see p. 31) or beef broth
1 can (15 ounces) red kidney beans, rinsed, drained
¼ cup tomato sauce
8 ounces reduced-fat smoked sausage, sliced
3 medium potatoes, peeled, cubed
1 cup chopped onion
½ cup chopped red bell pepper
2 tablespoons minced garlic
3 cups sliced kale or spinach
Salt and pepper, to taste
Hot pepper sauce, to taste

Per Serving:
Calories: 326
% calories from fat: 15
Protein (g): 18.7
Carbohydrate (g): 53
Fat (g): 5.7
Saturated fat (g): 1.2
Cholesterol (mg): 26.8
Sodium (mg): 850
Exchanges:
Milk: 0.0
Vegetable: 2.0
Fruit: 0.0
Bread: 3.0
Meat: 1.0
Fat: 0.5

1. Combine all ingredients, except kale, salt, pepper, and hot pepper sauce, in slow cooker; cover and cook on high 4 to 5 hours, adding kale during last 15 minutes. Season to taste with salt, pepper, and hot pepper sauce.

Pasta Fagioli Ole!

A traditional Pasta Fagioli, with some Mexican-style flavor twists!

6 first-course servings

3 cups Chicken Stock (see p. 30) or chicken broth
2 cans (15 ounces each) pinto beans, rinsed, drained
2½ cups diced tomatoes
1 cup each: chopped onions, green bell pepper,
    sliced carrots
½ cup chopped celery
1 clove garlic, minced
1 medium jalapeño chili, finely chopped
2 teaspoons dried oregano leaves
1 cup cooked elbow macaroni
¼ cup chopped cilantro
Salt and cayenne pepper, to taste

Per Serving:
Calories: 211
% calories from fat: 7
Protein (g): 11.3
Carbohydrate (g): 39.6
Fat (g): 1.7
Saturated fat (g): 0.3
Cholesterol (mg): 0.0
Sodium (mg): 725
Exchanges:
Milk: 0.0
Vegetable: 0.0
Fruit: 0.0
Bread: 2.5
Meat: 1.0
Fat: 0.0

1. Combine all ingredients, except macaroni, cilantro, salt, and cayenne pepper, in slow cooker. Cover and cook on high 4 to 5 hours, adding macaroni and cilantro during last 15 minutes. Season to taste with salt and cayenne pepper.

Italian Cannellini and Cabbage Soup

Any white bean, such as Great Northern or navy, may be substituted for the cannellini.

8 first-course servings

2 cans (14 ½ ounces each) reduced-sodium
   chicken broth
1 cup water
1 can (15 ounces) cannellini or Great Northern beans,
   rinsed, drained
3 cups thinly sliced or chopped cabbage
1 small onion, coarsely chopped
3 cloves garlic, minced
1 teaspoon crushed caraway seeds
½ cup cooked mostaccioli (penne)
Salt and pepper, to taste

Per Serving:
Calories: 107
% calories from fat: 7
Protein (g): 6.9
Carbohydrate (g): 21.9
Fat (g): 1
Saturated fat (g): 0.1
Cholesterol (mg): 0
Sodium (mg): 175
Exchanges:
Milk: 0.0
Vegetable: 1.0
Fruit: 0.0
Bread: 1.0
Meat: 0.5
Fat: 0.0

1. Combine all ingredients, except pasta, salt, and pepper, in slow cooker; cover and cook on high 4 to 5 hours, adding pasta during last 20 minutes. Season to taste with salt and pepper.

Sicilian Summer Tomato Soup

Perfect for a summer day when tomatoes are at their best. Orange zest adds a pleasant accent.

10 first-course servings

1 quart Chicken Stock (see p. 30) or chicken broth
½ cup dry white wine or Chicken Stock
¼ cup orange juice
2 tablespoons tomato paste
18 plum tomatoes, peeled, seeded, chopped
2 each: medium red and yellow onions, finely
   chopped
1 cup sliced mushrooms
½ cup each: chopped green onions, carrots, celery,
   parsley
¼ cup chopped garlic
1–2 tablespoons dried basil leaves
1 teaspoon sugar
Grated zest of 1 orange
1½ pounds spinach, coarsely chopped
Salt and pepper, to taste

Per Serving:
Calories: 146
% calories from fat: 22
Protein (g): 5.8
Carbohydrate (g): 22.2
Fat (g): 4.1
Saturated fat (g): 0.6
Cholesterol (mg): 0
Sodium (mg): 103
Exchanges:
Milk: 0.0
Vegetable: 4.0
Fruit: 0.0
Bread: 0.0
Meat: 0.0
Fat: 1.0

1. Combine all ingredients, except spinach, salt, and pepper, in 6-quart slow cooker; cover and cook on high 4 to 5 hours, adding spinach during last 30 minutes. Season to taste with salt and pepper.

Red and White Bean Soup with Bacon and Pasta

Any small soup pasta can be substituted for the orzo.

6 entrée servings

1½ quarts reduced-sodium fat-free chicken broth
1 can (19 ounces) cannellini beans, rinsed, drained
1 can (15 ounces) each: rinsed drained red kidney
   beans, tomato sauce
6 ounces Canadian bacon, thinly sliced
1 cup each: chopped onion, celery
2 teaspoons dried Italian seasoning
½ cup uncooked orzo
Salt and pepper, to taste

Per Serving:
Calories: 291
% calories from fat: 14
Protein (g): 18.9
Carbohydrate (g): 42.1
Fat (g): 4.3
Saturated fat (g): 0.8
Cholesterol (mg): 14.2
Sodium (mg): 1286
Exchanges:
Milk: 0.0
Vegetable: 0.0
Fruit: 0.0
Bread: 3.0
Meat: 1.5
Fat: 0.0

1. Combine all ingredients, except orzo, salt, and pepper, in 6-quart slow cooker; cover and cook on low 6 to 8 hours, adding orzo during last 20 minutes. Season to taste with salt and pepper.

Cannellini Bean and Pasta Soup

Garlic Croutons (see p. 51) would also be a flavorful garnish for this soup.

4 entrée servings

1 quart reduced-sodium fat-free chicken broth
1 can (19 ounces) cannellini beans, rinsed, drained
¾ cup diced Canadian bacon
⅓ cup diced red bell pepper
2 cloves garlic, minced
½ teaspoon each: dried marjoram and sage leaves
1 cup uncooked ditalini
Salt and pepper, to taste
Parmesan Croutons (see p. 73)

Per Serving:
Calories: 235
% calories from fat: 14
Protein (g): 18.2
Carbohydrate (g): 39.4
Fat (g): 4.2
Saturated fat (g): 0.7
Cholesterol (mg): 8.1
Sodium (mg): 731
Exchanges:
Milk: 0.0
Vegetable: 0.0
Fruit: 0.0
Bread: 2.5
Meat: 1.0
Fat: 0.0

1. Combine all ingredients, except ditalini, salt, pepper, and croutons, in slow cooker; cover and cook on low 6 to 8 hours, adding pasta during last 30 minutes. Season to taste with salt and pepper. Sprinkle each bowl of soup with Parmesan Croutons.

Italian Meatball Soup

Substitute other pastas for the spaghetti, if you like, such as orecchiette (little ears) or conchiglie (shells).

8 entrée servings

2 quarts reduced-sodium fat-free chicken broth
Italian Turkey Meatballs (recipe follows)
2 cups each: cut green beans, sliced carrots, chopped onions
5 plum tomatoes, coarsely chopped
2 cloves garlic, minced
1–2 teaspoons dried Italian seasoning
8 ounces thin spaghetti, broken into pieces (3-inch), cooked
Salt and pepper, to taste

Per Serving:
Calories: 270
% calories from fat: 28
Protein (g): 19
Carbohydrate (g): 30.2
Fat (g): 8.7
Saturated fat (g): 2
Cholesterol (mg): 31.7
Sodium (mg): 174
Exchanges:
Milk: 0.0
Vegetable: 1.0
Fruit: 0.0
Bread: 1.5
Meat: 2.0
Fat: 0.5

1. Combine all ingredients, except pasta, salt, and pepper, in 6-quart slow cooker; cover and cook on low 6 to 8 hours, adding pasta during last 15 to 20 minutes. Season to taste with salt and pepper.

Italian Turkey Meatballs

Makes 32

1½ pounds ground turkey
1 egg
¼ cup seasoned dry bread crumbs
2 cloves garlic, minced
1 tablespoon dried Italian seasoning
¾ teaspoon salt
½ teaspoon pepper

1. Mix all ingredients; shape into 32 meatballs.

Italian Mushroom-Barley Soup

For variation, substitute 1 can (15 ounces) drained, rinsed Great Northern beans for the barley.

6 first-course servings

1½ quarts chicken broth
2 cups each: tomato juice, chopped tomatoes
½ cup pearl barley
3 cups sliced mushrooms
¾ cup each: chopped carrots, onion
2 teaspoons minced garlic
1 teaspoon each: dried basil and oregano leaves
Salt and pepper, to taste
Reduced-fat sour cream, as garnish

Per Serving:
Calories: 126
% calories from fat: 7
Protein (g): 7.3
Carbohydrate (g): 25.3
Fat (g): 1.1
Saturated fat (g): 0.1
Cholesterol (mg): 2.5
Sodium (mg): 1196
Exchanges:
Milk: 0.0
Vegetable: 0.0
Fruit: 0.0
Bread: 1.5
Meat: 0.0
Fat: 0.5

1. Combine all ingredients, except salt, pepper, and sour cream, in 6-quart slow cooker; cover and cook on low 6 to 8 hours. Season to taste with salt and pepper. Top each bowl of soup with a dollop of sour cream.

Kale and Ravioli Soup

Fresh ravioli or tortellini can be cooked in the slow cooker or cooked in advance and added to the slow cooker near the end of cooking time.

6 first-course servings

1 quart reduced-sodium fat-free chicken broth
2 cups water
1 cup each: sliced carrots, chopped plum tomatoes, onions, celery
2 cloves garlic, minced
¾ teaspoon each: dried basil and rosemary leaves
½ package (9 ounce-size) fresh herb ravioli
3 cups coarsely chopped kale
2–3 teaspoons lemon juice
Salt and pepper, to taste

Per Serving:
Calories: 114
% calories from fat: 12
Protein (g): 7.7
Carbohydrate (g): 19.6
Fat (g): 1.6
Saturated fat (g): 0.8
Cholesterol (mg): 10.8
Sodium (mg): 206
Exchanges:
Milk: 0.0
Vegetable: 0.0
Fruit: 0.0
Bread: 1.0
Meat: 1.0
Fat: 0.0

1. Combine all ingredients, except ravioli, kale, lemon juice, salt, and pepper, in 6-quart slow cooker; cover and cook on high 3 to 4 hours. Add ravioli and kale, cooking until ravioli float to the top, about 10 to 15 minutes. Season to taste with lemon juice, salt, and pepper.

Mulligatawny

Colorful and lightly spiced with curry powder, this popular soup originated in India.

8 first-course servings

1¼ quarts Chicken Stock (see p. 30) or chicken broth
1 pound boneless, skinless chicken breast halves
1 can (14½ ounces) diced tomatoes, undrained
1½ cups each: coarsely chopped onions, tart apples
½ cup each: sliced celery, carrots, red bell pepper, diced peeled red potatoes
1 large clove garlic, minced
2½ teaspoons curry powder
1 teaspoon chili powder
½ teaspoon each: ground allspice, dried thyme leaves
¼ cup coarsely chopped parsley
Salt and pepper, to taste

Per Serving:
Calories: 95
% calories from fat: 9.5
Protein (g): 8.7
Carbohydrate (g): 11.1
Fat (g): 2
Saturated fat (g): 0.4
Cholesterol (mg): 16.8
Sodium (mg): 181
Exchanges:
Milk: 0.0
Vegetable: 0.0
Fruit: 0.5
Bread: 1.3
Meat: 1.0
Fat: 0.0

1. Combine all ingredients, except parsley, salt, and pepper, in 6-quart slow cooker; cover and cook on low 6 to 8 hours. Stir in parsley; season to taste with salt and pepper.

Indian-Style Potato-Spinach Soup with Chicken

An unusual combination of herbs and spices gives this hearty soup an exotic flavor and aroma.

6 entrée servings

3 cups Chicken Stock (see p. 30) or chicken broth
12 ounces boneless, skinless chicken breast, diced
1 can (14½ ounces) diced tomatoes, undrained
2 cups peeled cubed baking potatoes
1 cup chopped onion
2 large cloves garlic, minced
½ teaspoon each: caraway seeds, ground cardamom
1½ tablespoons mild or hot curry powder
2 teaspoons ground coriander
½ package (10 ounce-size) frozen chopped spinach, thawed, drained
Salt and pepper, to taste

Per Serving:
Calories: 209
% calories from fat: 13
Protein (g): 19.5
Carbohydrate (g): 23.9
Fat (g): 2.9
Saturated fat (g): 0.6
Cholesterol (mg): 42.9
Sodium (mg): 167
Exchanges:
Milk: 0.0
Vegetable: 0.0
Fruit: 0.0
Bread: 1.5
Meat: 2.0
Fat: 0.0

1. Combine all ingredients, except spinach, salt, and pepper, in slow cooker; cover and cook on low 6 to 8 hours, adding spinach during last 20 minutes. Season to taste with salt and pepper.

Curry Soup with Meatballs

This lightly thickened soup is delicately flavored with curry powder.

4 entrée servings

1¼ quarts Beef Stock (see p. 31) or beef broth
Curry Meatballs (recipe follows)
½ cup chopped onion
2 teaspoons each: minced garlic, curry powder
2 ounces vermicelli, broken into pieces (2-inch),
   cooked
Salt and pepper, to taste
¼ cup chopped mint

Per Serving:
Calories: 216
% calories from fat: 37
Protein (g): 13.8
Carbohydrate (g): 19.9
Fat (g): 8.8
Saturated fat (g): 3
Cholesterol (mg): 35.6
Sodium (mg): 49
Exchanges:
Milk: 0.0
Vegetable: 0.0
Fruit: 0.0
Bread: 1.0
Meat: 2.0
Fat: 0.5

1. Combine all ingredients, except pasta, salt, pepper, and mint, in slow cooker; cover and cook on high 4 to 5 hours, adding pasta during last 15 minutes. Season to taste with salt and pepper. Stir in mint.

Curry Meatballs

Makes 12 to 16

8 ounces lean ground beef
⅓ cup minced onion
1½ teaspoons curry powder
½ teaspoon salt
¼ teaspoon pepper

1. Combine all ingredients; shape into 12 to 16 meatballs.

Indian Lentil Soup

This soup from India, Dal Shorba, is flavored with curry powder and sweet coriander. Red, green, or brown lentils can be used.

8 entrée servings

1 quart reduced-sodium fat-free chicken broth
4 cups water
2 cups dried red or brown lentils
½ cup chopped onion
1 clove garlic, minced
2 teaspoons curry powder
1 teaspoon each: crushed coriander and cumin seeds
½ teaspoon ground turmeric
⅛–¼ teaspoon crushed red pepper
Salt and pepper, to taste
6 tablespoons reduced-fat plain yogurt

Per Serving:
Calories: 193
% calories from fat: 11
Protein (g): 16
Carbohydrate (g): 27.6
Fat (g): 2.4
Saturated fat (g): 0.3
Cholesterol (mg): 0.3
Sodium (mg): 121
Exchanges:
Milk: 0.0
Vegetable: 0.0
Fruit: 0.0
Bread: 2.0
Meat: 1.0
Fat: 0.0

1. Combine all ingredients, except salt, pepper, and yogurt, in 6-quart slow cooker; cover and cook on low 6 to 8 hours. Season to taste with salt and pepper. Top each bowl of soup with a tablespoon of yogurt.

Indian-Spiced Chicken Soup

This flavorful chicken soup is delicious with warm pita bread for a light lunch.

8 entrée servings

2 quarts reduced-sodium fat-free chicken broth
1 ½ pounds boneless skinless chicken breast, cubed
(¾-inch)
½ cup thinly sliced onion
6 peppercorns
2 teaspoons ground coriander
1 teaspoon each: ground turmeric, ginger
⅛–¼ teaspoon crushed red pepper
1½ teaspoons cider vinegar
Salt and pepper, to taste
Chopped cilantro, as garnish

Per Serving:
Calories: 179
% calories from fat: 26
Protein (g): 30.2
Carbohydrate (g): 1.4
Fat (g): 4.9
Saturated fat (g): 1.3
Cholesterol (mg): 82.1
Sodium (mg): 89
Exchanges:
Milk: 0.0
Vegetable: 0.0
Fruit: 0.0
Bread: 0.0
Meat: 3.0
Fat: 0.0

1. Combine all ingredients, except red pepper, vinegar, salt, pepper, and cilantro, in 6-quart slow cooker; cover and cook on high 3 to 4 hours, adding red pepper and vinegar during last 30 minutes. Season to taste with salt and pepper; garnish each bowl of soup with chopped cilantro.

Russian Cabbage Soup

Use red or green cabbage in this savory soup.

8 first-course servings

1½ quarts reduced-sodium fat-free beef broth
1 can (14½ ounces) diced tomatoes,
   undrained
6 cups thinly sliced red cabbage
4 large beets, peeled, cubed (½-inch)
1 cup each: sliced carrots, onions, cubed turnip,
   potato
1 tablespoon cider vinegar
Salt and pepper, to taste
8 tablespoons reduced-free sour cream

Per Serving:
Calories: 109
% calories from fat: 17
Protein (g): 4
Carbohydrate (g): 20.7
Fat (g): 2.2
Saturated fat (g): 0.4
Cholesterol (mg): 0
Sodium (mg): 91
Exchanges:
Milk: 0.0
Vegetable: 3.0
Fruit: 0.0
Bread: 0.5
Meat: 0.0
Fat: 0.0

1. Combine all ingredients, except salt, pepper, and sour cream, in 6-quart slow cooker; cover and cook on low 6 to 8 hours; season to taste with salt and pepper. Top each bowl of soup with a tablespoon of sour cream.

Hearty Cabbage and Vegetable Soup

A delicious and convenient use for leftover cooked beef. If using raw beef, add it at the beginning.

8 entrée servings

1 quart Fragrant Beef Stock (see p. 32) or beef broth
2 cups tomato juice
3 cups shredded green or red cabbage
1 cup each: thinly sliced onion, carrots, mushrooms, cubed unpeeled potatoes
1 teaspoon each: caraway seeds, paprika
4 cups cubed cooked lean beef
2 tablespoons raisins
1 tablespoon sugar
2–3 teaspoons vinegar
Salt and pepper, to taste
Dill Sour Cream (see p. 206)

Per Serving:
Calories: 214
% calories from fat: 28
Protein (g): 20.2
Carbohydrate (g): 18.7
Fat (g): 6.9
Saturated fat (g): 3
Cholesterol (mg): 51.1
Sodium (mg): 83
Exchanges:
Milk: 0.0
Vegetable: 2.0
Fruit: 0.0
Bread: 0.5
Meat: 2.0
Fat: 0.0

1. Combine stock, tomato juice, vegetables, caraway seeds, and paprika in 6-quart slow cooker; cover and cook on low 6 to 8 hours, adding beef, raisins, sugar, and vinegar during last 30 minutes. Season to taste with salt and pepper. Garnish bowls of soup with dollops of Dill Sour Cream.

Variation

Meatless Cabbage and Vegetable Soup—Make recipe as above, substituting Basic Vegetable Stock (see p. 34) or vegetable broth for the Beef Stock, and omitting beef. Add 1 can (15 ounces) each rinsed drained navy and kidney beans. Serve with Garlic Croutons (see p. 51).

Borscht

Use red or green cabbage in this soup.

8 entrée servings

2 quarts reduced-sodium fat-free beef broth
12 ounces boneless lean beef, cubed
1 pound beets, peeled, cubed
3 cups coarsely shredded cabbage
1½ cups sliced carrots
1 cup chopped onion
1 tablespoon dried dill weed
¼–⅓ cup cider vinegar
Salt and pepper, to taste
Reduced-fat sour cream, as garnish

Per Serving:
Calories: 121
% calories from fat: 14
Protein (g): 15.7
Carbohydrate (g): 9.5
Fat (g): 1.9
Saturated fat (g): 0.6
Cholesterol (mg): 23.4
Sodium (mg): 301
Exchanges:
Milk: 0.0
Vegetable: 2.0
Fruit: 0.0
Bread: 0.0
Meat: 1.5
Fat: 0.0

1. Combine all ingredients, except vinegar, salt, pepper, and sour cream, in 6-quart slow cooker; cover and cook on low 6 to 8 hours, adding vinegar during the last hour. Season to taste with salt and pepper. Garnish each bowl of soup with a dollop of sour cream.

Beet Borscht

This delicious soup is flavored in the traditional way, with Polish sausage.

8 first-course servings

1½ quarts reduced-sodium fat-free beef broth
8 ounce link reduced-fat smoked Polish sausage
1 small head red cabbage, thinly sliced
4 medium beets, peeled, cubed
2 carrots, sliced
1 clove garlic, minced
1 bay leaf
2–3 teaspoons sugar
2 tablespoons cider vinegar
Salt and pepper, to taste
Chopped dill weed, as garnish

Per Serving:
Calories: 120
% calories from fat: 25
Protein (g): 10.9
Carbohydrate (g): 13.1
Fat (g): 0.4
Saturated fat (g): 0.6
Cholesterol (mg): 17.2
Sodium (mg): 437
Exchanges:
Milk: 0.0
Vegetable: 3.0
Fruit: 0.0
Bread: 0.0
Meat: 1.0
Fat: 0.0

1. Combine all ingredients, except sugar, vinegar, salt, pepper, and dill weed, in 6-quart slow cooker; cover and cook on high 4 to 5 hours, adding sugar and vinegar during last hour. Remove sausage; slice and return to soup. Discard bay leaf. Season to taste with salt and pepper; sprinkle each bowl of soup with dill weed.

Russian Borscht

This Russian soup makes a hearty cold weather meal.

6 entrée servings

3 cans (14½ ounces each) reduced-sodium fat-free
beef broth
1 can (14½ ounces) diced tomatoes
1 pound lean beef stew meat, cubed
4 cups thinly sliced cabbage
2 cups each: shredded beets, carrots
1 cup each: chopped onion, shredded turnip
1 tablespoon sugar
2 bay leaves
1 teaspoon dried thyme leaves
3–4 tablespoons red wine vinegar
Salt and pepper, to taste
Dill Sour Cream (recipe follows)

Per Serving:
Calories: 137
% calories from fat: 21
Protein (g): 14.4
Carbohydrate (g): 12.8
Fat (g): 3.2
Saturated fat (g): 1.7
Cholesterol (mg): 28.7
Sodium (mg): 289
Exchanges:
Milk: 0.0
Vegetable: 3.0
Fruit: 0.0
Bread: 0.0
Meat: 1.0
Fat: 0.0

1. Combine all ingredients, except vinegar, salt, pepper, and Dill Sour
Cream, in 6-quart slow cooker; cover and cook on low 6 to 8 hours. Season
to taste with vinegar, salt, and pepper; discard bay leaves. Dollop each
bowl of soup with Dill Sour Cream.

Dill Sour Cream

Makes about ¾ cup

¾ cup reduced-fat sour cream
2 tablespoons fresh or 1 tablespoon dried dill weed
1–2 teaspoons lemon juice

1. Mix all ingredients.

Variation
Ukrainian Borscht—Make soup as above, substituting 8 ounces each lean
cubed pork and sliced, reduced-fat smoked sausage for the beef. Add 1 can
(15 ounces) rinsed, drained Great Northern beans.

Eastern European Borscht

Slow cooking enhances flavors in this favorite borscht.

12 entrée servings

2 quarts water
1 pound lean beef stew meat, cubed
1½ pounds reduced-fat smoked sausage, sliced
4 cups shredded cabbage
3½ cups cooked peeled coarsely shredded or cubed
   beets, divided
2 cups peeled shredded potatoes
1 cup each: shredded carrots, sliced onion
2 tablespoons red wine vinegar
1 teaspoon sugar
2 teaspoons each: dried marjoram leaves, dill weed
Salt and pepper, to taste
1 cup reduced-fat sour cream
¼ cup chopped fresh dill weed

Per Serving:
Calories: 224
% calories from fat: 22
Protein (g): 18.6
Carbohydrate (g): 24.3
Fat (g): 5.6
Saturated fat (g): 2.0
Cholesterol (mg): 48.5
Sodium (mg): 575
Exchanges:
Milk: 0.0
Vegetable: 0.0
Fruit: 0.0
Bread: 1.5
Meat: 2.0
Fat: 0.0

1. Combine all ingredients, except salt, pepper, sour cream, and dill weed, in 6-quart slow cooker; cover and cook on low 6 to 8 hours. Season to taste with salt and pepper. Garnish each bowl of soup with a generous dollop of sour cream; sprinkle with dill weed.

Goulash Soup

If desired, stir combined ¾ cup reduced-fat sour cream and 1 tablespoon cornstarch into soup at the end of cooking time; stir 2 to 3 minutes.

6 entrée servings

1½ quarts beef broth
1 pound lean beef round, cubed
2 cups peeled diced potatoes
1 cup each: chopped onion, cut green beans (¾-inch)
½ cup each: thinly sliced carrot, diced celery
2 large cloves garlic, minced
¼ cup pearl barley
1 bay leaf
1½ teaspoons paprika
½ teaspoon each: dried thyme leaves, dry mustard
1 can (15 ounces) tomato sauce
Salt and pepper, to taste

Per Serving:
Calories: 175
% calories from fat: 13
Protein (g): 13.9
Carbohydrate (g): 25.3
Fat (g): 2.5
Saturated fat (g): 0.7
Cholesterol (mg): 27.4
Sodium (mg): 547
Exchanges:
Milk: 0.0
Vegetable: 0.0
Fruit: 0.0
Bread: 1.5
Meat: 1.0
Fat: 0.0

1. Combine all ingredients, except tomato sauce, salt, and pepper, in 6-quart slow cooker; cover and cook on low 6 to 8 hours, adding tomato sauce during last hour. Discard bay leaf; season to taste with salt and pepper.

Goulash Bean Soup

Caraway seeds and paprika give a Hungarian accent to this vegetable and bean soup.

8 entrée servings

1 quart Beef Stock (see p. 31) or beef broth
2 cans (15 ounces each) light red kidney beans, rinsed, drained
1 can (14½ ounces) diced tomatoes, undrained
1½ pounds lean beef round steak, cubed
3 cups sliced cabbage
2 cups chopped onions
1 cup each: chopped carrots, red bell pepper
1 tablespoon each: minced garlic, paprika
2 teaspoons crushed caraway seeds
1 teaspoon dried thyme leaves
Salt and pepper, to taste
½ cup reduced-fat sour cream

Per Serving:
Calories: 253
% calories from fat: 13
Protein (g): 24.1
Carbohydrate (g): 31.6
Fat (g): 3.7
Saturated fat (g): 1.1
Cholesterol (mg): 41.4
Sodium (mg): 512
Exchanges:
Milk: 0.0
Vegetable: 0.0
Fruit: 0.0
Bread: 2.0
Meat: 2.0
Fat: 0.0

1. Combine all ingredients, except salt, pepper, and sour cream, in 6-quart slow cooker; cover and cook on low 6 to 8 hours. Season to taste with salt and pepper. Top each bowl of soup with dollops of sour cream.

Basque Vegetable Soup

A tasty chickpea soup with a Spanish accent!

8 entrée servings

2½ quarts reduced-sodium fat-free chicken broth
½ cup dry red wine or chicken broth
1¼ pounds boneless, skinless chicken breast, cubed
2 cans (15 ounces each) chickpeas, rinsed, drained
4 cups coarsely shredded cabbage
1 cup each: chopped onion, leeks (white parts only),
   cubed unpeeled potatoes
½ cup each: cubed turnip, chopped carrots, red and
   green bell peppers
5 large cloves garlic, chopped
2 teaspoons dried thyme leaves
Salt and pepper, to taste
1½ cups Garlic Croutons (see p. 51)

Per Serving:
Calories: 395
% calories from fat: 6
Protein (g): 29.7
Carbohydrate (g): 58.8
Fat (g): 2.7
Saturated fat (g): 0.5
Cholesterol (mg): 41.1
Sodium (mg): 1142
Exchanges:
Milk: 0.0
Vegetable: 0.0
Fruit: 0.0
Bread: 4.0
Meat: 3.0
Fat: 0.0

1. Combine all ingredients, except salt, pepper, and Garlic Croutons, in 6-quart slow cooker; cover and cook on low 6 to 8 hours. Season to taste with salt and pepper. Sprinkle each bowl of soup with Garlic Croutons.

Spicy North African-Style Chicken Soup

The tangy flavors and hearty textures of North African cuisine combine in this chicken soup.

6 entrée servings

1½ quarts Chicken Stock (see p. 30) or chicken
   broth
1 can (14½ ounces) stewed tomatoes,
   undrained
1 pound boneless, skinless chicken breast halves,
   cubed
3 cups coarsely chopped onions
½ cup each: sliced celery, bulgur wheat
2 large cloves garlic, minced
1 cinnamon stick
2 large bay leaves
¾ teaspoon each: dried marjoram and thyme leaves
⅛ teaspoon ground cloves
Salt and pepper, to taste

Per Serving:
Calories: 165
% calories from fat: 16
Protein (g): 17.5
Carbohydrate (g): 18.1
Fat (g): 3
Saturated fat (g): 0.6
Cholesterol (mg): 29.6
Sodium (mg): 335
Exchanges:
Milk: 0.0
Vegetable: 1.0
Fruit: 0.0
Bread: 1.0
Meat: 1.0
Fat: 0.0

1. Combine all ingredients, except salt and pepper, in 6-quart slow cooker; cover and cook on low 6 to 8 hours. Discard cinnamon stick and bay leaves; season to taste with salt and pepper.

Oriental Soup with Noodles and Chicken

The dried chow mein noodles in this soup are not the fried ones that have been used with chop suey for many years. Be sure to use the correct noodles.

4 entrée servings

1 ounce dried cloud ear or shiitake mushrooms
Hot water
2 cans (14½ ounces each) reduced-sodium fat-free
   chicken broth
2 tablespoons dry sherry (optional)
8 ounces boneless, skinless chicken breast, cubed
½ cup each: sliced white mushrooms, carrots
1½ teaspoons light soy sauce
½ teaspoon five-spice powder
2 ounces snow peas, trimmed
½ package (5 ounces) dried chow mein noodles
Salt and pepper, to taste

Per Serving:
Calories: 213
% calories from fat: 30
Protein (g): 16.4
Carbohydrate (g): 19.7
Fat (g): 7.6
Saturated fat (g): 1.2
Cholesterol (mg): 29.2
Sodium (mg): 259
Exchanges:
Milk: 0.0
Vegetable: 0.5
Fruit: 0.0
Bread: 1.0
Meat: 1.5
Fat: 1.0

1. Place dried mushrooms in bowl; pour hot water over to cover. Let stand until mushrooms are soft, about 15 minutes; drain. Slice mushrooms, discarding any tough parts.
2. Combine mushrooms and remaining ingredients, except snow peas, chow mein noodles, salt, and pepper, in slow cooker; cover and cook on high 4 to 5 hours, adding snow peas and chow mein noodles during last 20 minutes. Season to taste with salt and pepper.

East Meets West Soup

This creamy, hotly spiced soup is garnished with crisp Chili-Seasoned Wontons.

6 first-course servings

1 quart Chicken Stock (see p. 30) or chicken broth
2 cans (4 ounces each) chopped green chilies, drained
1 cup each: thinly sliced onions, celery
1 small jalapeño chili, minced
1 tablespoon each: minced gingerroot, garlic
1 teaspoon ground cumin
1 cup 2% reduced-fat milk
2 tablespoon cornstarch
Salt and pepper, to taste
¼ cup chopped cilantro
Chili-Seasoned Wontons (recipe follows)

Per Serving:
Calories: 192
% calories from fat: 18
Protein (g): 8.2
Carbohydrate (g): 31.2
Fat (g): 3.7
Saturated fat (g): 0.7
Cholesterol (mg): 5.7
Sodium (mg): 369
Exchanges:
Milk: 0.0
Vegetable: 0.0
Fruit: 0.0
Bread: 2.0
Meat: 0.0
Fat: 1.0

1. Combine all ingredients, except milk, cornstarch, salt, pepper, cilantro, and Chili-Seasoned Wontons, in slow cooker; cover and cook on high 3 to 4 hours. Stir in combined milk and cornstarch, stirring, 2 to 3 minutes. Season to taste with salt and pepper; stir in cilantro. Serve with Chili-Seasoned Wontons.

Chili-Seasoned Wontons

Makes 36

1 teaspoon hot chili powder
½ teaspoon garlic powder
¼ teaspoon cayenne pepper
2 teaspoons each: canola oil, water
18 wonton wrappers, cut diagonally into halves

1. Combine all ingredients, except wonton wrappers; brush both sides of wonton wrappers with mixture and place on cookie sheet. Bake at 375 degrees until crisp, about 5 minutes; cool on wire racks.

Chicken Wonton Soup

Ginger-spiced chicken wontons are a delicious addition to this soup. The wontons can be refrigerated, covered, several hours before cooking.

6 entrée servings

1 quart Chicken Stock (see p. 30) or chicken broth
1 can (8 ounces) baby corn, rinsed, drained
½ cup each: chopped red bell pepper, carrot
2 teaspoons each: minced gingerroot, soy sauce
1 teaspoon Asian sesame oil
1 cup sliced packed spinach leaves
Chicken Wontons (recipe follows)
Salt and cayenne pepper, to taste

Per Serving:
Calories: 187
% calories from fat: 13
Protein (g): 14.5
Carbohydrate (g): 25.1
Fat (g): 2.8
Saturated fat (g): 0.6
Cholesterol (mg): 28.2
Sodium (mg): 430
Exchanges:
Milk: 0.0
Vegetable: 2.0
Fruit: 0.0
Bread: 1.0
Meat: 1.0
Fat: 0.0

1. Combine all ingredients, except sesame oil, spinach, Chicken Wontons, salt, and cayenne pepper, in slow cooker; cover and cook on low 4 to 5 hours, adding spinach during last 10 minutes. Stir in Chicken Wontons; season to taste with salt and cayenne pepper.

Chicken Wontons

Makes 24 wontons

8 ounces boneless, skinless chicken breast
¼ cup sliced green onions
1 teaspoon minced gingerroot
24 wonton wrappers

1. Process all ingredients, except wonton wrappers, in food processor until finely chopped. Place 1 mounded teaspoon chicken mixture on each wonton wrapper; moisten edges with water, and fold in half diagonally to create triangles, sealing edges. Cook wontons in 2 to 3 quarts boiling water until they float to the top, 5 to 7 minutes. Drain.

Hot Sour Soup

The contrast in hot and sour flavors makes this Mandarin soup a unique offering. The hot chili sesame oil and Sour Sauce are intensely flavored, so use sparingly.

6 first-course servings

1 ounce dried Chinese black mushrooms
¾ cup boiling water
1 quart reduced-sodium fat-free chicken broth
1½ cups cubed tempeh or extra-firm light tofu
½ cup bamboo shoots
¼ cup distilled white vinegar
2 tablespoons tamari soy sauce
1 tablespoon each: finely chopped gingerroot, brown
   sugar, cornstarch
3 tablespoons water
Salt and pepper, to taste
1 egg, lightly beaten
1 teaspoon Asian sesame oil
12–18 drops hot chili sesame oil or Szechwan chili sauce
Sour Sauce (recipe follows)

Per Serving:
Calories: 176
% calories from fat: 28
Protein (g): 11
Carbohydrate (g): 21
Fat (g): 6
Saturated fat (g): 0.8
Cholesterol (mg): 35
Sodium (mg): 630
Exchanges:
Milk: 0.0
Vegetable: 0.0
Fruit: 0.0
Bread: 1.5
Meat: 1.5
Fat: 0.0

1. Combine mushrooms and boiling water in small bowl; let stand until mushrooms are softened, 15 to 20 minutes. Drain, reserving liquid. Slice mushrooms, discarding tough stems.
2. Combine mushrooms and reserved liquid, broth, tempeh, bamboo shoots, vinegar, soy sauce, gingerroot, and brown sugar in slow cooker; cover and cook on high 2 to 3 hours. Stir in combined cornstarch and water, stirring 2 to 3 minutes. Season to taste with salt and pepper. Slowly stir egg into soup; stir in sesame oil. Serve with hot chili oil and Sour Sauce.

Sour Sauce

Makes about ⅓ cup

3 tablespoons distilled white vinegar
1 tablespoon reduced-sodium tamari soy sauce
2 tablespoons packed light brown sugar

1. Mix all ingredients.

Asian Mushroom Soup with Soba Noodles

Thin egg noodles or spaghetti can be substituted for the soba noodles.

6 entrée servings

3 cups boiling water
1 ounce dried shiitake mushrooms
1 quart Chicken Stock (see p. 30) or chicken broth
1½ pounds cremini mushrooms, minced, divided
½ small onion, minced
1 clove garlic, minced
½ teaspoon dried thyme leaves
½ cup dry white wine (optional)
4 ounces soba noodles, cooked
8 ounces snow peas, trimmed
½ cup sliced radishes
1 tablespoon red wine vinegar
Salt and pepper, to taste

Per Serving:
Calories: 195
% calories from fat: 10
Protein (g): 11.3
Carbohydrate (g): 27.7
Fat (g): 2.3
Saturated fat (g): 0.5
Cholesterol (mg): 2.3
Sodium (mg): 118
Exchanges:
Milk: 0.0
Vegetable: 3.0
Fruit: 0.0
Bread: 1.0
Meat: 0.0
Fat: 1.0

1. Pour boiling water over shiitake mushrooms in bowl and let stand until softened, about 15 minutes. Drain; strain liquid through fine strainer and reserve. Finely chop mushrooms, discarding tough stems.
2. Combine shiitake mushrooms, reserved liquid, and remaining ingredients, except noodles, snow peas, radishes, vinegar, salt, and pepper, in 6-quart slow cooker; cover and cook on high 4 to 5 hours, adding noodles, snow peas, radishes, and vinegar during last 20 minutes. Season to taste with salt and pepper.

Asian Shiitake and Noodle Soup

Shiitake mushrooms and Japanese udon noodles give this soup its distinctive flavor.

6 first-course servings

1 quart reduced-sodium fat-free beef broth
2 cups thinly sliced shiitake or other wild
 mushrooms, tough stems discarded
1 cup each: chopped red bell pepper, carrots
2 green onions, sliced
1 teaspoon each: minced gingerroot, garlic, Asian
 sesame oil, tamari soy sauce
1 cup sliced packed fresh spinach
Salt and pepper, to taste
1 package (8½ ounces) Japanese udon noodles,
 cooked, warm

Per Serving:
Calories: 208
% calories from fat: 10
Protein (g): 10.7
Carbohydrate (g): 38
Fat (g): 2.4
Saturated fat (g): 0.1
Cholesterol (mg): 0
Sodium (mg): 215
Exchanges:
Milk: 0.0
Vegetable: 1.0
Fruit: 0.0
Bread: 2.0
Meat: 0.0
Fat: 0.5

1. Combine all ingredients, except sesame oil, soy sauce, spinach, salt, pepper, and noodles, in slow cooker; cover and cook on high 4 to 6 hours, adding sesame oil, soy sauce, and spinach during last 10 minutes. Season to taste with salt and pepper. Place noodles in bowls and ladle soup over.

SEVEN

Fish and Seafood Soups

- - - - - - - - - - - - -

Fish Soup with Vegetables

This soup is delicious served with warm crusty bread.

8 entrée servings

2 cans (28 ounces each) crushed tomatoes
1 can (16 ounces) tomato juice
¾ cup each: clam juice, dry white wine or water
1 cup chopped onion
3 medium potatoes, peeled, diced
½ cup each: chopped celery, sliced bell pepper,
   carrots, mushrooms
4 cloves garlic, minced
1 teaspoon dried oregano leaves
8 ounces each: cubed skinless halibut, sole, snapper
Salt and pepper, to taste

Per Serving:
Calories: 245
% calories from fat: 19
Protein (g): 20.3
Carbohydrate (g): 25.1
Fat (g): 5.2
Saturated fat (g): 0.8
Cholesterol (mg): 32.8
Sodium (mg): 275
Exchanges:
Milk: 0.0
Vegetable: 2.5
Fruit: 0.0
Bread: 1.0
Meat: 2.0
Fat: 0.0

1. Combine all ingredients, except fish, salt, and pepper, in 6-quart slow cooker; cover and cook on low 6 to 8 hours, adding fish during last 15 to 20 minutes. Season to taste with salt and pepper.

Hearty Fish Soup

This soup makes a hearty meal when served with salad and warm garlic bread.

6 entrée servings

3 cans (14½ ounces each) diced tomatoes, undrained
1 cup clam juice
½ cup dry white wine or clam juice
3 medium potatoes, peeled, diced
1 cup whole kernel corn
⅓ cup each: finely chopped onion, carrots,
   green bell pepper
2 teaspoons dried basil leaves
1 teaspoon dried oregano leaves
8 ounces each: cubed, skinless cod, flounder and
   orange roughy fillets
Salt and pepper, to taste

Per Serving:
Calories: 242
% calories from fat: 6
Protein (g): 23.3
Carbohydrate (g): 28.6
Fat (g): 1.7
Saturated fat (g): 0.3
Cholesterol (mg): 46.7
Sodium (mg): 204
Exchanges:
Milk: 0.0
Vegetable: 2.0
Fruit: 0.0
Bread: 1.0
Meat: 2.0
Fat: 0.0

1. Combine all ingredients, except fish, salt, and pepper, in slow cooker; cover and cook on low 6 to 8 hours, adding fish during last 15 to 20 minutes. Season to taste with salt and pepper.

Shortcut Fish Soup

This easy soup has a base of prepared spaghetti sauce.

6 entrée servings

1 jar (20 ounces) spaghetti sauce with herbs
1 cup each: clam juice, water
½ cup dry white wine or water
1 medium onion, thinly sliced
2 cloves garlic, minced
⅛–¼ teaspoon crushed red pepper
1 pound assorted skinless lean fish fillets
   (whitefish, cod, snapper, or flounder)
1 can (6 ounces) whole clams, undrained
Salt and pepper, to taste

Per Serving:
Calories: 227
% calories from fat: 24
Protein (g): 22.4
Carbohydrate (g): 17.6
Fat (g): 6.1
Saturated fat (g): 0.9
Cholesterol (mg): 49.4
Sodium (mg): 695
Exchanges:
Milk: 0.0
Vegetable: 3.0
Fruit: 0.0
Bread: 0.0
Meat: 3.0
Fat: 0.0

1. Combine all ingredients, except fish, clams, salt, and pepper, in slow cooker; cover and cook on high 3 to 4 hours, adding fish and clams with liquor during last 15 minutes. Season to taste with salt and pepper.

Fisherman's Catch

Choose two or three kinds of fish for this soup, selecting from cod, flounder, red snapper, salmon, halibut, or haddock.

6 entrée servings

1 can (14½ ounces) diced tomatoes, undrained
1 cup each: clam juice, dry white wine or clam juice
½ cup each: chopped onion, celery, carrot
1 teaspoon dried rosemary leaves
1½ pounds skinless fish fillets or steaks, cubed
⅓ cup each: chopped parsley, 2% reduced-fat milk
1 tablespoon cornstarch
Salt and pepper, to taste
6 slices Italian bread, toasted

Per Serving:
Calories: 302
% calories from fat: 13
Protein (g): 26.4
Carbohydrate (g): 25.1
Fat (g): 4.2
Saturated fat (g): 0.9
Cholesterol (mg): 48.7
Sodium (mg): 662
Exchanges:
Milk: 0.0
Vegetable: 2.0
Fruit: 0.0
Bread: 1.0
Meat 3.0
Fat: 0.0

1. Combine tomatoes with liquid, clam juice, wine, vegetables and rosemary in slow cooker; cover and cook on high 4 to 5 hours, adding fish and parsley during last 15 minutes. Stir in combined milk and cornstarch, stirring 2 to 3 minutes. Season to taste with salt and pepper. Place bread in soup bowls; ladle soup over.

Variation

Pesto Fish Soup—Make soup as above, adding 1 cup cooked cannellini or Great Northern beans, and omitting milk. Stir ¼ cup Basil Pesto (see p. 74) into soup before serving.

Light Salmon Bisque with Dill

Dill weed compliments the flavor of fresh salmon in this light, tempting bisque.

4 entrée servings

3 cups Fish Stock (see p. 33) or clam juice, divided
1½ cups peeled chopped potatoes
1 cup chopped onion
½ cup each: finely chopped celery, carrot
1 tablespoon tomato paste
1½ teaspoons dried dill weed
¼–½ teaspoon dry mustard
8–12 ounces skinless salmon steaks
1¼ cups whole milk, divided
2 tablespoons cornstarch
2–3 teaspoons lemon juice
Salt and white pepper, to taste

Per Serving:
Calories: 213
% calories from fat: 28
Protein (g): 20.3
Carbohydrate (g): 22.5
Fat (g): 6.7
Saturated fat (g): 2
Cholesterol (mg): 38.7
Sodium (mg): 508
Exchanges:
Milk: 0.0
Vegetable: 0.0
Fruit: 0.0
Bread: 1.5
Meat: 2.0
Fat: 0.0

1. Combine stock, vegetables, tomato paste, dill weed, and dry mustard in slow cooker; cover and cook on low 6 to 8 hours, adding salmon steaks and 1 cup milk during last 15 minutes. Remove salmon and reserve. Process soup in food processor or blender until smooth; return to slow cooker.
2. Flake reserved salmon into small pieces with a fork; add to slow cooker. Cover and cook on high 10 minutes; stir in combined remaining ¼ cup milk and cornstarch, stirring 2 to 3 minutes. Season to taste with lemon juice, salt, and white pepper.

Salmon–Wild Rice Soup

A very special soup—the rich flavors of salmon and wild rice are perfect complements to one another.

6 entrée servings

3 cups Easy Fish Stock (see p. 34) or chicken broth
1½ cups sliced mushrooms
¾ cup chopped onion
½ cup sliced celery
1 teaspoon minced garlic
½ teaspoon each: dry mustard, dried rosemary leaves
1 cup each: cooked wild rice, 2% reduced-fat milk, divided
1 pound skinless salmon steaks, cubed
1 tablespoon cornstarch
Salt and cayenne pepper, to taste
2 slices bacon, fried crisp, crumbled

Per Serving:
Calories: 200
% calories from fat: 20
Protein (g): 20.3
Carbohydrate (g): 15.5
Fat (g): 3.9
Saturated fat (g): 0.8
Cholesterol (mg): 44.7
Sodium (mg): 142
Exchanges:
Milk: 0.0
Vegetable: 0.0
Fruit: 0.0
Bread: 1.0
Meat: 2.0
Fat: 0.0

1. Combine stock, vegetables, garlic, dry mustard and rosemary in slow cooker; cover and cook on low 6 to 8 hours, adding wild rice and ½ cup milk during last 20 minutes. Add salmon; cover and cook on high 10 to 15 minutes. Stir in combined remaining ½ cup milk and cornstarch, stirring 2 to 3 minutes. Season to taste with salt and cayenne pepper. Sprinkle each bowl of soup with bacon.

Variation

Tuna–Rice Soup—Make soup as above, substituting tarragon for the rosemary, tuna steaks for the salmon, and white rice for the wild rice. Omit dry mustard; season to taste with lemon juice.

Zucchini and Tuna Soup

An easy soup, made with canned tuna—also delicious with canned salmon.

4 entrée servings

5 cups Chicken Stock (see p. 30) or chicken broth
2 cups chopped zucchini
1 cup each: finely chopped onion, celery
1 tablespoon minced garlic
2 cans (6½ ounces each) tuna in water, drained
2 cups whole milk, divided
2 tablespoons cornstarch
1–2 teaspoons lemon juice
1–1½ cups (4–6 ounces) shredded Cheddar cheese
Salt and pepper, to taste
Hot pepper sauce

Per Serving:
Calories: 224
% calories from fat: 33
Protein (g): 25.5
Carbohydrate (g): 11.6
Fat (g): 8.2
Saturated fat (g): 4.9
Cholesterol (mg): 42.3
Sodium (mg): 822
Exchanges:
Milk: 0.0
Vegetable: 0.0
Fruit: 0.0
Bread: 1.0
Meat: 3.0
Fat: 0.0

1. Combine stock, vegetables, and garlic in slow cooker; cover and cook on high 4 hours, adding tuna and 1 cup milk during last 30 minutes. Stir in combined remaining 1 cup milk and cornstarch, stirring 2 to 3 minutes. Season to taste with lemon juice; add cheese, stirring until melted. Season to taste with salt, pepper, and hot pepper sauce.

Maryland Crab Soup

Shrimp can be substituted for crabmeat for a delicious variation of this soup.

6 entrée servings

1½ quarts fat-free beef broth
2½ cups each: clam juice, coarsely chopped
   canned undrained plum tomatoes
3 cups peeled diced red potatoes
1 cup whole kernel corn
2 each: finely chopped large onions, carrots, ribs
   celery
2 bay leaves
½ teaspoon dry mustard
1–2 tablespoons Old Bay seasoning
12 ounces fresh crabmeat, cartilage and shell
   discarded, cut into pieces (½-inch)
2 slices bacon, fried crisp, crumbled
½ cup finely chopped parsley
Salt and pepper, to taste

Per Serving:
Calories: 206
% calories from fat: 12
Protein (g): 22.8
Carbohydrate (g): 29.7
Fat (g): 3.0
Saturated fat (g): 0.6
Cholesterol (mg): 36.7
Sodium (mg): 1371
Exchanges:
Milk: 0.0
Vegetable: 0.0
Fruit: 0.0
Bread: 2.0
Meat: 2.0
Fat: 0.0

1. Combine all ingredients, except crab, bacon, parsley, salt, and pepper, in 6-quart slow cooker; cover and cook on low 6 to 8 hours, adding crab, bacon, and parsley during last 20 minutes. Discard bay leaves; season to taste with salt and pepper.

Georgia Fish Soup

Peanut butter is the surprise ingredient in this unusual fish soup.

6 entrée servings

1½ cups each: clam juice, water
1 can (28 ounces) diced tomatoes, undrained
1 cup thinly sliced onion
½ cup chopped green bell pepper
2 teaspoons each: minced garlic, chili powder
½ teaspoon dried thyme leaves
⅓–½ cup peanut butter
1 package (10 ounces) frozen sliced okra, thawed
1 pound skinless cod fillets, cubed
Salt and pepper, to taste
Hot pepper sauce

Per Serving:
Calories: 210
% calories from fat: 28
Protein (g): 19.9
Carbohydrate (g): 19.2
Fat (g): 6.7
Saturated fat (g): 1.3
Cholesterol (mg): 32.4
Sodium (mg): 166
Exchanges:
Milk: 0.0
Vegetable: 3.0
Fruit: 0.0
Bread: 0.0
Meat: 2.0
Fat: 0.5

1. Combine all ingredients, except peanut butter, okra, cod, salt, pepper, and hot pepper sauce, in slow cooker; cover and cook on high 4 hours, adding peanut butter and okra during last 30 minutes and cod during last 15 minutes. Season to taste with salt and pepper; serve with hot pepper sauce.

Cioppino

Our version of this California-style soup is made with shellfish.

6 entrée servings

1 can (14½ ounces) diced tomatoes, undrained
1 cup each: clam juice, water
½ cup dry white wine or clam juice
1 cup each: thinly sliced onion, green onions,
  green bell pepper
1 tablespoon each: minced garlic, olive oil
½ teaspoon each: dried tarragon, thyme, and
  rosemary leaves
1 bay leaf
1 pound crabmeat or firm white fish, cubed
12 ounces shrimp, peeled, deveined
18 clams in shells, scrubbed
Salt and pepper, to taste

Per Serving:
Calories: 210
% calories from fat: 19
Protein (g): 24.1
Carbohydrate (g): 10.2
Fat (g): 4.3
Saturated fat (g): 0.6
Cholesterol (mg): 130.6
Sodium (mg): 276
Exchanges:
Milk: 0.0
Vegetable: 2.0
Fruit: 0.0
Bread: 0.0
Meat: 3.0
Fat: 0.0

1. Combine all ingredients, except seafood, salt, and pepper, in slow cooker; cover and cook on low 6 to 8 hours, adding seafood during last 15 to 20 minutes. Discard bay leaf and any clams that have not opened; season to taste with salt and pepper.

Cioppino Mediterranean

The popular California fish soup is given an Italian accent.

6 entrée servings

2 cans (14½ ounces each) diced tomatoes, undrained
1 can (6 ounces) tomato paste
1 cup clam juice or water
½ cup dry red wine or clam juice
¼ cup each: chopped green bell pepper, onion
1 clove garlic, minced
1 teaspoon each: dried oregano and basil leaves
2 cans (6½ ounces each) minced clams, undrained
8 ounces each: cubed skinless sole fillet, peeled
  deveined shrimp
Salt and pepper, to taste

Per Serving:
Calories: 206
% calories from fat: 19
Protein (g): 24.5
Carbohydrate (g): 14.9
Fat (g): 4.3
Saturated fat (g): 0.6
Cholesterol (mg): 95.3
Sodium (mg): 345
Exchanges:
Milk: 0.0
Vegetable: 0.0
Fruit: 0.0
Bread: 1.0
Meat: 3.0
Fat: 0.0

1. Combine all ingredients, except seafood, salt, and pepper, in slow cooker; cover and cook on low 6 to 8 hours, adding clams and liquor during last hour and remaining seafood during last 15 to 20 minutes. Season to taste with salt and pepper.

Shrimp Bisque

If you're in a hurry, substitute 1½ cups each clam juice and water for the Fish Stock.

4 entrée servings

1½ quarts Fish Stock (see p. 33) or chicken broth
¼ cup tomato paste
1½ cups chopped onion
3–4 teaspoons curry powder
½ teaspoon paprika
1 cup 2% reduced-fat milk
2 tablespoons cornstarch
1½ pounds shrimp, peeled, deveined
1½ cups finely chopped tomatoes
Salt and cayenne pepper, to taste
Garlic Croutons (see p. 51)

Per Serving:
Calories: 219
% calories from fat: 17
Protein (g): 23.0
Carbohydrate (g): 20.8
Fat (g): 4.1
Saturated fat (g): 0.8
Cholesterol (mg): 134.3
Sodium (mg): 482
Exchanges:
Milk: 0.0
Vegetable: 0.0
Fruit: 0.0
Bread: 1.5
Meat: 2.0
Fat: 0.0

1. Combine all ingredients, except shrimp, tomatoes, salt, cayenne pepper and Garlic Croutons, in 6-quart slow cooker; cover and cook on high 4 hours. Stir in combined milk and cornstarch, stirring 2 to 3 minutes; add shrimp and cook 10 minutes. Process soup in food processor or blender until smooth; return to slow cooker and add tomatoes. Cover and cook on high 10 minutes. Season to taste with salt and pepper; sprinkle each bowl of soup with Garlic Croutons.

Southern Gumbo with Shrimp

Enjoy this lighter version of the classic Southern soup.

6 entrée servings

1 quart Fish Stock (see p. 33) or chicken broth
3 cups finely chopped tomatoes
2 cups sliced okra
¾ cup each: sliced onion, green bell pepper
1 bay leaf
⅛–¼ teaspoon crushed red pepper
12 ounces each: cubed, skinless red snapper fillets,
   peeled deveined large shrimp
1 teaspoon gumbo file powder
Salt and pepper, to taste
2 cups cooked rice, warm

Per Serving:
Calories: 239
% calories from fat: 8
Protein (g): 25.9
Carbohydrate (g): 26
Fat (g): 2
Saturated fat (g): 0.4
Cholesterol (mg): 111.8
Sodium (mg): 146
Exchanges:
Milk: 0.0
Vegetable: 2.0
Fruit: 0.0
Bread: 1.0
Meat: 2.0
Fat: 0.0

1. Combine stock, vegetables, bay leaf, and crushed red pepper in 6-quart slow cooker; cover and cook on high 4 hours, adding seafood and file powder during last 10 minutes. Discard bay leaf; season to taste with salt and pepper. Serve over rice in bowls.

Mexican Corn and Shrimp Soup

Epazote is a popular Mexican herb that can be purchased in Mexican groceries. If using dried epazote, add to the slow cooker at the beginning of cooking; add fresh epazote at the end. A combination of fresh cilantro and oregano makes a flavorful substitute.

4 entrée servings

2 cups reduced-sodium vegetable broth
5 cups whole kernel corn
¾ cup chopped onion
1 each: minced medium jalapeño chili, clove garlic
2 tablespoons chopped fresh or 2 teaspoons dried
   epazote leaves
12 ounces shrimp, peeled, deveined
Salt and cayenne pepper, to taste
Roasted Red Pepper Sauce (see p. 66)

Per Serving:
Calories: 190
% calories from fat: 14
Protein (g): 22.6
Carbohydrate (g): 19.3
Fat (g): 3.1
Saturated fat (g): 0.5
Cholesterol (mg): 130.8
Sodium (mg): 332
Exchanges:
Milk: 0.0
Vegetable: 0.0
Fruit: 0.0
Bread: 1.0
Meat: 2.0
Fat: 0.0

1. Combine all ingredients, except epazote, shrimp, salt, cayenne pepper, and Roasted Red Pepper Sauce, in slow cooker; cover and cook on high 4 to 5 hours. Process soup and epazote in food processor or blender until smooth; return to slow cooker. Add shrimp; cover and cook on high 10 minutes. Season to taste with salt and cayenne pepper. Serve warm or refrigerate and serve chilled; swirl about 3 tablespoons Roasted Red Pepper Sauce into each bowl of soup.

Caribbean-Style Flounder Soup

Annatto seeds, which are often used in Caribbean and Mexican cooking, impart a subtle flavor and deep yellow color to foods they are cooked with. They're available in Mexican groceries and in many large supermarkets.

4 entrée servings

2 teaspoons canola oil
1 tablespoon annatto seeds (optional)
1 medium onion, thinly sliced
2 cups reduced-sodium fat-free chicken broth
1 can (14½ ounces) diced tomatoes, undrained
1 sweet potato, peeled, cubed
1 teaspoon dried thyme leaves
1 cup frozen peas, thawed
1 pound skinless flounder fillets, cubed (¾-inch)
3–4 teaspoons lemon juice
Salt and pepper, to taste

Per Serving:
Calories: 240
% calories from fat: 16
Protein (g): 28.5
Carbohydrate (g): 21.4
Fat (g): 4.2
Saturated fat (g): 0.8
Cholesterol (mg): 60.1
Sodium (mg): 227
Exchanges:
Milk: 0.0
Vegetable: 0.0
Fruit: 0.0
Bread: 1.0
Meat: 3.0
Fat: 0.0

1. Heat oil in large saucepan over medium-high heat; add annatto seeds and cook until oil is bright yellow, about 3 minutes. Remove seeds with slotted spoon and discard. Add onion to saucepan; sauté 2 minutes.
2. Combine onion mixture, broth, tomatoes with liquid, sweet potato, and thyme in slow cooker; cover and cook on high 4 to 5 hours, adding peas and flounder during last 15 minutes. Season to taste with lemon juice, salt, and pepper.

Niçoise Fish Soup

Fennel seeds add a special flavor dimension to this great soup.

8 entrée servings

3 cups water
1 cup clam juice
2 cups chopped tomatoes
1 cup chopped onion
1 tablespoon minced garlic
½ teaspoon each: dried thyme leaves, crushed
    fennel seeds, ground turmeric
1 bay leaf
2 pounds assorted lean skinless fish fillets or steaks
    (halibut, haddock, red snapper, cod, etc.), cubed
Salt and cayenne pepper, to taste
Bruschetta (see p. 43)

Per Serving:
Calories: 240
% calories from fat: 20
Protein (g): 27
Carbohydrate (g): 19.9
Fat (g): 5.4
Saturated fat (g): 0.8
Cholesterol (mg): 36.1
Sodium (mg): 309
Exchanges:
Milk: 0.0
Vegetable: 1.0
Fruit: 0.0
Bread: 1.0
Meat: 2.5
Fat: 0.0

1. Combine all ingredients, except fish, salt, cayenne pepper, and Bruschetta, in slow cooker; cover and cook on high 4 to 5 hours, adding fish during last 15 to 20 minutes. Discard bay leaf; season to taste with salt and cayenne pepper. Serve with Bruschetta.

Fish Soup Marseilles

Fresh fennel gives this soup its authentic "south of France" flavor; substitute 2 teaspoons fennel seeds if you prefer.

6 entrée servings

3–4 cups Mediterranean Stock (see p. 36)
    or vegetable broth
1 can (14½ ounces) Italian-style stewed tomatoes
½ cup each: chopped onion, sliced fennel bulb
1 tablespoon minced garlic
1 cup uncooked orzo or other small soup pasta
8 ounces each: cubed skinless whitefish fillets,
    peeled deveined shrimp
Salt and pepper, to taste

Per Serving:
Calories: 231
% calories from fat: 14
Protein (g): 16.5
Carbohydrate (g): 29.9
Fat (g): 3.4
Saturated fat (g): 0.5
Cholesterol (mg): 63.4
Sodium (mg): 227
Exchanges:
Milk: 0.0
Vegetable: 0.0
Fruit: 0.0
Bread: 2.0
Meat: 2.0
Fat: 0.0

1. Combine stock, tomatoes, onion, fennel, and garlic
in slow cooker; cover and cook on high 4 to 5 hours, adding orzo during last 20 minutes and seafood during last 10 minutes. Season to taste with salt and pepper.

Tuscan Fish Soup

Along the Tuscan coast, each town boasts its own incomparable fish soup.

6 entrée servings

1 quart chicken broth
½ cup dry red wine or chicken broth
3 pounds tomatoes, peeled, seeded, chopped
2 medium onions, chopped
3 cloves garlic, minced
1 teaspoon each: dried oregano, sage, and
   rosemary leaves
⅛–¼ teaspoon crushed red pepper
1¼ pounds assorted skinless fish fillets or steaks
   (sole, salmon, red snapper, tuna, or halibut), cubed
6 ounces shrimp, peeled, deveined
Salt and pepper, to taste
6 slices Italian bread, toasted
2 cloves garlic, halved

Per Serving:
Calories: 337
% calories from fat: 19
Protein (g): 28.6
Carbohydrate (g): 33.7
Fat (g): 7.1
Saturated fat (g): 1.1
Cholesterol (mg): 82.2
Sodium (mg): 337
Exchanges:
Milk: 0.0
Vegetable: 2.5
Fruit: 0.0
Bread: 1.5
Meat: 3.0
Fat: 0.0

1. Combine all ingredients, except seafood, salt, pepper, bread, and halved garlic cloves, in slow cooker; cover and cook on high 4 to 5 hours, adding seafood during last 15 minutes. Season to taste with salt and pepper. Rub bread with garlic cloves; place in soup bowls and ladle soup over.

Mediterranean-Style Shrimp and Vegetable Soup

A fragrant vegetable soup with a citrus accent.

6 first-course servings

1 can (14½ ounces) diced tomatoes, undrained
1 can (8 ounces) tomato sauce
2 cups vegetable broth
½ cup dry white wine or orange juice
2 cups sliced mushrooms
½ cup each: chopped onion, green bell pepper
3 cloves garlic, minced
2 strips orange zest (3 x ½ inches)
2 bay leaves
¾ teaspoon each: dried marjoram and savory leaves
½ teaspoon crushed fennel seeds
1 pound shrimp, peeled, deveined
Salt and pepper, to taste

Per Serving:
Calories: 121
% calories from fat: 8
Protein (g): 14.8
Carbohydrate (g): 10.7
Fat (g): 1.1
Saturated fat (g): 0.2
Cholesterol (mg): 115.6
Sodium (mg): 211
Exchanges:
Milk: 0.0
Vegetable: 2.0
Fruit: 0.0
Bread: 0.0
Meat: 1.0
Fat: 0.0

1. Combine all ingredients, except shrimp, salt, and pepper, in slow cooker; cover and cook on high 3 to 4 hours, adding shrimp last 15 minutes. Discard bay leaves; season to taste with salt and pepper.

Kakavia

Kakavia is the Greek version of the French bouillabaisse.

12 entrée servings

1 can (28 ounces) crushed tomatoes
1 quart clam juice
½ cup dry white wine or clam juice
2 cups chopped onions
2 ribs celery, chopped
1 tablespoon minced garlic
2 leeks (white parts only), sliced
3 large carrots, chopped
3 bay leaves
1 teaspoon dried thyme leaves
3 to 4 tablespoons lemon juice
2 pounds skinless fish fillets (halibut, salmon, cod, or red snapper), cubed
12 each: clams and mussels, scrubbed
12 ounces shrimp, peeled, deveined
Salt and pepper, to taste

Per Serving:
Calories: 203
% calories from fat: 14
Protein (g): 32.6
Carbohydrate (g): 11.2
Fat (g): 3.3
Saturated fat (g): 0.6
Cholesterol (mg): 121.0
Sodium (mg): 805
Exchanges:
Milk: 0.0
Vegetable: 0.0
Fruit: 0.0
Bread: 0.5
Meat: 4.0
Fat: 0.0

1. Combine all ingredients, except seafood, salt, and pepper, in 6-quart slow cooker; cover and cook on low 6 to 8 hours, adding seafood during last 15 to 20 minutes. Discard bay leaves and any clams or mussels that have not opened; season to taste with salt and pepper.

Spanish Fish Soup

This unique soup is flavored with ground almonds and thickened with bread.

8 entrée servings

1 quart clam juice
½ cup dry white wine or clam juice
1 cup chopped onion
1 teaspoon paprika
½ teaspoon crushed cumin seeds
¾ cup fresh bread crumbs
⅓ cup ground almonds
2 pounds skinless halibut, cubed
2 hard-cooked egg yolks, finely chopped
1 cup 2% reduced-fat milk
2 tablespoons cornstarch
Salt and cayenne pepper, to taste
8 thin slices lemon
Chopped parsley, as garnish

Per Serving:
Calories: 275
% calories from fat: 23
Protein (g): 28.1
Carbohydrate (g): 11.5
Fat (g): 6.5
Saturated fat (g): 1
Cholesterol (mg): 90
Sodium (mg): 356
Exchanges:
Milk: 0.0
Vegetable: 0.0
Fruit: 0.0
Bread: 1.0
Meat: 3.0
Fat: 1.0

1. Combine clam juice, wine, onion, paprika, cumin seeds, bread crumbs, and almonds in slow cooker; cover and cook on high 3 to 4 hours, adding fish and egg yolks the last 10 minutes. Stir in combined milk and cornstarch, stirring 2 to 3 minutes. Season to taste with salt and pepper. Garnish each bowl of soup with a lemon slice; sprinkle with parsley.

Portuguese-Style Fisherman's Soup

This soup is attractive and robustly seasoned.

6 entrée servings

2 cans (14½ ounces each) diced tomatoes, undrained
1½ cups reduced-sodium fat-free chicken broth
¾ cup dry white wine or water
2 large onions, finely chopped
⅓ cup each: chopped carrot, celery, red bell pepper
1 large clove garlic, minced
3–4 medium red potatoes, unpeeled, cubed
1 bay leaf
2 teaspoons each: chili powder, paprika
Pinch saffron threads, crumbled (optional)
½ teaspoon each: celery seeds, dried thyme leaves
Pinch crushed red pepper
24 fresh mussels, scrubbed
1½ pounds skinless cod, haddock, or whitefish fillets, cubed
8 ounces shrimp, peeled, deveined
Salt and cayenne pepper, to taste

Per Serving:
Calories: 362
% calories from fat: 16
Protein (g): 43.1
Carbohydrate (g): 27.3
Fat (g): 6.4
Saturated fat (g): 1.1
Cholesterol (mg): 132.5
Sodium (mg): 736
Exchanges:
Milk: 0.0
Vegetable: 0.0
Fruit: 0.0
Bread: 2.0
Meat: 4.0
Fat: 0.0

1. Combine all ingredients, except seafood, salt, and cayenne pepper, in 6-quart slow cooker; cover and cook on low 6 to 8 hours, adding seafood last 15 to 20 minutes. Discard bay leaf; season to taste with salt and cayenne pepper.

Caldo de Pescado

This South American fish soup includes a medley of vegetables and seafood, with a flavor accent of orange.

10 entrée servings

4 cups Easy Fish Stock (see p. 34) or 2 cups each
   clam juice and water
1 can (28 ounce) crushed tomatoes, undrained
2 cups each: chopped onions, peeled sliced potatoes
1 large red bell pepper, chopped
2 large ears corn, cut into pieces (1-inch)
3 cloves garlic, minced
1 teaspoon each: grated orange zest, ground turmeric
1 pound skinless red snapper fillets, cubed
12 ounces large shrimp, peeled, deveined
Salt and cayenne pepper, to taste

Per Serving:
Calories: 173
% calories from fat: 15
Protein (g): 19.4
Carbohydrate (g): 17.9
Fat (g): 2.8
Saturated fat (g): 0.5
Cholesterol (mg): 68
Sodium (mg): 389
Exchanges:
Milk: 0.0
Vegetable: 0.0
Fruit: 0.0
Bread: 1.0
Meat: 2.0
Fat: 0.0

1. Combine all ingredients, except seafood, salt, and cayenne pepper, in 6-quart slow cooker; cover and cook on low 6 to 8 hours, adding seafood during last 15 minutes. Season to taste with salt and cayenne pepper.

Sea Scallop and Pasta Soup

Small bay scallops or other seafood can be used in this colorful soup.

6 entrée servings

2 cups reduced-sodium fat-free chicken broth
1 can (14½ ounces) Italian plum tomatoes,
   undrained, chopped
½ cup each: dry white wine or chicken broth,
   chopped onion, diced green and red pepper
½ teaspoon minced garlic
8 ounces mushrooms, sliced
4 ounces uncooked small soup pasta
1 pound sea scallops, halved
¼–½ cup (1–2 ounces) grated Parmesan cheese
Salt and pepper, to taste

Per Serving:
Calories: 323
% calories from fat: 20
Protein (g): 24.1
Carbohydrate (g): 37.4
Fat (g): 74
Saturated fat (g): 1.3
Cholesterol (mg): 34.8
Sodium (mg): 382
Exchanges:
Milk: 0.0
Vegetable: 1.0
Fruit: 0.0
Bread: 2.0
Meat: 2.5
Fat: 0.0

1. Combine all ingredients, except pasta, scallops, cheese, salt, and pepper, in slow cooker; cover and cook on low 6 to 8 hours, adding pasta during last 30 minutes and scallops during last 15 minutes. Stir in cheese; season to taste with salt and pepper.

Squash and Scallop Soup

Acorn or butternut squash can also be used in this recipe.

6 entrée servings

1 cup reduced-sodium fat-free chicken broth
2 cups peeled cubed butternut squash
1 cup chopped celery
½ cup chopped onion
¼ teaspoon minced gingerroot
2 cups whole milk, divided
1 pound bay scallops
2 tablespoons cornstarch
1–2 teaspoons Worcestershire sauce
Salt and white pepper, to taste

Per Serving:
Calories: 161
% calories from fat: 17
Protein (g): 19.3
Carbohydrate (g): 14.5
Fat (g): 3.1
Saturated fat (g): 0.5
Cholesterol (mg): 33.6
Sodium (mg): 276
Exchanges:
Milk: 0.0
Vegetable: 0.0
Fruit: 0.0
Bread: 1.0
Meat: 2.0
Fat: 0.0

1. Combine broth, vegetables, and gingerroot in slow cooker; cover and cook on high 3 to 4 hours, adding 1½ cups milk and scallops during last 15 minutes. Stir in combined remaining ½ cup milk and cornstarch, stirring 2 to 3 minutes. Season to taste with Worcestershire sauce, salt, and white pepper.

Oyster and Mushroom Bisque

A creamy mushroom soup is enhanced with oysters and sherry.

4 first-course servings

1 cup reduced-sodium fat-free chicken broth
1 pint oysters, drained, liquor reserved
8 ounces mushrooms, sliced
1 cup whole milk
¼ cup dry sherry or water
2 tablespoons cornstarch
Salt and white pepper, to taste
Oyster crackers

Per Serving:
Calories: 140
% calories from fat: 23
Protein (g): 8.6
Carbohydrate (g): 14.2
Fat (g): 3.4
Saturated fat (g): 0.9
Cholesterol (mg): 67.4
Sodium (mg): 219
Exchanges:
Milk: 0.0
Vegetable: 0.0
Fruit: 0.0
Bread: 1.0
Meat: 0.5
Fat: 1.0

1. Combine broth, reserved oyster liquor, and mushrooms in slow cooker; cover and cook on high 2 to 3 hours, adding milk during last 30 minutes and oysters during last 15 minutes. Stir in combined sherry and cornstarch, stirring 2 to 3 minutes. Season to taste with salt and white pepper. Serve with oyster crackers (not included in nutritional data).

Mardi Gras Oyster Soup

Oysters, a New Orleans favorite, are combined with clam juice and wine in this special celebration soup.

6 first-course servings

1 quart clam juice
1½ pounds shucked fresh or canned oysters,
   liquor reserved
⅔ cup chopped onion
½ cup dry white wine or clam juice
2 tablespoons cornstarch
Salt and cayenne pepper, to taste
Chopped chives, as garnish

Per Serving:
Calories: 208
% calories from fat: 19
Protein (g): 32.3
Carbohydrate (g): 13.4
Fat (g): 5.2
Saturated fat (g): 1.2
Cholesterol (mg): 113.4
Sodium (mg): 1309
Exchanges:
Milk: 0.0
Vegetable: 0.0
Fruit: 0.0
Bread: 1.0
Meat: 3.0
Fat: 0.0

1. Combine clam juice, reserved oyster liquor, and onion in slow cooker; cover and cook on high 2 to 3 hours. Stir in oysters and combined wine and cornstarch; cover and cook 15 minutes. Season to taste with salt and cayenne pepper. Sprinkle each bowl of soup with chives.

Chinese Oyster Soup

Enjoy the Oriental flavor accents in this oyster soup.

4 first-course servings

2½ cups Oriental Stock (see p. 36) or chicken broth
2 tablespoons soy sauce
2 cups sliced Napa cabbage
8 ounces mushrooms, sliced
½ cup fresh or canned bean sprouts
4 green onions, sliced
1 tablespoon minced gingerroot
1 pint fresh or canned oysters, shucked, undrained
Salt and pepper, to taste

Per Serving:
Calories: 72
% calories from fat: 15
Protein (g): 6.2
Carbohydrate (g): 10.2
Fat (g): 1.3
Saturated fat (g): 0.3
Cholesterol (mg): 14.2
Sodium (mg): 444
Exchanges:
Milk: 0.0
Vegetable: 0.0
Fruit: 0.0
Bread: 0.5
Meat: 1.0
Fat: 0.0

1. Combine all ingredients, except oysters, salt, and pepper, in slow cooker; cook on low 6 to 8 hours, adding oysters and liquor during last 10 to 15 minutes. Season to taste with salt and pepper.

Clam Soup

You can make this dish with mussels as well, or make the soup with 1 pound peeled deveined shrimp, adding during the last 10 minutes of cooking.

4 entrée servings

1 cup each: clam juice or chicken broth, tomato
   sauce, dry white wine or clam juice
3 large cloves garlic
⅛–¼ teaspoon crushed red pepper
1 teaspoon each: dried oregano and thyme leaves
4 dozen clams (littlenecks or cherrystones), scrubbed
¼ cup minced parsley
Salt and pepper, to taste
4 slices Italian bread, toasted

Per Serving:
Calories: 275
% calories from fat: 26
Protein (g): 15.2
Carbohydrate (g): 25.9
Fat (g): 7.9
Saturated fat (g): 1.1
Cholesterol (mg): 28.9
Sodium (mg): 575
Exchanges:
Milk: 0.0
Vegetable: 0.0
Fruit: 0.0
Bread: 2.0
Meat: 2.0
Fat: 0.5

1. Combine all ingredients, except clams, parsley,
salt, pepper, and bread, in slow cooker; cover and cook on high 4 hours,
adding clams and parsley during last 15 minutes. Discard any clams that
have not opened; season soup to taste with salt and pepper. Serve broth
and clams in shallow bowls with toasted bread.

Mussel Soup with Saffron

Brightly colored bits of vegetables and a savory broth complement the flavor of the mussels in this tempting, attractive soup.

4 first-course servings

2 cups clam juice
¾ cup dry white wine or water
½ cup each: finely chopped carrot, celery, tomato
4 green onions, sliced
1 large clove garlic, minced
1 bay leaf
10 saffron threads, crumbled (optional)
2 pounds mussels, scrubbed
Salt and cayenne pepper, to taste

Per Serving:
Calories: 146
% calories from fat: 25
Protein (g): 16
Carbohydrate (g): 5.8
Fat (g): 3.9
Saturated fat (g): 0.3
Cholesterol (mg): 58.3
Sodium (mg): 402
Exchanges:
Milk: 0.0
Vegetable: 0.0
Fruit: 0.0
Bread: 0.5
Meat: 2.0
Fat: 0.0

1. Combine all ingredients, except mussels, salt, and cayenne pepper, in slow cooker; cover and cook on high 4 hours, adding mussels during last 15 minutes. Discard bay leaf and any mussels that have not opened; season to taste with salt and cayenne pepper.

Potato-Mussel Saffron Soup

Saffron lends a beautiful color and flavor to this soup.

8 first-course servings

1 quart water
1 can (14½ ounces) crushed tomatoes
3 each: medium peeled diced potatoes, thinly sliced
   carrots, small leeks (white parts only), minced
   cloves garlic, shallots
2 bay leaves
1 teaspoon fennel seeds
¼ teaspoon saffron (optional)
½ cup chopped parsley
32 mussels, scrubbed
Salt and white pepper, to taste

Per Serving:
Calories: 222
% calories from fat: 30
Protein (g): 8.3
Carbohydrate (g): 31.4
Fat (g): 7.6
Saturated fat (g): 1.9
Cholesterol (mg): 45.9
Sodium (mg): 401
Exchanges:
Milk: 0.0
Vegetable: 3.0
Fruit: 0.0
Bread: 1.0
Meat: 0.0
Fat: 1.5

1. Combine all ingredients, except parsley, mussels, salt, and pepper; cover and cook on low 6 to 7 hours. Turn heat to high and cook 10 minutes; add parsley and mussels. Cover and cook 15 minutes; discard bay leaves and any mussels that have not opened. Season to taste with salt and pepper.

EIGHT

Vegetarian
Soups

- - - - - - - - - - - - -

Cream of Artichoke and Mushroom Soup

L *Shiitake or cremini mushrooms can be substituted for the portobello mushrooms.*

4 first-course servings

2 cups vegetable broth
1 package (9 ounces) frozen artichoke hearts,
    thawed, finely chopped
¾ cup chopped portobello mushrooms
2 tablespoons chopped onion
1 cup light cream or whole milk
2 tablespoons cornstarch
Salt and white pepper, to taste
Paprika, as garnish

Per Serving:
Calories: 239
% calories from fat: 46
Protein (g): 9.0
Carbohydrate (g): 23.6
Fat (g): 12.1
Saturated fat (g): 7.3
Cholesterol (mg): 43.3
Sodium (mg): 393
Exchanges:
Milk: 0.0
Vegetable: 0.0
Fruit: 0.0
Bread: 1.5
Meat: 1.0
Fat: 1.5

1. Combine all ingredients, except cream, cornstarch,
salt, white pepper, and paprika, in slow cooker; cover and cook on high 3
to 4 hours. Stir in combined cream and cornstarch, stirring 2 to 3 minutes.
Season to taste with salt and white pepper. Sprinkle each bowl of soup
with paprika.

Brussels Sprouts Soup

L *A perfect fall soup, when tiny fresh Brussels sprouts are available.*

4 first-course servings

1 pound Brussels sprouts, halved
½ cup chopped onion
2 teaspoons minced garlic
½ teaspoon dried rosemary leaves
1 cup each: vegetable broth, 2% reduced-fat milk
Salt and white pepper, to taste
Ground nutmeg, as garnish

Per Serving:
Calories: 136
% calories from fat: 23
Protein (g): 7.6
Carbohydrate (g): 21.3
Fat (g): 3.8
Saturated fat (g): 0.9
Cholesterol (mg): 1.9
Sodium (mg): 113
Exchanges:
Milk: 0.0
Vegetable: 4.0
Fruit: 0.0
Bread: 0.0
Meat: 0.0
Fat: 0.5

1. Combine Brussels sprouts, onion, garlic, rosemary,
and broth in slow cooker; cover and cook on high
until Brussels sprouts are very tender, 2 to 4 hours.
Process soup and milk in food processor or blender until smooth;
season to taste with salt and white pepper. Sprinkle each bowl of
soup lightly with nutmeg.

Cabbage Soup

L

Easy to make and satisfying to eat.

6 entrée servings

4 cups vegetable broth
1 small head cabbage, thinly sliced
2 large onions, thinly sliced
2 carrots, sliced
1 large potato, peeled, sliced
1 bay leaf
½ teaspoon each: dried dill weed, rosemary leaves
1 cup reduced-fat sour cream
2 tablespoons cornstarch
Salt and pepper, to taste

Per Serving:
Calories: 146
% calories from fat: 20
Protein (g): 8.4
Carbohydrate (g): 24.2
Fat (g): 3.7
Saturated fat (g): 2.2
Cholesterol (mg): 11.2
Sodium (mg): 436
Exchanges:
Milk: 0.0
Vegetable: 0.0
Fruit: 0.0
Bread: 1.5
Meat: 0.0
Fat: 1.0

1. Combine all ingredients, except sour cream, cornstarch, salt, and pepper, in 6-quart slow cooker; cover and cook on low 6 to 8 hours. Discard bay leaf; stir in combined sour cream and cornstarch, stirring until thickened, 2 to 3 minutes. Season to taste with salt and pepper.

Variation

Cabbage and White Bean Soup—Make recipe as above, adding 1 can (15 ounces) rinsed drained Great Northern beans and 1 can (14½ ounces) undrained diced tomatoes. Reduce vegetable broth to 3 cups and omit sour cream and cornstarch.

Creamed Corn Soup

L

Garnish bowls of soup generously with finely chopped cilantro or parsley.

4 entrée servings

3½ cups vegetable broth
½ cup chopped onion
1 medium Idaho potato, peeled, cubed
2 cloves garlic, minced
½ teaspoon ground coriander
1 can (15½ ounces) whole kernel corn, drained
2 medium tomatoes, chopped
1 cup reduced-fat milk
2 tablespoons cornstarch
Salt and cayenne pepper, to taste
Paprika, as garnish

Per Serving:
Calories: 238
% calories from fat: 8
Protein (g): 7.7
Carbohydrate (g): 45.7
Fat (g): 2.3
Saturated fat (g): 0.4
Cholesterol (mg): 1
Sodium (mg): 443
Exchanges:
Milk: 0.0
Vegetable: 3.0
Fruit: 0.0
Bread: 2.0
Meat: 0.0
Fat: 0.5

1. Combine broth, onion, potato, garlic, and coriander in slow cooker; cover and cook on high 4 hours. Process soup in food processor or blender until almost smooth; return to slow cooker. Add corn and tomatoes; cover and cook on high 30 minutes. Stir in combined milk and cornstarch, stirring 2 to 3 minutes. Season to taste with salt and pepper; sprinkle each bowl of soup with paprika.

Variation

Latin-American Corn and Avocado Soup—Make soup as above, omitting tomatoes and adding ½ teaspoon crushed saffron with the broth. Beat 2 eggs with 4 ounces reduced-fat cream cheese and 2 tablespoons chili sauce. Whisk into puréed soup. Garnish each bowl of soup with avocado slices.

Easy Mexican Corn and Bean Soup

V

This spicy soup is quick and easy to prepare.

4 entrée servings

2½ cups tomato juice
1 can (14½ ounces) diced tomatoes, undrained, puréed
2 cups each: whole kernel corn, canned kidney beans
¾ cup each: finely chopped large onion, green bell pepper
1 clove garlic, minced
1 tablespoon chili powder
1 teaspoon each: ground cumin, sugar
Salt and pepper, to taste

Per Serving:
Calories: 232
% calories from fat: 14
Protein (g): 10.6
Carbohydrate (g): 44.2
Fat (g): 3.8
Saturated fat (g): 0.3
Cholesterol (mg): 0
Sodium (mg): 45
Exchanges:
Milk: 0.0
Vegetable: 2.0
Fruit: 0.0
Bread: 2.0
Meat: 0.0
Fat: 0.5

1. Combine all ingredients, except salt and pepper, in slow cooker; cover and cook on high 3 to 4 hours. Season to taste with salt and pepper.

Black Magic Garlic Chowder

L *Garlic lovers take note—this is a colorful chowder with plenty of palate-appealing garlic flavor.*

4 first-course servings

1 can (15 ounces) black beans, rinsed, drained, divided
1 can (14 ounces) reduced-sodium vegetable broth, divided
1 garlic bulb, cloves peeled, thinly sliced or chopped
2 small serrano chilies, seeded, minced
1 pound plum tomatoes, coarsely chopped
Salt and pepper, to taste
Chili Croutons (recipe follows)
¼ cup each: chopped parsley, reduced-fat sour cream

Per Serving:
Calories: 195
% calories from fat: 15
Protein (g): 9.2
Carbohydrate (g): 39.9
Fat (g): 3.9
Saturated fat (g): 0.4
Cholesterol (mg): 0
Sodium (mg): 503
Exchanges:
Milk: 0.0
Vegetable: 1.0
Fruit: 0.0
Bread: 2.0
Meat: 0.0
Fat: 0.5

1. Process ¾ cup beans and ¾ cup broth in food processor or blender until smooth. Combine puréed and whole black beans with remaining broth, garlic, chilies, and tomatoes in slow cooker; cover and cook on low 6 to 8 hours. Season to taste with salt and pepper. Top each bowl of chowder with Chili Croutons, parsley, and a dollop of sour cream.

Chili Croutons

Makes 1½ cups

1½ cups cubed firm or day-old French bread (½-inch)
Vegetable cooking spray
Chili powder

1. Spray bread cubes with cooking spray; sprinkle lightly with chili powder and toss. Arrange in single layer in baking pan; bake at 375 degrees until browned, 8 to 10 minutes, stirring occasionally.

Garlic Vegetable Soup

v

A real garlic lover's soup—add more garlic, if you like!

8 entrée servings

2 quarts water
1 can (15 ounces) navy or Great Northern beans,
  rinsed, drained
1 pound tomatoes, peeled, seeded, coarsely chopped
1 cup each: diced new potatoes, coarsely chopped
  carrots, cut green beans (½-inch), chopped leeks
  (white parts only)
½ cup chopped celery
6 large cloves garlic, minced
2 tablespoons each: tomato paste, dried basil leaves
Salt and pepper, to taste

Per Serving:
Calories: 148
% calories from fat: 14
Protein (g): 6.4
Carbohydrate (g): 27.5
Fat (g): 2.4
Saturated fat (g): 0.4
Cholesterol (mg): 0
Sodium (mg): 222
Exchanges:
Milk: 0.0
Vegetable: 2.0
Fruit: 0.0
Bread: 2.0
Meat: 0.0
Fat: 0.5

1. Combine all ingredients, except salt and pepper, in 6-quart slow cooker; cover and cook on low 6 to 8 hours. Season to taste with salt and pepper.

Savory Mushroom and Barley Soup

v

Use of quick-cooking barley speeds preparation. Other grains, such as wild rice or oat groats, can be substituted for the barley; cook according to package directions and add to soup during the last 30 minutes of cooking time.

4 entrée servings

3 cups water
1 can (14½ ounces) diced tomatoes,
  undrained
¾ cup each: chopped onion, celery, carrots
1 teaspoon dried savory leaves
¾ teaspoon crushed fennel seeds
2 cups sliced cremini or white mushrooms
½ cup quick-cooking barley
Salt and pepper, to taste

Per Serving:
Calories: 151
% calories from fat: 8
Protein (g): 5.6
Carbohydrate (g): 32.1
Fat (g): 1.4
Saturated fat (g): 0.1
Cholesterol (mg): 0
Sodium (mg): 53
Exchanges:
Milk: 0.0
Vegetable: 2.0
Fruit: 0.0
Bread: 1.5
Meat: 0.0
Fat: 0.0

1. Combine all ingredients, except barley, salt, and pepper, in slow cooker; cook on high 4 to 6 hours, adding barley during last 30 minutes. Season to taste with salt and pepper.

Variations

Savory Mushroom and Kale Soup—Make recipe above, adding 2 to 3 cloves sliced garlic. Omit barley; add 3 cups torn spinach during last 15 minutes of cooking time.

Maple Bean and Mushroom Soup—Make recipe above, adding 2 cloves minced garlic, 1 to 2 tablespoons maple syrup, and 1 can (15 ounces) drained Great Northern beans; omit barley.

Shiitake-Portobello Chowder

L

Celebrate the rich mushroom, cheese, and wine flavors in this chowder.

4 entrée servings

3 cups reduced-sodium vegetable broth
4 shallots, thinly sliced
2 large potatoes, cubed (¼-inch)
2 cups each: sliced shiitake mushroom caps, cubed
  portobello mushrooms
2 tablespoons Marsala wine (optional)
Salt and white pepper, to taste
¼ cup (1 ounce) shredded Gruyère or Swiss cheese

Per Serving:
Calories: 162
% calories from fat: 26
Protein (g): 5.6
Carbohydrate (g): 24.7
Fat (g): 5
Saturated fat (g): 1.8
Cholesterol (mg): 7.8
Sodium (mg): 114
Exchanges:
Milk: 0.0
Vegetable: 2.0
Fruit: 0.0
Bread: 1.0
Meat: 0.0
Fat: 1.0

1. Combine all ingredients, except wine, salt, white pepper, and cheese, in slow cooker; cover and cook on high to 4 to 5 hours. Stir in wine; season to taste with salt and white pepper. Sprinkle each bowl of soup with cheese.

Sweet Red Pepper Soup

L

Use jarred roasted peppers for this soup, or roast 3 medium red bell peppers.

4 first-course servings

1 can (14½ ounces) vegetable broth
1 jar (15 ounces) roasted red bell peppers, drained
1 cup tomato juice
1 medium onion, chopped
½ small jalapeño chili, seeded, minced
1 clove garlic, minced
½ teaspoon dried marjoram leaves
Salt and pepper, to taste
¼–½ cup reduced-fat sour cream
Sliced green onions, as garnish

Per Serving:
Calories: 92
% calories from fat: 3
Protein (g): 2.2
Carbohydrate (g): 21.8
Fat (g): 0.3
Saturated fat (g): 0
Cholesterol (mg): 2.5
Sodium (mg): 465
Exchanges:
Milk: 0.0
Vegetable: 0.0
Fruit: 0.0
Bread: 1.5
Meat: 0.0
Fat: 0.0

1. Combine all ingredients, except salt, pepper, sour cream, and green onions, in slow cooker; cover and cook on high 2 to 3 hours. Process soup in food processor or blender; season to taste with salt and pepper. Serve warm or refrigerate and serve chilled; top each bowl of soup with a dollop of sour cream and sprinkle with green onions.

Potato Pistou

A rich and flavorful soup with a velvety texture.

6 entrée servings

2 quarts water
2 cups chopped onions
5 tomatoes, peeled, seeded, chopped
4 red potatoes, peeled, diced
¾ cup halved green beans
2 medium zucchini, sliced
½ teaspoon dried marjoram leaves
1½ cups packed basil leaves
5 cloves garlic, halved
¼ cup (1 ounce) grated Parmesan cheese
Salt and pepper, to taste

Per Serving:
Calories: 136
% calories from fat: 10
Protein (g): 5.1
Carbohydrate (g): 28.4
Fat (g): 1.6
Saturated fat (g): 0.7
Cholesterol (mg): 2.6
Sodium (mg): 106
Exchanges:
Milk: 0.0
Vegetable: 2.0
Fruit: 0.0
Bread: 1.0
Meat: 0.0
Fat: 0.0

1. Combine water, vegetables, and marjoram in 6-quart slow cooker; cover and cook on high 3 to 4 hours. Process soup in food processor or blender until smooth; add basil, garlic, and cheese, processing until smooth. Return soup to slow cooker; cover and cook on high 15 minutes; season to taste with salt and pepper.

Vichyssoise

L *This classic French potato soup is traditionally served chilled, but it's good warm, too!*

4 entrée servings

6 cups reduced-sodium vegetable broth
2 pounds Idaho potatoes, peeled, cubed
¾ cup each: sliced leeks or green onions, celery
½ teaspoon dried thyme leaves
Salt and white pepper, to taste
6 tablespoons reduced-fat sour cream
Snipped chives, as garnish

Per Serving:
Calories: 282
% calories from fat: 20
Protein (g): 6.2
Carbohydrate (g): 51.5
Fat (g): 6.6
Saturated fat (g): 1.2
Cholesterol (mg): 0
Sodium (mg): 134
Exchanges:
Milk: 0.0
Vegetable: 1.0
Fruit: 0.0
Bread: 3.0
Meat: 0.0
Fat: 1.0

1. Combine all ingredients, except salt, white pepper, sour cream, and chives, in slow cooker; cover and cook on high 4 to 5 hours. Process soup in food processor or blender until smooth; season to taste with salt and white pepper. Serve warm, or refrigerate and serve chilled; top each bowl of soup with 1 tablespoon sour cream and sprinkle with chives.

Cucumber Vichyssoise with Roasted Red Pepper Swirl

L *Yogurt gives this soup a refreshing tang and roasted peppers add a flavor perk.*

4 first-course servings

1½ cups Basic Vegetable Stock (see p. 34)
  or vegetable broth
1 cup water
1 cup each: chopped onion, cubed peeled
  potato, sliced peeled cucumber
1 teaspoon ground cumin
1½ cups plain yogurt
2 tablespoons cornstarch
Salt and white pepper, to taste
Roasted Red Pepper Swirl (recipe follows)

Per Serving:
Calories: 87
% calories from fat: 7
Protein (g): 3.3
Carbohydrate (g): 17.7
Fat (g): 0.7
Saturated fat (g): 0.3
Cholesterol (mg): 1.4
Sodium (mg): 49
Exchanges:
Milk: 0.0
Vegetable: 2.0
Fruit: 0.0
Bread: 0.5
Meat: 0.0
Fat: 0.0

1. Combine all ingredients, except yogurt, cornstarch, salt, pepper, and Roasted Red Pepper Swirl, in slow cooker; cover and cook on high 2 to 3 hours. Stir in combined yogurt and cornstarch, stirring, 2 to 3 minutes. Process mixture in food processor or blender until smooth; season to taste with salt and white pepper. Serve warm or refrigerate and serve chilled. Spoon 2 tablespoons Roasted Red Pepper Swirl into each bowl of soup and swirl with knife.

Roasted Red Pepper Swirl

Makes about ¾ cup

¾ cup jarred roasted red peppers
½ small pickled jalapeño chili
1 clove garlic
2 teaspoons balsamic vinegar
2 to 4 tablespoons water

1. Process all ingredients, except water, in food processor or blender until smooth; add water, if needed, to make desired consistency.

Variation

Avocado and Chipotle Vichyssoise—Make recipe as above, omitting cucumber. Add 2 medium avocados, ¼–½ small chipotle chili in adobo, and 2 tablespoons dry sherry to soup in food processor. Garnish each bowl of soup with 1 tablespoon each crumbled feta cheese and chopped cilantro.

Hot Bean Gazpacho

L

Enjoy this hot bean soup, served gazpacho-style.

8 entrée servings

2 cans (15 ounces each) pinto beans, rinsed,
    drained
1 quart tomato juice
1 cup each: thick and chunky salsa, sliced celery
½ cup each: sliced green onions, chopped
    green bell pepper
2 teaspoons minced roasted garlic
3–4 tablespoons lime juice
Salt and pepper, to taste
½ cup each: chopped avocado, peeled seeded
    cucumber, reduced-fat sour cream, Croutons
    (see p. 38)

Per Serving:
Calories: 260
% calories from fat: 13
Protein (g): 12.9
Carbohydrate (g): 47.1
Fat (g): 3.8
Saturated fat (g): 0.2
Cholesterol (mg): 0
Sodium (mg): 642
Exchanges:
Milk: 0.5
Vegetable: 2.0
Fruit: 0.0
Bread: 2.5
Meat: 0.5
Fat: 0.0

1. Combine all ingredients, except lime juice, salt, pepper, avocado, cucumber, sour cream, and Croutons, in slow cooker; cover and cook on high 3 to 4 hours. Season to taste with lime juice, salt, and pepper. Process soup in food processor or blender until smooth. Serve hot or refrigerate and serve chilled. Mix avocado and cucumber into soup; garnish each bowl of soup with a dollop of sour cream and Croutons.

Tomato-Vegetable Soup with Sour Cream

Homemade croutons are delicious and easy to make (see Index).

L

6 entrée servings

1¼ quarts vegetable broth
½ cup dry white wine or water
8 large tomatoes, peeled, quartered
1 large onion, thinly sliced
1 cup each: cubed peeled cooked potatoes
  and butternut squash
1 bay leaf
2 teaspoons dried basil leaves
½ cup frozen peas, thawed
1½ cups reduced-fat sour cream, divided
2 tablespoons cornstarch
Salt and pepper, to taste
Plain croutons, as garnish

Per Serving:
Calories: 302
% calories from fat: 10
Protein (g): 12.2
Carbohydrate (g): 54.3
Fat (g): 3.8
Saturated fat (g): 0.6
Cholesterol (mg): 0.1
Sodium (mg): 684
Exchanges:
Milk: 0.0
Vegetable: 2.0
Fruit: 0.0
Bread: 3.0
Meat: 2.0
Fat: 0.5

1. Combine all ingredients, except peas, sour cream, cornstarch, salt, pepper, and croutons, in 6-quart slow cooker; cover and cook on high 4 to 5 hours, adding peas during last 20 minutes. Stir in combined 1 cup sour cream and cornstarch, stirring 2 to 3 minutes. Discard bay leaf; season to taste with salt and pepper. Garnish each bowl of soup with remaining ½ cup sour cream and croutons.

Orange-Scented Squash Soup

L

Subtly seasoned with orange and spices, this delicious soup can be served warm or chilled.

6 first-course servings

1½ cups water
½ cup orange juice
¾ cup chopped onion
3 pounds winter yellow squash (hubbard, butternut, or acorn), peeled, cubed
1 large, tart cooking apple, peeled, cubed
1 strip orange zest (3 x ½-inch)
1 teaspoon ground cinnamon
¼ teaspoon each: ground nutmeg, cloves
1½–2 cups 2% reduced-fat milk
2 tablespoons cornstarch
Salt and white pepper, to taste
6 thin orange slices
Snipped chives, as garnish

Per Serving:
Calories: 144
% calories from fat: 8
Protein (g): 4.1
Carbohydrate (g): 30.2
Fat (g): 1.4
Saturated fat (g): 0.3
Cholesterol (mg): 0
Sodium (mg): 64
Exchanges:
Milk: 0.0
Vegetable: 0.0
Fruit: 0.0
Bread: 2.0
Meat: 0.0
Fat: 0.0

1. Combine all ingredients, except milk, cornstarch, salt, white pepper, orange slices, and chives, in slow cooker; cover and cook on high 3 to 4 hours, adding 1 cup milk during last 30 minutes. Stir in remaining ½ cup milk and cornstarch, stirring 2 to 3 minutes; discard orange zest. Process soup in food processor or blender until smooth; season to taste with salt and white pepper. Serve warm or refrigerate and serve chilled; garnish each bowl of soup with an orange slice and chives.

Variation

Winter Squash Soup—Make recipe as above, omitting cloves, orange zest, and orange juice. Add ¼ teaspoon each ground ginger and cumin, and 1 cup apple cider; reduce reduced-fat milk to ½–1 cup.

Sherried Winter Squash Soup

Any type of winter squash can be used in this Italian-accented soup.

4 entrée servings

1¼ quarts Roasted Vegetable Stock (see p. 35) or
   vegetable broth
1 can (28 ounces) diced tomatoes, undrained
1 large butternut squash, peeled, seeded, cubed
4 medium potatoes, cubed
½ cup chopped onion
2 cloves garlic, minced
1 teaspoon dried basil leaves
½ teaspoon dried thyme leaves
½ cup chopped parsley
2 to 4 tablespoons dry sherry (optional)
Salt and pepper, to taste

Per Serving:
Calories: 260
% calories from fat: 10
Protein (g): 5.9
Carbohydrate (g): 51.4
Fat (g): 2.9
Saturated fat (g): 0.4
Cholesterol (mg): 0
Sodium (mg): 51
Exchanges:
Milk: 0.0
Vegetable: 1.0
Fruit: 0.0
Bread: 3.0
Meat: 0.0
Fat: 0.5

1. Combine all ingredients, except parsley, sherry, salt and pepper, in slow cooker; cover and cook on high 4 to 5 hours, adding parsley during last 20 minutes. Season to taste with dry sherry, salt, and pepper.

Cider Soup

An unusual soup, and a great choice for sipping when you come in from the winter cold!

6 first-course servings

1½ cups reduced-sodium vegetable broth
1 cup apple cider
2½ cups thinly sliced leeks (white part only)
¼ cup chopped celery
2 tablespoons chopped green bell pepper
½ teaspoon dried thyme leaves
¼ teaspoon dry mustard
2–3 teaspoons Worcestershire sauce
⅓ cup 2% reduced-fat milk
2 tablespoons cornstarch
1 cup (4 ounces) shredded reduced-fat Cheddar cheese
Salt and white pepper, to taste
Finely chopped thyme or parsley

Per Serving:
Calories: 123
% calories from fat: 35
Protein (g): 8.6
Carbohydrate (g): 11.4
Fat (g): 4.8
Saturated fat (g): 2.6
Cholesterol (mg): 13.5
Sodium (mg): 234
Exchanges:
Milk: 0.0
Vegetable: 0.0
Fruit: 1.0
Bread: 0.0
Meat: 1.0
Fat: 0.5

1. Combine all ingredients, except milk, cornstarch, cheese, salt, pepper, and thyme, in slow cooker; cook on high 2 to 3 hours. Stir in combined milk and cornstarch, stirring 2 to 3 minutes. Add cheese, stirring until melted; season to taste with salt and white pepper. Sprinkle each bowl of soup with thyme.

Variation

Caramel Apple Soup—Make soup as above. Sauté 2 cups peeled sliced apples in 1 to 2 tablespoons margarine 2 minutes; sprinkle with ⅓ cup packed light brown sugar. Cook over medium heat, stirring occasionally, until apples are tender, 3 to 4 minutes. Spoon apples into bottoms of soup bowls; ladle warm soup over.

Green Vegetable Soup

 Sun-dried tomato pesto is an excellent alternative to basil pesto in this colorful soup.

6 first-course servings

1 quart vegetable broth
½ cup each: thinly sliced green cabbage, chopped
   celery, onion, broccoli florets, cut green beans,
   cubed zucchini, potato
½ cup uncooked ditalini
Salt and pepper, to taste
¼ cup basil pesto

1. Combine all ingredients, except ditalini, salt, pepper, and pesto, in slow cooker; cover and cook on high 4 to 5 hours, adding ditalini during last 30 minutes. Season to taste with salt and pepper. Stir in basil pesto.

Per Serving:
Calories: 196
% calories from fat: 34
Protein (g): 6.2
Carbohydrate (g): 26.6
Fat (g): 7.4
Saturated fat (g): 1.6
Cholesterol (mg): 5
Sodium (mg): 620
Exchanges:
Milk: 0.0
Vegetable: 0.0
Fruit: 0.0
Bread: 2.0
Meat: 0.0
Fat: 1.5

Mother Hubbard's Soup

 Use this opportunity to clean out the refrigerator and pantry!

8 entrée servings

4 cans (14½ ounces each) reduced-sodium
vegetable broth
1 can (14½ ounces) diced tomatoes with
roasted garlic, undrained
2 cups each: cubed potatoes, sliced cabbage, small
broccoli florets
1 cup each: sliced carrots, cubed peeled sweet potato
2 ribs celery, sliced
½ teaspoon each: dried thyme, rosemary, and
oregano leaves
1 cup each: frozen thawed peas, whole kernel corn
Salt and pepper, to taste

Per Serving:
Calories: 172
% calories from fat: 2
Protein (g): 6.4
Carbohydrate (g): 37.9
Fat (g): 0.5
Saturated fat (g): 0.1
Cholesterol (mg): 0
Sodium (mg): 337
Exchanges:
Milk: 0.0
Vegetable: 1.0
Fruit: 0.0
Bread: 2.0
Meat: 0.0
Fat: 0.0

1. Combine all ingredients, except peas, corn, salt, and pepper, in 6-quart
slow cooker; cover and cook on low 6 to 8 hours, adding peas and corn
during last 30 minutes. Season to taste with salt and pepper.

Everything-but-Cabbage Soup

 *Load your shopping cart with healthy vegetables to make this tasty soup—
it's OK to add cabbage too!*

6 entrée servings

1½ quarts vegetable broth
1 can (14½ ounces) petite-diced tomatoes,
undrained, coarsely chopped
3 cups peeled diced baking potatoes
¾ cup each: cut green beans, chopped onion,
carrots, celery, sweet potatoes, butternut squash,
zucchini
1 tablespoon tomato paste
1 teaspoon each: white wine vinegar, sugar
1 bay leaf
¾ teaspoon each: dried thyme and marjoram leaves
½ cup each: whole kernel corn, frozen thawed peas
Salt and pepper, to taste

Per Serving:
Calories: 324
% calories from fat: 10
Protein (g): 9.9
Carbohydrate (g): 70
Fat (g): 4
Saturated fat (g): 0.6
Cholesterol (mg): 0
Sodium (mg): 567
Exchanges:
Milk: 0.0
Vegetable: 5.0
Fruit: 0.0
Bread: 2.5
Meat: 0.0
Fat: 0.0

1. Combine all ingredients, except corn, peas, salt, and pepper, in 6-quart slow cooker; cover and cook on low 6 to 8 hours, adding corn and peas during last 20 minutes. Discard bay leaf; season to taste with salt and pepper.

Mediterranean Vegetable Soup

V

A fragrant vegetable soup with a citrus accent.

6 first-course servings

1 quart Mediterranean Stock (see p. 36) or
  vegetable broth
1 can (14½ ounces) diced tomatoes, undrained
1 can (8 ounces) tomato sauce
1 pound light firm tofu, drained, cubed (¾-inch)
2 cups sliced mushrooms
½ cup each: chopped onion, green bell pepper
3 cloves garlic, minced
2 strips orange zest (3 x ½ inch)
2 bay leaves
1 teaspoon dried marjoram leaves
¼–½ teaspoon crushed fennel seeds
Salt and pepper, to taste

Per Serving:
Calories: 94
% calories from fat: 14
Fat (g): 1.5
Saturated fat (g): 0.2
Cholesterol (mg): 0.0
Sodium (mg): 296
Protein (g): 7
Carbohydrate (g):11.3
Exchanges:
Milk: 0.0
Vegetable: 0.0
Fruit: 0.0
Bread: 1.0
Meat: 1.0
Fat: 0.0

1. Combine all ingredients, except salt and pepper, in 6-quart slow cooker; cover and cook on low 6 to 8 hours. Discard bay leaves; season to taste with salt and pepper.

Vegetarian Chili

V *Cooked, crumbled vegetarian burgers can be added to this chili for additional texture.*

6 entrée servings

2 cans (15 ounces each) kidney beans, rinsed, drained
1 can (15 ounces) garbanzo beans, rinsed, drained
1 cup tomato purée
2 large tomatoes, peeled, seeded
1 cup each: chopped onion, carrots, mushrooms
½ cup each: chopped green bell pepper, celery
2 cloves garlic, minced
1 teaspoon ground cumin
1–2 tablespoons chili powder
Salt and pepper, to taste

Per Serving:
Calories: 266
% calories from fat: 13
Protein (g): 12.8
Carbohydrate (g): 47.5
Fat (g): 4.1
Saturated fat (g): 0.5
Cholesterol (mg): 0
Sodium (mg): 646
Exchanges:
Milk: 0.0
Vegetable: 1.0
Fruit: 0.0
Bread: 3.0
Meat: 0.0
Fat: 0.5

1. Combine all ingredients, except salt and pepper, in slow cooker; cover and cook on high 3 to 4 hours. Season to taste with salt and pepper.

Vegetable-Lentil Chili

V *Lentils add great texture to this meatless chili.*

4 entrée servings

1 quart vegetable broth
1 cup water
1 can (14½ ounces) diced tomatoes,
  undrained
¾ cup dried brown lentils
1 cup each: whole kernel corn, chopped onion,
  red or green bell pepper
⅓ cup each: sliced carrot, celery
1 clove garlic, minced
1 tablespoon chili powder
¾ teaspoon ground cumin
1 bay leaf
Salt and pepper, to taste

Per Serving:
Calories: 271
% calories from fat: 13
Protein (g): 13.3
Carbohydrate (g): 48.4
Fat (g): 3.9
Saturated fat (g): 0.5
Cholesterol (mg): 0
Sodium (mg): 541
Exchanges:
Milk: 0.0
Vegetable: 0.0
Fruit: 0.0
Bread: 3.0
Meat: 1.0
Fat: 0.0

1. Combine all ingredients, except salt and pepper, in slow cooker; cover and cook on high 3 to 4 hours. Discard bay leaf; season to taste with salt and pepper.

Vegetarian Chili in Black and White

 Black and white beans give this vegetarian chili a great texture. Its warm flavor comes from toasted cumin seeds.

4 entrée servings

2 cups tomato juice
1 cup vegetable broth
2 tablespoons tomato paste
1 can (15 ounces) each: rinsed drained black beans,
   Great Northern or navy beans
1 medium onion, chopped
1 anaheim chili, seeded, minced
1 teaspoon each: paprika, toasted cumin seeds
1½ cups cooked wild rice
Salt and pepper, to taste

Per Serving:
Calories: 300
% calories from fat: 6
Protein (g): 16.3
Carbohydrate (g): 60.6
Fat (g): 2.2
Saturated fat (g): 0.4
Cholesterol (mg): 0
Sodium (mg): 427
Exchanges:
Milk: 0.0
Vegetable: 0.0
Fruit: 0.0
Bread: 4.0
Meat: 0.0
Fat: 0.5

1. Combine all ingredients, except wild rice, salt, and pepper, in slow cooker; cover and cook on low 6 to 8 hours, adding wild rice during last 30 minutes. Season to taste with salt and pepper.

Chili-Bean and Corn Chili

This easy chili is spicy! For a less spicy chili, substitute 1 can rinsed drained pinto or kidney beans for the chili beans.

4 first-course servings

1 can (15 ounces) chili beans, undrained
1 cup reduced-sodium vegetable broth
1 can (14½ ounces) Italian-style diced
   tomatoes, undrained, chopped
1 cup each: chopped green bell peppers,
   whole kernel corn
1 medium onion, chopped
2 teaspoons minced garlic
2–3 teaspoons chili powder
Salt and pepper, to taste

Per Serving:
Calories: 150
% calories from fat: 7
Protein (g): 8.8
Carbohydrate (g): 31.5
Fat (g): 1.3
Saturated fat (g): 0.1
Cholesterol (mg): 0
Sodium (mg): 524
Exchanges:
Milk: 0.0
Vegetable: 0.0
Fruit: 0.0
Bread: 2.0
Meat: 0.0
Fat: 0.0

1. Combine all ingredients, except salt and pepper, in slow cooker; cover and cook on low 6 to 8 hours. Season to taste with salt and pepper.

Black Bean, Rice, and Corn Chowder

v *This vegetarian chili is simple, speedy, and tastes superb.*

4 entrée servings

1 can (28 ounces) crushed tomatoes, undrained
1 can (16 ounces) black beans, rinsed, drained
½ cup whole kernel corn
1½ cups chopped onions
1 each: large chopped red bell pepper, minced jalapeño chili
1 tablespoon each: minced garlic, chili powder
1 teaspoon ground allspice
½ cup cooked rice
Salt and pepper, to taste

Per Serving:
Calories: 219
% calories from fat: 9
Protein (g): 10.1
Carbohydrate (g): 49.2
Fat (g): 2.7
Saturated fat (g): 0.3
Cholesterol (mg): 0
Sodium (mg): 726
Exchanges:
Milk: 0.0
Vegetable: 3.0
Fruit: 0.0
Bread: 3.0
Meat: 0.0
Fat: 0.0

1. Combine all ingredients, except rice, salt, and pepper, in slow cooker; cover and cook on high 4 to 5 hours, adding rice during last 15 minutes. Season to taste with salt and pepper.

Pigeon Pea Chowder with Spanish Onions

v *This hearty chowder reflects the Spanish colonial culinary tradition that makes Cuban and Puerto Rican cooking delightfully distinctive. Sofrito, a popular Cuban seasoning, can be found in the ethnic section of many supermarkets.*

4 entrée servings

2 cups reduced-sodium vegetable broth
1 can (15 ounces) green pigeon peas, rinsed, drained
2 cups shredded zucchini
6 tomatillos, husked, diced
1 large potato, unpeeled, cubed
1 large Spanish onion, coarsely chopped
4 shallots, thinly sliced
¼ cup sofrito sauce (optional)
Salt and pepper, to taste

Per Serving:
Calories: 262
% calories from fat 22
Protein (g): 10.7
Carbohydrate (g): 42.1
Fat (g): 6.7
Saturated fat (g): 1.7
Cholesterol (mg): 5
Sodium (mg): 350
Exchanges:
Milk: 0.0
Vegetable: 0.0
Fruit: 0.0
Bread: 3.0
Meat: 0.0
Fat: 1.0

1. Combine all ingredients, except sofrito sauce, salt, and pepper, in slow cooker; cover and cook on low 6 to 8 hours. Stir in sofrito sauce; season to taste with salt and pepper.

Southwest-Style Potato-Corn Chowder con Queso

L

Add 1 teaspoon minced jalapeño chili to this satisfying soup, if you like!

4 entrée servings

3 cups Basic Vegetable Stock (see p. 34) or vegetable
   broth
3½ cups peeled cubed potatoes
⅔ cup chopped onion
1 package (10 ounces) frozen whole kernel corn
1 can (4 ounces) chopped mild green chilies, drained
1 bay leaf
½ teaspoon each: dry mustard, dried marjoram leaves
2 cups 2% reduced-fat milk
3 tablespoons cornstarch
¾ cup (3 ounces) shredded reduced-fat sharp
   Cheddar cheese
Salt and white pepper, to taste
Chopped chives, as garnish

Per Serving:
Calories: 324
% calories from fat: 18
Protein (g): 12.8
Carbohydrate (g): 55.3
Fat (g): 6.8
Saturated fat (g): 3
Cholesterol (mg): 18.1
Sodium (mg): 648
Exchanges:
Milk: 0.5
Vegetable: 0.0
Fruit: 0.0
Bread: 3.0
Meat: 0.0
Fat: 1.0

1. Combine all ingredients, except milk, cornstarch, cheese, salt, white pepper, and chives, in slow cooker; cook on high 3 to 4 hours. Stir in combined milk and cornstarch; stirring 2 to 3 minutes. Discard bay leaf; add cheese, stirring until melted. Season to taste with salt and pepper. Garnish each bowl of soup with chives.

French Vegetable Chowder with Pistou

L *Pistou, the French version of Italy's pesto, gives this chowder a lively flavor boost. Bon appétit!*

4 entrée servings

1 can (14½ ounces) vegetable broth, divided
1 can (15 ounces) Great Northern or navy beans, rinsed, drained
1 cup each: cut wax beans, small cauliflower florets, cubed zucchini, and potato
2 carrots, thinly sliced
3 plum tomatoes, coarsely chopped
4 scallions, sliced
1 cup cooked elbow macaroni
Pistou (recipe follows)
Salt and pepper, to taste

Per Serving:
Calories: 254
% calories fromo;; fat: 17
Protein (g): 12
Carbohydrate (g): 46.7
Fat (g): 5.2
Saturated fat (g): 1.8
Cholesterol (mg): 5.3
Sodium (mg): 581
Exchanges:
Milk: 0.0
Vegetable: 3.0
Fruit: 0.0
Bread: 2.0
Meat: 0.0
Fat: 1.0

1. Combine all ingredients, except macaroni, Pistou, salt, and pepper, in slow cooker; cover and cook on low 6 to 8 hours, adding macaroni and Pistou during last 15 minutes. Season to taste with salt and pepper.

Pistou

Makes about ⅔ cup

1 tablespoon minced garlic
2 teaspoons olive oil
½ cup finely chopped basil
¼ cup (1 ounce) crumbled blue cheese

1. Combine all ingredients in bowl; mash with fork.

Chili Sin Carne

L

The variety of toppings makes this chili fun to serve—add other toppings, too, such as chopped bell peppers and tomatoes, and chopped fresh oregano or cilantro.

6–8 entrée servings

6 cans (14½ ounces each) diced tomatoes, undrained
1 can (15 ounces) red kidney beans, rinsed, drained
1 can (6 ounces) tomato paste
¾ cup beer or water
⅔ package (12-ounce size) vegetarian ground beef
1 cup each: chopped onions, green bell pepper
2 cloves garlic, minced
1 tablespoon each: packed light brown sugar, unsweetened cocoa
1–2 tablespoons chili powder
1–2 teaspoons each: ground cumin, dried oregano leaves
¼ teaspoon ground cloves
Salt and pepper, to taste
Toppings: shredded reduced-fat Cheddar cheese, sour cream, thinly sliced green onions

Per Serving:
Calories: 245
% calories from fat: 5
Protein (g): 19.2
Carbohydrate (g): 40.3
Fat (g): 1.4
Saturated fat (g): 0.2
Cholesterol (mg): 0
Sodium (mg): 723
Exchanges:
Milk: 0.0
Vegetable: 2.0
Fruit: 0.0
Bread: 2.0
Meat: 1.0
Fat: 0.0

1. Combine all ingredients, except salt, pepper, and toppings, in 6-quart slow cooker; cover and cook on low 6 to 8 hours. Season to taste with salt and pepper. Serve with toppings (not included in nutritional data).

Variations

Veggie Mac—Make recipe as above, adding 1½ cups cooked elbow macaroni or chili mac pasta during last 30 minutes of cooking time. Omit toppings.

Southwest Chili—Make recipe as above, substituting black or pinto beans for the kidney beans and adding 1 minced jalapeño chili. Garnish each serving with a sprinkling of crushed tortilla chips and chopped cilantro leaves.

Sweet Potato Chipotle Chili

V

Chipotle chilies are dried, smoked jalapeño chilies. When canned, they are in adobo sauce, which is made with ground chilies and spices. The chilies have a distinctive smoky flavor; taste before adding more, as they can be fiercely hot!

4 entrée servings

2 cans (15 ounces each) black beans, rinsed, drained
1 can (14 ½ ounces) chili-style chunky tomatoes, undrained
1 cup water or vegetable broth
3 cups peeled cubed sweet potatoes
1 cup each: chopped onion, green bell pepper
2 teaspoons minced gingerroot
1 teaspoon each: minced garlic, crushed cumin seeds
½–1 small chipotle chili in adobo sauce, chopped
Salt, to taste

Per Serving:
Calories: 213
% calories from fat: 14
Protein (g): 8.6
Carbohydrate (g): 44.8
Fat (g): 3.9
Saturated fat (g): 0.6
Cholesterol (mg): 0
Sodium (mg): 452
Exchanges:
Milk: 0.0
Vegetable: 0.0
Fruit: 0.0
Bread: 3.0
Meat: 0.0
Fat: 0.5

1. Combine all ingredients, except chipotle chili and salt, in slow cooker; cover and cook on low 6 to 8 hours, adding chipotle chili during last 30 minutes. Season to taste with salt.

Cincinnati Chili with an Attitude

L

Midwesterners have a penchant for chili that's thick and spicy and served over spaghetti. This vegetarian version uses lentils, tomatoes, and easy-to-find seasonings.

6 entrée servings

2 cups vegetable broth
1 can (14½ ounces) crushed tomatoes
½ cup dried lentils
1 medium onion, chopped
1 tablespoon minced garlic
1 teaspoon olive oil
1 tablespoon each: chili powder, unsweetened cocoa
½ teaspoon ground cinnamon
¼ teaspoon ground allspice
Salt and pepper, to taste
12 ounces linguine, cooked, warm
Toppings: kidney beans, chopped onion and bell pepper, shredded reduced-fat Cheddar cheese

Per Serving:
Calories: 277
% calories from fat: 7
Protein (g): 13.4
Carbohydrate (g): 53
Fat (g): 2.5
Saturated fat (g): 0.2
Cholesterol (mg): 0
Sodium (mg): 308
Exchanges:
Milk: 0.0
Vegetable: 2.0
Fruit: 0.0
Bread: 3.0
Meat: 0.0
Fat: 0.0

1. Combine all ingredients, except salt, pepper, linguine, and toppings, in slow cooker; cover and cook on low 6 to 8 hours; if thicker consistency is desired, cook, uncovered, on high last 30 minutes. Season to taste with salt and pepper. Serve over linguine with a choice of toppings (not included in nutritional data).

Sagebrush Chili with Fresh Tomatoes

V

For a fresh take on an old Southwestern favorite, this full-flavored chili sports ripe tomatoes and sage leaves.

4 entrée servings

2 cans (15 ounces each) pinto beans, rinsed, drained
1 quart tomato wedges
4 scallions, sliced
8 cloves garlic, thinly sliced
1 large cayenne chili, roasted, seeded, minced
2 tablespoons chili powder
1 teaspoon each: ground cumin and coriander
¾ teaspoon dried sage leaves
Salt and pepper, to taste

Per Serving:
Calories: 269
% calories from fat: 17
Protein (g): 13.4
Carbohydrate (g): 46.1
Fat (g): 5.2
Saturated fat (g): 0.9
Cholesterol (mg): 0
Sodium (mg): 680
Exchanges:
Milk: 0.0
Vegetable: 0.0
Fruit: 0.0
Bread: 3.0
Meat: 1.0
Fat: 0.0

1. Combine all ingredients, except salt and pepper, in slow cooker; cover and cook on high 4 to 5 hours. Season to taste with salt and pepper.

Monterey Chili Acini de Pepe

LO

One-half cup of any cooked grain, such as barley, wheat berries, or millet, can be substituted for the pasta in this flavorful chili.

4 entrée servings

1 can (15 ounces) pinto beans, rinsed, drained
1 can (14½ ounces) diced tomatoes,
    undrained
½ cup each: chopped onion, green bell pepper
1 tablespoon chili powder
1 teaspoon each: dried oregano leaves,
    unsweetened cocoa
½ cup cooked acini de pepe
¼ cup chopped cilantro
Salt and pepper, to taste
¾ cup (3 ounces) shredded reduced-fat Monterey Jack
    cheese

Per Serving:
Calories: 275
% calories from fat: 29
Protein (g): 14
Carbohydrate (g): 36
Fat (g): 9.2
Saturated fat (g): 4.5
Cholesterol (mg): 18.9
Sodium (mg): 461
Exchanges:
Milk: 0.0
Vegetable: 1.0
Fruit: 0.0
Bread: 2.0
Meat: 1.0
Fat: 1.0

1. Combine all ingredients, except pasta, cilantro, salt, pepper, and cheese, in slow cooker; cover and cook on high 3 to 4 hours, adding pasta and cilantro during last 15 minutes. Season to taste with salt and pepper. Sprinkle each bowl of chili with cheese.

Salsa Chili

L *Salsa seasons this healthy, meatless chili.*

4 entrée servings

1 can (16 ounces) crushed tomatoes, undrained
1 can (15½ ounces) red kidney beans, rinsed, drained
1 cup water
½ cup each: medium or hot salsa, whole kernel corn
1 tablespoon chili powder
½–1 teaspoon minced jalapeño chili
½ cup quick-cooking barley
Salt and pepper, to taste
½ cup (2 ounces) shredded extra-sharp Cheddar
    cheese

Per Serving:
Calories: 317
% calories from fat: 16
Protein (g): 14.8
Carbohydrate (g): 55.2
Fat (g): 5.8
Saturated fat (g): 3.2
Cholesterol (mg): 14.9
Sodium (mg): 790
Exchanges:
Milk: 0.0
Vegetable: 2.0
Fruit: 0.0
Bread: 3.0
Meat: 0.0
Fat: 1.0

1. Combine all ingredients, except barley, salt, pepper, and cheese, in slow cooker; cover and cook on high 3 to 4 hours, adding barley during last 20 minutes. Season to taste with salt and pepper. Sprinkle each bowl of chili with shredded cheese.

Caribbean Chili

V

This hearty meatless three-bean chili is accented with Mango Salsa; serve with brown rice if you like.

6 entrée servings

2 cans (14½ ounces each) diced tomatoes, undrained
1 can (15 ounces) each: rinsed, drained pinto, Great Northern, and black beans
2 cups chopped red or green bell peppers
1 cup chopped onion
1 jalapeño chili, chopped
2 teaspoons each: minced gingerroot, sugar
1 tablespoon each: minced garlic, ground cumin
2 tablespoons each: paprika, chili powder
¼ teaspoon ground cloves
1 tablespoon lime juice
Salt and pepper, to taste
Mango Salsa (recipe follows)

Per Serving:
Calories: 331
% calories from fat: 13
Protein (g): 15.2
Carbohydrate (g): 67
Fat (g): 5.2
Saturated fat (g): 0.8
Cholesterol (mg): 0
Sodium (mg): 442
Exchanges:
Milk: 0.0
Vegetable: 3.0
Fruit: 0.0
Bread: 3.0
Meat: 0.0
Fat: 1.0

1. Combine all ingredients, except salt, pepper, and Mango Salsa, in 6-quart slow cooker; cover and cook on high 3 to 4 hours. Season to taste with salt and pepper; serve with Mango Salsa.

Mango Salsa

Makes about 2 cups

1 cup each: cubed mango, banana
¼ cup chopped cilantro
½ small jalapeño chili, finely chopped
1 tablespoon frozen pineapple or orange juice concentrate, thawed
1 teaspoon lime juice

1. Combine all ingredients.

Gingered Asian Noodle Soup

V *Asian flavors meld in this tempting soup.*

4 first-course servings

1 quart vegetable broth
1 cup sliced cremini mushrooms
½ cup each: chopped onion, sliced carrot
2 green onions, thinly sliced
1 teaspoon each: minced gingerroot, garlic
1 tablespoon soy sauce
⅛ teaspoon dried red pepper
1–2 teaspoons rice wine vinegar
1 cup each: lightly packed baby spinach
  leaves, snow peas
1 teaspoon Asian sesame oil
Salt, to taste
4 ounces cellophane noodles

Per Serving:
Calories: 175
% calories from fat: 10
Protein (g): 3.3
Carbohydrate (g): 36.2
Fat (g): 1.9
Saturated fat (g): 0.2
Cholesterol (mg): 0
Sodium (mg): 737
Exchanges:
Milk: 0.0
Vegetable: 1.0
Fruit: 0.0
Bread: 2.0
Meat: 0.0
Fat: 0.0

1. Combine all ingredients, except spinach, snow peas, sesame oil, salt, and noodles, in slow cooker. Cover and cook on high 2 to 3 hours, adding spinach and snow peas during last 15 minutes. Stir in sesame oil; season to taste with salt.
2. Pour boiling water over noodles to cover in large bowl; let stand 5 minutes, then drain. Spoon noodles into bowls and pour hot soup over.

Alsatian Peasant Soup

L

Root vegetables, cabbage, and beans combine for a robust soup that is almost a stew. Serve with a crusty rye bread and a good beer.

6 entrée servings

3 cups reduced-sodium vegetable broth
2 cans (15 ounces each) Great Northern beans, rinsed, drained
2 cups thinly sliced cabbage
1 cup each: cubed potato, parsnip, sliced carrots
½ cup each: chopped onion, celery
1 teaspoon dried thyme leaves
½ teaspoon crushed caraway seeds
1 bay leaf
Salt and pepper, to taste
¾ cup (3 ounces) shredded reduced-fat Swiss cheese
Croutons (see p. 38)

Per Serving:
Calories: 300
% calories from fat: 13
Protein (g): 17
Carbohydrate (g): 50
Fat (g): 4.3
Saturated fat (g): 1
Cholesterol (mg): 5
Sodium (mg): 352
Exchanges:
Milk: 0.0
Vegetable: 1.0
Fruit: 0.0
Bread: 3.0
Meat: 1.0
Fat: 0.0

1. Combine all ingredients, except salt, pepper, cheese, and croutons, in 6-quart slow cooker; cover and cook on low 6 to 8 hours. Discard bay leaf; season to taste with salt and pepper. Sprinkle each bowl of soup with 2 tablespoons shredded cheese and Croutons.

Tortellini Soup with Kale

LO

Fresh pasta can be cooked in the slow cooker if there is adequate broth and if it's added near the end of cooking time.

8 first-course servings

3 quarts Roasted Vegetable Stock (see p. 35) or vegetable broth
1 cup each: sliced mushrooms, leek (white part only) or green onions
3 cloves garlic, minced
½ package (9-ounce size) fresh mushroom or herb tortellini
2 cups coarsely chopped packed kale
Salt and pepper, to taste

Per Serving:
Calories: 105
% calories from fat: 24
Protein (g): 3
Carbohydrate (g): 11.6
Fat (g): 3.1
Saturated fat (g): 0.8
Cholesterol (mg): 8.4
Sodium (mg): 69
Exchanges:
Milk: 0.0
Vegetable: 2.0
Fruit: 0.0
Bread: 0.0
Meat: 0.0
Fat: 1.0

1. Combine stock, mushrooms, leek, and garlic in 6-quart slow cooker; cover and cook on high 3 to 4 hours. Add tortellini and kale; cover and cook until tortellini float to the top of the soup, about 20 minutes. Season to taste with salt and pepper.

Spinach and Tortellini Soup

LO *Fresh ravioli can be substituted for the tortellini in this great soup.*

6 entrée servings

2 cans (14 ½ ounces) reduced-sodium vegetable
   broth
1½ cups water
2 cups sliced carrots
¼ cup sliced green onions
2 cloves garlic, minced
1 teaspoon dried basil leaves
1 package (9 ounces) fresh tomato-cheese
   tortellini, cooked
3 cups spinach leaves, torn
2–3 teaspoons lemon juice
⅛–¼ teaspoon ground nutmeg
Salt and pepper, to taste

Per Serving:
Calories: 290
% calories from fat: 9
Protein (g): 12.1
Carbohydrate (g): 48
Fat (g): 2.8
Saturated fat (g): 1
Cholesterol (mg): 3.8
Sodium (mg): 395
Exchanges:
Milk: 0.0
Vegetable: 2.0
Fruit: 0.0
Bread: 2.5
Meat: 1.0
Fat: 0.0

1. Combine broth, water, vegetables, garlic, and basil in 6-quart slow cooker; cover and cook on high 3 to 4 hours, adding tortellini and spinach during the last 15 minutes. Season to taste with lemon juice, nutmeg, salt, and pepper.

Ditalini with White Beans and Collards

LO *Kale, cabbage, or mustard greens can be substituted for the collards.*

4 entrée servings

1 can (14 ounces) reduced-sodium vegetable broth
1 can (15 ounces) small white beans, rinsed, drained
1 can (14½ ounces) diced tomatoes, undrained
1 teaspoon olive oil
1 cup chopped onion
1 teaspoon dried oregano leaves
2 cups torn packed collard greens
⅔ cup uncooked ditalini
2 tablespoons shredded Provolone cheese
Salt and hot pepper sauce, to taste

Per Serving:
Calories: 234
% calories from fat: 14
Protein (g): 12.8
Carbohydrate (g): 44.1
Fat (g): 4
Saturated fat (g): 1.4
Cholesterol (mg): 4.9
Sodium (mg): 826
Exchanges:
Milk: 0.0
Vegetable: 3.0
Fruit: 0.0
Bread: 2.0
Meat: 0.0
Fat: 0.5

1. Combine all ingredients, except collard greens, ditalini, cheese, salt, and hot pepper sauce, in slow cooker; cover and cook on high 3 to 4 hours, adding collard greens and ditalini during last 20 minutes. Stir in Provolone cheese; season to taste with salt and hot pepper sauce.

Pasta e Fagioli

LO *Perhaps the only soup that's better than a good pasta e fagioli is e fagioli the second day. If you make it a day ahead, wait to add the pasta until just before you serve it.*

12 first-course servings

2½ quarts water
2 cups dried Great Northern or cannellini beans
4½ cups peeled seeded diced tomatoes
1 cup chopped onion
½ cup each: diced celery, carrot
1½ tablespoons minced garlic
5 ounces elbow macaroni, cooked
Salt and pepper, to taste
Grated Parmesan cheese, as garnish

Per Serving:
Calories: 124
% calories from fat: 21
Protein (g): 5
Carbohydrate (g): 20.4
Fat (g): 3.1
Saturated fat (g): 1.1
Cholesterol (mg): 10.2
Sodium (mg): 126
Exchanges:
Milk: 0.0
Vegetable: 1.0
Fruit: 0.0
Bread: 1.0
Meat: 0.0
Fat: 0.5

1. Combine all ingredients, except pasta, salt, pepper, and Parmesan cheese, in 6-quart slow cooker; cover and cook on low until beans are tender, 7 to 8 hours, adding pasta during last 20 minutes. Season to taste with salt and pepper. Sprinkle each bowl of soup with Parmesan cheese.

Green Vegetable Minestrone

LO *This green soup is wonderful in spring, when fresh asparagus and peas are in season, but make it whenever you're in the mood for delicious soup!*

6 entrée servings

1½ quarts Basic Vegetable Stock (see p. 34)
   or vegetable broth
2 cans (15 ounces each) Great Northern beans,
   rinsed, drained
2 cups sliced zucchini
1½ cups each: small broccoli florets, cut asparagus
   (1-inch)
1 cup each: thinly sliced onion, cut green beans
2 tablespoons chopped fresh or 2 teaspoons
   dried each: basil and rosemary leaves
2 large cloves garlic
2 ounces spinach fettuccine, broken into pieces (1-inch), cooked
1 cup frozen peas, thawed
Salt and pepper, to taste
Shredded Parmesan cheese, as garnish

Per Serving:
Calories: 186
% calories from fat: 6
Protein (g): 13.1
Carbohydrate (g): 38.8
Fat (g): 1.4
Saturated fat (g): 0.3
Cholesterol (mg): 14
Sodium (mg): 478
Exchanges:
Milk: 0.0
Vegetable: 2.0
Fruit: 0.0
Bread: 2.0
Meat: 0.0
Fat: 0.0

1. Combine all ingredients, except fettuccine, peas, salt, pepper, and Parmesan cheese, in 6-quart slow cooker; cover and cook on low 6 to 8 hours, adding fettuccine and peas during last 20 minutes. Season to taste with salt and pepper. Sprinkle each bowl of soup with Parmesan cheese.

Summer Minestrone

LO *Thick and savory, this traditional Italian soup is always a favorite.*

8 entrée servings

4 cups reduced-sodium vegetable broth
2 cups water
1 can (15 ounces) kidney beans, rinsed, drained
1 can (14½ ounces) stewed tomatoes
2 cups each: cubed potatoes, sliced carrots
1 cup each: halved green beans, sliced zucchini,
   carrots, cabbage, chopped onion
½ cup sliced celery
3–4 cloves garlic, minced
2 teaspoons dried Italian seasoning
1½ cups cooked mostaccioli
Salt and pepper, to taste
2 tablespoons grated Parmesan or Romano cheese

Per Serving:
Calories: 177
% calories from fat: 9
Protein (g): 8.1
Carbohydrate (g): 33.7
Fat (g): 1.8
Saturated fat (g): 0.6
Cholesterol (mg): 1.2
Sodium (mg): 256
Exchanges:
Milk: 0.0
Vegetable: 2.0
Fruit: 0.0
Bread: 1.5
Meat: 0.5
Fat: 0.0

1. Combine all ingredients, except pasta, salt, pepper, and Parmesan cheese, in 6-quart slow cooker; cover and cook on low 6 to 8 hours, adding pasta during last 20 minutes. Season to taste with salt and pepper; sprinkle each bowl of soup with Parmesan cheese.

Two-Bean Minestrone

LO *Cannellini beans and chickpeas enrich this nutritious soup.*

8 entrée servings

1½ quarts water
1 can (15 ounces) each: rinsed drained cannellini
   or Great Northern beans, chickpeas
1 can (14½ ounces) plum tomatoes, undrained,
   chopped
½ cup dry red wine
1½ cups each: sliced zucchini, shredded cabbage
1 cup each: diced potato, sliced leek
½ cup each: sliced carrots, celery, chopped onion,
   parsley
2 cloves garlic, minced
1 tablespoon each: dried oregano and basil leaves
½ cup cooked small elbow macaroni
Salt and pepper, to taste
8 teaspoons grated Parmesan cheese

Per Serving:
Calories: 267
% calories from fat: 17
Protein (g): 9
Carbohydrate (g): 43.1
Fat (g): 5.3
Saturated fat (g): 0.9
Cholesterol (mg): 1.3
Sodium (mg): 331
Exchanges:
Milk: 0.0
Vegetable: 2.0
Fruit: 0.0
Bread: 2.0
Meat: 0.0
Fat: 1.5

1. Combine all ingredients, except macaroni, salt, pepper, and cheese, in 6-quart slow cooker; cover and cook on high 4 to 5 hours, adding macaroni during last 20 minutes. Season to taste with salt and pepper. Sprinkle each bowl of soup with 1 teaspoon Parmesan cheese.

Italian Bean Soup

For a creamy textured soup, purée ½ the cooked bean mixture before adding the macaroni and garbanzo beans.

6 entrée servings

1½ quarts vegetable broth
1 quart water
1 cup dried cannellini or navy beans
1 cup each: chopped onion, green bell pepper, carrots
½ cup chopped celery
2 cloves garlic, minced
1 teaspoon each: dried basil and oregano leaves
¼ teaspoon dry mustard
2–3 cans (8 ounces) tomato sauce
½ cup cooked whole-wheat elbow macaroni
1 can (15 ounces) garbanzo beans, rinsed, drained
Salt and pepper, to taste

Per Serving:
Calories: 291
% calories from fat: 4
Protein (g): 14.1
Carbohydrate (g): 56.6
Fat (g): 1.4
Saturated fat (g): 0.2
Cholesterol (mg): 0
Sodium (mg): 280
Exchanges:
Milk: 0.0
Vegetable: 3.0
Fruit: 0.0
Bread: 3.0
Meat: 0.0
Fat: 0.0

1. Combine all ingredients, except tomato sauce, macaroni, garbanzo beans, salt, and pepper, in 6-quart slow cooker; cover and cook on low until beans are tender, 7 to 8 hours, adding tomato sauce, macaroni, and garbanzo beans during last 20 minutes. Season to taste with salt and pepper.

Tuscan Bean Soup

V

A hearty well-seasoned bean soup that is sure to please.

8 entrée servings

1¾ quarts reduced-sodium vegetable broth
2 cans (15 ounces each) cannellini or Great Northern
   beans, rinsed, drained
1 cup each: cubed unpeeled potato, sliced carrots,
   chopped onion
½ cup each: chopped celery, green bell pepper
2 teaspoons minced roasted garlic
2 tablespoons tomato paste
1½ teaspoons dried Italian seasoning
½ cup quick-cooking barley
1 cup packed baby spinach leaves
Salt and pepper, to taste

Per Serving:
Calories: 233
% calories from fat: 18
Protein (g): 10.7
Carbohydrate (g): 40.8
Fat (g): 5.6
Saturated fat (g): 0.7
Cholesterol (mg): 0
Sodium (mg): 245
Exchanges:
Milk: 0.0
Vegetable: 2.0
Fruit: 0.0
Bread: 2.0
Meat: 0.0
Fat: 1.0

1. Combine all ingredients, except barley, spinach, salt, and pepper, in 6-quart slow cooker; cover and cook on low 6 to 8 hours, adding barley and spinach during last 30 minutes. Season to taste with salt and pepper.

Chickpea and Pasta Soup

O

Use any fresh vegetables for the zucchini and celery in this soup—carrots, cauliflower or broccoli florets, mushrooms, peas, and green beans are possible choices.

4 entrée servings

1 can (15 ounces) each: reduced-sodium vegetable
   broth, rinsed drained chickpeas
1 can (14½ ounces) stewed tomatoes
¾ cup each: chopped onion, cubed zucchini,
   sliced celery
3–4 cloves garlic, minced
1 teaspoon each: dried rosemary and thyme leaves
⅛ teaspoon crushed red pepper
1 cup uncooked farfalle (bow ties)
2–3 teaspoons lemon juice
Salt, to taste

Per Serving:
Calories: 322
% calories from fat: 10
Protein (g): 11.5
Carbohydrate (g): 56.4
Fat (g): 3.7
Saturated fat (g): 0.5
Cholesterol (mg): 0
Sodium (mg): 514
Exchanges:
Milk: 0.0
Vegetable: 3.0
Fruit: 0.0
Bread: 3.0
Meat: 0.0
Fat: 0.5

1. Combine all ingredients, except pasta, lemon juice, and salt, in slow cooker; cover and cook on high 3 to 4 hours, adding pasta during last 20 minutes. Season to taste with lemon juice and salt.

Two-Bean and Pasta Soup

o *This substantial soup thickens upon standing; thin with additional broth or water, if necessary.*

6 entrée servings

2 cans (15 ounces each) reduced-sodium vegetable
  broth
1 cup water
1 can (14½ ounces) stewed tomatoes
1 can (15 ounces) each: cannellini and pinto beans,
  rinsed, drained
1½ cups cubed carrots
½ cup each: chopped green bell pepper, sliced green
  onions
3 cloves garlic, minced
2 teaspoons each: dried basil and oregano leaves
1½ cups cooked rigatoni
2–3 teaspoons lemon juice
Salt and pepper, to taste

Per Serving:
Calories: 225
% calories from fat: 7
Protein (g): 13.6
Carbohydrate (g): 45.7
Fat (g): 2
Saturated fat (g): 0
Cholesterol (mg): 0
Sodium (mg): 522
Exchanges:
Milk: 0.0
Vegetable: 2.0
Fruit: 0.0
Bread: 2.5
Meat: 0.0
Fat: 0.0

1. Combine all ingredients, except pasta, lemon juice, and salt, in 6-quart slow cooker; cover and cook on high 3 to 4 hours, adding pasta during last 15 minutes. Season to taste with lemon juice, salt, and pepper.

White Bean and Sweet Potato Soup with Cranberry Coulis

v *A wonderful combination of colors and flavors!*

6 entrée servings

3 cups reduced-sodium vegetable broth
2 cans (15 ounces each) navy or Great Northern
beans, rinsed, drained
1 pound sweet potatoes, peeled, cubed
1 cup each: chopped onion, peeled tart apple
1½ teaspoons minced gingerroot
½ teaspoon dried marjoram leaves
Salt and white pepper, to taste
Cranberry Coulis (recipe follows)

Per Serving:
Calories: 310
% calories from fat: 3
Protein (g): 12.6
Carbohydrate (g): 64.6
Fat (g): 1.2
Saturated fat (g): 0.3
Cholesterol (mg): 0
Sodium (mg): 650
Exchanges:
Milk: 0.0
Vegetable: 1.0
Fruit: 1.0
Bread: 3.0
Meat: 0.0
Fat: 0.0

1. Combine all ingredients, except salt, white pepper, and Cranberry Coulis, in 6-quart slow cooker; cover and cook on high 4 to 5 hours. Process soup in food processor or blender until smooth; season to taste with salt and white pepper. Swirl 2 tablespoons Cranberry Coulis into each bowl of soup.

Cranberry Coulis

Makes 6 servings (about 3 tablespoons each)

1½ cups fresh or frozen cranberries
1 cup orange juice
2 tablespoons each: sugar, honey

1. Heat cranberries and orange juice to boiling in small saucepan; reduce heat and simmer, covered, until cranberries are tender, 5 to 8 minutes. Process with sugar and honey in food processor or blender until almost smooth. Serve warm or room temperature.

Tangy Three-Bean Soup

V

The spicy barbecue flavor of this dish is a nice change of pace from the usual bean soups.

6 entrée servings

2 quarts water
½ cup each: dried black-eyed peas, baby lima and
   Great Northern beans, chopped onion, sliced
   carrot, celery
1 clove garlic, minced
⅛ teaspoon ground cloves
1 bay leaf
½ teaspoon each: dry mustard, chili powder
¼ teaspoon each: ground celery seeds, dried
   thyme leaves, paprika, black pepper
1 can (15 ounces) tomato sauce
1–2 tablespoons brown sugar
1 tablespoon each: apple cider vinegar, light molasses
Salt and cayenne pepper, to taste

Per Serving:
Calories: 167
% calories from fat: 5
Protein (g): 9.2
Carbohydrate (g): 33
Fat (g): 0.9
Saturated fat (g): 0.2
Cholesterol (mg): 0
Sodium (mg): 447
Exchanges:
Milk: 0.0
Vegetable: 1.0
Fruit: 0.0
Bread: 2.0
Meat: 0.0
Fat: 0.0

1. Combine all ingredients, except tomato sauce, brown sugar, vinegar, molasses, salt, and cayenne pepper, in slow cooker; cover and cook on low until beans are tender, 7 to 8 hours, adding remaining ingredients, except salt and cayenne pepper, during last 30 to 45 minutes. Discard bay leaf; season to taste with salt and cayenne pepper.

Black Bean Soup

L

Dried beans can be cooked in a slow cooker without soaking, saving advance preparation time. If you want them to cook more quickly than 7 to 8 hours, they will have to be soaked overnight, or "quick cooked."

4 entrée servings

1½ cups dried black beans
1½ quarts water
1 large onion, chopped
4 cloves garlic, minced
¾ teaspoon each: dried oregano and thyme leaves
1 large tomato, chopped
Salt and pepper, to taste
6 tablespoons reduced-fat sour cream
Chopped oregano or parsley, as garnish

Per Serving:
Calories: 200
% calories from fat: 4
Protein (g): 13.8
Carbohydrate (g): 39
Fat (g): 0.9
Saturated fat (g): 0.2
Cholesterol (mg): 0
Sodium (mg): 20
Exchanges:
Milk: 0.0
Vegetable: 1.0
Fruit: 0.0
Bread: 2.0
Meat: 0.5
Fat: 0.0

1. Combine beans, water, onion, garlic, and herbs in slow cooker; cover and cook on low until beans are tender, 7 to 8 hours, adding tomato during last 30 minutes. Process soup in food processor or blender until smooth; season to taste with salt and pepper. Top each bowl of soup with dollop of sour cream and sprinkle with oregano.

Variation

Bean Soup with Many Garnishes—Make soup as above, adding 1 tablespoon each dry sherry, soy sauce, and balsamic vinegar during last 15 minutes cooking time; do not purée. Serve soup over rice and serve with cubed avocado, sliced green onions, toasted pepitas, and lime wedges for garnishes.

Black Bean Soup with Sun-Dried Tomatoes and Cilantro-Lemon Cream

L

Cilantro-Lemon Cream adds a fresh accent to this south-of-the-border favorite.

4 entrée servings

3 cups Basic Vegetable Stock (see p. 34) or vegetable
   broth
2 cans (15 ounces each) black beans, rinsed, drained
1 cup chopped onion
2 cloves garlic, minced
1 jalapeño chili, minced
¾ cup sun-dried tomatoes (not in oil), room
   temperature
¾ teaspoon ground cumin, dried oregano leaves
¼–½ teaspoon hot pepper sauce
Salt and pepper, to taste
¼ cup cilantro, chopped
Cilantro-Lemon Cream (recipe follows)

Per Serving:
Calories: 239
% calories from fat: 5
Protein (g): 15.2
Carbohydrate (g): 44.0
Fat (g): 1.5
Saturated fat (g): 0.3
Cholesterol (mg): 0
Sodium (mg): 256
Exchanges:
Milk: 0.0
Vegetable: 1.0
Fruit: 0.0
Bread: 3.0
Meat: 0.0
Fat: 0.0

1. Combine all ingredients, except hot pepper sauce, salt, pepper, cilantro, and Cilantro-Lemon Cream, in slow cooker; cover and cook on high 3 to 4 hours. Process soup in food processor or blender until smooth. Season to taste with hot pepper sauce, salt, and pepper; stir in cilantro. Garnish each bowl of soup with dollops of Cilantro-Lemon Cream.

Cilantro-Lemon Cream

Makes about ⅓ cup

⅓ cup reduced-fat sour cream
2 tablespoons minced cilantro
1 teaspoon lemon or lime juice
¾ teaspoon ground coriander
2–3 dashes white pepper

1. Combine all ingredients.

Variation

Ancho Black Bean and Pumpkin Soup—Make soup as above, omitting sun-dried tomatoes and Cilantro-Lemon Cream. Heat 1 ancho chili in dry skillet over medium heat until softened; remove chili and discard veins and seeds. Purée chili and 1 can (15 ounces) pumpkin with the soup.

Pasilla Black Bean Soup

For a hot and smoky flavor accent, add 1 to 2 teaspoons chopped canned chipotle peppers in adobo sauce to the soup.

4 entrée servings

1 quart Basic Vegetable Stock (see p. 34) or vegetable broth
6 dried pasilla chilies, stems and seeds removed, torn into pieces
1 can (14½ ounces) diced tomatoes, undrained
1 can (15 ounces) black beans, rinsed, drained
1 cup each: chopped onion, carrots
2 teaspoons each: minced jalapeño chili, garlic
¾ teaspoon each: dried oregano leaves, ground cumin
¼ teaspoon dried thyme leaves
Salt and pepper, to taste
1 cup (4 ounces) shredded reduced-fat Mexican cheese blend
Chopped cilantro, as garnish

Per Serving:
Calories: 291
% calories from fat: 23
Protein (g): 16
Carbohydrate (g): 40
Fat (g): 7
Saturated fat (g): 4
Cholesterol (mg): 15
Sodium (mg): 1234
Exchanges:
Milk: 0.0
Vegetable: 0.0
Fruit: 0.0
Bread: 2.5
Meat: 2.0
Fat: 0.0

1. Combine all ingredients, except salt, pepper, cheese, and cilantro, in slow cooker; cover and cook on high 4 to 5 hours. Season to taste with salt and pepper. Sprinkle each bowl of soup with cheese and cilantro.

Cuban Black Bean Soup

The spicy, authentic Caribbean flavor is ample reward for making this soup.

8 entrée servings

2 cups dried black beans
2 quarts water
3 each: chopped medium onions, minced garlic cloves
4–5 drops hot pepper sauce
1 large green bell pepper, finely chopped
2 teaspoons each: ground cumin, dried oregano leaves
Salt and pepper, to taste
Cuban Rice, warm (recipe follows)

Per Serving:
Calories: 274
% calories from fat: 11
Protein (g): 11.8
Carbohydrate (g): 50.1
Fat (g): 3.5
Saturated fat (g): 0.5
Cholesterol (mg): 0
Sodium (mg): 480
Exchanges:
Milk: 0.0
Vegetable: 1.0
Fruit: 0.0
Bread: 3.0
Meat: 0.0
Fat: 0.5

1. Combine all ingredients, except salt, pepper, and Cuban Rice, in 6-quart slow cooker; cover and cook on low until beans are tender, 7 to 8 hours. Season to taste with salt and pepper. Serve soup over Cuban Rice in bowls.

Cuban Rice

Makes about 4 cups

1 cup uncooked long-grain white rice
1 tablespoon finely chopped onion
2 cups water
2 teaspoons olive oil
1½ tablespoons apple cider vinegar

1. Combine rice, onion, and water in large saucepan; heat to boiling. Reduce heat and simmer, covered, 20 minutes or until rice is tender. Stir in oil and vinegar.

Split Pea Soup with Three Accompaniments

V

This thick and beautiful green soup is served with cubed sweet potatoes, fresh peas, and croutons.

6 entrée servings

1½ quarts water
½ cup dry white wine or water
1 pound dried split peas
½ cup minced onion
1 rib celery, chopped
2 vegetable bouillon cubes
¾ teaspoon dried thyme leaves
1 bay leaf
Salt and pepper, to taste
1 cup each: cooked warm peas and cubed peeled
   sweet potatoes, plain croutons

Per Serving:
Calories: 374
% calories from fat: 8
Protein (g): 21.5
Carbohydrate (g): 60.7
Fat (g): 3.4
Saturated fat (g): 0.5
Cholesterol (mg): 0.1
Sodium (mg): 441
Exchanges:
Milk: 0.0
Vegetable: 0.0
Fruit: 0.0
Bread: 4.0
Meat: 1.0
Fat: 0.5

1. Combine all ingredients, except salt, pepper, peas, sweet potatoes, and croutons, in 6-quart slow cooker; cover and cook on low 6 to 8 hours. Process soup in food processor or blender until smooth. Discard bay leaf; season to taste with salt and pepper. Sprinkle each bowl of soup with peas, sweet potatoes, and croutons.

Easiest Black-Eyed Pea and Lentil Soup

V *Black-eyed peas and lentils combine in this satisfying soup.*

6 entrée servings

8 cups reduced-sodium vegetable broth
1½ cups dried lentils
¾ cup dried black-eyed peas
3 medium tomatoes, chopped
½ cup each: chopped carrots, celery, onion
1 teaspoon minced garlic
¾ teaspoon each: dried thyme and oregano leaves
1 bay leaf
Salt and pepper, to taste

Per Serving:
Calories: 356
% calories from fat: 14
Protein (g): 20.7
Carbohydrate (g): 58.3
Fat (g): 5.9
Saturated fat (g): 0.9
Cholesterol (mg): 0
Sodium (mg): 119
Exchanges:
Milk: 0.0
Vegetable: 2.0
Fruit: 0.0
Bread: 3.0
Meat: 1.0
Fat: 1.0

1. Combine all ingredients, except salt and pepper, in 6-quart slow cooker; cover and cook on low 6 to 8 hours. Discard bay leaf; season to taste with salt and pepper.

Country Lentil Soup

L *This soup is wholesome in flavor and texture.*

6 entrée servings

3 cups vegetable broth
2 cups water
1 cup dried lentils
1 can (14½ ounces) crushed tomatoes, undrained
1½ cups chopped onions
1 cup each: sliced celery, carrots
2 teaspoons minced garlic
½ teaspoon each: dried marjoram, oregano, and thyme leaves
Salt and pepper, to taste
6 tablespoons grated Parmesan cheese

Per Serving:
Calories: 275
% calories from fat: 14
Protein (g): 15.8
Carbohydrate (g): 42.8
Fat (g): 4.4
Saturated fat (g): 0.6
Cholesterol (mg): 0
Sodium (mg): 109
Exchanges:
Milk: 0.0
Vegetable: 3.0
Fruit: 0.0
Bread: 2.0
Meat: 0.5
Fat: 0.5

1. Combine all ingredients, except salt, pepper, and Parmesan cheese, in 6-quart slow cooker; cover and cook on low 6 to 8 hours. Season to taste with salt and pepper. Sprinkle each bowl of soup with 1 tablespoon cheese.

Easy Indian Lentil Soup

V

This hearty soup tastes best made with tiny beige Indian lentils, which are available in Indian food stores. However, regular brown lentils can also be used.

4 entrée servings

2½ quarts water
2 cups dried Indian lentils
1 large onion, finely chopped
⅓ cup each: thinly sliced celery, carrot
1 clove garlic, minced
2–3 teaspoons mild curry powder
1 teaspoon sugar
Salt and pepper, to taste

Per Serving:
Calories: 306
% calories from fat: 18
Protein (g): 20.8
Carbohydrate (g): 51.2
Fat (g): 3
Saturated fat (g): 2
Cholesterol (mg): 0
Sodium (mg): 28
Exchanges:
Milk: 0.0
Vegetable: 0.0
Fruit: 0.0
Bread: 4.0
Meat: 0.0
Fat: 0.0

1. Combine all ingredients, except salt and pepper, in 6-quart slow cooker; cover and cook on low 6 to 8 hours. Season to taste with salt and pepper.

Curried Lentil-Spinach Soup

V

Lentils and spinach lend delicious flavor and texture to this soup.

6 entrée servings

2 quarts reduced-sodium vegetable broth
1 can (14½ ounces) petite-diced tomatoes, undrained
1 cup dried brown lentils
2 cups chopped onions
¼ cup each: thinly sliced celery, carrot
2 large cloves garlic, minced
2–2½ teaspoons mild curry powder
1 teaspoon chili powder
1 package (10 ounces) frozen chopped spinach,
  thawed, drained
Salt and pepper, to taste

Per Serving:
Calories: 181
% calories from fat: 10
Protein (g): 10.5
Carbohydrate (g): 32.6
Fat (g): 2
Saturated fat (g): 0.3
Cholesterol (mg): 0
Sodium (mg): 104
Exchanges:
Milk: 0.0
Vegetable: 2.0
Fruit: 0.0
Bread: 1.5
Meat: 0.5
Fat: 1.0

1. Combine all ingredients, except spinach, salt, and pepper, in 6-quart slow cooker; cover and cook on low 6 to 8 hours, adding spinach during last 30 minutes. Season to taste with salt and pepper.

Bean and Barley Soup

A soup that can be easily increased, using a 6-quart slow cooker, to serve a crowd.

6 entrée servings

1½ quarts low-sodium vegetable broth
2 cans (15 ounces) cannellini or Great Northern
  beans, rinsed, drained
1 cup each: cubed unpeeled Idaho potato, sliced
  carrots
¾ cup each: chopped onion, red bell pepper
2 teaspoons minced garlic
2 tablespoons tomato paste
1½ teaspoons dried Italian seasoning
½ cup quick-cooking barley
1 cup packed baby spinach leaves
Salt and pepper, to taste

Per Serving:
Calories: 297
% calories from fat: 17
Protein (g): 10
Carbohydrate (g): 52.1
Fat (g): 5.6
Saturated fat (g): 0.7
Cholesterol (mg): 0
Sodium (mg): 325
Exchanges:
Milk: 0.0
Vegetable: 1.0
Fruit: 0.0
Bread: 3.0
Meat: 0.0
Fat: 1.0

1. Combine all ingredients, except barley, spinach, salt, and pepper, in 6-quart slow cooker; cover and cook on high 4 to 5 hours, adding spinach during last 15 minutes. Season to taste with salt and pepper.

Potato Barley Soup

You can vary the flavor of this homey soup by using different broths, as well as different vegetables.

8 entrée servings

3 cans (14½ ounces each) vegetable broth
1 cup each: tomato juice, chopped onion
3 cups peeled chopped potatoes
½ cup each: sliced carrot, celery, parsnip
1 clove garlic, minced
2 bay leaves
¼ teaspoon each: dried thyme and marjoram leaves
¾ cup quick-cooking barley
Salt and pepper, to taste

Per Serving:
Calories: 186
% calories from fat: 3
Protein (g): 5.1
Carbohydrate (g): 41.8
Fat (g): 0.7
Saturated fat (g): 0.1
Cholesterol (mg): 0
Sodium (mg): 285
Exchanges:
Milk: 0.0
Vegetable: 0.0
Fruit: 0.0
Bread: 2.5
Meat: 0.0
Fat: 0.0

1. Combine all ingredients, except barley, salt, and pepper, in 6-quart slow cooker; cover and cook on low 6 to 8 hours, stirring in barley during last 30 minutes. Discard bay leaves; season to taste with salt and pepper.

Variation
Potato and Portobello Mushroom Soup—Make recipe as above, omitting barley and tomato juice, and adding 2 cups chopped portobello mushrooms.

Polish-Style Mushroom-Barley Soup

L

Dried mushrooms add a woodsy flavor to the soup.

4–6 entrée servings

2 quarts vegetable broth
3 medium potatoes, peeled, diced
1 small onion, coarsely chopped
1 rib celery, sliced
½ cup each: halved baby carrots, pearl barley,
    dry white wine (optional)
¼ ounce dried mushrooms, coarsely chopped
1 cup frozen peas, thawed
Salt and white pepper, to taste
½ cup reduced-fat sour cream
Chopped fresh dill, as garnish

Per Serving:
Calories: 293
% calories from fat: 4
Protein (g): 9.9
Carbohydrate (g): 54.7
Fat (g): 1.5
Saturated fat (g): 0.1
Cholesterol (mg): 0
Sodium (mg): 777
Exchanges:
Milk: 0.0
Vegetable: 3.0
Fruit: 0.0
Bread: 3.0
Meat: 0.0
Fat: 0.0

1. Combine all ingredients, except peas, salt, white pepper, sour cream, and dill, in 6-quart slow cooker; cover and cook on low 6 to 8 hours, adding peas during last 20 minutes. Season to taste with salt and white pepper; garnish each bowl of soup with sour cream and dill.

Spicy Barley Soup

v *Herbs and dry mustard give this barley soup its savory flavor.*

6 first-course servings

2 quarts vegetable broth
1½ cups each: chopped onions, sliced mushrooms
½ cup each: sliced carrot, celery, turnip
1 large clove garlic, minced
3 tablespoons tomato paste
¼ cup pearl barley
2 bay leaves
1 teaspoon dried marjoram leaves
½ teaspoon each: dried thyme leaves, celery
   seeds, dry mustard
Salt and pepper, to taste

Per Serving:
Calories: 95
% calories from fat: 25
Protein (g): 2.6
Carbohydrate (g): 16.5
Fat (g): 2.8
Saturated fat (g): 0.2
Cholesterol (mg): 0
Sodium (mg): 492
Exchanges:
Milk: 0.0
Vegetable: 0.0
Fruit: 0.0
Bread: 1.0
Meat: 0.0
Fat: 0.5

1. Combine all ingredients, except salt and pepper, in 6-quart slow cooker; cover and cook on low 6 to 8 hours. Discard bay leaves; season to taste with salt and pepper.

NINE

Meat Stews

Family Beef Stew

A simple yet satisfying beef stew; serve over noodles, if you like.

4 entrée servings

1 pound beef round steak, cut into strips (½-inch)
1 cup reduced-sodium fat-free beef broth
½ cup dry red wine or beef broth
2 cups cut wax or green beans
2 each: cubed medium potatoes, small onions cut
   into wedges
3 carrots, thickly sliced
¾ teaspoon dried thyme leaves
Salt and pepper, to taste

Per Serving:
Calories: 292
% calories from fat: 16
Protein (g): 26
Carbohydrate (g): 29.7
Fat (g): 5.1
Saturated fat (g): 1.5
Cholesterol (mg): 55
Sodium (mg): 140
Exchanges:
Milk: 0.0
Vegetable: 0.0
Fruit: 0.0
Bread: 2.0
Meat: 3.0
Fat: 0.0

1. Combine all ingredients, except salt and pepper, in
slow cooker; cover and cook on low 6 to 8 hours.
Season to taste with salt and pepper.

Country Beef Stew

This slow cooked stew is delicious served over noodles or rice.

4 entrée servings

2 pounds lean beef stew meat, cubed
1 cup each: reduced-sodium beef broth,
   cubed parsnip, chopped onion, celery
½ cup dry red wine or beef broth
2 cups each: cubed unpeeled red potato,
   thickly sliced carrots
3 cloves garlic, minced
2 tablespoons tomato paste
½ teaspoon each: dried thyme and rosemary leaves
1 large bay leaf
½ cup frozen peas, thawed
2 tablespoons cornstarch
¼ cup cold water
Salt and pepper, to taste

Per Serving:
Calories: 326
% calories from fat: 16
Protein (g): 33.5
Carbohydrate (g): 29.6
Fat (g): 5.8
Saturated fat (g): 2
Cholesterol (mg): 70.9
Sodium (mg): 171
Exchanges:
Milk: 0.0
Vegetable: 2.0
Fruit: 0.0
Bread: 1.5
Meat: 3.0
Fat: 0.0

1. Combine all ingredients, except peas, cornstarch, water, salt, and pepper,
in 6-quart slow cooker; cover and cook on high 4 to 5 hours. Add peas,
turn heat to high, and cook 10 minutes; stir in combined cornstarch and
water, stirring 2 to 3 minutes. Discard bay leaf; season to taste with salt and
pepper.

Chuck Wagon Beef Stew

One of the heartiest stews you can rustle up! Serve with warm buttermilk biscuits.

6 entrée servings

1 pound lean beef round steak, cubed (¾-inch)
¾ cup reduced-sodium fat-free beef broth
1 can (14½ ounces) diced tomatoes, undrained
1 can (15 ounces) red kidney beans, rinsed, drained
½ cup chopped onion
3 each: cubed small unpeeled red potatoes, sliced
  carrots
1 tablespoon cornstarch
2 tablespoons cold water
2–3 teaspoons Worcestershire sauce
Salt and pepper, to taste

Per Serving:
Calories: 306
% calories from fat: 26
Protein (g): 22
Carbohydrate (g): 35
Fat (g): 8.8
Saturated fat (g): 3.3
Cholesterol (mg): 45.2
Sodium (mg): 383
Exchanges:
Milk: 0.0
Vegetable: 1.0
Fruit: 0.0
Bread: 2.0
Meat: 2.0
Fat: 1.0

1. Combine all ingredients, except cornstarch, water, Worcestershire sauce, salt, and pepper, in slow cooker; cover and cook on low 6 to 8 hours. Turn heat to high and cook 10 minutes; stir in combined cornstarch and water, stirring 2 to 3 minutes. Season to taste with Worcestershire sauce, salt, and pepper.

Simple Beef Stew

Serve this Italian-seasoned beef stew over noodles, rice, or Microwave Polenta (see p. 385).

6 entrée servings

2 pounds lean beef for stew, cubed (1-inch)
1 can (14½ ounces) Italian plum tomatoes,
  undrained, chopped
½ cup each: reduced-sodium beef broth,
  dry red wine or beef broth
2 each: chopped medium onions, minced
  cloves garlic
2 teaspoons dried Italian seasoning
Salt and pepper, to taste

Per Serving:
Calories: 290
% calories from fat: 34
Protein (g): 35.4
Carbohydrate (g): 8.6
Fat (g): 10.7
Saturated fat (g): 3.8
Cholesterol (mg): 103
Sodium (mg): 246
Exchanges:
Milk: 0.0
Vegetable: 1.5
Fruit: 0.0
Bread: 0.0
Meat: 5.0
Fat: 0.0

1. Combine all ingredients, except salt and pepper, in slow cooker; cover and cook on low 6 to 8 hours. Season to taste with salt and pepper.

Family Favorite Beef Stew

Use your family's favorite vegetables in this stew.

8 entrée servings

2 pounds lean beef stew meat, cubed (1-inch)
1 can (14½ ounces) diced tomatoes, undrained
1 cup reduced-sodium fat-free beef broth
2 cups each: cubed unpeeled medium potatoes,
   rutabaga or turnips
1½ cups chopped onions
1 cup thickly sliced carrots
2 large ribs celery, sliced
4 cloves garlic, minced
½–¾ teaspoon each: dried marjoram and
   thyme leaves
1 bay leaf
2 tablespoons cornstarch
¼ cup cold water
2–3 teaspoons Worcestershire sauce
Salt and pepper, to taste

Per Serving:
Calories: 314
% calories from fat: 22
Protein (g): 32.8
Carbohydrate (g): 28.5
Fat (g): 7.5
Saturated fat (g): 2.3
Cholesterol (mg): 70.9
Sodium (mg): 134
Exchanges:
Milk: 0.0
Vegetable: 0.0
Fruit: 0.0
Bread: 2.0
Meat: 3.0
Fat: 0.0

1. Combine all ingredients, except cornstarch, water, Worcestershire sauce, salt, and pepper, in 6-quart slow cooker; cover and cook on low 6 to 8 hours. Turn heat to high and cook 10 minutes; stir in combined cornstarch and water, stirring 2 to 3 minutes. Discard bay leaf; season to taste with Worcestershire sauce, salt, and pepper.

Beef and Vegetable Stew

This beef stew boasts an ample assortment of vegetables to make a well-rounded meal.

6 entrée servings

1½ pounds lean beef round steak, cubed (1-inch)
1 cup reduced-sodium fat-free beef broth
½ cup red wine or beef broth
6 medium carrots, quartered
4 each: quartered small potatoes, onions
2 small zucchini, sliced
1 cup small mushrooms
1 clove garlic, minced
1 teaspoon Worcestershire sauce
2 bay leaves
1 tablespoon cornstarch
¼ cup cold water
Salt and pepper, to taste

Per Serving:
Calories: 289
% calories from fat: 13
Protein (g): 24.5
Carbohydrate (g): 35.9
Fat (g): 4.1
Saturated fat (g): 1.4
Cholesterol (mg): 55
Sodium (mg): 96
Exchanges:
Milk: 0.0
Vegetable: 1.0
Fruit: 0.0
Bread: 1.5
Meat: 3.0
Fat: 0.0

1. Combine all ingredients, except cornstarch, water, salt, and pepper, in 6-quart slow cooker; cover and cook on low 6 to 8 hours. Turn heat to high and cook 10 minutes; stir in combined cornstarch and water, stirring 2 to 3 minutes. Discard bay leaves; season to taste with salt and pepper.

Beef and Mushroom Stew

A great thing about a slow cooker is that it can go to the table for serving!

6 entrée servings

1 pound lean beef round steak, cubed
2 cups reduced-sodium fat-free beef broth
½ cup dry white wine or beef broth
8 ounces mushrooms, thinly sliced
¼ cup chopped onion
1 clove garlic, minced
1 tablespoon dried Italian seasoning
2 tablespoons cornstarch
½ cup cold water
Salt and pepper, to taste
8 ounces wide noodles, cooked, warm

Per Serving:
Calories: 495
% calories from fat: 23
Protein (g): 36.4
Carbohydrate (g): 47.6
Fat (g): 12.5
Saturated fat (g): 1.9
Cholesterol (mg): 95.3
Sodium (mg): 264
Exchanges:
Milk: 0.0
Vegetable: 0.0
Fruit: 0.0
Bread: 3.0
Meat: 3.0
Fat: 1.5

1. Combine all ingredients, except cornstarch, water, salt, pepper, and noodles, in slow cooker; cover and cook on low 6 to 8 hours. Turn heat to high and cook 10 minutes; stir in combined cornstarch and water, stirring 2 to 3 minutes. Season to taste with salt and pepper; serve over noodles.

Beef and Cabbage Stew

A robust beef stew that includes both potatoes and rice. The potatoes add chunky texture and the rice helps thicken the flavorful sauce.

4 entrée servings

1 pound lean beef round steak, cubed
1½ cups each: reduced-sodium fat-free beef broth, coarsely shredded cabbage
2 small unpeeled potatoes, sliced
1 each: large finely chopped onion, sliced carrot
2 cloves garlic, minced
½ cup dry red wine or beef broth
¼ cup catsup
2 teaspoons brown sugar
1½ teaspoons each: cider vinegar, dried thyme leaves
½ teaspoon dry mustard
¼ cup uncooked converted long-grain rice
2 tablespoons cornstarch
¼ cup cold water
Salt and pepper, to taste

Per Serving:
Calories: 450
% calories from fat: 27
Protein (g): 28.5
Carbohydrate (g): 45.9
Fat (g): 13.4
Saturated fat (g): 5.0
Cholesterol (mg): 67.8
Sodium (mg): 397
Exchanges:
Milk: 0.0
Vegetable: 0.0
Fruit: 0.0
Bread: 3.0
Meat: 3.0
Fat: 1.0

1. Combine all ingredients, except rice, cornstarch, water, salt, and pepper, in slow cooker; cover and cook on low 6 to 8 hours, adding rice during last 2 hours. Turn heat to high and cook 10 minutes; stir in combined cornstarch and water, stirring 2 to 3 minutes. Season to taste with salt and pepper.

Harvest Stew

If you don't have a second slow cooker, the Polenta recipe can be made in the microwave (see p. 385), or you can cook polenta conventionally, following package directions.

8 entrée servings

2 pounds lean beef stew meat, cubed (1-inch)
1 cup reduced-sodium fat-free beef broth
3 cups cubed butternut squash
4 medium tomatoes, chopped
½ cup chopped onion
¾ teaspoon each: dried marjoram and savory leaves
3 medium zucchini, cubed
Salt and pepper, to taste
6 cups Polenta (see p. 520)

Per Serving:
Calories: 284
% calories from fat: 20
Protein (g): 25.2
Carbohydrate (g): 32.4
Fat (g): 6.6
Saturated fat (g): 1.7
Cholesterol (mg): 55
Sodium (mg): 84
Exchanges:
Milk: 0.0
Vegetable: 1.0
Fruit: 0.0
Bread: 1.5
Meat: 3.0
Fat: 0.0

1. Combine all ingredients, except zucchini, salt, pepper, and Polenta, in 6-quart slow cooker; cover and cook on low 6 to 8 hours, adding zucchini during last 45 minutes. Season to taste with salt and pepper. Serve over Polenta.

Wine-Braised Beef Stew

The slow cooking gives this dish a rich flavor. A good-quality Chianti would be an excellent wine choice.

6 entrée servings

1½ pounds boneless beef round steak, cubed
1 cup each: reduced-sodium fat-free beef broth,
   tomato sauce
½ cup dry red wine or beef broth
2 cups sliced mushrooms
1 cup chopped onion
½ cup thinly sliced celery
12 baby carrots
6 small potatoes, halved
1 teaspoon minced garlic
1 teaspoon dried thyme leaves
2 large bay leaves
1–2 tablespoons cornstarch
¼ cup cold water
Salt and pepper, to taste

Per Serving:
Calories: 366
% calories from fat: 18
Protein (g): 31.2
Carbohydrate (g): 36.9
Fat (g): 7.4
Saturated fat (g): 2.2
Cholesterol (mg): 55.9
Sodium (mg): 115
Exchanges:
Milk: 0.0
Vegetable: 2.0
Fruit: 0.0
Bread: 2.0
Meat: 3.0
Fat: 0.0

1. Combine all ingredients, except cornstarch, water, salt, and pepper, in 6-quart slow cooker; cover and cook on low 6 to 8 hours. Turn heat to high and cook 10 minutes; stir in combined cornstarch and water, stirring 2 to 3 minutes. Discard bay leaves; season to taste with salt and pepper.

Rosemary Beef Stew

Fragrant rosemary is the highlight of this delicious stew.

6 entrée servings

1½ pounds lean beef stew meat, cubed
1½ cups reduced-sodium fat-free beef broth
1 can (8 ounces) tomato sauce
2 tablespoons dry sherry (optional)
3 cups cut green beans
1 cup finely chopped onion
½ cup each: sliced carrots, celery
1 large clove garlic, minced
1 teaspoon dried rosemary leaves
1 bay leaf
1–2 tablespoons cornstarch
¼ cup cold water
Salt and pepper, to taste
4 cups cooked rice, warm

Per Serving:
Calories: 404
% calories from fat: 23
Protein (g): 30.9
Carbohydrate (g): 46.7
Fat (g): 10.1
Saturated fat (g): 3.4
Cholesterol (mg): 60.6
Sodium (mg): 596
Exchanges:
Milk: 0.0
Vegetable: 0.0
Fruit: 0.0
Bread: 3.0
Meat: 3.0
Fat: 0.0

1. Combine all ingredients, except cornstarch, water, salt, pepper, and rice, in 6-quart slow cooker; cover and cook on low 6 to 8 hours. Turn heat to high and cook 10 minutes; stir in combined cornstarch and water, stirring 2 to 3 minutes. Discard bay leaf; season to taste with salt and pepper; serve over rice.

Steak and Sweet Potato Stew

Apples give this autumn stew a touch of sweetness.

4 entrée servings

1 pound lean beef round steak, cubed (¾-inch)
1½ cups reduced-sodium fat-free beef broth
1 pound sweet potatoes, peeled, cubed
2 medium onions, cut into thin wedges
1 teaspoon dried savory leaves
2 medium apples, peeled, thickly sliced
½ cup frozen peas, thawed
2 tablespoons cornstarch
¼ cup cold water
Salt and pepper, to taste

Per Serving:
Calories: 442
% calories from fat: 13
Protein (g): 34.2
Carbohydrate (g): 62.3
Fat (g): 6.7
Saturated fat (g): 2.1
Cholesterol (mg): 55.9
Sodium (mg): 197
Exchanges:
Milk: 0.0
Vegetable: 0.0
Fruit: 1.0
Bread: 3.0
Meat: 3.0
Fat: 0.0

1. Combine all ingredients, except apples, peas, cornstarch, water, salt, and pepper, in slow cooker; cover and cook on low 6 to 8 hours, adding apples during last 15 minutes. Add peas, turn heat to high, and cook 10 minutes. Stir in combined cornstarch and water, stirring 2 to 3 minutes. Season to taste with salt and pepper.

Barbecued Beef and Bean Stew

This spicy barbecued beef and bean dinner is sure to please!

6 entrée servings

1 pound lean beef round steak, cut into strips
  (½-inch)
3 cans (15 ounces each) rinsed, drained kidney beans
1 can (8 ounces) tomato sauce
½ cup mild or medium salsa
1½ cups finely chopped onions
2 cloves garlic, minced
2 tablespoons cider vinegar
2–3 tablespoons brown sugar
2–3 teaspoons chili powder
2 teaspoons Worcestershire sauce
1 cup whole kernel corn
Salt and pepper, to taste

Per Serving:
Calories: 397
% calories from fat: 14
Protein (g): 29
Carbohydrate (g): 50.3
Fat (g): 9.6
Saturated fat (g): 3.4
Cholesterol (mg): 45
Sodium (mg): 1109
Exchanges:
Milk: 0.0
Vegetable: 1.0
Fruit: 0.0
Bread: 3.0
Meat: 3.0
Fat: 0.0

1. Combine all ingredients, except corn, salt, and pepper, in slow cooker; cover and cook on low 6 to 8 hours, stirring in corn last 30 minutes. Season to taste with salt and pepper.

Paprika-Sirloin Stew with Sour Cream

Enjoy tender beef and vegetables in a paprika-spiked sour cream sauce!

4 entrée servings

1 pound boneless beef sirloin steak, fat trimmed,
   cut into strips (1 x ½-inch)
1 cup reduced-sodium fat-free beef broth
1 can (14½ ounces) diced tomatoes, undrained
3 cups cubed red potatoes
8 ounces green beans, halved
4 ounces frozen pearl onions, thawed
2 bay leaves
1 tablespoon paprika
½ cup reduced-fat sour cream
1 tablespoon cornstarch
Salt and pepper, to taste

Per Serving:
Calories: 286
% calories from fat: 17
Protein (g): 27.4
Carbohydrate (g): 32.9
Fat (g): 5.4
Saturated fat (g): 2
Cholesterol (mg): 59.5
Sodium (mg): 768
Exchanges:
Milk: 0.0
Vegetable: 0.0
Fruit: 0.0
Bread: 2.0
Meat: 3.0
Fat: 0.0

1. Combine all ingredients, except sour cream, cornstarch, salt, and pepper, in slow cooker; cover and cook on low 6 to 8 hours. Stir in combined sour cream and cornstarch, stirring 2 to 3 minutes. Discard bay leaves; season to taste with salt and pepper.

Ground Beef and Vegetable Stroganoff

Sour cream and a medley of mushrooms contribute rich flavor and creamy texture to this favorite stew.

8 entrée servings

1½ pounds lean ground beef
½ cup water
¼ cup dry red wine or water
2 medium onions, thinly sliced
2 cloves garlic, minced
8 ounces sliced mixed wild mushrooms
   (shiitake, oyster, enoki, or cremini)
1½ teaspoons Dijon mustard
½ teaspoon dried dill weed
8 ounces broccoli florets
1 cup reduced-fat sour cream
2 tablespoons cornstarch
Salt and pepper, to taste
1 pound noodles, cooked, warm

Per Serving:
Calories: 414
% calories from fat: 21
Protein (g): 29.3
Carbohydrate (g): 49.8
Fat (g): 9.4
Saturated fat (g): 4.1
Cholesterol (mg): 110.4
Sodium (mg): 109
Exchanges:
Milk: 0.0
Vegetable: 1.0
Fruit: 0.0
Bread: 3.0
Meat: 3.0
Fat: 0.0

1. Cook ground beef in lightly greased large skillet over medium heat until browned, about 10 minutes, crumbling with a fork. Combine beef and remaining ingredients, except broccoli, sour cream, cornstarch, salt, pepper, and noodles, in slow cooker; cook on low 6 to 8 hours, adding broccoli during last 30 minutes. Stir in combined sour cream and cornstarch, stirring 2 to 3 minutes. Season to taste with salt and pepper; serve over noodles.

Beef and Ancho Chili Stew

Complement this delicious stew with sour cream; serve with warm tortillas.

8 entrée servings

2½ cups boiling water
4–6 ancho chilies, stems, seeds, and veins
  discarded
4 medium tomatoes, cut into wedges
2 pounds lean beef eye of round steak,
  cubed (¾-inch)
1 large onion, chopped
2 cloves garlic, minced
1 teaspoon each: minced jalapeño chili,
  dried oregano leaves, crushed cumin seeds
1 tablespoon cornstarch
3 tablespoons cold water
Salt and pepper, to taste
Red Pepper Rice (see p. 403)

Per Serving:
Calories: 393
% calories from fat: 31
Protein (g): 29.7
Carbohydrate (g): 38.5
Fat (g): 13.8
Saturated fat (g): 5.0
Cholesterol (mg): 67.8
Sodium (mg): 406
Exchanges:
Milk: 0.0
Vegetable: 2.0
Fruit: 0.0
Bread: 2.0
Meat: 3.0
Fat: 1.0

1. Pour boiling water over chilies in bowl; let stand until softened, about 10 minutes. Process chilies, water, and tomatoes in food processor or blender until smooth.
2. Combine chili mixture and remaining ingredients, except cornstarch, water, salt, pepper, and Red Pepper Rice, in slow cooker; cover and cook on low 6 to 8 hours. Turn heat to high and cook 10 minutes; stir in combined cornstarch and water, stirring 2 to 3 minutes. Season to taste with salt and pepper; serve over Red Pepper Rice.

Beef Stew da Vinci

A bounty of Italian flavors, served over linguine!

4 entrée servings

1¼ pounds lean beef round steak, cubed (1-inch)
1 can (14½ ounces) diced tomatoes, undrained
1 cup each: chopped onion, green bell peppers,
  sliced mushrooms
¼ cup chopped shallots or green onions
1 teaspoon each: beef bouillon crystals, dried basil
  leaves, garlic powder
2 tablespoons cornstarch
¼ cup cold water
Salt and pepper, to taste
6 ounces linguine, cooked, warm
¼ cup each: chopped parsley, grated Parmesan cheese

Per Serving:
Calories: 425
% calories from fat: 17
Protein (g): 41.3
Carbohydrate (g): 44.8
Fat (g): 7.9
Saturated fat (g): 3.0
Cholesterol (mg): 66.5
Sodium (mg): 479
Exchanges:
Milk: 0.0
Vegetable: 0.0
Fruit: 0.0
Bread: 3.0
Meat: 4.0
Fat: 0.0

1. Combine all ingredients, except cornstarch, water, salt, pepper, linguine, parsley, and cheese, in slow cooker; cover and cook on low 6 to 8 hours. Turn heat to high and cook 10 minutes; stir in combined cornstarch and water, stirring 2 to 3 minutes. Season to taste with salt and pepper. Serve over linguine; sprinkle with parsley and Parmesan cheese.

Beef Burgundy

This French-inspired stew is perfect for special occasions.

8 entrée servings

2 pounds lean beef stew meat
1 cup each: Burgundy or other red wine, reduced-
  sodium fat-free beef broth
1 tablespoon tomato paste
1 cup chopped onion
1 teaspoon each: thyme, rosemary, and
  tarragon leaves
1½ cups each: frozen thawed pearl onions,
  sliced mushrooms
2 tablespoons cornstarch
¼ cup cold water
½ cup chopped parsley
Salt and pepper, to taste

Per Serving:
Calories: 230
% calories from fat: 23
Protein (g): 30.4
Carbohydrate (g): 7.4
Fat (g): 5.6
Saturated fat (g): 2
Cholesterol (mg): 70.9
Sodium (mg): 98
Exchanges:
Milk: 0.0
Vegetable: 1.0
Fruit: 0.0
Bread: 0.0
Meat: 4.0
Fat: 0.0

1. Combine beef, wine, broth, tomato paste, chopped onion, and herbs in 6-quart slow cooker; cover and cook on low 6 to 8 hours, adding pearl onions and mushrooms during last 2 hours. Turn heat to high and cook 10 minutes; stir in combined cornstarch and water, stirring 2 to 3 minutes. Stir in parsley and season to taste with salt and pepper.

Beef Stroganoff

A favorite for buffet entertaining, this dish enjoys well-deserved popularity.

4 entrée servings

1 pound lean beef eye of round or sirloin steak, cut into strips (½-inch)
1 cup reduced-sodium fat-free beef broth
3 cups sliced mushrooms
½ cup sliced onion
2 cloves garlic, minced
1 teaspoon Dijon mustard
½ teaspoon dried thyme leaves
½ cup reduced-fat sour cream
1 tablespoon cornstarch
Salt and pepper, to taste
3 cups cooked noodles, warm

Per Serving:
Calories: 423
% calories from fat: 21
Protein (g): 39
Carbohydrate (g): 45.1
Fat (g): 10
Saturated fat (g): 2.2
Cholesterol (mg): 64
Sodium (mg): 167
Exchanges:
Milk: 0.0
Vegetable: 1.0
Fruit: 0.0
Bread: 2.5
Meat: 4.0
Fat: 0.0

1. Combine all ingredients, except sour cream, cornstarch, salt, pepper, and noodles, in slow cooker; cover and cook on low 6 to 8 hours. Stir in combined sour cream and cornstarch, stirring 2 to 3 minutes. Season to taste with salt and pepper; serve over noodles.

Creamy Beef Stroganoff with Rice

Horseradish adds a pleasant sharpness of flavor; increase the amount if you like.

4 entrée servings

1 pound lean beef top round steak, cubed (1-inch)
1 cup reduced-sodium fat-free beef broth
¼ cup red Burgundy wine (optional)
3 tablespoons tomato paste
8 ounces mushrooms, sliced
1 cup chopped onion
2 large cloves garlic, minced
1 teaspoon prepared horseradish
½ teaspoon dried thyme leaves
1 bay leaf
¾ cup reduced-fat sour cream
2 tablespoons cornstarch
Salt and pepper, to taste
1 cup cooked rice, warm

Per Serving:
Calories: 438
% calories from fat: 15
Protein (g): 36.1
Carbohydrate (g): 55.8
Fat (g): 6.9
Saturated fat (g): 2
Cholesterol (mg): 72.3
Sodium (mg): 412
Exchanges:
Milk: 0.0
Vegetable: 2.0
Fruit: 0.0
Bread: 3.0
Meat: 3.0
Fat: 0.0

1. Combine all ingredients, except sour cream, cornstarch, salt, pepper, and rice, in slow cooker; cover and cook on low 6 to 8 hours. Stir in combined sour cream and cornstarch, stirring 2 to 3 minutes. Discard bay leaf; season to taste with salt and pepper. Serve over rice.

Beef and Mushroom Stroganoff

Serve in shallow bowls with warm crusty bread to soak up the juices.

4 entrée servings

1 pound lean beef round steak, cut into strips
  (½-inch)
1½ cups reduced-sodium fat-free beef broth
8 ounces mushrooms, sliced
½ cup chopped onion
¼ cup chopped shallots or green onions
1 clove garlic, minced
½–1 cup reduced-fat sour cream
2 tablespoons cornstarch
Salt and pepper, to taste

Per Serving:
Calories: 281
% calories from fat: 30
Protein (g): 32.7
Carbohydrate (g): 15.4
Fat (g): 9.3
Saturated fat (g): 2.6
Cholesterol (mg): 69.5
Sodium (mg): 317
Exchanges:
Milk: 0.0
Vegetable: 0.0
Fruit: 0.0
Bread: 1.0
Meat: 4.0
Fat: 0.0

1. Combine all ingredients, except sour cream, cornstarch, salt, and pepper, in slow cooker; cover and cook on low 6 to 8 hours. Stir in combined sour cream and cornstarch, stirring 2 to 3 minutes. Season to taste with salt and pepper.

Beef Ragout

Serve this stew over rice, noodles, or a cooked grain, such as barley, wheat berries, or oat groats.

8 entrée servings

2 pounds lean beef stew meat, cubed (1-inch)
1½ cups reduced-sodium fat-free beef broth
2 cups each: sliced carrots, celery
8 ounces frozen pearl onions, thawed
1 clove garlic, chopped
1 teaspoon each: dried oregano and thyme leaves
2 tablespoons cornstarch
¼ cup cold water
Salt and pepper, to taste

Per Serving:
Calories: 215
% calories from fat: 35
Protein (g): 27.1
Carbohydrate (g): 7.2
Fat (g): 8.4
Saturated fat (g): 2.9
Cholesterol (mg): 77.2
Sodium (mg): 386
Exchanges:
Milk: 0.0
Vegetable: 1.0
Fruit: 0.0
Bread: 0.0
Meat: 3.5
Fat: 0.0

1. Combine all ingredients, except cornstarch, water, salt, and pepper, in 6-quart slow cooker; cover and cook on low 6 to 8 hours. Turn heat to high and cook 10 minutes; stir in combined cornstarch and water, stirring 2 to 3 minutes. Season to taste with salt and pepper.

Beef Goulash

In Hungary, this paprika-seasoned stew is called "gulyas," and it's often served with dollops of sour cream.

4 entrée servings

12–16 ounces lean beef round steak, cubed (¾-inch)
1 can (14½) diced tomatoes, undrained
2 cups cabbage, coarsely sliced
3 medium onions, cut into thin wedges
1 cup chopped portobello mushrooms
1 tablespoon paprika
2 teaspoons caraway seeds
1–2 tablespoons cornstarch
¼ cup cold water
Salt and pepper, to taste
8 ounces medium egg noodles, cooked, warm

Per Serving:
Calories: 407
% calories from fat: 17
Protein (g): 29.9
Carbohydrate (g): 55.2
Fat (g): 7.7
Saturated fat (g): 2
Cholesterol (mg): 90.9
Sodium (mg): 473
Exchanges:
Milk: 0.0
Vegetable: 2.0
Fruit: 0.0
Bread: 3.0
Meat: 2.0
Fat: 0.5

1. Combine all ingredients, except cornstarch, water, salt, pepper, and noodles, in slow cooker; cover and cook on low 6 to 8 hours. Turn heat to high and cook 10 minutes; stir in cornstarch and water, stirring 2 to 3 minutes. Season to taste with salt and pepper; serve over noodles.

Hungarian Goulash

Hungarian goulash is slow cooked to tender goodness.

6 entrée servings

2 pounds lean beef round steak, cubed (1-inch)
1 can (14½ ounces) diced tomatoes, undrained
1 medium onion, finely chopped
1 teaspoon minced garlic
1½ teaspoons paprika
1 bay leaf
1 cup reduced-fat sour cream
2 tablespoons cornstarch
Salt and pepper, to taste
12 ounces egg noodles, cooked, warm

Per Serving:
Calories: 471
% calories from fat: 17
Protein (g): 44.6
Carbohydrate (g): 50.5
Fat (g): 8.7
Saturated fat (g): 2.9
Cholesterol (mg): 123.5
Sodium (mg): 367
Exchanges:
Milk: 0.0
Vegetable: 1.0
Fruit: 0.0
Bread: 3.0
Meat: 4.0
Fat: 0.0

1. Combine all ingredients, except sour cream, cornstarch, salt, pepper, and noodles, in slow cooker; cover and cook on low 6 to 8 hours. Stir in combined sour cream and cornstarch, stirring 2 to 3 minutes. Discard bay leaf; season to taste with salt and pepper. Serve over noodles.

Hungarian-Style Beef Stew

Serve this rich-tasting stew with warm crusty bread to soak up the delicious sauce.

6 entrée servings

1 pound lean beef round steak, cut into thin strips
½ cup each: reduced-sodium fat-free beef broth,
  dry red wine or beef broth
1 can (8 ounces) tomato sauce
1 pound peeled potatoes, cubed
2 each: sliced large carrots, ribs celery
1 cup finely chopped onion
1 large clove garlic, minced
1 teaspoon each: dried thyme leaves, paprika
1 bay leaf
¼ teaspoon dry mustard
½ cup reduced-fat sour cream
1 tablespoon cornstarch
Salt and pepper, to taste

Per Serving:
Calories: 441
% calories from fat: 27
Protein (g): 30.6
Carbohydrate (g): 44.8
Fat (g): 13.2
Saturated fat (g): 4.9
Cholesterol (mg): 72.8
Sodium (mg): 724
Exchanges:
Milk: 0.0
Vegetable: 0.0
Fruit: 0.0
Bread: 3.0
Meat: 3.0
Fat: 1.0

1. Combine all ingredients, except sour cream, cornstarch, salt, and pepper, in slow cooker; cover and cook on low 6 to 8 hours. Stir in combined sour cream and cornstarch, stirring 2 to 3 minutes. Discard bay leaf; season to taste with salt and pepper.

Five-Spice Beef Stew

A simple-to-make stew with lots of Asian flavor, thanks to five-spice powder and Chinese chili sauces.

4 entrée servings

1 pound lean beef round steak, cubed (1-inch)
¾ cup each: orange juice, reduced-sodium fat-free
  beef broth
2 cups coarsely sliced Napa cabbage
1 each: medium onion cut into thin wedges, thinly
  sliced red bell pepper
1 tablespoon teriyaki sauce
1 teaspoon Chinese chili sauce with garlic
1¼ teaspoons five-spice powder
4 ounces bean thread noodles
Salt and pepper, to taste

Per Serving:
Calories: 321
% calories from fat: 14
Protein (g): 28.8
Carbohydrate (g): 39.3
Fat (g): 5
Saturated fat (g): 1.8
Cholesterol (mg): 55.9
Sodium (mg): 208
Exchanges:
Milk: 0.0
Vegetable: 1.0
Fruit: 0.0
Bread: 2.0
Meat: 3.0
Fat: 0.0

1. Combine all ingredients, except noodles, salt, and pepper, in slow cooker; cover and cook 6 to 8 hours.
2. During last hour of cooking time, soak bean thread noodles in hot water to cover in large bowl for 15 minutes; drain and stir into stew during last 30 minutes of cooking time. Season to taste with salt and pepper.

Asian Beef Stew with Sesame Noodles

Sesame Noodles are the perfect accompaniment for this fragrant stew.

8 entrée servings

2 pounds lean beef stew meat, cubed (1-inch)
1 cup water
2 each: thin slices gingerroot, halved cloves garlic, sliced green onions
3–4 tablespoons soy sauce
2–3 teaspoons sugar
3 tablespoons dry sherry (optional)
½ cup frozen peas, thawed
2 tablespoons cornstarch
¼ cup cold water
Salt and pepper, to taste
Sesame Noodles (recipe follows)
1 tablespoon sesame seeds, toasted
Finely chopped cilantro, as garnish

Per Serving:
Calories: 295
% calories from fat: 23
Protein (g): 26.8
Carbohydrate (g): 27.6
Fat (g): 7.3
Saturated fat (g): 1.7
Cholesterol (mg): 57.1
Sodium (mg): 518
Exchanges:
Milk: 0.0
Vegetable: 0.0
Fruit: 0.0
Bread: 2.0
Meat: 3.0
Fat: 0.0

1. Combine all ingredients, except peas, cornstarch, cold water, salt, pepper, noodles, sesame seeds, and cilantro, in slow cooker; cover and cook on low 6 to 8 hours. Add peas, turn heat to high, and cook 10 minutes; stir in combined cornstarch and water, stirring 2 to 3 minutes. Season to taste with salt and pepper. Serve over Sesame Noodles; sprinkle with sesame seeds and cilantro.

Sesame Noodles

Makes 8 servings

1 package (12 ounces) Asian or any thin noodles, cooked, warm
2–4 teaspoons soy sauce
2 teaspoons Asian sesame oil
2 green onions, thinly sliced

1. Toss warm noodles with remaining ingredients.

Teriyaki Beef and Broccoli Stew

The stew can also be served over rice, pasta, or any grain.

4 entrée servings

12–16 ounces lean beef round steak, cut into thin
  strips (½-inch)
1 cup reduced-sodium fat-free beef broth
1 medium onion, cut into thin wedges
2 carrots, sliced
1 tablespoon minced gingerroot
2 tablespoons teriyaki sauce
2 cups small broccoli florets
2 tablespoons cornstarch
¼ cup cold water
Salt and pepper, to taste
8 ounces noodles, cooked, warm

Per Serving:
Calories: 332
% calories from fat: 25
Protein (g): 26
Carbohydrate (g): 44.4
Fat (g): 10.3
Saturated fat (g): 1.7
Cholesterol (mg): 45.6
Sodium (mg): 1081
Exchanges:
Milk: 0.0
Vegetable: 1.0
Fruit: 0.0
Bread: 2.0
Meat: 3.0
Fat: 0.0

1. Combine all ingredients, except broccoli, cornstarch, water, salt, pepper, and noodles, to slow cooker; cover and cook on low 6 to 8 hours, adding broccoli during last 30 minutes. Turn heat to high and cook 10 minutes; stir in combined cornstarch and water, stirring 2 to 3 minutes. Season to taste with salt and pepper; serve over noodles.

Middle Eastern Beef and Bean Hot Pot

Sweet spices give Middle Eastern flavor accents to this stew.

8 entrée servings

1 pound lean beef stew meat, cubed
1 cup dried Great Northern beans
1 quart reduced-sodium fat-free beef broth
2 cups chopped onions
2 each: minced cloves garlic, bay leaves
1 teaspoon dried thyme leaves
½ teaspoon ground cinnamon
⅛ teaspoon ground cloves
1½ cups diced tomatoes
1¼ cups cooked rice
Salt and pepper, to taste

Per Serving:
Calories: 427
% calories from fat: 17
Protein (g): 35
Carbohydrate (g): 52
Fat (g): 8.1
Saturated fat (g): 4.4
Cholesterol (mg): 71
Sodium (mg): 595
Exchanges:
Milk: 0.0
Vegetable: 2.0
Fruit: 0.0
Bread: 3.0
Meat: 3.0
Fat: 0.0

1. Combine all ingredients, except rice, salt, and pepper, in 6-quart slow cooker; cover and cook on low until beans are tender, 7 to 8 hours, adding tomatoes and rice during last 30 minutes. Discard bay leaves; season to taste with salt and pepper.

Curried Beef Stew with Chive Biscuits

Part of the beef in this aromatic stew is coarsely chopped, giving the stew an extra-rich texture.

8 entrée servings

2 pounds lean beef stew meat
1½ cups each: reduced-sodium fat-free
  beef broth, chopped onions
1 large tomato, coarsely chopped
1½ teaspoons curry powder
2 bay leaves
Salt and pepper, to taste
1 package (10 ounces) frozen peas, thawed
4 biscuits, baked, halved
Melted margarine or cooking spray
Chopped fresh or dried chives

Per Serving:
Calories: 297
% calories from fat: 22
Protein (g): 27.1
Carbohydrate (g): 29.4
Fat (g): 7.3
Saturated fat (g): 1.9
Cholesterol (mg): 55.3
Sodium (mg): 416
Exchanges:
Milk: 0.0
Vegetable: 0.0
Fruit: 0.0
Bread: 2.0
Meat: 3.0
Fat: 0.0

1. Cut 1 pound beef into scant 1-inch cubes; coarsely chop remaining 1 pound beef. Combine beef and remaining ingredients, except salt, pepper, peas, biscuits, margarine, and chives, in slow cooker; cover and cook on low 6 to 8 hours. Discard bay leaves; season to taste with salt and pepper. Add peas and place biscuit halves, cut sides down, on stew. Brush biscuits lightly with margarine and sprinkle with chives; cover and cook 15 minutes.

Greek Beef and Lentil Stew

Lentils and fresh vegetables partner deliciously in this easy stew.

6 entrée servings

1 pound boneless beef eye of round, cubed (¾-inch)
3 cups reduced-sodium fat-free beef broth
1 can (14½ ounces) diced tomatoes, undrained
2 cups each: cubed Idaho potatoes, cut green beans
1 cup each: dried lentils, chopped onion, green bell
  pepper
2 teaspoons minced garlic
1 teaspoon each: dried oregano and mint leaves
½ teaspoon each: ground turmeric, coriander
1 cup cubed zucchini
Salt and pepper, to taste

Per Serving:
Calories: 302
% calories from fat: 7
Protein (g): 25.5
Carbohydrate (g): 46.7
Fat (g): 2.6
Saturated fat (g): 0.8
Cholesterol (mg): 27.5
Sodium (mg): 122
Exchanges:
Milk: 0.0
Vegetable: 3.0
Fruit: 0.0
Bread: 2.0
Meat: 1.5
Fat: 0.0

1. Combine all ingredients, except zucchini, salt, and pepper, in 6-quart slow cooker; cover and cook on low 6 to 8 hours, adding zucchini during last 30 minutes. Season to taste with salt and pepper.

Meatball and Pasta Stew

Romano Meatballs combine with vegetables and tricolor pasta in a delectable stew. Meatballs will be less fragile to handle if browned in a lightly greased skillet.

4 entrée servings

Romano Meatballs (recipe follows)
2 cans (14 ounces) reduced-sodium fat-free
  beef broth
1 can (14½ ounces) plum tomatoes, undrained,
  chopped
¼ cup chopped onion
1 teaspoon dried Italian seasoning
4 ounces tri-color corkscrew pasta, cooked
2 cups small broccoli florets
3 tablespoons cornstarch
⅓ cup cold water
Salt and pepper, to taste

Per Serving:
Calories: 337
% calories from fat: 22
Protein (g): 25.6
Carbohydrate (g): 39
Fat (g): 8.1
Saturated fat (g): 3.5
Cholesterol (mg): 98.4
Sodium (mg): 1023
Exchanges:
Milk: 0.0
Vegetable: 2.0
Fruit: 0.0
Bread: 2.0
Meat: 2.0
Fat: 0.5

1. Combine all ingredients, except pasta, broccoli, cornstarch, water, salt, and pepper, in slow cooker, making sure meatballs are submerged; cover and cook on low 6 to 8 hours, adding pasta and broccoli during the last 15 min-

utes. Turn heat to high and cook 10 minutes; stir in combined cornstarch and water, stirring 2 to 3 minutes. Season to taste with salt and pepper.

Romano Meatballs

Makes 16

8 ounces lean ground beef
1 egg white
½ cup quick-cooking oats
1 tablespoon dried minced onion
½ teaspoon dried Italian seasoning, divided
½ cup (2 ounces) grated Romano cheese

1. Combine all ingredients; shape mixture into 16 meatballs.

Cubed Steak Stew

The perfect stew for hearty appetites!

6 entrée servings

1½ pounds lean beef cubed steaks, cut into strips (2 x ½-inch)
1 can (14½ ounces) diced tomatoes with Italian herbs, undrained
1 can (8 ounces) tomato sauce
4 medium red potatoes, cubed
1 large onion, thinly sliced
½ teaspoon garlic powder
1 package (10 ounces) frozen peas and carrots, thawed
2 tablespoons cornstarch
¼ cup water
Salt and pepper, to taste

Per Serving:
Calories: 307
% calories from fat: 19
Protein (g): 26.6
Carbohydrate (g): 35.5
Fat (g): 6.3
Saturated fat (g): 1.6
Cholesterol (mg): 55
Sodium (mg): 372
Exchanges:
Milk: 0.0
Vegetable: 1.0
Fruit: 0.0
Bread: 2.0
Meat: 2.5
Fat: 0.0

1. Combine all ingredients, except frozen vegetables, cornstarch, water, salt, and pepper, in 6-quart slow cooker; cover and heat on low 6 to 8 hours, adding thawed frozen vegetables during last 10 minutes. Turn heat to high and cook 10 minutes; stir in combined cornstarch and water, stirring 2 to 3 minutes. Season to taste with salt and pepper.

Hearty Meatball 'n Veggie Stew

If meatballs are browned in a lightly greased large skillet, or baked at 350 degrees until browned, they will be less fragile and more attractive. Add meatballs to slow cooker carefully, so they don't break apart.

6 entrée servings

Hearty Meatballs (recipe follows)
1 cup reduced-sodium fat-free beef broth
1 can (28 ounces) diced tomatoes, undrained
3 carrots, thickly sliced
1 teaspoon dried basil leaves
2 small zucchini, sliced
½ cup frozen peas, thawed
2 tablespoons cornstarch
¼ cup cold water
Salt and pepper, to taste
12 ounces noodles or fettuccine, cooked, warm

Per Serving:
Calories: 554
% calories from fat: 26
Protein (g): 35.8
Carbohydrate (g): 65.3
Fat (g): 16
Saturated fat (g): 5.8
Cholesterol (mg): 105.8
Sodium (mg): 536
Exchanges:
Milk: 0.0
Vegetable: 2.0
Fruit: 0.0
Bread: 4.0
Meat: 3.0
Fat: 1.0

1. Combine all ingredients, except zucchini, peas, cornstarch, water, salt, pepper, and noodles, in 6-quart slow cooker, making sure meatballs are submerged; cover and cook on low 6 to 8 hours, adding zucchini and peas during last 20 minutes. Turn heat to high and cook 10 minutes; stir in combined cornstarch and water, stirring 2 to 3 minutes. Season to taste with salt and pepper; serve over noodles.

Hearty Meatballs

Makes 18

1½ pounds lean ground beef
⅓ cup finely chopped onion
1 egg
½ cup unseasoned dry bread crumbs
2 cloves garlic, minced
1–2 teaspoons beef-flavor bouillon crystals
½ teaspoon salt
¼ teaspoon pepper

1. Mix all ingredients in bowl; shape mixture into 18 meatballs.

Variation

Italian Meatball Stew—Make recipe as above, substituting dried Italian seasoning for the basil, adding 1 cup halved small mushrooms, and substituting Italian Turkey Meatballs (see p. 198) for the Hearty Meatballs.

Corned Beef and Red Cabbage Stew

Don't wait until St. Patrick's Day to enjoy this luck-of-the-Irish stew. It's fast, easy, and delicious.

4 entrée servings

1 pound each: cubed lean corned beef, coarsely
  sliced red or green cabbage
½ cup reduced-sodium fat-free chicken broth
4 medium red potatoes, cubed
1 cup each: sliced carrots, cubed turnips
1 tablespoon apple cider vinegar
1 teaspoon pickling spice
Salt and pepper, to taste

Per Serving:
Calories: 259
% calories from fat: 29
Protein (g): 13.6
Carbohydrate (g): 34.1
Fat (g): 8.5
Saturated fat (g): 2.8
Cholesterol (mg): 42.3
Sodium (mg): 646
Exchanges:
Milk: 0.0
Vegetable: 1.0
Fruit: 0.0
Bread: 2.0
Meat: 1.0
Fat: 1.0

1. Combine all ingredients, except salt and pepper, in slow cooker; cover and cook on low 6 to 8 hours. Season to taste with salt and pepper.

Veal Stew with Sage

Sage and dry white wine give this stew an Italian flair!

6 entrée servings

1¼ pounds boneless veal leg, cubed
1 cup reduced-sodium fat-free chicken broth
½ cup dry white wine or chicken broth
¾ cup chopped onion
2 each: sliced ribs celery, carrots, chopped cloves
  garlic
½ teaspoon each: dried sage and thyme leaves
Salt and pepper, to taste
12 ounces egg noodles, cooked, warm

Per Serving:
Calories: 389
% calories from fat: 14
Protein (g): 35.2
Carbohydrate (g): 43.3
Fat (g): 5.9
Saturated fat (g): 1.8
Cholesterol (mg): 144.3
Sodium (mg): 126
Exchanges:
Milk: 0.0
Vegetable: 0.0
Fruit: 0.0
Bread: 3.0
Meat: 3.0
Fat: 0.0

1. Combine all ingredients, except salt, pepper, and noodles, in slow cooker; cover and cook on low 6 to 8 hours. Season to taste with salt and pepper; serve over noodles.

Variation

Creamed Veal Stew with Peas and Mushrooms—Make recipe as above, adding 2 cups sliced mushrooms and omitting carrots and wine. Add ¾ cup frozen thawed petite peas and ¾ cup half-and-half or milk during last hour of cooking time. Turn heat to high and cook 10 minutes; stir in combined 2 tablespoons cornstarch and ¼ cup cold water, stirring 2 to 3 minutes.

Veal Stew Marsala

Chicken breast can be substituted for the veal in this stew; serve over rice, if desired.

4 entrée servings

1 pound lean veal leg, cubed
1 cup reduced-sodium fat-free chicken broth
¼–½ cup marsala wine or chicken broth
2 cups sliced mushrooms
2 cloves garlic, minced
¼–½ teaspoon crushed dried rosemary leaves
2 tablespoons cornstarch
¼ cup cold water
Salt and pepper, to taste

Per Serving:
Calories: 213
% calories from fat: 24
Protein (g): 32.4
Carbohydrate (g): 3.2
Fat (g): 5.6
Saturated fat (g): 1.8
Cholesterol (mg): 114.4
Sodium (mg): 74
Exchanges:
Milk: 0.0
Vegetable: 1.0
Fruit: 0.0
Bread: 0.0
Meat: 3.0
Fat: 0.0

1. Combine all ingredients, except cornstarch, water, salt, and pepper, in slow cooker; cover and cook on low 6 to 8 hours. Turn heat to high and cook 10 minutes; stir in combined cornstarch and water, stirring 2 to 3 minutes. Season to taste with salt and pepper.

Veal and Vegetable Paprikash

Your preference of hot or sweet paprika can be used in this recipe.

6 entrée servings

1½ pounds boneless veal leg, cubed (½-inch)
1 cup reduced-sodium fat-free chicken broth
2 cups thinly sliced cabbage
1 cup each: sliced onion, carrots, green bell
  peppers, mushrooms, chopped tomato
1 tablespoon paprika
1 cup sliced zucchini
½ cup reduced-fat sour cream
2 tablespoons cornstarch
Salt and pepper, to taste
12 ounces noodles, cooked, warm

Per Serving:
Calories: 419
% calories from fat: 20
Protein (g): 33.5
Carbohydrate (g): 49.8
Fat (g): 9.1
Saturated fat (g): 3.2
Cholesterol (mg): 138.5
Sodium (mg): 264
Exchanges:
Milk: 0.0
Vegetable: 2.0
Fruit: 0.0
Bread: 3.0
Meat: 3.0
Fat: 0.0

1. Combine all ingredients, except zucchini, sour cream, cornstarch, salt, pepper, and noodles, in 6-quart slow cooker; cover and cook on low 6 to 8 hours, adding zucchini during last 30 minutes. Stir in combined sour cream and cornstarch, stirring 2 to 3 minutes. Season to taste with salt and pepper. Serve over noodles.

Veal Stew with Wine

Chicken breast can be substituted for the veal in this recipe; serve over rice or pasta, with a green salad and warm crusty bread.

6 entrée servings

1½ pounds boneless veal leg, cubed (¾-inch)
½ cup each: chicken broth, tomato sauce,
   dry white wine or chicken broth
1 cup cubed sweet potatoes
1 each: large chopped onion, minced garlic clove
¼ cup each: chopped red and green bell pepper
1 cup frozen peas, thawed
2 tablespoons cornstarch
¼ cup cold water
Salt and pepper, to taste

Per Serving:
Calories: 256
% calories from fat: 31
Protein (g): 32.5
Carbohydrate (g): 4.3
Fat (g): 8.5
Saturated fat (g): 3.1
Cholesterol (mg): 128.1
Sodium (mg): 243
Exchanges:
Milk: 0.0
Vegetable: 1.0
Fruit: 0.0
Bread 0.0
Meat: 4.0
Fat: 0.0

1. Combine all ingredients, except peas, cornstarch, water, salt, and pepper, in slow cooker; cover and cook on low 6 to 8 hours. Add peas, turn heat to high and cook 10 minutes; stir in combined cornstarch and water, stirring 2 to 3 minutes. Season to taste with salt and pepper.

Savory Veal Stew

Caraway and anise seeds provide an unexpected flavor nuance in this stew.

8 entrée servings

2 pounds lean veal leg, cubed (¾-inch)
½ cup each: reduced-sodium fat-free chicken
   broth, dry white wine or chicken broth
1 small head cabbage, cut into 8 wedges
3 leeks (white parts only) thickly sliced
2 cups sliced mushrooms
3 cloves garlic, minced
1 teaspoon crushed caraway seeds
¾ teaspoon crushed anise seeds
2 bay leaves
1 tablespoon cornstarch
½ cup reduced-fat sour cream
Salt and pepper, to taste

Per Serving:
Calories: 284
% calories from fat: 28
Protein (g): 32.4
Carbohydrate (g): 16.5
Fat (g): 8.8
Saturated fat (g): 2.9
Cholesterol (mg): 104.5
Sodium (mg): 161
Exchanges:
Milk: 0.0
Vegetable: 3.0
Fruit: 0.0
Bread: 0.0
Meat: 4.0
Fat: 0.0

1. Combine all ingredients, except cornstarch, sour cream, salt, and pepper,

in 6-quart slow cooker; cover and cook on low 6 to 8 hours. Stir in combined cornstarch and sour cream, stirring 2 to 3 minutes. Discard bay leaves; season to taste with salt and pepper.

Veal Stew Sauvignon

This fragrant stew is also delicious served over an aromatic rice, such as basmati or jasmine.

4 entrée servings

1 pound boneless veal cutlets, cut into thin strips
½ cup each: reduced-sodium fat-free chicken broth, dry white wine or chicken broth
1 medium onion, halved, thinly sliced
1 teaspoon each: minced garlic, dried marjoram leaves
1 tablespoon tomato paste
2 cups each: small cauliflower florets, torn Swiss chard or spinach
Salt and pepper, to taste
8 ounces fettuccine, cooked, warm

Per Serving:
Calories: 427
% calories from fat: 15
Protein (g): 33.4
Carbohydrate (g): 51
Fat (g): 6.9
Saturated fat (g): 1.6
Cholesterol (mg): 90.5
Sodium (mg): 318
Exchanges:
Milk: 0.0
Vegetable: 1.0
Fruit: 0.0
Bread: 3.0
Meat: 3.0
Fat: 0.0

1. Combine all ingredients, except cauliflower, Swiss chard, salt, pepper, and pasta, in slow cooker; cover and cook on low 6 to 8 hours, adding cauliflower and Swiss chard during last 30 minutes. Season to taste with salt and pepper. Serve over fettuccine.

Mediterranean Veal Stew

Beef or pork can be substituted for the veal in this delicious recipe. If a thicker consistency stew is desired, thicken at the end of cooking time with combined 1 to 2 tablespoons cornstarch and ¼ cup cold water.

6 entrée servings

1½ pounds lean veal leg, cubed
1 cup reduced-sodium fat-free chicken broth
1 can (14½ ounces) petite-diced tomatoes, undrained
2 tablespoons tomato paste
½ cup each: coarsely chopped onion, carrots
2 cloves garlic, minced
¾ teaspoon each: dried thyme and basil leaves
1 bay leaf
⅓ cup olives, pitted
2 tablespoons drained capers
Salt and pepper, to taste
6 cups linguine, cooked, warm

Per Serving:
Calories. 458
% calories from fat: 28
Protein (g): 39
Carbohydrate (g): 43.2
Fat (g): 14.3
Saturated fat (g): 2.6
Cholesterol (mg): 114.4
Sodium (mg): 651
Exchanges:
Milk: 0.0
Vegetable: 2.0
Fruit: 0.0
Bread: 2.0
Meat: 4.0
Fat: 0.0

1. Combine all ingredients, except olives, capers, salt, pepper, and pasta, in slow cooker. Cover and cook on low 6 to 8 hours, adding olives and capers during last 30 minutes. Discard bay leaf; season to taste with salt and pepper. Serve over pasta.

Osso Bucco

Gremolata, a pungent mixture of finely chopped parsley, lemon zest, and garlic, is traditionally added to this classic northern Italian stew.

6 entrée servings

6 medium veal shanks (about 4 pounds), fat trimmed
2 cans (14½ ounces each) diced tomatoes, undrained
½ cup dry white wine or water
3 each: chopped medium carrots, minced cloves garlic
2 ribs celery, thinly sliced
1 medium onion, chopped
¾ teaspoon each: dried basil and thyme leaves
2 bay leaves
Gremolata (see p. 318), divided
Salt and pepper, to taste
4 cups cooked rice, warm

Per Serving:
Calories: 364
% calories from fat: 15
Protein (g): 28.8
Carbohydrate (g): 44.5
Fat (g): 6.2
Saturated fat (g): 1.7
Cholesterol (mg): 85.8
Sodium (mg): 91
Exchanges:
Milk: 0.0
Vegetable: 2.0
Fruit: 0.0
Bread: 2.0
Meat: 3.0
Fat: 0.0

1. Combine all ingredients, except Gremolata, salt, pepper, and rice, in 6-quart slow cooker; cover and cook on low 6 to 8 hours. Discard bay leaves; stir in ¼ cup Gremolata and season to taste with salt and pepper. Serve over rice; pass remaining Gremolata.

Pork and Squash Ragout

Garlic Bread is delicious with this hearty stew.

4 entrée servings

1 pound boneless pork loin, cubed (¾-inch)
2 cans (14½ ounces) diced tomatoes,
    undrained
1 can (15 ounces) red kidney beans,
    rinsed, drained
1 cup peeled cubed butternut or acorn squash
1½ cups each: chopped onions, green bell peppers
2 teaspoons each: minced roasted garlic, dried
    Italian seasoning
Salt and pepper, to taste
Garlic Bread (recipe follows)

Per Serving:
Calories: 344
% calories from fat: 10
Protein (g): 33.2
Carbohydrate (g): 46.2
Fat (g): 3.8
Saturated fat (g): 1.3
Cholesterol (mg): 73.1
Sodium (mg): 504
Exchanges:
Milk: 0.0
Vegetable: 0.0
Fruit: 0.0
Bread: 3.0
Meat: 3.0
Fat: 0.0

1. Combine all ingredients, except salt, pepper, and Garlic Bread, in slow cooker; cover and cook on low 6 to 8 hours. Season to taste with salt and pepper; serve with Garlic Bread.

Garlic Bread

Makes 4 servings

4 thick slices French or Italian bread
Olive oil cooking spray
2 cloves garlic, halved

1. Spray both sides of bread generously with cooking spray. Broil on cookie sheet 4 inches from heat source until browned, about 1 minute on each side. Rub both sides of hot toast with cut sides of garlic.

Pork Stew with Peppers and Zucchini

This delicious combination of pork and vegetables can be served over your choice of pasta.

4 entrée servings

1 pound pork tenderloin or boneless pork loin, cubed (1-inch)
1 can (8 ounces) tomato sauce
½ cup reduced-sodium fat-free chicken broth
3 tablespoons dry sherry (optional)
1 cup each: sliced red and green bell peppers
1 each: chopped large onion, minced garlic clove
¾ teaspoon each: dried basil and thyme leaves
1 bay leaf
1½ cups thinly sliced zucchini
1 tablespoon cornstarch
2 tablespoons cold water
Salt and pepper, to taste
8 ounces fusilli, cooked, warm

Per Serving:
Calories: 377
% calories from fat: 11
Fat (g): 4.6
Saturated fat (g): 1.5
Cholesterol (mg): 73.5
Sodium (mg): 472
Protein (g): 33
Carbohydrate (g):50.0
Exchanges:
Milk: 0.0
Vegetable: 0.0
Fruit: 0.0
Bread: 3.0
Meat: 3.0
Fat: 0.0

1. Combine all ingredients, except zucchini, cornstarch, water, salt, pepper, and fusilli, in slow cooker. Cover and cook on high 3 to 4 hours, adding zucchini during last 30 minutes. Stir in combined cornstarch and water, stirring, 2 to 3 minutes. Discard bay leaf; season to taste with salt and pepper. Serve over fusilli.

Pork, Artichoke, and White Bean Stew

An elegant and flavorful stew with Tuscan flavors.

6 entrée servings

1½ pounds boneless pork loin, cubed (¾-inch)
1 can (14½ ounces) diced tomatoes, undrained
1 can (15 ounces) cannellini or navy beans,
  rinsed, drained
⅔ cup reduced-sodium fat-free chicken broth
2 cloves garlic, minced
1 teaspoon each: dried rosemary leaves, grated
  orange zest
1 can (14 ounces) artichoke hearts, rinsed, drained,
  quartered
1 tablespoon cornstarch
2 tablespoons cold water
Salt and pepper, to taste

Per Serving:
Calories: 254
% calories from fat: 22
Protein (g): 29.3
Carbohydrate (g): 18.7
Fat (g): 5.9
Saturated fat (g): 1.6
Cholesterol (mg): 65.7
Sodium (mg): 341
Exchanges:
Milk: 0.0
Vegetable: 1.0
Fruit: 0.0
Bread: 1.0
Meat: 3.0
Fat: 0.0

1. Combine all ingredients, except artichokes, cornstarch, water, salt, and pepper, in slow cooker; cover and cook on low 6 to 8 hours, adding artichoke hearts during last 30 minutes. Turn heat to high and cook 10 minutes; stir in combined cornstarch and water, stirring 2 to 3 minutes. Season to taste with salt and pepper.

Peppered Pork and Wine Stew

Cubed boneless pork loin can be substituted for the tenderloin for a more economical stew.

4 entrée servings

1 pound pork tenderloin, sliced (½-inch)
1 cup reduced-sodium fat-free beef broth
½ cup dry white wine or water
1 medium onion, finely chopped
½ cup chopped red bell pepper
1 clove garlic, minced
2 teaspoons finely crushed peppercorns
1 tablespoon each: red wine vinegar, cornstarch
2 tablespoons cold water
Salt and pepper, to taste
¼ cup minced chives or parsley

Per Serving:
Calories: 214
% calories from fat: 18
Protein (g): 26.9
Carbohydrate (g): 11
Fat (g): 4.2
Saturated fat (g): 1.4
Cholesterol (mg): 65.7
Sodium (mg): 110
Exchanges:
Milk: 0.0
Vegetable: 2.0
Fruit: 0.0
Bread: 0.0
Meat: 3.0
Fat: 0.0

1. Combine all ingredients, except vinegar, cornstarch, water, salt, pepper, and chives, in slow cooker; cover and cook on high 3 to 4 hours. Stir in combined vinegar, cornstarch, and water, stirring 2 to 3 minutes. Season to taste with salt and pepper; sprinkle with chives.

Austrian Pork Stew with Apples and Cranberry Sauce

Enjoy this thyme-seasoned medley of lean pork and fruit.

4 entrée servings

1 pound boneless pork loin, cubed (¾-inch)
1 can (16 ounces) whole-berry cranberry sauce
1 cup chopped onion
2 large tart apples, peeled, cored, thinly sliced
1 tablespoon each: Worcestershire sauce, apple cider vinegar, brown sugar
½ teaspoon dried thyme leaves
Salt and pepper, to taste
8 ounces egg noodles, cooked, warm

Per Serving:
Calories: 460
% calories from fat: 17
Protein (g): 19
Carbohydrate (g): 79
Fat (g): 8.5
Saturated fat (g): 2.4
Cholesterol (mg): 77
Sodium (mg): 123
Exchanges:
Milk: 0.0
Vegetable: 0.0
Fruit: 3.0
Bread: 2.0
Meat: 2.0
Fat: 0.5

1. Combine all ingredients, except salt, pepper, and noodles, in slow cooker; cover and cook on low 6 to 8 hours. Season to taste with salt and pepper; serve over noodles.

Orange Pork Ragout

Orange juice and cloves give this easy dish a distinct flavor.

4 entrée servings

1 pound boneless pork loin, cubed (1-inch)
1 cup each: chicken broth, orange juice, sliced onion, red and green bell peppers
2 teaspoons sugar
1 teaspoon dried thyme leaves
¼ teaspoon ground cloves
2 tablespoons cornstarch
¼ cup cold water
Salt and pepper, to taste
3 cups cooked white or brown rice, warm

Per Serving:
Calories: 428
% calories from fat: 23
Protein (g): 25.5
Carbohydrate (g): 57.3
Fat (g): 10.8
Saturated fat (g): 3.1
Cholesterol (mg): 42.4
Sodium (mg): 50
Exchanges:
Milk: 0.0
Vegetable: 2.0
Fruit: 0.5
Bread: 2.5
Meat: 3.0
Fat: 0.0

1. Combine all ingredients, except cornstarch, water, salt, pepper, and rice, in slow cooker; cover and cook on low 6 to 8 hours. Turn heat to high and cook 10 minutes; stir in combined cornstarch and water, stirring 2 to 3 minutes. Season to taste with salt and pepper; serve over rice.

Barbecue Pork Stew

Barbecue sauce and apple cider are the flavor secrets in this tasty stew.

4 entrée servings

1 pound boneless pork loin, cubed (¾-inch)
1½ cups apple cider or apple juice, divided
½ cup honey-mustard barbecue sauce
4 cups thinly sliced cabbage
1 medium onion, coarsely chopped
1 large tart apple, peeled, coarsely chopped
1 teaspoon crushed caraway seeds
1 tablespoon cornstarch
3 tablespoons cold water
Salt and pepper, to taste
8 ounces noodles, cooked, warm

Per Serving:
Calories: 521
% calories from fat: 8
Protein (g): 34
Carbohydrate (g): 82.9
Fat (g): 5
Saturated fat (g): 1.4
Cholesterol (mg): 65.7
Sodium (mg): 444
Exchanges:
Milk: 0.0
Vegetable: 1.0
Fruit: 2.0
Bread: 3.0
Meat: 3.0
Fat: 0.0

1. Combine all ingredients, except cornstarch, water, salt, pepper, and noodles, in slow cooker; cover and cook on low 6 to 8 hours. Turn heat to high and cook 10 minutes; stir in combined cornstarch and water, stirring 2 to 3 minutes. Season to taste with salt and pepper; serve over noodles.

Pork Stew with Gremolata

Gremolata, a refreshing blend of garlic, lemon peel, and parsley, is often used to flavor stews and soups.

4 entrée servings

1 pound boneless pork loin, cubed (1-inch)
1 cup reduced-sodium fat-free beef broth
1 can (14½ ounces) diced tomatoes, undrained
2 medium potatoes, cubed
4 shallots, thinly sliced
2 cloves garlic, minced
1 teaspoon dried thyme leaves
1½ tablespoons cornstarch
¼ cup cold water
Salt and pepper, to taste
Gremolata (recipe follows)

Per Serving:
Calories: 289
% calories from fat: 17
Protein (g): 28.6
Carbohydrate (g): 31.2
Fat (g): 5.5
Saturated fat (g): 1.6
Cholesterol (mg): 65.7
Sodium (mg): 523
Exchanges:
Milk: 0.0
Vegetable: 0.0
Fruit: 0.0
Bread: 2.0
Meat: 3.0
Fat: 0.0

1. Combine all ingredients, except cornstarch, water, salt, pepper, and Gremolata, in slow cooker; cover and cook on low 6 to 8 hours. Turn heat to high and cook 10 minutes; stir in combined cornstarch and water, stirring 2 to 3 minutes. Season to taste with salt and pepper. Pass Gremolata to stir into stew.

Gremolata

Makes about ½ cup

1 cup packed parsley sprigs
1–2 tablespoons grated lemon zest
4 large cloves garlic, minced

1. Process all ingredients in food processor until finely minced.

Cantonese Pork Stew

Lean beef or boneless, skinless chicken breast can be substituted for the pork in this sweet–sour stew.

6 entrée servings

1½ pounds lean pork steak, cut into thin strips
1 can (8 ounces) tomato sauce
¾ cup each: sliced onion, red bell pepper, mushrooms
3 tablespoons brown sugar
1½ tablespoons cider vinegar
2 teaspoons Worcestershire sauce
1 tablespoon dry sherry (optional)
½ cup each: pineapple chunks, halved snow peas
2 tablespoons cornstarch
¼ cup cold water
Salt and pepper, to taste
3 cups cooked rice, warm

Per Serving:
Calories: 305
% calories from fat: 8
Fat (g): 2.7
Saturated fat (g): 1.0
Cholesterol (mg): 57.6
Sodium (mg): 277
Protein (g): 30
Carbohydrate (g):39.6
Exchanges:
Milk: 0.0
Vegetable: 1.0
Fruit: 0.0
Bread: 2.0
Meat: 3.0
Fat: 0.0

1. Combine all ingredients, except pineapple chunks, snow peas, cornstarch, water, salt, pepper, and rice, in slow cooker; cover and cook on low 6 to 8 hours, adding pineapple and snow peas during last 15 minutes. Turn heat to high and cook 10 minutes; stir in combined cornstarch and water, stirring until thickened, 2 to 3 minutes. Season to taste with salt and pepper; serve over rice.

Mediterranean Curried Stew

Brightly colored Turmeric Rice completes this dish perfectly.

6 entrée servings

1 pound pork tenderloin or boneless, skinless chicken breast, cubed (¾-inch)
1 can (15 ounces) garbanzo beans, rinsed, drained
2 cans (14½ ounces, each) diced tomatoes, undrained
1 small eggplant, unpeeled, cubed (1-inch)
½ cup each: sliced onion, chopped green bell pepper, celery
2 cloves garlic, minced
½ teaspoon each: ground cinnamon, nutmeg, curry powder, cumin
⅛ teaspoon cayenne pepper
1 cup each: cubed zucchini, butternut squash
1–2 tablespoons cornstarch
¼ cup cold water
Salt and pepper, to taste
Turmeric Rice (recipe follows)
3 tablespoons each: raisins, toasted slivered almonds

Per Serving:
Calories: 446
% calories from fat: 22
Protein (g): 25.3
Carbohydrate (g): 61.3
Fat (g): 11.1
Saturated fat (g): 2
Cholesterol (mg): 43.8
Sodium (mg): 427
Exchanges:
Milk: 0.0
Vegetable: 3.0
Fruit: 0.0
Bread: 3.0
Meat: 2.0
Fat: 1.0

1. Combine all ingredients, except zucchini and butternut squash, cornstarch, water, salt, pepper, Turmeric Rice, raisins, and almonds in 6-quart slow cooker; cover and cook on high 4 to 5 hours, adding zucchini and butternut squash during last 20 minutes. Stir in combined cornstarch and water, stirring 2 to 3 minutes. Season to taste with salt and pepper. Serve over Turmeric Rice and sprinkle with raisins and almonds.

Turmeric Rice

Makes 6 servings (about ⅔ cup each)

2¼ cups water
1 cup uncooked converted long-grain rice
½ teaspoon turmeric
⅛ teaspoon salt

1. Heat water to boiling in large saucepan; stir in rice, turmeric and salt; reduce heat and simmer, covered, until rice is tender, 20 to 25 minutes.

Caribbean Ginger, Bean, and Pork Stew

Fresh gingerroot accents the flavor contrasts in this colorful stew.

6 entrée servings

12–16 ounces lean pork loin, cubed
½ cup each: chicken broth, orange juice
1 can (15 ounces) each: black beans, black-eyed peas,
  rinsed, drained
1 cup each: chopped onion, red bell pepper
2 teaspoons each: minced garlic, jalapeño chili
1 tablespoon chopped gingerroot
½ teaspoon dried thyme leaves
¾ cup fresh or frozen thawed cut okra
⅓ cup jalapeño chili jelly or orange marmalade
1 can (11 ounces) Mandarin orange segments, drained
Salt and pepper, to taste
3 cups cooked brown or white rice

Per Serving:
Calories: 369
% calories from fat: 15
Protein (g): 18.9
Carbohydrate (g): 66.3
Fat (g): 6.8
Saturated fat (g): 1.6
Cholesterol (mg): 24.6
Sodium (mg): 704
Exchanges:
Milk: 0.0
Vegetable: 0.0
Fruit: 1.0
Bread: 3.0
Meat: 2.0
Fat: 0.0

1. Combine all ingredients, except okra, chili jelly, orange segments, salt, pepper, and rice, in slow cooker; cover and cook on low 6 to 8 hours, adding okra, and jelly during last 30 minutes. Stir in orange segments and season to taste with salt and pepper; serve over rice.

Savory Stewed Pork and Chorizo

This stewed pork dish makes delicious tacos too (see variation on next page).

6 entrée servings

Chorizo (see p. 166)
12 ounces boneless pork loin, cubed (1-inch)
2 large tomatoes, chopped
1 small red onion, sliced
1 clove garlic, minced
¼ teaspoon each: dried oregano and thyme leaves
1 bay leaf
2–3 pickled jalapeño chilies, finely chopped
1 tablespoon pickled jalapeño chili juice
Salt and pepper, to taste
4 cups cooked rice, warm

Per Serving:
Calories: 298
% calories from fat: 15
Protein (g): 27.2
Carbohydrate (g): 35
Fat (g): 4.7
Saturated fat (g): 1.5
Cholesterol (mg): 65.7
Sodium (mg): 313
Exchanges:
Milk: 0.0
Vegetable: 0.0
Fruit: 0.0
Bread: 2.0
Meat: 3.0
Fat: 0.0

1. Cook Chorizo in lightly greased medium skillet over medium heat until browned, crumbling with a fork. Combine Chorizo and remaining ingredi-

ents, except salt, pepper, and rice, in slow cooker; cover and cook on high 4 to 5 hours. Discard bay leaf; season to taste with salt and pepper. Serve over rice.

Variation

Pork and Chorizo Tacos—Make recipe as above, omitting rice and substituting 8 ounces purchased chorizo for the Chorizo recipe. At the end of cooking time, turn heat to high and cook 10 minutes; stir in combined 1 tablespoon cornstarch and 2 tablespoons water, stirring 2 to 3 minutes. Stir in ¼ cup chopped cilantro. Serve in warm crisp taco shells or roll up in warm flour or corn tortillas, topping with reduced-fat sour cream and shredded iceberg lettuce.

Tomatillo Pork Stew

Tomatillos add a special flavor to this south-of-the-border version of pork stew.

8 entrée servings

1½ pounds boneless lean pork loin, cubed (¾-inch)
½ cup reduced-sodium fat-free chicken broth
2 large tomatoes, chopped
12 ounces tomatillos, husked, chopped
1 cup chopped onion
1 small poblano chili or green bell pepper, chopped
4 cloves garlic, minced
¾ teaspoon each: dried oregano leaves, ground cumin
2 tablespoons cornstarch
¼ cup cold water
1–2 teaspoons lime juice
Salt and pepper, to taste
5 cups cooked rice
Minced cilantro and pine nuts, as garnish

Per Serving:
Calories: 284
% calories from fat: 14
Fat (g): 4.3
Saturated fat (g): 1.4
Cholesterol (mg): 54.9
Sodium (mg): 65
Protein (g): 23
Carbohydrate (g):37.6
Exchanges:
Milk: 0.0
Vegetable: 1.0
Fruit: 0.0
Bread: 2.0
Meat: 2.0
Fat: 0.0

1. Combine all ingredients, except cornstarch, water, lime juice, salt, pepper, rice, cilantro, and pine nuts, in slow cooker; cover and cook on low 6 to 8 hours. Turn heat to high and cook 10 minutes; stir in combined cornstarch and water, stirring 2 to 3 minutes. Season to taste with lime juice, salt, and pepper. Serve over rice; sprinkle with cilantro and pine nuts.

Pork, Potato, and Cabbage Stew

Serve this robust pork stew over noodles or rice.

4 entrée servings

1 pound boneless lean pork loin
1 can (14½ ounces) stewed tomatoes
1 can (8 ounces) tomato sauce
2 cups each: thinly sliced cabbage, cubed peeled
potatoes
1 large onion, finely chopped
2 cloves garlic, minced
1 tablespoon brown sugar
2 teaspoons each: balsamic vinegar, dried thyme
leaves
1 bay leaf
Salt and pepper, to taste

Per Serving:
Calories: 328
% calories from fat: 18
Protein (g): 23.4
Carbohydrate (g): 45.4
Fat (g): 6.8
Saturated fat (g): 2.2
Cholesterol (mg): 49.3
Sodium (mg): 101
Exchanges:
Milk: 0.0
Vegetable: 3.0
Fruit: 0.0
Bread: 2.0
Meat: 2.0
Fat: 0.0

1. Combine all ingredients, except salt and pepper, in slow cooker; cover and cook on low 6 to 8 hours. Discard bay leaf; season to taste with salt and pepper.

Pork and Sauerkraut Stew

Serve this delicious stew in shallow bowls with crusty rye rolls.

4 entrée servings

1 pound boneless lean pork loin, cubed (¾-inch)
1 can (14½ ounces) diced tomatoes, undrained
1 package (16 ounces) fresh sauerkraut, drained
12 ounces red potatoes, thinly sliced
1 large onion, finely chopped
1 teaspoon caraway seeds
½ cup reduced-fat sour cream
1 tablespoon cornstarch
Salt and pepper, to taste

Per Serving:
Calories: 245
% calories from fat: 25
Protein (g): 18.2
Carbohydrate (g): 28.5
Fat (g): 7
Saturated fat (g): 2
Cholesterol (mg): 39.7
Sodium (mg): 650
Exchanges:
Milk: 0.0
Vegetable: 2.0
Fruit: 0.0
Bread: 1.0
Meat: 2.0
Fat: 0.0

1. Combine all ingredients, except sour cream, cornstarch, salt, and pepper, in slow cooker; cover and cook on low 6 to 8 hours. Stir in combined sour cream and cornstarch, stirring 2 to 3 minutes. Season to taste with salt and pepper.

Finnish Pork Stew with Beets and Noodles

This Scandinavian dish is colorful and delicious.

4 entrée servings

1 can (16 ounces) cubed beets, undrained
1 pound boneless lean pork loin, cubed (2-inch)
½ cup reduced-sodium fat-free beef broth
3 tablespoons cider vinegar
1 cup chopped onion
1½ teaspoons prepared horseradish
½ teaspoon dried thyme leaves
2 teaspoons cornstarch
¼ cup cold water
Salt and pepper, to taste
8 ounces egg noodles, cooked, warm

Per Serving:
Calories: 291
% calories from fat: 21
Protein (g): 20
Carbohydrate (g): 38
Fat (g): 6.9
Saturated fat (g): 2.2
Cholesterol (mg): 78
Sodium (mg): 345
Exchanges:
Milk: 0.0
Vegetable: 1.5
Fruit: 0.0
Bread: 2.0
Meat: 2.0
Fat: 0.0

1. Drain beets, reserving ½ cup juice. Combine beet juice, pork, and remaining ingredients, except beets, cornstarch, water, salt, pepper, and noodles, in slow cooker; cover and cook on low 6 to 8 hours. Add beets, turn heat to high and cook 10 minutes; stir in combined cornstarch and water, stirring 2 to 3 minutes. Season to taste with salt and pepper. Serve over noodles.

German-Style Stew

Serve this stew over noodles with thick slices of warm rye bread.

4 entrée servings

1 pound boneless pork loin, cubed (1-inch)
1 cup each: apple cider, chopped onion, cubed,
   peeled rutabaga
2 cups each: drained fresh sauerkraut, thinly sliced
   peeled potatoes
2 bay leaves
1½ tablespoons brown sugar
2 medium apples, peeled, sliced
½ cup frozen peas, thawed
Salt and pepper, to taste

Per Serving:
Calories: 296
% calories from fat: 22
Fat (g): 7.1
Saturated fat (g): 2.5
Cholesterol (mg): 61.9
Sodium (mg): 510
Protein (g): 28
Carbohydrate (g):24.0
Exchanges:
Milk: 0.0
Vegetable: 2.0
Fruit: 0.0
Bread: 1.0
Meat: 3.0
Fat: 0.0

1. Combine all ingredients, except apples, peas, salt, and pepper, in slow cooker. Cover and cook on low 6 to 8 hours, adding apples and peas during last 30 minutes. Discard bay leaves; season to taste with salt and pepper.

Southern Stewed Black Eyes, Chickpeas, and Ham

Serve with warm biscuits or Roasted Chili Cornbread (see p. 529).

6 entrée servings

12–16 ounces baked ham, cubed
1 can (14½ ounces) stewed tomatoes
1 can (15 ounces) each: rinsed drained chickpeas
   and black-eyed peas
½ cup chopped onion
2 cloves garlic, minced
1 teaspoon each: dried marjoram and thyme leaves
¼ teaspoon hot pepper sauce
½ package (10-ounce size) frozen spinach,
   thawed, drained
2 cups frozen cut okra, thawed
Salt and pepper, to taste

Per Serving:
Calories: 320
% calories from fat: 23
Protein (g): 21.8
Carbohydrate (g): 41.6
Fat (g): 8.2
Saturated fat (g): 2
Cholesterol (mg): 32.3
Sodium (mg): 841
Exchanges:
Milk: 0.0
Vegetable: 2.0
Fruit: 0.0
Bread: 2.0
Meat: 0.5
Fat: 0.0

1. Combine all ingredients, except spinach, okra, salt, and pepper, in slow cooker; cover and cook on high 4 to 5 hours, adding spinach and okra during last 30 minutes. Season to taste with salt and pepper.

Ham and Pepper Stew with Polenta

The microwave method for cooking polenta eliminates the constant stirring necessary when polenta is made on the stovetop. Also consider making Polenta (see p. 520) in a slow cooker!

4 entrée servings

8 ounces ham steak, cubed
1 can (14½ ounces) diced tomatoes, undrained
1½ cups cubed mixed green, red, and yellow
   bell peppers (1-inch)
1 each: chopped medium onion, minced garlic clove
1 bay leaf
1–1½ teaspoons dried Italian seasoning
Salt and pepper, to taste
Microwave Polenta (see p. 385)
2 tablespoons grated Parmesan cheese

Per Serving:
Calories: 394
% calories from fat: 21
Protein (g): 21
Carbohydrate (g): 57.8
Fat (g): 9.2
Saturated fat (g): 2.7
Cholesterol (mg): 36.5
Sodium (mg): 687
Exchanges:
Milk: 0.0
Vegetable: 0.0
Fruit: 0.0
Bread: 4.0
Meat: 2.0
Fat: 0.0

1. Combine all ingredients, except salt, pepper, Microwave Polenta, and Parmesan cheese, in slow cooker; cover and cook on high 4 to 5 hours. Discard bay leaf; season to taste with salt and pepper. Serve over Microwave Polenta; sprinkle with Parmesan cheese.

Sausage and Bean Stew

Serve this hearty winter stew over noodles or rice, with warm Buttermilk Bread (see p. 524).

8 entrée servings

1 pound reduced-fat smoked sausage, sliced (¾-inch)
2 cans (15½ ounces each) light red kidney beans, rinsed, drained
1 can (15½ ounces) Great Northern beans, rinsed, drained
2 cans (14½ ounces each) diced tomatoes, undrained
½ cup water
1½ cups chopped onion
½ cup chopped green bell pepper
2 cloves garlic, minced
½ teaspoon each: dried thyme and savory leaves
1 bay leaf
Salt and pepper, to taste

Per Serving:
Calories: 255
% calories from fat: 15
Protein (g): 19.2
Carbohydrate (g): 39.4
Fat (g): 4.6
Saturated fat (g): 1.1
Cholesterol (mg): 26.5
Sodium (mg): 791
Exchanges:
Milk: 0.0
Vegetable: 1.0
Fruit: 0.0
Bread: 2.0
Meat: 2.0
Fat: 0.0

1. Combine all ingredients, except salt and pepper, in 6-quart slow cooker; cover and cook on high 4 to 5 hours. Discard bay leaf; season to taste with salt and pepper.

Acorn Squash Stew with Smoked Sausage

Smoked sausage adds great flavor to this chunky, vegetable-rich stew.

4 entrée servings

8 ounces reduced-fat smoked sausage, sliced (¾-inch)
1 can (14½ ounces) stewed tomatoes
½ cup reduced-sodium fat-free beef broth
4 cups peeled seeded cubed acorn or butternut squash (¾-inch)
1 medium onion, cut into thin wedges
1 cup frozen peas, thawed
Salt and pepper, to taste
3 cups cooked brown rice, warm (optional)

Per Serving:
Calories: 298
% calories from fat: 11
Protein (g): 17.2
Carbohydrate (g): 54.9
Fat (g): 4
Saturated fat (g): 1
Cholesterol (mg): 26.5
Sodium (mg): 709
Exchanges:
Milk: 0.0
Vegetable: 0.0
Fruit: 0.0
Bread: 3.0
Meat: 2.0
Fat: 0.0

1. Combine all ingredients, except peas, salt, pepper, and rice, in slow cooker; cover and cook on high 4 to 6 hours, adding peas during last 20 minutes. Season to taste with salt and pepper; serve over brown rice.

Irish Lamb Stew

An Irish comfort food, this simply seasoned stew is always welcome on cold winter evenings.

6 entrée servings

1½ pounds lamb cubes for stew
2 cups reduced-sodium fat-free chicken broth
2 medium onions, sliced
6 each: quartered medium potatoes, thickly sliced medium carrots
½ teaspoon dried thyme leaves
1 bay leaf
½ cup frozen peas, thawed
2 tablespoons cornstarch
¼ cup cold water
1–1½ teaspoons Worcestershire sauce
Salt and pepper, to taste

Per Serving:
Calories: 376
% calories from fat: 29
Fat (g): 12.2
Saturated fat (g): 5.0
Cholesterol (mg): 82.6
Sodium (mg): 241
Protein (g): 28
Carbohydrate (g):38.9
Exchanges:
Milk: 0.0
Vegetable: 0.0
Fruit: 0.0
Bread: 2.5
Meat: 3.0
Fat: 0.5

1. Combine all ingredients, except peas, cornstarch, water, Worcestershire sauce, salt, and pepper, in slow cooker; cover and cook on low 6 to 8 hours. Add peas, turn heat to high and cook 10 minutes; stir in combined cornstarch and water, stirring 2 to 3 minutes. Discard bay leaf; season to taste with Worcestershire sauce, salt, and pepper.

Hearty Rosemary Lamb Stew with Sweet Potatoes

The pairing of rosemary and lamb is classic, distinctive, and delightful.

4 entrée servings

1 pound boneless lamb shoulder, fat trimmed,
    cubed (¾-inch)
1½ cups reduced-sodium fat-free beef broth
1 pound sweet potatoes, peeled, cubed (¾-inch)
1½ cups cut green beans
1 large onion, cut into thin wedges
1 teaspoon dried rosemary leaves
2 bay leaves
1–2 tablespoons cornstarch
¼ cup cold water
Salt and pepper, to taste

Per Serving:
Calories: 285
% calories from fat: 23
Protein (g): 20.6
Carbohydrate (g): 34.7
Fat (g): 7.4
Saturated fat (g): 2.5
Cholesterol (mg): 47.2
Sodium (mg): 171
Exchanges:
Milk: 0.0
Vegetable: 1.0
Fruit: 0.0
Bread: 2.0
Meat: 2.0
Fat: 0.0

1. Combine all ingredients, except cornstarch, water, salt, and pepper, in slow cooker; cover and cook on low 6 to 8 hours. Turn heat to high and cook 10 minutes; stir in combined cornstarch and water, stirring 2 to 3 minutes. Discard bay leaves; season to taste with salt and pepper.

Lamb, White Bean, and Sausage Stew

Dried beans cook perfectly in the slow cooker—no need to soak or precook!

6 entrée servings

1 pound boneless lamb shoulder, cubed (1-inch)
8 ounces dried white beans (navy, Great Northern,
    or cannellini)
2 cups reduced-sodium fat-free chicken broth
½ cup dry white wine or chicken broth
8 ounces reduced-fat smoked sausage, sliced (1-inch)
1 cup chopped onion
3 carrots, thickly sliced
1 clove garlic, minced
¾ teaspoon each: dried rosemary and oregano leaves
1 bay leaf
1 can (16 ounces) petite-diced tomatoes, undrained
Salt and pepper, to taste

Per Serving:
Calories: 335
% calories from fat: 16
Fat (g): 5.9
Saturated fat (g): 1.9
Cholesterol (mg): 66
Sodium (mg): 912
Protein (g): 30
Carbohydrate (g):36.6
Exchanges:
Milk: 0.0
Vegetable: 1.0
Fruit: 0.0
Bread: 2.0
Meat: 3.0
Fat: 0.0

1. Combine all ingredients, except tomatoes, salt, and pepper, in 6-quart slow cooker. Cover and cook on low until beans are tender, 7 to 8 hours; adding tomatoes with liquid during last 30 minutes. Discard bay leaf; season to taste with salt and pepper.

Savory Lamb Stew

Enjoy this rich and flavorful combination of lamb shanks, lentils, vegetables, and spices.

6 entrée servings

2 pounds lamb shanks, fat trimmed
1½ cups reduced-sodium fat-free chicken broth
1 can (14½ ounces) diced tomatoes, undrained
½ cup each: brown dried lentils, sliced carrots,
   chopped green bell pepper
2 cups chopped onions
2 cloves garlic, minced
2 bay leaves
2 teaspoons dried thyme leaves
¼ teaspoon each: ground cinnamon and cloves
Salt and pepper, to taste
1¼ cups cooked brown rice, warm

Per Serving:
Calories: 325
% calories from fat: 26
Protein (g): 25
Carbohydrate (g): 40
Fat (g): 7.8
Saturated fat (g): 2.2
Cholesterol (mg): 56
Sodium (mg): 246
Exchanges:
Milk: 0.0
Vegetable: 1.5
Fruit: 0.0
Bread: 2.0
Meat: 2.0
Fat: 0.0

1. Combine all ingredients, except salt, pepper, and rice, in 6-quart slow cooker; cover and cook on low 6 to 8 hours. Discard bay leaves. Remove lamb shanks; remove lean meat and cut into bite-sized pieces. Return meat to stew; season to taste with salt and pepper. Serve over rice.

Lamb Stew with Chilies

For a variation on this stew, beef eye of round steak and beef broth can be substituted for the lamb and chicken broth.

4 entrée servings

1 pound boneless lamb shoulder, fat trimmed, cubed
  (¾-inch)
2 cans (14½ ounces each) diced tomatoes, undrained
½ cup reduced-sodium fat-free chicken broth
2–3 cans (4 ounces each) chopped mild green chilies
1 cup each: cubed potatoes, yellow summer squash,
  sliced onion
½ cup whole kernel corn
1 small jalapeño chili
4 cloves garlic, minced
1½ teaspoons dried Italian seasoning
2 tablespoons cornstarch
¼ cup cold water
Salt and pepper, to taste

Per Serving:
Calories: 293
% calories from fat: 15
Protein (g): 22.8
Carbohydrate (g): 41.6
Fat (g): 5.3
Saturated fat (g): 1.7
Cholesterol (mg): 48.5
Sodium (mg): 270
Exchanges:
Milk: 0.0
Vegetable: 2.0
Fruit: 0.0
Bread: 2.0
Meat: 2.0
Fat: 0.0

1. Combine all ingredients, except cornstarch, water, salt, and pepper, in slow cooker; cover and cook on low 6 to 8 hours. Turn heat to high and cook 10 minutes; stir in combined cornstarch and water, stirring 2 to 3 minutes. Season to taste with salt and pepper.

Lamb and Turnip Stew with Cilantro

This home-style lamb dish has been updated with fresh sage and cilantro; serve over white or brown rice.

4 entrée servings

1 pound boneless lamb shoulder, fat trimmed, cubed
  (1-inch)
1 cup tomato juice
½ cup dry red wine or tomato juice
2 cups each: cubed potatoes, turnips
1 medium onion, chopped
1 tablespoon minced garlic
1 tablespoon fresh or 1 teaspoon dried sage leaves
Salt and pepper, to taste
½ cup chopped cilantro

Per Serving:
Calories: 269
% calories from fat: 24
Protein (g): 17.4
Carbohydrate (g): 30
Fat (g): 7.3
Saturated fat (g): 2.4
Cholesterol (mg): 47.2
Sodium (mg): 81
Exchanges:
Milk: 0.0
Vegetable: 0.0
Fruit: 0.0
Bread: 2.0
Meat: 2.0
Fat: 0.0

1. Combine all ingredients, except salt, pepper, and cilantro, in slow cooker; cover and cook on low 6 to 8 hours. Season to taste with salt and pepper; stir in cilantro.

Moroccan Lamb Stew

Sweet spices season this stew and raisins, almonds, and hard-cooked eggs provide colorful garnish.

8 entrée servings

2 pounds boneless lean leg of lamb, cubed (¾-inch)
1 cup reduced-sodium fat-free chicken broth
1½ cups each: chopped onions, tomatoes
2 large cloves garlic, minced
2 teaspoons minced gingerroot
½ teaspoon ground cinnamon
¼ teaspoon ground turmeric
1 bay leaf
⅓ cup raisins
Salt and pepper, to taste
¼ cup whole almonds, toasted
2 hard-cooked eggs, chopped
Chopped cilantro, as garnish
5 cups cooked couscous or rice, warm

Per Serving:
Calories: 308
% calories from fat: 20
Protein (g): 23.8
Carbohydrate (g): 37.4
Fat (g): 6.6
Saturated fat (g): 2
Cholesterol (mg): 101.5
Sodium (mg): 103
Exchanges:
Milk: 0.0
Vegetable: 1.0
Fruit: 0.0
Bread: 2.0
Meat: 2.5
Fat: 0.0

1. Combine all ingredients, except raisins, salt, pepper, almonds, eggs, cilantro, and couscous, in 6-quart slow cooker; cover and cook on low 6 to 8 hours, adding raisins during last 30 minutes. Discard bay leaf, season to taste with salt and pepper. Spoon stew onto rimmed serving platter; sprinkle with almonds, hard-cooked eggs, and cilantro. Serve over couscous.

Lamb and Vegetable Tajine

Enjoy the fragrant flavors of Moroccan cuisine. Serve with warm pita bread.

6 entrée servings

1 pound lean lamb or beef, cubed
2 cans (14½ ounces each) diced tomatoes, undrained
1 can (15 ounces) garbanzo beans, rinsed, drained
1½ cups halved green beans
1 cup each: chopped butternut squash, turnip
½ cup each: chopped onion, sliced celery, carrot
1–2 teaspoons each: minced gingerroot, garlic
1 cinnamon stick
2 teaspoons each: paprika, ground cumin, coriander
1 cup prunes, pitted
¼ cup small black olives, pitted
Salt and pepper, to taste
4½ cups cooked couscous, warm

Per Serving:
Calories: 466
% calories from fat: 15
Protein (g): 24.8
Carbohydrate (g): 76.9
Fat (g): 8.4
Saturated fat (g): 2
Cholesterol (mg): 38.9
Sodium (mg): 580
Exchanges:
Milk: 0.0
Vegetable: 3.0
Fruit: 0.0
Bread: 4.0
Meat: 2.0
Fat: 0.0

1. Combine all ingredients, except prunes, olives, salt, pepper, and couscous, in 6-quart slow cooker; cover and cook on low 6 to 8 hours, adding prunes and olives during last 30 minutes. Season to taste with salt and pepper; serve over couscous.

Marrakech Lamb Stew

Three cans (15 ounces each) navy or Great Northern beans can be substituted for the dried beans, if you like.

8 entrée servings

2 pounds boneless lean leg of lamb, cubed (1-inch)
3 cups reduced-sodium fat-free chicken broth
4 ounces each: dried navy or Great Northern beans,
   coarsely chopped portobello or cremini mushrooms
½ cup each: sliced carrots, onion
3 large cloves garlic, minced
1 teaspoon ground cumin
½ teaspoon each: dried thyme and savory leaves
2 bay leaves
¾ cup sliced roasted red peppers
3 cups baby spinach leaves
½ cup dry white wine or chicken broth
2 tablespoons cornstarch
Salt and pepper, to taste
5 cups cooked couscous or rice, warm

Per Serving:
Calories: 463
% calories from fat: 40
Fat (g): 20.2
Saturated fat (g): 9.8
Cholesterol (mg): 71.8
Sodium (mg): 383
Protein (g): 29
Carbohydrate (g):36.7
Exchanges:
Milk: 0.0
Vegetable: 1.0
Fruit: 0.0
Bread: 2.0
Meat: 3.0
Fat: 3.0

1. Combine all ingredients, except roasted peppers, spinach, wine, cornstarch, salt, pepper, and couscous, in 6-quart slow cooker; cover and cook on low until beans are tender, 7 to 8 hours. Add roasted peppers and spinach, turn heat to high and cook 10 minutes; stir in combined wine and cornstarch, stirring until thickened, 2 to 3 minutes. Discard bay leaves; season to taste with salt and pepper. Serve over couscous.

Lamb Biriani

This traditional Indian meat and rice dish can also be made with chicken or beef.

4 entrée servings

1 pound boneless lean lamb leg, cubed (¾-inch)
1 cup reduced-sodium fat-free chicken broth
2 cups chopped onions
1 clove garlic, minced
1 teaspoon each: ground coriander, ginger
½ teaspoon chili powder
¼ teaspoon each: ground cinnamon, cloves
¾ cup reduced-fat plain yogurt
1 tablespoon cornstarch
Salt and pepper, to taste
3 cups cooked basmati or jasmine rice, warm

Per Serving:
Calories: 280
% calories from fat: 26
Protein (g): 22
Carbohydrate (g): 30
Fat (g): 82
Saturated fat (g): 2.1
Cholesterol (mg): 46
Sodium (mg): 332
Exchanges:
Milk: 0.0
Vegetable: 1.5
Fruit: 0.0
Bread: 1.5
Meat: 2.0
Fat: 0.5

1. Combine all ingredients, except yogurt, cornstarch, salt, pepper, and rice, in slow cooker; cover and cook on low 6 to 8 hours. Stir in combined yogurt and cornstarch, stirring 2 to 3 minutes. Season to taste with salt and pepper; serve over rice.

Lamb and Beef Stew with Cognac

The flavors of two meats, wine, and cognac blend uniquely in this elegant stew.

6 entrée servings

1 pound each: cubed (¾-inch) lean beef eye of
  round steak and leg of lamb
½ cup each: beef broth, dry white wine or beef broth
3 tablespoons cognac (optional)
2 cups baby carrots
½ teaspoon ground cinnamon
¼ teaspoon ground mace
2 cups each: small broccoli florets, frozen thawed
  pearl onions
Salt and pepper, to taste

Per Serving:
Calories: 314
% calories from fat: 25
Protein (g): 30.7
Carbohydrate (g): 19
Fat (g): 8.6
Saturated fat (g): 2.5
Cholesterol (mg): 74
Sodium (mg): 123
Exchanges:
Milk. 0.0
Vegetable: 4.0
Fruit 0.0
Bread: 0.0
Meat: 3.0
Fat: 0.0

1. Combine all ingredients, except broccoli, pearl onions, salt, and pepper, in slow cooker; cover and cook 6 to 8 hours, adding broccoli and onions during last 30 minutes. Season to taste with salt and pepper.

Two-Meat Goulash

The combination of caraway and fennel seeds adds interesting flavor to this distinctive goulash.

8 entrée servings

1 pound each: cubed (¾-inch) lean beef eye of round steak, lean pork loin
½ cup reduced-sodium fat-free beef broth
1 can (14½ ounces) diced tomatoes, undrained
2 tablespoons tomato paste
4 ounces small mushrooms, halved
1½ cups chopped onions
2 cloves garlic, minced
2 tablespoons paprika
½ teaspoon each: crushed caraway and fennel seeds
2 bay leaves
½ cup reduced-fat sour cream
2 tablespoons cornstarch
Salt and pepper, to taste
1 pound noodles, cooked, warm

Per Serving:
Calories: 443
% calories from fat: 16
Protein (g): 36.7
Carbohydrate (g): 53.9
Fat (g): 8.1
Saturated fat (g): 2.2
Cholesterol (mg): 59.7
Sodium (mg): 333
Exchanges:
Milk: 0.0
Vegetable: 1.0
Fruit: 0.0
Bread: 3.0
Meat: 4.0
Fat: 0.0

1. Combine all ingredients, except sour cream, cornstarch, salt, pepper, and noodles, in slow cooker; cover and cook on low 6 to 8 hours. Stir in combined sour cream and cornstarch, stirring 2 to 3 minutes. Discard bay leaves; season to taste with salt and pepper. Serve over noodles.

Two-Meat, Two-Mushroom Stew

Substitute any favorite dried and fresh mushrooms for the shiitake mushrooms in this richly flavored stew.

6 entrée servings

½ cup boiling water
3 medium dried shiitake mushrooms
12 ounces each: boneless cubed (¾-inch) pork loin,
  veal leg
½ cup each: dry white wine, reduced-sodium fat-free
  chicken broth
4 ounces small cremini or white button mushrooms,
  halved
1 cup chopped onion
½ teaspoon fennel seeds, lightly crushed
Salt and pepper, to taste
4 cups cooked brown or white rice

Per Serving:
Calories: 384
% calories from fat: 22
Protein (g): 33.9
Carbohydrate (g): 36.8
Fat (g): 9
Saturated fat (g): 2.7
Cholesterol (mg): 89.4
Sodium (mg): 221
Exchanges:
Milk: 0.0
Vegetable: 1.0
Fruit: 0.0
Bread: 2.0
Meat: 4.0
Fat: 0.0

1. Pour boiling water over dried mushrooms in small bowl; let stand until mushrooms are softened, 5 to 10 minutes. Drain, reserving liquid; strain liquid. Slice mushrooms into thin strips, discarding hard centers.
2. Combine dried mushrooms and reserved liquid, and remaining ingredients, except salt, pepper, and rice, in slow cooker; cover and cook on low 6 to 8 hours. Season to taste with salt and pepper. Serve over rice.

Karelian Ragout

Allspice gently seasons beef, pork, and lamb in this Finnish stew. Serve over cooked rice or noodles, if you wish.

12 entrée servings

1 pound each: cubed (1-inch) lean beef eye-of-round
  steak, lamb, pork loin
2 cups reduced-sodium fat-free beef broth
2 cups thinly sliced onions
½ teaspoon ground allspice
2 bay leaves
Salt and pepper, to taste
¼ cup finely chopped parsley

Per Serving:
Calories: 163
% calories from fat: 29
Protein (g): 23.5
Carbohydrate (g): 4.6
Fat (g): 5.1
Saturated fat (g): 1.8
Cholesterol (mg): 55.9
Sodium (mg): 107
Exchanges:
Milk: 0.0
Vegetable: 0.0
Fruit: 0.0
Bread: 0.0
Meat: 3.0
Fat: 0.0

1. Combine all ingredients, except salt, pepper, and parsley, in 6-quart slow cooker; cover and cook on low 6 to 8 hours. Discard bay leaves; season to taste with salt and pepper. Stir in parsley.

Three-Meat Goulash

The mingled juices of three kinds of meat yield unsurpassed flavor.

8 entrée servings

12 ounces each: cubed (¾-inch) boneless beef eye
 of round steak, pork loin, chicken breast
1 cup reduced-sodium fat-free beef broth
¼ cup tomato paste
3 large tomatoes, coarsely chopped
8 ounces mushrooms, sliced
½ cup each: thinly sliced green onions, chopped
 onion
1 tablespoon paprika
¾ teaspoon crushed caraway seeds
½ teaspoon dried dill weed
¾ cup reduced-fat sour cream
3 tablespoons cornstarch
Salt and pepper, to taste
1 pound noodles, cooked, warm

Per Serving:
Calories: 487
% calories from fat: 25
Fat (g): 13.2
Saturated fat (g): 5.0
Cholesterol (mg): 132.2
Sodium (mg): 148
Protein (g): 40
Carbohydrate (g):51.8
Exchanges:
Milk: 0.0
Vegetable: 1.0
Fruit: 0.0
Bread: 3.0
Meat: 4.0
Fat: 0.0

1. Combine all ingredients, except sour cream, cornstarch, salt, pepper, and noodles, in 6-quart slow cooker; cover and cook on low 6 to 8 hours. Stir in combined sour cream and cornstarch, stirring until thickened, 2 to 3 minutes. Season to taste with salt and pepper. Serve over noodles.

TEN

Poultry Stews

- - - - - - - - - - - - - - - -

Easy Chicken Stew

This stew can be made easily using convenient canned and frozen ingredients.

4 entrée servings

1 can (10¾ ounces) reduced-sodium 98% fat-free
   condensed cream of chicken soup
1¼ cups 2% reduced-fat milk
1 cup water
1 pound boneless skinless chicken breasts,
   cubed (¾-inch)
1 cup sliced onion
1 package (10 ounces) frozen mixed vegetables,
   thawed
2 tablespoons cornstarch
¼ cup cold water
Salt and pepper, to taste

Per Serving:
Calories: 293
% calories from fat: 15
Fat (g): 4.6
Saturated fat (g): 2.2
Cholesterol (mg): 79.6
Sodium (mg): 303
Protein (g): 34
Carbohydrate (g):27
Exchanges:
Milk: 0.0
Vegetable: 0.0
Fruit: 0.0
Bread: 2.0
Meat: 3.0
Fat: 0.0

1. Combine soup, milk, and water in slow cooker; stir in chicken and on-ion. Cover and cook on low 5 to 6 hours, adding mixed vegetables during last 20 minutes. Turn heat to high and cook 10 minutes; stir in combined cornstarch and water, stirring 2 to 3 minutes. Season to taste with salt and pepper.

Country Chicken Stew

This stew is also delicious served on warm biscuits or cornbread.

6 entrée servings

1½ pounds boneless, skinless chicken breast, cubed
  (1-inch)
1 cup reduced-sodium fat-free chicken broth
1 can (6 ounces) tomato paste
2 cups coarsely chopped cabbage
1 cup each: chopped onion, green bell pepper
2 large cloves garlic, minced
1 bay leaf
1 tablespoon each: lemon juice, Worcestershire sauce,
  sugar
2 teaspoons each: dried basil leaves, Dijon mustard
3–4 drops hot pepper sauce
Salt and pepper, to taste
4 cups cooked rice, warm

Per Serving:
Calories: 217
% calories from fat: 7
Protein (g): 29.5
Carbohydrate (g): 20.5
Fat (g): 1.7
Saturated fat (g): 0.4
Cholesterol (mg): 65.7
Sodium (mg): 430
Exchanges:
Milk: 0.0
Vegetable: 1.0
Fruit: 0.0
Bread: 1.0
Meat: 3.0
Fat: 0.0

1. Combine all ingredients, except salt, pepper, and rice, in slow cooker; cover and cook on low 6 to 8 hours. Discard bay leaf; season to taste with salt and pepper. Serve over rice.

Picnic Chicken Stew

Canned garbanzo and baked beans combine with chicken in a chili powder-spiked stew.

8 entrée servings

10 ounces boneless, skinless chicken breast, cubed
2 cans (15 ounces each) baked beans or pork and
  beans
1 can (15 ounces) garbanzo beans, rinsed, drained
1 can (14½ ounces) diced tomatoes, undrained
1 each: chopped large onion, red bell pepper
2 cloves garlic, minced
2–3 teaspoons chili powder
¾ teaspoon dried thyme leaves
Salt and pepper, to taste

Per Serving:
Calories: 251
% calories from fat: 14
Protein (g): 18.1
Carbohydrate (g): 39.1
Fat (g): 4.1
Saturated fat (g): 0.8
Cholesterol (mg): 25.9
Sodium (mg): 616
Exchanges:
Milk: 0.0
Vegetable: 2.0
Fruit: 0.0
Bread: 2.0
Meat: 1.0
Fat: 0.0

1. Combine all ingredients, except salt and pepper, in slow cooker; cover and cook on high 4 to 5 hours. Season to taste with salt and pepper.

Sweet Potato Chicken Stew

The stew is also delicious made with russet potatoes, or a combination of russet and sweet potatoes.

4 entrée servings

1 pound boneless, skinless chicken breast, cubed
    (1-inch)
1½ cups reduced-sodium fat-free chicken broth
12 ounces sweet potatoes, cubed (¾-inch)
1 large green bell pepper, sliced
2–3 teaspoons chili powder
½ teaspoon garlic powder
2 tablespoons cornstarch
¼ cup cold water
Salt and pepper, to taste

Per Serving:
Calories: 342
% calories from fat: 24
Protein (g): 30.7
Carbohydrate (g): 33.3
Fat (g): 9
Saturated fat (g): 2
Cholesterol (mg): 69
Sodium (mg): 261
Exchanges:
Milk: 0.0
Vegetable: 0.0
Fruit: 0.0
Bread: 2.0
Meat: 3.0
Fat: 0.5

1. Combine all ingredients, except cornstarch, water, salt, and pepper, in slow cooker; cover and cook on high 4 to 5 hours. Stir in combined cornstarch and water, stirring 2 to 3 minutes. Season to taste with salt and pepper.

Chicken and Mashed Potato Stew

The mounds of cheesy mashed potatoes that top this hearty stew are delicious; the potatoes can be made one day in advance and refrigerated, covered.

4 entrée servings

1 pound boneless, skinless chicken breast, cubed (¾-inch)
1 cup reduced-sodium fat-free chicken broth
⅔ cup each: chopped onion, carrots, celery, sliced mushrooms
½ teaspoon each: dried rosemary and thyme leaves
½ cup frozen petite peas, thawed
1–2 tablespoons cornstarch
3–4 tablespoons cold water
Salt and pepper, to taste
2 cups (½ recipe) Real Mashed Potatoes (see p. 475)
1 egg yolk
½ cup (2 ounces) shredded reduced-fat Cheddar cheese
1–2 tablespoons margarine or butter, melted

Per Serving:
Calories: 378
% calories from fat: 26
Protein (g): 29.9
Carbohydrate (g): 35.1
Fat (g): 10.7
Saturated fat (g): 2.1
Cholesterol (mg): 122.4
Sodium (mg): 420
Exchanges:
Milk: 0.0
Vegetable: 1.0
Fruit: 0.0
Bread: 2.0
Meat: 3.0
Fat: 1.0

1. Combine chicken, broth, onion, carrots, celery, mushrooms, and herbs in slow cooker; cover and cook on low 6 to 8 hours. Add peas, turn heat to high, and cook 10 minutes. Stir in combined cornstarch and water, stirring 2 to 3 minutes; season to taste with salt and pepper.
2. While stew is cooking, make Real Mashed Potatoes, mixing in egg yolk and cheese. Spoon potato mixture into 4 mounds on greased cookie sheet and refrigerate, covered, until chilled, about 30 minutes. Drizzle potatoes with margarine; bake at 425 degrees until browned, about 15 minutes. Top bowls of stew with potatoes.

Chicken and Mushroom Stew

Serve this stew with warm slices of Parmesan Bread (see pg. 530).

4 entrée servings

1 pound boneless, skinless chicken breast, cubed
    (¾-inch)
1 cup reduced-sodium fat-free chicken broth
1 can (6 ounces) tomato paste
1 tablespoon Worcestershire sauce
8 ounces mushrooms, thickly sliced
1 large onion, chopped
2 each: minced cloves garlic, coarsely
    shredded large carrots
1 bay leaf
1 teaspoon dried Italian seasoning
¼ teaspoon dry mustard
1–2 tablespoons cornstarch
2–4 tablespoons cold water
Salt and pepper, to taste
8 ounces spaghetti, cooked, warm

Per Serving:
Calories: 338
% calories from fat: 6
Protein (g): 29.5
Carbohydrate (g): 41.4
Fat (g): 2.1
Saturated fat (g): 0.5
Cholesterol (mg): 54.3
Sodium (mg): 300
Exchanges:
Milk: 0.0
Vegetable: 0.0
Fruit: 0.0
Bread: 3.0
Meat: 3.0
Fat: 0.0

1. Combine all ingredients, except cornstarch, water, salt, pepper, and spaghetti, in slow cooker; cover and cook on high 4 to 6 hours. Stir in combined cornstarch and water, stirring 2 to 3 minutes. Discard bay leaf; season to taste with salt and pepper. Serve over spaghetti.

Chicken and Wild Mushroom Stew

This richly flavored stew benefits from slow cooking.

4 entrée servings

1 pound boneless, skinless chicken breasts, cubed
½ cup each: reduced-sodium fat-free chicken broth,
    dry white wine or chicken broth
8 ounces mixed wild mushrooms, coarsely chopped
¼ cup each: thinly sliced green onions, leek
    (white part only)
1 tablespoon drained capers
1–2 tablespoons cornstarch
2–4 tablespoons cold water
Salt and pepper, to taste
3 cups cooked brown rice, warm

Per Serving:
Calories: 339
% calories from fat: 8
Protein (g): 32.4
Carbohydrate (g): 39.5
Fat (g): 2.9
Saturated fat (g): 0.7
Cholesterol (mg): 66
Sodium (mg): 206
Exchanges:
Milk: 0.0
Vegetable: 0.0
Fruit: 0.0
Bread: 2.5
Meat: 3.0
Fat: 0.0

1. Combine all ingredients, except capers, cornstarch, water, salt, pepper, and rice, in slow cooker; cover and cook on low 6 to 8 hours. Add capers, turn heat to high, and cook 10 minutes; stir in combined cornstarch and water, stirring 2 to 3 minutes. Season to taste with salt and pepper; serve over rice.

Chicken Stew with Spinach Rice

Spinach Rice is a flavorful accompaniment to this French-style stew.

6 entrée servings

1 chicken (about 2 pounds), cut up
1 cup reduced-sodium fat-free chicken broth
1 can (6 ounces) tomato paste
8 medium tomatoes, seeded, coarsely chopped
¾ cup each: chopped onion, red bell pepper,
   sliced mushrooms
1 clove garlic, minced
½ teaspoon each: dried basil, tarragon, and
   oregano leaves
Generous pinch ground nutmeg
2 medium zucchini, sliced
¼ cup pitted black olives
1–2 tablespoons cornstarch
2–4 tablespoons cold water
Salt and pepper, to taste
Spinach Rice (recipe follows)

Per Serving:
Calories: 491
% calories from fat: 29
Protein (g): 33.3
Carbohydrate (g): 54.7
Fat (g): 16.4
Saturated fat (g): 3.6
Cholesterol (mg): 67.5
Sodium (mg): 417
Exchanges:
Milk: 0.0
Vegetable: 2.0
Fruit: 0.0
Bread: 2.5
Meat: 4.0
Fat: 1.0

1. Combine all ingredients, except zucchini, black olives, cornstarch, water, salt, pepper, and Spinach Rice, in slow cooker; cover and cook on low 6 to 8 hours. Add zucchini and black olives during last 20 minutes. Turn heat to high and cook 10 minutes; stir in cornstarch and water, stirring 2 to 3 minutes. Season to taste with salt and pepper. Serve over Spinach Rice.

Spinach Rice

Makes 4 cups

¼ cup chopped onion
1¼ cups uncooked rice
2½ cups reduced-sodium fat-free chicken broth
2 cups sliced packed spinach leaves

1. Sauté onion in lightly greased medium saucepan until tender, 2 to 3 minutes; stir in rice and broth and heat to boiling. Reduce heat and simmer, covered, until rice is tender, about 25 minutes, stirring in spinach during last 10 minutes.

Lemon Chicken Stew

Fresh lemon juice and jalapeño chili are flavor accents in this delicious stew.

6 entrée servings

1 pound boneless, skinless chicken breast, cubed
2 cans (14½ ounces each) diced tomatoes, undrained
1 jalapeño chili, minced
2 cloves garlic, minced
1 teaspoon instant chicken bouillon crystals
2 teaspoons dried basil leaves
2 cups broccoli florets
¼–⅓ cup lemon juice
Salt and pepper, to taste
12 ounces angel hair pasta, cooked, warm
Shredded Parmesan cheese, as garnish

Per Serving:
Calories: 310
% calories from fat: 17
Protein (g): 26.2
Carbohydrate (g): 38.2
Fat (g): 5.8
Saturated fat (g): 1.5
Cholesterol (mg): 109.8
Sodium (mg): 783
Exchanges:
Milk: 0.0
Vegetable: 2.0
Fruit: 0.0
Bread: 2.0
Meat: 2.0
Fat: 0.0

1. Combine all ingredients, except broccoli, lemon juice, salt, pepper, pasta, and cheese, in slow cooker; cover and cook on high 4 to 5 hours, adding broccoli during last 20 minutes. Season to taste with lemon juice, salt, and pepper. Serve over pasta; sprinkle with Parmesan cheese.

Orange Chicken and Vegetable Stew

Both orange juice and zest are used to accent this flavorful stew. Serve over an aromatic rice.

6 entrée servings

2½ pounds boneless, skinless chicken breast halves
1½ cups each: orange juice, chopped tomatoes,
   unpeeled cubed potatoes
1 cup sliced onion
2 each: thickly sliced large carrots, minced
   cloves garlic
½ teaspoon each: dried marjoram and thyme leaves
2 teaspoons grated orange zest
1 piece cinnamon stick (1-inch)
2 tablespoons cornstarch
¼ cup cold water
Salt and pepper, to taste

Per Serving:
Calories: 318
% calories from fat: 10
Protein (g): 29.4
Carbohydrate (g): 42.4
Fat (g): 3.5
Saturated fat (g): 0.9
Cholesterol (mg): 69
Sodium (mg): 87
Exchanges:
Milk: 0.0
Vegetable: 2.0
Fruit: 0.5
Bread: 1.5
Meat: 2.5
Fat: 0.0

1. Combine all ingredients, except cornstarch, water, salt, and pepper, in 6-quart slow cooker; cover and cook on low 6 to 8 hours. Turn heat to high and cook 10 minutes; stir in combined cornstarch and water, stirring 2 to 3 minutes. Season to taste with salt and pepper.

Ginger-Orange Chicken and Squash Stew

Any winter squash, such as acorn, butternut, or hubbard, is appropriate for this orange and ginger-accented stew; sweet potatoes can be used too.

6 entrée servings

1½ pounds boneless, skinless chicken breast, cubed
1 cup reduced-sodium fat-free chicken broth
1 can (14½ ounces) diced tomatoes, undrained
½ cup orange juice
3 cups peeled cubed winter yellow squash
2 medium Idaho potatoes, peeled, cubed
¾ cup each: coarsely chopped onions, green
  bell peppers
2 cloves garlic, minced
1 tablespoon grated orange zest
½ teaspoon ground ginger
½ cup reduced-fat sour cream
1 tablespoon cornstarch
Salt and pepper, to taste
4 cups cooked noodles or brown basmati rice, warm

Per Serving:
Calories: 482
% calories from fat: 12
Protein (g): 38.7
Carbohydrate (g): 67.0
Fat (g): 6.6
Saturated fat (g): 1.4
Cholesterol (mg): 111.6
Sodium (mg): 264.5
Exchanges:
Milk: 0.0
Vegetable: 0.0
Fruit: 0.0
Bread: 4.0
Meat: 3.0
Fat: 0.0

1. Combine all ingredients, except sour cream, cornstarch, salt, pepper, and noodles, in 6-quart slow cooker; cover and cook on low 6 to 8 hours. Stir in combined sour cream and cornstarch, stirring 2 to 3 minutes. Season to taste with salt and pepper. Serve over noodles.

Apricot Chicken Stew

Apricot jam and Dijon mustard flavor the wine sauce in this stew.

6 entrée servings

1½ pounds boneless, skinless chicken breast
   halves, quartered
⅓ cup each: reduced-sodium fat-free chicken
   broth, dry white wine or chicken broth, apricot jam
½ cup each: chopped carrots, celery, sliced
   green onions
2 tablespoons Dijon mustard
1 teaspoon each: crushed dried rosemary
   leaves, paprika
½ cup frozen petite peas, thawed
1–2 tablespoons cornstarch
2–3 tablespoons cold water
Salt and pepper, to taste
4 cups cooked rice, warm

Per Serving:
Calories: 433
% calories from fat: 12
Protein (g): 31
Carbohydrate (g): 57
Fat (g): 5.7
Saturated fat (g): 1.2
Cholesterol (mg): 65.7
Sodium (mg): 299
Exchanges:
Milk: 0.0
Vegetable: 0.0
Fruit: 0.0
Bread: 4.0
Meat: 3.0
Fat: 0.0

1. Combine all ingredients, except peas, cornstarch, water, salt, pepper, and rice, in slow cooker; cover and cook on high 4 to 5 hours, adding peas during last 20 minutes. Stir in combined cornstarch and water, stirring 2 to 3 minutes. Season to taste with salt and pepper; serve over rice.

Chicken Stew with Dried Fruit

Dried fruits make a flavorful sweet broth for chicken stew. Thicken the stew with combined 1 to 2 tablespoons cornstarch and 2 to 3 tablespoons water, if thicker consistency is desired.

4 entrée servings

1 pound boneless, skinless chicken breast,
   cubed (1½-inch)
1¼ cups reduced-sodium fat-free chicken broth
¾ cup each: finely chopped onion, red bell pepper
1 clove garlic, minced
½ teaspoon ground ginger
1 bay leaf
1½ cups mixed raisins, coarsely chopped pitted
   prunes, and dried apricots
2–4 tablespoons light rum (optional)
Salt and pepper, to taste
1 cup cooked rice, warm

Per Serving:
Calories: 406
% calories from fat: 9
Protein (g): 19
Carbohydrate (g): 68
Fat (g): 4.2
Saturated fat (g): 0.8
Cholesterol (mg): 36
Sodium (mg): 105
Exchanges:
Milk: 0.0
Vegetable: 1.0
Fruit: 2.0
Bread: 2.5
Meat: 1.5
Fat: 0.0

1. Combine all ingredients, except dried fruit, rum, salt, pepper, and rice, in slow cooker; cover and cook on high 4 to 5 hours, adding dried fruit and rum during last 1½ hours. Discard bay leaf and season to taste with salt and pepper; serve over rice.

Chicken Stew Veronique

Red and green seedless grapes add flavor and color to this company fare. Serve over an aromatic rice, such as jasmine or basmati.

4 entrée servings

1 pound chicken tenders, halved
1¼ cups reduced-sodium fat-free chicken broth
¼ cup dry white wine (optional)
½ cup thinly sliced leek (white part only) or
    green onions
2 cloves garlic, minced
¾ teaspoon dried tarragon leaves
½ cup each: halved red and green seedless grapes
2 tablespoons cornstarch
¼ cup cold water
Salt and pepper, to taste

Per Serving:
Calories: 340
% calories from fat: 15
Protein (g): 28.5
Carbohydrate (g): 17.9
Fat (g): 4.9
Saturated fat (g): 0.6
Cholesterol (mg): 65.7
Sodium (mg): 274
Exchanges:
Milk: 0.0
Vegetable: 0.0
Fruit: 0.0
Bread: 1.0
Meat: 3.0
Fat: 2.0

1. Combine all ingredients, except grapes, cornstarch, water, salt, and pepper, in slow cooker; cover and cook on high 4 to 5 hours, adding grapes in the last 10 minutes. Stir in combined cornstarch and water, stirring 2 to 3 minutes. Season to taste with salt and pepper.

Tarragon-Mustard Chicken Stew

Tarragon and mustard combine for a sweet and tangy flavor in this stew.

4 entrée servings

1 pound boneless, skinless chicken breast, cubed
1 cup reduced-sodium fat-free chicken broth
1 cup each: chopped onion, sliced carrots,
   halved small Brussels sprouts
2 small ribs celery, chopped
1–2 tablespoons Dijon mustard
2 teaspoons dried tarragon leaves
2 teaspoons brown sugar
1 teaspoon lemon juice
2 tablespoons cornstarch
¼ cup water
Salt and pepper, to taste
3 cups cooked white rice, warm

Per Serving:
Calories: 252
% calories from fat: 17
Protein (g): 29.6
Carbohydrate (g): 19.7
Fat (g): 4.3
Saturated fat (g): 0.9
Cholesterol (mg): 75.1
Sodium (mg): 396
Exchanges:
Milk: 0.0
Vegetable: 0.0
Fruit: 0.0
Bread: 1.0
Meat: 3.0
Fat: 0.0

1. Combine all ingredients, except cornstarch, water, salt, pepper, and rice, in slow cooker; cover and cook on low 6 to 8 hours. Turn heat to high and cook 10 minutes; stir in combined cornstarch and water, stirring 2 to 3 minutes. Season to taste with salt and pepper; serve over rice.

Honey-Mustard Chicken Stew

The honey-mustard flavor of this delicious chicken recipe is enhanced by the addition of curry powder.

4 entrée servings

1 pound boneless, skinless chicken breast, cubed
1½ cups reduced-sodium fat-free chicken broth
2 cups small cauliflower florets
1 cup each: chopped onion, sliced carrots
2 tablespoons honey
1 tablespoon Dijon mustard
1–2 teaspoons curry powder
1–2 tablespoons cornstarch
2–4 tablespoons cold water
Salt and pepper, to taste
3 cups cooked white rice, warm

Per Serving:
Calories: 276
% calories from fat: 13
Protein (g): 30.3
Carbohydrate (g): 28.6
Fat (g): 4.0
Saturated fat (g): 0.8
Cholesterol (mg): 65.8
Sodium (mg): 430
Exchanges:
Milk: 0.0
Vegetable: 0.0
Fruit: 0.0
Bread: 2.0
Meat: 3.0
Fat: 0.0

1. Combine all ingredients, except cornstarch, water, salt, pepper, and rice, in slow cooker; cover and cook on high 4 to 5 hours. Stir in combined cornstarch and water, stirring 2 to 3 minutes. Season to taste with salt and pepper; serve over rice.

Sweet-Sour Chicken and Vegetable Stew

Chicken and vegetables are cooked in cider and seasoned with honey and vinegar for a refreshing sweet-sour flavor.

6 entrée servings

1 pound boneless, skinless chicken breast, cubed
½ cup apple cider or apple juice
1 can (4½ ounces) diced tomatoes, undrained
2 cups peeled cubed butternut or acorn yellow squash
1 cup each: peeled cubed Idaho and sweet
  potatoes, whole-kernel corn
½ cup each: chopped shallots, red bell pepper
2 cloves garlic, minced
1½ tablespoons each: honey, cider vinegar
1 bay leaf
¼ teaspoon ground nutmeg
1 cup peeled sliced tart apples
Salt and pepper, to taste
4 cups cooked basmati rice, warm

Per Serving:
Calories: 373
% calories from fat: 4
Protein (g): 23.3
Carbohydrate (g): 64.1
Fat (g): 1.8
Saturated fat (g): 0.3
Cholesterol (mg): 43.8
Sodium (mg): 85
Exchanges:
Milk: 0.0
Vegetable: 0.0
Fruit: 0.0
Bread: 4.0
Meat: 2.0
Fat: 0.0

1. Combine all ingredients, except apples, salt, pepper, and rice, in slow cooker; cover and cook on low 5 to 6 hours, adding apples during last 20 minutes. Discard bay leaf; season to taste with salt and pepper. Serve over rice.

Tomato-Chicken Stew

This recipe is great served over Polenta (see p. 520) or rice.

6 entrée servings

1½ pounds boneless, skinless chicken breast, cubed
1 can (14½ ounces) diced tomatoes, undrained
1 can (15 ounces) Great Northern beans, rinsed, drained
1 cup reduced-sodium fat-free chicken broth
½ cup dry white wine or chicken broth
¼ cup tomato paste
2 cups sliced mushrooms
1 cup sliced onion
2 cloves garlic, minced
2 teaspoons lemon juice
1 bay leaf
½ teaspoon dried oregano leaves
¼ teaspoon dried thyme leaves
Salt and pepper, to taste

Per Serving:
Calories: 253
% calories from fat: 19
Protein (g): 32
Carbohydrate (g): 18.1
Fat (g): 5.5
Saturated fat (g): 1
Cholesterol (mg): 69
Sodium (mg): 659
Exchanges:
Milk: 0.0
Vegetable: 1.0
Fruit: 0.0
Bread: 1.0
Meat: 3.0
Fat: 0.0

1. Combine all ingredients, except salt and pepper, in slow cooker; cover and cook on low 6 to 8 hours. Discard bay leaf; season to taste with salt and pepper.

Chicken Vegetable Stew with Lentils

This healthy stew combines chicken and lentils with a medley of vegetables; serve in shallow bowls.

6 entrée servings

1 chicken (about 3 pounds), cut up
1 can (14½ ounces) diced tomatoes, undrained
1½ cups reduced-sodium fat-free chicken broth
1 cup dried lentils
½ cup each: sliced celery, carrots, broccoli stalks, chopped onion
2 cloves garlic, minced
½ teaspoon dried marjoram leaves
3 slices bacon, cooked crisp, crumbled
Salt and pepper, to taste

Per Serving:
Calories: 344
% calories from fat: 18
Protein (g): 41.3
Carbohydrate (g): 24.6
Fat (g): 6.4
Saturated fat (g): 1.7
Cholesterol (mg): 104.5
Sodium (mg): 437
Exchanges:
Milk: 0.0
Vegetable: 0.0
Fruit: 0.0
Bread: 1.5
Meat: 4.0
Fat: 0.0

1. Combine all ingredients, except bacon, salt, and pepper, in 6-quart slow cooker; cover and cook on low 6 to 8 hours. Stir in bacon; season to taste with salt and pepper.

Garden Stew with Chicken and Couscous

Take advantage of your garden's bounty to make this stew, substituting vegetables you have in abundance.

6 entrée servings

2½ pounds boneless, skinless chicken breast
  halves, halved or quartered
1½ cups reduced-sodium fat-free chicken broth
4 medium tomatoes, coarsely chopped
8 ounces each: halved baby carrots, sliced
  shiitake or white mushrooms
  (tough stems discarded)
2 medium onions, thickly sliced
1 medium turnip, cubed
1 small jalapeño chili, finely chopped
2 medium zucchini, sliced
½ cup cilantro leaves, loosely packed
Salt and pepper, to taste
1½ cups cooked couscous, warm

Per Serving:
Calories: 397
% calories from fat: 6
Protein (g): 29
Carbohydrate (g): 63
Fat (g): 2.7
Saturated fat (g): 0.7
Cholesterol (mg): 46
Sodium (mg): 141
Exchanges:
Milk: 0.0
Vegetable: 3.0
Fruit: 0.0
Bread: 3.0
Meat: 2.0
Fat: 0.0

1. Combine all ingredients, except zucchini, cilantro, salt, pepper, and couscous, in 6-quart slow cooker; cover and cook on low 6 to 8 hours, adding zucchini during last 30 minutes. Stir in cilantro; season to taste with salt and pepper. Serve over couscous.

Chicken Fricassee

Cloves and bay leaves add a flavor update to this dish; the traditional herbs rosemary and thyme can be substituted.

6 entrée servings

1½ pounds boneless, skinless chicken breast halves, halved or quartered
1 can (14 ½ ounces) reduced-sodium fat-free chicken broth
1 cup each: onion wedges, sliced carrots, celery
2 cloves garlic, minced
16 whole cloves, tied in a cheesecloth bag
2 bay leaves
2 tablespoons cornstarch
¼ cup cold water
1–2 teaspoons lemon juice
Salt and pepper, to taste
12 ounces fettuccine, cooked, warm

Per Serving:
Calories: 361
% calories from fat: 13
Protein (g): 35.9
Carbohydrate (g): 41.5
Fat (g): 5.1
Saturated fat (g): 0.9
Cholesterol (mg): 78.6
Sodium (mg): 401
Exchanges:
Milk: 0.0
Vegetable: 2.0
Fruit: 0.0
Bread: 2.0
Meat: 3.0
Fat: 0.0

1. Combine all ingredients, except cornstarch, water, lemon juice, salt, pepper, and pasta, in slow cooker; cover and cook on low 6 to 8 hours. Turn heat to high and cook 10 minutes; stir in combined cornstarch and water, stirring 2 to 3 minutes. Discard cloves and bay leaves; season to taste with salt and pepper. Serve over fettuccine.

Chicken Gumbo

A delicious and easy gumbo that can't be beat!

4 entrée servings

1 pound chicken breast, cubed (¾-inch)
1 can (14 ½ ounces) stewed tomatoes
2 cups reduced-sodium fat-free chicken broth
1 cup chopped onion
½ cup chopped red or green bell pepper
2 cloves garlic, minced
½ teaspoon dried thyme leaves
⅛–¼ teaspoon crushed red pepper
8 ounces fresh or frozen thawed small okra, halved
Salt and pepper, to taste
3 cups cooked rice, warm

Per Serving:
Calories: 424
% calories from fat: 11
Protein (g): 42.5
Carbohydrate (g): 49.8
Fat (g): 5.2
Saturated fat (g): 1.4
Cholesterol (mg): 87.5
Sodium (mg): 413
Exchanges:
Milk: 0.0
Vegetable: 1.0
Fruit: 0.0
Bread: 3.0
Meat: 3.0
Fat: 0.0

1. Combine all ingredients, except okra, salt, pepper, and rice, in slow cooker; cover and cook on low 6 to 8 hours, adding okra during last 30 minutes. Season to taste with salt and pepper; serve over rice.

Chicken, Black-Eyed Pea, And Succotash Gumbo

Black-eyed peas, okra, and succotash—all Southern favorites—combine nicely in this nourishing gumbo. Serve with Spoon Bread (see pg. 525).

6 entrée servings

1 pound boneless, skinless chicken breast, cubed
2 cups reduced-sodium fat-free chicken broth
1 can (14 ½ ounces) diced tomatoes, undrained
1 package (10 ounces) each: frozen thawed
   black-eyed peas, succotash
1 medium ham hock (optional)
1 cup chopped onion
⅓ cup each: chopped celery, red or green bell pepper
1 bay leaf
¼ teaspoon dried thyme leaves
1 cup frozen sliced okra, thawed
Salt and pepper, to taste

Per Serving:
Calories: 269
% calories from fat: 7
Protein (g): 27.1
Carbohydrate (g): 36.6
Fat (g): 2.2
Saturated fat (g): 0.3
Cholesterol (mg): 44.7
Sodium (mg): 568
Exchanges:
Milk: 0.0
Vegetable: 1.0
Fruit: 0.0
Bread: 2.0
Meat: 3.0
Fat: 0.0

1. Combine all ingredients, except okra, salt, and pepper, in slow cooker; cover and cook on low 6 to 8 hours, adding okra during last 30 minutes. Discard ham hock and bay leaf; season to taste with salt and pepper.

El Paso Chicken Stew

Serve this stew over rice, sprinkled with tortilla chips and cheese.

4 entrée servings

1 pound boneless, skinless chicken breast, cubed
2 cans (14½ ounces each) Mexican-style stewed
   tomatoes, undrained
1 can (15 ounces) pinto beans, rinsed, drained
2 cups each: cut green beans, whole-kernel corn
½ package (1.25 ounce-size) reduced-sodium
   taco-seasoning mix
Salt and pepper, to taste

1. Combine all ingredients, except salt and pepper, in slow cooker; cover and cook on low 6 to 8 hours. Season to taste with salt and pepper.

Per Serving:
Calories: 407
% calories from fat: 16
Protein (g): 34.9
Carbohydrate (g): 51.1
Fat (g): 7.6
Saturated fat (g): 1.5
Cholesterol (mg): 69
Sodium (mg): 862
Exchanges:
Milk: 0.0
Vegetable: 1.0
Fruit: 0.0
Bread: 3.0
Meat: 3.0
Fat: 0.0

Creole Sausage and Corn Stew

Use any kind of sausage you like in this stew—vegetarian sausage links are delicious too. Serve over rice or cornbread to soak up juices.

4 entrée servings

12–16 ounces reduced-fat smoked or spicy turkey
   sausage links, sliced (1-inch)
1 can (28 ounces) diced tomatoes with roasted
   garlic, undrained
1 cup each: chopped onion, whole-kernel corn
½ cup chopped green bell pepper
2 cloves garlic, minced
½ teaspoon dried thyme leaves
Salt and pepper, to taste
Hot pepper sauce

Per Serving:
Calories: 254
% calories from fat: 14
Protein (g): 18.8
Carbohydrate (g): 41
Fat (g): 4.2
Saturated fat (g): 1.3
Cholesterol (mg): 39.7
Sodium (mg): 570
Exchanges:
Milk: 0.0
Vegetable: 0.0
Fruit: 0.0
Bread: 2.0
Meat: 2.0
Fat: 0.0

1. Combine all ingredients, except salt, pepper, and hot pepper sauce, in slow cooker; cover and cook on high 4 to 5 hours. Season to taste with salt and pepper; serve with hot pepper sauce.

Black Bean and Okra Gumbo

The gumbo is delicious served over warm cornbread.

8 entrée servings

1 pound smoked turkey sausage, sliced
1 can (14½ ounces) stewed tomatoes with chilies
2 cans (15 ounces each) black beans, rinsed, drained
1 cup vegetable or chicken broth
2 cups small mushrooms
1 cup each: chopped onion, red and
   green bell peppers, sliced carrots
1 tablespoon chili powder
1 teaspoon gumbo file
2 cups frozen cut okra, thawed
Salt and pepper, to taste

Per Serving:
Calories: 292
% calories from fat: 21
Protein (g): 24.3
Carbohydrate (g): 36.8
Fat (g): 7.4
Saturated fat (g): 1.7
Cholesterol (mg): 48.9
Sodium (mg): 1443
Exchanges:
Milk: 0.0
Vegetable: 0.0
Fruit: 0.0
Bread: 2.5
Meat: 2.0
Fat: 0.0

1. Combine all ingredients, except okra, salt, and pepper, in 6-quart slow cooker; cover and cook on low 6 to 8 hours, adding okra during last 30 minutes. Season to taste with salt and pepper Season to taste with salt and pepper.

Chicken Stew with Biscuits

For a meal another time, omit the biscuits and serve this savory stew over noodles or Real Mashed Potatoes (see p. 475).

6 entrée servings

1½ pounds boneless, skinless chicken breast, cubed
1½ cups reduced-sodium fat-free chicken
   broth, divided
1 cup chopped onion
3 carrots, thickly sliced
½ cup sliced celery
¾ teaspoon dried sage leaves
2 tablespoons cornstarch
¼ cup cold water
Salt and pepper, to taste
½ cup frozen peas, thawed
3 buttermilk biscuits, baked, halved

Per Serving:
Calories: 233
% calories from fat: 20
Protein (g): 19.2
Carbohydrate (g): 26.7
Fat (g): 5.1
Saturated fat (g): 1.4
Cholesterol (mg): 35.5
Sodium (mg): 383
Exchanges:
Milk: 0.0
Vegetable: 2.0
Fruit: 0.0
Bread: 1.0
Meat: 1.5
Fat: 0.5

1. Combine all ingredients, except cornstarch, water, salt, pepper, peas, and biscuits, in slow cooker; cover and cook on low 6 to 8 hours. Turn heat to high, and cook 10 minutes; stir in combined cornstarch and water, stirring to to 3 minutes. Season to taste with salt and pepper. Stir in peas and place biscuit halves, cut sides down, on stew; cover and cook 10 minutes.

Brunswick Stew

Serve with warm biscuits for real down-home taste.

4 entrée servings

1 pound boneless, skinless chicken breast, cubed (1-inch)
1 cup reduced-sodium fat-free chicken broth
1 can (15 ounces) butter beans, rinsed, drained
1 can (14½ ounces) diced tomatoes, undrained
1 cup whole-kernel corn
½ cup each: chopped onion, green bell pepper
⅛–¼ teaspoon crushed red pepper
½ cup sliced fresh or frozen thawed okra
1–2 tablespoons cornstarch
¼ cup cold water
Salt and pepper, to taste

Per Serving:
Calories: 348
% calories from fat: 27
Protein (g): 30.6
Carbohydrate (g): 37.5
Fat (g): 11.3
Saturated fat (g): 2.6
Cholesterol (mg): 51.7
Sodium (mg): 630
Exchanges:
Milk: 0.0
Vegetable: 1.0
Fruit: 0.0
Bread: 2.0
Meat: 3.0
Fat: 0.5

1. Combine all ingredients, except okra, cornstarch, water, salt, and pepper, in slow cooker; cover and cook on high 4 to 5 hours, adding okra during last 20 minutes. Stir in combined cornstarch and water, stirring 2 to 3 minutes. Season to taste with salt and pepper.

Green Salsa Chicken Stew

This delicious stew is served in shallow bowls over refried beans and rice.

6 entrée servings

1 cup reduced-sodium fat-free chicken broth
2 cups mild or hot green salsa
3 cups packed sliced romaine lettuce leaves
1½ pounds boneless, skinless chicken breast halves, halved or quartered
1/3 cup chopped onion
1 clove garlic, chopped
¼ cup reduced-fat sour cream
1 tablespoon cornstarch
¼ cup chopped cilantro
Salt and pepper, to taste
1 can (15 ounces) refried beans
3 cups cooked rice, warm

Per Serving:
Calories: 288
% calories from fat: 12
Protein (g): 29.7
Carbohydrate (g): 34.7
Fat (g): 3.9
Saturated fat (g): 0.3
Cholesterol (mg): 48.2
Sodium (mg): 537
Exchanges:
Milk: 0.0
Vegetable: 1.0
Fruit: 0.5
Bread: 1.0
Meat: 3.0
Fat: 0.0

1. Process broth, salsa, and lettuce in food processor or blender until almost smooth. Add to slow cooker with remaining ingredients, except sour cream, cornstarch, cilantro, salt, pepper, refried beans, and rice; cover and cook on high 3 to 4 hours. Stir in combined sour cream and cornstarch, stirring 2 to 3 minutes. Stir in cilantro; season to taste with salt and pepper. Serve over refried beans and rice.

Sweet-Sour Island Stew

Sweet and sour flavors team with chicken, pineapple, and beans for this island-inspired dish—delicious with jasmine rice or couscous.

6 entrée servings

1½ pounds chicken tenders, halved
2 cups reduced-sodium fat-free chicken broth
1 can (15 ounces) black beans, rinsed, drained
1 cup each: sliced onion, green and red bell peppers
2 teaspoons each: minced garlic, gingerroot,
    jalapeño chili
2 tablespoons each: light brown sugar,
    apple cider vinegar
2–3 teaspoons curry powder
1 can (20 ounces) unsweetened pineapple
    chunks, drained
2 tablespoons cornstarch
¼ cup cold water
Salt and pepper, to taste

Per Serving:
Calories: 288
% calories from fat: 12
Protein (g): 29.7
Carbohydrate (g): 34.7
Fat (g): 3.9
Saturated fat (g): 0.3
Cholesterol (mg): 48.2
Sodium (mg): 537
Exchanges:
Milk: 0.0
Vegetable: 1.0
Fruit: 0.5
Bread: 1.0
Meat: 3.0
Fat: 0.0

1. Combine all ingredients, except pineapple, cornstarch, water, salt, and pepper, in slow cooker; cover and cook on low 6 to 8 hours, adding pineapple during last 20 minutes. Turn heat to high and cook 10 minutes; stir in combined cornstarch and water, stirring 2 to 3 minutes. Season to taste with salt and pepper.

Coconut Chicken Stew

This spicy Indonesian-influenced stew is enhanced with the unique flavor of coconut milk.

6 entrée servings

1½ pounds boneless, skinless chicken breast, cubed
1 cup each: reduced-fat or regular coconut milk,
   reduced-sodium fat-free chicken broth
1 can (15 ounces) red beans, rinsed, drained
⅔ cup each: thinly sliced onion, green bell pepper
¼ cup sliced green onions
1 clove garlic, minced
2 teaspoons minced gingerroot
1 tablespoon cornstarch
2 tablespoons lime juice
Salt and cayenne pepper, to taste
4 cups cooked rice, warm
Finely chopped cilantro, as garnish

Per Serving:
Calories: 404
% calories from fat: 15
Protein (g): 35.1
Carbohydrate (g): 48
Fat (g): 7
Saturated fat (g): 1.1
Cholesterol (mg): 69
Sodium (mg): 333
Exchanges:
Milk: 0.0
Vegetable: 1.0
Fruit: 0.0
Bread: 3.0
Meat: 3.0
Fat: 0.0

1. Combine all ingredients, except cornstarch, lime juice, salt, cayenne pepper, rice, and cilantro, in slow cooker; cover and cook on low 6 to 8 hours. Turn heat to high and cook 10 minutes; stir in combined cornstarch and lime juice, stirring 2 to 3 minutes. Season to taste with salt and cayenne pepper. Serve over rice; sprinkle generously with cilantro.

Luau Chicken Stew

Pineapple juice gives this stew its delicious sweet-sour flavor.

6 entrée servings

1½ pounds boneless, skinless chicken breast, cubed
½ cup each: reduced-sodium fat-free chicken
  broth, unsweetened pineapple juice
8 ounces mushrooms, sliced
2 medium carrots, diagonally sliced
1 each: thinly sliced small red onion, minced
  clove garlic
2–3 tablespoons each: rice or cider vinegar,
  soy sauce
2 small tomatoes, cut into thin wedges
1 cup frozen peas, thawed
1–2 tablespoons cornstarch
2–4 tablespoons cold water
Salt and pepper, to taste
4 cups cooked rice, warm

Per Serving:
Calories: 381
% calories from fat: 14
Protein (g): 32.9
Carbohydrate (g): 47.1
Fat (g): 5.9
Saturated fat (g): 1.3
Cholesterol (mg): 69
Sodium (mg): 301
Exchanges:
Milk: 0.0
Vegetable: 0.0
Fruit: 0.0
Bread: 3.0
Meat: 3.0
Fat: 0.0

1. Combine all ingredients, except tomatoes, peas, cornstarch, water, salt, pepper, and rice, in slow cooker; cover and cook on low 6 to 8 hours, adding tomatoes during last 30 minutes. Add peas, turn heat to high and cook 10 minutes; stir in combined cornstarch and water, stirring 2 to 3 minutes. Season to taste with salt and pepper; serve over rice.

Island Chicken Stew

This curried chicken stew is creatively garnished with sliced plantain and cashews.

6 entrée servings

1½ pounds boneless, skinless chicken breast, cubed
1½ cups reduced-sodium fat-free chicken broth
½ cup each: dried apples, apricots, raisins
¼ cup sliced green onions
2–3 teaspoons curry powder
⅛–¼ teaspoon crushed red pepper
2–3 teaspoons lime juice
Salt and pepper, to taste
4 cups cooked rice, warm
1 ripe plantain or banana, sliced
¼ cup chopped cashews

Per Serving:
Calories: 485
% calories from fat: 23
Protein (g): 26.2
Carbohydrate (g): 68.7
Fat (g): 12.6
Saturated fat (g): 28
Cholesterol (mg): 51.7
Sodium (mg): 147
Exchanges:
Milk: 0.0
Vegetable: 0.0
Fruit: 2.0
Bread: 2.5
Meat: 3.0
Fat: 0.5

1. Combine all ingredients, except lime juice, salt, pepper, rice, plantain, and cashews, in slow cooker; cover and cook on high 3 to 4 hours. Season to taste with lime juice, salt, and pepper; serve over rice and top with plantain and cashews.

Caribbean Stewed Chicken with Black Beans

The flavors of the islands come alive in this chicken and black bean stew.

4 entrée servings

1 pound boneless, skinless chicken breast, cut
   into thin strips
1 cup reduced-sodium fat-free chicken broth
1 can (16 ounces) black beans, rinsed, drained
1 can (8 ounces) tomato sauce
⅔ cup each: chopped onion, green bell pepper
2 cloves garlic, minced
½ teaspoon ground cinnamon
¼ teaspoon ground cloves
2–4 tablespoons light rum (optional)
Salt and cayenne pepper; to taste
3 cups cooked rice, warm

Per Serving:
Calories: 336
% calories from fat: 9
Protein (g): 20
Carbohydrate (g): 50
Fat (g): 3.4
Saturated fat (g): 1.0
Cholesterol (mg): 32
Sodium (mg): 390
Exchanges:
Milk: 0.0
Vegetable: 0.5
Fruit: 0.0
Bread: 3.0
Meat: 2.0
Fat: 0.0

1. Combine all ingredients, except rum, salt, cayenne pepper, and rice, in slow cooker; cover and cook on high 4 to 5 hours. Season to taste with rum, salt, and cayenne pepper; serve over rice.

Chicken Stew with Vermouth

The flavor of vermouth adds a touch of elegance to this stew. At the end of cooking time, juices can be thickened with combined 2 tablespoons cornstarch and ¼ cup cold water.

8 entrée servings

3 pounds skinless chicken breasts and thighs
¾ cup reduced-sodium fat-free chicken broth
½ cup dry vermouth or chicken broth
4 each: cubed new potatoes, thickly sliced carrots
4 ounces small mushrooms, halved or quartered
1 large onion, thinly sliced
2 ribs celery, sliced
1 teaspoon minced garlic
½ teaspoon dried thyme leaves
Salt and pepper, to taste

Per Serving:
Calories: 306
% calories from fat: 13
Protein (g): 38.9
Carbohydrate (g): 22.6
Fat (g): 4.4
Saturated fat (g): 1.1
Cholesterol (mg): 120
Sodium (mg): 131
Exchanges:
Milk: 0.0
Vegetable: 0.0
Fruit: 0.0
Bread: 1.5
Meat: 4.0
Fat: 0.0

1. Combine all ingredients, except salt and pepper, in 6-quart slow cooker; cover and cook on low 6 to 8 hours. Season to taste with salt and pepper.

Chicken Stew with White Wine

Serve this stew with rice and Italian bread to soak up the delicious broth.

4 entrée servings

1 pound boneless, skinless chicken breast, cubed
½ cup each: reduced-sodium fat-free chicken
  broth, dry white wine or chicken broth
1 medium onion, chopped
2 large cloves garlic, minced
1 bay leaf
1 teaspoon each: dried oregano and thyme leaves
1 cup each: small broccoli florets, cubed yellow
  summer squash
Salt and pepper, to taste

Per Serving:
Calories: 224
% calories from fat: 16
Protein (g): 29.1
Carbohydrate (g): 8.3
Fat (g): 3.8
Saturated fat (g): 0.7
Cholesterol (mg): 68.5
Sodium (mg): 194
Exchanges:
Milk: 0.0
Vegetable: 1.0
Fruit: 0.0
Bread: 0.0
Meat: 3.0
Fat: 0.0

1. Combine all ingredients, except broccoli, squash, salt, and pepper, in slow cooker; cover and cook on high 4 to 5 hours, adding broccoli and squash during last 20 minutes. Discard bay leaf; season to taste with salt and pepper.

Sherried Chicken Stew

Chicken is simmered in a delicious ginger, sherry, and soy-accented broth.

4 entrée servings

1 pound boneless, skinless chicken breast, cubed
1 cup reduced-sodium fat-free chicken broth
1 cup chopped onion
½ cup chopped red bell pepper
1 teaspoon each: minced garlic, gingerroot
1 cup sliced snow peas
1½ tablespoons cornstarch
2 tablespoons dry sherry (optional)
3–4 tablespoons soy sauce
1–2 teaspoons Asian sesame oil
Salt and pepper, to taste
12 ounces Chinese egg noodles or vermicelli, cooked, warm
¼ cup sliced green onions

Per Serving:
Calories: 366
% calories from fat: 8
Protein (g): 35.1
Carbohydrate (g): 44.2
Fat (g): 3.0
Saturated fat (g): 0.5
Cholesterol (mg): 65.7
Sodium (mg): 871
Exchanges:
Milk: 0.0
Vegetable: 0.0
Fruit: 0.0
Bread: 3.0
Meat: 3.0
Fat: 0.0

1. Combine chicken, broth, onion, bell pepper, garlic, and gingerroot in slow cooker; cover and cook on high 3 to 4 hours, adding snow peas during last 20 minutes. Stir in combined cornstarch, sherry, and soy sauce, stirring 2 to 3 minutes. Season to taste with sesame oil, salt, and pepper. Serve over noodles; sprinkle with green onions.

Burgundy Chicken Stew

Serve over noodles or rice with a green salad and warm bread to complete the meal.

6 entrée servings

1 chicken (about 2½ pounds), cut up
½ cup each: reduced-sodium fat-free chicken
   broth, Burgundy wine or chicken broth
8 ounces small mushrooms, halved
6 small new potatoes, unpeeled, scrubbed
1 cup frozen pearl onions, thawed
⅔ cup sliced green onions
1 clove garlic, crushed
¾ teaspoon dried thyme leaves
1–2 tablespoons cornstarch
2 –4 tablespoons water
Salt and pepper, to taste

Per Serving:
Calories: 292
% calories from fat: 16
Protein (g): 24.2
Carbohydrate (g): 30.5
Fat (g): 5.2
Saturated fat (g): 1.4
Cholesterol (mg): 60.2
Sodium (mg): 91
Exchanges:
Milk: 0.0
Vegetable: 0.0
Fruit: 0.0
Bread: 2.0
Meat: 3.0
Fat: 0.0

1. Combine all ingredients, except cornstarch, water, salt, and pepper, in 6-quart slow cooker; cover and cook on low 6 to 8 hours. Turn heat to high and cook 10 minutes; stir in combined cornstarch and water, stirring 2 to 3 minutes. Season to taste with salt and pepper.

Chicken Stew Provençal

Bursting with garlic and herb flavors, this stew is reminiscent of dishes from the Provence region of France.

4 entrée servings

1 pound boneless, skinless chicken breast, cubed
   (¾-inch)
1 can (28 ounces) diced tomatoes, undrained
½ cup each: dry white wine, chicken broth
4 medium potatoes, peeled, thinly sliced
4 teaspoons minced garlic
1½–2 teaspoons herbs de Provence or bouquet garni
2 tablespoons cornstarch
¼ cup cold water
Salt and pepper, to taste
Finely chopped basil, as garnish

Per Serving:
Calories: 352
% calories from fat: 14
Protein (g): 29.6
Carbohydrate (g): 37.2
Fat (g): 5.6
Saturated fat (g): 1.2
Cholesterol (mg): 69
Sodium (mg): 364
Exchanges:
Milk: 0.0
Vegetable: 2.0
Fruit: 1.0
Bread: 2.0
Meat: 3.0
Fat: 0.0

1 Combine all ingredients, except cornstarch, water, salt, pepper, and basil, in slow cooker; cover and cook on low 6 to 8 hours. Turn heat to high and cook 10 minutes; stir in combined cornstarch and water, stirring 2 to 3 minutes. Season to taste with salt and pepper; sprinkle generously with basil.

Coq au Vin

This easy version of the French classic is perfect for the slow cooker.

6 entrée servings

6 boneless, skinless chicken breast halves
   (4 ounces each), halved
½ cup each: chicken broth, Burgundy wine or
   chicken broth
4 slices bacon, diced
3 green onions, sliced
1 cup frozen pearl onions, thawed
8 ounces small mushrooms
6 small new potatoes, halved
1 teaspoon minced garlic
½ teaspoon dried thyme leaves
1–2 tablespoon cornstarch
2–4 tablespoons cold water
Salt and pepper, to taste

Per Serving:
Calories: 343
% calories from fat: 13
Protein (g): 31.2
Carbohydrate (g): 39.3
Fat (g): 4.9
Saturated fat (g): 1.5
Cholesterol (mg): 73.2
Sodium (mg): 357
Exchanges:
Milk: 0.0
Vegetable: 1.0
Fruit: 0.0
Bread: 2.0
Meat: 3.0
Fat: 0.0

1. Combine all ingredients, except cornstarch, water, salt, and pepper, in slow cooker; cover and cook on low 6 to 8 hours. Turn heat to high and cook 10 minutes; stir in combined cornstarch and water, stirring 2 to 3 minutes. Season to taste with salt and pepper.

Chicken Stew Paprikash

Serve this stew with thick slices of warm sourdough bread.

4 entrée servings

1 pound chicken tenders, halved
1 can (14½ ounces) stewed tomatoes
½ cup reduced-sodium fat-free chicken broth
2 each: finely chopped medium onions,
   minced cloves garlic
1 medium green bell pepper, chopped
1 cup sliced mushrooms
2½–3 teaspoons paprika
1 teaspoon poppy seeds
½ cup reduced-fat sour cream
1 tablespoon cornstarch
Salt and pepper, to taste
4 cups cooked noodles, warm

Per Serving:
Calories: 468
% calories from fat: 17
Protein (g): 38
Carbohydrate (g): 58.1
Fat (g): 8.9
Saturated fat (g): 2.2
Cholesterol (mg): 74
Sodium (mg): 331
Exchanges:
Milk: 0.0
Vegetable: 3.0
Fruit: 0.0
Bread: 3.0
Meat: 3.0
Fat: 0.0

1. Combine all ingredients, except sour cream, cornstarch, salt, pepper, and noodles, in slow cooker; cover and cook on low 6 to 8 hours. Stir in combined sour cream and cornstarch, stirring 2 to 3 minutes. Season to taste with salt and pepper; serve over noodles.

Kashmir Chicken Stew

This hearty stew is flavored with sweet Middle Eastern spices and raisins.

6 entrée servings

12–16 ounces boneless, skinless chicken breast,
  cubed (1-inch)
2 cans (15 ounces each) navy beans, rinsed, drained
1 can (14½ ounces) Italian-style stewed tomatoes
1½ cups chopped onions
¾ cup chopped red bell pepper
2 teaspoons minced garlic
⅛–¼ teaspoon crushed red pepper
1 teaspoon each: ground cumin, cinnamon
⅓ cup raisins
Salt and pepper, to taste
4 cups cooked couscous, warm

Per Serving:
Calories: 470
% calories from fat: 13
Protein (g): 29.3
Carbohydrate (g): 72.9
Fat (g): 7
Saturated fat (g): 1.2
Cholesterol (mg): 34.5
Sodium (mg): 614
Exchanges:
Milk: 0.0
Vegetable: 2.0
Fruit: 0.0
Bread: 4.0
Meat: 2.0
Fat: 0.0

1. Combine all ingredients, except raisins, salt, pepper, and couscous, in slow cooker; cover and cook on high 4 to 5 hours, adding raisins during last 30 minutes. Season to taste with salt and pepper; serve over couscous.

Chicken Curry Stew

Apple and raisins flavor this delicious curry.

4 entrée servings

1 pound boneless, skinless chicken breast, cubed
1 cup reduced-sodium fat-free chicken broth
1 cup sliced carrots
¼ cup each: chopped onion, sliced green onions
1 clove garlic, minced
1–2 teaspoons curry powder
½ teaspoon ground ginger
1 medium apple, peeled, sliced
¼ cup raisins
¾ cup 2% reduced-fat milk
1 tablespoon cornstarch
Salt and pepper, to taste
3 cups cooked rice, warm

Per Serving:
Calories: 419
% calories from fat: 20
Protein (g): 23.5
Carbohydrate (g): 58.1
Fat (g): 9.2
Saturated fat (g): 2.1
Cholesterol (mg): 43.5
Sodium (mg): 132
Exchanges:
Milk: 0.0
Vegetable: 0.0
Fruit: 1.0
Bread: 3.0
Meat: 2.0
Fat: 0.5

1. Combine chicken, broth, carrots, onions, garlic, and spices, in slow cooker; cover and cook on high 4 to 5 hours, adding apple and raisins during last 30 minutes. Stir in combined milk and cornstarch, stirring 2 to 3 minutes. Season to taste with salt and pepper; serve over rice.

Thai-Spiced Chicken and Carrot Stew

One tablespoon peanut butter and ¼–½ teaspoon crushed red pepper can be substituted for the Thai peanut sauce.

4 entrée servings

1 pound boneless, skinless chicken breast, cubed
1¼ cups reduced-sodium fat-free chicken broth
4 carrots, diagonally sliced
¾ cup sliced scallions
1 tablespoon each: minced gingerroot, garlic,
  soy sauce, Thai peanut sauce
1 teaspoon sugar
½–1 teaspoon Asian sesame oil
Salt and pepper, to taste
3 cups cooked rice, warm

Per Serving:
Calories: 358
% calories from fat: 11
Protein (g): 32.8
Carbohydrate (g): 44.4
Fat (g): 4.3
Saturated fat (g): 1.3
Cholesterol (mg): 69
Sodium (mg): 371
Exchanges:
Milk: 0.0
Vegetable: 2.0
Fruit: 0.0
Bread: 2.0
Meat: 3.0
Fat: 0.0

1. Combine all ingredients, except sesame oil, salt, and pepper, in slow cooker; cover and cook on high 3 to 4 hours. Season to taste with sesame oil, salt, and pepper; serve over rice.

Indian Curry Chicken and Vegetable Stew

The mixture of spices in the Curry Seasoning gives this stew a unique flavor;
however, 3 tablespoons of curry powder can be substituted.

6 entrée servings

1 pound chicken tenders, halved
¾ cup each: reduced-sodium vegetable broth,
   reduced-fat or regular coconut milk
1 can (14½ ounces) crushed tomatoes
1 can (6 ounces) tomato paste
8 ounces mushrooms, coarsely chopped
1 cup each: cubed potato, sliced carrots, small
   cauliflower florets, cut green beans, finely
   chopped onion
2 tablespoons each: white wine vinegar, brown sugar
1–2 tablespoons Curry Seasoning (recipe follows)
1 cup fresh or frozen thawed cut okra
Salt, to taste
3 cups cooked brown rice, warm

Per Serving:
Calories: 509
% calories from fat: 12
Protein (g): 38.7
Carbohydrate (g): 76.7
Fat (g): 6.8
Saturated fat (g): 2.8
Cholesterol (mg): 65.7
Sodium (mg): 861
Exchanges:
Milk: 0.0
Vegetable: 0.0
Fruit: 0.0
Bread: 5.0
Meat: 3.0
Fat: 0.0

1. Combine all ingredients, except okra, salt, and rice, in 6-quart slow cooker; cover and cook on low 6 to 8 hours, adding okra during last 30 minutes. Season to taste with salt; serve with rice.

Curry Seasoning

Makes about 2 tablespoons

2 teaspoons ground coriander
1 teaspoon ground turmeric, chili powder
½ teaspoon each: ground cumin, dry mustard, ground ginger, black pepper

1. Combine all ingredients.

Curried Chicken and Vegetable Stew

A variety of spices and herbs are combined to make the fragrant curry that seasons this dish.

4 entrée servings

12–16 ounces boneless, skinless chicken
    breast, cubed
1 cup reduced-sodium fat-free chicken broth
½ small head cauliflower, cut into florets
2 each: cubed medium potatoes, thickly
    sliced carrots
1 large tomato, chopped
½ cup chopped onion
2 cloves garlic
¾ teaspoon ground turmeric
½ teaspoon each: dry mustard, ground
    cumin, coriander
1–2 tablespoons lemon juice
Salt and cayenne pepper, to taste

Per Serving:
Calories: 250
% calories from fat: 11
Protein (g): 28.4
Carbohydrate (g): 29
Fat (g): 3.1
Saturated fat (g): 0.7
Cholesterol (mg): 51.7
Sodium (mg): 203
Exchanges:
Milk: 0.0
Vegetable: 2.0
Fruit: 0.0
Bread: 1.0
Meat: 2.0
Fat: 0.0

1. Combine all ingredients, except lemon juice, salt, and cayenne pepper, in slow cooker; cover and cook on low 5 to 6 hours. Season to taste with lemon juice, salt, and cayenne pepper.

Curry-Ginger Chicken Stew

This stew is seasoned with a great-tasting Curry-Ginger Spice Blend.

10 entrée servings

2 chickens (about 2½ pounds each), cut up
1½ cups reduced-sodium fat-free chicken broth
2 cups chopped onions
1 cup peeled seeded chopped tomatoes
2 cloves garlic, finely chopped
Curry-Ginger Spice Blend (recipe follows)
1½ cups frozen peas, thawed
¼ cup chopped cilantro
½–1 cup reduced-fat sour cream
2 tablespoons cornstarch
Salt and pepper, to taste
5 cups cooked rice, warm

Per Serving:
Calories: 334
% calories from fat: 27
Protein (g): 28.8
Carbohydrate (g): 31.3
Fat (g): 9.8
Saturated fat (g): 2.2
Cholesterol (mg): 73
Sodium (mg): 328
Exchanges:
Milk: 0.0
Vegetable: 0.0
Fruit: 0.0
Bread: 2.0
Meat: 3.0
Fat: 0.5

1. Combine chicken, broth, onions, tomatoes, garlic, and Curry-Ginger Spice Blend in 6-quart slow cooker; cover and cook on low 6 to 8 hours, adding peas during last 20 minutes. Stir in cilantro and combined sour cream and cornstarch, stirring 2 to 3 minutes. Season to taste with salt and pepper; serve over rice.

Curry-Ginger Spice Blend

Makes about ¼ cup

2 tablespoons finely chopped gingerroot
1 tablespoon sesame seeds
2 teaspoons coriander seeds
1 teaspoon each: cumin seeds, ground turmeric, salt
¼ teaspoon each: peppercorns, fennel seeds
⅛–¼ teaspoon crushed red pepper

1. Process all ingredients in spice mill or food processor until finely ground.

Curried Chicken and Apple Stew

The flavors of apple and ginger make this stew a special treat. Serve with Spinach Rice (see p. 345).

6 entrée servings

1½ pounds boneless, skinless chicken breast
  halves, halved or quartered
1½ cups reduced-sodium fat-free chicken broth
1 cup each: chopped onion, sliced carrots
1 teaspoon minced garlic
1½ tablespoons curry powder
1 teaspoon ground ginger
1 cup each: peeled sliced cooking apples,
  reduced-fat sour cream
2 tablespoons cornstarch
Salt and pepper, to taste

Per Serving:
Calories: 232
% calories from fat: 22
Protein (g): 30.7
Carbohydrate (g): 13.9
Fat (g): 5.6
Saturated fat (g): 1.2
Cholesterol (mg): 66.5
Sodium (mg): 336
Exchanges:
Milk: 0.0
Vegetable: 0.0
Fruit: 1.0
Bread. 0.0
Meat: 3.0
Fat: 0.0

1. Combine all ingredients, except apples, sour cream, cornstarch, salt, and pepper, in slow cooker; cover and cook on low 5 to 6 hours, adding apples during last 30 minutes. Stir in combined sour cream and cornstarch, stirring 2 to 3 minutes; season to taste with salt and pepper.

Moroccan Chicken Stew with Couscous

Tantalize your taste buds with this version of a Middle Eastern stew.

4 entrée servings

1 pound boneless, skinless chicken breast, cubed
  (¾-inch)
2 cans (14½ ounces each) stewed tomatoes
¼ cup finely chopped onion
2 teaspoons minced garlic
½ teaspoon each: ground cinnamon, coriander
⅛–¼ teaspoon crushed red pepper
½ cup each: quartered dried apricots, currants
½ teaspoon cumin seeds, lightly crushed
Salt and pepper, to taste
1 cup cooked couscous, warm

Per Serving:
Calories: 499
% calories from fat: 8
Protein (g): 34.5
Carbohydrate (g): 80.1
Fat (g): 4.8
Saturated fat (g): 1.1
Cholesterol (mg): 69
Sodium (mg): 498
Exchanges:
Milk: 0.0
Vegetable: 2.0
Fruit: 0.0
Bread: 2.5
Meat: 3.0
Fat: 0.0

1. Combine all ingredients, except salt, pepper, and couscous, in slow cooker; cover and cook on high 3 to 4 hours. Season to taste with salt and pepper; serve over couscous.

Moroccan Chicken and Chickpea Stew

This dish is great for entertaining because it serves eight and can be doubled easily for a 7-quart slow cooker.

8 entrée servings

8 boneless, skinless chicken breast halves
   (4 ounces each), halved or quartered
1 can (15 ounces) chickpeas, rinsed, drained
½ cup reduced-sodium fat-free chicken broth
¾ cup chopped onion
4 cloves garlic, crushed
2 teaspoons ground ginger
1 teaspoon ground turmeric
1 cinnamon stick
½ cup raisins
2–3 tablespoons lemon juice
Salt and pepper, to taste

Per Serving:
Calories: 357
% calories from fat: 23
Protein (g): 42.9
Carbohydrate (g): 24.3
Fat (g): 9
Saturated fat (g): 2.4
Cholesterol (mg): 115.7
Sodium (mg): 254
Exchanges:
Milk: 0.0
Vegetable: 0.0
Fruit: 0.0
Bread: 2.0
Meat: 4.0
Fat: 0.0

1. Combine all ingredients, except raisins, lemon juice, salt, and pepper, in 6-quart slow cooker; cover and cook on high 4 to 5 hours, adding raisins during last 30 minutes. Discard cinnamon stick; season to taste with lemon juice, salt, and pepper.

Middle Eastern-Style Chicken Stew

Couscous cooks quickly and lends a uniquely pleasing texture to this stew.

4 entrée servings

1 pound boneless, skinless chicken breast,
  cubed (1-inch)
1½ cups reduced-sodium fat-free chicken broth
1 can (15 ounces) garbanzo beans, rinsed, drained
2 cups chopped tomatoes
¾ cup each: chopped onion, green bell pepper
2 cloves garlic, minced
1 bay leaf
1½ teaspoons dried thyme leaves
1 teaspoon ground cumin
¼ teaspoon ground allspice
1 cup couscous
¼ cup raisins
Salt and pepper, to taste

Per Serving:
Calories: 389
% calories from fat: 12
Protein (g): 24
Carbohydrate (g): 63
Fat (g): 5.4
Saturated fat (g): 1
Cholesterol (mg): 34
Sodium (mg): 235
Exchanges:
Milk: 0.0
Vegetable: 1.0
Fruit: 1.0
Bread: 3.0
Meat: 1.5
Fat: 0.0

1. Combine all ingredients, except couscous, raisins, salt, and pepper, in slow cooker; cover and cook on high 4 to 5 hours, adding couscous and raisins during last 5 to 10 minutes. Discard bay leaf; season to taste with salt and pepper.

Chicken Stew Marengo

The orange-scented tomato sauce, lightly seasoned with herbs and wine, benefits from slow cooking to meld flavors.

6 entrée servings

6 small boneless, skinless chicken breast halves
   (4 ounces each), quartered
1 cup reduced-sodium fat-free chicken broth
½ cup dry white wine or chicken broth
3 tablespoons tomato paste
2 cups sliced mushrooms
1 cup sliced carrots
1 small onion, chopped
3 cloves garlic, minced
2 tablespoons grated orange zest
1 teaspoon each: dried tarragon and thyme leaves
⅓ cup frozen peas, thawed
Salt and pepper, to taste
12 ounces linguine or other flat pasta, cooked, warm

Per Serving:
Calories: 343
% calories from fat: 16
Protein (g): 25 4
Carbohydrate (g): 42.7
Fat (g): 6.1
Saturated fat (g): 1.1
Cholesterol (mg): 43.5
Sodium (mg): 133
Exchanges:
Milk: 0.0
Vegetable: 1.0
Fruit: 0.0
Bread: 2.5
Meat: 2.5
Fat: 0.0

1. Combine all ingredients, except salt, pepper, and pasta, in slow cooker; cover and cook on high 4 to 5 hours. Season to taste with salt and pepper; serve over pasta.

Chicken Stew with Artichokes

Serve Red Pepper Rice (see p. 403) as a flavorful complement to this chicken stew.

4 entrée servings

1 pound boneless, skinless chicken breast, cubed
   (1-inch)
1 can (14½ ounces) petite-diced tomatoes, undrained
½ can (15 ounces) quartered canned artichoke hearts
½ cup each: chopped onion, thinly sliced celery
1 teaspoon dried oregano leaves
½ cup halved ripe olives
Salt and pepper, to taste

Per Serving:
Calories: 228
% calories from fat: 27
Protein (g): 29.3
Carbohydrate (g): 11.3
Fat (g): 6.8
Saturated fat (g): 1.1
Cholesterol (mg): 73
Sodium (mg): 223
Exchanges:
Milk: 0.0
Vegetable: 2.0
Fruit: 0.0
Bread: 0.0
Meat: 3.0
Fat: 0.0

1. Combine all ingredients, except olives, salt, and pepper, in slow cooker; cover and cook on high 4 to 5 hours, adding olives during last 30 minutes. Season to taste with salt and pepper.

Chicken Stew Athenos

Cinnamon, lemon, and feta cheese give this tomato-based stew the signature flavors of Greece.

4 entrée servings

1 pound boneless, skinless chicken breast,
    cubed (¾-inch)
1 can (14½ ounces) stewed tomatoes, undrained
½ cup reduced-sodium fat-free chicken broth
½ cup each: canned artichoke quarters, finely
    chopped onion
1 tablespoon lemon juice
2 teaspoons minced garlic
1 each: cinnamon stick, bay leaf
1–2 tablespoons dry sherry (optional)
Salt and pepper, to taste
8 ounces egg noodles, cooked, warm
¼ cup (1 ounce) crumbled feta cheese

Per Serving:
Calories: 412
% calories from fat: 17
Protein (g): 34.4
Carbohydrate (g): 46
Fat (g): 7.9
Saturated fat (g): 2.5
Cholesterol (mg): 124.2
Sodium (mg): 370
Exchanges:
Milk: 0.0
Vegetable: 2.0
Fruit: 0.0
Bread: 2.0
Meat: 4.0
Fat: 0.0

1. Combine all ingredients, except sherry, salt, pepper, noodles, and cheese, in slow cooker; cover and cook on high 4 to 5 hours. Discard cinnamon stick and bay leaf; season to taste with sherry, salt, and pepper. Serve over noodles with feta cheese.

Spanish Chicken and Rice Stew

The Spanish name of this dish, arroz con pollo, translates as "rice with chicken."

6 entrée servings

1 pound boneless, skinless chicken breast, cubed
  (1½-inch)
3 cups reduced-sodium fat-free chicken broth
1 cup each: chopped onion, green and red
  bell pepper
2 cloves garlic, minced
¼ teaspoon crushed saffron threads (optional)
1 cup uncooked converted long-grain rice
1–2 tablespoons dry sherry (optional)
1 cup frozen peas, thawed
Salt and cayenne pepper, to taste

Per Serving:
Calories: 246
% calories from fat: 12
Protein (g): 15
Carbohydrate (g): 35
Fat (g): 3.1
Saturated fat (g): 1.0
Cholesterol (mg): 30
Sodium (mg): 255
Exchanges:
Milk: 0.0
Vegetable: 1.0
Fruit: 0.0
Bread: 2.0
Meat: 1.5
Fat: 0.0

1. Combine all ingredients, except rice, sherry, peas, salt, and cayenne pepper, in slow cooker; cover and cook on low 5 to 6 hours, adding rice during last 2 hours and sherry and peas during last 20 minutes. Season to taste with salt and cayenne pepper.

Mediterranean Chicken Stew

Thicken this flavorful stew with cornstarch if a thicker consistency is desired; serve over couscous or rice.

6 entrée servings

1½ pounds boneless, skinless chicken breast, cubed
  (1-inch)
1 cup reduced-sodium fat-free chicken broth
½ cup dry white wine or chicken broth
¼ cup balsamic vinegar
8 ounces small mushrooms, halved
6 plum tomatoes, chopped
¼ cup halved Greek or black olives
3 cloves garlic, minced
1 teaspoon each: dried rosemary and thyme leaves
Salt and pepper, to taste

Per Serving:
Calories: 201
% calories from fat: 11
Protein (g): 29.5
Carbohydrate (g): 11.2
Fat (g): 2.4
Saturated fat (g): 0.6
Cholesterol (mg): 65.7
Sodium (mg): 258
Exchanges:
Milk: 0.0
Vegetable: 0.0
Fruit: 0.0
Bread: 1.0
Meat: 3.0
Fat: 0.0

1. Combine all ingredients, except salt and pepper, in slow cooker; cover and cook on high 4 to 5 hours. Season to taste with salt and pepper.

Med-Rim Chicken Stew

Serve this excellent Mediterranean-style stew over Red Pepper Rice or Polenta (see p. 403, 520).

4 entrée servings

1 pound boneless, skinless chicken breast,
  cubed (1½-inch)
½ cup each: reduced-sodium fat-free chicken
  broth, dry white wine or chicken broth
4 medium tomatoes, quartered
1 cup sliced mushrooms
½ cup chopped onion
1 clove garlic, minced
1 teaspoon each: dried thyme, rosemary, and
  tarragon leaves
1 cup canned quartered artichoke hearts, drained
¼ cup sliced black or Greek olives
Salt and pepper, to taste
¼ cup crumbled feta cheese

Per Serving:
Calories: 32.8
% calories from fat 27
Protein (g): 29
Carbohydrate (g): 20.9
Fat (g): 10
Saturated fat (g): 1.7
Cholesterol (mg): 69
Sodium (mg): 376
Exchanges:
Milk: 0.0
Vegetable: 2.0
Fruit: 0.0
Bread: 0.5
Meat: 3.0
Fat: 1.5

1. Combine all ingredients, except artichoke hearts, olives, salt, pepper, and feta cheese, in slow cooker; cover and cook on high 4 to 5 hours, adding artichoke hearts and olives during last hour. Season to taste with salt and pepper; sprinkle each serving with feta cheese.

Italian-Style Bean and Vegetable Stew with Polenta

This colorful mélange can also be served over pasta, rice, or squares of warm cornbread.

6 entrée servings

10 ounces Italian-style turkey sausage, casing removed
1 can (14½ ounces) diced tomatoes, undrained
1 can (15 ounces) each: rinsed drained garbanzo and red kidney beans
1½ cups each: chopped onions, portobello mushrooms
4 cloves garlic, minced
1½ teaspoons dried Italian seasoning
⅛–¼ teaspoon crushed red pepper
2 cups broccoli florets and sliced stems
1 cup sliced yellow summer squash
Salt and pepper, to taste
1 package (16 ounces) prepared Italian herb polenta, warm

Per Serving:
Calories: 380
% calories from fat: 27
Protein (g): 21.7
Carbohydrate (g): 49.6
Fat (g): 11.9
Saturated fat (g): 2.5
Cholesterol (mg): 30.4
Sodium (mg): 833
Exchanges:
Milk: 0.0
Vegetable: 3.0
Fruit: 0.0
Bread: 3.0
Meat: 1.0
Fat: 1.0

1. Cook Italian sausage in greased medium skillet until browned, crumbling with a fork. Combine Italian sausage with remaining ingredients, except broccoli, squash, salt, pepper, and polenta, in 6-quart slow cooker; cover and cook on low 6 to 8 hours, adding broccoli and squash during last 30 minutes. Season to taste with salt and pepper. Serve over polenta.

Chicken Stew Peperonata

Serve this very simple but delicious Tuscan stew over rice or your favorite pasta.

4 entrée servings

1 pound boneless, skinless chicken breast, cubed (1-inch)
1 can (14½ ounces) chunky Italian-seasoned crushed tomatoes
1 cup each: sliced onion, red and green bell pepper
½ teaspoon minced garlic
Salt and pepper, to taste
4 tablespoons grated Parmesan cheese

Per Serving:
Calories: 215
% calories from fat: 29
Protein (g): 28.5
Carbohydrate (g): 9.7
Fat (g): 7
Saturated fat (g): 1.8
Cholesterol (mg): 71
Sodium (mg): 674
Exchanges:
Milk: 0.0
Vegetable: 2.0
Fruit: 0.0
Bread: 0.0
Meat: 3.0
Fat: 0.0

1. Combine all ingredients, except salt, pepper, and cheese, in slow cooker; cover and cook on high 4 to 5 hours. Season to taste with salt and pepper; sprinkle each serving with Parmesan cheese.

Chicken, Vegetable, and Pasta Stew

Sun-dried tomatoes and black olives lend an earthy flavor to this colorful stew.

4 entrée servings

1 pound boneless, skinless chicken breast, cubed (1-inch)
1 can (14½ ounces) Italian-seasoned diced tomatoes, undrained
¾ cup reduced-sodium fat-free chicken broth
1 cup sliced carrots
½ cup each: chopped onion, green bell pepper
2 teaspoons minced garlic
2 bay leaves
1 teaspoon dried marjoram leaves
3 tablespoons chopped sun-dried tomatoes (not in oil)
¼ cup pitted halved Greek olives
2 medium yellow summer squash, cubed
1 cup small broccoli florets
4 ounces rigatoni, cooked, warm
Salt and pepper, to taste

Per Serving:
Calories: 330
% calories from fat: 25
Protein (g): 30.9
Carbohydrate (g): 30.7
Fat (g): 9.1
Saturated fat (g): 1.6
Cholesterol (mg): 69
Sodium (mg): 761
Exchanges:
Milk: 0.0
Vegetable: 1.0
Fruit: 0.0
Bread: 2.0
Meat: 3.0
Fat: 0.0

1. Combine all ingredients, except olives, squash, broccoli, rigatoni, salt, and pepper, in slow cooker; cover and cook on high 4 to 5 hours, adding squash, broccoli, and rigatoni during the last 20 minutes. Discard bay leaves; season to taste with salt and pepper.

Stewed Chicken Marinara

Team this stew with focaccia and a salad for an easy Italian meal.

4 entrée servings

1 pound boneless, skinless chicken breast, cubed
1 can (14½ ounces) crushed tomatoes
½ cup reduced-sodium fat-free chicken broth
1½ cups chopped onions
1 cup quartered medium mushrooms
½ cup each: finely chopped celery, carrot
2 cloves garlic, minced
1 teaspoon dried Italian seasoning
1 cup chopped zucchini
Salt and pepper, to taste
8 ounces ziti, cooked, warm

Per Serving:
Calories: 356
% calories from fat: 16
Protein (g): 28.1
Carbohydrate (g): 48.6
Fat (g): 6.8
Saturated fat (g): 1.5
Cholesterol (mg): 51.7
Sodium (mg): 544
Exchanges:
Milk: 0.0
Vegetable: 2.0
Fruit: 0.0
Bread: 2.0
Meat: 3.0
Fat: 0.0

1. Combine all ingredients, except zucchini, salt, pepper, and ziti, in slow cooker; cover and cook on high 4 to 5 hours, adding zucchini during last 20 minutes. Season to taste with salt and pepper; serve over ziti.

Chicken, Mushroom, and Tomato Stew with Polenta

Cooking polenta in the microwave is easy and fast, but it can also be made in the slow cooker (see p. 520).

4 entrée servings

1 pound boneless, skinless chicken breast, cubed
(1-inch)
2 cans (14½ ounces each) Italian plum tomatoes,
undrained, coarsely chopped
1 can (8 ounces) tomato sauce
2 tablespoons tomato paste
8 ounces mushrooms, sliced
½ cup each: sliced carrot, chopped onion
2 cloves garlic, minced
1 teaspoon each: sugar, dried basil and thyme leaves
Salt and pepper, to taste
Microwave Polenta (recipe follows)

Per Serving:
Calories: 403
% calories from fat: 17
Protein (g): 38
Carbohydrate (g): 46
Fat (g): 7.8
Saturated fat (g): 1.9
Cholesterol (mg): 85
Sodium (mg): 691
Exchanges:
Milk: 0.0
Vegetable: 3.0
Fruit: 0.0
Bread: 1.5
Meat: 4.0
Fat: 0.0

1. Combine all ingredients, except salt, pepper, and Microwave Polenta, in slow cooker; cover and cook on high 4 to 5 hours. Season to taste with salt and pepper; serve over Microwave Polenta.

Microwave Polenta

Makes about 3 cups

1⅓ cups yellow cornmeal
½ teaspoon salt
3 cups water
1 cup 2% reduced-fat milk
1 medium onion, diced

1. Combine all ingredients in 2½-quart glass casserole. Cook, uncovered, on high power 8 to 9 minutes, whisking halfway through cooking time. Whisk until smooth, cover, and cook on high 6 to 7 minutes. Remove from microwave, whisk, and let stand, covered, 3 to 4 minutes.

Chicken Cacciatore

Traditionally, this stew was made from any game brought back from the day's hunt and would vary slightly from kitchen to kitchen.

4 entrée servings

8 ounces each: cubed (¾-inch) boneless skinless
   chicken breast, thighs
2 cans (14½ ounces each) diced tomatoes, undrained
½ cup dry red wine or water
3 cups quartered medium mushrooms
1 cup each: chopped onion, green bell pepper
6 cloves garlic, minced
2 teaspoons dried oregano leaves
½ teaspoon garlic powder
1 bay leaf
1–2 tablespoons cornstarch
2–4 tablespoons water
Salt and pepper, to taste
3 cups cooked noodles, warm

Per Serving:
Calories: 411
% calories from fat: 15
Protein (g): 30.9
Carbohydrate (g): 53.7
Fat (g): 7.2
Saturated fat (g): 1.7
Cholesterol (mg): 65.5
Sodium (mg): 199
Exchanges:
Milk: 0.0
Vegetable: 4.0
Fruit: 0.0
Bread: 2.0
Meat: 3.0
Fat: 0.0

1. Combine all ingredients, except cornstarch, water, salt, pepper, and noodles, in slow cooker; cover and cook on low 6 to 8 hours. Turn heat to high and cook 10 minutes; stir in combined cornstarch and water, stirring 2 to 3 minutes. Discard bay leaf; season to taste with salt and pepper and serve over noodles.

Chicken and Ravioli Stew

Use any favorite flavor of refrigerated fresh ravioli in this quick and nutritious bean stew.

4 entrée servings

1 pound chicken tenders, quartered
2 cans (15 ounces each) kidney beans, rinsed, drained
1 can (14½ ounces) diced tomatoes, undrained
½ cup reduced-sodium fat-free chicken broth
¾ cup chopped onion
4 teaspoons minced garlic
½ teaspoon dried thyme leaves
½ package (9 ounce-size) fresh sun-dried tomato
   ravioli, cooked, warm
Salt and pepper, to taste

Per Serving:
Calories: 410
% calories from fat: 12
Protein (g): 39.1
Carbohydrate (g): 53.3
Fat (g): 5.7
Saturated fat (g): 2.4
Cholesterol (mg): 63.5
Sodium (mg): 984
Exchanges:
Milk: 0.0
Vegetable: 1.0
Fruit: 0.0
Bread: 3.0
Meat: 3.0
Fat: 0.0

1. Combine all ingredients, except ravioli, salt, and pepper, in slow cooker; cover and cook on high 4 to 5 hours, adding ravioli during last 10 minutes. Season to taste with salt and pepper.

Alfredo Chicken Stew

A creamy alfredo sauce makes this stew especially good.

4 entrée servings

1 pound boneless, skinless chicken breast, cubed
   (¾-inch)
2 cups reduced-sodium fat-free chicken broth
¼ cup sliced green onions
1 teaspoon each: minced garlic, dried basil leaves
4 ounces asparagus, sliced (1½-inch)
⅓ cup frozen petite peas, thawed
2 tablespoons cornstarch
½ cup each: 2% reduced-fat milk, shredded Parmesan
   cheese
Salt and pepper, to taste
8 ounces fettuccine, cooked, warm

Per Serving:
Calories: 448
% calories from fat: 11
Protein (g): 42
Carbohydrate (g): 54
Fat (g): 5.3
Saturated fat (g): 2.1
Cholesterol (mg): 80
Sodium (mg): 604
Exchanges:
Milk: 0.5
Vegetable: 2.0
Fruit: 0.0
Bread: 2.0
Meat: 3.0
Fat: 0.0

1. Combine chicken, broth, green onions, garlic, and basil, in slow cooker; cover and cook on high 4 to 5 hours, adding asparagus and peas during last 20 minutes. Stir in combined cornstarch and milk, stirring 2 to 3 minutes; add cheese, stirring melted. Season to taste with salt and pepper. Serve over fettuccine.

Tuscan Chicken Stew

Serve this hearty Tuscan stew over rice or pasta.

6 entrée servings

1 cup reduced-sodium fat-free chicken broth, boiling
1 ounce dried porcini or shiitake mushrooms
1½ pounds boneless, skinless chicken breast, cubed (1-inch)
1 can (14 ounces) Italian-seasoned diced tomatoes, undrained
1 can (15 ounces) cannellini or other white beans, rinsed, drained
½ cup dry white wine or chicken broth
¾ cup chopped onion
3 cloves garlic, minced
2 tablespoons cornstarch
¼ cup cold water
Salt and pepper, to taste

Per Serving:
Calories: 233
% calories from fat: 29
Protein (g): 28.3
Carbohydrate (g): 9.2
Fat (g): 7.5
Saturated fat (g): 1.4
Cholesterol (mg): 69
Sodium (mg): 439
Exchanges:
Milk: 0.0
Vegetable: 2.0
Fruit: 0.0
Bread: 0.0
Meat: 3.0
Fat: 0.0

1. Pour broth over mushrooms in small bowl; let stand until mushrooms are softened, about 10 minutes. Drain mushrooms; strain and reserve broth. Slice mushrooms, discarding any tough pieces.
2. Combine mushrooms, reserved broth, and remaining ingredients, except cornstarch, water, salt, and pepper, in slow cooker, cover and cook on high 4 to 5 hours. Stir in combined cornstarch and water, stirring 2 to 3 minutes. Season to taste with salt and pepper.

Home-Style Turkey Stew

A great family meal!

4 entrée servings

12–16 ounces turkey breast, cubed (¾-inch)
1 can (14½ ounces) reduced-sodium fat-free
   chicken broth
1 cup each: sliced carrots, unpeeled cubed
   potatoes, chopped onion
4 ounces mushrooms, halved
1 teaspoon each: dried thyme leaves, celery seeds
1 cup frozen peas, thawed
Salt and pepper, to taste

Per Serving:
Calories: 158
% calories from fat: 26
Protein (g): 21.1
Carbohydrate (g): 7
Fat (g): 4.5
Saturated fat (g): 1
Cholesterol (mg): 44.7
Sodium (mg): 63
Exchanges:
Milk: 0.0
Vegetable: 0.0
Fruit: 0.0
Bread: 0.5
Meat: 3.0
Fat: 0.0

1. Combine all ingredients, except peas, salt, and
pepper, in slow cooker; cover and cook on low 6 to 8 hours, adding peas
during last 20 minutes. Season to taste with salt and pepper.

Sausage, Potato, and Bell Pepper Stew

An attractive stew with the vibrant colors of bell peppers.

4 entrée servings

8–12 ounces smoked turkey sausage, thinly sliced
¾ cup reduced-sodium fat-free chicken broth
4 cups thinly sliced red potatoes
3 cups thinly sliced mixed red, green, and yellow
   bell peppers
1 cup thinly sliced onion
¼–½ cup quartered sun-dried tomatoes (not in oil)
1 teaspoon each: dried thyme and marjoram leaves
1–2 tablespoons cornstarch
¼ cup cold water
Salt and pepper, to taste

Per Serving:
Calories: 258
% calories from fat: 19
Protein (g): 13.7
Carbohydrate (g): 42.8
Fat (g): 5.7
Saturated fat (g): 1.4
Cholesterol (mg): 28.2
Sodium (mg): 736
Exchanges:
Milk: 0.0
Vegetable: 3.0
Fruit: 0.0
Bread: 3.0
Meat: 1.0
Fat: 0.0

1. Combine all ingredients, except cornstarch, water, salt, and pepper,
in slow cooker; cover and cook on high 4 to 5 hours. Stir in combined
cornstarch and water, stirring 2 to 3 minutes. Season to taste with salt and
pepper.

Turkey Ragout with White Wine

Turkey simmers with white wine and herbs to make a flavorful stew; delicious over rice or Polenta (see p. 520).

6 entrée servings

1½ pounds turkey breast, cubed (1-inch)
1 can (14½ ounces) Italian plum tomatoes,
   undrained, chopped
½ cup dry white wine or chicken broth
2½ cups sliced mushrooms
1 cup chopped onion
½ cup each: sliced carrots, celery
2 large cloves garlic, minced
½ teaspoon each: dried rosemary and sage leaves
1–2 tablespoons cornstarch
2–4 tablespoons cold water
Salt and pepper, to taste

Per Serving:
Calories: 226
% calories from fat: 24
Protein (g): 30
Carbohydrate (g): 8.1
Fat (g): 5.8
Saturated fat (g): 1.0
Cholesterol (mg): 71.3
Sodium (mg): 97
Exchanges:
Milk: 0.0
Vegetable: 0.0
Fruit: 0.0
Bread: 0.5
Meat: 3.0
Fat: 0.0

1. Combine all ingredients, except cornstarch, water, salt, and pepper, in slow cooker; cover and cook on low 6 to 8 hours. Turn heat to high and cook 10 minutes; stir in combined cornstarch and water, stirring 2 to 3 minutes. Season to taste with salt and pepper.

Turkey-Wild Rice Stew

Turkey, vegetables, and wild rice combine to create a delicious supper stew.

4 entrée servings

1 pound turkey breast, cubed
2 cups reduced-sodium fat-free chicken broth
½ cup chopped onion
1 teaspoon dried sage leaves
1½ cups sliced carrots
½ cup uncooked wild rice
1½ cups small broccoli florets
Salt and pepper, to taste

Per Serving:
Calories: 250
% calories from fat: 13
Protein (g): 29
Carbohydrate (g): 24.6
Fat (g): 3.8
Saturated fat (g): 0.9
Cholesterol (mg): 44.7
Sodium (mg): 196
Exchanges:
Milk: 0.0
Vegetable: 1.0
Fruit: 0.0
Bread: 1.0
Meat: 3.0
Fat: 0.0

1. Combine all ingredients, except rice, broccoli, salt, and pepper, in slow cooker; cover and cook on low 6 to 8 hours, stirring in rice during last 2 hours and broccoli during last 30 minutes. Season to taste with salt and pepper.

Turkey Stew with Apricots

Serve with jasmine or basmati rice to complement the subtle apricot flavor in the stew.

4 entrée servings

1 pound turkey breast, cubed (1-inch)
1¾ cups reduced-sodium fat-free chicken broth
1 cup each: chopped onion, tomato
2 cloves garlic, minced
1 teaspoon ground cumin
½ teaspoon ground allspice
10 dried apricot halves, quartered
2 tablespoons cornstarch
¼ cup water
¼ cup chopped cilantro
Salt and pepper, to taste
1 cup cooked rice, warm

Per Serving:
Calories: 319
% calories from fat: 7
Protein (g): 27
Carbohydrate (g): 46
Fat (g): 2.6
Saturated fat (g): 0.7
Cholesterol (mg): 65
Sodium (mg): 260
Exchanges:
Milk: 0.0
Vegetable: 0.0
Fruit: 0.5
Bread: 2.0
Meat: 3.0
Fat: 0.0

1. Combine all ingredients, except cornstarch, water, cilantro, salt, pepper, and rice, in slow cooker; cook, covered, 5 to 6 hours. Turn heat to high and cook 10 minutes; stir in combined cornstarch and water, stirring 2 to 3 minutes. Stir in cilantro; season to taste with salt and pepper. Serve over rice.

Southwest Turkey Stew

This stew is spicy! For less heat, the jalapeño chili can be omitted.

6 entrée servings

1½ pounds turkey breast, cubed (1-inch)
1 can (15 ounces) chili beans in spicy sauce, undrained
1 can (14½ ounces) stewed tomatoes
½ cup reduced-sodium fat-free chicken broth
¾ cup each: chopped green and red bell pepper, onion
1 small jalapeño chili, minced
2 cloves garlic, minced
1 tablespoon chili powder
1 teaspoon ground cumin
Salt and pepper to taste

Per Serving:
Calories: 352
% calories from fat: 25
Protein (g): 30
Carbohydrate (g): 37.7
Fat (g): 10.2
Saturated fat (g): 2.7
Cholesterol (mg): 48.5
Sodium (mg): 786
Exchanges:
Milk: 0.0
Vegetable: 2.0
Fruit: 0.0
Bread: 2.0
Meat: 3.0
Fat: 0.0

1. Combine all ingredients, except salt and pepper, in slow cooker; cover and cook on high 3 to 4 hours. Season to taste with salt and pepper.

Latin American Turkey Stew

Enjoy this hearty stew with a Latin American flair; serve over rice.

4 entrée servings

1 pound turkey breast, cubed (¾-inch)
1 can (15 ounces) black beans, rinsed, drained
1 can (14½ ounces) reduced-sodium fat-free chicken broth
1 can (8 ounces) tomato paste
2 cups peeled cubed butternut squash
1 cup each: peeled cubed sweet and white potato, chopped onion
1 jalapeño chili, minced
1 teaspoon cumin seeds, toasted
Salt and pepper, to taste
¼ cup coarsely chopped cashews

Per Serving:
Calories: 324
% calories from fat: 18
Protein (g): 29.6
Carbohydrate (g): 43.7
Fat (g): 7.2
Saturated fat (g): 1.5
Cholesterol (mg): 44.7
Sodium (mg): 652
Exchanges:
Milk: 0.0
Vegetable: 0.0
Fruit: 0.0
Bread: 2.5
Meat: 2.0
Fat: 0.0

1. Combine all ingredients, except salt, pepper, and cashews; cover and cook on low 6 to 8 hours. Season to taste with salt and pepper. Sprinkle each serving with cashews.

Italian Sausage Stew with Hot Peppers

The flavors of this stew will remind you of a sassy Italian hot sausage and pepper sandwich!

4 entrée servings

12–16 ounces Italian-style turkey sausage, sliced (1-inch)
1 can (14½ ounces) diced tomatoes, undrained
1 cup reduced-sodium fat-free chicken broth
2 small onions, cut into thin wedges
1 tablespoon chopped garlic
½–1 small jalapeño chili, thinly sliced
1½ teaspoons dried Italian seasoning
⅛–¼ teaspoon crushed red pepper
1 zucchini, halved lengthwise, thickly sliced
4 ounces rigatoni, cooked
Salt and pepper, to taste
¼ cup (1 ounce) shredded Parmesan cheese

Per Serving:
Calories: 317
% calories from fat: 16
Protein (g): 24.8
Carbohydrate (g): 43.1
Fat (g): 5.8
Saturated fat (g): 2.2
Cholesterol (mg): 43.6
Sodium (mg): 738
Exchanges:
Milk: 0.0
Vegetable: 2.0
Fruit: 0.0
Bread: 2.0
Meat: 2.0
Fat: 0.0

1. Combine all ingredients, except zucchini, pasta, salt, pepper, and cheese, in slow cooker; cover and cook on high 4 to 5 hours, adding zucchini and pasta during last 20 minutes. Season to taste with salt and pepper; sprinkle each serving with 1 tablespoon cheese.

Turkey Stew Cacciatore

Boneless, skinless chicken breasts can be substituted for the turkey in this simple stew.

4 entrée servings

1 pound turkey breast cutlets, sliced (2-inch)
1 can (14½ ounces) stewed tomatoes
⅓ cup water
¾ cup sliced mushrooms
¾ teaspoon dried oregano leaves
2 small zucchini, cubed
Salt and pepper, to taste
4 cups cooked pasta or rice, warm

Per Serving:
Calories: 579
% calories from fat: 16
Protein (g): 32.4
Carbohydrate (g): 87.7
Fat (g): 10.6
Saturated fat (g): 1.8
Cholesterol (mg): 44.7
Sodium (mg): 265
Exchanges:
Milk: 0.0
Vegetable: 3.0
Fruit: 0.0
Bread: 4.0
Meat: 3.0
Fat: 1.0

1. Combine all ingredients, except zucchini, salt, pepper, and pasta, in slow cooker; cover and cook on high 4 to 5 hours, adding zucchini during last 30 minutes. Season to taste with salt and pepper; serve over pasta.

Italian-Style Turkey Sausage and Fennel Stew

Use your preference of sweet or hot sausage in this harvest stew.

4 entrée servings

10 ounces Italian-style turkey sausage, sliced
1 can (14½ ounces) diced tomatoes, undrained
1 cup reduced-sodium fat-free chicken broth
1 pound butternut squash, peeled, cubed
8 small Brussels sprouts, halved
1 medium onion, cut into thin wedges
2 parsnips, sliced
1 small fennel bulb, sliced
Pinch crushed red pepper
1 teaspoon dried Italian seasoning
1–2 tablespoons cornstarch
2–4 tablespoons cold water
Salt and pepper, to taste

Per Serving:
Calories: 310
% calories from fat: 26
Protein (g): 21.8
Carbohydrate (g): 39.4
Fat (g): 9.7
Saturated fat (g): 2.6
Cholesterol (mg): 45.6
Sodium (mg): 780
Exchanges:
Milk: 0.0
Vegetable: 2.0
Fruit: 0.0
Bread: 2.0
Meat: 2.0
Fat: 0.0

1. Combine all ingredients, except cornstarch, water, salt, and pepper, in slow cooker; cover and cook on low 5 to 6 hours. Turn heat to high and cook 10 minutes; stir in combined cornstarch and water, stirring 2 to 3 minutes Season to taste with salt and pepper.

Smoky Garbanzo Bean Stew

Smoked turkey sausage gives this stew lots of flavor; the beans and vegetables make it extra-nutritious.

6 entrée servings

1 pound smoked turkey sausage, sliced
1 can (28 ounces) diced tomatoes, undrained
2 cans (15 ounces each) garbanzo beans, rinsed, drained
1 cup each: chopped onion, green bell pepper, cut green beans
2 cloves garlic, minced
2 teaspoons dried oregano leaves
2 medium zucchini, sliced
Salt and pepper, to taste

Per Serving:
Calories: 298
% calories from fat: 17
Protein (g): 15.9
Carbohydrate (g): 48.9
Fat (g): 5.8
Saturated fat (g): 1.1
Cholesterol (mg): 17.6
Sodium (mg): 556
Exchanges:
Milk: 0.0
Vegetable: 1.0
Fruit: 0.0
Bread: 2.0
Meat: 1.0
Fat: 0.5

1. Combine all ingredients, except zucchini, salt, and pepper, in 6-quart slow cooker; cover and cook on high 4 to 5 hours, adding zucchini during last 30 minutes. Season to taste with salt and pepper.

ELEVEN

Fish and Seafood Stews

Savory Fish Stew

Serve with generous squares of warm Roasted Chili Cornbread (see p. 529).

8 entrée servings

1 can (28 ounces) stewed tomatoes
1 cup clam juice or water
½ cup dry white wine or water
1 cup finely chopped onion
4 cloves garlic, minced
1 teaspoon each: dried basil and oregano leaves
½ teaspoon ground turmeric
2 bay leaves
1 pound cod or other whitefish fillets, sliced (1-inch)
8 ounces each: peeled deveined shrimp, bay scallops
Salt and pepper, to taste

Per Serving:
Calories: 175
% calories from fat: 20
Protein (g): 21.5
Carbohydrate (g): 10.2
Fat (g): 4
Saturated fat (g): 0.7
Cholesterol (mg): 79.7
Sodium (mg): 539
Exchanges:
Milk: 0.0
Vegetable: 2.0
Fruit: 0.0
Bread: 0.0
Meat: 2.0
Fat: 0.0

1. Combine all ingredients, except seafood, salt, and pepper, in slow cooker; cover and cook on high 3 to 4 hours; adding seafood during last 10 to 15 minutes. Discard bay leaves; season to taste with salt and pepper.

Fennel-Scented Fish Stew

Flavors of fennel seeds, orange zest, and white wine meld in this fish stew.

8 entrée servings

1 quart Fish Stock (see p. 33) or clam juice
½ cup dry white wine (optional)
5 medium tomatoes, peeled, chopped
1 cup each: chopped carrots, onion
3 cloves garlic, minced
1 tablespoon minced orange zest
1 teaspoon fennel seeds, lightly crushed
2 pounds firm fish fillets (cod, red snapper, salmon, orange roughy halibut), cut into pieces (1½-inch)
¼ cup chopped parsley
Salt and pepper, to taste

Per Serving:
Calories: 174
% calories from fat: 14
Protein (g): 22.8
Carbohydrate (g): 10.1
Fat (g): 2.6
Saturated fat (g): 0.5
Cholesterol (mg): 51.9
Sodium (mg): 110
Exchanges:
Milk: 0.0
Vegetable: 2.0
Fruit: 0.0
Bread: 0.0
Meat: 2.0
Fat: 0.0

1. Combine all ingredients, except fish, parsley, salt, and pepper, in slow cooker; cover and cook on low 6 to 8 hours, adding fish during last 15 minutes. Stir in parsley; season to taste with salt and pepper.

Variation

Fish Stew Salsa Verde—Make recipe as above, decreasing tomatoes to 3 and adding 1 pound chopped husked tomatillos, 1 minced small jalapeño chili, ½ teaspoon crushed cumin seeds, and ½ teaspoon dried oregano leaves. Omit fennel seeds, orange zest, and parsley. Sprinkle each serving generously with chopped cilantro.

Fish and Sun-Dried Tomato Stew

Add 1 tablespoon drained capers to this rich tomato-based stew, if you like, and serve over Polenta (see p. 520), pasta, or rice.

4 entrée servings

1 cup clam juice or reduced-fat chicken broth
1 can (8 ounces) tomato sauce
2 cups chopped tomatoes
1 large onion, chopped
½ cup each: chopped green bell pepper, carrots
3 tablespoons chopped sun-dried tomatoes
   (not in oil), room temperature
1 teaspoon each: minced garlic, dried
   marjoram leaves
½ teaspoon dried oregano leaves
1 pound halibut or other firm-fleshed whitefish
   steaks, sliced (1-inch)
Salt and pepper, to taste

Per Serving:
Calories: 204
% calories from fat: 30
Protein (g): 25.4
Carbohydrate (g): 9.6
Fat (g): 6.8
Saturated fat (g): 0.9
Cholesterol (mg): 36.1
Sodium (mg): 232
Exchanges:
Milk: 0.0
Vegetable: 2.0
Fruit: 0.0
Bread: 0.0
Meat: 3.0
Fat: 0.0

1. Combine all ingredients, except fish, salt, and pepper, in slow cooker; cover and cook on low 6 to 8 hours, adding fish during last 10 to 15 minutes. Season to taste with salt and pepper.

Cioppino with Pasta

A California favorite! Substitute other kinds of fresh fish, according to availability and price.

6 entrée servings

½ cup each: clam juice, dry white wine or clam juice
3 cups chopped tomatoes
1 cup each: chopped green bell pepper, onion,
    sliced mushrooms
4 cloves garlic, minced
1 tablespoon tomato paste
2 teaspoons each: dried oregano and basil leaves
1 teaspoon ground turmeric
8 ounces each: sea scallops, sliced crabmeat (½-inch)
4 ounces halibut or haddock steak, cubed (1-inch)
12 mussels, scrubbed
Salt and pepper, to taste
12 ounces fettuccine, cooked, warm

Per Serving:
Calories: 516
% calories from fat: 24
Protein (g): 32.6
Carbohydrate (g): 63
Fat (g): 13.6
Saturated fat (g): 2.8
Cholesterol (mg): 107.8
Sodium (mg): 685
Exchanges:
Milk: 0.0
Vegetable: 3.0
Fruit: 0.0
Bread: 3.0
Meat: 3.0
Fat: 1.0

1. Combine all ingredients, except seafood, salt, pepper, and fettuccine, in 6-quart slow cooker; cover and cook on low 6 to 8 hours, adding seafood during last 15 minutes. Discard any mussels that have not opened; season to taste with salt and pepper. Serve over fettuccine.

Georgia Fish and Vegetable Stew

Serve with Spinach Rice (see p. 345).

6 entrée servings

1 cup each: fat-free chicken broth, clam juice
3 cups peeled cubed (¾-inch)potatoes
2 cups chopped onions
1 large clove garlic, minced
1–2 tablespoons dry sherry (optional)
1 bay leaf
½–¾ teaspoon each: dried thyme and basil leaves
¼ teaspoon dry mustard
2 cups small broccoli florets
¾ cup 2% reduced-fat milk
1 tablespoon cornstarch
8 ounces each: cubed (1½-inch) lean whitefish (flounder, turbot, or haddock), medium peeled deveined shrimp, bay scallops
2–3 teaspoons lemon juice
Salt and white pepper, to taste

Per Serving:
Calories: 288
% calories from fat: 13
Protein (g): 31.5
Carbohydrate (g): 29.4
Fat (g): 4.4
Saturated fat (g): 0.9
Cholesterol (mg): 101
Sodium (mg): 793
Exchanges:
Milk: 0.0
Vegetable: 0.0
Fruit: 0.0
Bread: 2.0
Meat: 3.0
Fat: 0.0

1. Combine all ingredients, except broccoli, milk, cornstarch, seafood, lemon juice, salt, and white pepper, in 6-quart slow cooker; cover and cook on high 4 to 6 hours, adding broccoli during last 20 minutes. Stir in combined milk and cornstarch, stirring 2 to 3 minutes. Add whitefish, shrimp and scallops; cover and cook 5 to 10 minutes. Discard bay leaf; season to taste with lemon juice, salt, and white pepper.

Creole Fish Stew

Rich flavors and easy preparation—who could ask for more?

4 entrée servings

1 can (28 ounces) diced tomatoes, undrained
¼ cup dry white wine or water
2 cups chopped onions
1 cup each: chopped green bell pepper, celery
½ teaspoon dried thyme leaves
⅛–¼ teaspoon crushed red pepper
2 teaspoons minced garlic
2 tablespoons soy sauce
1 tablespoon paprika
2 bay leaves
1 pound cod fillets, cubed
Salt and pepper, to taste
3 cups cooked rice, warm

Per Serving:
Calories: 378
% calories from fat: 10
Protein (g): 28
Carbohydrate (g): 56.1
Fat (g): 4.1
Saturated fat (g): 0.7
Cholesterol (mg): 48.6
Sodium (mg): 385
Exchanges:
Milk: 0.0
Vegetable: 1.0
Fruit: 0.0
Bread: 3.0
Meat: 3.0
Fat: 0.0

1. Combine all ingredients, except cod, salt, pepper, and rice, in slow cooker; cover and cook on high 4 to 5 hours, adding cod during last 10 to 15 minutes. Discard bay leaves; season to taste with salt and pepper; serve over rice.

Bayou Snapper Stew

Serve this Southern-style favorite with Roasted Chili Cornbread (see p. 529). Flounder, sole, or whitefish fillets can be substituted for the red snapper.

4 entrée servings

1 can (14½ ounces) stewed tomatoes
1 cup clam juice or water
½ cup each: chopped medium onion, green bell
  pepper, carrot
2 cloves garlic, minced
2–3 teaspoons Worcestershire sauce
1 cup frozen cut okra, thawed
1 pound red snapper fillets, cut into pieces (1-inch)
Salt and cayenne pepper, to taste
3–6 cups cooked rice, warm
Hot pepper sauce

Per Serving:
Calories: 414
% calories from fat: 13
Protein (g): 29.8
Carbohydrate (g): 59.2
Fat (g): 5.9
Saturated fat (g): 0.9
Cholesterol (mg): 41.6
Sodium (mg): 184
Exchanges:
Milk: 0.0
Vegetable: 2.0
Fruit: 0.0
Bread: 3.0
Meat: 3.0
Fat: 0.0

1. Combine tomatoes, clam juice, vegetables, garlic, and Worcestershire sauce in slow cooker; cover and cook on high 4 to 6 hours, adding okra during last 30 minutes and fish during last 10 to 15 minutes. Season to taste with salt and cayenne pepper. Serve over rice with hot pepper sauce.

Gulf Coast Snapper Stew

This Gulf Coast favorite has a robust sauce with just a hint of cayenne heat. Red Pepper Rice is the perfect accompaniment.

6 entrée servings

1 can (14½ ounces) diced tomatoes, undrained
½ cup clam juice or chicken broth
2–3 tablespoons tomato paste
½ cup each: chopped medium onion, green bell pepper
4 green onions, sliced
1 rib celery, thinly sliced
4 cloves garlic, minced
¾ teaspoon dried oregano leaves
1 bay leaf
1½ pounds red snapper fillets, cut into pieces (2-inch)
Salt and hot pepper sauce, to taste
Red Pepper Rice (recipe follows)

Per Serving:
Calories: 445
% calories from fat: 18
Protein (g): 21.4
Carbohydrate (g): 70.4
Fat (g): 9.1
Saturated fat (g): 2.5
Cholesterol (mg): 25.2
Sodium (mg): 303
Exchanges:
Milk: 0.0
Vegetable: 2.0
Fruit: 0.0
Bread: 4.0
Meat: 2.0
Fat: 0.0

1. Combine all ingredients, except fish, salt, red pepper sauce, and Red Pepper Rice, in slow cooker; cover and cook on high 4 to 5 hours, adding fish during last 15 minutes. Discard bay leaf; season to taste with salt and hot pepper sauce. Serve over Red Pepper Rice.

Red Pepper Rice

Makes 6 servings

1½ cups uncooked long-grain rice
¼ teaspoon ground turmeric
½ teaspoon paprika
1 roasted red pepper, coarsely chopped

1. Cook rice according to package directions, stirring turmeric into cooking water. Stir paprika and roasted red pepper into cooked rice.

Variation

Catfish Creole—Make recipe as above, substituting catfish fillets for the red snapper, and ½ teaspoon each dried marjoram and thyme leaves, celery seeds, and ground cumin for the oregano and bay leaf. Serve over cooked rice.

Caribbean Sweet-Sour Salmon Stew

Sweet and sour flavors team with salmon, pineapple, and beans in this island-inspired stew.

4 entrée servings

1 can (15 ounces) black beans, rinsed, drained
1 can (8 ounces) pineapple tidbits in juice, undrained
1 cup each: coarsely chopped onion, sliced red and green bell peppers
4 cloves garlic, minced
2 teaspoons minced gingerroot
1 jalapeño chili, finely chopped
2–3 tablespoons each: light brown sugar, cider vinegar
2–3 teaspoons curry powder
¼ cup cold water
1½ tablespoons cornstarch
1 pound salmon steaks, cubed (1½-inch)
Salt and pepper, to taste
4 cups cooked rice, warm

Per Serving:
Calories: 516
% calories from fat: 9
Protein (g): 33
Carbohydrate (g): 86.9
Fat (g): 5.1
Saturated fat (g): 1.2
Cholesterol (mg): 83.7
Sodium (mg): 469
Exchanges:
Milk: 0.0
Vegetable: 0.0
Fruit: 0.0
Bread: 5.0
Meat: 3.0
Fat: 0.0

1. Combine all ingredients, except water, cornstarch, salmon, salt, pepper, and rice, in slow cooker; cover and cook on high 4 to 5 hours. Stir in combined water and cornstarch, stirring 2 to 3 minutes. Add salmon; cook 10 to 15 minutes. Season to taste with salt and pepper. Serve over rice.

Easy Bouillabaisse

This version of bouillabaisse is easy to assemble.

8 entrée servings

1 cup each: clam juice, dry white wine or clam juice
2 cans (14½ ounces each) diced tomatoes, undrained
1 cup chopped onion
½ cup thinly sliced fennel or celery
2 leeks (white parts only), thinly sliced
1 clove garlic, minced
1 bay leaf
½ teaspoon each: dried thyme and rosemary leaves,
  grated orange zest
1 pound salmon steaks, cubed (1½-inch)
8 ounces each: peeled deveined medium shrimp,
  bay scallops
12 mussels, scrubbed
¼ cup chopped parsley
Salt and pepper, to taste

Per Serving:
Calories: 221
% calories from fat: 17
Protein (g): 28
Carbohydrate (g): 12.5
Fat (g): 4
Saturated fat (g): 0.7
Cholesterol (mg): 106
Sodium (mg): 219
Exchanges:
Milk: 0.0
Vegetable: 2.0
Fruit: 0.0
Bread: 0.0
Meat: 3.0
Fat: 0.0

1. Combine all ingredients, except seafood, parsley, salt, and pepper, in 6-quart slow cooker; cover and cook on high 4 to 5 hours; adding seafood during last 15 minutes. Discard bay leaf and any mussels that do not open; stir in parsley and season to taste with salt and pepper.

Bouillabaisse St. Tropez

The love for bouillabaisse is universal; aioli sauce adds the finishing touch.

8 entrée servings

1 can (28 ounces) diced tomatoes, undrained
2 cups clam juice
½ cup chopped onion
2 cloves garlic, minced
½ teaspoon each: dried basil and thyme leaves
⅛ teaspoon each: crushed saffron threads
   (optional), fennel seeds
1 bay leaf
⅛–¼ teaspoon crushed red pepper
8 ounces each: haddock or halibut fillets, sole or
   flounder fillets, cubed crabmeat or lobster meat,
   shucked oysters
2 tablespoons cornstarch
¼ cup water
Salt and pepper, to taste
8 slices each: lemon, French bread
Aioli (recipe follows)

Per Serving:
Calories: 290
% calories from fat: 18
Protein (g): 30.2
Carbohydrate (g): 27.7
Fat (g): 5.7
Saturated fat (g): 1.2
Cholesterol (mg): 116.3
Sodium (mg): 701
Exchanges:
Milk: 0.0
Vegetable: 1.0
Fruit: 0.0
Bread: 1.5
Meat: 3.0
Fat: 0.0

1. Combine all ingredients, except seafood, cornstarch, water, salt, pepper, lemon, bread, and Aioli, in slow cooker; cover and cook on high 4 to 5 hours, adding seafood during last 10 to 15 minutes. Stir in combined cornstarch and water, stirring 2 to 3 minutes. Discard bay leaf; season to taste with salt and pepper. Stir in lemon slices.
2. Spread bread slices with Aioli and place in bottoms of soup bowls; ladle stew over bread. Serve with remaining Aioli.

Aioli

Makes about ¾ cup

¾ cup reduced-fat mayonnaise
1 teaspoon each: tarragon vinegar, lemon juice
½–1 teaspoon Dijon mustard
3 cloves garlic, minced
Salt and white pepper, to taste

1. Mix all ingredients, except salt and white pepper; season to taste with salt and white pepper.

Fish Stew Marsala

Marsala wine adds a distinctive, appealing note to this simple Italian fish stew.

4 entrée servings

2½ cups reduced-sodium fat-free chicken broth
⅓ cup dry Marsala wine or chicken broth
¼ cup tomato paste
1 cup each: chopped onion, red and green bell
  peppers
½ cup chopped celery
1 teaspoon minced garlic
1 teaspoon dried thyme leaves
1 pound haddock steaks, cubed (2-inch)
2 cups cooked medium pasta shells, warm
2–3 tablespoons lemon juice
Salt and pepper, to taste

Per Serving:
Calories: 409
% calories from fat: 15
Protein (g): 33
Carbohydrate (g): 49
Fat (g): 7
Saturated fat (g): 1
Cholesterol (mg): 65.2
Sodium (mg): 206
Exchanges:
Milk: 0.0
Vegetable: 1.0
Fruit: 0.0
Bread: 3.0
Meat: 3.0
Fat: 0.0

1. Combine all ingredients, except fish, pasta, lemon juice, salt, and pepper, in slow cooker; cover and cook on high 4 to 5 hours, adding fish and pasta during last 10 to 15 minutes. Season to taste with lemon juice, salt and pepper.

Seafood Stew with Risotto, Milanese-Style

An easy-to-make Microwave Risotto is stirred into this stew for a delicious gourmet touch. If you prefer, the stew can be served over cooked rice instead.

4 entrée servings

1 can (14½ ounces) diced tomatoes, undrained
½–1 cup reduced-sodium fat-free chicken broth
1 medium onion, chopped
1 clove garlic, minced
¼ teaspoon crushed saffron threads (optional)
1 cup sliced zucchini
8 ounces each: bay scallops, peeled deveined
    medium shrimp
Microwave Risotto (recipe follows), warm
¼ cup (1 ounce) grated Parmesan cheese
Salt and pepper, to taste

Per Serving:
Calories: 353
% calories from fat: 17
Protein (g): 31.8
Carbohydrate (g): 39.7
Fat (g): 6.9
Saturated fat (g): 1.9
Cholesterol (mg): 114.7
Sodium (mg): 527
Exchanges:
Milk: 0.0
Vegetable: 2.0
Fruit: 0.0
Bread: 2.0
Meat: 3.0
Fat: 0.0

1. Combine tomatoes with liquid, ½ cup broth, onion, garlic, and saffron in slow cooker; cover and cook on high 3 to 4 hours, adding zucchini during last 30 minutes and seafood during last 10 minutes. Stir in Microwave Risotto and Parmesan cheese, adding remaining ½ cup broth, if desired. Season to taste with salt and pepper.

Microwave Risotto

About 3 cups

¾ cup uncooked arborio rice
2 teaspoons olive oil
2⅔ cups reduced-sodium fat-free chicken broth
½ teaspoon dried thyme leaves
Salt and white pepper

1. Combine rice and oil in 2½-quart glass casserole; microwave, uncovered, on high 1 minute. Stir in remaining ingredients, except salt and white pepper; microwave, covered, on high, 7 to 8 minutes, turning casserole ½ turn after 4 minutes. Stir and microwave, uncovered, on high, 11 to 13 minutes or until broth is absorbed. Let stand, covered, 2 to 3 minutes. Season to taste with salt and pepper.

Scallop Stew, Italian-Style

Scallops make an easy, healthy stew.

4 entrée servings

1 can (14½ ounces) Italian-style plum tomatoes,
    undrained, chopped
1 cup reduced-sodium fat-free chicken broth
1 each: chopped medium onion, chopped
    medium green bell pepper, minced clove garlic
1 bay leaf
1 teaspoon dried basil leaves
2 cups small broccoli florets
12–16 ounces bay or sea scallops
2 teaspoons cornstarch
¼ cup cold water
2–4 tablespoons dry sherry (optional)
Salt and pepper, to taste
1 cup cooked white or brown rice, warm

Per Serving:
Calories: 339
% calories from fat: 9
Protein (g): 22
Carbohydrate (g): 50
Fat (g): 3.5
Saturated fat (g): 0.4
Cholesterol (mg): 37
Sodium (mg): 352
Exchanges:
Milk: 0.0
Vegetable: 2.0
Fruit: 0.0
Bread: 2.5
Meat: 2.0
Fat: 0.0

1. Combine tomatoes with liquid, broth, onion, bell pepper, garlic, and herbs in slow cooker; cover and cook on high 4 to 5 hours, adding broccoli during last 30 minutes and scallops during last 5 to 10 minutes. Stir in combined cornstarch and water, stirring 2 to 3 minutes. Discard bay leaf and season to taste with sherry, salt, and pepper; serve over rice.

Italian-Style Fish Stew

Enjoy the flavors of Italy in this well-seasoned fish stew.

4 entrée servings

1 cup reduced-sodium fat-free chicken broth or
   clam juice
½ cup dry white wine or chicken broth
1½ pounds tomatoes, peeled, chopped
1 cup halved small mushrooms
3 large cloves garlic, minced
2 teaspoons dried Italian seasoning
⅛–¼ teaspoon crushed red pepper
1 pound grouper or other firm-fleshed fish steaks,
   thinly sliced
½ cup chopped parsley
Salt and pepper, to taste

Per Serving:
Calories: 201
% calories from fat: 23
Protein (g): 24.1
Carbohydrate (g): 10.5
Fat (g): 5.3
Saturated fat (g): 0.9
Cholesterol (mg): 41.6
Sodium (mg): 67
Exchanges:
Milk: 0.0
Vegetable: 2.0
Fruit: 0.0
Bread: 0.0
Meat: 3.0
Fat: 0.0

1. Combine all ingredients, except fish, parsley, salt, and pepper, in slow cooker; cover and cook on high 4 to 5 hours, adding fish and parsley during last 10 minutes. Season to taste with salt and pepper.

Mediterranean Fishermen's Stew

Bottled clam juice makes a quick and easy alternative to homemade fish stock in this recipe.

4 entrée servings

1 can (28 ounces) Italian plum tomatoes,
   undrained, chopped
1 cup clam juice
1 large onion, chopped
½ cup sliced carrots
4 teaspoons minced garlic
1 teaspoon dried basil leaves
½ teaspoon lemon pepper
2 medium zucchini, cubed
1 pound cod, cubed (1-inch)
½ cup chopped parsley
Salt and pepper, to taste

Per Serving:
Calories: 192
% calories from fat: 12
Protein (g): 23.9
Carbohydrate (g): 19.9
Fat (g): 2.9
Saturated fat (g): 0.4
Cholesterol (mg): 48.6
Sodium (mg): 282
Exchanges:
Milk: 0.0
Vegetable: 2.0
Fruit: 0.0
Bread: 0.0
Meat: 3.0
Fat: 0.0

1. Combine all ingredients, except zucchini, cod, parsley, salt, and pepper, in slow cooker; cover and cook on high 4 to 5 hours, adding zucchini during last 45 minutes and cod during last 10 minutes. Stir in parsley; season to taste with salt and pepper.

Paella

Paella, a staple of Spanish cookery, was traditionally prepared with whatever seafood and ingredients the cook had on hand, so the recipe can vary.

4 entrée servings

8 ounces chicken tenders, halved
3 ounces Canadian bacon, cut into thin strips
2½ cups reduced-sodium fat-free chicken broth
1 can (14½ ounces) Italian-style diced tomatoes, undrained
1 can (14¾ ounces) artichoke hearts, drained, halved
1 cup each: chopped onion, red and green bell pepper
2 cloves garlic, minced
¾ teaspoon each: dried thyme and basil leaves
¼ teaspoon crushed saffron threads (optional)
1¼ cups uncooked converted long-grain rice
8 ounces medium shrimp, peeled, deveined
Salt and cayenne pepper, to taste

Per Serving:
Calories: 371
% calories from fat: 11
Protein (g): 28
Carbohydrate (g): 56
Fat (g): 4.6
Saturated fat (g): 1.2
Cholesterol (mg): 101
Sodium (mg): 678
Exchanges:
Milk: 0.0
Vegetable: 2.0
Fruit: 0.0
Bread: 3.0
Meat: 2.0
Fat: 0.0

1. Combine all ingredients, except rice, shrimp, salt, and cayenne pepper, in slow cooker; cover and cook on low 6 to 8 hours, adding rice during last 2 hours, and shrimp during last 10 minutes. Season to taste with salt and cayenne pepper.

Thai-Style Shrimp Stew

Chinese chili sauce is HOT, so use cautiously!

4 entrée servings

2 cups each: reduced-sodium fat-free chicken
  broth, chopped bok choy
1 cup each: sliced red bell pepper, sliced scallions,
  fresh or canned rinsed drained bean sprouts
4 ounces bean threads or cellophane noodles, cut
  (2-inch)
¼ cup rice wine vinegar
½–1 teaspoon Chinese chili sauce with garlic
1 pound medium shrimp, peeled, deveined
Soy sauce, to taste
Salt and pepper, to taste

Per Serving:
Calories: 236
% calories from fat: 5
Protein (g): 23.7
Carbohydrate (g): 31.2
Fat (g): 1.2
Saturated fat (g): 0.3
Cholesterol (mg): 173.3
Sodium (mg): 395
Exchanges:
Milk: 0.0
Vegetable: 3.0
Fruit: 0.0
Bread: 1.0
Meat: 1.5
Fat: 0.0

1. Combine broth and vegetables in slow cooker; cover and cook on high 4 to 5 hours.
2. While stew is cooking, soak cellophane noodles in hot water until softened; drain. Add noodles, vinegar, chili sauce, and shrimp to slow cooker during last 10 minutes. Season to taste with soy sauce, salt, and pepper.

Shrimp and Vegetable Stew

Smoked sausage adds a hearty flavor to this easy stew.

4 entrée servings

1 can (14½ ounces) stewed tomatoes
4 ounces smoked turkey sausage, thickly sliced
1 cup each: halved baby carrots, small Brussels sprouts,
  whole-kernel corn
1 medium onion, cut into thin wedges
1 teaspoon chili powder
12–16 ounces medium shrimp, peeled, deveined
Salt and pepper, to taste
3 cups cooked rice, warm

Per Serving:
Calories: 361
% calories from fat: 7
Protein (g): 25.6
Carbohydrate (g): 59.6
Fat (g): 2.8
Saturated fat (g): 0.8
Cholesterol (mg): 143.2
Sodium (mg): 594
Exchanges:
Milk: 0.0
Vegetable: 3.0
Fruit: 0.0
Bread: 3.0
Meat: 1.0
Fat: 0.0

1. Combine all ingredients, except shrimp, salt, pepper, and rice, in slow cooker; cover and cook on high 4 to 5 hours, adding shrimp during last 10 to 15 minutes. Season to taste with salt and pepper; serve over rice.

Herbed Shrimp Stew

Enjoy an herb-seasoned stew with a bounty of perfectly cooked shrimp.

4 entrée servings

1 can (28 ounces) diced tomatoes with garlic, undrained
1 cup clam juice or vegetable broth
1 each: finely chopped medium onion, rib celery
2 cloves garlic, minced
1 teaspoon each: dried thyme and basil leaves
½ cup chopped parsley
1 pound medium shrimp, peeled, deveined
3 cups cooked rice, warm
Salt and pepper, to taste

Per Serving:
Calories: 367
% calories from fat: 14
Protein (g): 32.1
Carbohydrate (g): 47.7
Fat (g): 5.9
Saturated fat (g): 1.0
Cholesterol (mg): 172.4
Sodium (mg): 618
Exchanges:
Milk: 0.0
Vegetable: 0.0
Fruit: 0.0
Bread: 3.0
Meat: 3.0
Fat: 0.0

1. Combine all ingredients, except parsley, shrimp, rice, salt, and pepper, in slow cooker; cover and cook on high 3 to 4 hours, adding parsley, shrimp, and rice during last 10 minutes. Season to taste with salt and pepper.

Spicy Shrimp and Rice Stew

This full-bodied shrimp and rice stew is seasoned with a creative combination of spices.

6 entrée servings

2 cups reduced-sodium fat-free chicken broth
1 can (14½ ounces) diced tomatoes, undrained
1 each: chopped large onion, carrot, rib celery, medium green bell pepper
2 large cloves garlic, minced
1 bay leaf
1½ teaspoons dried thyme leaves
¾ teaspoon paprika
3 cups cooked white rice, warm
1 pound medium shrimp, peeled, deveined
Salt, cayenne, and black pepper, to taste

Per Serving:
Calories: 217
% calories from fat: 9
Protein (g): 14.2
Carbohydrate (g): 34.6
Fat (g): 2.1
Saturated fat (g): 0.4
Cholesterol (mg): 87.5
Sodium (mg): 217
Exchanges:
Milk: 0.0
Vegetable: 1.0
Fruit: 0.0
Bread: 2.0
Meat: 1.0
Fat: 0.0

1. Combine all ingredients, except rice, shrimp, salt, and pepper, in slow cooker; cover and cook on high 4 to 5 hours, adding rice and shrimp during last 10 to 15 minutes. Discard bay leaf; season to taste with salt, cayenne, and black pepper.

Shrimp, Artichoke, and Pepper Stew

This easy stew is brimming with flavor.

4 entrée servings

1 can (14½ ounces) reduced-sodium chunky tomato
   sauce
1 can (14 ounces) quartered artichoke hearts, drained
¾ cup each: chicken or vegetable broth, thinly
   sliced onion, red and green bell pepper
1 teaspoon minced garlic
12 ounces medium shrimp, peeled, deveined
1–2 tablespoons dry sherry (optional)
Salt and pepper, to taste
8 ounces penne, cooked, warm

Per Serving:
Calories: 415
% calories from fat: 11
Protein (g): 26.1
Carbohydrate (g): 60.8
Fat (g): 5.1
Saturated fat (g): 0.8
Cholesterol (mg): 130
Sodium (mg): 438
Exchanges:
Milk: 0.0
Vegetable: 3.0
Fruit: 0.0
Bread: 3.0
Meat: 2.0
Fat: 0.0

1. Combine all ingredients, except shrimp, sherry, salt, pepper, and penne, in slow cooker; cover and cook on low 5 to 6 hours, adding shrimp during last 10 minutes. Season to taste with sherry, salt, and pepper. Serve over penne.

Variation

Shrimp and Okra Stew—Make recipe as above, omitting bell pepper, dry sherry, and penne and substituting 2 cups fresh or frozen thawed cut okra for the artichoke hearts. Serve over Polenta (see p. 520) or rice and sprinkle with parsley.

Scallop, Shrimp, and Pepper Stew with Pasta

A light, colorful stew that's simple to make.

4 entrée servings

1½ cups clam juice or reduced-sodium fat-free
   chicken broth
2 cups diced mixed red, yellow, and green bell
   peppers (1-inch)
1 cup each: coarsely chopped onion, tomato
2 large cloves garlic, minced
1 teaspoon grated lemon zest
½ teaspoon dried thyme leaves
Pinch crushed red pepper
8 ounces each: peeled deveined medium shrimp,
   bay scallops
⅓ cup chopped fresh parsley
2–3 teaspoons lemon juice
Salt and pepper, to taste
8 ounces vermicelli, cooked, warm

Per Serving:
Calories: 434
% calories from fat: 20
Protein (g): 39.2
Carbohydrate (g): 52.0
Fat (g): 9.8
Saturated fat (g): 1.3
Cholesterol (mg): 116.2
Sodium (mg): 987
Exchanges:
Milk: 0.0
Vegetable: 1.0
Fruit: 0.0
Bread: 3.0
Meat: 3.0
Fat: 0.0

1. Combine all ingredients, except seafood, parsley, lemon juice, salt, pepper, and pasta, in slow cooker; cover and cook on high 4 to 5 hours, adding seafood and parsley during last 10 minutes. Season to taste with lemon juice, salt, and pepper. Serve over pasta.

Creole Stew with Shrimp and Ham

Crisply cooked strips of ham and dry sherry add complementary flavors to this stew.

6 entrée servings

4 ounces lean ham, cut into thin strips
1–2 tablespoons canola oil
1 can (28 ounces) stewed tomatoes
½ cup clam juice or water
2–3 tablespoons tomato paste
½ cup each: finely chopped onion, celery, red or
   green bell pepper
3 cloves garlic, minced
1–1½ pounds shrimp, peeled, deveined
2–4 tablespoons dry sherry (optional)
¼–½ teaspoon hot pepper sauce
Salt and pepper, to taste
4 cups cooked rice, warm

Per Serving:
Calories: 301
% calories from fat: 14
Protein (g): 22
Carbohydrate (g): 43
Fat (g): 4.5
Saturated fat (g): 0.9
Cholesterol (mg): 126
Sodium (mg): 778
Exchanges:
Milk: 0.0
Vegetable: 2.0
Fruit: 0.0
Bread: 2.0
Meat: 2.0
Fat: 0.0

1. Cook ham in oil in small skillet over medium-high heat until browned and crisp, 3 to 4 minutes; remove and reserve.
2. Combine tomatoes, clam juice, vegetables, and garlic in slow cooker; cover and cook on high 3 to 4 hours, adding reserved ham, shrimp, sherry and hot pepper sauce during last 10 minutes. Season to taste with salt and pepper; serve over rice.

Cajun Shrimp, Corn, and Bean Stew

A shrimp stew with a spicy tang! Serve this stew over Spoon Bread (see pg. 525).

4 entrée servings

1 can (15 ounces) red beans, rinsed, drained
1 can (16 ounces) cream-style corn
1 cup clam juice or chicken broth
1 each: finely chopped medium onion, minced
   jalapeño chili
2 cloves garlic, minced
1 teaspoon dried thyme leaves
½ teaspoon dried oregano leaves
1 cup each: small broccoli florets, whole milk
2 tablespoons cornstarch
12–16 ounces shrimp, peeled, deveined
Salt, to taste
Hot pepper sauce, to taste

Per Serving:
Calories: 272
% calories from fat: 13
Protein (g): 29.3
Carbohydrate (g): 33.7
Fat (g): 4.2
Saturated fat (g): 1.4
Cholesterol (mg): 135.4
Sodium (mg): 1126
Exchanges:
Milk: 0.0
Vegetable: 2.0
Fruit: 0.0
Bread: 2.0
Meat: 3.0
Fat: 0.0

1. Combine beans, corn, clam juice, onion, jalapeño chili, garlic, and herbs in slow cooker; cover and cook on high 3 to 4 hours, adding broccoli during last 20 minutes. Stir in combined milk and cornstarch, stirring 2 to 3 minutes. Add shrimp; cook 5 to 10 minutes. Season to taste with salt and hot pepper sauce.

Shrimp and Sausage Gumbo

Okra thickens the gumbo while giving it a characteristic Creole flavor.

4 entrée servings

2 cans (14 ounces each) stewed tomatoes
4 ounces reduced-fat smoked sausage thickly sliced
1 large red bell pepper, finely chopped
1 clove garlic, minced
⅛ teaspoon crushed red pepper
8 ounces fresh or frozen thawed sliced okra
8–12 ounces shrimp, peeled, deveined
Salt, to taste
3 cups cooked rice, warm

Per Serving:
Calories: 316
% calories from fat: 14
Protein (g): 19.9
Carbohydrate (g): 48.9
Fat (g): 5
Saturated fat (g): 1.2
Cholesterol (mg): 104.4
Sodium (mg): 395
Exchanges:
Milk: 0.0
Vegetable: 3.0
Fruit: 0.0
Bread: 2.0
Meat: 2.0
Fat: 0.0

1. Combine all ingredients, except okra, shrimp, salt, and rice, in slow cooker; cover and cook on low 6 to 7 hours, adding okra during last 30 minutes and shrimp during last 10 minutes. Season to taste with salt; serve over rice.

TWELVE

Vegetarian Stews

- - - - - - - - - - - - -

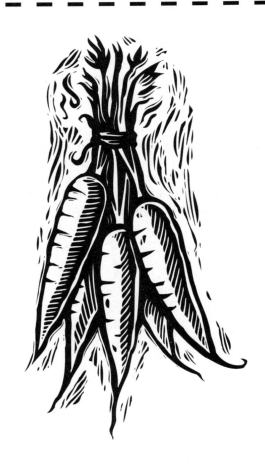

Any-Season Vegetable Stew

V *Use any vegetables in season for this healthy veggie stew.*

4 entrée servings

1½ cups reduced-sodium vegetable broth, divided
2 medium tomatoes, chopped
8 ounces each: green beans and small new
   potatoes, halved
2 each: sliced small carrots, turnips
4 green onions, sliced
½ teaspoon dried marjoram leaves
¼ teaspoon dried thyme leaves
4 slices vegetarian bacon, fried crisp, crumbled
1 cup each: frozen thawed peas and artichoke hearts
8 asparagus spears, cut (2-inch)
2 tablespoons cornstarch
¼ cup cold water
Salt and pepper, to taste
3 cups cooked rice, warm

Per Serving:
Calories: 431
% calories from fat: 7
Protein (g): 13.9
Carbohydrate (g): 89.5
Fat (g): 3.3
Saturated fat (g): 0.5
Cholesterol (mg): 0.0
Sodium (mg): 391
Exchanges:
Milk: 0.0
Vegetable: 0.0
Fruit: 0.0
Bread: 6.0
Meat: 0.0
Fat: 0.0

1. Combine all ingredients, except vegetarian bacon, peas, artichoke hearts, asparagus, cornstarch, water, salt, pepper, and rice, in slow cooker; cover and cook on high 3 to 4 hours, adding bacon, peas, artichoke hearts, and asparagus during last 30 minutes. Stir in combined cornstarch and water, stirring 2 to 3 minutes. Season to taste with salt and pepper; serve over rice.

Veggie Stew with Chili-Cheese Biscuits

L *Poblano chilies can be hot! One green bell pepper and one small jalapeño chili can be substituted.*

6 entrée servings

2 cans (14½ ounces each) diced tomatoes, undrained
1 can (15 ounces) each: black-eyed peas and red
  beans, rinsed, drained
2 cups chopped onions
1½ cups peeled cubed butternut or acorn squash
1 cup each: coarsely chopped poblano chilies, red
  and yellow bell peppers
3 cloves garlic, minced
2–3 tablespoons chili powder
1½–2 teaspoons ground cumin
¾ teaspoon each: dried oregano and marjoram leaves
1 cup fresh or frozen thawed okra
Salt and pepper, to taste
3 large buttermilk biscuits, baked, halved
Chili powder
½ cup (2 ounces) shredded reduced-fat Cheddar cheese

Per Serving:
Calories: 433
% calories from fat: 29
Protein (g): 17.4
Carbohydrate (g): 65.9
Fat (g): 14.9
Saturated fat (g): 2.7
Cholesterol (mg): 3.7
Sodium (mg): 713
Exchanges:
Milk: 0.0
Vegetable: 3.0
Fruit: 0.0
Bread: 3.0
Meat: 1.0
Fat: 2.0

1. Combine all ingredients, except okra, salt, pepper, biscuits, chili powder, and cheese, in 6-quart slow cooker; cover and cook on low 6 to 8 hours, adding okra during last 30 minutes. Season to taste with salt and pepper.
2. Place biscuits, cut sides down, on stew; sprinkle with chili powder and cheese. Cover and cook until cheese is melted, about 5 minutes.

Vegetable Garden Stew

V *Made with vegetables from your garden or greengrocer, this colorful stew is served over healthful millet.*

4 entrée servings

2 cups vegetable broth
8 ounces each: sliced mushrooms, cauliflower
   florets, cubed potatoes
2 each: medium onions and tomatoes, cut into
   wedges
2 cloves garlic, minced
1 teaspoon dried savory leaves
1 bay leaf
2 small zucchini, sliced
Salt and pepper, to taste
3 cups cooked millet or couscous, warm

Per Serving:
Calories: 404
% calories from fat: 6
Protein (g): 13.4
Carbohydrate (g): 84.6
Fat (g): 2.6
Saturated fat (g): 0.4
Cholesterol (mg): 0
Sodium (mg): 116
Exchanges:
Milk: 0.0
Vegetable: 3.0
Fruit: 0.0
Bread: 4.5
Meat: 0.0
Fat: 0.0

1. Combine all ingredients, except zucchini, salt, pepper, and millet, in slow cooker; cover and cook on low 6 to 8 hours, adding zucchini during last 30 minutes. Discard bay leaf and serve over millet in shallow bowls.

Sweet-Sour Squash and Potato Stew

V *The stew is cooked in cider and seasoned with honey and vinegar for a refreshing sweet-sour flavor.*

6 entrée servings

1 can (14½ ounces) diced tomatoes, undrained
1 cup apple cider or apple juice
3 cups each: peeled cubed butternut or acorn
    squash, Idaho potatoes
2 cups each: peeled cubed sweet potatoes, sliced
    unpeeled tart green apples
1½ cups whole-kernel corn
½ cup each: chopped shallots, red bell pepper
2 cloves garlic, minced
1½ tablespoons each: honey, cider vinegar
1 bay leaf
¼ teaspoon ground nutmeg
2 tablespoons cornstarch
¼ cup cold water
Salt and pepper, to taste
4 cups cooked basmati or jasmine rice, warm

Per Serving:
Calories: 411
% calories from fat: 4
Protein (g): 9.7
Carbohydrate (g): 95.9
Fat (g): 1.8
Saturated fat (g): 0.2
Cholesterol (mg): 0
Sodium (mg): 52
Exchanges:
Milk: 0.0
Vegetable: 3.0
Fruit: 1.0
Bread: 3.5
Meat: 0.0
Fat: 0.0

1. Combine all ingredients, except cornstarch, water, salt, pepper, and rice, in 6-quart slow cooker; cover and cook on low 6 to 8 hours. Turn heat to high and cook 10 minutes; stir in combined cornstarch and water, stirring 2 to 3 minutes. Discard bay leaf; season stew to taste with salt and pepper. Serve over rice.

Wild Mushroom Stew

V

This stew includes three flavorful varieties of fresh mushrooms. Dried mushrooms, softened in hot water, can be substituted for some of the fresh mushrooms for an even richer taste.

6 entrée servings

3 cans (15 ounces each) Great Northern beans,
    rinsed, drained
1 cup reduced-sodium vegetable broth
½ cup dry white wine or vegetable broth
2 cups each: chopped portobello mushrooms, sliced
    shiitake, cremini, or white mushrooms
1 cup each: sliced leeks (white parts only), chopped
    red bell pepper
½ cup chopped onion
1 tablespoon minced garlic
½ teaspoon each: dried rosemary and thyme leaves
⅛–¼ teaspoon crushed red pepper
4 cups sliced Swiss chard or spinach
Salt and pepper, to taste
Polenta (see p. 520)

Per Serving:
Calories: 341
% calories from fat: 13
Protein (g): 16.3
Carbohydrate (g): 63
Fat (g): 5.5
Saturated fat (g): 0.8
Cholesterol (mg): 0
Sodium (mg): 758
Exchanges:
Milk: 0.0
Vegetable: 3.0
Fruit: 0.0
Bread: 3.0
Meat: 1.0
Fat: 1.0

1. Combine all ingredients, except Swiss chard, salt, pepper, and Polenta in 6-quart slow cooker; cover and cook on high 3 to 4 hours, adding Swiss chard during last 15 minutes. Season to taste with salt and pepper; serve over Polenta.

Veggie Stew with Bulgur

Nutritious bulgur helps thicken this stew. Serve with warm Parmesan Bread (see p. 530).

4 entrée servings

1 can (14½ ounces) diced tomatoes, undrained
1 cup spicy tomato juice
2 cups each: thickly sliced carrots, halved cremini
  mushrooms
1 cup each: chopped unpeeled Idaho potatoes, onion
1 each: thickly sliced medium red and green
  bell pepper
2–3 cloves garlic, minced
½ cup bulgur
1 teaspoon each: dried thyme and oregano leaves
2 medium zucchini, cubed
1 medium yellow summer squash, cubed
Salt and pepper, to taste

Per Serving:
Calories: 259
% calories from fat: 5
Protein (g): 9.9
Carbohydrate (g): 57.4
Fat (g): 1.4
Saturated fat (g): 0.2
Cholesterol (mg): 0
Sodium (mg): 694
Exchanges:
Milk: 0.0
Vegetable: 5.0
Fruit: 0.0
Bread: 2.0
Meat: 0.0
Fat: 0.0

1. Combine all ingredients, except zucchini, summer squash, salt, and pepper, in slow cooker; cover and cook on high 4 to 5 hours, adding zucchini and summer squash during last 30 minutes. Season to taste with salt and pepper.

Wheat Berry and Lentil Stew

v

Wheat berries and lentils are a healthy and flavorful grain combination you'll enjoy.

8 entrée servings

3 cups reduced-sodium vegetable broth
1 cup wheat berries
½ cup dried lentils
1½ pounds russet potatoes, unpeeled, cubed
1 cup chopped onion
½ cup each: sliced carrots, celery
4 cloves garlic, minced
1 teaspoon dried savory leaves
Salt and pepper, to taste

Per Serving:
Calories: 150
% calories from fat: 8
Protein (g): 7.2
Carbohydrate (g): 28.9
Fat (g): 1.4
Saturated fat (g): 0.1
Cholesterol (mg): 0.0
Sodium (mg): 123
Exchanges:
Milk: 0.0
Vegetable: 0.0
Fruit: 0.0
Bread: 1.5
Meat: 1
Fat: 0.0

1. Combine all ingredients, except salt and pepper, in 6-quart slow cooker; cover and cook on low 6 to 8 hours. Season to taste with salt and pepper.

Lentil and Vegetable Stew

L

This lentil stew is flavored with chili peppers, ginger, and lots of garlic. It's very spicy; adjust the seasoning according to your taste, but remember that the flavors will mellow as the stew cooks.

8 entrée servings

2 cups vegetable broth
8 small potatoes, cubed
3 cups each: sliced onions, chopped tomatoes
8 ounces each: chopped carrots, green beans
½ cup dried lentils
2–4 small jalapeño or other hot chilies, mashed
    into a paste, or 1–2 teaspoons cayenne pepper
1 tablespoon minced gingerroot
1 stick cinnamon
10 cloves garlic
6 each: whole cloves, crushed cardamom pods
1 teaspoon ground turmeric
½ teaspoon crushed dried mint leaves
Salt, to taste
2 cups each: frozen thawed peas, cooked warm couscous
Reduced-fat plain yogurt, as garnish

Per Serving:
Calories: 380
% calories from fat: 2
Protein (g): 14.4
Carbohydrate (g): 79.7
Fat (g): 1
Saturated fat (g): 0.2
Cholesterol (mg): 0
Sodium (mg): 55
Exchanges:
Milk: 0.0
Vegetable: 4.0
Fruit: 0.0
Bread: 4.0
Meat: 0.0
Fat: 0.0

1. Combine all ingredients, except salt, peas, couscous, and yogurt in 6-quart slow cooker; cover and cook on low 6 to 8 hours, adding peas during last 15 minutes. Season to taste with salt; serve over couscous and garnish with dollops of yogurt.

Lentil Stew with Spiced Couscous

V *Lentils cook perfectly in the slow cooker—any leftover soup freezes well.*

6 entrée servings

1 can (14½ ounces) diced tomatoes, undrained
3 cups reduced-sodium vegetable broth
2 cups dried lentils
1 cup each: chopped onion, red or green bell pepper, celery, carrots
1 teaspoon each: minced garlic, dried oregano leaves
½ teaspoon ground turmeric
Salt and pepper, to taste
Spiced Couscous (recipe follows)

Per Serving:
Calories: 420
% calories from fat: 9
Protein (g): 24
Carbohydrate (g): 74
Fat (g): 4.1
Saturated fat (g): 0.6
Cholesterol (mg): 0
Sodium (mg): 355
Exchanges:
Milk: 0.0
Vegetable: 3.0
Fruit: 0.0
Bread: 4.0
Meat: 0.0
Fat: 1.0

1. Combine all ingredients, except salt, pepper, and couscous, in 6-quart slow cooker; cover and cook on low 6 to 8 hours. Season to taste with salt and pepper; serve over Spiced Couscous.

Spiced Couscous

Makes about 3 cups

⅓ cup sliced green onions
1 clove garlic, minced
⅛–¼ teaspoon crushed red pepper
½ teaspoon ground turmeric
1 teaspoon olive oil
1⅔ cups reduced-sodium vegetable broth
1 cup couscous

1. Sauté green onions, garlic, red pepper, and turmeric in oil in medium saucepan until onions are tender, about 3 minutes. Stir in broth; heat to boiling. Stir in couscous; remove from heat and let stand, covered, 5 minutes or until broth is absorbed.

Bean-Thickened Vegetable Stew

Puréed beans provide the perfect thickening for this stew.

6 entrée servings

1½ cups Basic Vegetable Stock (see p. 34) or
   vegetable broth
1 can (15 ounces) each: rinsed drained black and
   puréed navy beans
2 cups chopped tomatoes
1½ cups sliced mushrooms
1 yellow summer squash, sliced
½ cup each: sliced carrots, chopped onion
3 cloves garlic, minced
2 bay leaves
¾ teaspoon each: dried thyme and oregano leaves
1 cup frozen peas, thawed
Salt and pepper, to taste
4 cups cooked noodles, warm

Per Serving:
Calories: 348
% calories from fat: 5
Protein (g): 18.3
Carbohydrate (g): 71.8
Fat (g): 1.9
Saturated fat (g): 0.2
Cholesterol (mg): 0
Sodium (mg): 589
Exchanges:
Milk: 0.0
Vegetable: 2.0
Fruit: 0.0
Bread: 4.0
Meat: 0.0
Fat: 0.0

1. Combine all ingredients, except peas, salt, pepper, and noodles, in slow cooker; cover and cook on high 4 to 5 hours, adding peas during last 15 minutes. Discard bay leaves; season to taste with salt and pepper. Serve over noodles.

Bean and Squash Stew

This delicious stew cooks slowly to savory goodness. Serve with Buttermilk Bread (see p. 524).

6 entrée servings

2 cans (14½ ounces each) diced tomatoes, undrained
1 can (15 ounces) red kidney beans, rinsed, drained
1 can (13¼ ounces) baby lima beans, rinsed, drained
2 cups peeled cubed butternut or acorn squash
1½ cups each: chopped onions, green bell peppers
2 teaspoons minced roasted garlic
½–¾ teaspoon dried Italian seasoning
Salt and pepper, to taste

Per Serving:
Calories: 239
% calories from fat: 5
Protein (g): 14
Carbohydrate (g): 50.5
Fat (g): 1.4
Saturated fat (g): 0.2
Cholesterol (mg): 0
Sodium (mg): 160
Exchanges:
Milk: 0.0
Vegetable: 3.0
Fruit: 0.0
Bread: 2.0
Meat: 0.5
Fat: 0.0

1. Combine all ingredients, except salt and pepper, in slow cooker; cover and cook on high 4 to 5 hours. Season to taste with salt and pepper.

Hearty Bean Stew with Greens

Warm crusty bread and fresh fruit would be perfect accompaniments to this stew.

6 entrée servings

2 quarts reduced-sodium vegetable broth
½ cup each: dried garbanzo and kidney beans,
   thinly sliced carrots
¼ cup pearl barley
1 cup each: cubed potatoes, zucchini
1 medium onion, sliced
2 cloves garlic, minced
½ cup cooked elbow macaroni
2 cups sliced spinach or watercress
2–4 tablespoons lemon juice
Salt and pepper, to taste

Per Serving:
Calories: 230
% calories from fat: 7
Protein (g): 10 6
Carbohydrate (g): 44.6
Fat (g): 1.7
Saturated fat (g): 0.2
Cholesterol (mg): 0
Sodium (mg): 279
Exchanges:
Milk: 0.0
Vegetable: 3.0
Fruit: 0.0
Bread: 2.0
Meat: 0.0
Fat: 0.0

1. Combine all ingredients, except macaroni, spinach, lemon juice, salt, and pepper, in 6-quart slow cooker; cover and cook on low until beans are tender 6 to 8 hours, stirring in macaroni and spinach during last 20 minutes. Season to taste with lemon juice, salt, and pepper.

Sweet Bean Stew

This vegetable stew is a sweet, chili-flavored treat! Serve with Spoon Bread (see p. 525).

8 entrée servings

3 cans (15 ounces each) pinto beans, rinsed, drained
2 cans (14½ ounces each) chili-seasoned diced
   tomatoes, undrained
¾ cup apple cider or apple juice
2 cups diced red or green bell peppers
1½ cups each: chopped onions, peeled cubed sweet
   potatoes, zucchini
2 teaspoons each: minced garlic, chili powder
1 teaspoon cumin seeds, lightly crushed
½ teaspoon ground cinnamon
½ cup raisins
Salt and pepper, to taste

Per Serving:
Calories: 371
% calories from fat: 15
Protein (g): 13.6
Carbohydrate (g): 69.8
Fat (g): 6.4
Saturated fat (g): 1.7
Cholesterol (mg): 4
Sodium (mg): 717
Exchanges:
Milk: 0.0
Vegetable: 2.0
Fruit: 0.0
Bread: 4.0
Meat: 0.0
Fat: 1.0

1. Combine all ingredients, except raisins, salt, and pepper, in 6-quart slow cooker; cover and cook on low 6 to 8 hours, adding raisins during last 30 minutes. Season to taste with salt and pepper.

Black Bean and Spinach Stew

The amount of chilies and gingerroot in this heartily spiced dish can be decreased if less hotness is desired.

8 entrée servings

3 cans (15 ounces each) black beans, rinsed, drained
1 can (14½ ounces) diced tomatoes, undrained
1 cup each: chopped onion, red bell pepper,
   cubed zucchini
2 jalapeño chilies, finely chopped
2 teaspoons minced garlic
1 tablespoon chopped gingerroot
2–3 teaspoons chili powder
1 teaspoon ground cumin
½ teaspoon cayenne pepper
3 cups sliced spinach
Salt, to taste
4 cups cooked rice, warm

Per Serving:
Calories: 237
% calories from fat: 11
Protein (g): 10.2
Carbohydrate (g): 53.8
Fat (g): 3.6
Saturated fat (g): 0.3
Cholesterol (mg): 0
Sodium (mg): 789
Exchanges:
Milk: 0.0
Vegetable: 1.0
Fruit: 0.0
Bread: 3.0
Meat: 0.0
Fat: 0.0

1. Combine all ingredients, except spinach, salt, and rice, in slow cooker; cover and cook on high 3 to 4 hours, adding spinach during last 15 minutes. Season to taste with salt; serve over rice.

Sweet 'N Hot Spicy Bean and Vegetable Stew

V

Sweet spices and fiery chilies combine nicely in this hearty stew.

6 entrée servings

2 cans (14½ ounces each) diced tomatoes, undrained
1 can (15 ounces) each: rinsed drained black and
    pinto beans
1½ cups Basic Vegetable Stock (see p. 34) or
    vegetable broth
6 each: sliced carrots, cubed unpeeled red potatoes
1½ cups chopped onions
2–3 teaspoons each: minced serrano chilies, garlic
1½ teaspoons dried oregano leaves
¾ teaspoon ground cinnamon
½ teaspoon ground cloves
1 bay leaf
1 tablespoon red wine vinegar
Salt and pepper, to taste

Per Serving:
Calories: 284
% calories from fat: 5
Protein (g): 15.4
Carbohydrate (g): 60.8
Fat (g): 2
Saturated fat (g): 0.1
Cholesterol (mg): 0
Sodium (mg): 527
Exchanges:
Milk: 0.0
Vegetable: 3.0
Fruit: 0.0
Bread: 3.0
Meat: 0.0
Fat: 0.0

1. Combine all ingredients, except salt and pepper, in 6-quart slow cooker; cover and cook on low 6 to 8 hours. Discard bay leaf; season to taste with salt and pepper.

Winter Bean and Vegetable Stew

v *Serve this satisfying stew with Garlic Bread (see p. 313).*

6 entrée servings

1 can (15 ounces) black beans, rinsed, drained
1 can (13¼ ounces) baby lima beans, rinsed, drained
1½ cups reduced-sodium vegetable broth
1 cup each: chopped onion, peeled cubed Idaho
   and sweet potato
1 large tomato, cut into wedges
½ cup each: sliced carrot, parsnip, chopped green
   bell pepper
2 cloves garlic, minced
¾ teaspoon dried sage leaves
2 tablespoons cornstarch
¼ cup cold water
Salt and pepper, to taste

Per Serving:
Calories: 238
% calories from fat: 20
Protein (g): 10.8
Carbohydrate (g): 42.4
Fat (g): 5.7
Saturated fat (g): 0.7
Cholesterol (mg): 0
Sodium (mg): 399
Exchanges:
Milk: 0.0
Vegetable: 2.0
Fruit: 0.0
Bread: 2.0
Meat: 0.0
Fat: 1.0

1. Combine all ingredients, except cornstarch, water, salt, and pepper, in slow cooker; cover and cook on high 3 to 4 hours. Stir in combined cornstarch and water, stirring 2 to 3 minutes. Season to taste with salt and pepper.

Tofu and Vegetable Stew

V | *As with most stews, vegetables in this dish can vary according to season and availability.*

4 entrée servings

4 cups Rich Mushroom Stock (see p. 37) or
    vegetable broth
1 package (10½ ounces) firm light tofu or tempeh,
    cubed (½-inch)
2 cups each: sliced peeled red potatoes, sliced carrots
½ cup each: sliced onion, celery
3 cloves garlic, minced
1 bay leaf
1 teaspoon ground cumin
½ teaspoon dried thyme leaves
1 package (10 ounces) frozen chopped spinach,
    thawed
¼ cup minced parsley
Salt and pepper, to taste

Per Serving:
Calories: 239
% calories from fat: 8
Protein (g): 11.1
Carbohydrate (g): 43.8
Fat (g): 2.3
Saturated fat (g): 0.2
Cholesterol (mg): 0
Sodium (mg): 182
Exchanges:
Milk: 0.0
Vegetable: 4.0
Fruit: 0.0
Bread: 1.5
Meat: 0.5
Fat: 0.0

1. Combine all ingredients, except spinach, parsley, salt, and pepper, in slow cooker; cover and cook on high 3 to 4 hours, adding spinach during last 20 minutes. Discard bay leaf; season to taste with salt and pepper.

Southern Vegetable Stew

V *Team this Southern favorite with rice and Roasted Chili Cornbread (see p. 529).*

4 entrée servings

1 can (14½ ounces) diced tomatoes, undrained
1 cup each: reduced-sodium vegetable broth, thickly sliced carrots, zucchini
1 small eggplant, peeled, cubed (1-inch)
¾ cup each: coarsely chopped green and red bell pepper
¼ cup sliced green onions
4 cloves garlic, minced
1 package (8 ounces) frozen pearl onions, thawed
4 ounces fresh or frozen thawed sliced okra
2–3 teaspoons coarse-grain mustard
Hot pepper sauce, to taste
Salt and pepper, to taste

Per Serving:
Calories: 170
% calories from fat: 8
Protein (g): 5.7
Carbohydrate (g): 34.4
Fat (g): 1.6
Saturated fat (g): 0.2
Cholesterol (mg): 0
Sodium (mg): 94
Exchanges:
Milk: 0.0
Vegetable: 6.0
Fruit: 0.0
Bread: 0.0
Meat: 0.0
Fat: 0.0

1. Combine all ingredients, except pearl onions, okra, mustard, hot pepper sauce, salt, and pepper, in slow cooker; cover and cook on low 6 to 8 hours, adding pearl onions and okra during last 30 minutes. Season to taste with mustard, hot pepper sauce, salt, and pepper.

Tex-Mex Vegetable Stew

Poblano chilies range from mild to very hot in flavor, so taste a tiny bit before using. If the chili is very hot, you may want to use less or substitute some sweet green bell pepper.

6 entrée servings

2 cans (14½ ounces each) tomatoes with chilies, undrained
1 can (15 ounces) black beans, rinsed, drained
1 cup reduced-sodium vegetable broth
12 small new potatoes, halved
4 medium carrots, thickly sliced
½ cup each: chopped red onion, seeded poblano chili
3 cloves garlic, minced
2 tablespoons balsamic vinegar
1 tablespoon chili powder
2 teaspoons ground cumin
½ teaspoon dried oregano leaves
3 ears corn, cut into pieces (2-inch)
2 cups frozen peas, thawed
½ cup finely chopped cilantro
Salt and pepper, to taste

Per Serving:
Calories: 423
% calories from fat: 5
Protein (g): 16.7
Carbohydrate (g): 92.5
Fat (g): 2.4
Saturated fat (g): 0.2
Cholesterol (mg): 0
Sodium (mg): 793
Exchanges:
Milk: 0.0
Vegetable: 3.0
Fruit: 0.0
Bread: 5.0
Meat: 0.0
Fat: 0.0

1. Combine all ingredients, except corn, peas, cilantro, salt, and pepper, in 6-quart slow cooker; cover and cook on high 4 to 5 hours, adding corn and peas during last 20 minutes. Stir in cilantro; season to taste with salt and pepper.

Mexi-Beans 'N Greens Stew

V

Four cans (15 ounces each) pinto beans, rinsed and drained, can be substituted for the dried beans.

8 entrée servings

2 quarts water
2 cups dried pinto beans
½ cup each: coarsely chopped onion, poblano chili,
    red bell pepper
4 cloves garlic, minced
1 tablespoon finely chopped gingerroot
1–2 teaspoons minced serrano chilies
2 teaspoons each: chili powder, dried oregano leaves
1 teaspoon ground cumin
1 can (14½ ounces) diced tomatoes, undrained
2 cups coarsely chopped turnip or mustard greens
Salt and cayenne pepper, to taste

Per Serving:
Calories: 228
% calories from fat: 16
Protein (g): 11 7
Carbohydrate (g): 37.9
Fat (g): 4.4
Saturated fat (g): 0.6
Cholesterol (mg): 0
Sodium (mg): 233
Exchanges:
Milk: 0.0
Vegetable: 2.0
Fruit: 1.0
Bread: 2.0
Meat: 0.0
Fat: 1.0

1. Combine all ingredients, except tomatoes, greens, salt, and cayenne pepper, in 6-quart slow cooker; cover and cook on low until beans are tender, 7 to 8 hours, adding tomatoes with liquid and greens during last 30 minutes. Season to taste with salt and cayenne pepper.

Colombian-Style Vegetable Stew

V

Cilantro is an important flavor element in this delicious stew.

8 entrée servings

2 cans (14½ ounces each) diced tomatoes, undrained
1 can (15 ounces) chickpeas, rinsed, drained
1½ cups reduced-sodium vegetable broth
½ cup dry white wine or vegetable broth
4 each: peeled cubed medium potatoes, thickly
   sliced carrots, ribs celery
1 cup each: chopped onion, whole-kernel corn
4 cloves garlic, minced
2 bay leaves
1 teaspoon dried cumin
¾ teaspoon dried oregano leaves
1½ tablespoons white wine vinegar
1 cup frozen peas, thawed
½ cup chopped cilantro
Salt and pepper, to taste

Per Serving:
Calories: 240
% calories from fat: 4
Protein (g): 7.2
Carbohydrate (g): 48.1
Fat (g): 1.2
Saturated fat (g): 0.1
Cholesterol (mg): 0
Sodium (mg): 472
Exchanges:
Milk: 0.0
Vegetable: 0.0
Fruit: 0.0
Bread: 3.0
Meat: 0.0
Fat: 0.5

1. Combine all ingredients, except peas, cilantro, salt, and pepper, in 6-quart slow cooker; cover and cook on high 4 to 5 hours, adding peas during last 15 minutes. Stir in cilantro; discard bay leaves. Season to taste with salt and pepper.

Argentinean Stew

V *This stew is traditionally made with meat and served in a baked pumpkin shell. This meatless version is delicious and beautiful.*

12 entrée servings

2 cans (14½ ounces each) diced tomatoes, undrained, coarsely chopped
2 cups reduced-sodium vegetable broth
½ cup dry white wine (optional)
3 cups each: peeled cubed potatoes, sweet potatoes or butternut squash
2 cups coarsely chopped red onions
1 large green bell pepper, chopped
5 cloves garlic, minced
2 tablespoons each: brown sugar, white wine vinegar
2 bay leaves
1 teaspoon dried oregano leaves
6 ears corn, cut into pieces (1½-inches)
1 pound zucchini, thickly sliced
6 small peaches, peeled, halved
Salt and pepper, to taste

Per Serving:
Calories: 205
% calories from fat: 4
Protein (g): 5.2
Carbohydrate (g): 47.3
Fat (g): 1.0
Saturated fat (g): 0.1
Cholesterol (mg): 0
Sodium (mg): 294
Exchanges:
Milk: 0.0
Vegetable: 0.0
Fruit: 0.0
Bread: 3.0
Meat: 0.0
Fat: 0.0

1. Combine all ingredients, except corn, zucchini, peaches, salt, and pepper, in 6-quart slow cooker; cover and cook on low 6 to 8 hours, adding corn, zucchini, and peaches during last 20 minutes. Discard bay leaves; season to taste with salt and pepper.

Vegetable Stew with Cheese Tortellini

LO   *Serve this simple vegetable stew over your favorite kind of tortellini.*

4 entrée servings

1 can (14½ ounces) each: stewed tomatoes,
   reduced-sodium vegetable broth
1 cup each: sliced mushrooms, green bell pepper
½ cup finely chopped onion
¼ teaspoon allspice
½ teaspoon each: dried chervil and basil leaves
4 small green or yellow zucchini, cubed
Salt and pepper, to taste
1 package (9 ounces) fresh cheese tortellini,
   cooked, warm

Per Serving:
Calories: 276
% calories from fat: 15
Protein (g): 13.4
Carbohydrate (g): 47.3
Fat (g): 5
Saturated fat (g): 2
Cholesterol (mg): 33.9
Sodium (mg): 511
Exchanges:
Milk: 0.0
Vegetable: 3.0
Fruit: 0.0
Bread: 2.0
Meat: 0.0
Fat: 1.0

1. Combine all ingredients, except zucchini, salt, pepper, and tortellini, in slow cooker; cover and cook on high 4 to 5 hours, adding zucchini during last 30 minutes. Season to taste with salt and pepper; serve over tortellini in shallow bowls.

Italian Bean and Pasta Stew

LO   *This traditional dish is a cross between a soup and a stew—thick, rich, and flavorful.*

6 entrée servings

1 can (19 ounces) cannellini or Great Northern
   beans, drained
1 can (14½ ounces) Italian plum tomatoes,
   undrained, chopped
2 cups reduced-sodium vegetable broth
1 cup each: sliced carrot, celery, chopped onion
1 clove garlic, minced
½ teaspoon each: dried oregano and basil leaves
3 ounces elbow macaroni, cooked
Salt and pepper, to taste
Grated Parmesan cheese

Per Serving:
Calories: 212
% calories from fat: 9
Protein (g): 10.6
Carbohydrate (g): 37.8
Fat (g): 2.0
Saturated fat (g): 0.3
Cholesterol (mg): 0
Sodium (mg): 356
Exchanges:
Milk: 0.0
Vegetable: 1.0
Fruit: 0.0
Bread: 2.0
Meat: 1.0
Fat: 0.0

1. Combine all ingredients, except macaroni, salt, pepper, and cheese, in slow cooker; cover and cook on high 4 to 5 hours, adding macaroni during last 15 minutes. Season to taste with salt and pepper. Pass Parmesan cheese to sprinkle on stew.

Chickpea and Roasted Pepper Stew with Creamy Polenta

L

The slow cooker Polenta can also be used in this recipe (see pg. 520).

4 entrée servings

1 can (15 ounces) each: rinsed drained chickpeas, tomato sauce
1 can (14½ ounces) stewed tomatoes
1 jar (7 ounces) roasted red peppers, drained, chopped
1 medium onion, chopped
1 clove garlic, minced
1 teaspoon dried Italian seasoning
1 medium zucchini, cubed
Salt and pepper, to taste
¼ cup (1 ounce) grated Parmesan cheese
Microwave Polenta (see p. 385)

Per Serving:
Calories: 471
% calories from fat: 14
Protein (g): 16.3
Carbohydrate (g): 88.9
Fat (g): 7.3
Saturated fat (g): 1.9
Cholesterol (mg): 7.5
Sodium (mg): 601
Exchanges:
Milk: 0.0
Vegetable: 2.0
Fruit: 0.0
Bread: 5.0
Meat: 0.0
Fat: 1.0

1. Combine all ingredients, except zucchini, salt, pepper, cheese, and Microwave Polenta, in slow cooker; cover and cook on high 2 to 3 hours, adding zucchini during last 30 minutes. Season to taste with salt and pepper. Stir Parmesan cheese into Microwave Polenta; serve stew over Microwave Polenta.

Ratatouille with Feta Aioli

LO *Greek feta cheese imparts a welcome tang to this Mediterranean stew.*

4 entrée servings

1 can (28 ounces) petite-diced tomatoes, undrained
1 medium eggplant, peeled, cubed
1 cup each: finely chopped onion, sliced yellow
   bell pepper
3 teaspoons minced garlic
2 teaspoons dried Italian seasoning
2 small zucchini, halved, thinly sliced
Salt and pepper, to taste
Feta Aioli (recipe follows)

Per Serving:
Calories: 164
% calories from fat: 15
Protein (g): 6.7
Carbohydrate (g): 31.7
Fat (g): 3.1
Saturated fat (g): 0.5
Cholesterol (mg): 0
Sodium (mg): 522
Exchanges:
Milk: 0.0
Vegetable: 3.0
Fruit: 0.0
Bread: 1.0
Meat: 0.0
Fat: 0.5

1. Combine all ingredients, except zucchini, salt, and pepper, in slow cooker; cover and cook on high 4 to 5 hours, adding zucchini during last 30 minutes. Season to taste with salt and pepper; serve with Feta Aioli.

Feta Aioli

Makes about ½ cup

¼ cup each: crumbled feta cheese (1 ounce), reduced-fat mayonnaise
2–3 cloves garlic, minced

1. Process all ingredients in food processor until smooth.

Curried Mediterranean Stew with Couscous

Serve this stew with a selection of condiments to provide flavor accents.

L

4 entrée servings

1 cup reduced-sodium vegetable broth
8 ounces fresh or frozen thawed whole okra
1 cup each: whole-kernel corn, sliced mushrooms,
    chopped onion
2 each: sliced medium carrots, chopped tomato
1 teaspoon minced garlic
1½ teaspoons curry powder
⅔ cup uncooked couscous
Salt and pepper, to taste
Condiments: reduced-fat plain yogurt, raisins,
    chopped cucumber, peanuts, and tomato

Per Serving:
Calories: 280
% calories from fat: 24
Protein (g): 7.9
Carbohydrate (g): 47.8
Fat (g): 7.7
Saturated fat (g): 1
Cholesterol (mg): 0
Sodium (mg): 46
Exchanges:
Milk: 0.0
Vegetable: 3.0
Fruit: 0.0
Bread: 2.0
Meat: 0.0
Fat: 1.5

1. Combine all ingredients, except couscous, salt, pepper, and condiments, in slow cooker; cover and cook on high 4 to 5 hours. Stir in couscous and turn heat off; cover and let stand 5 to 10 minutes. Season to taste with salt and pepper. Serve stew with condiments (not included in nutritional data).

Vegetable Tajine

v

In Moroccan cuisine, tajines are traditionally cooked in earthenware pots. Serve with couscous and pita bread.

6 entrée servings

2 cans (14½ ounces each) diced tomatoes, undrained
1 can (15 ounces) garbanzo beans, rinsed, drained
½ cup vegetable broth or orange juice
1½ cups cut green beans
1 cup each: chopped butternut or acorn squash, turnip or rutabaga, pitted prunes
½ cup each: chopped onion, sliced carrot, celery
1–2 teaspoons minced gingerroot
1 teaspoon minced garlic
1 cinnamon stick
2 teaspoons each: paprika, ground cumin and coriander
¼ cup small pitted black olives
Salt and pepper, to taste
4 cups cooked couscous, warm

Per Serving:
Calories: 386
% calories from fat: 10
Protein (g): 12.5
Carbohydrate (g): 78.7
Fat (g): 4.6
Saturated fat (g): 0.6
Cholesterol (mg): 0
Sodium (mg): 540
Exchanges:
Milk: 0.0
Vegetable: 3.0
Fruit: 1.0
Bread: 3.0
Meat: 0.0
Fat: 1.0

1. Combine all ingredients, except black olives, salt, pepper, and couscous, in 6-quart slow cooker; cover and cook on high 4 to 5 hours, adding olives during last 30 minutes. Season to taste with salt and pepper. Serve over couscous.

Vegetable Stew Marengo

V

A delicious dish that picks up the colors and flavors of the Mediterranean.

4 entrée servings

1 can (14½ ounces) diced tomatoes, undrained
¾ cup vegetable broth
1 package (10½ ounces) firm light tofu, cubed
  (1-inch)
1 cup each: chopped onion, diced zucchini,
  whole small mushrooms, sliced carrots
1 teaspoon minced garlic
1 strip orange zest (3 x 1 inch)
½ teaspoon each: dried thyme and oregano leaves
2 tablespoons cornstarch
¼ cup water
Salt and pepper, to taste
3 cups cooked couscous or rice, warm

Per Serving:
Calories: 349
% calories from fat: 27
Protein (g): 16.7
Carbohydrate (g): 48.4
Fat (g): 10.8
Saturated fat (g): 1
Cholesterol (mg): 0
Sodium (mg): 608
Exchanges:
Milk: 0.0
Vegetable: 3.0
Fruit: 0.0
Bread: 2.0
Meat: 1.0
Fat: 1.5

1. Combine all ingredients, except cornstarch, water, salt, pepper, and couscous, in slow cooker; cover and cook on high 3 to 4 hours. Stir in combined cornstarch and water, stirring 2 to 3 minutes. Season to taste with salt and pepper. Serve over couscous.

Many-Vegetable Stew with Couscous

V

A Moroccan favorite that will please family or guests.

12 entrée servings

3 cans (15 ounces each) garbanzo beans, rinsed,
    drained
2–3 cups reduced-sodium vegetable broth
1 small cabbage, cut into 12 wedges
1 large eggplant, cubed
8 ounces each: sliced carrots, cubed small potatoes,
    turnips, cut green beans, cubed peeled pumpkin or
    butternut squash
4 medium tomatoes, quartered
1½ cups chopped onions
3 cloves garlic, minced
2 teaspoons ground cinnamon
1 teaspoon paprika
½ teaspoon each: ground ginger and turmeric
1 package (10 ounces) frozen artichoke hearts, thawed, quartered
½ cup each: raisins, chopped parsley
Salt and cayenne pepper, to taste
8 cups cooked couscous, warm

Per Serving:
Calories: 495
% calories from fat: 11
Protein (g): 17.6
Carbohydrate (g): 97.5
Fat (g): 64
Saturated fat (g): 1.7
Cholesterol (mg): 0
Sodium (mg): 295
Exchanges:
Milk: 0.0
Vegetable: 6.0
Fruit: 0.0
Bread: 5.0
Meat: 0.0
Fat: 1.0

1. Combine beans, broth, fresh vegetables, garlic, and spices in 6-quart
slow cooker; cover and cook on low 5 to 7 hours, adding artichoke hearts,
raisins, and parsley during last 30 minutes. Season to taste with salt and
cayenne pepper. Serve over couscous.

African Sweet Potato Stew

v *A spicy garlic paste seasons this delicious stew.*

6 entrée servings

2 cans (15 ounces each) chickpeas, rinsed, drained
1 can (28 ounces) diced tomatoes, undrained
1½ cups reduced-sodium vegetable broth
1½ pounds sweet potatoes, peeled, cubed
1 cup thinly sliced onion
Garlic Seasoning Paste (recipe follows)
1½ cups fresh or frozen thawed cut okra
Salt and pepper, to taste
Hot pepper sauce, to taste
3 cups cooked couscous, warm

Per Serving:
Calories: 517
% calories from fat: 8
Protein (g): 15.7
Carbohydrate (g): 104.8
Fat (g): 4.9
Saturated fat (g): 0.6
Cholesterol (mg): 0
Sodium (mg): 544
Exchanges:
Milk: 0.0
Vegetable: 0.0
Fruit: 0.0
Bread: 7.0
Meat: 0.0
Fat: 0.5

1. Combine all ingredients, except okra, salt, pepper, hot pepper sauce, and couscous, in 6-quart slow cooker; cover and cook on high 4 to 5 hours, adding okra during 45 minutes. Season to taste with salt, pepper, and hot pepper sauce. Serve over couscous.

Garlic Seasoning Paste

Makes about 3 tablespoons

6 cloves garlic
2 slices gingerroot (¼-inch)
2 teaspoons each: paprika, cumin seeds
½ teaspoon ground cinnamon
1–2 tablespoons olive oil

1. Process all ingredients in food processor until smooth, or mince garlic and mash with other ingredients to make a paste.

Vegetable Stew Stroganoff

LO *A warming stew for cold winter evenings. Substitute turnips, parsnips, or rutabagas for one of the potatoes, if you like.*

6 entrée servings

1½ cups vegetable broth
8 ounces mushrooms, halved
3 medium onions, thinly sliced
2 each: peeled cubed medium Idaho and sweet
   potatoes
1 tablespoon each: dry mustard, sugar
1 cup frozen peas, thawed
1 cup reduced-fat sour cream
2 tablespoons cornstarch
Salt and pepper, to taste
4 cups cooked wide noodles, warm

Per Serving:
Calories: 414
% calories from fat: 13
Protein (g): 14.4
Carbohydrate (g): 78.9
Fat (g): 6.1
Saturated fat (g): 1
Cholesterol (mg): 39.8
Sodium (mg): 653
Exchanges:
Milk: 0.0
Vegetable: 2.0
Fruit: 0.0
Bread: 4.5
Meat: 0.0
Fat: 1.0

1. Combine all ingredients, except peas, sour cream, cornstarch, salt, pepper, and noodles, in 6-quart slow cooker; cover and cook on low 6 to 8 hours, adding peas during last 30 minutes. Stir in combined sour cream and cornstarch, stirring 2 to 3 minutes. season to taste with salt and pepper; serve over noodles.

Cabbage Ragout with Real Mashed Potatoes

L

Fresh fennel, gingerroot, and apple lend aromatic highlights to this cabbage stew. If the eggplant is really fresh, it will not need to be salted.

6 entrée servings

1 medium eggplant (about 1¼ pounds), unpeeled, cubed (1-inch)
2 cups reduced-sodium vegetable broth
8 cups thinly sliced cabbage
1 cup chopped onion
½ cup thinly sliced fennel bulb or celery
1 tablespoon each: minced garlic, gingerroot
1 teaspoon crushed fennel seeds
2 medium apples, peeled, coarsely chopped
1 cup reduced-fat sour cream
2 tablespoons cornstarch
Salt and pepper, to taste
Real Mashed Potatoes (see p. 475)

Per Serving:
Calories: 249
% calories from fat: 10
Protein (g): 8.5
Carbohydrate (g): 50
Fat (g): 3
Saturated fat (g): 0.5
Cholesterol (mg): 8.8
Sodium (mg): 255
Exchanges:
Milk: 0.0
Vegetable: 0.0
Fruit: 0.0
Bread: 3.0
Meat: 0.0
Fat: 0.5

1. Lightly salt eggplant and let stand in colander 15 minutes; rinse well and dry.
2. Combine eggplant and remaining ingredients, except apples, sour cream, cornstarch, salt, pepper, and Real Mashed Potatoes, in 6-quart slow cooker; cover and cook on low 6 to 8 hours, adding apples during last 20 minutes. Turn heat to high and cook 10 minutes; stir in combined sour cream and cornstarch, stirring 2 to 3 minutes. Season to taste with salt and pepper; serve over Real Mashed Potatoes in shallow bowls.

Squash and Potato Goulash

LO *This goulash would also be delicious with Spinach Rice (see p. 345).*

6 entrée servings

1 can (14½ ounces) diced tomatoes, undrained
1 cup vegetable broth
½ cup dry white wine or vegetable broth
3 cups each: peeled cubed butternut squash,
   Idaho potatoes
1½ cups each: diced red and green bell pepper
2 medium onions, coarsely chopped
1 clove garlic, minced
1–2 teaspoons caraway seeds, lightly crushed
3 tablespoons paprika
1 cup reduced-fat sour cream
2 tablespoons cornstarch
Salt and pepper, to taste
4 cups cooked wide noodles, warm

Per Serving:
Calories: 491
% calories from fat: 9
Protein (g): 15.3
Carbohydrate (g): 95.8
Fat (g): 5
Saturated fat (g): 0.9
Cholesterol (mg): 39.8
Sodium (mg): 533
Exchanges:
Milk: 0.0
Vegetable: 3.0
Fruit: 0.0
Bread: 5.0
Meat: 0.0
Fat: 1.0

1. Combine all ingredients, except paprika, sour cream, cornstarch, salt, pepper, and noodles, in 6-quart slow cooker; cover and cook on low 6 to 8 hours. Stir in paprika and combined sour cream and cornstarch, stirring 2 to 3 minutes. Season to taste with salt and pepper; serve over noodles.

Mexican Ancho Chili Stew

This stew has lots of delicious sauce, so serve with crusty warm rolls or tortillas. Vary the amount of ancho chilies to taste.

4 entrée servings

4–6 ancho chilies, stems, seeds, and veins discarded
2 cups boiling water
4 medium tomatoes, cut into wedges
6–8 Mexican-style vegetarian burgers, crumbled
1 large onion, chopped
2 cloves garlic, minced
1 teaspoon each: minced serrano or jalapeño chili,
    dried oregano leaves, crushed cumin seeds
Salt, to taste

Per Serving:
Calories: 275
% calories from fat: 13
Protein (g): 11.9
Carbohydrate (g): 50.9
Fat (g): 4.3
Saturated fat (g): 0.1
Cholesterol (mg): 0
Sodium (mg): 735
Exchanges:
Milk: 0.0
Vegetable: 2.0
Fruit: 0.0
Bread: 2.5
Meat: 0.5
Fat: 0.5

1. Place ancho chilies in bowl; pour boiling water over. Let stand until chilies are softened, about 10 minutes. Process chilies mixture and tomatoes in food processor or blender until smooth.
2. Combine chili mixture and remaining ingredients, except salt, in slow cooker; cover and cook on high 3 to 4 hours. Season to taste with salt.

THIRTEEN

Other

Entrées

Beef Round Roast with Fettuccine

Slice this perfectly cooked roast and serve with fettuccine.

8 servings

1 boneless top or beef bottom round roast
  (about 3 pounds)
Salt and pepper
1 cup sliced onion
½ cup beef broth
1 tablespoon cornstarch
2 tablespoons water
½ cup frozen thawed petite peas
½ cup (2 ounces) grated Romano cheese
1 pound fettuccine, cooked, warm

Per Serving:
Calories: 509
% calories from fat: 26
Protein (g): 45.7
Carbohydrate (g): 46.1
Fat (g): 14.2
Saturated fat (g): 5.4
Cholesterol (mg): 68.6
Sodium (mg): 208.9
Exchanges:
Milk: 0.0
Vegetable: 0.0
Fruit: 0.0
Bread: 3.0
Meat: 5.0
Fat: 0.0

1. Sprinkle beef lightly with salt and pepper; place in slow cooker with onion and broth; insert meat thermometer so tip is in center of roast. Cover and cook on low until meat thermometer registers 155 degrees for medium doneness, about 4 hours. Remove to serving platter and cover loosely with foil.

2. Add peas to slow cooker; cover and cook on high 10 minutes; stir in combined cornstarch and water, stirring 2 to 3 minutes. Stir in Romano cheese; season to taste with salt and pepper. Toss with fettuccine and serve with beef.

Variation

Beef Round Roast with Horseradish Sauce—Make recipe as above, omitting fettucine. To make Horseradish Sauce, mix 2 tablespoons prepared horseradish and generous pinch cayenne pepper into 1 cup whipped cream.

Sauerbraten

The longer you can marinate the beef, the more flavorful it will be. Many Sauerbraten recipes do not include sour cream—omit it if you want.

8–10 servings

2 cups water
1 cup dry red wine
1 large onion, thinly sliced
2 tablespoons pickling spice
12 each: whole cloves, peppercorns
2 bay leaves
1½ teaspoons salt
1 boneless beef top or bottom round roast
   (about 3 pounds)
⅔ cup each: finely crushed gingersnaps,
   reduced-fat sour cream
2 tablespoons cornstarch

Per Serving:
Calories: 314
% calories from fat: 30
Protein (g): 40.6
Carbohydrate (g): 11.5
Fat (g): 8.3
Saturated fat (g): 3.2
Cholesterol (mg): 83.8
Sodium (mg): 614.9
Exchanges:
Milk: 0.0
Vegetable: 0.0
Fruit: 0.0
Bread: 0.5
Meat: 5.0
Fat: 0.0

1. Heat water, wine, onion, seasonings, and salt to boiling in large sauce-pan; cool. Pour mixture over beef in slow cooker crock; refrigerate crock, covered, at least 1 day.
2. Place crock in slow cooker; cover and cook on low 6 to 8 hours. Remove meat to serving platter and keep warm. Stir gingersnaps into broth; stir in combined sour cream and cornstarch, stirring 2 to 3 minutes. Serve sauce over sliced meat.

Pot Roast

Pot roast with vegetables can't be beat for a cold weather meal—add the wine, or not, for extra flavor.

8 servings

1 beef chuck roast (about 3 pounds)
2 large onions, halved and sliced
1 package (1 ounce) onion soup mix
1 pound carrots, thickly sliced
6–8 medium red potatoes, unpeeled
½ small head cabbage, cut into 6–8 wedges
Salt and pepper, to taste
½ cup dry red wine or beef broth

Per Serving:
Calories: 331
% calories from fat: 16
Protein (g): 42.5
Carbohydrate (g): 26.6
Fat (g): 6.0
Saturated fat (g): 2.2
Cholesterol (mg): 59.5
Sodium (mg): 492
Exchanges:
Milk: 0.0
Vegetable: 0.0
Fruit: 0.0
Bread: 2.0
Meat: 4.0
Fat: 0.0

1. Place beef on onions in 6-quart slow cooker and sprinkle with soup mix. Arrange vegetables around beef and sprinkle lightly with salt and pepper; add wine, cover and cook on low 6 to 8 hours. Serve beef and vegetables with broth, or make gravy.

Note: To make gravy, measure broth and pour into small saucepan; heat to boiling. For every cup of broth, whisk in 2 tablespoons flour mixed with ¼ cup cold water, whisking until thickened, about 1 minute.

Coffee Pot Roast

A favorite recipe of a good friend, Judy Pompei—it will be your favorite too!

10 servings

2 large onions, sliced
1 beef rump roast (about 3 pounds)
1 cup strong coffee
¼ cup soy sauce
1 clove garlic, minced
1 teaspoon dried oregano leaves
2 bay leaves

Per Serving:
Calories: 243
% calories from fat: 26
Protein (g): 39.6
Carbohydrate (g): 3.6
Fat (g): 6.8
Saturated fat (g): 2.2
Cholesterol (mg): 89.3
Sodium (mg): 604.1
Exchanges:
Milk: 0.0
Vegetable: 0.0
Fruit: 0.0
Bread: 0.0
Meat: 5.0
Fat: 0.0

1. Place half the onions in slow cooker; top with roast and remaining onions. Add remaining ingredients; cover and cook on low 6 to 8 hours. Serve beef with broth.

Barbecued Brisket

This delicious brisket is prepared with an easy spice rub, and slow cooked to perfection with barbecue sauce.

10 servings

1 beef brisket, fat trimmed (about 3 pounds)
Spice Rub (recipe follows)
2 cups barbecue sauce
¼ cup red wine vinegar
¼ cup packed light brown sugar
2 medium onions, sliced
½ cup water
1 pound fettuccine, cooked, warm

Per Serving:
Calories: 494
% calories from fat: 22
Protein (g): 34.3
Carbohydrate (g): 59.7
Fat (g): 11.8
Saturated fat (g): 3.4
Cholesterol (mg): 83.5
Sodium (mg): 744.4
Exchanges:
Milk: 0.0
Vegetable: 0.0
Fruit: 0.0
Bread: 4.0
Meat: 4.0
Fat: 0.0

1. Rub brisket with Spice Rub and place in slow cooker; pour in combined remaining ingredients, except fettuccine. Cover and cook on low 6 to 8 hours, turning heat to high during last 20 to 30 minutes. Remove brisket to serving platter and let stand, covered with foil, 10 minutes. Slice and serve with barbecue sauce and onions over fettuccine.

Spice Rub

Makes about 2 tablespoons

2 tablespoons minced parsley
1 teaspoon minced garlic
½ teaspoon each: seasoned salt, ground ginger, nutmeg, and pepper

1. Mix all ingredients.

Variations

Barbecued Beef Sandwiches—Make recipe as above, omitting fettuccine; shred brisket with a fork and mix with barbecue mixture; spoon beef on bottoms of toasted hoagie rolls and top with cole slaw and bun tops.
Pulled Pork Sandwiches—Make recipe as above, substituting boneless pork loin for the brisket and omitting noodles; shred pork with a fork and mix with barbecue mixture. Serve in toasted burger buns with dill pickles.

Mushroom-Stuffed Flank Steak

An impressive meat dish that's very easy to make!

6 servings

3 slices bacon
8 ounces cremini mushrooms, sliced
¼ cup chopped onion
¾ teaspoon dried thyme leaves
Salt and pepper, to taste
1 beef flank steak (about 1½ pounds)
¾ cup dry red wine or beef broth
4 cups cooked rice

Per Serving:
Calories: 353
% calories from fat: 26
Protein (g): 30.4
Carbohydrate (g): 31.8
Fat (g): 9.8
Saturated fat (g): 3
Cholesterol (mg): 49.9
Sodium (mg): 168.7
Exchanges:
Milk: 0.0
Vegetable: 0.0
Fruit: 0.0
Bread: 2.0
Meat: 4.0
Fat: 0.0

1. Cook bacon in large skillet until crisp; drain and crumble. Discard all but 1 tablespoon bacon fat; add mushrooms, onion and thyme to skillet and sauté until tender, 5 to 8 minutes. Mix in bacon; season to taste with salt and pepper.
2. Pound meat with meat mallet, if necessary, to make even in thickness. Spoon stuffing over meat and roll up, beginning from long side. Secure with short skewers and place in slow cooker; add wine. Cover and cook on low 6 to 8 hours. Slice and serve over rice, spooning juices over.

Variation
Vegetable-Stuffed Flank Steak—Make recipe above, omitting bacon; substitute olive oil for the bacon fat. Use ½ cup sliced mushrooms, and sauté with ¼ cup each chopped carrots, zucchini, and whole-kernel corn, substituting rosemary for the thyme. Omit wine; add 1 can (16 ounces) undrained petite-diced tomatoes to the slow cooker with the flank steak.

Rouladen

Thin sandwich steaks make easy work of Rouladen.

4 servings

4 small or 2 large thin beef sandwich steaks
  (about 1 pound)
Salt and pepper, to taste
4 slices smoked ham (about 1 ounce each)
1 cup finely chopped mushrooms
¼ cup each: finely chopped dill pickle, onion
1–2 tablespoons Dijon mustard
1 teaspoon dried dill weed
½ cup beef broth

Per Serving:
Calories: 208
% calories from fat: 29
Protein (g): 30.3
Carbohydrate (g): 4.2
Fat (g): 6.2
Saturated fat (g): 2.1
Cholesterol (mg): 60.1
Sodium (mg): 603
Exchanges:
Milk: 0.0
Vegetable: 0.0
Fruit: 0.0
Bread: 0.0
Meat: 4.0
Fat: 0.0

1. Sprinkle sandwich steaks lightly with salt and
pepper; top each steak with ham slice. Mix remaining
ingredients, except broth, and spread over ham slices. Roll up steaks, securing with toothpicks; place, seam sides down, in slow cooker. Add broth;
cover and cook on low 5 to 6 hours.

Variations

Italian-Style Rouladen—Make recipe as above, omitting mushrooms,
pickle, onion, mustard, and dill weed. Top each ham slice with a 1-ounce
slice reduced-fat Provolone cheese; sprinkle with 1 tablespoon chopped
sun-dried tomato and ½ teaspoon dried dill weed.

Greek-Style Rouladen—Make recipe as above, omitting ham, mushrooms,
pickle, onion, mustard, and dill weed. Mash ½ cup feta cheese and mix
with 2 finely chopped green onions, and ¼ cup each chopped sun-dried
tomatoes and sliced Greek olives. Spread mixture on beef steaks.

Braised Short Ribs

You'll find these short ribs especially tasty and juicy—nibbling on the bones is allowed!

4 servings

1 cup dry red wine or beef broth
4 large carrots, thickly sliced
1 large onion, cut into wedges
2 bay leaves
1 teaspoon dried marjoram
2 pounds beef short ribs

Per Serving:
Calories: 246
% calories from fat: 38
Protein (g): 19.7
Carbohydrate (g): 10.2
Fat (g): 9
Saturated fat (g): 3.7
Cholesterol (mg): 43.9
Sodium (mg): 109.4
Exchanges:
Milk: 0.0
Vegetable: 2.0
Fruit: 0.0
Bread: 0.0
Meat: 2.0
Fat: 1.0

1. Combine all ingredients in slow cooker, placing short ribs on the top; cover and cook on low 7 to 8 hours.

Just Plain Meat Loaf

Moist, the way meat loaf should be, with plenty of leftovers for sandwiches, too! Serve with Real Mashed Potatoes (see p. 475).

6 servings

1½ pounds lean ground beef
1 cup quick-cooking oats
½ cup 2% reduced-fat milk
1 egg
¼ cup catsup or chili sauce
½ cup each: chopped onion, green bell pepper
1 teaspoon each: minced garlic, dried Italian seasoning
1 teaspoon salt
½ teaspoon pepper

Per Serving:
Calories: 241
% of calories from fat: 21
Fat (gm): 5.5
Saturated fat (gm): 1.8
Cholesterol (mg): 64.3
Sodium (mg): 489
Protein (gm): 31.2
Carbohydrate (gm): 15.3
Exchanges:
Milk: 0.0
Vegetable: 0.0
Fruit: 0.0
Bread: 1.0
Meat: 3.0
Fat: 0.0

1. Make foil handles (see p. vi) and fit into slow cooker. Mix all ingredients until blended; pat mixture into a loaf shape and place in slow cooker, making sure sides of loaf do not touch crock. Insert meat thermometer so tip is in center of loaf; cover and cook on low until meat thermometer registers 170 degrees, 6 to 7 hours. Remove, using foil handles, and let stand, loosely covered with foil, 10 minutes.

Note: Meat loaf can also be cooked in a 9 x 5-inch loaf pan or two smaller loaf pans, if they fit in your slow cooker; place pans on a rack or tuna cans with the ends removed.

Variations

Italian Meat Loaf—Make recipe as above, adding ¼ cup (1 ounce) grated Parmesan cheese, ½ cup (2 ounces) shredded reduced-fat mozzarella cheese, and 2 tablespoons chopped pitted ripe olives. At the end of cooking time, top with 2 tablespoons seasoned tomato sauce or catsup and sprinkle with 2 tablespoons each grated Parmesan and shredded reduced-fat mozzarella cheeses; cover and cook until cheeses are melted, 5 to 10 minutes.

Savory Cheese Meat Loaf—Make recipe as above, substituting ½ pound ground lean pork for ½ pound of the beef, and adding 4 ounces reduced-fat cream cheese, ½ cup (2 ounces) shredded reduced-fat Cheddar cheese, and 2 tablespoons Worcestershire sauce. At the end of cooking time, sprinkle ¼ cup (1 ounce) shredded reduced-fat Cheddar cheese over top of meat loaf; cover and cook until cheese is melted, 5 to 10 minutes.

Chutney-Peanut Meat Loaf—Make recipe as above, substituting ½ cup chopped chutney for the catsup, and adding ⅓ cup chopped peanuts, 1 teaspoon curry powder, and ½ teaspoon ground ginger.

Lemon Meat Loaf

Meat loaf takes on a new dimension with a lemon accent and a smooth egg lemon sauce.

6 servings

1½ pounds lean ground beef
1 cup fresh bread crumbs
1 egg
⅓ cup each: chopped onion, green bell pepper
1 clove garlic, minced
1 tablespoon each: lemon juice, grated lemon zest
1 teaspoon Dijon mustard
½ teaspoon each: dried savory leaves, pepper
¾ teaspoon salt
Egg Lemon Sauce (recipe follows)

Per Serving:
Calories: 228
% of calories from fat: 29
Fat (gm): 7.2
Saturated fat (gm): 2.2
Cholesterol (mg): 94.4
Sodium (mg): 463
Protein (gm): 29.4
Carbohydrate (gm): 10.2
Exchanges:
Milk: 0.0
Vegetable: 0.0
Fruit: 0.0
Bread: 1.0
Meat: 3.0
Fat: 0.0

1. Make foil handles (see p. vi) and fit into slow cooker. Mix all ingredients until blended; pat mixture into a loaf shape and place in slow cooker, making sure sides of loaf do not touch crock. Insert meat thermometer so tip is in center of loaf; cover and cook on low until meat thermometer registers 170 degrees, 6 to 7 hours. Remove, using foil handles, and let stand, loosely covered with foil, 10 minutes. Serve with Egg Lemon Sauce.

Egg Lemon Sauce

Makes about 1¼ cups

1 tablespoon margarine or butter
2 tablespoons flour
½ cup each: reduced-sodium fat-free chicken broth, 2% reduced-fat milk
1 egg, lightly beaten
3–4 tablespoons lemon juice
1 teaspoon grated lemon zest
Salt and white pepper, to taste

1. Melt margarine in medium saucepan; whisk in flour and cook 1 minute. Whisk in broth and milk; heat to boiling, whisking until thickened, about 1 minute. Whisk about ½ the broth mixture into the egg; whisk mixture back into saucepan. Whisk over medium heat 1 minute. Add lemon juice and zest; season to taste with salt and white pepper.

Note: Meat loaf can also be cooked in a 9 x 5-inch loaf pan or two smaller loaf pans, if they fit in your slow cooker; place pans on a rack or on tuna cans with the ends removed.

Variation
Sweet-Sour Ham Loaf—Make recipe as above, substituting ½ pound ground smoked ham for ½ pound of the ground beef, and omitting lemon juice and zest, savory, and Egg Lemon Sauce. Add 2 chopped sweet pickles, ⅓ cup each coarsely chopped almonds, mixed dried fruit, apricot preserves, 1 tablespoon cider vinegar, and 2 teaspoons soy sauce.

Stuffed Cabbage Leaves

You'll enjoy this hearty dish that's stuffed with ground beef and rice and sauced with tomatoes.

4 servings

8 large cabbage leaves
1 pound lean ground beef
¼ cup each: finely chopped onion, green bell
   pepper, cooked rice, water
1 teaspoon salt
¼ teaspoon pepper
1 can (14 ounces) tomato sauce
1 can (16 ounces) petite-diced tomatoes, undrained

Per Serving:
Calories: 319
% calories from fat: 35
Protein (g): 27.4
Carbohydrate (g): 25.7
Fat (g): 12.6
Saturated fat (g): 4.8
Cholesterol (mg): 73.7
Sodium (mg): 1123
Exchanges:
Milk: 0.0
Vegetable: 0.0
Fruit: 0.0
Bread: 1.5
Meat: 3.0
Fat: 1.0

1. Place cabbage leaves in boiling water until softened, 1 to 2 minutes; drain well. Trim thick veins from leaves so they lay flat.
2. Mix ground beef and remaining ingredients, except tomato sauce and diced tomatoes. Divide meat mixture into 8 equal parts, shaping each into a loaf shape; wrap each in a cabbage leaf, folding ends and sides over. Pour half the combined tomato sauce and diced tomatoes with liquid into slow cooker; add cabbage rolls, seam sides down. Pour remaining tomato mixture over; cover and cook on low 6 to 8 hours.

Meatballs Florentine

This hearty entrée celebrates flavors of the Mediterranean.

4 servings

1 cup spinach leaves
½ cup ricotta cheese
1 egg
¼ cup chopped green onions
2 cloves garlic
2 teaspoon dried oregano leaves
½ teaspoon each: dried dill leaves, ground nutmeg,
   salt, pepper
1 pound lean ground beef
½ cup fresh bread crumbs
4 cups spaghetti sauce with herbs
8 ounces fettuccine, cooked, warm

Per Serving:
Calories: 584
% calories from fat: 24
Protein (g): 41.6
Carbohydrate (g): 70.4
Fat (g): 15.3
Saturated fat (g): 5.6
Cholesterol (mg): 138.9
Sodium (mg): 1434.3
Exchanges:
Milk: 0.0
Vegetable: 0.0
Fruit: 0.0
Bread: 4.5
Meat: 4.0
Fat: 1.0

1. Process spinach, ricotta cheese, egg, green onions, garlic, seasonings, salt, and pepper in food processor until smooth; mix with ground beef and bread crumbs. Shape mixture into 8 to 12 meatballs. Combine meatballs and spaghetti sauce in slow cooker, covering meatballs with sauce. Cover and cook on low 5 to 6 hours. Serve on fettuccine.

Ziti with Eggplant Meatballs

Eggplant is a surprise ingredient in these fabulous meatballs!

6 servings

Eggplant Meatballs (recipe follows)
12 ounces ziti or other shaped pasta, cooked, warm
2–3 tablespoons olive oil
2 tablespoons drained capers
¼ cup chopped Italian parsley

1. Make Eggplant Meatballs. Toss ziti with oil, capers, and parsley; serve with meatballs.

Per Serving:
Calories: 560
% calories from fat: 26
Protein (g): 39.8
Carbohydrate (g): 63.3
Fat (g): 16
Saturated fat (g): 5.4
Cholesterol (mg): 149.5
Sodium (mg): 1337.7
Exchanges:
Milk: 0.0
Vegetable: 0.0
Fruit: 0.0
Bread: 4.0
Meat: 4.0
Fat: 1.0

Eggplant Meatballs

Makes 18

1 small eggplant (about 12 ounces), peeled, cubed
1½ pounds lean ground beef
½ cup each: grated Romano cheese (2 ounces), unseasoned
   dry bread crumbs
2 eggs
1½ teaspoons dried Italian seasoning
1 teaspoon salt
½ teaspoon pepper
1 jar (26 ounces) spaghetti sauce

1. Cook eggplant in 2 inches simmering water in medium saucepan until tender, about 10 minutes; drain, cool, and mash. Combine eggplant with remaining ingredients, except spaghetti sauce; shape into 18 meatballs. Combine meatballs and spaghetti sauce in slow cooker, covering meatballs with sauce. Cover and cook on high 3 to 4 hours.

Veal Meatballs with Sour-Cream Mushroom Sauce

Ground chicken, pork, or beef can be substituted for the veal in this recipe.

4 servings

8 ounces sliced mushrooms
Veal Meatballs (recipe follows)
½ cup chicken broth
1 cup reduced-fat sour cream
3 tablespoons cornstarch
Salt and pepper, to taste
8 ounces fettuccine, cooked, warm

Per Serving:
Calories: 650
% calories from fat: 30
Protein (g): 48.7
Carbohydrate (g): 63.6
Fat (g): 21
Saturated fat (g): 8.8
Cholesterol (mg): 262.4
Sodium (mg): 1052.4
Exchanges:
Milk: 0.0
Vegetable: 0.0
Fruit: 0.0
Bread: 4.0
Meat: 6.0
Fat: 0.5

1. Place ¾ of the mushrooms in bottom of slow cooker; top with meatballs and remaining mushrooms. Pour broth over; cover and cook on low 5 to 6 hours. Remove meatballs and keep warm. Stir combined sour cream and cornstarch into broth, stirring 2 to 3 minutes. Season to taste with salt and pepper. Serve meatballs and sauce over fettuccine.

Veal Meatballs

Makes 8 large meatballs

1½ pounds ground veal
¼ cup finely chopped green onions
1 clove garlic
2 eggs
¼ cup chicken broth or milk
½ cup unseasoned dry bread crumbs
1 teaspoon salt
¼ teaspoon pepper

1. Mix all ingredients; shape into 8 meatballs.

Fruit-Stuffed Pork Loin

Any desired dried fruit can be used in the fragrant filling.

6–8 servings

¾ cup pitted prunes
1 boneless pork loin roast (about 2 pounds)
½ cup chopped peeled apple
½ teaspoon each: dried marjoram and sage leaves
Salt and pepper, to taste
½ cup dry white wine or apple juice
2 tablespoons each: cornstarch, honey
¾ cup whole milk or light cream

Per Serving:
Calories: 326
% calories from fat: 25
Protein (g): 34.5
Carbohydrate (g): 23.9
Fat (g): 9.1
Saturated fat (g): 3.3
Cholesterol (mg): 86.2
Sodium (mg): 82.4
Exchanges:
Milk: 0.0
Vegetable: 0.0
Fruit: 1.5
Bread: 0.0
Meat: 4.0
Fat: 0.0

1. Soak prunes in hot water to cover until softened, 10 to 15 minutes. Drain well; chop coarsely. Push the handle of a long wooden spoon through the center of the roast to make an opening for the stuffing.
2. Combine prunes, apple, and herbs; push mixture through meat, using the handle of a wooden spoon. Sprinkle outside of roast lightly with salt and pepper; place meat thermometer in roast, making sure tip does not rest in stuffing.
3. Place pork and wine in slow cooker; cover and cook on low until temperature registers 160 degrees, about 3 hours. Remove meat to platter and keep warm; turn heat to high and cook 10 minutes. Stir in combined cornstarch, honey, and milk, stirring 2 to 3 minutes.

Pork Loin Braised in Milk

Pork is exceedingly tender and moist when roasted in milk. The milk will curdle; however, the juices can be strained, discarding the milk curds, to make a flavorful gravy.

8 servings

1 boneless pork loin roast (about 3 pounds)
Salt and pepper, to taste
½ cup whole milk
¼ cup dry white wine or milk
2 each: large rosemary and sage sprigs
2 cloves garlic, minced

Per Serving:
Calories: 279
% calories from fat: 45
Protein (g): 33.4
Carbohydrate (g): 1.4
Fat (g): 13.3
Saturated fat (g): 4.9
Cholesterol (mg): 109.2
Sodium (mg): 98
Exchanges:
Milk: 0.0
Vegetable: 0.0
Fruit: 0.0
Bread: 6.0
Meat: 0.0
Fat: 0.0

1. Sprinkle pork lightly with salt and pepper; insert meat thermometer in center of roast so tip is in center of meat. Place meat and remaining ingredients in slow cooker; cover and cook on low until meat thermometer registers 160 degrees, about 4 hours. Remove to serving platter. Strain broth, discarding milk curds and herbs; make gravy with broth or reserve for another use.

Note: To make gravy, measure strained broth and pour into small saucepan; heat to boiling. For every cup of broth, whisk in 2 tablespoons flour mixed with ¼ cup cold water, whisking until thickened, about 1 minute.

Pork Roast with Mango Chutney

Make the chutney in advance; it can be refrigerated for several weeks. It's also excellent served with chicken.

8 servings

½ cup finely chopped onion
½ cup chicken broth
1 boneless pork loin roast (about 3 pounds)
Paprika
Salt and pepper
Mango Chutney (recipe follows)

Per Serving:
Calories: 404
% calories from fat: 18
Protein (g): 38.2
Carbohydrate (g): 43
Fat (g): 8.1
Saturated fat (g): 2.9
Cholesterol (mg): 106.8
Sodium (mg): 163.5
Exchanges:
Milk: 0.0
Vegetable: 0.0
Fruit: 3.0
Bread: 4.0
Meat: 0.0
Fat: 0.0

1. Place onion and broth in slow cooker. Sprinkle pork lightly with paprika, salt, and pepper; insert meat thermometer in center of roast so tip is in center of meat. Place pork in slow cooker; cover and cook on low until meat thermometer registers

160 degrees, about 4 hours. Remove pork to serving platter and let stand, loosely covered with foil, 10 minutes. Make gravy with broth mixture or reserve for soup or another use. Serve pork with Mango Chutney.

Mango Chutney

Makes about 2 cups

3 cups chopped mango (about 3 mangoes)
1 cup packed light brown sugar
½ cup cider vinegar
¼ cup white raisins
2 teaspoons minced jalapeño chili
1½ tablespoons minced gingerroot
1 large clove garlic, minced
4 cardamom pods, crushed
1 small stick cinnamon
2 cloves
Salt, to taste

1. Combine all ingredients in slow cooker; cover and cook on high 3½ hours. Uncover and cook until thickened to desired consistency, about 2 hours. Cool; refrigerate. Season to taste with salt.

Note: To make gravy, measure broth mixture and pour into small saucepan; heat to boiling. For every cup of broth mixture, whisk in 2 tablespoons flour mixed with ¼ cup cold water, whisking until thickened, about 1 minute.

Pork Loin with Mustard Sauce

This pork loin cooks to perfect doneness in about 4 hours and can be carved at the dinner table. The mustard sauce is superb!

8 servings

1 cup chopped onion
½ cup chicken broth
1 boneless pork loin roast (about 3 pounds)
Paprika
Salt and pepper
Mustard Sauce (recipe follows)

1. Place onion and broth in slow cooker. Sprinkle pork lightly with paprika, salt, and pepper; insert meat thermometer in center of roast so tip is in center of

Per Serving:
Calories: 359
% calories from fat: 22
Protein (g): 39.4
Carbohydrate (g): 28
Fat (g): 8.7
Saturated fat (g): 2.5
Cholesterol (mg): 170
Sodium (mg): 150.8
Exchanges:
Milk: 0.0
Vegetable: 0.0
Fruit: 0.0
Bread: 2.0
Meat: 4.0
Fat: 0.0

meat. Place pork in slow cooker; cover and cook on low until meat thermometer registers 160 degrees, about 4 hours. Remove pork to serving platter and let stand, loosely covered with foil, 10 minutes. Strain broth and onions; spoon onions around pork. Reserve the broth for soup or another use. Serve pork with Mustard Sauce.

Mustard Sauce

Makes about 1½ cups

1 cup sugar
¼ cup dry mustard
1 tablespoon flour
½ cup cider vinegar
2 eggs
1 tablespoon margarine or butter

1. Mix sugar, dry mustard, and flour in small saucepan; whisk in vinegar and eggs. Cook over low heat until thickened, about 10 minutes; stir in margarine.

Variations
Roast Pork with Marmalade Sauce—Make recipe above, omitting onion and Mustard Sauce; reserve broth another use. For Marmalade Sauce: Heat 1½ cups orange marmalade, 2 tablespoons margarine and 2 tablespoons orange liqueur or water in small saucepan until hot; serve with pork.
Pork Loin with Onion Gravy—Make recipe as above, omitting Mustard Sauce. Measure broth mixture and heat to boiling in medium saucepan. For each cup broth mixture, stir in combined 2 tablespoons flour combined with ¼ cup cold water or half-and-half, stirring until thickened, about 1 minute. Season to taste with salt and pepper; serve gravy with pork.
Pork Loin with Gingered Tomato Relish— Make recipe as above, omitting Mustard Sauce. Strain broth mixture, reserving broth for soup or another use. To make Gingered Tomato Relish: Heat reserved onions, 1½ cups chopped tomato, ½ cup each finely chopped zucchini and carrot, and 1 tablespoon minced gingerroot in medium skillet, covered, over medium-high heat until tomatoes are soft and mixture is bubbly, 3 to 4 minutes. Simmer rapidly, uncovered, until excess liquid is gone, about 5 minutes. Season to taste with salt and pepper; serve relish with pork.
Pork Loin with Cranberry Coulis—Make recipe as above, omitting Mustard Sauce and onion and reserving broth for soup or another use. To make Cranberry Coulis, heat 1½ cups fresh or frozen cranberries, 1 cup orange juice, ¼ cup sugar and 2–3 tablespoons honey to boiling in medium saucepan; reduce heat and simmer, covered, until cranberries are tender, 5 to 8 minutes. Process in food processor or blender until almost smooth. Serve coulis with pork.

Pork Loin with Brandied Cherry Sauce—Make recipe as above, omitting Mustard Sauce and onion and reserving broth for soup or another use. To make Brandied Cherry Sauce: Mix 2 tablespoons sugar, 2 teaspoons cornstarch, ¼ teaspoon ground allspice, and ½ cup cold water in medium saucepan; stir in 1 cup fresh or frozen, thawed pitted dark sweet cherries. Heat to boiling, stirring until thickened, about 1 minute. Stir in 1 tablespoon brandy or ½ teaspoon brandy extract; season to taste with lemon juice. Serve sauce with pork.

Pork Shoulder Roast with Noodles

This pork roast cooks to "falling-apart tenderness," perfect for Savory Herb-Rubbed Pork, Teriyaki Pork, or Pork Tacos (see variations below).

8 servings

1 cup each: chopped onion, chicken broth
1 boneless pork shoulder roast (about 3 pounds)
Salt and pepper
3 tablespoons cornstarch
⅓ cup water
4–6 cups cooked noodles or rice, warm

Per Serving:
Calories: 378
% calories from fat: 35
Protein (g): 36.9
Carbohydrate (g): 22.1
Fat (g): 14
Saturated fat (g): 4.9
Cholesterol (mg): 138
Sodium (mg): 220
Exchanges:
Milk: 0.0
Vegetable: 0.0
Fruit: 0.0
Bread: 1.5
Meat: 5.0
Fat: 0.0

1. Place onion and broth in slow cooker. Sprinkle pork lightly with salt and pepper and place in slow cooker; cover and cook on low 7 to 8 hours. Remove pork and shred.
2. Turn slow cooker to high; cook 10 minutes. Stir in combined cornstarch and water, stirring 2 to 3 minutes. Return pork to slow cooker and toss; serve over noodles or rice.

Variations
Savory Herb-Rubbed Pork—Make recipe as above, adding 1 cup sliced green bell pepper and omitting salt and pepper. Rub roast with 1 package (1.06 ounces) zesty herb marinade mix. Serve pork and broth mixture over noodles or rice, or use for sandwiches in buns.

Teriyaki Pork—Make recipe as above through step 1, omitting cornstarch, water, and noodles. Mix shredded pork with ½ to 1 package (1.06 ounces) teriyaki marinade mix, adding enough broth and onion mixture to moisten pork. Serve on noodles or rice, or roll up in warm flour tortillas.

Pork Tacos—Make recipe as above through step 1, omitting onion, cornstarch, water, and noodles. Mix shredded pork with ½ to 1 package (1.25 ounces) taco seasoning mix, adding enough broth to moisten pork. Serve in warm taco shells or flour tortillas with shredded lettuce, chopped tomato and avocado, and sour cream.

Herbed Pork Chops

Enjoy the convenience of canned soup in making these delectable pork chops.

4 servings

4 boneless loin pork chops (4 ounces each)
1 teaspoon dried thyme leaves
Salt and pepper, to taste
1 small onion, halved, sliced
4 green onions, thinly sliced
1 small rib celery, sliced
1 can (10 ounces) 98% fat-free cream of celery soup
½ cup 2% reduced fat milk

Per Serving:
Calories: 243
% calories from fat: 42
Protein (g): 24.1
Carbohydrate (g): 10.2
Fat (g): 11
Saturated fat (g): 4.1
Cholesterol (mg): 75.9
Sodium (mg): 531
Exchanges:
Milk: 0.0
Vegetable: 0.0
Fruit: 0.0
Bread: 0.5
Meat: 3.0
Fat: 1.0

1. Sprinkle pork chops with thyme, salt, and pepper; place in slow cooker, adding onions and celery. Pour combined soup and milk over; cover and cook on low 4 to 5 hours.

Variation

Portobello Pork Chops—Make recipe as above, omitting small onion and celery, adding 1 cup chopped portobello mushrooms, and substituting 98% fat-free cream of mushroom soup for the celery soup.

Pork Chops with Apricot-Hoisin Sauce

The easiest of dinners, slow cooker-style! Serve over rice, if you like.

6 servings

6 boneless loin pork chops (about 4 ounces each)
Salt and pepper, to taste
¼ cup chicken broth
½ cup apricot preserves
3 tablespoons hoisin sauce
2–3 teaspons cornstarch
2 tablespoons finely chopped cilantro or parsley

Per Serving:
Calories: 271
% calories from fat: 31
Protein (g): 22.3
Carbohydrate (g): 22.8
Fat (g): 9
Saturated fat (g): 3.2
Cholesterol (mg): 72.3
Sodium (mg): 239
Exchanges:
Milk: 0.0
Vegetable: 0.0
Fruit: 0.0
Bread: 1.5
Meat: 3.0
Fat: 0.0

1. Sprinkle pork chops very lightly with salt and pepper and place in slow cooker; add chicken broth. Cover and cook on low until pork chops are tender, about 3 hours; remove pork chops and keep warm. Turn heat to high and cook 10 minutes; stir combined remaining ingredients into broth, stirring 2 to 3 minutes. Serve sauce over pork chops.

Pork Chops with Sage

Sage is a perfect complement to pork and mustard adds a finishing accent.

4 servings

4 boneless loin pork chops (about 4 ounces each)
¼ cup chopped onion
½ cup each: chicken broth, dry white wine or
   chicken broth
1 tablespoon cornstarch
2 tablespoons each: honey, water
1–2 tablespoons each: Dijon mustard, lemon juice
Salt and pepper, to taste

Per Serving:
Calories: 242
% calories from fat: 36
Protein (g): 22.1
Carbohydrate (g): 10.8
Fat (g): 8.7
Saturated fat (g): 3.1
Cholesterol (mg): 72.3
Sodium (mg): 269
Exchanges:
Milk: 0.0
Vegetable: 0.0
Fruit: 0.0
Bread: 0.5
Meat: 3.0
Fat: 0.0

1. Combine pork chops, onion, broth, and wine in slow cooker; cover and cook on low until pork chops are tender, 3 to 4 hours. Remove pork chops and keep warm; turn heat to high. Stir combined cornstarch, honey and water into broth; cook, uncovered, until juices are a thin sauce consistency, about 5 minutes. Season to taste with mustard, lemon juice, salt, and pepper.

Pork Stewed with Prunes

A simple dish with rich flavor.

6–8 servings

2 pounds boneless pork loin, cubed (1½-inch)
8 ounces pitted prunes
1½ cups chicken broth
½ cup dry white wine or chicken broth
Grated zest of 1 lemon
2 tablespoons cornstarch
¼ cup cold water
1–2 teaspoons lemon juice
Salt and pepper, to taste
4 cups cooked rice or couscous, warm

Per Serving:
Calories: 462
% calories from fat: 17
Protein (g): 36.9
Carbohydrate (g): 54.8
Fat (g): 8.6
Saturated fat (g): 2.9
Cholesterol (mg): 83.8
Sodium (mg): 311
Exchanges:
Milk: 0.0
Vegetable: 0.0
Fruit: 0.5
Bread: 3.0
Meat: 4.0
Fat: 0.0

1. Combine all ingredients, except cornstarch, water, lemon juice, salt, pepper, and rice, in slow cooker; cover and cook on low 6 to 8 hours. Turn heat to high and cook 10 minutes; stir in combined cornstarch and water, stirring 2 to 3 minutes. Season to taste with lemon juice, salt, and pepper; serve over rice.

Variation

Pork Stewed with Pears and Apricots—Make recipe as above, substituting 4 ounces each dried pears and apricots for the prunes, orange juice for the wine, and 2 tablespoons grated orange zest for the lemon zest.

Country-Style Ribs with Plum Sauce

Plum sauce and honey make these ribs sweet eating! If you want, ribs can be browned under the broiler before serving.

4 servings

3 pounds country-style pork ribs, cut into servings
1 jar (7 ounces) plum sauce
½ cup honey
1 tablespoon soy sauce
2 tablespoons cornstarch
¼ cup orange juice
Salt and pepper, to taste

Per Serving:
Calories: 353
% calories from fat: 25
Protein (g): 25.7
Carbohydrate (g): 40.6
Fat (g): 9.7
Saturated fat (g): 3.5
Cholesterol (mg): 80.6
Sodium (mg): 404
Exchanges:
Milk: 0.0
Vegetable: 0.0
Fruit: 3.0
Bread: 0.0
Meat: 3.0
Fat: 0.0

1. Arrange ribs in slow cooker; pour combined plum sauce, honey, and soy sauce over ribs. Cover and cook on low 6 to 8 hours. Remove ribs to platter; keep warm. Turn heat to high and cook 10 minutes; stir in combined cornstarch and orange juice, stirring 2 to 3 minutes. Season it with salt and pepper; serve sauce over ribs.

Orange-Honey Ham

This easy-to-make ham is subtly flavored with orange and honey!

8–10 servings

3 pounds boneless smoked ham
⅓ cup each orange juice, honey
½ teaspoon ground cloves
1½ tablespoons cornstarch
¼ cup cold water
2 tablespoons dry sherry (optional)

Per Serving:
Calories: 374
% calories from fat: 23
Protein (g): 42.9
Carbohydrate (g): 28.5
Fat (g): 9.4
Saturated fat (g): 3.1
Cholesterol (mg): 93.6
Sodium (mg): 2259
Exchanges:
Milk: 0.0
Vegetable: 0.0
Fruit: 0.0
Bread: 2.0
Meat: 4.0
Fat: 0.0

1. Place meat thermometer in ham so tip is near the center; place in slow cooker. Add remaining ingredients, except cornstarch, water, and sherry. Cover and cook on low until temperature registers 155 degrees, about 3 hours. Remove ham to platter and keep warm.

2. Measure 1½ cups broth into saucepan and heat to boiling; whisk in combined cornstarch, water, and sherry, whisking until thickened, about 1 minute. Serve sauce over ham.

Roast Chicken with Cranberry-Orange Relish

Using a meat thermometer assures that the chicken will be cooked to the correct doneness for perfect slicing. The Cranberry-Orange Relish recipe makes an ample amount; it can be made in advance and refrigerated for several weeks.

6 servings

1 whole chicken (about 3 pounds)
Paprika
Salt and pepper
½ cup chicken broth
1½ cups Cranberry-Orange Relish (recipe follows)

Per Serving:
Calories: 561
% calories from fat: 44
Protein (g): 32
Carbohydrate (g): 46.5
Fat (g): 27.7
Saturated fat (g): 7.5
Cholesterol (mg): 120.9
Sodium (mg): 140
Exchanges:
Milk: 0.0
Vegetable: 0.0
Fruit: 3.0
Bread: 0.0
Meat: 4.0
Fat: 3.0

1. Make foil handles (see p. vi) and fit into slow cooker. Sprinkle chicken lightly with paprika, salt, and pepper; insert meat thermometer so tip is in thickest part of inside thigh, not touching bone. Place chicken in slow cooker; add broth. Cover and cook on low until thermometer registers 175 degrees, 4 to 5 hours. Remove chicken, using foil handles; place on serving platter and cover loosely with foil. Reserve broth for soup or another use. Serve chicken with Cranberry-Orange Relish.

Cranberry-Orange Relish

Makes about 4 cups

5 large navel oranges
1 cup water
3 cups sugar, divided
1 package (12 ounces) cranberries
½ cup coarsely chopped walnuts

1. Grate zest from 3 oranges; reserve. Peel oranges and cut into sections. Combine all ingredients in slow cooker; cover and cook on low 6 to 7 hours. If thicker consistency is desired, cook uncovered until thickened.

Roast Chicken with Mashed Potatoes and Gravy

You'll never taste a more delicious, moist, perfectly cooked chicken!

6 servings

1 whole chicken (about 3 pounds)
Paprika
Salt and pepper
½ cup chicken broth or water
¼ cup all-purpose flour
½ cup cold water
Salt and pepper, to taste
Real Mashed Potatoes (recipe follows)

Per Serving:
Calories: 550
% calories from fat: 49
Protein (g): 33.4
Carbohydrate (g): 35.8
Fat (g): 29.5
Saturated fat (g): 8.6
Cholesterol (mg): 119.9
Sodium (mg): 188
Exchanges:
Milk: 0.0
Vegetable: 0.0
Fruit: 0.0
Bread: 2.0
Meat: 4.0
Fat: 4.0

1. Make foil handles (see p. vi) and fit into slow cooker. Sprinkle chicken lightly with paprika, salt, and pepper; insert meat thermometer so tip is in thickest part of inside thigh, not touching bone. Place chicken in slow cooker; add broth. Cover and cook on low until thermometer registers 175 degrees, 4 to 5 hours. Remove chicken, using foil handles; place on serving platter and cover loosely with foil.
2. Pour broth into measuring cup; spoon off fat. Measure 2 cups broth into small saucepan and heat to boiling. Whisk in combined flour, whisking until thickened, about 1 minute. Season to taste with salt and pepper. Serve chicken with Real Mashed Potatoes and gravy.

Real Mashed Potatoes

6 servings

2 pounds Idaho potatoes, peeled, cooked, warm
⅓ cup each: 2% reduced-fat milk and sour cream
2 tablespoons margarine or butter
Salt and pepper, to taste

1. Mash potatoes or beat until smooth, adding milk, sour cream, and margarine; season to taste with salt and pepper.

Chicken Breasts with Vegetable Melange

Orange, rosemary, and fennel accent the root vegetables that top tender chicken breasts.

4 servings

4 skinless chicken breast halves (about 6 ounces each)
12 baby carrots
8 small red potatoes, quartered
8 ounces white or cremini mushrooms, quartered
3 cloves garlic, thinly sliced
1–2 teaspoons grated orange zest
1 teaspoon each: crushed fennel seeds, dried
  rosemary leaves
1 bay leaf
½ cup each: chicken broth, orange juice, dry white
  wine or chicken broth
2 tablespoons orange liqueur (optional)
1 tablespoon cornstarch
2 tablespoons water
Salt and pepper, to taste

Per Serving:
Calories: 435.3
% calories from fat: 6
Protein (g): 46.6
Carbohydrate (g): 49.3
Fat (g): 2.9
Saturated fat (g): 0.7
Cholesterol (mg): 98.9
Sodium (mg): 258
Exchanges:
Milk: 0.0
Vegetable: 0.0
Fruit: 0.0
Bread: 3.0
Meat: 4.0
Fat: 0.0

1. Place all ingredients, except cornstarch, water, salt, and pepper in slow cooker. Cover and cook on low 6 to 8 hours; remove chicken and vegetables to serving platter and keep warm.

2. Measure 2 cups broth into small saucepan; whisk in combined cornstarch and water, whisking until thickened, about 1 minute. Season to taste with salt and pepper; serve gravy over vegetables and chicken breasts.

Sherried Chicken

A lovely dish for entertaining or for special family meals. Serve over an aromatic rice to absorb flavorful juices.

4 servings

¼ cup dry sherry
1 cup golden raisins
4 skinless chicken breast halves (about 6 ounces each)
½ cup coarsely chopped walnuts
1 tart cooking apple, peeled, chopped
1 small red onion, sliced
2 cloves garlic, minced
1 cup chicken broth
Salt and pepper, to taste

Per Serving:
Calories: 486
% calories from fat: 22
Protein (g): 44.6
Carbohydrate (g): 45.6
Fat (g): 12
Saturated fat (g): 1.5
Cholesterol (mg): 99.5
Sodium (mg): 456
Exchanges:
Milk: 0.0
Vegetable: 0.0
Fruit: 0.0
Bread: 3.0
Meat: 5.0
Fat: 0.0

1. Pour sherry over raisins in bowl; let stand 15 to 30 minutes. Place all ingredients, except salt and pepper, in slow cooker; cover and cook on high until chicken is tender, 3 to 4 hours. Season to taste with salt and pepper.

Mediterranean Chicken

Chicken breasts are topped with Mediterranean flavors in a flavorful tomato-based sauce.

4 servings

4 skinless chicken breast halves (about 6 ounces each)
1 can (16 ounces) petite-diced tomatoes, undrained
½ cup each: chicken broth, dry white wine or chicken broth
1 medium zucchini, sliced
¾ cup each: chopped onion, sliced fennel bulb
1 teaspoon dried oregano leaves
1 bay leaf
¼ cup pitted sliced Greek olives
1–2 teaspoons lemon juice
Salt and pepper, to taste
3 cups cooked rice

Per Serving:
Calories: 423
% calories from fat: 8
Protein (g): 44.8
Carbohydrate (g): 45.1
Fat (g): 3.7
Saturated fat (g): 0.8
Cholesterol (mg): 99
Sodium (mg): 798
Exchanges:
Milk: 0.0
Vegetable: 0.0
Fruit: 0.0
Bread: 1.5
Meat: 3.0
Fat: 0.0

1. Place all ingredients, except olives, lemon juice, salt, pepper, and rice, in slow cooker; cover and cook on low 6 to 8 hours, adding olives during last 30 minutes. Season to taste with lemon juice, salt, and pepper; discard bay leaf. Serve chicken and tomato mixture over rice.

Indonesian Chicken with Zucchini

You'll enjoy the subtle blending of coconut milk, gingerroot, garlic, cilantro, and cumin in this dish.

6 servings

3 large skinless chicken breasts (6 to 8 ounces each), halved
1 can (15 ounces) light coconut milk
¼ cup each: water, lemon juice
1 medium onion, finely chopped
1 clove garlic, minced
3 tablespoons minced gingerroot or 2 teaspoons ground ginger
2 teaspoons ground coriander
1 teaspoon ground cumin
1 pound zucchini, halved lengthwise, seeded, sliced
1 tablespoon cornstarch
2 tablespoons water
⅓ cup chopped cilantro
Salt and pepper, to taste
4 cups cooked rice, warm

Per Serving:
Calories: 339
% calories from fat: 16
Protein (g): 30.4
Carbohydrate (g): 39.5
Fat (g): 5.7
Saturated fat (g): 3
Cholesterol (mg): 65.7
Sodium (mg): 98
Exchanges:
Milk: 0.0
Vegetable: 1.0
Fruit: 0.0
Bread: 2.0
Meat: 3.0
Fat: 0.0

1. Place all ingredients, except zucchini, cornstarch, water, cilantro, salt, pepper, and rice, in slow cooker; cover and cook on low 3½ to 4 hours, adding zucchini during last 30 minutes. Remove chicken breasts and keep warm. Turn heat to high and cook 10 minutes; stir in combined cornstarch and 2 tablespoons water, stirring 2 to 3 minutes. Stir in cilantro; season to taste with salt and pepper. Serve chicken and broth over rice in shallow bowls.

Chicken Breasts with Figs

Figs and orange juice complement tender chicken breasts.

4 servings

4 skinless chicken breast halves (6 to 8 ounces each)
8 dried figs, quartered
2 tablespoons each: soy sauce, dry sherry
¾ cup orange juice
Grated zest of 1 orange
2 tablespoons each: cornstarch, cold water, honey
Salt and pepper, to taste
3 cups cooked rice, warm

Per Serving:
Calories: 461
% calories from fat: 5
Protein (g): 42.4
Carbohydrate (g): 63.3
Fat (g): 2.5
Saturated fat (g): 0.6
Cholesterol (mg): 94.5
Sodium (mg): 597
Exchanges:
Milk: 0.0
Vegetable: 0.0
Fruit: 0.0
Bread: 4.0
Meat: 4.0
Fat: 0.0

1. Place all ingredients, except cornstarch, water, honey, salt, pepper, and rice, in slow cooker; cover and cook on high 4 to 6 hours. Remove chicken and keep warm. Turn heat to high and cook 10 minutes; stir in combined cornstarch, water, and honey, stirring 2 to 3 minutes. Season to taste with salt and pepper. Serve chicken breasts and sauce over rice.

Chicken Mole

This easy mole sauce is made with canned chili beans!

4 servings

Mole Sauce (recipe follows)
4 skinless chicken breast halves (about 4 ounces each)
3 cups cooked rice, warm
Chopped cilantro, as garnish
½ cup reduced-fat sour cream

Per Serving:
Calories: 497
% calories from fat: 22
Protein (g): 38.5
Carbohydrate (g): 57.4
Fat (g): 12.2
Saturated fat (g): 4.5
Cholesterol (mg): 76.2
Sodium (mg): 544
Exchanges:
Milk: 0.0
Vegetable: 0.0
Fruit: 0.0
Bread: 4.0
Meat: 4.0
Fat: 0.0

1. Spoon 1 cup Mole Sauce into slow cooker; top with chicken breasts and remaining sauce. Cover and cook on low 4 to 6 hours. Serve over rice; sprinkle generously with cilantro and serve with sour cream.

Mole Sauce

Makes about 2½ cups

1 can (15 ounces) beans in hot chili sauce, undrained
½ cup coarsely chopped onion
2 cloves garlic
¼ cup tomato sauce
1 tablespoon Worcestershire sauce
½ teaspoon ground cinnamon
½ ounce unsweetened chocolate, finely chopped
¼ cup slivered almonds

1. Process all ingredients in food processor until smooth.

Chicken Divan

This rich, sherry-laced sauce nicely complements tender chicken breasts.

6 servings

Sauce Divan (recipe follows)
6 boneless, skinless chicken breast halves
   (3–4 ounces each), halved
3 cups broccoli florets and sliced stems
4 cups cooked brown rice, warm
Grated Parmesan cheese, as garnish
Paprika, as garnish

Per Serving:
Calories: 480
% calories from fat: 37
Protein (g): 27.4
Carbohydrate (g): 42.8
Fat (g): 19.6
Saturated fat (g): 8.8
Cholesterol (mg): 86.3
Sodium (mg): 174
Exchanges:
Milk: 0.0
Vegetable: 0.0
Fruit: 0.0
Bread: 3.0
Meat: 3.0
Fat: 2.0

1. Spoon 1 cup Sauce Divan into slow cooker; top with chicken and remaining sauce. Cover and cook on low 4 to 5 hours, stirring in broccoli during last 30 minutes. Serve over rice; sprinkle with Parmesan cheese and paprika.

Sauce Divan

3 tablespoons margarine or butter
¼ cup all-purpose flour
2½ cups half-and-half or light cream
¼ cup dry sherry or half-and-half
Salt and pepper, to taste

1. Melt margarine in medium saucepan; stir in flour and cook 1 to 2 minutes. Whisk in half-and-half and heat to boiling, whisking until thickened, about 1 minute. Whisk in sherry; season to taste with salt and pepper.

Apricot-Glazed Cornish Hens

Cornish hens, cooked to moist tenderness, are topped with an herb-infused apricot sauce.

4 servings

2 frozen thawed Cornish hens (about 1¼ pounds
  each)
Paprika
Salt and pepper
⅓ cup chicken broth
Apricot Glaze (recipe follows)
2 tablespoons cornstarch
¼ cup water

Per Serving:
Calories: 315
% calories from fat: 12
Protein (g): 26.2
Carbohydrate (g): 44.1
Fat (g): 4.4
Saturated fat (g): 1.1
Cholesterol (mg): 116.6
Sodium (mg): 94
Exchanges:
Milk: 0.0
Vegetable: 0.0
Fruit: 3.0
Bread: 0.0
Meat: 3.0
Fat: 0.0

1. Sprinkle Cornish hens with paprika, salt, and
pepper; place in slow cooker and add broth. Cover
and cook on low until legs move freely, 5½ to 6 hours, brushing with
Apricot Glaze 2 to 3 times during cooking. Remove hens to serving platter
and cover loosely with aluminum foil.
2. Stir any remaining Apricot Glaze into slow cooker; cover and cook on
high 10 minutes. Stir in combined cornstarch and water, stirring 2 to 3
minutes; spoon sauce over Cornish hens.

Apricot Glaze

Makes about ¾ cup

¾ cup apricot preserves
2 tablespoons orange juice
Finely shredded zest from ½ orange
½ teaspoon each: dried thyme and rosemary leaves

1. Mix all ingredients.

Turkey Meat Loaf

The meat loaf can also be formed into a loaf in the slow cooker; see Just Plain Meat Loaf (see p. 460) for directions.

6–8 servings

1½ pounds ground turkey breast
½ cup each: finely chopped onion, red or green pepper
1 egg
½ cup each: chicken broth, unseasoned dry bread crumbs
3 tablespoons steak sauce
1 teaspoon each: dried thyme leaves, salt
½ teaspoon pepper
½ cup chili sauce

Per Serving:
Calories: 204
% calories from fat: 14
Protein (g): 29.3
Carbohydrate (g): 14.1
Fat (g): 3
Saturated fat (g): 0.9
Cholesterol (mg): 80.5
Sodium (mg): 1010
Exchanges:
Milk: 0.0
Vegetable: 0.0
Fruit: 0.0
Bread: 1.0
Meat: 3.0
Fat: 0.0

1. Mix all ingredients, except chili sauce; pack mixture
into greased 9 x 5-inch loaf pan and top with chili sauce. Insert meat thermometer so tip is in center of meatloaf. Place pan on rack in 6-quart slow cooker; cover and cook on low until thermometer registers 170 degrees, 6 to 7 hours.

Poached Salmon with Lemon-Caper Sauce

Slow cooking gives this delicious salmon extra moistness.

Makes 4 servings

½ cup each: water, dry white wine
1 thin slice yellow onion
1 bay leaf
½ teaspoon salt
4 salmon steaks (about 4 ounces each)
Lemon-Caper Sauce (recipe follows)

Per Serving:
Calories: 703
% calories from fat: 26
Protein (g): 47.7
Carbohydrate (g): 75.4
Fat (g): 19.5
Saturated fat (g): 3.6
Cholesterol (mg): 66.3
Sodium (mg): 3137
Exchanges:
Milk: 0.0
Vegetable: 0.0
Fruit: 0.0
Bread: 5.0
Meat: 3.0
Fat: 2.0

1. Combine all ingredients, except salmon and
Lemon-Caper Sauce, in slow cooker; cover and cook on high 20 minutes. Add salmon; cover and cook on high until salmon is tender and flakes with a fork, about 20 minutes. Serve with Lemon-Caper Sauce.

Lemon-Caper Sauce

2–3 tablespoons margarine or butter
3 tablespoons flour
1 can (14½ ounces) reduced-sodium fat-free chicken broth
2–3 teaspoons lemon juice
3 tablespoons capers
¼ teaspoon salt
⅛ teaspoon white pepper

1. Melt margarine in small saucepan; stir in flour and cook over medium heat 1 minute. Whisk in chicken broth and lemon juice; heat to boiling, whisking until thickened, about 1 minute. Stir in capers, salt, and white pepper.

Salmon Loaf with Cucumber Sauce

Salmon loaf, always a favorite, makes a perfect lunch or light dinner.

4 servings

1 can (7½ ounces each) salmon, drained
1 cup fresh whole-wheat bread crumbs
¼ cup each: chopped green onions, milk
1 egg
2 tablespoons each: lemon juice, capers
1 tablespoon dried dill weed
½ teaspoon salt
¼ teaspoon pepper
Cucumber Sauce (recipe follows)

Per Serving:
Calories: 236
% calories from fat: 33.6
Protein (g): 27.8
Carbohydrate (g): 10.9
Fat (g): 8.7
Saturated fat (g): 2.6
Cholesterol (mg): 97.5
Sodium (mg): 1066
Exchanges:
Milk: 0.0
Vegetable: 0.0
Fruit: 0.0
Bread: 1.0
Meat: 3.0
Fat: 0.0

1. Make foil handles (see p. vi) and fit into slow cooker. Combine all ingredients, except Cucumber Sauce; form into loaf in bottom of slow cooker. Cover and cook on low 4 to 5 hours; remove loaf, using foil handles. Slice and serve with Cucumber Sauce.

Cucumber Sauce

Makes about 1 cup

½ cup each: reduced-fat plain yogurt, chopped cucumber
½ teaspoon dill weed
Salt and white pepper, to taste

1. Mix all ingredients.

Halibut Fillets in Romaine Leaves

An attractive presentation for a delicious fish dish!

4 servings

1 cup dry white wine or chicken broth
8–12 large romaine leaves
4 halibut steaks (4 ounces each)
1 teaspoon bouquet garni or dried tarragon leaves
Salt and pepper, to taste
½ cup thinly sliced spinach

Per Serving:
Calories: 179
% calories from fat: 17
Protein (g): 24.1
Carbohydrate (g): 2.5
Fat (g): 2.7
Saturated fat (g): 0.3
Cholesterol (mg): 36.2
Sodium (mg): 69
Exchanges:
Milk: 0.0
Vegetable: 0.0
Fruit: 0.0
Bread: 0.0
Meat: 3.0
Fat: 0.0

1. Pour wine into slow cooker; cover and cook on high 20 minutes. Cut large center vein from romaine leaves, leaving leaves intact; immerse in boiling water just until leaves are wilted, about 30 seconds. Drain well.
2. Sprinkle fish with herbs; sprinkle lightly with salt, pepper, and spinach. Wrap fish in romaine leaves, using 2 to 3 leaves for each; place, seam sides down, in slow cooker. Cover and cook on high until fish is tender and flakes with a fork, about 1 hour.

Red Snapper with Caramelized Garlic Sauce

The garlic sauce is equally delicious with salmon or any firm fleshed white fish, such as halibut or haddock.

4 servings

1 red snapper fillet (about 1¼ pounds)
Salt and pepper, to taste
¼–½ cup clam juice or vegetable broth
Caramelized Garlic Sauce (recipe follows)

Per Serving:
Calories: 181
% calories from fat: 25
Protein (g): 30.2
Carbohydrate (g): 4.7
Fat (g): 5.2
Saturated fat (g): 0.7
Cholesterol (mg): 35.5
Sodium (mg): 282
Exchanges:
Milk: 0.0
Vegetable: 0.0
Fruit: 0.0
Bread: 0.0
Meat: 4.0
Fat: 0.0

1. Line slow cooker with aluminum foil or make foil handles (see p. vi). Sprinkle fish lightly with salt and pepper; place in slow cooker. Add clam juice; cover and cook on high until fish is tender and flakes with a fork, about 30 minutes. Remove fish, using foil handles; serve with Caramelized Garlic Sauce.

Caramelized Garlic Sauce

Makes 1 cup

12 cloves garlic, peeled
1–2 tablespoons olive oil
¾ cup chicken broth, divided
2 tablespoons dry white wine (optional)
1 tablespoon each: flour, finely chopped parsley
Salt and white pepper, to taste

1. Cook garlic in oil in medium skillet, covered, over medium to medium-low heat until tender, about 10 minutes. Cook, uncovered, over medium-low to low heat until garlic cloves are golden brown, about 10 minutes. Mash cloves slightly with a fork. Add combined broth, wine, and flour; heat to boiling, stirring until thickened, about 1 minute. Stir in parsley; season to taste with salt, and pepper.

Tuna-Stuffed Spaghetti Squash

The spaghetti squash can also be cooked plain in the slow cooker; fluff strands of squash with a fork and toss with melted margarine and herbs or spaghetti sauce.

4 servings

1 can (14 ounces) diced tomatoes, undrained
½ cup sliced ripe olives
2 cans (6 ounces each) white tuna in water, drained, flaked
1 teaspoon dried oregano leaves
Salt and pepper, to taste
1 small to medium spaghetti squash (2 to 2½ pounds), halved lengthwise, seeded
½ cup water
¼ cup (1 ounce) shredded Parmesan cheese

Per Serving:
Calories: 269
% calories from fat: 30
Protein (g): 25.6
Carbohydrate (g): 17.3
Fat (g): 8.6
Saturated fat (g): 2.9
Cholesterol (mg): 43.3
Sodium (mg): 1038.5
Exchanges:
Milk: 0.0
Vegetable: 0.0
Fruit: 0.0
Bread: 1.0
Meat: 3.0
Fat: 0.0

1. Combine tomatoes and liquid, olives, tuna, oregano, salt, and pepper; spoon into squash halves and place in slow cooker. Add water; cover and cook on high until squash is fork-tender, 3 to 4 hours on high or 6 to 8 hours on low. Fluff strands of squash with a fork, combining with tuna mixture. Sprinkle with Parmesan cheese.

Macaroni-Tomato Casserole

LO *Yummy comfort food, any time!*

6 servings

8 ounces small elbow macaroni, cooked
1 can (16 ounces) petite-diced tomatoes, drained
½ cup chopped onion
2 cups reduced-fat evaporated milk
1 tablespoon cornstarch
3 eggs, lightly beaten
½ cup (2 ounces) grated Parmesan cheese
½ teaspoon each: ground cinnamon and nutmeg, salt
Paprika, as garnish

Per Serving:
Calories: 312
% calories from fat: 33
Protein (g): 14
Carbohydrate (g): 38.2
Fat (g): 11.5
Saturated fat (g): 4.3
Cholesterol (mg): 119.8
Sodium (mg): 617
Exchanges:
Milk: 0.0
Vegetable: 0.0
Fruit: 0.0
Bread: 2.5
Meat: 1.0
Fat: 1.5

1. Combine macaroni, tomatoes, and onion in slow cooker. Mix remaining ingredients, except paprika, and pour over macaroni mixture. Cover and cook on low until custard is set, about 3 hours; sprinkle with paprika.

Ultimate Mac 'n Cheese

LO *A combination of four cheeses makes this the best mac 'n' cheese ever!*

8 servings

3 cups whole milk
⅓ cup all-purpose flour
1 cup (4 ounces) each: shredded reduced-fat
   mozzarella and Cheddar cheese, crumbled blue
   cheese
½ cup (2 ounces) Parmesan cheese, divided
1 pound ziti or penne, cooked al dente

Per Serving:
Calories: 439
% calories from fat: 31
Protein (g): 22
Carbohydrate (g): 52.1
Fat (g): 14.5
Saturated fat (g): 8.9
Cholesterol (mg): 43.6
Sodium (mg): 673
Exchanges:
Milk: 0.0
Vegetable: 0.0
Fruit: 0.0
Bread: 3.5
Meat: 2.0
Fat: 2.0

1. Mix milk and flour until smooth in large bowl; add remaining ingredients, except ¼ cup Parmesan cheese and ziti. Mix in ziti and spoon into slow cooker; sprinkle with remaining ¼ cup Parmesan cheese. Cover and cook on low 3 hours.

Tuna-Noodle Casserole

Comfort food at its finest! It's important not to overcook the noodles.

6 servings

1 can (10 ounces) 98% fat-free cream of mushroom soup
¾ cup 2% reduced-fat milk
½ cup reduced-fat mayonnaise
1 cup (4 ounces) shredded reduced-fat processed cheese
⅓ cup each: chopped celery, green bell pepper, finely chopped onion
Salt and pepper
6 ounces medium egg noodles, cooked al dente
2 cans (7 ounces each) white tuna in water, drained
½ cup frozen, thawed peas
1–2 tablespoons margarine or butter
⅓ cup each: fresh bread crumbs, slivered almonds

Per Serving:
Calories: 423
% calories from fat: 39
Protein (g): 27.2
Carbohydrate (g): 36.3
Fat (g): 18.3
Saturated fat (g): 4.6
Cholesterol (mg): 68.3
Sodium (mg): 1183
Exchanges:
Milk: 0.0
Vegetable: 0.0
Fruit: 0.0
Bread: 2.5
Meat: 3.0
Fat: 1.5

1. Mix soup, milk, mayonnaise, cheese, celery, bell pepper, and onion in slow cooker; season to taste with salt and pepper. Mix in noodles and tuna; cover and cook on low 4 to 5 hours, adding peas during last 30 minutes.
2. Melt margarine in small skillet over medium heat; mix in bread crumbs and almonds, cooking until browned, about 5 minutes. Sprinkle over tuna mixture.

Pasta Bolognese

Bolognese sauce is no doubt the favorite of pasta sauces—enjoy this savory and healthful version!

6 servings

1 pound lean ground beef
¼ cup each: chopped onion, carrot, celery
3 cloves garlic, minced
1½ teaspoons dried Italian seasoning
⅛ teaspoon ground nutmeg
1 can (8 ounces) each: tomato sauce, undrained, diced tomatoes
¼ cup dry red wine or tomato juice
½ teaspoon salt
¼ teaspoon pepper
12 ounces spaghetti, cooked, warm

Per Serving:
Calories: 361
% of calories from fat: 16
Fat (gm): 6.2
Saturated fat (gm): 2.2
Cholesterol (mg): 28.2
Sodium (mg): 287
Protein (gm): 24.6
Carbohydrate (gm): 50.2
Exchanges:
Milk: 0.0
Vegetable: 1.0
Fruit: 0.0
Bread: 3.0
Meat: 2.0
Fat: 0.0

1. Cook ground beef in lightly greased medium saucepan over medium heat until browned, 5 to 8 minutes, crumbling with a fork. Combine ground beef and remaining ingredients, except spaghetti, in slow cooker. Cover and cook on low 6 to 7 hours. If thicker consistency is desired, cook uncovered, turning heat to high, during last 30 minutes. Serve sauce over spaghetti.

Pasta with Fresh Tomato-Herb Sauce

V *Prepare and enjoy this dish when garden tomatoes are at peak ripeness.*

6 servings

5 cups chopped tomatoes
½ cup each: finely chopped onion, dry red wine or water
2 tablespoons each: tomato paste, minced garlic
1 tablespoon sugar
2 bay leaves
2 teaspoons dried basil leaves
1 teaspoon dried thyme leaves
⅛ teaspoon crushed red pepper
Salt, to taste
12 ounces flat or shaped pasta, cooked, warm

Per Serving:
Calories: 278
% calories from fat: 4
Protein (g): 13
Carbohydrate (g): 55
Fat (g): 1.3
Saturated fat (g): 0.2
Cholesterol (mg): 0
Sodium (mg): 56
Exchanges:
Milk: 0.0
Vegetable: 2.0
Fruit: 0.0
Bread: 3.0
Meat: 0.0
Fat: 0.0

1. Combine all ingredients, except salt and pasta, in slow cooker; cover and cook on low 6 to 7 hours. If thicker consistency is desired, cook uncovered, on high, during last 30 minutes. Serve sauce over pasta.

Risi Bisi

v *Opinions vary as to whether Risi Bisi is a risotto or a thick soup. If you agree with the latter definition, use an additional ½ to 1 cup of broth to make the mixture a thick soup consistency.*

4 entrée servings

3 cups vegetable broth
1 small onion, chopped
3 cloves garlic, minced
1½ cups arborio rice
2 teaspoons dried basil leaves
8 ounces frozen, thawed petite peas
¼–½ cup (1–2 ounces) grated Parmesan cheese
Salt and pepper, to taste

Per Serving:
Calories: 407
% of calories from fat: 6
Fat (gm): 2.5
Saturated fat (gm): 1.3
Cholesterol (mg): 4.9
Sodium (mg): 291
Protein (gm): 12.2
Carbohydrate (gm): 82.1
Exchanges:
Milk: 0.0
Vegetable: 1.0
Fruit: 0.0
Bread: 5.0
Meat: 0
Fat: 0.5

1. Heat broth to boiling in small saucepan; pour into slow cooker. Add remaining ingredients, except peas, Parmesan cheese, salt, and pepper; cover and cook on high until rice is al dente and liquid is almost absorbed, about 1¼ hours, adding peas the last 15 minutes (watch carefully so rice does not overcook). Stir in cheese; season to taste with salt and pepper.

Variations
Chicken Risotto—Make recipe as above, substituting 1 teaspoon dried marjoram leaves for the basil and Asiago cheese for the Parmesan cheese, and adding 1 chopped medium tomato. Add 1½ cups cooked, cubed chicken breast with the peas.
Porcini Risotto—Place ¼ to ½ ounce dried porcini or other dried mushrooms in bowl and pour 1 cup boiling water over; let stand until softened, about 15 minutes. Drain, reserving liquid. Make recipe as above, substituting reserved porcini liquid for 1 cup of the broth, 1 chopped small tomato for 4 ounces of the peas, and ½ teaspoon each dried sage and thyme leaves for the basil.
Broccoli, and Pine Nut Risotto—Make recipe as above, substituting 1 teaspoon dried Italian seasoning for the basil and 1 cup small broccoli florets for the peas. Add ¼ cup each raisins and toasted pine nuts with the broccoli during last 20 minutes of cooking time.

Winter Vegetable Risotto

L

*Arborio rice is a short-grain rice grown in the Arborio region of Italy. It's espe-
cially suited for making risotto, as it cooks to a wonderful creaminess.*

4 entrée servings

3 cups vegetable broth
1 small onion, chopped
3 cloves garlic, minced
1 cup sliced cremini or white mushrooms
1 teaspoon each: dried rosemary and thyme leaves
1½ cups arborio rice
1 cup each: halved small Brussels sprouts,
   peeled cubed sweet potato
¼ cup (1 ounce) grated Parmesan cheese
Salt and pepper, to taste

Per Serving:
Calories: 384
% of calories from fat: 8
Fat (gm): 3.3
Saturated fat (gm): 1.4
Cholesterol (mg): 4.9
Sodium (mg): 153
Protein (gm): 11
Carbohydrate (gm): 77.3
Exchanges:
Milk: 0.0
Vegetable: 3.0
Fruit: 0.0
Bread: 4.0
Meat: 0.0
Fat: 0.5

1. Heat broth to boiling in small saucepan; pour into slow cooker. Add remaining ingredients, except Parmesan cheese, salt, and pepper; cover and
cook on high until rice is al dente and liquid is almost absorbed, about 1¼
hours (watch carefully so rice does not overcook). Stir in cheese; season to
taste with salt and pepper.

Variations
Summer Vegetable Risotto—Make recipe as above, substituting 4 sliced
green onions for the chopped onion, 1 cup chopped plum tomatoes for
the mushrooms, and ¾ cup each cubed zucchini and summer yellow
squash for the Brussels sprouts and sweet potato.
Italian Sausage and Vegetable Risotto—Make recipe as above, substituting
1 cup each cubed butternut squash and cooked sliced Italian sausage for
the Brussels sprouts and sweet potato.
Shrimp Risotto—Make recipe as above, omitting rosemary, Brussels
sprouts, and sweet potato; add 1 chopped medium tomato. Stir in ½ cup
frozen thawed peas and 8 to 12 ounces peeled, deveined shrimp during the
last 15 minutes of cooking time.

Mushroom-Basil Egg Pie

LO

Perfect for brunch, this dish is like quiche without a crust!

4 servings

5 eggs
¼ cup all-purpose flour
⅓ teaspoon baking powder
¼ teaspoon each: salt, pepper
2 cups (8 ounces) shredded reduced-fat Monterey
    Jack cheese
1 cup reduced-fat large curd cottage cheese
1 cup sliced mushrooms
¾ teaspoon dried basil leaves

Per Serving:
Calories: 324
% calories from fat: 51
Protein (g): 29.8
Carbohydrate (g): 11
Fat (g): 19
Saturated fat (g): 9.3
Cholesterol (mg): 306.3
Sodium (mg): 984.2
Exchanges:
Milk: 0.0
Vegetable: 0.0
Fruit: 0.0
Bread: 0.5
Meat: 4.0
Fat: 0.5

1. Beat eggs in large bowl until foamy; mix in combined flour, baking powder, salt, and pepper. Mix in remaining ingredients and pour into greased slow cooker; cover and cook on low until set, about 4 hours. Serve from the slow cooker or remove crock, let stand on wire rack 5 minutes, and invert onto serving plate.

Note: This dish can also be cooked in a 1-quart soufflé dish or casserole; place on rack in 6-quart slow cooker and cook until set, about 4½ hours.

Seven-Layer Lasagne

L

It's easy to make lasagne using the "oven-ready" noodles and prepared sauce. This lasagne is delicate in texture, rich in flavor.

6 servings

3 cups tomato-basil spaghetti sauce
8 oven-ready lasagne noodles (4 ounces)
2½ cups each: reduced-fat ricotta cheese, shredded
    reduced-fat mozzarella cheese (10 ounces)
1 egg
1 teaspoon dried basil leaves
¼ cup (1 ounce) shredded Parmesan cheese

Per Serving:
Calories: 427
% calories from fat: 32
Protein (g): 32
Carbohydrate (g): 40.7
Fat (g): 15.5
Saturated fat (g): 8.2
Cholesterol (mg): 52.9
Sodium (mg): 1054
Exchanges:
Milk: 0.0
Vegetable: 0.0
Fruit: 0.0
Bread: 3.0
Meat: 3.0
Fat: 1.0

1. Spread ⅓ cup sauce on bottom of 9 x 5-inch bread pan. Top with 1 lasagne noodle and ⅓ cup each ricotta and mozzarella cheese. Repeat layers, ending with ⅓ cup sauce on top; sprinkle with Parmesan cheese. Place pan on rack in 6-quart slow cooker; cover and cook on low 4 hours. Remove pan and

cool on wire rack 10 minutes. The lasagne may look sunken in the center, but will become more even as it cools.

Variations

Sausage Lasagne—Make recipe above, adding ¼ cup each sautéed sliced mushrooms and cooked, crumbled Italian sausage between each layer.

Pasta Salad with Eggplant

Serve this pasta dish warm or at room temperature.

6 servings

1 medium eggplant (about 1 pound)
1 cup coarsely chopped tomato
3 green onions, sliced
2 tablespoons balsamic or red wine vinegar
1 tablespoon olive oil
1–2 teaspoons lemon juice
Salt and pepper, to taste
12 ounces whole-wheat spaghetti, cooked, room temperature
½ cup (2 ounces) shredded Parmesan cheese

Per Serving:
Calories: 221
% of calories from fat: 15
Fat (gm): 4
Saturated fat (gm): 0.7
Cholesterol (mg): 2
Sodium (mg): 242
Protein (gm): 16
Carbohydrate (gm): 32
Exchanges:
Milk: 0.0
Vegetable: 0.0
Fruit: 0.0
Bread: 2.0
Meat: 1.5
Fat: 0.0

1. Pierce eggplant 6 to 8 times with fork and place in slow cooker; cover and cook on low until tender, about 4 hours. Let stand until cool enough to handle. Cut eggplant in half; scoop out pulp and cut into ¾-inch pieces. Toss eggplant, tomato, onions, vinegar, oil, and lemon juice; season to taste with salt and pepper. Toss with pasta and Parmesan cheese.

Brunch Bread Pudding

Like a strata, this bread pudding is assembled in advance and refrigerated overnight before cooking. Make the pudding in a soufflé dish, or cook it directly in the crock.

6 servings

6 cups cubed stale French bread (½-inch)
½ cup each: chopped dried apricots, slivered almonds
3 eggs
½ cup sugar
2½ cups milk
1 teaspoon each: vanilla, ground cinnamon
Warm maple syrup

Per Serving:
Calories: 325
% calories from fat: 26
Protein (g): 13
Carbohydrate (g): 48.8
Fat (g): 9.7
Saturated fat (g): 2.6
Cholesterol (mg): 113.9
Sodium (mg): 286
Exchanges:
Milk: 0.0
Vegetable: 0.0
Fruit: 0.0
Bread: 1.5
Meat: 3.0
Fat: 0.0

1. Combine bread cubes, apricots, and almonds in large bowl. Beat eggs in large bowl until thick and lemon colored, about 5 minutes; beat in sugar, milk, vanilla, and cinnamon. Pour over bread mixture and toss; spoon into 1½-quart soufflé dish or casserole. Refrigerate, covered, overnight.
2. Place soufflé dish on rack in 6-quart slow cooker; cover and cook on high until pudding is set, about 5 hours. Serve warm with maple syrup.

Welsh Rarebit

Rarebit is also delicious served over sliced ham or chicken breast and asparagus on toast.

6 servings (about ½ cup each)

2 cups (8 ounces) shredded reduced-fat Cheddar
  cheese
8 ounces reduced-fat cream cheese, room
  temperature
1 cup beer
½ teaspoon each: dry mustard, Worcestershire
  sauce
Cayenne pepper, to taste
6 slices multigrain bread, toasted
12 slices tomato
Paprika and chopped chives, as garnish

Per Serving:
Calories: 302
% calories from fat: 41
Protein (g): 18.4
Carbohydrate (g): 25.1
Fat (g): 14.4
Saturated fat (g): 8.9
Cholesterol (mg): 44.4
Sodium (mg): 602
Exchanges:
Milk: 0.0
Vegetable: 0.0
Fruit: 0.0
Bread: 2.0
Meat: 2.0
Fat: 1.0

1. Combine cheeses, beer, dry mustard, and Worcestershire sauce in slow cooker; cover and cook on low until cheeses are melted, about 2 hours, stirring twice during cooking. Season to taste with cayenne pepper. Place toasted bread on serving plates; top with sliced tomatoes. Spoon Welsh Rarebit over; sprinkle with paprika and chopped chives.

Variations

Eggs Rarebit—Make recipe as above, omitting tomato. Top each toast slice with 1 ounce slice warm ham and a poached egg; spoon Welsh Rarebit over. Sprinkle with crisp crumbled bacon, paprika, and chopped chives.

Crab and Shrimp Rarebit—Make recipe as above, stirring in ½ to ¾ cup coarsely chopped crabmeat. Top each toast slice with 2 tomato slices and 3 or 4 cooked asparagus spears. Spoon Rarebit over; top each serving with 3 large cooked shrimp and sprinkle with chopped parsley.

Maple-Fruit Steel Cut Oatmeal

V *Let breakfast cook while you're sleeping—this is the best breakfast ever!*

4–6 servings

1 cup steel-cut oats
4½ cups water
½ cup each: maple syrup, chopped dried fruit
3 tablespoons margarine or butter
½ teaspoon salt

1. Combine all ingredients in slow cooker; cover and cook on low 6 to 8 hours.

Per Serving:
Calories: 271
% calories from fat: 31
Protein (g): 22.3
Carbohydrate (g): 22.8
Fat (g): 9
Saturated fat (g): 3.2
Cholesterol (mg): 72.3
Sodium (mg): 238.6
Exchanges:
Milk: 0.0
Vegetable: 0.0
Fruit: 0.0
Bread: 1.5
Meat: 3.0
Fat: 0.0

Variation

Multigrain Breakfast Cereal—Make recipe as above, substituting ¼ cup each whole oats and hard or soft wheat berries for ½ cup of the steel-cut oats. Toast ¼ cup millet or quinoa in small skillet over medium heat; stir into cereal mixture during last hour of cooking.

FOURTEEN

Side

Dishes

Chunky Applesauce

Great served warm, or chilled, as an accompaniment to entrées, or as a topping for Spiced Pudding Cake (see p. 560).

6 servings

3 pounds Jonathan apples, peeled, coarsely chopped
⅔ cup water
½ cup sugar
Ground cinnamon

1. Combine all ingredients, except cinnamon, in slow cooker; cover and cook on high until apples are very soft, and form applesauce when stirred, 2 to 2½ hours. Sprinkle with cinnamon when serving.

Per Serving:
Calories: 183
% calories from fat: 2
Protein (g): 5.9
Carbohydrate (g): 48
Fat (g): 0.4
Saturated fat (g): 0.1
Cholesterol (mg): 0.0
Sodium (mg): 2
Exchanges:
Milk: 0.0
Vegetable: 0.0
Fruit: 3.0
Bread: 0.0
Meat: 0.0
Fat: 0.0

Artichokes with Mock Hollandaise Sauce

The Mock Hollandaise Sauce is excellent served over asparagus spears, broccoli, or cauliflower too.

4 servings

4 whole small artichokes, stems removed
1 lemon, quartered
¾ cup water
Mock Hollandaise Sauce (recipe follows)

1. Cut 1 inch from tops of artichokes and discard; squeeze a wedge of lemon over each artichoke and place in slow cooker; add 1 inch water to slow cooker. Cover and cook on high until artichokes are tender (bottom leaves will pull out easily), 3½ to 4 hours. Remove artichokes and cover with foil to keep warm. Discard water in slow cooker; make Mock Hollandaise Sauce and serve with artichokes for dipping.

Per Serving:
Calories: 114
% of calories from fat: 2
Protein (gm): 11.9
Carbohydrate (gm): 17.5
Fat (gm): 0.3
Saturated fat (gm): 0.1
Cholesterol (mg): 0.2
Sodium (mg): 396
Exchanges:
Milk: 0.5
Vegetable: 2.0
Fruit: 0.0
Bread: 0.0
Meat: 0.5
Fat: 0.0

Mock Hollandaise Sauce

Makes about 1¼ cups

6 ounces reduced-fat cream cheese, room temperature
⅓ cup reduced-fat sour cream
3–4 tablespoons 2% reduced-fat milk
1–2 teaspoons lemon juice
½–1 teaspoon Dijon mustard
⅛ teaspoon ground turmeric (optional)

1. Add all ingredients to slow cooker; cover and cook on high until cream cheese is melted and mixture is warm, about 10 minutes, stirring once or twice to blend.

Note: Mock Hollandaise Sauce can also be made on the stovetop. Combine all ingredients in small saucepan; cook over medium-low to low heat, stirring until melted and smooth.

Asparagus and White Beans, Italian-Style

A substantial side dish to serve with grilled or roasted meat, this recipe will also serve 4 as a meatless entrée.

8 servings

1 can (15 ounces) cannellini or Great Northern beans, rinsed, drained
¾ cup vegetable broth
2 cups chopped plum tomatoes
1 cup carrots
1 teaspoon dried rosemary leaves
1 pound asparagus, sliced (2-inch pieces)
Salt and pepper, to taste
8 ounces linguine or thin spaghetti, cooked, warm
¼–½ cup (1–2 ounces) shredded Parmesan cheese

Per Serving:
Calories: 169
% of calories from fat: 16
Protein (gm): 7.9
Carbohydrate (gm): 29.4
Fat (gm): 3.1
Saturated fat (gm): 0.7
Cholesterol (mg): 2
Sodium (mg): 229
Exchanges:
Milk: 0.0
Vegetable: 1.0
Fruit: 0.0
Bread: 1.0
Meat: 0.0
FAT: 0.5

1. Combine beans, broth, tomatoes, carrots, and rosemary in slow cooker; cover and cook on high until carrots are tender, about 3 hours, adding asparagus during last 30 minutes. Season to taste with salt and pepper; toss with linguine and cheese.

Greek-Style Green Beans

Fresh green beans are slow cooked with tomatoes, herbs, and garlic in traditional Greek style.

8–10 servings

1 pound green beans
1 can (28 ounces) petite-diced tomatoes, undrained
½ cup chopped onion
4 cloves garlic, minced
¾ teaspoon each: dried oregano and basil leaves
Salt and pepper, to taste

1. Combine all ingredients, except salt and pepper, in slow cooker; cover and cook on high until beans are tender, about 4 hours. Season to taste with salt and pepper.

Per Serving:
Calories: 123
% of calories from fat: 28
Protein (gm): 4.5
Carbohydrate (gm): 20.5
Fat (gm): 4.3
Saturated fat (gm): 0.6
Cholesterol (mg): 0
Sodium (mg): 30
Exchanges:
Milk: 0.0
Vegetable: 4.0
Fruit: 0.0
Bread: 0.0
Meat: 0.0
Fat: 0.5

Oriental Green Beans

Serve these beans as a flavorful accompaniment to any meat or poultry entrée.

4 servings

2 cups halved green beans
¼ cup each: chopped onion, red bell pepper
2 teaspoons each: finely chopped gingerroot, garlic
½ cup water
1 cup canned drained black or adzuki beans
½ cup sliced water chestnuts
1 tablespoon rice wine vinegar
1–2 teaspoons tamari soy sauce
Salt and pepper, to taste

1. Combine green beans, onion, bell pepper, gingerroot, garlic, and water in slow cooker; cover and cook on high until green beans are crisp-tender, about 1½ hours; drain. Add remaining ingredients, except salt and pepper; cover and cook on high 30 minutes. Season to taste with salt and pepper.

Per Serving:
Calories: 109
% of calories from fat: 2
Protein (gm): 5.8
Carbohydrate (gm): 22.5
Fat (gm): 0.2
Saturated fat (gm): 0
Cholesterol (mg): 0
Sodium (mg): 64
Exchanges:
Milk: 0.0
Vegetable: 1.5
Fruit: 0.0
Bread: 1.0
Meat: 0.0
Fat: 0.0

Green Bean Casserole

L

Reduced-fat ingredients make this old favorite possible in a healthier form.

6 servings

1 can (10¾ ounces) 98% fat-free cream of
   mushroom soup
½ cup reduced-fat sour cream
¼ cup 2 % reduced-fat milk
1 package (10 ounces) frozen French-style
   green beans, thawed
Salt and pepper, to taste
½ cup canned French-fried onions

Per Serving:
Calories: 81
% of calories from fat: 31
Protein (gm): 3
Carbohydrate (gm): 11.6
Fat (gm): 2.9
Saturated fat (gm): 0.8
Cholesterol (mg): 1.3
Sodium (mg): 172
Exchanges:
Milk: 0.0
Vegetable: 2.0
Fruit: 0.0
Bread: 0.0
Meat: 0.0
Fat: 0.5

1. Mix soup, sour cream, and milk in slow cooker; stir
in green beans. Cover and cook on low 4 to 6 hours.
Season to taste with salt and pepper; stir in onions just
before serving.

Variation

Green Beans Supreme—Make recipe as above, adding 1 cup sliced sautéed
cremini mushrooms and ¼ cup thinly sliced green onions. Omit French-
fried onions; stir in 4 slices crumbled cooked bacon just before serving.

Santa Fe Baked Beans

L

*These baked beans boast flavors of the great Southwest; modify the amounts
of chilies for desired hotness!*

8 servings

1 cup chopped onion
¼–½ cup chopped poblano chili or green
   bell pepper
½–1 serrano or jalapeño chili, finely chopped
2 cans (15 ounces each) pinto beans, rinsed,
   drained
1 cup whole-kernel corn
6 sun-dried tomatoes (not in oil), softened, sliced
2–3 tablespoons honey
½ teaspoon each: ground cumin, dried thyme
   leaves
3 bay leaves
Salt and pepper, to taste
½ cup (2 ounces) crumbled Mexican white or farmer's cheese
¼ cup finely chopped cilantro

Per Serving:
Calories: 166
% of calories from fat: 13
Protein (gm): 8.3
Carbohydrate (gm): 29.5
Fat (gm): 2.5
Saturated fat (gm): 1.0
Cholesterol (mg): 5.1
Sodium (mg): 367
Exchanges:
Milk: 0.0
Vegetable: 1.0
Fruit: 0.0
Bread: 2.0
Meat: 1.0
Fat: 0.0

1. Combine all ingredients, except salt, pepper, cheese, and cilantro, in slow cooker; season to taste with salt and pepper. Cover and cook on low until beans are desired consistency, 5 to 6 hours, sprinkling with cheese and cilantro during last 30 minutes.

Tuscan Bean Bake

v *Easy to make, these beans are lemon-scented and seasoned with sun-dried tomatoes, garlic, and herbs.*

6 servings

3 cans (15 ounces each) cannellini or Great
  Northern beans
1 cup vegetable broth
½ cup each: chopped onion, red bell pepper
2 teaspoons minced garlic
1 teaspoon each: dried sage and rosemary leaves
2–3 teaspoons grated lemon zest
6 sun-dried tomatoes (not in oil), softened, sliced
Salt and pepper, to taste

Per Serving:
Calories: 186
% of calories from fat: 1
Protein (gm): 14.0
Carbohydrate (gm): 37.4
Fat (gm): 0.3
Saturated fat (gm): 0.1
Cholesterol (mg): 0
Sodium (mg): 677
Exchanges:
Milk: 0.0
Vegetable: 0.0
Fruit: 0.0
Bread: 2.5
Meat: 1.0
Fat: 0.0

1. Combine all ingredients, except salt and pepper, in slow cooker; cover and cook on low until beans are desired consistency, 5 to 6 hours.

Brazilian Black Bean Bake

v *Festive flavors of Brazil combine in this irresistible dish!*

12 servings

2 cups chopped onions
1–2 tablespoons each: minced jalapeño chili,
  gingerroot
4 cans (15 ounces each) black beans, rinsed, drained
2 cans (14½ ounces each) petite-diced tomatoes,
  undrained
½ cup each: honey, packed light brown sugar
¾ teaspoon each: dried thyme leaves, ground cumin
Salt and pepper, to taste
½ cup each: sliced mango, banana

Per Serving:
Calories: 223
% of calories from fat: 0.5
Protein (gm): 7.8
Carbohydrate (gm): 48.2
Fat (gm): 0.1
Saturated fat (gm): 0.0
Cholesterol (mg): 0.0
Sodium (mg): 673
Exchanges:
Milk: 0.0
Vegetable: 0.0
Fruit: 0.0
Bread: 3.0
Meat: 0.0
Fat: 0.0

1. Combine all ingredients, except salt, pepper, mango, and banana, in slow cooker; season to taste with salt and pepper. Cover and cook on low until beans are desired consistency, 5 to 6 hours. Top with mango and banana before serving.

Ginger-Baked Beans

V

Slow baking adds goodness to this special ginger and sweet-spiced bean dish.

24 servings

1½ cups chopped onions
2–3 tablespoons finely chopped gingerroot
3–4 cloves garlic, minced
4 cans (15 ounces each) Great Northern, Beans, rinsed, drained
½ cup packed light brown sugar
1 can (6 ounces) tomato sauce
½ cup light molasses
1 teaspoon each: dry mustard, ground ginger, dried thyme leaves
¼ teaspoon each: ground cinnamon and allspice
2 bay leaves
Pepper, to taste
½ cup coarsely ground gingersnap crumbs

Per Serving:
Calories: 170
% of calories from fat: 12
Protein (gm): 16.3
Carbohydrate (gm): 32.5
Fat (gm): 2.4
Saturated fat (gm): 0.4
Cholesterol (mg): 0
Sodium (mg): 30
Exchanges:
Milk: 0.0
Vegetable: 1.0
Fruit: 0.0
Bread: 2.0
Meat: 0.0
Fat: 0.5

1. Combine all ingredients, except pepper and gingersnap crumbs, in slow cooker; season to taste with pepper. Cover and cook on low until thickened to desired consistency, about 6 hours, mixing in gingersnap crumbs during last hour. Discard bay leaves.

Beets Dijon

L

Try different mustards in this recipe, such as horseradish, whole grain, or honey mustard.

4 servings

1 pound beets, peeled, cubed (½-inch)
⅓ cup finely chopped onion
2 cloves garlic, minced
⅓ cup sour cream
1 tablespoon cornstarch
2 tablespoons Dijon mustard
2–3 teaspoons lemon juice
Salt and white pepper, to taste

Per Serving:
Calories: 71
% of calories from fat: 7
Protein (gm): 3.5
Carbohydrate (gm): 13.8
Fat (gm): 0.6
Saturated fat (gm): 0.1
Cholesterol (mg): 0
Sodium (mg): 185
Exchanges:
Milk: 0.0
Vegetable: 3.0
Fruit: 0.0
Bread: 0.0
Meat: 0.0
Fat: 0.0

1. Combine beets, onion, garlic, and sour cream in slow cooker; cover and cook on high until beets are tender, about 2 hours. Stir in combined cornstarch, mustard, and lemon juice, stirring 2 to 3 minutes. Season to taste with salt and pepper.

Honeyed Beets

V

Beets are easy to peel if cooked with their skins on—just rinse under cool water and the skins can be rubbed off. This sweet and sour beet dish is sure to please!

6 servings

1½ pounds medium beets
2 cups hot water
¼ cup very finely chopped red or yellow onion
2 cloves garlic, minced
¼ cup currants or raisins
3–4 tablespoons toasted walnuts
¼ cup honey
2–3 tablespoons red wine vinegar
1 tablespoon margarine
Salt and pepper, to taste

Per Serving:
Calories: 94
% of calories from fat: 18
Protein (gm): 1.1
Carbohydrate (gm): 19.3
Fat (gm): 1.9
Saturated fat (gm): 0.4
Cholesterol (mg): 0
Sodium (mg): 70
Exchanges:
Milk: 0.0
Vegetable: 2.0
Fruit: 0.0
Bread: 0.5
Meat: 0.0
Fat: 0.0

1. Combine beets and water in slow cooker; cover and cook on high until beets are tender, 2 to 2½ hours. Drain; peel beets and cut into ¾-inch cubes. Combine beets and remaining ingredients, except salt and pepper, in slow cooker; cover and cook on high 20 to 30 minutes. Season to taste with salt and pepper.

Sugar-Glazed Brussels Sprouts and Pearl Onions

v *Large Brussels sprouts can be cut into halves for faster cooking and easier eating.*

4–6 servings

8 ounces each: small Brussels sprouts, frozen,
    thawed pearl onions
1½ cups hot water
1 tablespoon margarine
¼ cup sugar
Salt and white pepper, to taste

Per Serving:
Calories: 107
% of calories from fat: 25
Protein (gm): 2.3
Carbohydrate (gm): 19.7
Fat (gm): 3.2
Saturated fat (gm): 0.6
Cholesterol (mg): 0
Sodium (mg): 48
Exchanges:
Milk: 0.0
Vegetable: 2.0
Fruit: 0.0
Bread: 0.5
Meat: 0.0
Fat: 0.5

1. Combine Brussels sprouts, onions, and water in slow cooker; cover and cook on high until Brussels sprouts are tender, about 2 hours; drain. Add margarine and sugar; cover and cook on high until glazed, about 10 minutes. Season to taste with salt and pepper.

Wine-Braised Cabbage

You'll enjoy the combination of aromatic anise and caraway seeds in this cabbage dish.

4–6 servings

1 medium head cabbage, thinly sliced
¾ cup chopped onion
½ cup chopped green bell pepper
3 cloves garlic, minced
½ teaspoon each: crushed caraway and anise seeds
¼ cup each: canned vegetable broth, dry white wine
2 slices diced bacon, cooked crisp, drained
Salt and pepper, to taste

Per Serving:
Calories: 118
% of calories from fat: 10
Protein (gm): 6.4
Carbohydrate (gm): 19.3
Fat (gm): 1.5
Saturated fat (gm): 0.1
Cholesterol (mg): 0
Sodium (mg): 148
Exchanges:
Milk: 0.0
Vegetable: 3.0
Fruit: 0.0
Bread: 0.5
Meat: 0.0
Fat: 0.0

1. Combine all ingredients, except bacon, salt, and pepper, in slow cooker; cover and cook on high until cabbage is tender, 3 to 4 hours. Stir in bacon; season to taste with salt and pepper.

Variation

Creamed Cabbage—Make recipe as above, omitting bacon. Stir in combined ½ cup reduced-fat sour cream and 1 tablespoon cornstarch; cover and cook on low 5 to 10 minutes.

Gingered Carrot Purée

L

This traditional French vegetable purée can easily be made in the slow cooker! You'll enjoy the intense flavor and velvety texture.

6–8 servings

2 pounds carrots, sliced
2 cups peeled cubed Idaho potato
1 cup water
1–2 tablespoons margarine or butter
¼–½ cup 2% reduced-fat milk, warm
½ teaspoon ground ginger
Salt and pepper, to taste

Per Serving:
Calories: 122
% of calories from fat: 16
Protein (gm): 2.4
Carbohydrate (gm): 24.1
Fat (gm): 2.2
Saturated fat (gm): 0.4
Cholesterol (mg): 0
Sodium (mg): 132
Exchanges:
Milk: 0.0
Vegetable: 2.5
Fruit: 0.0
Bread: 0.5
Meat: 0.0
Fat: 0.5

1. Combine carrots, potato, and water in slow cooker; cover and cook on high until vegetables are very tender, about 3 hours. Drain well. Process carrots and potato in food processor until smooth; return to slow cooker. Cook on high, uncovered, until mixture is very thick, about 30 minutes, stirring occasionally. Beat margarine and enough milk into mixture to make a creamy consistency. Stir in ground ginger; season to taste with salt and pepper.

Variations
Cauliflower-Fennel Purée—Make recipe as above, substituting cauliflower for the carrots, omitting the ground nutmeg, and adding 1–1½ teaspoons crushed fennel or caraway seeds.
Celery Root Purée—Make recipe as above, substituting celery root for the carrots and omitting ground ginger.
Herbed Broccoli Purée—Make recipe as above, substituting broccoli for the carrots, omitting ground ginger, and adding ½ teaspoon each dried marjoram and savory leaves.

Orange-Glazed Baby Carrots

V

The sweet-spiced orange glaze is also delicious over sweet potatoes or beets.

4 servings

1 pound baby carrots
¾ cup orange juice
1 tablespoon margarine
½ cup packed light brown sugar
½ teaspoon ground cinnamon
¼ teaspoon ground mace
2 tablespoons cornstarch
¼ cup water
Salt and white pepper, to taste

Per Serving:
Calories: 191
% of calories from fat: 13
Protein (gm): 1.8
Carbohydrate (gm): 42.4
Fat (gm): 3
Saturated fat (gm): 0.6
Cholesterol (mg): 0
Sodium (mg): 145
Exchanges:
Milk: 0.0
Vegetable: 2.0
Fruit: 2.0
Bread: 0.0
Meat: 0.0
Fat: 0.5

1. Combine all ingredients, except cornstarch, water, salt, and white pepper, in slow cooker; cover and cook on high until carrots are crisp-tender, about 3 hours. Turn heat to high and cook 10 minutes. Stir in combined cornstarch and water, stirring 2 to 3 minutes; season to taste with salt and pepper.

Cauliflower with Creamy Cheese Sauce

L

For flavor variations, make the cheese sauce with other reduced-fat cheeses, such as Havarti, Gruyère, American, or blue.

6 servings

1 medium head cauliflower (1–1¼ pounds)
1½ cups water
Creamy Cheese Sauce (recipe follows)
Paprika, as garnish

Per Serving:
Calories: 102
% of calories from fat: 31
Protein (gm): 6.5
Carbohydrate (gm): 11.7
Fat (gm): 3.6
Saturated fat (gm): 1.5
Cholesterol (mg): 5.7
Sodium (mg): 194
Exchanges:
Milk: 0.0
Vegetable: 2.0
Fruit: 0.0
Bread: 0.0
Meat: 0.5
Fat: 0.5

1. Place cauliflower in slow cooker and add water; cover and cook on high until cauliflower is tender, about 2 hours. Place cauliflower on serving plate; spoon Creamy Cheese Sauce over and sprinkle with paprika.

Creamy Cheese Sauce

Makes about 1¼ cups

2 tablespoons minced onion
1 tablespoon margarine or butter
2 tablespoons flour
1 cup 2% reduced-fat milk
½ cup (2 ounces) cubed reduced-fat processed cheese
¼ teaspoon dry mustard
2–3 drops red pepper sauce
Salt and white pepper, to taste

1. Sauté onion in margarine in small saucepan 2 to 3 minutes. Stir in flour; cook 1 minute. Whisk in milk and heat to boiling, stirring until thickened, about 1 minute. Reduce heat to low; add cheese, dry mustard, and pepper sauce, whisking until cheese is melted. Season to taste with salt and white pepper.

Variation

Easy Three-Cheese Cauliflower—Make recipe as above, omitting Creamy Cheese Sauce. Return drained cauliflower to slow cooker; sprinkle with ½ cup (2 ounces) each shredded reduced-fat brick and Cheddar cheese and ¼ cup (1 ounce) crumbled blue cheese; cover and cook on low until cheese is melted, about 5 minutes.

Corn Flan

Whole-kernel and creamed corn are combined in a delicate custard.

6 servings

1 cup whole milk
3 eggs, lightly beaten
1 teaspoon sugar
1 can (14¾ ounces) creamed corn
1 package (10 ounces) frozen, thawed whole-kernel corn
½ teaspoon salt
¼ teaspoon pepper

Per Serving:
Calories: 151
% calories from fat: 24
Protein (g): 6.9
Carbohydrate (g): 24.3
Fat (g): 4.4
Saturated fat (g): 1.6
Cholesterol (mg): 109.8
Sodium (mg): 441
Exchanges:
Milk: 0.0
Vegetable: 0.0
Fruit: 0.0
Bread: 1.5
Meat: 0.0
Fat: 0.5

1. Mix milk and eggs until well blended; mix in remaining ingredients and pour into greased 1½-quart soufflé dish or casserole. Place soufflé dish on rack in 6-quart slow cooker; cover and cook on low until custard is set, about 3 hours.

Note: The recipe can be made without a soufflé dish; pour mixture into greased 3-quart slow cooker. Cover and cook on high until set and sharp knife inserted between center and edge comes out clean, 2½ to 3 hours.

Corn Pudding

LO *A great tasting corn pudding, spiked with jalapeño chilies!*

6 servings

1 package (10 ounces) frozen, thawed whole-kernel corn, divided
1 cup whole milk
3 eggs
2 tablespoons flour
½ teaspoon ground cumin
1 teaspoon salt
¼ teaspoon pepper
2 cups (8 ounces) shredded reduced-fat Monterey Jack cheese
¼ cup finely chopped green bell pepper
½–1 small jalapeño chili, minced

Per Serving:
Calories: 216
% calories from fat: 48
Protein (g): 15.1
Carbohydrate (g): 14.9
Fat (g): 12.2
Saturated fat (g): 6.3
Cholesterol (mg): 136.5
Sodium (mg): 760
Exchanges:
Milk: 0.0
Vegetable: 0.0
Fruit: 0.0
Bread: 1.0
Meat: 1.0
Fat: 2.0

1. Process ¾ cup corn, milk, eggs, flour, cumin, salt, and pepper in food processor or blender until smooth. Pour into greased slow cooker; mix in remaining corn, cheese, bell pepper, and jalapeño chili. Cover and cook on low until pudding is set, about 3 hours.

Leek Custard

LO *A unique vegetable dish that will complement any entrée.*

6 servings

4 large leeks (white parts only), thinly sliced
2 tablespoons each: finely chopped shallots or onion, olive oil
1 cup whole milk
2 eggs, lightly beaten
⅛ teaspoon ground nutmeg
¼ teaspoon each: salt, white pepper
½ cup (2 ounces) shredded reduced-fat Jarlsberg or Swiss cheese
2 tablespoons grated Parmesan cheese

Per Serving:
Calories: 136
% calories from fat: 48
Protein (g): 6.8
Carbohydrate (g): 11.2
Fat (g): 7.4
Saturated fat (g): 3.1
Cholesterol (mg): 80.5
Sodium (mg): 214
Exchanges:
Milk: 0.0
Vegetable: 0.0
Fruit: 0.0
Bread: 1.0
Meat: 0.0
Fat: 1.5

1. Sauté leeks and shallots in oil in small skillet until tender, about 8 minutes. Combine leek mixture and remaining ingredients, except Parmesan cheese and pour into 1-quart soufflé dish; place on rack in 6-quart slow cooker. Cover and cook on low 3½ hours; sprinkle custard with Parmesan cheese. Cover and cook until custard is set and sharp knife inserted halfway between center and edge comes out clean, about 30 minutes longer.

Savory Stuffed Onions

Goat cheese, sun-dried tomatoes, and pine nuts combine deliciously in the stuffing.

6 servings

3 medium Vidalia or other sweet onions, peeled
½ cup each: fresh Italian bread crumbs, crumbled
   goat cheese
4 sun-dried tomato halves (not in oil), chopped
2 tablespoons pine nuts
2 cloves garlic, minced
½ teaspoon dried thyme leaves
¼ teaspoon each: salt, pepper
1 egg white
½ cup chicken broth, hot

Per Serving:
Calories: 118
% calories from fat: 40
Protein (g): 5
Carbohydrate (g): 13.4
Fat (g): 5.4
Saturated fat (g): 2.1
Cholesterol (mg): 7.7
Sodium (mg): 505
Exchanges:
Milk: 0.0
Vegetable: 0.0
Fruit: 0.0
Bread: 1.1
Meat: 0.0
Fat: 1.0

1. Boil onions in water to cover 10 minutes; drain and cool. Cut onions crosswise into halves and remove centers, leaving a shell several layers thick. Reserve centers for soup or another use.
2. Combine remaining ingredients, except chicken broth; fill onion halves with mixture. Add chicken broth and onions to slow cooker; cover and cook on high until onions are very tender, but hold their shape, about 4 hours.

Candied Yams

o *Whether they're called yams or sweet potatoes in your family, the sweet goodness of this dish is the same!*

8–10 servings

2 pounds sweet potatoes, peeled, sliced (¼-inch)
⅔ cup packed light brown sugar
Salt and pepper, to taste
2 tablespoons cold margarine or butter, cut into
 small pieces
½ cup water
2 tablespoons cornstarch

Per Serving:
Calories: 176
% of calories from fat: 8
Protein (gm): 1.5
Carbohydrate (gm): 39.5
Fat (gm): 1.5
Saturated fat (gm): 0.3
Cholesterol (mg): 0
Sodium (mg): 63
Exchanges:
Milk: 0.0
Vegetable: 0.0
Fruit: 0.0
Bread: 2.5
Meat: 0.0
Fat: 0.0

1. Layer sweet potatoes in slow cooker, sprinkling each layer with brown sugar, salt, and pepper, and dotting with margarine. Combine water and cornstarch and pour over the top. Cover and cook on low 3 hours; increase heat to high and cook until potatoes are tender, about 1 hour.

Variation

Fruit and Nut Sweet Potatoes—Make recipe as above, sprinkling ¼ cup each currants or raisins and toasted pecans between layers of potatoes. Sprinkle top of potatoes with ½ cup miniature marshmallows during last 5 to 10 minutes of cooking time.

Sweet Potato Loaf with Apple-Cranberry Relish

Perfect for the winter holidays—but this loaf is so delicious and easy to make, you'll want to serve it year-round.

6 servings

1¼ cups coarsely grated, peeled sweet potatoes
⅓ cup each: finely chopped onion, shredded tart
   apple
¼ cup raisins
½ teaspoon dried thyme leaves
¼ teaspoon ground cinnamon
⅛ teaspoon ground nutmeg
¼ cup all-purpose flour
¼ cup orange juice
Salt and pepper, to taste
1 egg
Apple-Cranberry Relish (recipe follows)

Per Serving:
Calories: 421
% of calories from fat: 12
Protein (gm): 7.3
Carbohydrate (gm): 88.9
Fat (gm): 5.6
Saturated fat (gm): 1
Cholesterol (mg): 71
Sodium (mg): 63.6
Exchanges:
Milk: 0.0
Vegetable: 0.0
Fruit: 3.0
Bread: 3.0
Meat: 0.0
Fat: 0.5

1. Mix all ingredients, except salt, pepper, egg, and Apple-Cranberry Relish; season to taste with salt and pepper. Mix in egg. Pack mixture in greased 5½ x 3-inch loaf pan and cover securely with aluminum foil; place on rack in 6-quart slow cooker. Add 2 inches hot water; cover and cook at high until sweet potatoes are tender, about 3 hours. Remove from slow cooker and let stand on wire rack 5 minutes; invert onto serving plate. Slice loaf and serve with Apple-Cranberry Relish.

Apple-Cranberry Relish

Makes about 1 cup

½ cup whole-berry cranberry sauce
¼ cup each: chopped tart apple, orange segments
2 tablespoons chopped pecans or walnuts
2–4 tablespoons sugar
1 tablespoon grated orange or lemon zest

1. Combine all ingredients.

Sweet Potato Pudding

LO *This comfort food will become a favorite. Drizzle with warm maple syrup, if you like.*

6 servings

Vegetable cooking spray
4 medium sweet potatoes, peeled, cubed
¼ cup orange juice
1–2 tablespoons margarine or butter
¼ cup packed light brown sugar
1 tablespoon grated orange zest
¼ teaspoon each: ground cinnamon, cloves, salt
3 eggs, lightly beaten
1 cup miniature marshmallows

Per Serving:
Calories: 179
% of calories from fat: 16
Protein (gm): 5.5
Carbohydrate (gm): 27.7
Fat (gm): 3.1
Saturated fat (gm): 0.7
Cholesterol (mg): 1.0
Sodium (mg): 303
Exchanges:
Milk: 0.0
Vegetable: 0.5
Fruit: 0.0
Bread: 1.0
Meat: 0.5
Fat: 0.0

1. Spray bottom and side of slow cooker with cooking spray and add sweet potatoes; cover and cook on high until potatoes are tender, about 3 hours. Remove potatoes and mash with remaining ingredients, except eggs and marshmallows; mix in eggs. Return potatoes to slow cooker; cover and cook on high 30 minutes, sprinkling with marshmallows during last 5 minutes.

Variation

Sweet Autumn Pudding—Make recipe as above, using 1½ cups each peeled cubed sweet potatoes, hubbard squash, and sliced carrots; substitute ½ teaspoon ground mace for the cinnamon and cloves and omit marshmallows.

Potatoes Gratin

 These potatoes taste so rich and creamy you'll never imagine they were made without heavy cream!

8 servings

2 pounds Idaho potatoes, peeled, sliced (¼-inch)
¼ cup thinly sliced onion
Salt and pepper to taste
Cheddar Cheese Sauce (recipe follows)
Ground nutmeg, to taste

Per Serving:
Calories: 202
% of calories from fat: 23
Protein (gm): 7.6
Carbohydrate (gm): 31.7
Fat (gm): 5.1
Saturated fat (gm): 1.7
Cholesterol (mg): 8.5
Sodium (mg): 259
Exchanges:
Milk: 0.0
Vegetable: 0.0
Fruit: 0.0
Bread: 2.0
Meat: 0.5
Fat: 0.5

1. Layer half the potatoes and onion in slow cooker; sprinkle lightly with salt and pepper. Pour half the cheese sauce over; repeat layers. Cover and cook on high until potatoes are tender, about 3½ hours. Sprinkle with nutmeg.

Cheddar Cheese Sauce

Makes about 2 cups

2 tablespoons margarine or butter
3 tablespoons each: finely chopped onion, flour
1½ cups 2% reduced-fat milk
2 ounces reduced-fat processed cheese, cubed
¾ cup (3 ounces) shredded reduced-fat Cheddar cheese
½ teaspoon dry mustard
Salt and pepper, to taste

1. Melt margarine in small saucepan; add onion and flour and cook 1 to 2 minutes. Gradually whisk in milk; heat to boiling, stirring until thickened, 2 to 3 minutes. Reduce heat to low; add cheeses and dry mustard, stirring until melted. Season to taste with salt and pepper.

Variations

Easy Potatoes Gratin—Make recipe as above, omitting Cheddar Cheese Sauce and dividing ¾ cup (3 ounces) shredded reduced-fat Cheddar cheese equally between each layer of potatoes. Pour ½ cup water over and cook as above.

Scalloped Potatoes—Make sauce as above, omitting cheeses and increasing margarine to 3 tablespoons, flour to ¼ cup, and milk to 2 cups.

Creamy Potatoes and Ham

A very easy dish to make, using prepared foods—no potatoes to peel or cube!

8 servings

1 package (28 ounces) frozen O'Brien potatoes, thawed and separated
12 ounces cubed smoked ham
1 can (10 ounces) 98% fat-free cream of mushroom soup
1 cup 2% reduced-fat milk
1½ cups (6 ounces) shredded reduced-fat Cheddar cheese
¼ teaspoon pepper

Per Serving:
Calories: 317
% of calories from fat: 32
Protein (gm): 25.4
Carbohydrate (gm): 29.0
Fat (gm): 11.3
Saturated fat (gm): 6.0
Cholesterol (mg): 56.4
Sodium (mg): 1336
Exchanges:
Milk: 0.0
Vegetable: 0.0
Fruit: 0.0
Bread: 2.0
Meat: 2.0
Fat: 0.5

1. Combine potatoes and ham in slow cooker; mix in combined remaining ingredients. Cover and cook on high 3 to 4 hours.

Winter Vegetables Baked in Cream

Winter's root vegetables, slow cooked in half-and-half, are a delicious treat.

6 servings

4 small red potatoes, sliced
2 medium parsnips, sliced
2–3 small leeks (white parts only), sliced
1 medium fennel bulb, sliced
2 cloves garlic, minced
½ teaspoon dried thyme leaves
1 cup each: chicken broth, half-and-half or
  light cream
1 cup reduced-fat sour cream
2 tablespoons cornstarch
Salt and pepper, to taste

Per Serving:
Calories: 214
% of calories from fat: 34
Protein (gm): 5.2
Carbohydrate (gm): 31.1
Fat (gm): 8.4
Saturated fat (gm): 5.0
Cholesterol (mg): 26.4
Sodium (mg): 233
Exchanges:
Milk: 0.0
Vegetable: 0.0
Fruit: 0.0
Bread: 2.0
Meat: 0.0
Fat: 1.5

1. Combine all ingredients, except sour cream, cornstarch, salt, and pepper, in slow cooker; cover and cook on high until vegetables are tender, about 5 hours. Stir in combined sour cream and cornstarch, stirring 2 to 3 minutes. Season to taste with salt and pepper.

Spinach Bake

LO *Slow cooked and delicious, this humble spinach recipe makes a great side dish.*

4–6 servings

1 package (10 ounces) frozen spinach, thawed,
  undrained
1 small onion, coarsely chopped
1 rib celery, thickly sliced
1 clove garlic
2 tablespoons olive oil
½ teaspoon each: dried basil and thyme leaves
⅛ teaspoon ground nutmeg
Salt and pepper, to taste
2 eggs
½ cup (2 ounces) shredded reduced-fat Swiss cheese
¼ cup (1 ounce) grated Parmesan cheese

Per Serving:
Calories: 174
% calories from fat: 60
Protein (g): 11.3
Carbohydrate (g): 6
Fat (g): 11.4
Saturated fat (g): 3.1
Cholesterol (mg): 115.1
Sodium (mg): 256
Exchanges:
Milk: 0.0
Vegetable: 1.0
Fruit: 0.0
Bread: 1.5
Meat: 1.0
Fat: 2.0

1. Process spinach, onion, celery, garlic, oil, herbs, and nutmeg in food processor until very finely chopped. Season to taste with salt and pepper; add eggs and process until smooth. Stir in Swiss cheese; spoon mixture into greased 1-quart soufflé dish and sprinkle with Parmesan cheese. Place soufflé dish on rack in 6-quart slow cooker; cover and cook on low until mixture is set and sharp knife inserted halfway between center and edge comes out clean, about 4 hours.

Spaghetti Squash Parmesan

L

The delicate flavor of the squash is complemented by the combination of Italian seasoning and Parmesan cheese.

4 servings

1 spaghetti squash (about 2 pounds)
¼ cup sliced green onions
1 teaspoon minced garlic
1 tablespoon margarine or butter
¼ cup vegetable broth
1½ teaspoons dried Italian seasoning
½ cup (2 ounces) Parmesan cheese
Salt and pepper, to taste

Per Serving:
Calories: 99
% of calories from fat: 29
Fat (gm): 3.6
Saturated fat (gm): 0.7
Cholesterol (mg): 0
Sodium (mg): 102
Protein (gm): 5.1
Carbohydrate (gm): 14.3
Exchanges:
Milk: 0.0
Vegetable: 2.0
Fruit: 0.0
Bread: 0.0
Meat: 0.5
Fat: 0.5

1. Cut about 1-inch off ends of squash and place squash in slow cooker; cover and cook on high until fork-tender, 3 to 4 hours on high or 6 to 8 hours on low. Cut squash lengthwise into halves; scoop out and discard seeds. Fluff strands of squash with tines of fork, leaving squash in shells.
2. Sauté green onions and garlic in margarine in small saucepan until tender, 3 to 4 minutes. Stir in broth and Italian seasoning; heat to boiling. Spoon half the mixture into each squash half and toss; sprinkle with Parmesan cheese and toss. Season to taste with salt and pepper.

Zucchini-Mushroom Soufflé

LO *Serve the soufflé immediately, as it soars above the dish!*

8 servings

4 eggs
¾ cup whole milk
¼ cup all-purpose flour
1 pound zucchini, finely chopped
4 ounces sliced mushrooms
2 tablespoons snipped chives or parsley
1 clove garlic, minced
½ teaspoon dried Italian seasoning
¾ teaspoon salt
⅛ teaspoon pepper
½ cup (2 ounces) shredded Parmesan cheese, divided
Paprika

Per Serving:
Calories: 96
% calories from fat: 42
Protein (g): 7.1
Carbohydrate (g): 7
Fat (g): 4.6
Saturated fat (g): 2
Cholesterol (mg): 112
Sodium (mg): 345
Exchanges:
Milk: 0.0
Vegetable: 1.0
Fruit: 0.0
Bread: 0.0
Meat: 1.0
Fat: 0.0

1. Beat eggs, milk, and flour in bowl until smooth; mix in remaining ingredients, except ¼ cup Parmesan cheese and paprika. Pour mixture into 1½-quart soufflé dish or casserole; sprinkle with remaining ¼ cup Parmesan cheese and paprika. Place soufflé dish on rack in 6-cup slow cooker; cover and cook on high until puffed and set, about 4 hours. Serve immediately.

Zucchini-Corn Timbale with Roasted Red Pepper Sauce

LO *A summer treat, made with fresh garden vegetables!*

6 servings

4 medium zucchini, coarsely shredded
2 cups whole-kernel corn
¼ cup each: chopped onion, cilantro, dry white wine
5 eggs
⅔ cup reduced-fat evaporated milk
¾ cup (3 ounces) shredded reduced-fat Chedddar cheese
½ teaspoon salt
⅛ teaspoon pepper
Roasted Red Pepper Sauce (recipe follows)

Per Serving:
Calories: 224
% calories from fat: 34
Protein (g): 13.0
Carbohydrate (g): 22.8
Fat (g): 8.4
Saturated fat (g): 3.5
Cholesterol (mg): 187.4
Sodium (mg): 398
Exchanges:
Milk: 0.0
Vegetable: 0.0
Fruit: 0.0
Bread: 1.5
Meat: 1.0
Fat: 1.0

1. Combine all ingredients, except Roasted Red Pepper Sauce, in 1-quart casserole or soufflé dish. Place on rack in 6-quart slow cooker; cover and cook on high until vegetables are tender, about 4 hours. Serve with Roasted Red Pepper Sauce.

Roasted Red Pepper Sauce

Makes about 1½ cups

4 large red bell peppers, halved
1 teaspoon sugar

1. Place peppers, skin sides up, on broiler pan. Broil 4 to 6 inches from heat source until skins are blistered and blackened, about 5 minutes. Place peppers in plastic bag 5 minutes; remove and peel off skins. Process in food processor or blender until smooth.

Notes: This recipe can also be cooked in a 3-quart slow cooker, without using a casserole; cooking time will be 3 to 3½ hours.
One jar (12 ounces) roasted red peppers, drained, can be substituted for the fresh bell peppers in the Roasted Red Pepper Sauce.

Tomato Pudding

V

Purchased croutons can be substituted for homemade.

6 servings

½ cup each: finely chopped celery, onion, green bell pepper
1 can (16 ounces) diced tomatoes, undrained
½ teaspoon each: celery seeds, dried marjoram leaves
1 tablespoon light brown sugar
Salt and pepper, to taste
1 tablespoon cornstarch
2 tablespoons cold water
Croutons (see p. 38)

Per Serving:
Calories: 85
% of calories from fat: 9
Fat (gm): 0.9
Saturated fat (gm): 0.1
Cholesterol (mg): 0
Sodium (mg): 88
Protein (gm): 2.6
Carbohydrate (gm): 17.9
Exchanges:
Milk: 0.0
Vegetable: 2.0
Fruit: 0.0
Bread: 0.5
Meat: 0.0
Fat: 0.0

1. Combine chopped vegetables, tomatoes with liquid, herbs, and brown sugar in slow cooker; season to taste with salt and pepper. Cover and cook on high 2 hours; stir in combined cornstarch and water, stirring 2 to 3 minutes. Stir in Croutons; cover and cook on high 15 minutes.

Spinach-Cheese Noodle Pudding

Be forewarned—everyone will want seconds!

8 servings

1 cup reduced-fat small curd cottage cheese
3 ounces reduced-fat cream cheese, room temperature
3 large eggs, lightly beaten
1¼ cups whole milk
½ cup raisins
½ teaspoon ground cinnamon
¼ package (10-ounce size) frozen spinach, thawed, undrained
4 ounces egg noodles, cooked, al dente
½ teaspoon salt
Parmesan cheese and paprika, as garnish

Per Serving:
Calories: 194
% calories from fat: 35
Protein (g): 10.3
Carbohydrate (g): 21.2
Fat (g): 10.3
Saturated fat (g): 4.0
Cholesterol (mg): 97.1
Sodium (mg): 346
Exchanges:
Milk: 0.0
Vegetable: 0.0
Fruit: 0.0
Bread: 1.5
Meat: 1.0
Fat: 1.0

1. Combine cottage cheese and cream cheese; mix in eggs, blending well. Mix in remaining ingredients, except Parmesan cheese and paprika; spoon into 1-quart soufflé dish or casserole and sprinkle with Parmesan cheese and paprika. Place soufflé dish on rack in 6-quart slow cooker; cover and cook on low until set, about 4 hours.

Note: This recipe can also be cooked in a 3-quart slow cooker, without using a soufflé dish; cooking time will be about 3½ hours.

Hungarian Noodle Pudding

This kugel, flavored with raspberry preserves and almonds, can also be served as a dessert!

10 servings

4 eggs, separated
½ cup sugar
1 cup reduced-fat sour cream
1 tablespoon grated orange zest
2 teaspoons ground cinnamon
8 ounces egg noodles or small elbow macaroni, cooked
2 tablespoons margarine or butter
½ cup each: melted seedless raspberry preserves, chopped almonds

Per Serving:
Calories: 269
% calories from fat: 29
Fat (gm): 8.6
Saturated fat (gm): 1.5
Cholesterol (mg): 108.9
Sodium (mg): 106
Protein (gm): 8.1
Carbohydrate (gm): 40
Exchanges:
Milk: 0.0
Vegetable: 0.0
Fruit: 1.0
Bread: 2.0
Meat: 0.0
Fat: 2.0

1. Beat egg yolks and sugar in small bowl until thick and lemon-colored, about 5 minutes. Beat in sour cream, orange zest, and cinnamon. Beat egg whites in clean large bowl with clean beaters, until stiff peaks form. Fold yolk mixture into egg whites.

2. Mix noodles, margarine, and egg mixture in large bowl; spoon half the mixture into greased slow cooker. Spoon preserves over noodles and sprinkle with ¼ cup almonds. Top with remaining noodle mixture and remaining ¼ cup almonds. Cover and cook on high until set, about 1 hour. Serve from slow cooker or invert onto serving platter.

Variation

Cherry-Peach Dessert Kugel—Make recipe as above, omitting raspberry preserves and stirring 1 cup reduced-fat cottage cheese, 1 can (8 ounces) drained chopped peaches, and ⅓ cup dried cherries into noodle mixture.

Mushroom Bread Pudding

LO

This savory version of bread pudding is the perfect accompaniment to any meat or poultry. It can be cooked after assembling, but is more flavorful if refrigerated overnight.

8 servings

8 ounces Italian or sourdough bread, cubed (1-inch)
Olive oil cooking spray
1 teaspoon dried thyme leaves
8 ounces cremini mushrooms, thinly sliced
¾ cup each: thinly sliced celery, onion, bell pepper
1 clove garlic, minced
1–2 tablespoons olive oil
1 cup each: light cream, whole milk
4 eggs, lightly beaten
½ teaspoon salt
⅛ teaspoon pepper
¼ cup (1 ounce) finely shredded asiago cheese

Per Serving:
Calories: 242
% calories from fat: 49
Protein (g): 10.0
Carbohydrate (g): 21.1
Fat (g): 13.2
Saturated fat (g): 6.1
Cholesterol (mg): 131.1
Sodium (mg): 432
Exchanges:
Milk: 0.0
Vegetable: 0.0
Fruit: 0.0
Bread: 1.5
Meat: 1.0
Fat: 2.0

1. Spray bread cubes lightly with cooking spray; sprinkle with thyme and toss. Bake on cookie sheet at 375 degrees until just beginning to brown, about 15 minutes. Sauté mushrooms, celery, onion, bell pepper, and garlic in oil in large skillet until tender, about 8 minutes.

2. Mix cream, milk, eggs, salt, and pepper until well blended in large bowl; mix in bread cubes and sautéed vegetables. Spoon into greased slow cooker crock and sprinkle with cheese; refrigerate overnight. Place crock in slow cooker; cover and cook on high until set, 4½ to 5 hours.

Note: The bread pudding can also be cooked in a greased 6-cup soufflé dish or casserole; place on rack in 6-quart slow cooker. Cover and cook on high 5 hours.

Savory Steel-Cut Oats

Thank you, Chef Kevin Stantz, for sharing this fabulous recipe! The perfect side-dish for any meat, poultry, or fish entrée.

1 cup steel cut oats
3½ cups chicken broth
1 cup dry white wine
6 ounces baby bella mushrooms, sliced
1 leek (white part only), halved, thinly sliced
1 teaspoon minced garlic
1 teaspoon each: dried basil, oregano, thyme leaves
1 teaspoon each: salt, pepper
½–¾ cup (2–3 ounces) grated Parmesan cheese

1. Combine all ingredients, except cheese, in slow cooker; cover and cook on low 6 to 8 hours. Stir in cheese.

Per Serving:
Calories: 185
% calories from fat: 18
Protein (g): 8.5
Carbohydrate (g): 23.8
Fat (g): 3.9
Saturated fat (g): 1.5
Cholesterol (mg): 7.3
Sodium (mg): 1058
Exchanges:
Milk: 0.0
Vegetable: 0.0
Fruit: 0.0
Bread: 1.5
Meat: 0.0
Fat: 1.5

Polenta

L

Creamy polenta is a wonderful side dish—this basic recipe has many possible variations (see below).

6 servings

¾ cup yellow cornmeal
2 cups water
2 tablespoons margarine or butter
½ cup (2 ounces) grated Parmesan cheese
Salt and pepper, to taste

Per Serving:
Calories: 63
% calories from fat: 4
Protein (g): 1.5
Carbohydrate (g): 13
Fat (g): 0.3
Saturated fat (g): 0.0
Cholesterol (mg): 0.0
Sodium (mg): 0.5
Exchanges:
Milk: 0.0;
Vegetable: 0.0
Fruit: 0.0
Bread: 1.0
Meat: 0.0
Fat: 0.0

1. Mix cornmeal and water in slow cooker; cover and cook on high 1½ hours, stirring once after 45 minutes. Stir in margarine and cheese; cover and cook 15 minutes (Polenta should be soft, but should hold its shape). Season to taste with salt and pepper.

Variations

Blue Cheese Polenta—Make recipe as above, substituting ½ cup (2 ounces) crumbled blue cheese for the Parmesan cheese.

Goat Cheese Polenta—Make recipe as above, substituting ¼ to ½ cup (1 to 2 ounces) crumbled goat cheese for the Parmesan cheese.

Garlic Polenta—Sauté ¼ cup finely chopped onion and 4 to 6 cloves minced garlic in 1 tablespoon olive oil in small skillet until tender, 2 to 3 minutes. Make recipe as above, adding sautéed vegetables during last 30 minutes cooking time; omit Parmesan cheese.

Roasted Pepper-Goat Cheese Polenta—Make recipe as above, omitting Parmesan cheese, and gently stirring ¼ to ½ cup crumbled goat cheese and ⅓ cup coarsely chopped roasted red pepper into polenta during last 15 minutes cooking time.

Basil Polenta—Sauté 3 sliced green onions, 2 cloves garlic, and 1 teaspoon dried basil leaves in 2 teaspoons olive oil in large saucepan until tender, about 2 minutes. Make recipe above, adding sautéed mixture during last 30 minutes cooking time.

Cheesy Rice Torta

LO

A unique rice dish you're sure to enjoy!

6 servings

1 cup arborio rice, cooked until al dente
½ package (10-ounce size) frozen spinach, thawed, squeezed dry
2 eggs, lightly beaten
½ cup each: finely chopped onion, halved cherry tomatoes
¾ cup (3 ounces) shredded reduced-fat mozzarella cheese
¼ cup sliced ripe olives
½ teaspoon salt
⅛ teaspoon pepper

Per Serving:
Calories: 184
% calories from fat: 25
Protein (g): 8.9
Carbohydrate (g): 26.7
Fat (g): 5.3
Saturated fat (g): 2.4
Cholesterol (mg): 78
Sodium (mg): 395
Exchanges:
Milk: 0.0
Vegetable: 0.0
Fruit: 0.0
Bread: 1.5
Meat: 1.0
Fat: 0.5

1. Combine rice, spinach, and eggs in bowl; mix in remaining ingredients. Spoon into greased 7-inch springform pan; place pan on rack in 6-quart slow cooker. Cover and cook on low until set, about 3 hours. Remove springform pan and cool on wire rack 5 to 10 minutes; loosen side of pan and cut into wedges.

FIFTEEN

Breads and Sandwiches

Buttermilk Bread

L

Yummy with soups and stews—serve warm with butter.

8 servings

1½ cups all-purpose flour
2 teaspoons baking powder
⅛ teaspoon baking soda
½ teaspoon salt
4 tablespoons cold margarine or butter, cut into
   pieces
¾ cup low-fat buttermilk
1 tablespoon dried parsley

Per Serving:
Calories: 146
% calories from fat: 40
Protein (g): 1.4
Carbohydrate (g): 19.5
Fat (g): 6.1
Saturated fat (g): 1.3
Cholesterol (mg): 0.9
Sodium (mg): 378.7
Exchanges:
Milk: 0.0
Vegetable: 0.0
Fruit: 0.0
Bread: 1.0
Meat: 0.0
Fat: 1.5

1. Combine flour, baking powder, baking soda, and salt in bowl; cut in margarine until mixture resembles small crumbs. Stir in buttermilk and parsley.
2. Knead dough on floured surface 1 to 2 minutes; pat dough into greased 7-inch springform pan and place on rack in 6-quart slow cooker. Cover and cook on high until toothpick inserted in center comes out clean, 2 to 2½ hours. Cool in pan on wire rack 10 minutes. Remove side of pan; break off pieces to serve.

Variations

Pepper and Herb Bread—Make recipe as above, omitting parsley and adding 1 teaspoon each coarse ground pepper, dried dill weed, and chives. Sprinkle top of bread with 1 tablespoon dried chives.

Rosemary-Raisin Bread—Make recipe as above, adding ⅓ cup golden raisins and ½ teaspoon dried crushed rosemary.

Spoon Bread

LO

Spoon this bread into shallow bowls and top with stew, or invert the bread onto a serving plate and break into pieces to serve with soups or stews.

6–8 servings

¾ cup boiling water
½ cup yellow cornmeal
2 teaspoons margarine or butter, room temperature
2 egg yolks
⅓ cup low-fat buttermilk
½ teaspoon each: salt, sugar, baking powder
¼ teaspoon baking soda
2 egg whites, beaten to stiff peaks

Per Serving:
Calories: 87
% calories from fat: 27
Protein (g): 3.5
Carbohydrate (g): 13.9
Fat (g): 2.9
Saturated fat (g): 0.9
Cholesterol (mg): 70.5
Sodium (mg): 337
Exchanges:
Milk: 0.0
Vegetable: 0.0
Fruit: 0.0
Bread: 1.0
Meat: 0.5
Fat: 0.0

1. Stir boiling water into cornmeal in bowl; let cool until barely warm, stirring occasionally. Stir in margarine and egg yolks, blending well. Mix in buttermilk and combined remaining ingredients, except egg whites; fold in egg whites.
2. Pour batter into greased 7-inch springform pan; place pan on rack in 6-quart slow cooker. Cover and cook on high until toothpick inserted in center of bread comes out clean, 2½ to 2¾ hours. Serve immediately.

Fruited Bran Bread

LO

Delicious served warm with honey or fruit jam!

1 loaf (16 servings)

1¼ cups all-purpose flour
½ cup whole-wheat flour
2 teaspoons baking powder
½ teaspoon each: baking soda, salt
1½ cups whole-bran cereal flakes
1⅓ cups low-fat buttermilk
¾ cup packed light brown sugar
3 tablespoons margarine or butter, melted
1 egg
1 cup coarsely chopped mixed dried fruit
¼–½ cup chopped walnuts

Per Serving:
Calories: 169
% calories from fat: 20
Protein (g): 4.1
Carbohydrate (g): 33.1
Fat (g): 4.2
Saturated fat (g): 0.8
Cholesterol (mg): 14.1
Sodium (mg): 261
Exchanges:
Milk: 0.0
Vegetable: 0.0
Fruit: 0.0
Bread: 2.0
Meat: 0.0
Fat: 0.5

1. Combine flours, baking powder, baking soda, salt, and bran cereal in medium bowl. Add buttermilk, brown sugar, margarine, and egg, mixing just until dry ingredients are moistened. Gently fold in dried fruit and walnuts.

2. Pour batter into greased and floured 9 x 5-inch loaf pan. Place pan on rack in 6-quart slow cooker; cover and cook on high until toothpick inserted in center of loaf comes out clean, 2 to 3 hours. Cool in pan on wire rack 5 minutes; remove from pan and cool on wire rack.

Variation

Apricot-Date Bran Bread—Make recipe above, substituting ¼ cup each chopped dates and dried apricots for the mixed dried fruit, and pecans for the walnuts.

Pumpkin-Pecan Bread

LO *Using canned pumpkin makes this bread extra easy.*

1 loaf (16 servings)

1 cup canned pumpkin
4 tablespoons margarine or butter, room
   temperature
½ cup each: granulated and packed light brown
   sugar, 2% reduced-fat milk
2 eggs
2 cups all-purpose flour
2 teaspoons baking powder
½ teaspoon baking soda
¾ teaspoon salt
1½ teaspoons ground cinnamon
¼–½ teaspoon ground mace
½ cup chopped toasted pecans

Per Serving:
Calories: 150
% calories from fat: 21
Protein (g): 1.9
Carbohydrate (g): 27.4
Fat (g): 3.4
Saturated fat (g): 0.6
Cholesterol (mg): 27.0
Sodium (mg): 225
Exchanges:
Milk: 0.0
Vegetable: 0.0
Fruit: 0.0
Bread: 2.0
Meat: 0.0
Fat: 0.5

1. Beat pumpkin, margarine, and sugars in bowl until well blended; mix in milk and eggs. Mix in combined dry ingredients; mix in pecans.

2. Spoon batter into greased 9 x 5-inch loaf pan and place on rack in 6-quart slow cooker. Cover and cook on high until toothpick inserted in center of bread comes out clean, about 3½ hours. Cool in pan on wire rack 5 minutes; remove from pan and cool on wire rack.

Brown Sugar Banana Bread

LO *Brown sugar gives this banana bread a caramel flavor; the applesauce adds moistness.*

1 loaf (16 servings)

4 tablespoons margarine or butter, room temperature
¼ cup applesauce
2 eggs
2 tablespoons 2% reduced-fat milk or water
¾ cup packed light brown sugar
1 cup mashed ripe bananas (2–3 medium bananas)
1¾ cups all-purpose flour
2 teaspoons baking powder
½ teaspoon baking soda
¼ teaspoon salt
¼ cup coarsely chopped walnuts or pecans

Per Serving:
Calories: 146
% calories from fat: 30
Protein (g): 1.6
Carbohydrate (g): 23.7
Fat (g): 4.9
Saturated fat (g): 0.9
Cholesterol (mg): 26.6
Sodium (mg): 184
Exchanges:
Milk: 0.0
Vegetable: 0.0
Fruit: 0.0
Bread: 1.5
Meat: 0.0
Fat: 1.0

1. Beat margarine, applesauce, eggs, milk, and brown sugar in large bowl until smooth. Add bananas and mix at low speed; beat at high speed 1 to 2 minutes. Mix in combined flour, baking powder, baking soda, and salt; mix in walnuts.
2. Pour batter into greased 9 x 5-inch loaf pan. Place pan on rack in 6-quart slow cooker; cover and cook on high until toothpick inserted in center of bread comes out clean, 2 to 3 hours. Cool in pan on wire rack 5 minutes; remove bread from pan and cool on wire rack.

Fruit and Nut Banana Bread

LO *Use any dried fruit or nut that you want in this tasty bread.*

1 loaf (12 servings)

6 tablespoons margarine or butter, room temperature
½ cup sugar
2 eggs
1 cup mashed ripe bananas
1¾ cups self-rising flour
½ teaspoon salt
½ cup each: chopped dried apples, chopped pecans

Per Serving:
Calories: 211
% calories from fat: 42
Protein (g): 3.5
Carbohydrate (g): 27.9
Fat (g): 10
Saturated fat (g): 1.7
Cholesterol (mg): 35.3
Sodium (mg): 410
Exchanges:
Milk: 0.0
Vegetable: 0.0
Fruit: 0.0
Bread: 2.0
Meat: 0.0
Fat: 2.0

1. Beat margarine and sugar in large bowl until fluffy; beat in eggs and bananas. Mix in flour and salt; mix in dried apples and pecans.
2. Pour batter into greased 9 x 5-inch loaf pan; place on rack in 6-quart slow cooker; cover and cook on high until wooden skewer inserted in center of bread comes out clean, about 3½ hours. Cool on wire rack 5 minutes; remove from pan and cool.

Boston Brown Bread

The slow cooker is perfect for steamed breads!

2 loaves (6–8 servings each)

⅔ cup whole-wheat flour
⅓ cup each: yellow cornmeal, chopped walnuts, raisins
2 tablespoons light brown sugar
¾ teaspoon baking soda
½ teaspoon salt
⅔ cup 2% reduced-fat milk
¼ cup light molasses
1 tablespoon lemon juice

Per Serving:
Calories: 104
% calories from fat: 22
Protein (g): 2.3
Carbohydrate (g): 19.1
Fat (g): 2.7
Saturated fat (g): 0.4
Cholesterol (mg): 1.1
Sodium (mg): 188
Exchanges:
Milk: 0.0
Vegetable: 0.0
Fruit: 0.0
Bread: 1.0
Meat: 0.0
Fat: 0.5

1. Combine all ingredients, except milk, molasses, and lemon juice, in bowl. Add combined milk, molasses, and lemon juice, mixing well; spoon mixture into two greased and floured 16-ounce cans. Cover tops of cans with greased aluminum foil, securing with rubber bands.
2. Stand cans in slow cooker; add enough boiling water to come halfway up sides of cans, making sure foil does not touch water. Cover and cook on high 2 hours; turn heat to low and cook until wooden skewer inserted in breads comes out clean, about 4 hours. Uncover cans and stand on wire rack to cool 10 minutes. Loosen sides of bread by gently rolling cans on counter, or remove bottoms of cans and push breads through.

Roasted Chili Cornbread

This cornbread is extra moist and "chili hot!" Omit or reduce the amount of poblano chili for less hotness.

8 servings (1 piece each)

¼ each: chopped small red bell pepper, poblano and jalapeño chili
1 large green onion, chopped
¾ cup all-purpose flour
¼ cup yellow cornmeal
2 tablespoons light brown sugar
1½ teaspoons baking powder
¼ teaspoon each: ground cumin, dried oregano leaves, salt
1 egg, lightly beaten
½ cup low-fat buttermilk
¼ cup whole-kernel corn
2 tablespoons minced cilantro

Per Serving:
Calories: 155
% calories from fat: 9
Protein (g): 4.1
Carbohydrate (g): 32.8
Fat (g): 1.6
Saturated fat (g): 0.4
Cholesterol (mg): 27
Sodium (mg): 194
Exchanges:
Milk: 0.0
Vegetable: 0.0
Fruit: 0.0
Bread: 2.0
Meat: 0.0
Fat: 0.0

1. Cook bell pepper, chilies, and green onion in lightly greased skillet over medium heat until tender, about 5 minutes; reserve. Combine flour, cornmeal, brown sugar, baking powder, herbs, and salt in medium bowl; add combined egg and buttermilk, mixing just until combined. Stir in sautéed vegetables, corn, and cilantro.
2. Pour batter into greased and floured 7-inch springform pan; place pan on rack in 6-quart slow cooker. Cover and cook on high until toothpick inserted in center of bread comes out clean, about 2 hours. Cool in pan on wire rack 10 minutes; serve warm.

Parmesan Bread

L

This melty cheese bread is a perfect accompaniment to soups and stews. Choose an oval or round loaf that will fit your slow cooker.

6–8 servings

1 small loaf Italian bread (10–12 ounces)
6 tablespoons margarine or butter, room temperature
⅓ cup grated Parmesan cheese

1. Cut bread into 6 to 8 slices, cutting to but not through bottom of loaf. Spread both sides of bread slices with combined margarine and Parmesan cheese. Wrap loaf securely in aluminum foil. Place in slow cooker and cook on low 2 hours.

Note: The bread can also be baked at 350 degrees until warm, about 20 minutes.

Per Serving:
Calories: 249
% calories from fat: 52
Protein (g): 6.0
Carbohydrate (g): 23.9
Fat (g): 14.3
Saturated fat (g): 3.4
Cholesterol (mg): 3.9
Sodium (mg): 477
Exchanges:
Milk: 0.0
Vegetable: 0.0
Fruit: 0.0
Bread: 1.5
Meat: 0.0
Fat: 3.0

Sour Cream Coffee Cake with Cranberry Filling

LO

An irresistible offering, this moist cake boasts a flavorful cranberry filling.

8 servings

3 tablespoons margarine or butter, room temperature
2 tablespoons unsweetened applesauce
⅓ cup granulated sugar
¼ cup packed light brown sugar
1 egg
1 teaspoon vanilla
1 cup plus 2 tablespoons all-purpose flour
¾ teaspoon each: baking powder, baking soda
½ teaspoon ground cinnamon
¼ teaspoon salt
½ cup reduced-fat sour cream
Cranberry Filling (recipe follows)
Powdered sugar, as garnish

Per Serving:
Calories: 244
% calories from fat: 24
Protein (g): 2.3
Carbohydrate (g): 43.6
Fat (g): 6.5
Saturated fat (g): 1.8
Cholesterol (mg): 31.4
Sodium (mg): 345
Exchanges:
Milk: 0.0
Vegetable: 0.0
Fruit: 0.0
Bread: 3.0
Meat: 0.0
Fat: 1.0

1. Beat margarine, applesauce, and sugars until smooth. Beat in egg and vanilla. Mix in combined flour, baking powder, baking soda, cinnamon, and salt alternately with sour cream, beginning and ending with dry ingredients.

2. Spoon ⅓ of batter into greased and floured 6-cup fluted cake pan; spoon ½ the Cranberry Filling over batter. Repeat layers, ending with batter. Place pan on rack in 6-quart slow cooker; cover and cook on high until toothpick inserted in center of cake comes out clean, about 3 hours. Cool cake on wire rack 10 minutes; invert onto serving plate. Sprinkle generously with powdered sugar and serve warm.

Cranberry Filling

Makes about 1 cup

¾ cup each: dried cranberries, water
2 tablespoons sugar
1 tablespoon flour
⅛ teaspoon salt

1. Combine all ingredients in small saucepan and heat to boiling; reduce heat and simmer, uncovered, until mixture is thick, 5 to 8 minutes. Cool.

Almond Coffee Cake

LO *The Sweet Topping disappears into the cake during cooking, creating a rich texture. Serve this delicious coffee cake for brunch, or enjoy with afternoon tea.*

8 servings

1 cup all-purpose flour
½ cup sugar
1½ teaspoons baking powder
½ teaspoon salt
4 tablespoons margarine or butter, room temperature
½ cup plus 2% reduced-fat milk
1 egg
½ teaspoon almond extract
Sweet Topping (recipe follows)
⅓ cup powdered sugar
1–2 teaspoons 2% reduced-fat milk
3 tablespoons toasted sliced or slivered almonds

Per Serving:
Calories: 241
% calories from fat: 39
Protein (g): 2.2
Carbohydrate (g): 34.3
Fat (g): 10.2
Saturated fat (g): 2.1
Cholesterol (mg): 27.8
Sodium (mg): 344
Exchanges:
Milk: 0.0
Vegetable: 0.0
Fruit: 0.0
Bread: 2.0
Meat: 0.0
Fat: 1.0

1. Beat all ingredients, except Sweet Topping, powdered sugar, 1–2 teaspoons milk, and almonds, in bowl until blended; beat on medium speed 2 minutes. Pour batter into greased 7-inch springform pan; sprinkle with Sweet Topping. Place pan on rack in 6-quart slow cooker; cover, placing 3 layers of paper towels under lid, and cook on high until toothpick inserted in center comes out clean, 3 to 3½ hours. Cool on wire rack; remove side of pan and place coffee cake on serving plate.

2. Mix powdered sugar with 1 to 2 teaspoons milk to make thin glaze consistency; drizzle glaze over top of cake. Sprinkle with almonds.

Sweet Topping

1½ tablespoons cold margarine or butter
2 tablespoons flour
2 tablespoons sugar

1. Cut margarine into combined flour and sugar until crumbly.

Sloppy Joes

A great sandwich for kids of all ages! Serve with lots of pickles and fresh vegetable relishes.

6–8 servings

1 pound ground beef
1 cup each: chopped onion, green or red bell pepper
2 teaspoons minced garlic
1 cup catsup
½ cup water
¼ cup packed light brown sugar
2 tablespoons prepared mustard
2 teaspoons each: celery seeds, chili powder
Salt and pepper, to taste
6–8 whole-wheat hamburger buns, toasted
8 sweet or dill pickle spears

Per Serving:
Calories: 278
% of calories from fat: 23
Protein (gm): 19.1
Carbohydrate (gm): 35.8
Fat (gm): 7.3
Saturated fat (gm): 2.6
Cholesterol (mg): 41.6
Sodium (mg): 265
Exchanges:
Milk: 0.0
Vegetable: 1.0
Fruit: 0.0
Bread: 2.0
Meat: 2.0
Fat: 0.0

1. Cook ground beef in lightly greased skillet until browned, crumbling with a fork. Combine ground beef and remaining ingredients, except salt, pepper, buns, and pickles, in slow cooker; cover and cook on high 2 to 3 hours. Season to taste with salt and pepper. Serve in buns with pickles.

Variation

Vegetarian Joes—Make recipe as above, omitting ground beef; add 1 cup each textured vegetable protein and sliced mushrooms, and increase water to 1½ cups.

Cheeseburger Joes

A cheeseburger deluxe, made sloppy joe-style! Everyone will stand in line for this cheesy sandwich!

12 servings

2 pounds lean ground beef
¾ cup each: chopped onion, green bell pepper
8 ounces sliced mushrooms
1 tablespoon minced garlic
½ cup each: crumbled fried bacon, sweet pickle relish, yellow mustard
¾ cup catsup
1 tablespoon Worcestershire sauce
8 ounces reduced-fat processed cheese, cubed
Salt and pepper, to taste
12 hamburger buns, toasted

Per Serving:
Calories: 333
% calories from fat: 28
Protein (g): 27.2
Carbohydrate (g): 32.7
Fat (g): 10.2
Saturated fat (g): 4.2
Cholesterol (mg): 31.4
Sodium (mg): 1005
Exchanges:
Milk: 0.0
Vegetable: 0.0
Fruit: 0.0
Bread: 2.0
Meat: 3.0
Fat: 0.5

1. Cook beef, onion, and bell pepper over medium heat in large skillet until beef is browned, crumbling with a fork; transfer to slow cooker. Add remaining ingredients, except salt, pepper, and buns; cover and cook on low 2 to 3 hours. Season to taste with salt and pepper; serve on buns.

Vino Joes

An "adult" version of a sloppy joe!

12 servings

1 pound lean ground beef
¾ cup each: chopped onion, green bell pepper
2 teaspoons minced garlic
1 can (14½ ounces) diced tomatoes, drained
½ cup dry red wine
2 tablespoons Worcestershire sauce
¼ cup packed light brown sugar
2 tablespoons Dijon mustard
2 teaspoons celery seeds
Salt and pepper, to taste
12 Italian rolls, toasted

Per Serving:
Calories: 399
% calories from fat: 16
Protein (g): 21.3
Carbohydrate (g): 58.0
Fat (g): 6.7
Saturated fat (g): 1.8
Cholesterol (mg): 35.2
Sodium (mg): 694
Exchanges:
Milk: 0.0
Vegetable: 0.0
Fruit: 0.0
Bread: 4.0
Meat: 2.0
Fat: 0.0

1. Cook ground beef, onion, bell pepper, and garlic over medium heat in large skillet until beef is browned, crumbling with a fork; transfer to slow cooker. Add remaining ingredients, except salt, pepper, and rolls; cover and cook on high 2 to 3 hours. Season to taste with salt and pepper; serve in rolls.

Pulled Chicken Sandwiches

Friends will ask for this tangy barbecue recipe!

8 servings

1 pound boneless, skinless chicken breasts, quartered
1 can (12 ounces) cola
1 cup catsup
⅓ cup yellow mustard
¼ cup packed light brown sugar
½ cup chopped onion
1 teaspoon minced garlic
2 tablespoons cornstarch
¼ cup cold water
Salt and pepper, to taste
8 hamburger buns

Per Serving:
Calories: 275
% calories from fat: 10
Protein (g): 18.3
Carbohydrate (g): 44.1
Fat (g): 3.0
Saturated fat (g): 0.7
Cholesterol (mg): 44.1
Sodium (mg): 691
Exchanges:
Milk: 0.0
Vegetable: 0.0
Fruit: 0.0
Bread: 3.0
Meat: 2.0
Fat: 0.0

1. Combine all ingredients, except cornstarch, water, salt, pepper, and buns, in slow cooker; cover and cook on low 6 to 8 hours. Turn heat to high and cook 10 minutes; stir in combined cornstarch and cold water, stirring 2 to 3 minutes. Stir to shred chicken; season to taste with salt and pepper. Serve in buns.

Pulled Pork Sandwiches, Southern-Style

White Barbecue Sauce is popular in the South; the sandwiches can be served either on biscuits or small buns.

12 servings

1 boneless pork loin roast (about 2 pounds)
Brown Sugar Rub (recipe follows)
½ cup chicken broth
12 biscuits or small buns
White Barbecue Sauce (recipe follows)

1. Rub pork loin with Brown Sugar Rub; place in slow cooker with broth. Cover and cook on low 6 to 8 hours. Remove pork and shred; reserve cooking liquid for soup or another use. Spoon meat onto bottoms of biscuits and top with White Barbecue Sauce and biscuit tops.

Per Serving:
Calories: 418
% calories from fat: 46
Protein (g): 20.7
Carbohydrate (g): 34.9
Fat (g): 21.3
Saturated fat (g): 4.4
Cholesterol (mg): 43.5
Sodium (mg): 650
Exchanges:
Milk: 0.0
Vegetable: 0.0
Fruit: 0.0
Bread: 2.0
Meat: 2.0
Fat: 3.0

Brown Sugar Rub

Makes about ¼ cup

¼ cup packed light brown sugar
1 teaspoon garlic powder
½ teaspoon each: ground cumin, salt, pepper

1. Mix all ingredients.

White Barbecue Sauce

Makes about 2½ cups

1½ cups reduced-fat mayonnaise
¼ cup apple cider vinegar
1 tablespoon sugar
1 clove garlic, minced
2 teaspoons horseradish (optional)
1–2 tablespoons lemon juice

1. Mix all ingredients, adding lemon juice to taste.

Pork and Chutney Sandwiches

Easy sandwiches for a crowd! You can make your own Mango Chutney, if you want (see p. 468).

12 servings

1 boneless pork loin roast (about 2 pounds)
Curry Spice Rub (recipe follows)
½ cup chicken broth
1½ cups mango chutney
48 slices sourdough bread

Per Serving:
Calories: 500
% calories from fat: 14
Protein (g): 40.4
Carbohydrate (g): 69.4
Fat (g): 7.9
Saturated fat (g): 2.6
Cholesterol (mg): 62.5
Sodium (mg): 823
Exchanges:
Milk: 0.0
Vegetable: 0.0
Fruit: 0.5
Bread: 4.0
Meat: 3.0
Fat: 0.0

1. Rub pork loin with Curry Spice Rub; insert meat thermometer in center of roast so tip is in center of meat. Place pork in slow cooker and add broth; cover and cook on low until meat thermometer registers 160 degrees, about 3 hours. Remove pork to cutting board and let stand, loosely covered with foil, 10 minutes. Reserve broth for soup or another use. Slice pork and make sandwiches, spooning about 2 tablespoons chutney into each sandwich.

Curry Spice Rub

Makes about 2 tablespoons

1½ teaspoons each: curry powder, paprika
¾ teaspoon each: ground cinnamon, garlic powder, salt
½ teaspoon each: ground nutmeg and ginger

1. Combine all ingredients.

French Dip Sandwich

Tender beef, served in a bun, with flavorful broth for dipping—let guests make their own sandwiches.

12 servings

1 boneless beef chuck roast (about 3 pounds)
Pepper, to taste
2 cups reduced-sodium beef broth
1 cup dry red wine or beef broth
1 package (1 ounce) onion soup mix
1 teaspoon minced garlic
12 hard rolls
6 ounces sliced reduced-fat provolone cheese

Per Serving:
Calories: 384
% calories from fat: 22
Protein (g): 36.2
Carbohydrate (g): 33.7
Fat (g): 9.1
Saturated fat (g): 3.3
Cholesterol (mg): 47.2
Sodium (mg): 969
Exchanges:
Milk: 0.0
Vegetable: 0.0
Fruit: 0.0
Bread: 2.0
Meat: 4.0
Fat: 0.0

1. Sprinkle chuck roast lightly with pepper and place in slow cooker; add remaining ingredients, except rolls and cheese. Cover and cook on low 6 to 8 hours. Remove chuck roast and slice thinly; return to slow cooker and turn heat to warm. Serve beef on hard rolls with provolone cheese; serve broth for dipping.

Philly Cheese Steak Sandwiches

Sandwiches can be briefly put under the broiler to melt the cheese.

6–8 servings

1 pound boneless round steak, thinly sliced
1 cup each: thinly sliced onion, green bell pepper,
    reduced-sodium beef broth
1 teaspoon minced garlic
1 tablespoon Worcestershire sauce
Salt and pepper, to taste
6–8 hard or hoagie rolls
1–1½ cups (6 to 8 ounces) shredded reduced-fat
    mozzarella cheese

Per Serving:
Calories: 568
% calories from fat: 24
Protein (g): 2.3
Carbohydrate (g): 43.6
Fat (g): 6.5
Saturated fat (g): 1.8
Cholesterol (mg): 31.4
Sodium (mg): 345
Exchanges:
Milk: 0.0
Vegetable: 0.0
Fruit: 0.0
Bread: 3.0
Meat: 0.0
Fat: 1.0

1. Combine all ingredients, except salt, pepper, rolls, and cheese, in slow cooker; cover and cook on low 6 to 8 hours. Season to taste with salt and pepper. Top rolls with meat and vegetable mixture; sprinkle with cheese. If desired, broil 6 inches from heat source until cheese is melted, 3 to 4 minutes.

Hot Muffuletta

A new version of a New Orleans favorite! Make sure the size of the bread will fit in your slow cooker.

6 servings

Olive Relish (recipe follows)
1 round loaf sourdough bread or focaccia (about 8 inches diameter), halved
4 ounces each: thinly sliced Italian salami, smoked ham, reduced-fat provolone or fontina cheese

Per Serving:
Calories: 482
% calories from fat: 43
Protein (g): 24.7
Carbohydrate (g): 46.2
Fat (g): 23.9
Saturated fat (g): 6.6
Cholesterol (mg): 29.2
Sodium (mg): 1528
Exchanges:
Milk: 0.0
Vegetable: 0.0
Fruit: 0.0
Bread: 3.0
Meat: 2.0
Fat: 3.0

1. Spread ½ the Olive Relish on bottom of bread; top with salami, ham, cheese, remaining Olive Relish, and top of bread. Press sandwich together firmly and wrap securely in aluminum foil. Line bottom of slow cooker with large piece of aluminum foil; place sandwich in slow cooker. Cover and cook on low 2 hours. Cut into wedges to serve.

Olive Relish

Makes about 1 cup

½ cup each: chopped pitted black and green olives, tomatoes
¼ cup each: chopped parsley, olive oil
1 anchovy fillet, mashed (optional)
Juice of ½ lemon
Pepper, to taste

1. Mix all ingredients, except pepper; season to taste with pepper.

Brat Sandwiches with Peppers and Onions

Brats cooked in beer, served in buns, and heaped with savory bell peppers, onions, and mushrooms—a sandwich that's hard to beat! The brats can be briefly browned in a skillet or under the broiler before serving, if you like.

6–8 servings

6–8 fresh bratwurst (1½ pounds)
2–3 bottles (12 ounces each) beer
1 cup each: chopped onion, sliced red and green bell
    pepper
8 ounces sliced baby bella mushrooms
2 teaspoons minced garlic
Salt and pepper, to taste
6–8 hot dog buns

Per Serving:
Calories: 616
% calories from fat: 55
Protein (g): 27.7
Carbohydrate (g): 33.3
Fat (g): 37.0
Saturated fat (g): 13.5
Cholesterol (mg): 92.7
Sodium (mg): 1361
Exchanges:
Milk: 0.0
Vegetable: 0.0
Fruit: 0.0
Bread: 2.0
Meat: 3.0
Fat: 7.0

1. Combine all ingredients, except salt, pepper, and buns, in slow cooker; cover and cook on low 6 to 8 hours. Season with salt and pepper. Serve brats in buns with vegetable mixture spooned over.

Polish Sausage and Sauerkraut Sandwiches

Double or triple the recipe to serve a crowd—easy to keep warm on a buffet table!

4–6 servings

4–6 Polish sausages (1 pound)
8–12 ounces sauerkraut, rinsed, drained
1 medium onion, thinly sliced
1 small tart apple, peeled, thinly sliced
1 teaspoon each: fennel and caraway seeds
½ cup reduced-sodium chicken broth
Pepper, to taste
4–6 hot dog buns or rolls
Whole grain mustard

Per Serving:
Calories: 538
% calories from fat: 59
Protein (g): 22.5
Carbohydrate (g): 33.1
Fat (g): 34.8
Saturated fat (g): 12.3
Cholesterol (mg): 80.6
Sodium (mg): 1652
Exchanges:
Milk: 0.0
Vegetable: 0.0
Fruit: 0.0
Bread: 2.0
Meat: 2.0
Fat: 6.0

1. Place sausages in slow cooker; top with combined remaining ingredients, except pepper, buns, and mustard. Cover and cook on low 6 to 8 hours. Season to taste with pepper. Serve sausages and sauerkraut on buns with mustard.

Italian Beef Sandwiches

Slow cooked to savory goodness!!

12 servings

1 boneless beef rump roast (about 3 pounds)
3 cups beef broth
1 package (.7 ounce) Italian salad dressing mix
1 bay leaf
1 teaspoon pepper
12 buns or Italian rolls

1. Combine all ingredients, except buns, in slow cooker; cover and cook on low 10 to 12 hours. Remove meat and shred; return to slow cooker. Serve meat and juices in buns.

Per Serving:
Calories: 266
% calories from fat: 17
Protein (g): 23.6
Carbohydrate (g): 30.7
Fat (g): 5.1
Saturated fat (g): 1.0
Cholesterol (mg): 39.7
Sodium (mg): 489
Exchanges:
Milk: 0.0
Vegetable: 0.0
Fruit: 0.0
Bread: 2.0
Meat: 3.0
Fat: 0.0

Grinders

A sandwich to rave about—the meatballs are extra special!

6 servings

Eggplant Meatballs (see p. 464)
2 cups sliced red and green bell peppers
1½–2 cups prepared spaghetti sauce, warm
6 hoagie buns, toasted

1. Make Eggplant Meatballs, shaping into 24 meatballs. Combine meatballs, bell peppers, and spaghetti sauce in slow cooker; cover and cook on high 3 to 4 hours. Serve 4 meatballs with sauce in each bun.

Per Serving:
Calories: 565
% calories from fat: 23
Protein (g): 40.3
Carbohydrate (g): 69.0
Fat (g): 14.1
Saturated fat (g): 5.2
Cholesterol (mg): 149.5
Sodium (mg): 1559
Exchanges:
Milk: 0.0
Vegetable: 2.0
Fruit: 0.0
Bread: 4.0
Meat: 4.0
Fat: 0.0

Turkey Pitas

Fill pita halves with this zesty mixture, or serve in buns.

8–12 servings

1 pound boneless, skinless turkey breast or thighs, cubed (2-inch)
1 can (14½ ounces) diced tomatoes, undrained
½ can (6 ounce-size) tomato sauce
2 cups sliced mushrooms
½ cup each: chopped onion, sliced green olives, hot pepper rings
1 tablespoon prepared mustard
1 teaspoon dried oregano leaves
Salt and pepper, to taste
4–8 large pitas, halved

Per Serving:
Calories: 183
% calories from fat: 10
Protein (g): 18.2
Carbohydrate (g): 22.3
Fat (g): 2.1
Saturated fat (g): 0.3
Cholesterol (mg): 35.2
Sodium (mg): 708
Exchanges:
Milk: 0.0
Vegetable: 0.0
Fruit: 0.0
Bread: 1.5
Meat: 2.0
Fat: 0.0

1. Combine all ingredients, except salt, pepper, and pitas, in slow cooker; cover and cook on low 6 to 8 hours. Season to taste with salt and pepper; stir to shred turkey. Serve in pita halves.

Greek Pitas

Ground beef, or a mixture of lamb and beef can be used in these flavorful meatballs.

4 servings

1 pound ground lamb
¾ cup fresh bread crumbs
1 egg
¼ cup finely chopped onion
1 teaspoon each: dried oregano and mint leaves
¾ teaspoon salt
½ teaspoon pepper
¾ cup chicken broth
2 pita breads, halved
Cucumber-Yogurt Sauce (recipe follows)
4 tablespoons crumbled feta cheese

Per Serving:
Calories: 489
% calories from fat: 53
Protein (g): 26.7
Carbohydrate (g): 24.3
Fat (g): 25.5
Saturated fat (g): 11.1
Cholesterol (mg): 140.0
Sodium (mg): 1021
Exchanges:
Milk: 0.0
Vegetable: 0.0
Fruit: 0.0
Bread: 1.5
Meat: 3.0
Fat: 3.5

1. Combine lamb, bread crumbs, egg, onion, oregano, mint, salt and pepper; shape into 16 meatballs. Place in slow cooker with chicken broth; cover and cook on low 4 hours. Drain and discard juices, or save for another use.

2. Spoon 4 meatballs into each pita half; top meatballs in each pita with 2 tablespoons Cucumber-Yogurt sauce and 1 tablespoon feta cheese.

Cucumber-Yogurt Sauce

Makes about ½ cup

¼ cup each: reduced-fat yogurt, finely chopped seeded cucumber
1 teaspoon dried mint leaves

1. Mix all ingredients.

Moo Shu Wraps

Enjoy traditional flavors of moo shu pork in a wrap!

6 servings

1 pound pork tenderloin
2 teaspoons each: five-spice powder, minced garlic
½ cup plum sauce
¼ cup water
1 tablespoon soy sauce
2 teaspoons minced gingerroot
⅓ cup julienned bamboo shoots
Salt and pepper, to taste
6 flour tortillas (6-inch) warm
½–¾ cup hoisin sauce
6 small green onions

Per Serving:
Calories: 255
% calories from fat: 18
Protein (g): 16.6
Carbohydrate (g): 34.7
Fat (g): 5.1
Saturated fat (g): 1.2
Cholesterol (mg): 36.6
Sodium (mg): 856
Exchanges:
Milk: 0.0
Vegetable: 0.0
Fruit: 0.0
Bread: 2.0
Meat: 2.0
Fat: 0.0

1. Rub pork with five-spice powder and garlic; let stand 30 minutes. Place pork in slow cooker; add combined plum sauce, water, soy sauce, and gingerroot. Cover and cook on low until pork is very tender, about 3 hours; remove pork and shred with 2 forks. Return to slow cooker; add bamboo shoots and cover and cook on low 30 minutes. Season to taste with salt and pepper.
2. Spread each tortilla with 1 tablespoon hoisin sauce and lay a green onion in the center. Spoon generous ¼ cup pork mixture on each tortilla and roll up.

Picadillo Tacos

These soft tacos are perfect party fare!

6 servings

12 ounces pork tenderloin
¼ cup each: water, thinly sliced green onion
1 teaspoon each: minced garlic, jalapeño chili,
   ground cinnamon
¼ teaspoon dried oregano leaves
1–2 teaspoons cider vinegar
¼ cup each: raisins, slivered almonds
Salt and pepper, to taste
6 flour tortillas (6-inch), warm
¾ cup each: chopped tomato, avocado
Cilantro sprigs, as garnish
Salsa

Per Serving:
Calories: 247
% calories from fat: 33
Protein (g): 16.5
Carbohydrate (g): 25.4
Fat (g): 9.1
Saturated fat (g): 1.8
Cholesterol (mg): 36.6
Sodium (mg): 230
Exchanges:
Milk: 0.0
Vegetable: 0.0
Fruit: 0.0
Bread: 1.5
Meat: 2.0
Fat: 0.5

1. Combine pork, water, green onion, garlic, jalapeño chili, cinnamon, oregano, and vinegar in slow cooker; cover and cook on low 3 hours. Remove pork and shred with 2 forks; return to slow cooker; add raisins and almonds. Cover and cook on low 1 hour; season to taste with salt and pepper.
2. Top each tortilla with about ¼ cup pork mixture; sprinkle with 1 tablespoon each tomato and avocado and several sprigs cilantro. Roll up and serve with salsa.

Sandwich Melts

Serve melty warm sandwiches from the slow cooker for delicious party fare. Make a medley of sandwiches from the recipes below and label them for guests to choose from. A 3-quart slow cooker will easily hold 10 to 12 of these small sandwiches—a 6-quart slow cooker will hold many more!

Ham, Cheese, and Pesto Melts

4 servings

2–4 tablespoons basil pesto
4 small buns or hard rolls, halved
4 ounces thinly sliced ham
2 ounces thinly sliced reduced-fat provolone cheese

1. Spread pesto on bottoms of buns; top with ham, cheese, and bun tops. Wrap each sandwich in aluminum foil. Place in slow cooker; cover and cook on low 2 hours. Turn heat to warm for serving.

Per Serving:
Calories: 190
% calories from fat: 34
Protein (g): 13.1
Carbohydrate (g): 20.0
Fat (g): 7.5
Saturated fat (g): 2.6
Cholesterol (mg): 23.6
Sodium (mg): 678
Exchanges:
Milk: 0.0
Vegetable: 0.0
Fruit: 0.0
Bread: 1.0
Meat: 1.5
Fat: 0.5

Turkey Chutney Melts

4 servings

2 ounces reduced-fat cream cheese, room temperature
1 tablespoon chopped pecans or walnuts
4 small buns, halved
4 ounces thinly sliced turkey
4 tablespoons whole cranberry sauce

1. Spread combined cream cheese and nuts on bottoms of buns; top with turkey, cranberry sauce, and bun tops. Wrap each sandwich in aluminum foil. Place in slow cooker; cover and cook on low 2 hours. Turn heat to warm for serving.

Per Serving:
Calories: 176
% calories from fat: 24
Protein (g): 10.0
Carbohydrate (g): 25.6
Fat (g): 4.9
Saturated fat (g): 1.9
Cholesterol (mg): 20.3
Sodium (mg): 504
Exchanges:
Milk: 0.0
Vegetable: 0.0
Fruit: 0.0
Bread: 2.0
Meat: 1.0
Fat: 0.0

Goat Cheese and Salami Melts

4 servings

2 ounces each: goat cheese, reduced-fat
cream cheese, room temperature
4 small buns or hard rolls
2–4 tablespoons sun-dried tomato pesto
2–3 ounces thinly sliced salami

1. Spread combined goat and cream cheese on
bottoms of buns; top with pesto, salami, and bun
tops. Wrap each sandwich in aluminum foil.
Place in slow cooker; cover and cook on low 2
hours. Turn heat to warm for serving.

Per Serving:
Calories: 269
% calories from fat: 46
Protein (g): 12.3
Carbohydrate (g): 24.1
Fat (g): 13.5
Saturated fat (g): 6.9
Cholesterol (mg): 30.9
Sodium (mg): 515
Exchanges:
Milk: 0.0
Vegetable: 0.0
Fruit: 0.0
Bread: 1.5
Meat: 1.0
Fat: 2.0

Reuben Melts

4 servings

2–4 tablespoons thousand-island salad dressing
4 small rye buns, halved
4 ounces thinly sliced corned beef
4–6 tablespoons well drained sauerkraut
2 ounces thinly sliced reduced-fat Swiss cheese

1. Spread salad dressing on bottoms of buns; top
with corned beef, sauerkraut, cheese, and bun tops.
Wrap each sandwich in aluminum foil. Place in
slow cooker; cover and cook on low 2 hours. Turn
heat to warm for serving.

Per Serving:
Calories: 249
% calories from fat: 38
Protein (g): 13.6
Carbohydrate (g): 24.6
Fat (g): 10.4
Saturated fat (g): 2.9
Cholesterol (mg): 34.9
Sodium (mg): 862
Exchanges:
Milk: 0.0
Vegetable: 0.0
Fruit: 0.0
Bread: 2.0
Meat: 1.0
Fat: 1.0

L Cucumber Cheese Melts

4 servings

2 ounces reduced-fat cream cheese, room temperature
1 tablespoon crumbled blue cheese
4 small multigrain buns, halved
8 thin cucumber slices
2 tablespoons apricot jam

1. Spread combined cream cheese and blue cheese
on bottoms of buns; top with cucumber slices, jam,
and bun tops. Wrap each sandwich in aluminum
foil. Place in slow cooker; cover and cook on low
2 hours. Turn heat to warm for serving.

Per Serving:
Calories: 172
% calories from fat: 26
Protein (g): 6.0
Carbohydrate (g): 26.7
Fat (g): 5.2
Saturated fat (g): 2.3
Cholesterol (mg): 8.2
Sodium (mg): 297
Exchanges:
Milk: 0.0
Vegetable: 0.0
Fruit: 0.0
Bread: 2.0
Meat: 0.0
Fat: 1.0

L

Blue Cheese and Pear Melts

4 servings

2 ounces thinly sliced reduced-fat brick cheese
4 small sourdough buns
¼ cup orange marmalade
½ small pear, thinly sliced
2 tablespoons crumbled blue cheese

1. Place cheese on bottoms of buns; top with marmalade, pear, blue cheese, and bun tops. Wrap each sandwich in aluminum foil. Place in slow cooker; cover and cook on low 2 hours. Turn heat to warm for serving.

Per Serving:
Calories: 226
% calories from fat: 19
Protein (g): 11
Carbohydrate (g): 37.9
Fat (g): 5.2
Saturated fat (g): 2.1
Cholesterol (mg): 9.9
Sodium (mg): 334
Exchanges:
Milk: 0.0
Vegetable: 0.0
Fruit: 0.0
Bread: 2.5
Meat: 1.0
Fat: 0.0

SIXTEEN

Desserts

Lemony Carrot Cake with Cream Cheese Glaze

LO

A carrot cake with a difference! Filled with raisins and walnuts, you'll enjoy the fresh lemon zest accent.

12 servings

12 tablespoons margarine or butter, room temperature
¾ cup packed light brown sugar
3 eggs
2 cups shredded carrots
⅓ cup each: raisins, coarsely chopped walnuts
Grated zest of 1 lemon
1½ cups self-rising flour
1 teaspoon baking powder
¼ teaspoon salt
Cream Cheese Glaze (recipe follows)

Per Serving:
Calories: 337
% calories from fat: 43
Protein (g): 4.5
Carbohydrate (g): 44.3
Fat (g): 16.6
Saturated fat (g): 3.5
Cholesterol (mg): 55.1
Sodium (mg): 491
Exchanges:
Milk: 0.0
Vegetable: 0.0
Fruit: 0.0
Bread: 3.0
Meat: 0.0
Fat: 3.0

1. Beat margarine and brown sugar in large bowl until fluffy; beat in eggs one at a time, beating well after each addition. Mix in carrots, raisins, walnuts, and lemon zest. Fold in combined flour, baking powder and salt.
2. Pour batter into greased and floured 7-cup springform pan; place on rack in slow cooker. Cover and cook on high until toothpick inserted in center of cake comes out clean, about 3½ hours. Cool pan on wire rack 10 minutes; remove side of pan and cool. Drizzle cake with Cream Cheese Glaze.

Cream Cheese Glaze

Makes about ¾ cup

2 ounces reduced-fat cream cheese, room temperature
1 tablespoon margarine or butter, room temperature
½ teaspoon vanilla
1½ cups powdered sugar
Milk

1. Beat cream cheese, margarine, and vanilla in medium bowl until smooth; beat in powdered sugar and enough milk to make thick glaze consistency.

Pumpkin Ginger Cake Rounds with Warm Rum Sauce

LO

Baked in cans, this spiced cake is sliced into rounds and served with warm rum sauce.

2 cakes (4 to 6 servings each)

½ cup each: canned pumpkin, packed light brown
   sugar
¼ cup each: room temperature margarine or butter,
   light molasses
1 egg
1½ cups all-purpose flour
½ teaspoon each: baking powder, baking soda,
   ground allspice, cloves, and ginger
Warm Rum Sauce (recipe follows)

Per Serving:
Calories: 212
% calories from fat: 27
Protein (gm): 3.3
Carbohydrate (gm): 35.5
Fat (gm): 6.5
Saturated fat (gm): 1.3
Cholesterol (mg): 21.6
Sodium (mg): 177
Exchanges:
Milk: 0.0
Vegetable: 0.0
Fruit: 0.0
Bread: 2.5
Meat: 0.0
Fat: 1.0

1. Combine pumpkin, brown sugar, margarine,
molasses, and egg in large mixer bowl; beat at medium speed until well
blended. Mix in combined flour, baking powder, baking soda, allspice,
cloves, and ginger, blending at low speed until moistened.
2. Pour batter into two greased and floured 16-ounce cans. Stand cans
in slow cooker; cover and cook on high until wooden skewer inserted in
cakes comes out clean, about 2½ hours. Stand cans on wire rack to cool
10 minutes. Loosen sides of cakes by gently rolling cans on counter, or
remove bottom ends of cans and push cakes through. Slice and serve with
Warm Rum Sauce.

Warm Rum Sauce

Makes 1½ cups

¼ cup sugar
1 tablespoon cornstarch
1¼ cups 2% reduced-fat milk
2 tablespoons each: rum or ½ teaspoon rum extract, margarine or butter
½ teaspoon vanilla
⅛ teaspoon ground nutmeg

1. Mix sugar and cornstarch in small saucepan; whisk in milk and rum.
Whisk over medium heat until mixture boils and thickens, 1 to 2 minutes.
Remove from heat; stir in margarine, vanilla, and nutmeg. Serve warm.

Variation

Date and Nut Ginger Slices—Make recipe as above, adding ¼ cup each
chopped dates and walnuts; omit Warm Rum Sauce. Spread cake slices
with softened cream cheese and apricot preserves.

Gingerbread Cake

LO

Enjoy this perfectly spiced cake all year, but especially during the winter holidays.

12 servings

1½ cups self-rising flour
½ cup all-purpose flour
1 teaspoon ground cinnamon
½ teaspoon ground ginger
¼ teaspoon each: ground allspice, salt
8 tablespoons margarine or butter, room temperature
⅔ cup light molasses
¾ cup packed light brown sugar
1 egg, lightly beaten
½ cup 2% reduced-fat milk
½ teaspoon baking soda
Cream Cheese Glaze (see p. 548)

Per Serving:
Calories: 315
% calories from fat: 29
Protein (gm): 2.8
Carbohydrate (gm): 53.4
Fat (gm): 10.0
Saturated fat (gm): 2.4
Cholesterol (mg): 20.7
Sodium (mg): 410
Exchanges:
Milk: 0.0
Vegetable: 0.0
Fruit: 0.0
Bread: 3.5
Meat: 0.0
Fat: 1.5

1. Combine flours, spices, and salt in large bowl. Combine margarine, molasses, and brown sugar in 4-cup glass measure; microwave on high until margarine is melted, about 2 minutes, stirring to blend. Whisk margarine mixture into flour mixture, blending well; whisk in egg. Whisk in combined milk and baking soda until blended.
2. Pour batter into greased and floured 7-inch springform pan; place on rack in slow cooker. Cover and cook on high until toothpick inserted in center of cake comes out clean, about 5 hours. Cool in pan on wire rack 10 minutes; remove side of pan and cool. Drizzle with Cream Cheese Glaze.

Applesauce Cake with Buttery Glaze

LO *Oatmeal adds to the homey goodness of this dessert. Serve warm with ice cream or frozen yogurt.*

12 servings

½ cup margarine or butter, room temperature
¾ cup packed light brown sugar
1 egg
¾ cup applesauce
1 teaspoon vanilla
1 cup all-purpose flour
½ cup each: whole-wheat flour, quick-cooking oats
2 teaspoons baking powder
½ teaspoon each: salt, ground cinnamon
¼ teaspoon each: baking soda, ground cloves
Buttery Glaze (recipe follows)

Per Serving:
Calories: 242
% calories from fat: 31
Protein (gm): 2.1
Carbohydrate (gm): 39.5
Fat (gm): 8.4
Saturated fat (gm): 1.7
Cholesterol (mg): 17.7
Sodium (mg): 306
Exchanges:
Milk: 0.0
Vegetable: 0.0
Fruit: 1.5
Bread: 1.0
Meat: 0.0
Fat: 1.5

1. Beat margarine and sugar in large bowl until blended; beat in egg, applesauce, and vanilla. Mix in combined remaining ingredients, except Buttery Glaze, stirring until well blended.
2. Pour batter into greased and floured 6-cup fluted cake pan; place pan on rack in 6-quart slow cooker. Cover and cook on high until toothpick inserted in center of cake comes out clean, 2½ to 3 hours. Cool cake on wire rack 10 minutes; invert onto rack and cool.

Buttery Glaze

Makes about ⅓ cup

1 cup powdered sugar
½ teaspoon butter extract
Milk

1. Mix powdered sugar and butter extract with enough milk to make a glaze consistency.

Red Velvet Cake

LO

Also known as Waldorf Astoria Cake, this colorful red dessert is reputed to trace its origins to the famed New York hotel.

8 servings

¾ cup sugar
3 tablespoons vegetable shortening
1 egg
1 teaspoon vanilla
1 bottle (1 ounce) red food color
¼ cup unsweetened cocoa
1 cup plus 2 tablespoons all-purpose flour
1 teaspoon baking soda
½ teaspoon salt
½ cup low-fat buttermilk
1½ teaspoons white distilled vinegar
Buttercream Frosting (recipe follows)

Per Serving:
Calories: 265
% calories from fat: 21
Protein (gm): 3.4
Carbohydrate (gm): 48.8
Fat (gm): 6.3
Saturated fat (gm): 1.6
Cholesterol (mg): 27.2
Sodium (mg): 185
Exchanges:
Milk: 0.0
Vegetable: 0.0
Fruit: 0.0
Bread: 3.0
Meat: 0.0
Fat: 1.0

1. Beat sugar and shortening until well blended in large bowl. Add egg and vanilla, blending well; beat in food color and cocoa until well blended. Mix in combined flour, baking soda, and salt alternately with combined buttermilk and vinegar, beginning and ending with dry ingredients.
2. Pour batter into greased and floured 1-quart soufflé dish; place on rack in 6-quart slow cooker. Cover and cook on high until toothpick inserted in center of cake comes out clean, 2 to 2¾ hours; remove to wire rack and cool 10 minutes. Invert onto rack and cool; frost with Buttercream Frosting.

Buttercream Frosting

Makes about 1½ cups

2½ cups powdered sugar
1 tablespoon margarine or butter, room temperature
½ teaspoon vanilla
1–2 tablespoons milk

1. Mix powdered sugar, margarine, vanilla, and enough milk to make spreading consistency.

Chocolate Chip Peanut Butter Cake

LO *Chocolate and peanut butter—a comfort food combination that can't be beat!!*

8 servings

⅓ cup each: room temperature margarine or
  butter, granulated and packed light brown sugar
2 eggs
½ cup each: chunky peanut butter, reduced-fat
  sour cream
1⅔ cups self-rising flour
¼ teaspoon salt
½ cup semi-sweet chocolate morsels
Hot fudge or chocolate sauce (optional)

Per Serving:
Calories: 352
% calories from fat: 52
Protein (gm): 7.4
Carbohydrate (gm): 36.4
Fat (gm): 21.4
Saturated fat (gm): 5.9
Cholesterol (mg): 57.1
Sodium (mg): 402
Exchanges:
Milk: 0.0
Vegetable: 0.0
Fruit: 0.0
Bread: 2.5
Meat: 0.0
Fat: 4.0

1. Beat margarine and sugars in bowl until fluffy;
beat in eggs, blending well. Mix in peanut butter
and sour cream; mix in flour, salt, and chocolate morsels.
2. Pour batter into greased and floured 6-cup fluted cake pan; place on rack
in 6-quart slow cooker. Cover and cook on high until toothpick inserted in
center of cake comes out clean, 2 to 2½ hours. Cool cake on wire rack 10
minutes; invert onto rack and cool. Serve with hot fudge sauce.

Chocolate Sauerkraut Cake

LO

Is the secret ingredient in this moist chocolate cake the sauerkraut or the beer?

8 servings

¾ cup sugar
¼ cup vegetable shortening
1 egg
1 teaspoon vanilla
¼ cup unsweetened cocoa
1 cup plus 2 tablespoons all-purpose flour
½ teaspoon each: baking powder, baking soda
¼ teaspoon salt
½ cup beer or water
⅓ cup finely chopped sauerkraut, well-drained, rinsed
Chocolate Glaze (recipe follows)

Per Serving:
Calories: 210
% calories from fat: 30
Protein (gm): 3.1
Carbohydrate (gm): 32.9
Fat (gm): 6.9
Saturated fat (gm): 2
Cholesterol (mg): 23.2
Sodium (mg): 229
Exchanges:
Milk: 0.0
Vegetable: 0.0
Fruit: 0.0
Bread: 2.0
Meat: 0.0
Fat: 1.0

1. Beat sugar and shortening in large bowl until blended; beat in egg, vanilla, and cocoa. Mix in combined flour, baking powder, baking soda, and salt alternately with beer, beginning and ending with dry ingredients; mix in sauerkraut.
2. Pour batter into greased and floured 6-cup fluted cake pan; place on rack in 6-quart slow cooker. Cover and cook on high until toothpick inserted in center of cake comes out clean, 2½ to 3 hours. Cool cake on wire rack 10 minutes; invert onto rack and cool. Drizzle Chocolate Glaze over.

Chocolate Glaze

Makes about ⅓ cup

¾ cup powdered sugar
2 tablespoons unsweetened cocoa
½ teaspoon vanilla
Milk

1. Mix powdered sugar, cocoa, vanilla, and enough milk to make glaze consistency.

Chocolate Zucchini Cake

LO

The cake can also be glazed with Chocolate Glaze (see p. 554).

8 servings

¼ cup each: room temperature margarine or
  butter, applesauce
¾ cup sugar
1 egg
¼ cup low-fat buttermilk
1 teaspoon vanilla
1¼ cups all-purpose flour
2 tablespoons unsweetened cocoa
½ teaspoon each: baking soda, baking powder
¼ teaspoon each: salt, ground cinnamon and cloves
1 cup finely chopped or shredded zucchini
¼ cup semisweet chocolate morsels
Powdered sugar, as garnish

Per Serving:
Calories: 291
% calories from fat: 25
Protein (gm): 4
Carbohydrate (gm): 51.8
Fat (gm): 8.4
Saturated fat (gm): 2.4
Cholesterol (mg): 26.9
Sodium (mg): 189
Exchanges:
Milk: 0.0
Vegetable: 0.0
Fruit: 0.0
Bread: 3.0
Meat: 0.0
Fat: 1.5

1. Beat margarine, applesauce, and sugar in large bowl until smooth. Mix in egg, buttermilk, and vanilla. Mix in combined flour, cocoa, baking soda, baking powder, salt, and spices; mix in zucchini and chocolate morsels.
2. Pour batter into greased and floured 6-cup fluted cake pan; place pan on rack in 6-quart slow cooker. Cover and cook on high until toothpick inserted in center of cake comes out clean, 3 to 4 hours. Cool cake on wire rack 10 minutes; invert cake onto rack and cool. Sprinkle generously with powdered sugar.

Chocolate-Coffee Cake

LO

This cake can also be baked in a 3-quart slow cooker; pour batter into greased slow cooker. Cooking time will be about 2½ hours. Using foil handles (see p. vi) will make this cake easier to remove from the slow cooker.

12 servings

6 tablespoons margarine or butter, room temperature
1⅓ cups sugar
2 eggs
1 cup all-purpose flour
⅓ cup Dutch process cocoa
½ teaspoon baking soda
¼ teaspon each: baking powder, salt
1–2 tablespoons each: instant espresso or coffee, boiling water
⅓ cup reduced-fat sour cream
Coffee Glaze (recipe follows)

Per Serving:
Calories: 208
% calories from fat: 29
Protein (gm): 2.8
Carbohydrate (gm): 34.4
Fat (gm): 6.7
Saturated fat (gm): 1.4
Cholesterol (mg): 30.4
Sodium (mg): 177
Exchanges:
Milk: 0.0
Vegetable: 0.0
Fruit: 0.0
Bread: 2.0
Meat: 0.0
Fat: 1.0

1. Beat margarine and sugar in bowl until fluffy; beat in eggs one at a time, beating well after each addition. Mix in combined dry ingredients alternately with combined espresso, boiling water, and sour cream, beginning and ending with dry ingredients.
2. Pour batter into greased and floured 6-cup fluted cake pan; place pan on rack in 6-quart slow cooker. Cover and cook on high until toothpick inserted in center of cake comes out clean, 4 to 4½ hours. Cool cake on wire rack 10 minutes; invert cake onto rack and cool. Drizzle cake with Coffee Glaze.

Coffee Glaze

Makes about ⅓ cup

¾ cup powdered sugar
1 tablespoon margarine or butter, melted
2–3 tablespoons strong brewed coffee

1. Mix powdered sugar, margarine, and enough coffee to make glaze consistency.

Flourless Mocha Mousse Cake

LO *This sinfully rich cake has a light mousse-like texture. Cut with a sharp knife, wetting the knife between every slice.*

8 servings

½ cup Dutch process cocoa
¾ cup packed light brown sugar
3 tablespoons flour
2 teaspoons instant espresso powder
⅛ teaspoon salt
¾ cup 2% reduced-fat milk
1 teaspoon vanilla
2 ounces each: coarsely chopped semi-sweet and
   bittersweet chocolate
1 egg
3 egg whites
⅛ teaspoon cream of tartar
⅓ cup granulated sugar
Cocoa or powdered sugar, as garnish

Per Serving:
Calories: 251
% calories from fat: 23
Protein (gm): 4.8
Carbohydrate (gm): 45.8
Fat (gm): 6.8
Saturated fat (gm): 3.2
Cholesterol (mg): 21.7
Sodium (mg): 79
Exchanges:
Milk: 0.0
Vegetable: 0.0
Fruit: 0.0
Bread: 3.0
Meat: 0.0
Fat: 1.0

1. Combine cocoa, brown sugar, flour, espresso powder, and salt in medium saucepan; gradually whisk in milk and vanilla to make smooth mixture. Whisk over medium heat until mixture is hot and sugar dissolved (do not boil). Remove saucepan from heat; add chocolate, whisking until melted. Whisk about ½ cup chocolate mixture into egg; whisk egg mixture back into saucepan. Cool to room temperature.

2. Beat egg whites and cream of tartar to soft peaks; beat to stiff peaks, gradually adding granulated sugar. Stir about ¼ of the egg whites into cooled chocolate mixture; fold chocolate mixture into remaining egg whites.

3. Pour batter into lightly greased 7-inch springform pan; place on rack in 6-quart slow cooker. Cover, placing 3 layers of paper toweling under lid, and cook on high until toothpick inserted ½-inch from edge of cake comes out clean (cake will look moist and will be soft in the center), 2¼ to 3¼ hours. Remove pan to wire rack and cool completely; refrigerate, loosely covered, 8 hours or overnight. Remove side of pan and place cake on serving plate; sprinkle top of cake generously with cocoa.

Marble Pound Cake

LO *This delicious, tender cake can also be dusted with powdered sugar and/or cocoa.*

8 servings

¾ cup low-fat buttermilk
1 teaspoon vanilla
½ teaspoon baking soda
6 tablespoons margarine or butter, room temperature
1 cup sugar
1 egg
1½ cups cake flour
⅛ teaspoon salt
1½ ounces semisweet chocolate, melted
Chocolate Glaze (see p. 554)

Per Serving:
Calories: 232
% calories from fat: 28
Protein (gm): 2.9
Carbohydrate (gm): 39.4
Fat (gm): 7.3
Saturated fat (gm): 1.8
Cholesterol (mg): 0.7
Sodium (mg): 161
Exchanges:
Milk: 0.0
Vegetable: 0.0
Fruit: 0.0
Bread: 2.5
Meat: 0.0
Fat: 1.0

1. Mix buttermilk, vanilla, and baking soda in bowl; let stand 2 to 3 minutes. Beat margarine and sugar until fluffy in large bowl. Beat in egg, blending well. Mix in combined flour and salt alternately with buttermilk mixture, beginning and ending with flour mixture. Reserve 1½ cups batter; stir melted chocolate into remaining batter.
2. Spoon batters alternately into greased and floured 9 x 5-inch loaf pan; swirl gently with knife. Place pan on rack in 6-quart slow cooker; cover, placing 3 layers of paper toweling under lid, and cook on high until toothpick inserted in center of cake comes out clean, 4 to 4½ hours. Remove pan and cool on wire rack 10 minutes; invert onto rack and cool. Drizzle with Chocolate Glaze.

Variation

Orange-Glazed Pound Cake—Make recipe as above, omitting chocolate and vanilla and adding 1 teaspoon orange extract. Pierce top of warm cake at 1-inch intervals with long-tined fork; spoon Orange Syrup over cake. To make Orange Syrup: Heat ¾ cup powdered sugar and ½ cup orange juice to boiling in small saucepan, stirring until sugar is dissolved. Cool slightly.

Hot Fudge Pudding Cake

L

Part cake, part pudding—the ultimate treat! Use a springform pan that has a tight seal to prevent the batter from leaking. A 1-quart soufflé dish that measures 7 inches in diameter can also be used.

6 servings

1 cup all-purpose flour
½ cup packed light brown sugar
6 tablespoons Dutch process cocoa, divided
1½ teaspoons baking powder
¼ teaspoon salt
½ cup 2% reduced-fat milk
2 tablespoons vegetable oil
1 teaspoon vanilla
⅓ cup granulated sugar
1½ cups boiling water

Per Serving:
Calories: 192
% calories from fat: 18
Protein (gm): 2.9
Carbohydrate (gm): 36.6
Fat (gm): 4
Saturated fat (gm): 0.5
Cholesterol (mg): 0.3
Sodium (mg): 178
Exchanges:
Milk: 0.0
Vegetable: 0.0
Fruit: 0.0
Bread: 2.5
Meat: 0.0
Fat: 0.0

1. Wrap bottom of springform pan in aluminum foil. Combine flour, brown sugar, 3 tablespoons cocoa, baking powder, and salt in medium bowl. Whisk combined milk, oil, and vanilla into flour mixture, mixing well.
2. Spoon batter into greased 7-inch springform pan. Mix remaining 3 tablespoons cocoa and granulated sugar; sprinkle over cake batter. Slowly pour boiling water over the back of a large spoon or spatula over batter; do not stir. Place pan on rack in 6-cup slow cooker; cover and cook on high until cake springs back when touched, about 2 hours. Cool pan on wire rack 10 minutes; remove side of pan and serve warm.

Variation

Mocha Latte Pudding Cake—Make recipe as above, substituting granulated sugar for the brown sugar and adding 1 tablespoon instant espresso powder and ½ teaspoon ground cinnamon to flour mixture. Serve warm pudding cake with a scoop of vanilla or chocolate ice cream and light whipped topping.

Spice Pudding Cake

LO

Thank you, Merri-Lu Bourbonnais, for this fabulous, moist pudding-style cake! Serve warm with ice cream and enjoy!

12 servings

Vegetable cooking spray
1 package (18.25 ounces) spice cake mix
1 package (1 ounce) instant butterscotch pudding
1 cup each: reduced-fat sour cream, water
¾ cup canola oil
1 egg
1 can (8 ounces) crushed pineapple, undrained

Per Serving:
Calories: 353
% calories from fat: 49
Protein (gm): 2.9
Carbohydrate (gm): 41.6
Fat (gm): 19.2
Saturated fat (gm): 3.6
Cholesterol (mg): 24.3
Sodium (mg): 337
Exchanges:
Milk: 0.0
Vegetable: 0.0
Fruit: 0.0
Bread: 3.0
Meat: 0.0
Fat: 3.0

1. Spray bottom and side of slow cooker with vegetable spray. Combine remaining ingredients in bowl; beat at medium speed until combined, about 2 minutes.
2. Pour into slow cooker; cover and cook on low 5 to 6 hours. The cake will rise almost to the top of the slow cooker; it will bubble slowly and is done when bubbling stops and the cake begins to pull away from the side of the slow cooker. Spoon warm cake onto plates.

Variations

Carrot Pudding Cake—Make recipe as above, substituting carrot cake mix for the spice cake mix and instant vanilla pudding for the butterscotch pudding.

Triple-Chocolate Pudding Cake—Make recipe as above, substituting chocolate fudge cake mix for the spice cake mix and instant chocolate pudding for the butterscotch pudding; omit pineapple. Cover and cook on low 3½ to 4 hours; serve warm with chocolate syrup or hot fudge sauce.

New York-Style Cheesecake

LO

There are only accolades for this version of the famous cheesecake.

8 servings

1 pound reduced-fat cream cheese, room temperature
½ cup sugar
2 eggs
1½ tablespoons cornstarch
¼ teaspoon salt
¾ cup reduced-fat sour cream
1 teaspoon vanilla
Graham Cracker Crumb Crust (recipe follows)

Per Serving:
Calories: 335
% calories from fat: 46
Protein (gm): 10.1
Carbohydrate (gm): 35.4
Fat (gm): 17.0
Saturated fat (gm): 8.1
Cholesterol (mg): 86.6
Sodium (mg): 546
Exchanges:
Milk: 0.0
Vegetable: 0.0
Fruit: 0.0
Bread: 2.5
Meat: 0.0
Fat: 3.0

1. Beat cream cheese and sugar in large bowl until light and fluffy; beat in eggs, cornstarch, and salt, blending well. Mix in sour cream and vanilla; pour into crust in springform pan.
2. Place pan on rack in 6-quart slow cooker; cover, placing 3 layers of paper towels under lid, and cook on high until cheesecake is set, but still slightly soft in the center, 2 to 3 hours. Turn off heat and let stand, covered, in slow cooker 1 hour. Remove from slow cooker and cool on wire rack. Refrigerate, covered, 8 hours or overnight.

Graham Cracker Crumb Crust

Makes one 7-inch crust

1¼ cups graham cracker crumbs
2 tablespoons sugar
3 tablespoons margarine or butter, melted
1–2 tablespoons honey

1. Combine graham crumbs, sugar, and margarine in 7-inch springform pan; add enough honey for mixture to stick together. Pat mixture evenly on bottom and 1-inch up side of pan.

Variations

Latte Cheesecake—Make recipe as above, adding ⅓ cup espresso or double-strength coffee, 2 egg yolks, and ⅛ teaspoon ground nutmeg. Spread top of chilled cheesecake with 2 cups light whipped topping; sprinkle lightly with cinnamon and chocolate shavings.

Chocolate Chip–Pecan Cheesecake—Make recipe as above, adding ⅓ cup each mini-chocolate morsels and chopped pecans. Garnish top of cheesecake with chocolate curls.

Pear Cheesecake

LO *The Gingersnap Crust adds flavor contrast to the pears in this creamy cheesecake.*

8 servings

8 ounces reduced-fat cream cheese, room temperature
½ cup sugar
2 tablespoons flour
¼ teaspoon salt
1 cup reduced-fat sour cream
1 egg
1 teaspoon vanilla extract
1 medium pear, peeled, thinly sliced
Gingersnap Crumb Crust (recipe follows)
Chopped candied ginger, as garnish

Per Serving:
Calories: 270
% calories from fat: 37
Protein (gm): 5.5
Carbohydrate (gm): 37.6
Fat (gm): 13.2
Saturated fat (gm): 5.9
Cholesterol (mg): 58.3
Sodium (mg): 329
Exchanges:
Milk: 0.0
Vegetable: 0.0
Fruit: 0.0
Bread: 3.0
Meat: 0.0
Fat: 3.0

1. Beat cream cheese, sugar, flour, and salt in large bowl until smooth; beat in sour cream, egg, and vanilla. Arrange pear slices on crust in springform pan; pour filling over pears.
2. Place cheesecake on rack in 6-quart slow cooker; cover, placing 3 layers of paper towels under lid and cook on high until cheesecake is just set in the center, 3½ to 4 hours. Turn off heat and let stand, covered, in slow cooker 1 hour. Remove from slow cooker and cool on wire rack. Refrigerate, covered, 8 hours or overnight. Garnish with candied ginger.

Gingersnap Crumb Crust

Makes one 7-inch crust

½ cup graham cracker crumbs
½ cup gingersnap cookie crumbs
2–3 tablespoons each: melted margarine or butter, honey

1. Combine graham crumbs, gingersnap crumbs, and margarine in 7-inch springform pan; add enough honey for mixture to stick together. Pat mixture evenly on bottom and 1-inch up side of pan.

Raspberry Swirl Cheesecake

LO

Top this fabulous cheesecake with fresh raspberries for an added treat.

8 servings

1 pound reduced-fat cream cheese, room temperature
1 cup reduced-fat sweetened condensed milk
2 eggs
1 teaspoon vanilla
¼ teaspoon salt
Vanilla Cookie-Pecan Crust (recipe follows)
½ cup seedless raspberry preserves

Per Serving:
Calories: 348
% calories from fat: 39
Protein (gm): 7.7
Carbohydrate (gm): 39.5
Fat (gm): 13.2
Saturated fat (gm): 5.9
Cholesterol (mg): 58.3
Sodium (mg): 329
Exchanges:
Milk: 0.0
Vegetable: 0.0
Fruit: 0.0
Bread: 3.0
Meat: 0.0
Fat: 3.0

1. Beat cream cheese in large bowl until fluffy; beat in sweetened condensed milk, eggs, vanilla, and salt. Pour mixture into crust in springform pan. Swirl in raspberry preserves.
2. Place pan on rack in 6-quart slow cooker; cover, placing 3 layers of paper towels under lid, and cook on high until cheesecake is set, but still slightly soft in the center, about 3 hours. Remove from slow cooker and cool on wire rack. Refrigerate, covered, 8 hours or overnight.

Vanilla Cookie-Pecan Crust

Makes one 7-inch crust

1 cup vanilla wafer cookie crumbs
¼ cup ground toasted pecans
2–3 tablespoons each: melted margarine or butter, honey

1. Combine vanilla crumbs, pecans, and margarine in 7-inch springform pan; add enough honey for mixture to stick together. Pat mixture evenly on bottom and 1-inch up side of 7-inch springform pan.

Variation

Blueberry Cheesecake—Make recipe as above, substituting blueberry preserves for the raspberry preserves, brown sugar for the granulated sugar, and orange extract for the vanilla. Add 1 tablespoon grated orange zest to the cheesecake mixture.

Chocolate Cheese Pie

LO *A chocolate lover's dream!*

10 servings

1 pound reduced-fat cream cheese, room temperature
¾ cup sugar
2 eggs
1 teaspoon vanilla
¼ teaspoon salt
1 ounce bittersweet chocolate, melted
¼ cup Dutch process cocoa
Chocolate Cookie Crumb Crust (recipe follows)
1½–2 cups whipped topping or whipped cream
Chocolate curls, as garnish

Per Serving:
Calories: 225
% calories from fat: 32
Protein (gm): 7.7
Carbohydrate (gm): 30.3
Fat (gm): 8
Saturated fat (gm): 3.4
Cholesterol (mg): 38.6
Sodium (mg): 311
Exchanges:
Milk: 0.0
Vegetable: 0.0
Fruit: 0.0
Bread: 2.0
Meat: 0.0
Fat: 1.5

1. Beat cream cheese until fluffy in large bowl; beat in sugar, eggs, vanilla, and salt. Mix in melted chocolate and cocoa. Pour filling into crust in springform pan.
2. Place pan on rack in 6-quart slow cooker; cover, placing 3 layers of paper towels under lid and cook on high until cheesecake is just set in the center, 2½ to 3 hours. Turn off heat and let stand, covered, in slow cooker 1 hour. Remove from slow cooker and cool on wire rack. Refrigerate, covered, 8 hours or overnight. Spread whipped topping over cheesecake and garnish with chocolate curls.

Chocolate Cookie Crumb Crust

Makes one 7-inch crust

1¼ cups chocolate cookie crumbs
2 tablespoons sugar
3 tablespoons margarine or butter, melted
1–2 tablespoons honey

1. Combine cookie crumbs, sugar, and margarine in 7-inch springform pan; add enough honey for mixture to stick together. Pat mixture evenly on bottom and 1-inch up side of pan.

Variation

Black Forest Cheesecake—Make recipe as above, increasing chocolate to 2 ounces and substituting 2 tablespoons brandy or 1 teaspoon brandy extract for the vanilla. Spoon cherry pie filling over slices.

Chocolate Chip Bar Cookies

 Can't stop eating them!

16 servings

8 tablespoons margarine or butter, room temperature
1 egg
1 teaspoon vanilla
¼ cup each: granulated sugar, packed light brown
   sugar
1 cup all-purpose flour
½ teaspoon baking soda
¼ teaspoon salt
½ cup each: semi-sweet chocolate morsels, coarsely
   chopped walnuts
Vegetable cooking spray

Per Serving:
Calories: 169
% calories from fat: 55
Protein (gm): 1.4
Carbohydrate (gm): 17.6
Fat (gm): 10.5
Saturated fat (gm): 2.7
Cholesterol (mg): 13.2
Sodium (mg): 148
Exchanges:
Milk: 0.0
Vegetable: 0.0
Fruit: 0.0
Bread: 1.0
Meat: 0.0
Fat: 2.0

1. Beat margarine, egg, and vanilla in bowl until fluffy; mix in combined sugars. Mix in combined flour, baking soda, and salt. Mix in chocolate morsels and walnuts. Spread dough evenly in bottom of greased 7-inch springform pan. Cover and cook on high until toothpick inserted in center comes out clean, 3 to 3½ hours. Turn lid askew and cook 20 minutes longer. Cool in pan on wire rack 5 minutes; remove side of pan. Cut into bars while warm.

Five-Layer Bars

You'll love these moist chewy cookies—delicious!!

16 servings

1½ cups graham cracker crumbs
1 tablespoon each: melted margarine or butter, honey
⅔ cup semi-sweet chocolate morsels
⅓ cup each: flaked coconut, chopped toasted
   walnuts
1 can (15 ounces) reduced-fat sweetened condensed
   milk

Per Serving:
Calories: 204
% calories from fat: 26
Protein (gm): 4.4
Carbohydrate (gm): 34.0
Fat (gm): 6.0
Saturated fat (gm): 2.3
Cholesterol (mg): 4.4
Sodium (mg): 120
Exchanges:
Milk: 0.0
Vegetable: 0.0
Fruit: 0.0
Bread: 2.0
Meat: 0.0
Fat: 1.5

1. Press combined graham cracker crumbs, margarine, and honey in bottom of 7-inch springform pan; sprinkle with chocolate morsels, coconut, and walnuts; drizzle condensed milk over the top. Place pan on rack in 6-quart slow cooker; cover and cook on low until milk is absorbed and cookies are almost firm to touch, 3 to 3½ hours. Cool on wire rack 5 minutes for cookies to firm; remove side of pan. Cut into wedges or squares while still slightly warm.

Chocolate Indulgence Brownies

LO *Chocolatey and moist, you'll enjoy these brownies!*

24 servings

3 eggs
¾ cup packed light brown sugar
2 teaspoons vanilla
2 cups chocolate cookie crumbs
3 tablespoons unsweetened cocoa
¼ teaspoon salt
⅔ cup chopped dates
½ cup reduced-fat semisweet chocolate morsels

Per Serving:
Calories: 124
% calories from fat: 26
Protein (gm): 1.8
Carbohydrate (gm): 22.7
Fat (gm): 3.8
Saturated fat (gm): 1.7
Cholesterol (mg): 26.5
Sodium (mg): 129
Exchanges:
Milk: 0.0
Vegetable: 0.0
Fruit: 0.0
Bread: 1.5
Meat: 0.0
Fat: 0.5

1. Beat eggs, brown sugar, and vanilla in large bowl until thick, about 2 minutes. Fold in cookie crumbs, cocoa, and salt; fold in dates and chocolate morsels.
2. Pour batter into greased and floured 9 x 5-inch loaf pan; place on rack in 6-quart slow cooker. Cover and cook on high until toothpick inserted in center comes out almost clean, about 3 hours. Cool on wire rack 10 minutes; invert onto wire rack and cool. Cut into ¾-inch slices; cut slices into halves.

Easy Brownies

LO *Fudgey, rich, and simple to make with a brownie mix!*

16 servings

1 package (19.8 ounces) brownie mix
4 tablespoons margarine or butter, melted
½ to 1 cup chopped walnuts

Per Serving:
Calories: 249
% calories from fat: 43
Protein (gm): 3.1
Carbohydrate (gm): 34.3
Fat (gm): 12.7
Saturated fat (gm): 2.0
Cholesterol (mg): 25.0
Sodium (mg): 171
Exchanges:
Milk: 0.0
Vegetable: 0.0
Fruit: 0.0
Bread: 2.0
Meat: 0.0
Fat: 2.5

1. Make brownie mix according to package directions, adding margarine and walnuts. Pour batter in greased 7-inch springform pan and place on rack in 6-quart slow cooker; cover and cook on high until toothpick inserted in center comes out almost clean, about 6 hours. Cool on wire rack; remove side of pan and cut into squares or wedges.

Variation

Warm Caramel Brownie Bars—Make recipe as above, omitting walnuts. Spoon warm caramel ice cream sauce over warm brownies; sprinkle with chocolate covered raisins, chopped walnuts, and flaked coconut.

Carrot Cake Snackers

LO *When you crave a snack, this is a delicious way to indulge!*

16 servings

4 tablespoons margarine or butter, room temperature
¾ cup each: packed light brown sugar,
  2% reduced-fat milk
1 egg
1 tablespoon lemon juice
1 teaspoon vanilla
1¼ cups quick-cooking oats
½ cup all-purpose flour
¼ cup whole-wheat flour
2 teaspoons baking powder
¼ teaspoon baking soda
1 teaspoon ground cinnamon
¼ teaspoon salt
1 cup shredded carrots
½ cup each: raisins, chopped pecans or walnuts
Orange Glaze (recipe follows)

Per Serving:
Calories: 173
% calories from fat: 32
Protein (gm): 2.4
Carbohydrate (gm): 27.7
Fat (gm): 6.4
Saturated fat (gm): 1.1
Cholesterol (mg): 14.1
Sodium (mg): 170
Exchanges:
Milk: 0.0
Vegetable: 0.0
Fruit: 0.0
Bread: 2.0
Meat: 0.0
Fat: 1.0

1. Beat margarine and brown sugar in large bowl until blended; beat in milk, egg, lemon juice, and vanilla. Mix in combined oats, flours, baking powder, baking soda, cinnamon, and salt; mix in carrots, raisins, and pecans.
2. Pour batter into greased and floured 7-inch springform pan; place pan on rack in 6-quart slow cooker. Cover and cook on high until toothpick inserted in center of cake comes out clean, about 3 hours. Cool cake in pan on wire rack 10 minutes; remove side of pan and cool. Drizzle with Orange Glaze; cut into squares or wedges.

Orange Glaze

Makes about ¼ cup

½ cup powdered sugar
1 teaspoon grated orange zest
2–4 teaspoons orange juice

1. Mix powdered sugar, orange zest, and enough orange juice to make glaze consistency.

Note: Be sure to use a springform pan that does not leak, or line bottom of pan with aluminum foil.

Lemon Cream Cheese Bites

These lemony treats will disappear in a hurry!!

LO

12 servings

1 package (9 ounces) yellow cake mix
1 egg
1 tablespoon margarine or butter, room temperature
2 ounces reduced-fat cream cheese, room temperature
¼ cup sugar
½ teaspoon vanilla
1 tablespoon each: finely grated lemon zest, flour
¼ teaspoon salt
Lemon Glaze (recipe follows)

Per Serving:
Calories: 143
% calories from fat: 27
Protein (gm): 2.0
Carbohydrate (gm): 24
Fat (gm): 4.4
Saturated fat (gm): 1.1
Cholesterol (mg): 19.8
Sodium (mg): 180
Exchanges:
Milk: 0.0
Vegetable: 0.0
Fruit: 0.0
Bread: 1.5
Meat: 0.0
Fat: 1.0

1. Mix cake mix, egg, and margarine in bowl; reserve 1 cup dough. Pat remaining dough evenly in bottom of greased 7-inch springform pan. Bake at 350 degrees until lightly browned, about 10 minutes.
2. Beat cream cheese, sugar, and vanilla in bowl until smooth; mix in combined lemon zest, flour, and salt. Pour into pan and spoon teaspoons of reserved dough over the top. Place pan on rack in 6-quart slow cooker; cover and cook on high until set, 2½ to 3½ hours. Cool in pan on wire rack; drizzle with Lemon Glaze. Cut into squares or wedges.

Lemon Glaze

Makes about ¼ cup

½ cup powdered sugar
2 teaspoons finely grated lemon zest
3–4 teaspoons lemon juice

1. Mix powdered sugar and lemon zest, adding enough lemon juice to make a thick glaze consistency.

Caramel Flan

LO

This delicate flan is one you'll serve over and over again.

4–6 servings

⅔ cup sugar, divided
2½ cups whole milk
3 eggs, lightly beaten
2 teaspoons vanilla

Per Serving:
Calories: 186
% calories from fat: 34
Protein (gm): 7.9
Carbohydrate (gm): 22.7
Fat (gm): 7.1
Saturated fat (gm): 3.2
Cholesterol (mg): 144.4
Sodium (mg): 93
Exchanges:
Milk: 0.0
Vegetable: 0.0
Fruit: 0.0
Bread: 1.5
Meat: 0.0
Fat: 1.5

1. Heat ⅓ cup sugar in small skillet over medium-high heat until sugar melts and turns golden, stirring occasionally (watch carefully, as the sugar can burn easily!). Quickly pour syrup into bottom of 1-quart soufflé dish or casserole and tilt bottom to spread caramel. Set aside to cool.
2. Heat milk and remaining ⅓ cup sugar until steaming and just beginning to bubble at edges. Whisk mixture into eggs; add vanilla. Strain into soufflé dish over caramel. Place soufflé dish on rack in 6-quart slow cooker; add 1-inch hot water to slow cooker and cover dish with a plate, lid, or aluminum foil. Cover and cook on low until custard is set and a sharp knife inserted halfway between center and edge comes out clean, 1½ to 2 hours. Remove soufflé dish to wire rack, uncover, and cool. Refrigerate 8 hours or overnight.
3. To unmold, loosen edge of custard with sharp knife. Place rimmed serving dish over soufflé dish and invert.

Variations

Rosemary Flan—Make recipe as above, adding 1 teaspoon dried rosemary leaves to milk mixture and heating to boiling; let stand 10 minutes before straining into soufflé dish.

Steamed Marmalade Pudding

LO

Steamed puddings are traditional celebration desserts in England. They can be made in a 1-quart casserole, soufflé dish, or pudding mold.

8 servings

½ cup sugar
5 tablespoons margarine or butter, room temperature
2 eggs, lightly beaten
1⅓ cups all-purpose flour
1½ teaspoons baking powder
2 tablespoons orange juice or milk
¾ cup orange marmalade
Orange Marmalade Sauce (recipe follows)

Per Serving:
Calories: 191
% calories from fat: 32
Protein (gm): 3.3
Carbohydrate (gm): 29.3
Fat (gm): 7
Saturated fat (gm): 1.5
Cholesterol (mg): 42.6
Sodium (mg): 155
Exchanges:
Milk: 0.0
Vegetable: 0.0
Fruit: 0.0
Bread: 2.0
Meat: 0.0
Fat: 1.0

1. Beat sugar and margarine in bowl until fluffy; beat in eggs. Stir in combined flour and baking powder; stir in orange juice. Spread marmalade in bottom of greased 1-quart bowl, soufflé dish or pudding mold and spoon batter over; cover tightly with aluminum foil or lid. Place bowl on rack in 6-quart slow cooker; pour boiling water into cooker to come about ⅔ up side of bowl. Cover and cook on low until toothpick inserted in center of pudding comes out clean, about 1½ hours. Remove from slow cooker; remove foil and cool on wire rack about 30 minutes. Loosen edge of pudding with knife; invert onto serving platter. Serve warm with Orange Marmalade Sauce.

Orange Marmalade Sauce

Makes about 1½ cups

¾ cup orange marmalade
2 teaspoons cornstarch
⅔ cup cold water

1. Heat marmalade to boiling in small saucepan over medium heat; stir in combined cornstarch and water, stirring until thickened, about 1 minute.

Cranberry Toffee Bread Pudding with Toffee Sauce

This recipe is destined to become a holiday favorite! Warm maple syrup can be substituted for the Toffee Sauce, if you like.

6 servings

1½ cups whole milk
2 eggs
⅓ cup packed light brown sugar
½ cup each: dried cranberries, toffee chips
2 cups cubed day-old sourdough bread
⅓ cup coarsely chopped walnuts
Toffee Sauce (recipe follows)

Per Serving:
Calories: 362
% calories from fat: 30
Protein (gm): 6.8
Carbohydrate (gm): 58.3
Fat (gm): 12.7
Saturated fat (gm): 4.8
Cholesterol (mg): 84.1
Sodium (mg): 162
Exchanges:
Milk: 0.0
Vegetable: 0.0
Fruit: 1.0
Bread: 3.0
Meat: 0.0
Fat: 2.0

1. Whisk milk and eggs in large bowl until well blended; mix in brown sugar, cranberries, and toffee chips. Gently mix in bread and walnuts; spoon mixture into 9 x 5-inch loaf pan or 1-quart soufflé dish. Cover securely with aluminum foil. Set pan on rack in slow cooker; cover and cook on high until pudding is set and toothpick inserted in center comes out clean, about 2 hours. Serve warm with Toffee Sauce.

Toffee Sauce

Makes about ½ cup

½ cup each: packed light or dark brown sugar, water
2 tablespoons light corn syrup
½ teaspoon vanilla

1. Combine sugar, water, and corn syrup in small saucepan; heat to boiling, stirring until sugar is dissolved. Reduce heat and simmer until sauce is the consistency of maple syrup, about 10 minutes; stir in vanilla.

Variations

Old-Fashioned Raisin Bread Pudding—Make recipe as above, omitting toffee chips. Substitute raisins for the dried cranberries; add ½ cup coarsely chopped pecans, ¾ teaspoon ground cinnamon, and ⅛ teaspoon ground nutmeg. Add 1–2 tablespoons light rum, or ½ teaspoon rum extract to the Toffee Sauce, if desired.

Blueberry Bread Pudding with Lemon Sauce—Make recipe as above, omitting dried cranberries, toffee chips, and Toffee Sauce. Add 1 cup fresh or thawed frozen blueberries. To make Lemon Sauce: Melt 2 tablespoons margarine or butter in small skillet; add ⅔ to 1 cup sugar and 1 cup lemon juice, stirring over medium heat until sugar is dissolved. Whisk about ½ cup lemon mixture into 2 lightly beaten eggs; whisk mixture back into saucepan. Whisk over low heat until mixture coats the back of a spoon, 2 to 3 minutes. Makes about 1½ cups sauce.

Chocolate-Mandarin Bread Pudding

LO *Bread puddings are perfect slow-cooker desserts!*

8 servings

6 cups cubed day-old whole-wheat bread
1 can (11 ounces) Mandarin oranges, drained, halved
1 can (12 ounces) reduced-fat evaporated milk
1½ cups packed dark brown sugar
1 cup unsweetened cocoa
1 egg

Per Serving:
Calories: 315
% calories from fat: 11
Protein (gm): 8.3
Carbohydrate (gm): 68.1
Fat (gm): 4.2
Saturated fat (gm): 1.2
Cholesterol (mg): 34.0
Sodium (mg): 173
Exchanges:
Milk: 0.0
Vegetable: 0.0
Fruit: 0.0
Bread: 4.0
Meat: 0.0
Fat: 1.0

1. Toss bread and Mandarin oranges in lightly greased slow cooker. Heat evaporated milk, brown sugar, and cocoa in large saucepan over medium-high heat, stirring until brown sugar is melted, about 5 minutes. Whisk about half the mixture into eggs; whisk egg mixture back into saucepan. Pour mixture over bread, making sure bread is covered. Cover and cook on high until pudding is set and toothpick inserted in center comes out clean, about 4 hours. Serve warm.

Pineapple Custard Bread Pudding

Other bread choices for this delicious pudding include multigrain or sour-dough—day-old bread is best.

8 servings

8 tablespoons margarine or butter, room temperature
½ cup each: granulated sugar, packed light brown
  sugar
½ teaspoon ground cinnamon
2 eggs
1 can (15½ ounces) crushed pineapple, drained
2½ cups cubed French bread, lightly toasted
6 tablespoons coarsely chopped macadamia nuts
  or slivered almonds

Per Serving:
Calories: 319
% calories from fat: 46
Protein (gm): 4.0
Carbohydrate (gm): 40.5
Fat (gm): 17.1
Saturated fat (gm): 3.3
Cholesterol (mg): 26.4
Sodium (mg): 250
Exchanges:
Milk: 0.0
Vegetable: 0.0
Fruit: 1.0
Bread: 2.0
Meat: 0.0
Fat: 3.0

1. Beat margarine, sugars, and cinnamon in large
bowl until fluffy; beat in eggs. Mix in pineapple and bread cubes. Spoon
mixture into slow cooker; cover and cook on high until pudding is set
and sharp knife inserted in center comes out clean, about 1½ hours. Serve
warm; sprinkle each serving with macadamia nuts.

Creamy Rice Pudding

*For a summer treat, mix raspberries, strawberries, or blueberries into this
tasty rice pudding before serving.*

6 servings

4 cups whole milk, divided
½ cup sugar
½ teaspoon salt
¾ cup converted long-grain rice, cooked
1½ tablespoons cornstarch
Ground cinnamon, as garnish

Per Serving:
Calories: 255
% calories from fat: 19
Protein (gm): 6.9
Carbohydrate (gm): 44.5
Fat (gm): 5.4
Saturated fat (gm): 3.1
Cholesterol (mg): 16.3
Sodium (mg): 260
Exchanges:
Milk: 0.0
Vegetable: 0.0
Fruit: 0.0
Bread: 3.0
Meat: 0.0
Fat: 1.0

1. Heat 3 cups milk, sugar, and salt to boiling in
medium saucepan; combine with rice in slow cooker.
Stir in combined remaining 1 cup milk and
cornstarch. Cover and cook on high until pudding
is thick and creamy, about 2 hours. Serve warm or
refrigerate and serve cold. Sprinkle with cinnamon.

Variations
Apple Rice Pudding—Make recipe as above, substituting brown sugar for the granulated sugar. Sauté 1 cup coarsely chopped unpeeled apple in 1 tablespoon margarine in large skillet until lightly browned. Stir apples and 1 teaspoon vanilla into rice pudding at the end of cooking time.

Almond Rice Pudding—Make recipe as above, adding 1 cinnamon stick and reducing sugar to ¼ cup. Stir ⅔ cup finely chopped toasted almonds, 2 teaspoons vanilla, and 1 teaspoon almond extract into pudding at the end of cooking time. Cool to room temperature; fold in 2 cups light whipped topping or whipped cream and refrigerate until chilled.

Cranberry-Apple Tart

V *Perfect for fall, with the combination of apples and cranberries.*

8 servings

Frozen pastry for 9-inch pie crust, thawed
¾ cup sugar
2 tablespoons flour
⅓ cup water
2 teaspoons grated orange zest
⅛ teaspoon ground nutmeg
3 cups peeled sliced apples
1 cup fresh or frozen cranberries
Powdered sugar, as garnish

Per Serving:
Calories: 216
% calories from fat: 26
Protein (gm): 5.2
Carbohydrate (gm): 35.3
Fat (gm): 6.4
Saturated fat (gm): 1.3
Cholesterol (mg): 0.5
Sodium (mg): 283
Exchanges:
Milk: 0.0
Vegetable: 0.0
Fruit: 0.5
Bread: 2.0
Meat: 0.0
Fat: 1.0

1. Roll pastry on floured surface into a 10-inch round; fit into bottom and 1½ inches up side of 7-inch springform pan. Bake at 375 degrees until lightly browned, about 15 minutes.
2. Mix sugar and flour in large saucepan; add water, orange zest, and nutmeg. Heat to boiling, stirring to dissolve sugar; add apples and cranberries. Simmer 10 minutes or until cranberries pop, stirring occasionally. Spoon fruit mixture into crust, spreading evenly. Place pan on rack in 6-quart slow cooker; cover and cook on high 2½ hours. Cool on wire rack. Sprinkle with powdered sugar before serving.

Baked Stuffed Apples

V

Apples are filled with fragrant fruit and perfectly baked. Serve warm with ice cream for a special treat.

4 servings

4 medium baking apples
½ cup chopped mixed dried fruit
2–4 tablespoons chopped toasted pecans
3 tablespoons sugar
½ teaspoon ground cinnamon
⅛ teaspoon ground nutmeg
2–3 tablespoons cold margarine, cut into pieces

1. Core apples, cutting to, but not through, bottoms; peel 1 inch skin from tops. Fill apples with combined remaining ingredients and place in slow cooker; cover and cook on high until tender, 1½ to 2 hours.

Per Serving:
Calories: 241
% calories from fat: 30
Protein (gm): 1.2
Carbohydrate (gm): 44
Fat (gm): 8.7
Saturated fat (gm): 1.4
Cholesterol (mg): 0
Sodium (mg): 68
Exchanges:
Milk: 0.0
Vegetable: 0.0
Fruit: 3.0
Bread: 0.0
Meat: 0.0
Fat: 1.5

Pears Belle Hélène

L

Tuck a buttery cookie beside each dish to complete this elegant offering.

4 servings

4 medium pears, peeled with stems intact
1½ cups each: apple juice, water
¼ cup sugar
1½ cups frozen vanilla yogurt
Bittersweet Chocolate Sauce (recipe follows)

1. Stand pears upright in slow cooker. Heat apple juice, water, and sugar to boiling in small saucepan; pour over pears. Cover and cook on high until pears are tender, 1½ to 2 hours. Drain; serve warm with Bittersweet Chocolate Sauce, or cool pears in syrup and refrigerate until chilled.

2. To serve, flatten a scoop of yogurt in each of 6 dessert dishes. Place a pear on top and drizzle with Bittersweet Chocolate Sauce.

Per Serving:
Calories: 243
% calories from fat: 11
Protein (gm): 4.2
Carbohydrate (gm): 54.9
Fat (gm): 3.1
Saturated fat (gm): 0.4
Cholesterol (mg): 1.6
Sodium (mg): 48
Exchanges:
Milk: 0.0
Vegetable: 0.0
Fruit: 2.0
Bread: 1.5
Meat: 0.0
Fat: 0.5

Bittersweet Chocolate Sauce

Makes about ¾ cup

⅓ cup unsweetened cocoa
¼ cup sugar
⅓ cup 2% reduced-fat milk
1 tablespoon margarine or butter
1 teaspoon vanilla
¼ teaspoon ground cinnamon

1. Mix cocoa and sugar in small saucepan; stir in milk and add margarine. Stir over medium heat until boiling; reduce heat and simmer until sauce is smooth and slightly thickened, 3 to 4 minutes. Stir in vanilla and cinnamon. Serve warm or at room temperature.

Poached Pears with Fruit in Rosemary Syrup

V

Perfectly poached pears combine with fresh fruit in a fragrant herbed sugar syrup.

4 servings

2 large pears, peeled, cored
Rosemary Syrup (recipe follows)
1 cup each: raspberries, fresh or frozen, thawed
    blueberries
1 large orange, peeled, cut into segments
Mint sprigs, as garnish

Per Serving:
Calories: 204
% calories from fat: 3
Protein (gm): 1
Carbohydrate (gm): 46.9
Fat (gm): 0.7
Saturated fat (gm): 0.1
Cholesterol (mg): 0 1
Sodium (mg): 4
Exchanges:
Milk: 0.0
Vegetable: 0.0
Fruit: 3.0
Bread: 0.0
Meat: 0.0
Fat: 0.0

1. Stand pears upright in slow cooker; pour Rosemary Syrup over. Cover and cook on high until pears are tender, 1½–2 hours. Remove pears to shallow bowl; strain syrup over pears and cool. Refrigerate until chilled, 1 to 2 hours.
2. Cut pears into halves; arrange pears and remaining fruit in shallow serving bowls. Spoon Rosemary Syrup over fruit; garnish with mint.

Rosemary Syrup

Makes about 1 cup

⅔ cup each: sugar, dry white wine or apple juice
1 tablespoon each: balsamic vinegar, dried rosemary leaves
1 bay leaf
1 teaspoon grated orange or lemon zest

1. Heat all ingredients to boiling in small saucepan.

Blueberry-Pear Compote

L *Poaching fruit is easy with a slow cooker!*

6 servings

4 medium pears, peeled, with stems intact
⅔ cup packed light brown sugar
½ cup water
1 tablespoon lemon juice
1 teaspoon grated lemon zest
2 tablespoons margarine or butter
2 cups fresh or frozen thawed blueberries
Cinnamon Sour Cream (recipe follows)

Per Serving:
Calories: 207
% calories from fat: 14
Protein (gm): 1.7
Carbohydrate (gm): 45.4
Fat (gm): 3.4
Saturated fat (gm): 0.6
Cholesterol (mg): 0
Sodium (mg): 58
Exchanges:
Milk: 0.0
Vegetable: 0.0
Fruit: 2.0
Bread: 1.0
Meat: 0.0
Fat: 0.5

1. Stand pears upright in slow cooker. Heat brown sugar, water, lemon juice and zest, and margarine in small saucepan to boiling; pour over pears. Cover and cook on high until pears are tender, about 2 hours. Remove pears to serving dish. Turn slow cooker to high and cook, uncovered, until liquid is a syrup consistency, about 15 minutes; stir in blueberries. Spoon warm blueberry mixture around pears in shallow bowls. Serve with Cinnamon Sour Cream.

Cinnamon Sour Cream

½ cup reduced-fat sour cream
1 tablespoon light brown sugar
¼ teaspoon ground cinnamon

1. Mix all ingredients.

Rhubarb-Strawberry Compote

v

Two of spring's most awaited treasures, cooked to tender goodness. Frozen thawed fruit can also be used, so you can enjoy this dessert all year

6 servings

1 pound each: quartered strawberries, thickly sliced
   rhubarb
½ cup sugar
¼ cup water

1. Combine all ingredients in slow cooker; cover and cook on high until fruit is soft, about 1½ hours. Cook, uncovered, if thicker consistency is desired, about 30 minutes.

Per Serving:
Calories: 105
% calories from fat: 3
Protein (gm): 1.2
Carbohydrate (gm): 26.0
Fat (gm): 0.4
Saturated fat (gm): 0.1
Cholesterol (mg): 0
Sodium (mg): 4
Exchanges:
Milk: 0.0
Vegetable: 0.0
Fruit: 2.0
Bread: 0.0
Meat: 0.0
Fat: 0.0

Winter Fruit Compote

v

Serve over slices of pound cake or over ice cream.

6 servings

1 package (7 ounces) mixed dried fruit
1 package (6 ounces) dried peaches or pears
½ lemon, thinly sliced
⅔ cup each: sweet red wine or apple juice, sugar
½ cup apple juice
½ stick cinnamon
6 whole cloves
⅛ teaspoon salt

1. Combine all ingredients in slow cooker; cover and cook on high 2 to 3 hours, stirring after 1 hour. Serve warm or room temperature.

Per Serving:
Calories: 294
% calories from fat: 2
Protein (gm): 2.4
Carbohydrate (gm): 71.3
Fat (gm): 0.5
Saturated fat (gm): 0.1
Cholesterol (mg): 0
Sodium (mg): 61
Exchanges:
Milk: 0.0
Vegetable: 0.0
Fruit: 4.5
Bread: 0.0
Meat: 0.0
Fat: 0.0

Apple-Cranberry Compote

 You'll serve this autumn dessert offering often!

6 servings

4 cups peeled cored sliced apples
½ cup dried cranberries
⅓ cup packed light brown sugar
2 tablespoons margarine (optional)
1 teaspoon ground cinnamon
¼ teaspoon each: ground nutmeg, salt
¾ cup granola with nuts

1. Combine all ingredients, except granola, in slow cooker; cover and cook on high until apples are tender, 1½ to 2 hours. Sprinkle each serving with granola.

Per Serving:
Calories: 175
% calories from fat: 10
Protein (gm): 3.3
Carbohydrate (gm): 40.2
Fat (gm): 2.3
Saturated fat (gm): 0.1
Cholesterol (mg): 0
Sodium (mg): 125
Exchanges:
Milk: 0.0
Vegetable: 0.0
Fruit: 1.5
Bread: 1.0
Meat: 0.0
Fat: 0.5

Autumn Fruit Crisp

 Late harvest peaches and tart apples combine for flavors of fall.

6 servings

8 cups sliced fresh or drained canned peaches
2 cups peeled sliced tart baking apples
⅓ cup raisins
¼ cup honey
Almond Streusel (recipe follows)

1. Combine peaches, apples, raisins, and honey in slow cooker; cover and cook on high until apples are tender, about 1½ hours. Serve warm, sprinkling each serving with Almond Streusel.

Per Serving:
Calories: 275
% calories from fat: 31
Protein (gm): 2.3
Carbohydrate (gm): 46.6
Fat (gm): 9.8
Saturated fat (gm): 1.7
Cholesterol (mg): 0.0
Sodium (mg): 91
Exchanges:
Milk: 0.0
Vegetable: 0.0
Fruit: 2.0
Bread: 1.0
Meat: 0.0
Fat: 2.0

Almond Streusel

Makes about 1 cup

¾ cup all-purpose flour
¼ cup each: sugar, chopped almonds, melted margarine
Pinch salt

1. Mix all ingredients with fork until mixture is crumbly. Using hands, squeeze mixture into "clumps," using 2 to 3 tablespoons for each; place on cookie sheet. Bake at 350 degrees until lightly browned, about 10 minutes; break into medium to large pieces with a fork.

Peach and Apple Cobbler

L

Baked biscuits make a perfect cobbler topping—serve with generous dollops of whipped topping or scoops of vanilla ice cream.

8 servings

4 cups each: peeled sliced baking apples, fresh or drained, canned peaches
⅔ cup each: granulated sugar, packed light brown sugar
2 tablespoons flour
½ teaspoon ground cinnamon
¼ teaspoon ground nutmeg
3 tablespoons margarine or butter, cut into pieces
4 buttermilk biscuits, baked, halved
2 teaspoons margarine or butter, melted
1 tablespoon cinnamon sugar

Per Serving:
Calories: 280
% calories from fat: 10
Protein (gm): 3.0
Carbohydrate (gm): 64.3
Fat (gm): 3.4
Saturated fat (gm): 0.6
Cholesterol (mg): 0
Sodium (mg): 136
Exchanges:
Milk: 0.0
Vegetable: 0.0
Fruit: 4.0
Bread: 0.0
Meat: 0.0
Fat: 0.5

1. Toss fruit with combined sugars, flour, and spices and spoon into slow cooker. Cover and cook on high until fruit is tender, about 2 hours. Arrange biscuit halves, cut sides down, on fruit during last 30 minutes of cooking, dot with cold margarine. Brush biscuits lightly with margarine and sprinkle with cinnamon sugar. Serve warm.

Chocolate Fondue

L

For the chocoholic!

16 servings (about ¼ cup each)

32 ounces dark chocolate, coarsely chopped
¾–1 cup half-and-half or light cream
3–4 tablespoons rum or brandy (optional)
Dippers: whole strawberries, fruit pieces, angel
  food cake

1. Combine chocolate and half-and-half in 1½-quart
slow cooker; cover and cook until chocolate is
melted, 30 to 45 minutes. Whisk in rum; serve with
dippers (not included in nutritional analysis).

Per Serving:
Calories: 314
% calories from fat: 54
Protein (gm): 3.4
Carbohydrate (gm): 34.1
Fat (gm): 19.5
Saturated fat (gm): 0.7
Cholesterol (mg): 6.5
Sodium (mg): 8
Exchanges:
Milk: 0.0
Vegetable: 0.0
Fruit: 2.0
Bread: 0.0
Meat: 0.0
Fat: 4.0

Variations

Chocolate–Orange Fondue—Make recipe as above, substituting semi-sweet
chocolate for the dark chocolate and orange liqueur for the rum; add 1 to
2 tablespoons grated orange zest.

Chocolate–Coconut Fondue—Make recipe as above, omitting rum, substituting 16 ounces semi-sweet chocolate for 16 ounces of the dark chocolate,
and adding 1 can (15 ounces) cream of coconut. After chocolate is melted,
stir in ¼ cup flaked coconut and 1 teaspoon vanilla.

Chocolate–Cream Cheese Fondue—Make recipe as above, omitting rum,
substituting 16 ounces semi-sweet chocolate for 16 ounces of the dark
chocolate, and adding 2 cups half-and-half and 6 ounces room temperature reduced-fat cream cheese.

White Chocolate Fondue—Make recipe as above, omitting rum and substituting white chocolate morsels for the dark chocolate. Add ¾ cup chopped
toasted almonds.

Rum Raisin Caramel Fondue

L

Favorite flavors, ready for dipping at party time!

12 servings (¼ cup each)

2½ cups caramel ice cream topping
½ cup marshmallow cream
⅓ cup chopped raisins
1–2 tablespoons light rum or ½ teaspoon rum extract
Dippers: vanilla wafers, pretzels, apple slices,
  banana pieces

1. Combine all ingredients, except dippers, in
1½-quart slow cooker; cover and cook until hot,
1 to 1½ hours. Serve with dippers (not included in
nutritional analysis).

Per Serving:
Calories: 222
% calories from fat: 0
Protein (gm): 3.4
Carbohydrate (gm): 51.7
Fat (gm): 0
Saturated fat (gm): 0
Cholesterol (mg): 0
Sodium (mg): 152
Exchanges:
Milk: 0.0
Vegetable: 0.0
Fruit: 0.0
Bread: 3.0
Meat: 0.0
Fat: 0.0

Variation
Peanut Butter Caramel Fondue—Make recipe as above, omitting raisins
and rum. Stir in ½ cup peanut butter and ⅓ cup coarsely chopped toasted
peanuts.

Index

METRIC GUIDELINES

With the tables below and a little common sense, you'll have no trouble making these recipes using metric measuring instruments. We have rounded off the liters, milliliters, centimeters, and kilos to make conversion as simple as possible.

SOME BENCHMARKS—ALL YOU REALLY NEED TO KNOW

Water boils at 212°F
Water freezes at 32°F
325°F is the oven temperature for roasting
Your 250 mL measure replaces one 8 oz cup
Your 15 mL measure replaces one tablespoon
Your 5 mL measure replaces one teaspoon
A 20 cm x 20 cm baking pan replaces a U.S. 8" x 8"
A 22.5 cm x 22.5 cm baking pan replaces a U.S. 9" x 9"
A 30 cm x 20 cm baking pan replaces a U.S. 12" x 8"
A 22.5 cm pie pan replaces a 9" pie pan
A 21.25 cm x 11.25 cm loaf pan replaces an 8" x 4" loaf pan
A 1.5 liter casserole, sauce pan, or soufflé dish replaces a 1 ½ qt dish
A 3 liter casserole, sauce pan, or soufflé dish replaces a 3 qt dish
5 cm is about 2 inches
1 pound is a little less than 500 gm
2 pounds is a little less than 1 kg

OVEN TEMPERATURES

175°F............80°C	350°F..........180°C
200°F..........100°C	375°F..........190°C
225°F..........110°C	400°F..........200°C
250°F..........120°C	425°F..........220°C
275°F..........140°C	450°F..........240°C
300°F..........150°C	500°F..........260°C

FAHRENHEIT TO U.K. GAS STOVE MARKS

275°F.........mark 1	425°F.........mark 7
300°F.........mark 2	450°F.........mark 8
325°F.........mark 3	475°F.........mark 9
350°F.........mark 4	
375°F.........mark 5	
400°F.........mark 6	

VOLUME

¼ cup..50 mL	4 cups (1 quart)..........................0.95 L
½ cup..125 mL	1.06 quarts......................................1 L
1/3 cup ....75 mL	4 quarts (1 gallon)......................3.8 L
¾ cup..175 mL	
1 cup...250 mL	1 teaspoon ....5 mL
1 ¼ cups ....300 mL	½ teaspoon ....2 mL
1 ½ cups ....375 mL	¼ teaspoon ....1 mL
2 cups ....500 mL	1 tablespoon ....15 mL
2½ cups ....625 mL	2 tablespoons ....30 mL
3 cups ....750 mL	3 tablespoons ....45 mL

WEIGHT

1 oz.................................. 28 gm	
2 oz.................................. 56 gm	
¼ pound .... 125 gm (4 oz)	
1 pound ....500 grams	
2 pounds.............................1 kg	
5 pounds .... 2½ kg	

LENGTH

½ inch...................................... 1 cm
1 inch...................................... 2.5 cm
4 inches.................................... 10 cm

This material was prepared with the assistance of the Canadian Home Economics Association and the American Association of Family and Consumer Services.